ATLA BIBLIOGRAPHY SERIES
edited by Dr. Kenneth E. Rowe

1. *A Guide to the Study of the Holiness Movement,* by Charles Edwin Jones. 1974.
2. *Thomas Merton: A Bibliography,* by Marquita E. Breit. 1974.
3. *The Sermon on the Mount: A History of Interpretation and Bibliography,* by Warren S. Kissinger. 1975.
4. *The Parables of Jesus: A History of Interpretation and Bibliography,* by Warren S. Kissinger. 1979.
5. *Homosexuality and the Judeo-Christian Tradition: An Annotated Bibliography,* by Tom Horner. 1981.
6. *A Guide to the Study of the Pentecostal Movement,* by Charles Edwin Jones. 1983.
7. *The Genesis of Modern Process Thought: A Historical Outline with Bibliography,* by George R. Lucas, Jr. 1983.
8. *A Presbyterian Bibliography,* by Harold B. Prince. 1983.
9. *Paul Tillich: A Comprehensive Bibliography . . .* by Richard C. Crossman. 1983.

A PRESBYTERIAN BIBLIOGRAPHY

The Published Writings of Ministers Who Served
in the Presbyterian Church in the United States
During Its First Hundred Years, 1861-1961,
And Their Locations in Eight Significant
Theological Collections in the U.S.A.

compiled and edited by

Harold B. Prince

ATLA Bibliography Series, No. 8

The Scarecrow Press, Inc. and
The American Theological Library Association
Metuchen, N.J., & London • 1983

Library of Congress Cataloging in Publication Data

Prince, Harold B.
    A Presbyterian bibliography.

    (ATLA bibliography series ; no. 8)
    Includes index.
    1. Presbyterian Church in the U.S.--Clergy--
Bibliography--Union lists. 2. Presbyterian Chruch in
the U.S.--Bibliography--Union lists. 3. Presbyterian
Church--Clergy--Bibliography--Union lists.
4. Presbyterian Church--Bibliography--Union lists.
5. Theology--Bibliography--Union lists. 6. Catalogs,
Union--United States. I. Title. II. Series.
Z7845.P9P83   1983   [BX8965]   016.285'173   83-10116
ISBN 0-8108-1639-3

DEDICATED

to the

Prophets who wrote

so that

We who run today may read*

*Habakkuk 2:2

CONTENTS

EDITOR'S NOTE

The American Theological Library Association Bibliography Series is designed to stimulate and encourage the preparation of reliable bibliographies and guides to the literature of religious studies in all of its scope and variety. Compilers are free to define their field, make their own selections, and work out internal organization as the unique demands of the subject require. We are pleased to publish Harold Prince's bibliography of the ministers who served in the Presbyterian Church in the United States during its first hundred years as Number 8 in our series.

Harold B. Prince retired in 1982 after thirty-one years of service at Columbia Theological Seminary in Decatur, Georgia. Mr. Prince held the post of librarian from 1951 until 1976 and then continued to serve the library in several special assignments. He held the title of Professor of Bibliography from 1961 until his retirement. A member of the American Theological Library Association since 1951, Mr. Prince served as treasurer of the Association from 1956 until 1964, as Vice-president in 1968-69, and as President in 1969-70.

Kenneth E. Rowe
Series Editor

Drew University Library
Madison, New Jersey

PREFACE

A Presbyterian Bibliography is the culmination of an effort
begun in 1955 by librarians of the Presbyterian Educational Association of the South--an association of official and church-related educational institutions of the Presbyterian Church in the United States
(PCUS)--to compile a union list of their holdings of Presbyterian
materials that would be useful for research.   Presbyterian materials
were defined, at the time, as books, parts of books, pamphlets, and
separately published reprints of periodical articles, by and about
ministers of the Presbyterian Church in the United States, from the
beginning of the denomination in 1861 to date.   The editor of this
bibliography was chairman of the committee which began the work.

The initial effort, bravely undertaken by all the Association
librarians before the day of photocopy machines, was carried forward by them for a few years in their spare time; subsequently, it
became the particular concern of the heads of the four theological
seminary libraries of the Presbyterian Church in the United States
and the director of the Historical Foundation of the Presbyterian
and Reformed Churches.   By the late 1960s, cards had been gathered
together, and the bibliographical information on them was typed into
manuscript form.

In 1972, the Board of Directors of Columbia Theological
Seminary gave the editor a sabbatical leave of two quarters; and
during this time the bibliography manuscript was checked in the
card catalogs of the PCUS theological seminary libraries and the
Historical Foundation.   Additional entries were made, and the project appeared ready for mimeographing and distributing to the libraries involved.

When a suggestion was made, however, that the bibliography
might be submitted to the American Theological Library Association
Bibliography Series Committee for consideration for publication, it
was immediately apparent that additional editorial work and research
would be required.   Loose parameters needed to be more precisely
defined; the inclusive-exclusive aspect needed to be guarded more
carefully; duplications needed to be eradicated; and a consistent, ap-
propriate, bibliographic style needed to be developed and observed.
Thus, more editing and a second checking of the libraries were
obligatory.

The Board of Directors of Columbia Theological Seminary

generously granted the editor an additional year of sabbatical leave, beginning February 1, 1981, to complete the project and prepare the manuscript for publication. With the able assistance of Evelyn Prince, wife of the editor, the second checking of the libraries was completed in February, 1982. During this time, the collections of Reformed Theological Seminary, the Presbyterian Historical Society, and Princeton Theological Seminary were added to the survey. Thus, with the addition of one independent theological seminary and two institutions of the United Presbyterian Church in the United States of America, the Bibliography provides access to eight of the more significant--perhaps the eight most significant--collections of Presbyterian Church in the United States materials in the nation.

A Presbyterian Bibliography is a main entry listing--with 4,187 entries--of published (i. e., printed) works both by and about, in whole or in part, ministers of the Presbyterian Church who formed the Presbyterian Church of the Confederate States of America on December 4, 1861, and by and about all ministers who were ordained by, or received into, it and its successor, the Presbyterian Church in the United States, from December 4, 1861 through December 31, 1961; so far as these works have been located in the eight collections surveyed. The Bibliography includes works published before 1861 for all ministers who served in the early years of the denomination, and it includes works published after 1961 for ministers who were ordained by, or received into, the Presbyterian Church in the United States through December 31, 1961. All extant editions and imprint variations are shown.

In the Bibliography, manuscript, mimeographed, typed, and microform materials are not included, except in the few instances where the only copy available was in microform, or where the microform copy was a supplemental holding of a published copy of a work. Personal, corporate, and title entries are used; entries for persons not ministers of the Presbyterian Church in the United States are indicated with an asterisk by the author's name. For many books, contents notes and annotations are provided to indicate individual minister contributions to the work. The index leads to each listing of a minister's name, and to the main entries for persons not ministers of the Presbyterian Church in the United States. For each entry, the symbols of the institutions which hold it are indicated. The eight collections surveyed are those of Austin Presbyterian Theological Seminary, Columbia Theological Seminary, The Historical Foundation of the Presbyterian and Reformed Churches, Louisville Presbyterian Theological Seminary, The Presbyterian Historical Society, Reformed Theological Seminary, and Union Theological Seminary in Virginia.

A person who reads through A Presbyterian Bibliography will see that ministers of the Presbyterian Church in the United States became, at times, authors, editors, translators, illustrators, poets, dramatists, composers, and essayists. They wrote sermons, polemics, commentaries, Bible studies, Sunday School lessons, theologies, histories, music, letters to Presidents. They translated, and their writings were translated into, various languages of Africa,

Asia, Europe, North America, and South America. Their works show that these ministers reacted to, and interacted with, life in their times and in the Church; their literary production reflects the evolving, growing, re-forming life of their denomination and of the Church. Some of the persons included in the Bibliography served much of their ministry in Presbyterian denominations other than the Presbyterian Church in the United States; one of them--William Swan Plumer--was elected moderator of the General Assembly of the Presbyterian Church in the United States of America (Old School) in 1838, and was elected moderator of the General Assembly of the Presbyterian Church in the United States in 1871.

The termination of this survey with ministers ordained by or received into the denomination through 1961 does not allow the including of women ministers, since ordination of women as ministers in the Presbyterian Church in the United States began in 1965. The strong participation of women in the life of the denomination may be seen, however, in the index which lists persons not ministers of the Presbyterian Church in the United States. There, names like Carolyn Philips Blackwood, Janie W. McGaughey, Catherine Wood Marshall, Dorothy Mallett Slusser, Margaret Wilson Taylor, and Ethel Taylor Wharton appear among such other non-PCUS-minister names as Karl Barth, Martin Butzer, John Calvin, Toyohiko Kagawa, Francis Makemie, and Albert Schweitzer.

The editor is grateful for the opportunity afforded him to make the bibliographic acquaintance of these persons who are a part of our Presbyterian history and heritage. As this effort is brought to a close, he is aware that many people must share the credit for its completion, though they should not be blamed for its shortcomings. It would be difficult to name them all, but it is a pleasure to note a few of them here. Henry M. Brimm, of Union Theological Seminary in Virginia, gave the vision to the librarians of the Presbyterian Educational Association of the South in 1955. The Association librarians launched the effort. The PCUS theological seminary librarians and the director of the Historical Foundation--Norman D. Dow, Jr., at Austin; myself at Columbia; Ernest M. White at Louisville; Henry M. Brimm at Union; and Thomas H. Spence, Jr., at the Historical Foundation--cooperated in carrying the work forward. Successors--Calvin C. Klemt at Austin; James A. Overbeck at Columbia; John B. Trotti at Union; Jerrold L. Brooks at the Historical Foundation--continued this assistance. In the final, expanded checking, Sharon Taylor at Reformed Theological Seminary; Gerald W. Gillette at the Presbyterian Historical Society; and Charles Willard of Princeton Theological Seminary were also fully cooperative. Presidents J. McDowell Richards, C. Benton Kline, and J. Davison Philips, of Columbia Theological Seminary, gave personal encouragement. The Boards of Directors of Columbia Theological Seminary granted helpful sabbatical leaves. Ernest M. White, Henry M. Brimm, and John B. Trotti made valuable suggestions for the preface. And, above all, Sarah Evelyn Houck Prince, my wife --in reality, co-compiler and co-editor--provided meaningful support all the way; and, in the final checking and typing, assumed a share of the work that hastened its completion by many months.

Decatur, Georgia
November, 1982

Harold B. Prince, Librarian
Professor of Bibliography Emeritus,
Columbia Theological Seminary,
Editor

ABBREVIATIONS AND SYMBOLS

A   Austin Presbyterian Theological Seminary, 106 W. 27th St., Austin, TX 78705

C   Columbia Theological Seminary, Box 520, Decatur, GA 30031

H   The Historical Foundation of the Presbyterian and Reformed Churches, Box 847, Montreat, NC 28757

L   Louisville Presbyterian Theological Seminary, 1044 Alta Vista Rd., Louisville, KY 40205

PH   The Presbyterian Historical Society, 425 Lombard St., Philadelphia, PA 19147

PT   Princeton Theological Seminary, P.O. Box 111, Princeton, NJ 08540

R   Reformed Theological Seminary, 5422 Clinton Blvd., Jackson, MS 39209

U   Union Theological Seminary in Virginia, 3401 Brook Rd., Richmond, VA 23227

The Smyth Lectures   The Thomas Smyth Foundation Lectures, Columbia Theological Seminary

The Sprunt Lectures   The James A. Sprunt Lectures, Union Theological Seminary in Virginia

* Not a minister of the Presbyterian Church in the United States

01 ACREY, Oliver Chauncey, 1905-
    Tribute to John B. McLane, January 12, 1935. Cameron,
    Tex., [S. Brooks McLane, 1935]. unpaged. H

02 ADAMS, Lane Goldman, 1924-
    Come fly with me. Glendale, Calif., Gospel Light Publica-
    tions, © 1973. 117 p. C R

03 ADAMS, Lane Goldman, 1924-
    How come it's taking me so long to get better? Wheaton,
    Ill., Tyndale House, © 1975. 159 p. C PT U

04 ADDRESSES at the inauguration of the Rev. G. Wilson McPhail,
    D. D., as President of Lafayette College and Professor of
    Mental and Moral Philosophy. Delivered at Easton, Pennsyl-
    vania, July 28th, 1858. Philadelphia, William S. & Alfred
    Martien, 1858. 28 p. PH

05 ADDRESSES delivered at the inauguration of Rev. Wm. S. Plum-
    er, D. D., as Professor of Didactic and Pastoral Theology
    in the Western Theological Seminary: comprising the charge
    to the professor, by Rev. E. P. Swift, D. D., and the in-
    augural address. Pittsburgh, W. S. Haven, 1854. 32 p.
    PH

06 ADDRESSES of Rev. R. L. Dabney, D. D., LL. D., Hon. Gus-
    tave Cook, Hon. H. Teichmueller, Rev. G. W. Briggs, de-
    livered before the San Marcos Sunday School Assembly and
    Summer Institute, 1886. n. p., n. d. 39 p. U

07 ADGER, John Bailey, 1810-1899, comp.
    The child's entertainer, consisting chiefly of religious pieces,
    with a few articles on nat. history ... compiled and translated
    into modern Armenian. Smyrna, A. B. C. F. M., 1838. 288 p.
    PT

08 ADGER, John Bailey, 1810-1899.
    Christian missions and African colonization. Columbia, S. C.,
    E. H. Britton, 1857. 53 p. PH

09 ADGER, John Bailey, 1810-1899.
    Church power: a sermon preached by appointment before

1

the Presbytery of South Carolina. Columbia, S. C., Presbyterian Publishing House, 1874. 17 p. PH

10 ADGER, John Bailey, 1810-1899.
Farewell letter. Charleston, Observer Office Press, 1834. 30 p. PT U

11 ADGER, John Bailey, 1810-1899.
Inaugural discourse ... delivered at his inauguration as Professor of Ecclesiastical History and Church Polity in the Theological Seminary of the Synod of South Carolina & Georgia, at Sumterville, S. C., on Friday evening, Oct. 29, 1858. Columbia, S. C., R. W. Gibbes, 1859. 44 p. C PT

12 ADGER, John Bailey, 1810-1899.
My life and times, 1810-1899. Richmond, Presbyterian Committee of Publication, © 1899. 681 p. A C H L PH PT R U

13 ADGER, John Bailey, 1810-1899.
The pastoral relation and the support of the ministry: a sermon preached by appointment before the Synod of South Carolina. Columbia, S. C., Presbyterian Publishing House, 1875. 20 p. C

14 ALDRIDGE, John William, 1929-1976.
The hermeneutic of Erasmus. Richmond, John Knox Press, © 1966. 134 p. A C H L PT R U

15 ALEXANDER, Eugene, 1890-1958, comp.
The Query history, biographical and historical data of pioneers in Cabarrus and Mecklenburg counties. Distributed at annual reunion at Back Creek Church, Mecklenburg County, August 8, 1934. n. p., n. d. 50 p. H

16 ALEXANDER, Hasell Norwood, 1889-1968.
The keeper of the door. The house of Christian living. n. p., n. d. 12 p. Cover-title. PH PT

17 ALEXANDER, Henry Carrington, 1835-1894.
Class papers on apologetics. A syllabus and an epitome of lectures on atheism, agnosticism, pantheism and evolution. Hampden Sidney, Va., A. D. Brydone, n. d. unpaged. U

18 ALEXANDER, Henry Carrington, 1835-1894.
The doctrine of inspiration considered on its divine and human side. n. p., n. d. 190-208 p. Reprinted from the Presbyterian Quarterly, April, 1891. PT U

19 ALEXANDER, Henry Carrington, 1835-1894.
The life of Joseph Addison Alexander. New York, Charles Scribner & Co., 1870. 2 v. A C H PH PT U ... L PH: New York, Scribner, Armstrong & Co., 1875. 917 p.

20 ALEXANDER, Samuel Caldwell, 1830-1907.
The covenant and its seals; or, Children of believers are members of the church, and our Saviour commands that they be baptized. Richmond, Presbyterian Committee of Publication, © 1886. 55 p. C

21 ALEXANDER, Samuel Caldwell, 1830-1907.
The Gospel in Genesis and an exposition of the beginnings. A text book for Bible students. St. Louis, J. T. Smith, 1893. 257 p. H

22 ALEXANDER, Samuel Caldwell, 1830-1907.
An historical address, delivered at the centennial celebration of Thyatira Church, Rowan County, N. C., October 19, 1855. Salisbury, N. C., J. J. Bruner, 1855. 27 p. H PH

23 ALEXANDER, Samuel Caldwell, 1830-1907.
An historical address, delivered at the dedication of Back Creek Church, March 21st, 1857. Salisbury, "Herald" Office, 1857. 20 p. H PH

24 ALEXANDER, Samuel Caldwell, 1830-1907.
History of Back Creek Presbyterian Church, Rowan County, N.C., for 100 years: September 1805 to March 1857 by Rev. S. C. Alexander and March 1857 to September 1905 by John K. Goodman. Mooresville, N. C., Enterprise Prtg., n. d. 34 p. Contains historical address delivered at dedication, March 21st, 1857. H PH

25 ALEXANDER, Samuel Caldwell, 1830-1907.
Miracles and events; or, Some things that God wrought during fifty years of my ministry, from A. D. 1853 to 1903. Pine Bluff, Ark., Commercial Printing Co., n. d. 141 p. A H R

26 ALEXANDER, Samuel Caldwell, 1830-1907.
The stone kingdom; or, the United States and America as seen by the prophets. St. Louis, Farris, Smith & Co., 1885. 231 p. H U ... R: St. Louis, J. T. Smith, 1892.

27 ALEXANDER, William Addison, 1857-1909.
Card playing. Richmond, Presbyterian Committee of Publication, 1892. 29 p. U

28 ALEXANDER, William McFaddin, 1861-1944.
Many infallible proofs of the resurrection of Christ, a sermon ... preached in Prytania Street Presbyterian Church, New Orleans, La., January 27, 1901. [New Orleans, E S. Upton], n. d. 16 p. U

29 ALEXANDER, William Mortimer, 1928-
Johann Georg Hamann: philosophy and faith. The Hague, Martinus Nijhoff, 1966. 212 p. L U

30 ALFORD, Charles McMillan, 1858-1921.
"What kind of a church would our church be, if all of its
members were just like me?" A sermon. Philadelphia, James
W. Britton, 1907. 12 p. PH

31 ALLEN, Donald Ray, 1930-
Barefoot in the church. Richmond, John Knox Press, © 1972.
187 p. A C L PT R U

32 ALLEN, Elliott Douglass, 1874-1964.
Armageddon: studies in the Revelation of St. John. Philadelphia, Presbyterian and Reformed Publishing Co., © 1964.
116 p. PT R

33 ALLEN, Horace Thaddeus, 1933-
A handbook for the lectionary ... developed by the Joint Office of Worship of the Presbyterian Church in the United States
and the United Presbyterian Church in the United States of
America. [1st ed.] Philadelphia, Geneva Press, © 1980. 254
p. A C L U

34 ALLEN, James Woodruff, 1885-1980.
Dikuatshisha dia kuyila lumu luimpe luakafundabo kudi Yone.
Luebo, Congo Belge, J. Leighton Wilson Press, 1950. 397 p.
Outlines and comments on the Gospel of John in Baluba lan-
guage. H

35 ALLEN, James Woodruff, 1885-1980.
Kulondolola kua malu a mu mukanda wa Lewitiki. Luebo,
Congo Belge, J. Leighton Wilson Press, A.P.C.M., 1931.
184 p. Outlines and comments on Leviticus in Baluba language.
H

36 ALLEN, James Woodruff, 1885-1980.
Kulondolola kua malu a mu mukanda wa Nomba. Luebo,
Congo Belge, J. Leighton Wilson Press, A.P.C.M., 1931.
152 p. Outlines and comments on Numbers in Baluba language.
H

37 ALLEN, James Woodruff, 1885-1980.
Kulondolola kua malu a mu mikanda ya Genese, Elesode,
Matayo, Bienzedi, Lomo, I ne II Kolinto. Published for Bulape
Bible School, Belgian Congo Mission of the Presbyterian Church,
U.S., n.d. 514 p. Outlines and comments on Genesis, Exo-
dus, Matthew, Acts, Romans, I and II Corinthians in Baluba
language. H

38 ALLEN, James Woodruff, 1885-1980.
Our work in Congo; a symposium, by James W. Allen [and
others]. Nashville, Tenn., Executive Committee of Foreign
Missions, Presbyterian Church in the U.S., [1945?]. 40 p.
U

39 ALLISON, John Lee, 1863-1946.
... History of Westminster Presbyterian Church, cor. Fayette and Greene streets, Baltimore. n.p., 1902. 24 p. [At head of title: 1852-1902.] PH

40 ALLISON, John Lee, 1863-1946.
Vital truths; briefs of sermons and addresses. Richmond, Presbyterian Committee of Publication, © 1916. 155 p. C H U

41 ALLSUP, Herbert Justin, 1884-
A brief history of church life in Franklin, New Jersey ... upon the occasion of the one hundred eleventh anniversary of the first church organization: the fortieth anniversary of Presbyterianism: the twentieth anniversary of the erection of the present Presbyterian church building: and the tenth anniversary of the present pastorate in the Franklin Presbyterian Church. n.p., 1934. 50 p. PT

42 ALSTON, Wallace McPherson, 1906-
Break up the night! Richmond, John Knox Press, © 1947. 158 p. A C H L U

43 ALSTON, Wallace McPherson, 1906-
Mirrors of the soul; practical and devotional studies of selected Psalms. Atlanta, Board of Women's Work, Presbyterian Church in the U.S., n.d. 59 p. C U

44 ALSTON, Wallace McPherson, 1906-
The throne among the shadows. Richmond, John Knox Press, 1945. 157 p. A C H L R U

45 ANDERSON, Archer E., 1899-
Why do the Godly suffer? Grand Rapids, Mich., Zondervan Publishing House, © 1960. 14 p. PH

46 ANDERSON, John Franklin, 1920-
"Metaphors for missions." Richmond, St. Giles Presbyterian Church, 1968. 37 p. (J. Blanton Belk Lectures, first series.) A C

47 ANDERSON, John Gray, 1850-1944.
The mode of baptism. Richmond, Presbyterian Committee of Publication, n.d. 15 p. U

48 ANDERSON, John Monroe, 1821-1879.
Christ our life, light, and glory. A sermon preached at Ebenezer, York Dist., S.C., the first Sabbath of September, 1860. Columbia, S.C., Robert M. Stokes, 1860. 26 p. PH

49 ANDERSON, Neal Larkin, 1865-1931.
A brief study of the First Presbyterian Church Ephesus; its polity and doctrine. n.p., n.d. 7 p. PT U

50 ANDERSON, Neal Larkin, 1865-1931.
The deacon: a plea and an appeal. Address ... before the convention of the Layman's Missionary Movement, at Chattanooga, Feb. 8, 1912. Richmond Presbyterian Committee of Publication, n.d. 8 p.   U

51 ANDERSON, Neal Larkin, 1865-1931.
God's world and word: addresses for today. New York, Fleming H. Revell Co., © 1926. 160 p.   A C H PT R U

52 ANDERSON, Neal Larkin, 1865-1931.
The race problems in the South; fallacies and the duty of the church. [Tuscaloosa, Ala., General Assembly, Presbyterian Church in the U.S., 1907]. 24 p. A sermon preached at the Montreat Conference on the Colored Evangelistic Work of the Southern Presbyterian Church, Aug. 4, 1907.   H

53 ANDERSON, Neal Larkin, 1865-1931.
The recoil of evolution's assault upon teleology--a review of the "argument to design." n.p., n.d. 268-280 p. Reprinted from the Presbyterian Quarterly, April, 1899.   PT

54 ANDERSON, Neal Larkin, 1865-1931.
What our Lord teaches concerning his second coming. [Savannah, Ga.], n.p., n.d. 8 p. Reprinted from the Christian Observer.   C

55 ANDERSON, Neal Larkin, 1865-1931.
With wings; a bird's eye view of Western Europe. Richmond, Presbyterian Committee of Publication, © 1928. 72 p.   C H R

56 ANDERSON, Robert Campbell, 1864-1955.
The story of Montreat from its beginning, 1897-1947. Montreat, N.C., Robert Campbell Anderson, © 1949. 237 p.
A C H L PT R U

57 ANDERSON, Vernon Andy, 1896-
Still led in triumph. Illustrations by Claire Randall. [Nashville, Tenn.], Board of World Missions, Presbyterian Church in the U.S., [1959]. 55 p. Sequel to Ethel Taylor Wharton's "Led in triumph."   C R U

58 ANDERSON, William Madison, 1889-1935.
The faith that satisfies: sermons. New York, Loizeaux Brothers, © 1948. 247 p.   A L U ... C: [1949].

59 ANDERSON, William Madison, 1889-1935.
Our defensible faith. A sermon delivered ... Dallas, Texas, March 16, 1930. n.p., n.d. unpaged.   PH

60 ANDERSON, William Madison, 1889-1935.
Over fool hill. Binghamton, Vail-Ballou Press, © 1924. 184 p.
H

61 APPLEBY, James Mourning, 1904-1977.
Field work and evangelism. Inaugural address, delivered
September 10, 1947, in Schauffler Hall, Union Theological Semi-
nary. Richmond, Union Theological Seminary, 1947. 17 p.
A C H U

62 APPLEBY, James Mourning, 1904-1977.
The glory of the church. A study based on Ephesians. [At-
lanta, Board of Women's Work, Presbyterian Church in the
U.S., 1954]. 47 p. A L U

63 An APPRECIATION of C. Darby Fulton, D.D., LL.D., Executive
Secretary, Board of World Missions, Presbyterian Church,
U.S., May, 1932-October, 1961. [Nashville, Tenn., Board
of World Missions, Presbyterian Church in the U.S., 1961].
unpaged. C

64 ARMISTEAD, Jessie Scott, 1795-1869.
The work of the Holy Spirit on the hearts of men. Philadelphia, Presbyterian Board of Publication, n.d. 16 p. PH PT

65 ARMSTRONG, George Dodd, 1813-1899.
A centennial discourse, delivered before the Presbytery of
Lexington, Synod of Virginia, at Timber-Ridge Church, September 25th, 1886, the one hundredth anniversary of its organization. Staunton, Va., Valley Virginian Power Press, 1887.
20 p. H U

66 ARMSTRONG, George Dodd, 1813-1899.
The Christian doctrine of slavery. New York, Charles Scrib-
ner, 1857. 148 p. C H L PH PT U ... R: microfiche ... A L R:
New York, Negro Universities Press, [1969].

67 ARMSTRONG, George Dodd, 1813-1899.
A defence of the "deliverance" on evolution, adopted by the
General Assembly of the Presbyterian Church in the United
States, May 26th, 1886. Norfolk, Va., John D. Ghiselin, n.d.
18 p. C U

68 ARMSTRONG, George Dodd, 1813-1899.
A discussion on slaveholding. Three letters to a conservative, by George D. Armstrong, D.D., of Virginia, and Three
conservative replies, by C. Van Rensselaer, D.D., of New
Jersey.... Together with Two rejoinders on slaveholding,
schemes of emancipation, colonization, etc. Philadelphia, Joseph M. Wilson, 1858. 137 p. H U

69 ARMSTRONG, George Dodd, 1813-1899.
The doctrine of baptisms. Scriptural examination of the questions respecting: I. The translation of baptizo, II. The mode of
baptism, III. The subjects of baptism. New York, Charles
Scribner, 1857. 322 p. A C H L PH PT R U

70 ARMSTRONG, George Dodd, 1813-1899.
"The election of grace," as set forth in the Word of God and
the Confession of Faith. Richmond, Presbyterian Committee of
Publication, 1890. 30 p. C PH U

71 ARMSTRONG, George Dodd, 1813-1899.
Evolution. The substance of two lectures. Norfolk, Va.,
John D. Ghiselin, n.d. 22 p. H U

72 ARMSTRONG, George Dodd, 1813-1899.
The good hand of our God upon us; a thanksgiving sermon,
preached on occasion of the victory of Manassas, July 21st,
1861, in the Presbyterian Church, Norfolk, Va. Norfolk, John
D. Ghiselin, 1861. 15 p. H U

73 ARMSTRONG, George Dodd, 1813-1899.
A half hour with Robert Elsmere. Norfolk, Va., T. O. Wise
& Son, 1889. 20 p. PT U

74 ARMSTRONG, George Dodd, 1813-1899.
Higher criticism and its conclusions. Norfolk, Va., n.p.,
1885. U

75 ARMSTRONG, George Dodd, 1813-1899.
"Jesus Christ and him crucified": a semi-centenary discourse, preached in the First Presbyterian Church, Norfolk,
Va., September 16, 1888. Richmond, Jenkins & Walthall, 1889.
17 p. PT

76 ARMSTRONG, George Dodd, 1813-1899.
The lesson of the pestilence. A discourse preached in the
Presbyterian Church, Norfolk, Va., on Sabbath, Dec. 2nd, 1855.
Richmond, Charles H. Wynne, 1855. 19 p. PH

77 ARMSTRONG, George Dodd, 1813-1899.
The nature of conversion to God, as exhibited in Christian
experience. Philadelphia, Presbyterian Board of Publication,
n.d. 24 p. (Presbyterian Tracts, no. 225.) H PH PT R U

78 ARMSTRONG, George Dodd, 1813-1899.
The nature of infant baptism. New York, M. W. Dodd, 1852.
16 p. U

79 ARMSTRONG, George Dodd, 1813-1899.
The Pentateuchal story of creation. n.p., n.d. 345-368 p.
Reprinted from the Presbyterian Quarterly, October, 1888. PT

80 ARMSTRONG, George Dodd, 1813-1899.
Politics and the pulpit, a sermon. Norfolk, Va., John D.
Ghiselin, 1856. 40 p. PH U

81 ARMSTRONG, George Dodd, 1813-1899.
The sacraments of the New Testament as instituted by Christ.

New York, A. C. Armstrong & Son, 1880. 232, 314 p. ["The doctrine of the Lord's Supper ..." has special half-title and separate pagination.] H PT ... A C H L R: Richmond, Presbyterian Committee of Publication, 1884.

82 ARMSTRONG, George Dodd, 1813-1899.
The Scripture-warrant for infant baptism. New York, M. W. Dodd, 1852. 26 p. U

83 ARMSTRONG, George Dodd, 1813-1899.
The study of natural science. Lynchburg, Fletcher & Toler, 1841. 16 p. PT U

84 ARMSTRONG, George Dodd, 1813-1899.
The summer of the pestilence. A history of the ravages of the yellow fever in Norfolk, Va., A.D. 1855. Philadelphia, J. B. Lippincott & Co., 1856. 192 p. H PH U ... PH PT: 2d ed.

85 ARMSTRONG, George Dodd, 1813-1899.
The theology of Christian experience, designed as an exposition of the "common faith" of the church of God. New York, Charles Scribner, 1858. 342 p. A C H L PH PT R U

86 ARMSTRONG, George Dodd, 1813-1899.
The two books of nature and revelation collated. New York, Funk & Wagnalls, 1886. 213 p. A C H PT R U

87 ARMSTRONG, George Dodd, 1813-1899.
Two discourses on infant baptism: I. The Scripture-warrant for infant baptism. II. The nature of infant baptism. New York, M. W. Dodd, 1852. 52 p. H PH PT U

88 ARMSTRONG, George Dodd, 1813-1899.
What hath God wrought? A historical discourse preached June 25th, 1876, on the completion of a twenty-five years' ministry in the First Presbyterian Church, Norfolk, Va. Norfolk, Published by the Congregation, 1876. 22 p. PT U

89 ARMSTRONG, John Irvine, 1872-1924.
Elders that rule well; the nature, duties and rewards of the office of ruling elder in the Presbyterian Church. Richmond, Presbyterian Committee of Publication, 1922. 32 p. A

90 ARMSTRONG, Oscar Vance, 1876-1941, comp.
Comfort for those who mourn; Bible, poetry, prose. Nashville, Tenn., Cokesbury Press, © 1930. 97 p. A H L R U

91 ARMSTRONG, Oscar Vance, 1876-1941, comp.
Prayer poems, compiled by O. V. and Helen Armstrong. New York, Abingdon-Cokesbury Press, © 1942. 256 p. C H L PT R U

92 ARROWOOD, William Butler, 1850-1919.
   The polity of the Presbyterian Church. A sermon preached
   before the Presbytery of Fayetteville, North Carolina. Richmond, Presbyterian Committee of Publication, 1895. 43 p.
   C U

93 ATKINS, Alexander Harrison, 1860-1933.
   The fundamentals. Richmond, Whittet & Shepperson, 1924.
   110 p. A C H R U

94 ATKINS, Alexander Harrison, 1860-1933.
   The law and the gospel. [Richmond, Whittet & Shepperson,
   1915]. 151 p. A C H PT

95 ATKINSON, Joseph Mayo, 1820-1891.
   Casting your burden on the Lord. Richmond, Presbyterian
   Committee of Publication, n.d. 8 p. U

96 ATKINSON, Joseph Mayo, 1820-1891.
   The true path, or the young man invited to the Saviour.
   Philadelphia, Presbyterian Board of Publication, © 1860.
   300 p. PH PT U

97 *ATKINSON, William Mayo, 1796-1849.
   A sermon delivered at the installation of the Rev. John M.
   P. Atkinson, as pastor of the church at Warrenton, Fauquier
   County, September 15, 1844. n.p., n.d. 24 p. H PH PT U

98 AXSON, Samuel Edward, 1833-1884.
   Difficulties of the immersion theory. Adopted by the Com-
   mittee of Publication at Richmond, Va. Rome, Ga., Albin
   Omberg, 1879. 113 p. A H U

99 AXSON, Samuel Edward, 1833-1884.
   ... Twelve years of church work in the Rome Presbyterian
   Church. A sermon. Rome, Ga., Albin Omberg, 1878. 18 p.
   [At head of title: February 1866 to February 1878.] PH

100 BACHMAN, George Oliver, 1854-1939.
    A world: without the Bible; outline studies in the book of
    Job. Nashville, Tenn., Presbyterian Bible Training School
    for Christian Workers, © 1910. 44 p. A H R U

101 *BAHA ULLAH, 1817-1892.
    al-Kitāb al-aqdas; or, The most holy book, by Mīrzā Husayn
    'Alī Bahā'u'llāh. Translated from the original Arabic and
    edited by Earl E. Elder and William McE. Miller. London,
    Royal Asiatic Society, 1961. 74 p. C L PT U

102 BAILEY, John Crooks, 1870-1962.
    History of Ebenezer Presbyterian Church. n.p., n.d. 58 p.
    C

103 BAILEY, Rufus William, 1793-1863.
An address, delivered at the close of the Sabbath school on
Norwich Plain, November 9, 1819. Woodstock, [Conn.], David
Watson, 1820. 12 p. C

104 BAILEY, Rufus William, 1793-1863.
Daughters at school instructed in a series of letters. Phila-
delphia, Presbyterian Board of Publication, © 1857. 252 p.
C H PH PT R U

105 BAILEY, Rufus William, 1793-1863.
Domestic duties; or, The family, a nursery for earth and
heaven. Philadelphia, Presbyterian Board of Publication, n.d.
120 p. A shortened form of "The family preacher." C H
PH PT

106 BAILEY, Rufus William, 1793-1863.
English grammar: a simple, concise, and comprehensive
manual of the English language.... 2d ed. Philadelphia,
Clark & Hesser, 1853. 239 p. H

107 BAILEY, Rufus William, 1793-1863.
The family preacher; or, Domestic duties illustrated and
enforced in eight discourses. New York, John S. Taylor,
1837. 158 p. C H PH R U

108 BAILEY, Rufus William, 1793-1863.
God the proper object of gratitude; and thanksgiving a necessary evidence of its sincerity. A sermon, preached in Pittsfield, Mass., on the day of the state thanksgiving, December
3, 1824. Pittsfield, Phinehas Allen, 1825. 20 p. C PT

109 BAILEY, Rufus William, 1793-1863.
The issue, presented in a series of letters on slavery.
New York, John S. Taylor, 1837. 110 p. C

110 BAILEY, Rufus William, 1793-1863.
The magnitude of the ministerial office illustrated from the
value of the soul. A sermon delivered July 4, 1821, at the
ordination of Rev. Dana Clayes, to the pastoral care of the
church and society in Meriden parish, Plainfield, N.H. Hanover, N.H., Ridley Bannister, 1821. 32 p. C PT

111 BAILEY, Rufus William, 1793-1863.
The scholar's companion; containing exercises in the orthog-
raphy, derivation, and classification of English words. New
ed., thoroughly rev. Philadelphia, J. H. Butler & Co., 1876.
312 p. R

112 BAIN, Bernard Edwin, 1906-1981.
My one hundred children, by Bernard E. Bain, with Dale
Kramer. New York, Simon and Schuster, 1954. 210 p.
H R U

113 BAIRD, Ebenezer Thompson, 1821-1887.
An essay on the pastoral duties of ruling elders: read before the Presbytery of Tombeckbee, Mississippi, and ordered to be published, April 7, 1860. Columbia, S.C., Southern Guardian Steam-power Press, 1860. 22 p. PH U

114 BAIRD, Ebenezer Thompson, 1821-1887.
The religious instruction of our colored population. A pastoral letter from the Presbytery of Tombeckbee to the churches and people under its care. Columbia, S.C., R. W. Gibbes, 1859. 19 p. U

115 BAIRD, Ebenezer Thompson, 1821-1887.
Songs of praise, for Sabbath schools. Rev. ed. Richmond, Presbyterian Committee of Publication, © 1867. 126 p. A H PT U

116 BAIRD, Ebenezer Thompson, 1821-1887, ed.
The voice of praise: a selection of hymns and tunes for the Sabbath school, prayer meeting, and family circle. Edited by E. T. Baird and Karl Reden [pseud.]. Richmond, E. Thompson Baird, © 1872. 216 p. H PT U

117 BAIRD, James H., ca. 1830-1900.
The Century Magazine versus John Bunyan and evangelicalism, and the Bible of our fathers. n.p., n.d. 16 p. PH

118 BAIRD, James H., ca. 1830-1900.
Neglect of infant baptism. Philadelphia, William S. & Alfred Martien, 1857. 29 p. Reprinted from the Princeton Review, January, 1857. PH PT U

119 BAIRD, Joseph Simon, 1869-1957.
A brief history of the Baird and McLain families of Scotland, Ireland, and America. Atlanta, Joseph S. Baird, 1952. 16 p. H

120 BAIRD, Samuel John, 1817-1893.
The Bible history of baptism. Richmond, Presbyterian Committee of Publication, n.d. 36 p. Reprinted from the Southern Presbyterian Review, July, 1870. PH

121 BAIRD, Samuel John, 1817-1893.
Christ's own mode of baptism. Clarksburg, W.Va., J. H. Baird, 1887. 16 p. PH PT U

122 BAIRD, Samuel John, 1817-1893.
The church of Christ: its construction and order. A manual for the instruction of families, Sabbath-schools, and Bible classes. Philadelphia, Presbyterian Board of Publication, © 1864. 144 p. C H PH PT U

123 BAIRD, Samuel John, 1817-1893, comp.
A collection of the acts, deliverances, and testimonies of

the supreme judicatory of the Presbyterian Church from its origin in America to the present time. With notes and documents, explanatory and historical: constituting a complete illustration of her polity, faith, and history. Philadelphia, Presbyterian Board of Publication, 1856. 856 p. A C H L PH PT R U ... A L PH PT U: 2d ed. [1858]. 880 p.

124 BAIRD, Samuel John, 1817-1893.
The discussion on reunion: a review. Richmond, Whittet & Shepperson, 1887. 34 p. H PH PT U ... A: microfilm ... C H PT U: 2d ed., enl. 1888. 50 p.

125 BAIRD, Samuel John, 1817-1893.
The first Adam and the second. The Elohim revealed in the creation and redemption of man. Philadelphia, Parry & McMillan, 1860. 688 p. A C H PH U ... PT R: Philadelphia, Lindsay & Blakiston.

126 BAIRD, Samuel John, 1817-1893.
The great baptizer. A Bible history of baptism. Richmond, Presbyterian Committee of Publication, 1882. 489 p. PT R ... A C H PH R U: Philadelphia, James H. Baird ... H L U: 2d ed. Richmond, Presbyterian Committee of Publication, 1892.

127 BAIRD, Samuel John, 1817-1893.
A history of the early policy of the Presbyterian Church in the training of her ministry; and of the first years of the Board of Education. Philadelphia, Published by the Board, 1865. 37 p. PH PT

128 BAIRD, Samuel John, 1817-1893.
A history of the New School, and of the questions involved in the disruption of the Presbyterian Church in 1838. Philadelphia, Claxton, Remsen & Haffelfinger, 1868. 564 p. A C H PH PT R U

129 BAIRD, Samuel John, 1817-1893.
A rejoinder to the Princeton Review, upon The Elohim revealed, touching the doctrine of imputation and kindred topics. Philadelphia, Joseph M. Wilson, 1860. 40 p. C H PH PT U

130 BAIRD, Samuel John, 1817-1893.
The Socinian apostasy of the English Presbyterian churches. A discourse, delivered on behalf of the Presbyterian Historical Society, before the General Assembly of the Presbyterian Church, in the First Presbyterian Church, New York, May 16th, 1856. Philadelphia, Presbyterian Historical Society, 1857. 34 p. C PH PT U

131 BAIRD, Samuel John, 1817-1893.
Southern rights and Northern duties in the present crisis. A letter to Hon. William Pennington. Philadelphia, Lindsay & Blakiston, 1861. 32 p. H PH U

132 BAIRD, Samuel John, 1817-1893.
      Training of the children. n.p., n.d. 78-95 p. Reprinted
      from the Princeton Review, January, 1863. PH PT

133 BAIRD, Washington, -1868.
      A discourse on ordination and church polity; in which it is
      shown, that the arrogant assumptions of high-churchism are
      inconsistent with scripture, with reason, and with facts. New
      York, J. F. Trow & Co., 1844. 31 p. C PH PT U

134 BAIRD, Washington, -1868.
      Duty and reward; or, The blessedness of doing good. New
      York, Anson D. F. Randolph, 1859. 77 p. H PH

135 BAKER, Daniel Summer, 1823-1900.
      Points about Sunday Schools: Romanism and the Columbian
      exhibition at Chicago, in 1893. n.p., n.d. 30 p. PT

136 BAKER, Daniel Summer, 1823-1900.
      The sovereignty of God. n.p., n.d. 20 p. (Presbyterian
      Tracts, no. 78) C H L PH PT R U

137 BAKER, Daniel Summer, 1823-1900.
      The standards of the Presbyterian Church, a faithful mirror
      of Bible truth. n.p., n.d. 27 p. (Presbyterian Tracts, no.
      87) C H L PH PT R U

138 BAKER, Frank Fisher, 1890-1979.
      Memoirs. Recollections of a ... member of the East Bra-
      zil mission, 1913-1961. Mount Airy, N.C., n.p., 1965.
      112 p. H U

139 BAKER, William Elliott, 1830-1906.
      Collision between a Sunday train and an angry God. Staun-
      ton, Vindicator, Print., n.d. 11 p. PT

140 BAKER, William Mumford, 1825-1885.
      Funeral discourse delivered on the occasion of the death of
      Joseph Wade Hampton, a ruling elder in the Austin City Pres-
      byterian Church. Austin, "Texas State Times" Office, 1855.
      16 p. PH

141 BAKER, William Mumford, 1825-1885.
      The life and labours of the Rev. Daniel Baker, D.D., pas-
      tor and evangelist. Prepared by his son. Philadelphia, Wil-
      liam S. & Alfred Martien, 1858. 573 p. A C H PT R U ...
      L PH U: 1859 ... C H U: 3d ed. Philadelphia, Presbyterian
      Board of Publication, © 1858. 560 p.

142 BAKER, William Mumford, 1825-1885.
      The new Timothy. New York, Harper & Brothers, 1870.
      344 p. A novel. H

143 BAKER, William Mumford, 1825-1885.
Oak-Mot. Philadelphia, Presbyterian Board of Publication
and Sabbath-school Work, © 1868. 226 p.   H PH PT R

144 BAKER, William Mumford, 1825-1885.
The ten theophanies; or, The appearances of our Lord to
men before his birth in Bethlehem. New York, Anson D. F.
Randolph & Co., © 1883. 247 p.   A C H PH PT R U

145 *BALCH, Lewis Penn Witherspoon, 1814-1875.
God in the storm: a narrative by the Rev. L. P. W.
Balch; an address, by the Rev. Lyman Beecher, D.D., and
a sermon, by the Rev. Thomas Smyth, D.D. Prepared on
board the Great Western, after the storm encountered on her
recent voyage. New-York, Robert Carter, 1846. 29, 24,
42 p.   R ... C PT: 1847 ... PH: 1851.

146 BALCH, Thomas Bloomer, 1793-1878.
Christianity and literature in a series of discourses. Philadelphia, E. Littell, 1826. 233 p.   C

147 BALCH, Thomas Bloomer, 1793-1878.
The office and work of a bishop. A discourse preached at
the installation of Rev. G. Wilson McPhail as pastor of the
Presbyterian Church of Fredericksburg, Va., June 12th, 1842.
Fredericksburg, Virginia Herald, 1842. 28 p.   H PH

148 BALCH, Thomas Bloomer, 1793-1878.
Reminiscences of Georgetown, D.C. A lecture delivered
in the Methodist Protestant Church, Georgetown, D.C., January 20, 1859. Washington, Henry Polkinhorn, 1859. 28 p.
PT

149 BALES, Tipton Clinton, 1884-
Landmarks of faith; a history of the Clifton Forge Presbyterian Church, 1881-1957. Clifton Forge, Va., n.p., © 1959.
107 p.   H U

150 BALNICKY, Robert Gabriel, 1922-
Why I cannot be a Roman Catholic. n.p., n.d. 8 ℓ.   U

151 BANKHEAD, Robert Crawford, 1933-
Liturgical formulae in the New Testament. Clinton, S.C.,
Jacobs Press, 1971. 205 p. Diss.--Univ. of Basel.   C U

152 BARBOUR, John, 1849-1929.
Ministers and music: Princeton lectures. [Maysville, Ky.,
Printed for the author], n.d. 128 p.   PT

153 BARBOUR, Lewis Green, 1829-1907.
The end of time, a poem of the future. New York, G. P.
Putnam's Sons, 1892. 191 p.   U

154 BARKS, Herbert Bernard, 1933-
     Prime time. [1st ed.] Nashville, Thomas Nelson, © 1978.
     134 p. U

155 BARKS, Herbert Bernard, 1933-
     Words are no good if the game is solitaire. Waco, Tex.,
     Word Books, © 1971. 96 p. C

156 BARLOW, James Stanley, 1924-
     The fall into consciousness. Philadelphia, Fortress Press,
     © 1973. 148 p. A C L PT U

157 BARNES, George Owen, 1827-1908.
     A lost people and A vanished sceptre. New York, The
     Shakespeare Press, 1911. 62 p. R

158 BARR, John Tilman, 1886-1963.
     A treasure hunt: a study of baptism. Richmond, Executive
     Committee of Religious Education and Publication, n.d. 40 p.
     U

159 BARR, Thomas Calhoun, 1904-
     The story of the Presbyteries of Columbia and Nashville:
     from early settlement to 1972, by Thomas C. Barr, Robert E.
     Cogswell, Spencer C. Murray, George T. Wingard [and others].
     Brentwood, Presbytery of Middle Tennessee, Presbyterian
     Church in the U.S., 1976. 278 p. R

160 BARR, Thomas Calhoun, 1904-
     The Ten Commandments, and other sermons. n.p., 1940.
     72 p. U

161 BARRET, Thomas Carr, 1841-1916.
     History of Bellevue Presbyterian Church, Caledonia, Mo.
     A sermon, preached by Rev. T. C. Barrett in the Presby-
     terian Church in Caledonia, Mo., August 5th, 1877. Potosi,
     Mo., "Independent," 1877. 24 p. PH .PT

162 BARRIER, Thomas Franklin, 1865-
     An essay on necessity and character of public education.
     n.p., n.d. 20 p. PT

163 BARRON, Luther Wiggins, 1869-1905.
     Killed in a saloon. Richmond, Presbyterian Committee of
     Publication, © 1901. 19 p. PT U

164 BARRON, Vance, 1916-
     Sermons for the celebration of the Christian year. Nash-
     ville, Abingdon, © 1977. 95 p. A C L PT U

165 *BARTH, Karl, 1886-1968.
     The Heidelberg catechism for today. Translated by Shirley

C. Guthrie, Jr. Richmond, John Knox Press, © 1964. 141 p.
A C H L PT R U

166 *BARTH, Karl, 1886-1968.
Die Theologie Schleiermachers: Vorlesung Göttingen Win-
tersemester 1923-24; herausgegeben von Dietrich Ritschl.
Zürich, Theologischer Verlag, © 1978. 480 p. L U

167 BARTLETT, William Frederick Vincent, 1831-1903.
The Sabbath day. A sermon preached before the Synod of
Kentucky, (October 10, 1895). [Lexington, Ky.], n.p., n.d.
unpaged. PH

168 A BASIS for study, a theological prospectus for the campus
ministry. A symposium by Presbyterian university pastors.
Richmond, Board of Christian education, Presbyterian Church
in the U.S., and Philadelphia, Board of Christian Education,
United Presbyterian Church in the U.S.A., © 1959. 153 p.
Chapters by Neely McCarter, Harry Smith, William W. Rogers, and others. C U

169 BATCHELOR, Alexander Ramsay, 1891-1955.
Jacob's ladder: Negro work of the Presbyterian Church in
the United States. Atlanta, Board of Church Extension, Presbyterian Church in the U.S., © 1953. 158 p. C H L R U

170 BATEMAN, Thomas Douglas, 1884-1944.
Fountains of faith; prayers and talks. New Orleans, Peli-
can Publishing Co., © 1957. 157 p. R

171 BAYLESS, John Clark, 1809-1875.
The errors of education, delivered before the patrons and
students of Marshall Academy and Seminary, near Guyandotte,
Cabell County, Va., on the 27th day of August, 1857. Guyandotte, Western Virginian Print., 1858. 23 p. PH

172 BEALL, Benjamin Leander, 1827-1913.
The Lord's Supper. n.p., [1910?]. 32 p. U

173 BEAN, William Smith, 1849-1920.
Teachings of the Lord Jesus.... With an introduction by
Prof. C. R. Hemphill. Philadelphia, Presbyterian Board of
Publication and Sabbath-school Work, 1903. 105 p. A H L

174 BEAR, James Edwin, 1893-1977.
Dispensationalism and the covenant of grace. n.p., n.d.
285-307 p. Reprinted from the Union Seminary Review, July,
1938. A U

175 BEAR, James Edwin, 1893-1977.
The Kingdom of God or world revolution. [Richmond, Presbyterian Outlook], n.d. 14 p. U

176 BEAR, James Edwin, 1893-1977.
A literal vs. a spiritual interpretation of the Bible. Richmond, Presbyterian Committee of Publication, n.d. 27 p.
A C PT R U

177 BEAR, James Edwin, 1893-1977.
Mission to Brazil. n.p., Board of World Missions, Presbyterian Church in the U.S., © 1961. 240 p.   C H L PT R U

178 BEAR, James Edwin, 1893-1977.
The Presbyterian standards vs. the Scofield Bible. [Richmond], Presbyterian of the South, 1941. 9 ℓ.   U

179 BEATIE, Arthur Young, 1872-1945.
Walter W. Moore and Union Seminary; a short story of the life of a truly great man, a brief record of the growth of a vitally important institution under his administration, and an approved plan for establishing the work of his hands. Richmond, Union Theological Seminary, 1927. 48 p.   PT U

180 BEATTIE, Francis Robert, 1848-1906.
Apologetics; or, The rational vindication of Christianity....
With an introduction by Benjamin B. Warfield. Vol. I. Richmond, Presbyterian Committee of Publication, © 1903. 605 p.
A C H L PT R U

181 BEATTIE, Francis Robert, 1848-1906.
Calvinism and modern thought. Philadelphia, Westminster Press, 1901. 48 p.   PH ... PT U: 1902

182 BEATTIE, Francis Robert, 1848-1906.
Christian apologetics. Inaugural address ... on the occasion of his installation as Professor in the Theological Seminary at Columbia, S.C., May, 1890. n.p., n.d. 337-370 p.
Reprinted from the Presbyterian Quarterly, July, 1890.   PT

183 BEATTIE, Francis Robert, 1848-1906.
Christian unity: a sermon ... 1899. n.p., [Christian Observer], n.d. 22 p.   PT U

184 BEATTIE, Francis Robert, 1848-1906.
An examination of the utilitarian theory of morals. Brantford, J. & J. Sutherland, 1885. 222 p.   H

185 BEATTIE, Francis Robert, 1848-1906.
The higher criticism; or modern critical theories as to the origin and contents of the literature and religion in the Holy Scriptures. Toronto, William Briggs, 1888. 56 p.   PH PT U

186 BEATTIE, Francis Robert, 1848-1906.
The methods of theism. Brantford, [Ont.], Watt & Shenston, 1887. 138 p.   C H R

187 BEATTIE, Francis Robert, 1848-1906.
Presbyterian educational work in Kentucky. Richmond,
Whittet & Shepperson, 1903. 15 p. PT

188 BEATTIE, Francis Robert, 1848-1906.
The Presbyterian standards: an exposition of the Westminster Confession of Faith and catechisms. Richmond, Presbyterian Committee of Publication, © 1896. 431 p. A C H
L PH PT R U

189 BEATTIE, Francis Robert, 1848-1906.
Radical criticism; an exposition and examination of the radi-
cal critical theory concerning the literature and religious system
of the Old Testament scriptures.... With an introduction by W.
W. Moore. Chicago, Fleming H. Revell Co., © 1894. 323 p.
A C H L PT R U

190 BEATTIE, Francis Robert, 1848-1906.
A reply to Col. Bennett H. Young's "Suggestions touching
organic union." Louisville, Ky., n.p., n.d. 22 p. U

191 BEATTIE, Francis Robert, 1848-1906.
The second advent of Christ ... published by special request of the graduating class of 1895. Louisville, Ky., Converse & Co., 1895. 30 p. PH PT U

192 *BECK, Madeline Hulse, 1923-
Mastering New Testament facts. Programmed reading, art,
and activity tests to get it all down pat, by Madeline H. Beck
[and] Lamar Williamson, Jr. Richmond, John Knox Press,
© 1973. 4 v. A C L R U

193 BECKMAN, Ludwig Armstrong, 1897- , comp.
Alexander Thompson of Fairfield District, South Carolina;
the genealogical record of his descendants. [Ellisville, Miss.,
n.p., 1950]. 56 p. H

194 BECKMAN, Ludwig Armstrong, 1897-
The autobiography of Rev. Ludwig Armstrong Beckman, Jr.,
of Louisville, Mississippi. Fulton, Miss., Itawamba County
Times, [1978]. 250 p. C H L

195 BECKMAN, Ludwig Armstrong, 1897-
Junior sermons to children; here are sixty sermons which
have been preached to boys and girls in Sunday morning services. Fulton, Miss., Itawamba County Times, [1969].
129 p. H

196 BECKMAN, Ludwig Armstrong, 1897-
South Santee stories for children. New York, Vantage
Press, © 1955. 79 p. C U

197 BEDINGER, Robert Dabney, 1885-1970.

Triumphs of the Gospel in the Belgian Congo. Being some account of the mission work ... by the Presbyterian Church in the United States. Richmond, Presbyterian Committee of Publication, [1920]. 218 p. A C H R U

198 BEDINGER, William Lucas, 1856-1932.
Affusion vs. immersion. Lynchburg, Va., Liggan & Holt, n.d. 26 p. U

199 BEDINGER, William Lucas, 1856-1932.
Soul food: discourses on topics from the teachings of Paul the apostle. Grand Rapids, Mich., Reformed Press, n.d. 316 p. C H R U

200 BELK, George Washington, 1859-1925.
The baptism of John: was it from heaven? 2d ed. Richmond, Whittet & Shepperson, 1899. 20 p. U

201 BELK, George Washington, 1859-1925.
The Presbyterian faith founded upon divine authority. A summary of the things most surely believed among us. 3d ed. [Charlotte, N.C., Presbyterian Standard Publishing Co.], n.d. 102 p. C H ... A L: 4th ed. 100 p.

202 BELK, John Blanton, 1893-1972.
A faith to move nations. n.p., [Moral Re-Armament], © 1969. 124 p. U

203 BELK, John Blanton, 1893-1972.
Our fighting faith. Richmond, John Knox Press, 1944. 89 p. A H PT U

204 BELL, Benjamin Charles, 1876-1940, comp.
Presbyterianism in north Louisiana to 1929 ... approved by the Presbytery of Red River, April 16th, 1930, in session at Alabama Church. [Shreveport, La., Presbyterian Board of Publications of the Synod of Louisiana, 1930]. 131 p. A C PT U

205 BELLINGRATH, George Council, 1897-1977.
Qualities associated with leadership in the extra-curricular activities of the high school. New York, Teachers College, Columbia University, 1930. 57 p. U

206 BENFIELD, William Avery, 1915-
A Bible study on the position of women in the church. [Atlanta, Board of Women's Work, Presbyterian Church in the U.S., 1963]. 15 p. U

207 BENFIELD, William Avery, 1915-
Youth entering into covenants, for parents. Richmond, CLC Press, © 1965. 48 p. (The Covenant Life Curriculum.) C U ... L: [1968].

208 BENSON, Clarence Herbert, 1879-1954.
The Christian teacher. Chicago, Moody Press, 1950.
288 p.   L R U

209 BENSON, Clarence Herbert, 1879-1954.
The church at work: practical methods for building up the
church and increasing its efficiency. Los Angeles, Bible Institute of Los Angeles, © 1929. 155 p.   C R U

210 BENSON, Clarence Herbert, 1879-1954.
The earth, the theater of the universe; a scientific and
scriptural study of the earth's place and purpose in the divine
program. Chicago, Bible Institute Colportage Ass'n., © 1929.
140 p.   R

211 BENSON, Clarence Herbert, 1879-1954.
The greatness and grace of God, conclusive evidence that
refutes evolution; arranged to be used as a textbook in Christian evidences. Chicago, Scripture Press, © 1953. 224 p.
R

212 BENSON, Clarence Herbert, 1879-1954.
A guide for Bible doctrine: the doctrines of God, Christ,
and the Holy Spirit. Wheaton, Ill., Evangelical Teacher Training Association, © 1949. 89 p.   R

213 BENSON, Clarence Herbert, 1879-1954.
A guide for Bible doctrine: the doctrines of salvation, in-
spiration, the church, angels, and last things. Wheaton, Ill.,
Evangelical Teacher Training Association, © 1949. 83 p.   R

214 BENSON, Clarence Herbert, 1879-1954.
A guide for Bible study. Unit I, Old Testament law and
history. Wheaton, Ill., Evangelical Teacher Training Association, [1956]. 81 p.   R ... A R: Unit II, Old Testament
poetry and prophecy. [1956]. 91 p.

215 BENSON, Clarence Herbert, 1879-1954.
A guide for child study. Wheaton, Ill., Evangelical Teacher Training Association, © 1950. 87 p.   R

216 BENSON, Clarence Herbert, 1879-1954.
Immensity; God's greatness seen in creation. Chicago, Van
Kampen Press, © 1937. 140 p.   R ... PT: Scripture Press.

217 BENSON, Clarence Herbert, 1879-1954.
An introduction to child study. Chicago, Bible Institute Colportage Ass'n., © 1927. 240 p.   L U ... C R: [Rev.] Chicago, Moody Press, © 1942.

218 BENSON, Clarence Herbert, 1879-1954.
Old Testament survey: poetry and prophecy (Job-Malachi).

Rev. ed. Wheaton, Ill., Evangelical Teacher Training Association, [1970]. 92 p. R

219 BENSON, Clarence Herbert, 1879-1954.
A popular history of Christian education. Chicago, Moody Press, © 1943. 355 p. A C L PT R U

220 BENSON, Clarence Herbert, 1879-1954.
The Sunday school in action. Chicago, Bible Institute Colportage Ass'n., © 1932. 327 p. A PT

221 BENSON, Clarence Herbert, 1879-1954.
Sunday school success. Wheaton, Ill., Evangelical Teacher Training Association, © 1958. 95 p. R

222 BENSON, Clarence Herbert, 1879-1954.
Techniques of a working church. Chicago, Moody Press, © 1946. 266 p. C L PT U

223 BENSON, Clarence Herbert, 1879-1954.
Understanding children and youth; an introductory study of human development. [4th ed.] Wheaton, Ill., Evangelical Teacher Training Association, [1969]. 93 p. R

224 BERRY, Robert Taylor, 1812-1877.
A discourse commemorative of the history of the Bridge Street Church, Georgetown, D.C., delivered September 8, 1848. Washington, J. and G. S. Gideon, 1848. 24 p. PH PT

225 BERRYVILLE, Va. Stone's Chapel Presbyterian Church.
Yearbook of the Berryville, Stone's Chapel, and Clearbrook Presbyterian churches. David Howard Scanlon, minister, Winchester Presbytery, 1905-1906. n.p., 1906. 22 p. U

226 BEVERIDGE, John, -1881 or '82.
The baptism of the soul.... Edited by H. F. Hoyt. Richmond, Whittet & Shepperson, 1884. 533 p. C H U

227 BEVERIDGE, John, -1881 or '82.
Typical character of the old and new dispensations.... Edited by H. F. Hoyt. Richmond, Whittet & Shepperson, 1883. 533 p. A C R U

228 BEVERLEY, James Andrew, 1929-
A history of the communion token, by James Andrew Beverley; and The story of the formation of the token collection located at the Austin Presbyterian Theological Seminary Library, related to Oliver Keith Rumbel. Austin, Tex., n.p., 1961. 20 p. A C H PH PT U

229 BEVERLY, Harry Black, 1934-
Harry Emerson Fosdick's Predigtweise, its significance

(for America), its limits, its overcoming. Winterthur, Switzerland, P. G. Keller, 1965. 108 p. A C PT

230 BIBLE. English. Authorized. 1917.
The Scofield reference Bible. The Holy Bible, containing the Old and New Testaments. Authorized Version, with a new system of connected topical references to all the greater themes of Scripture ... edited by C. I. Scofield. New York, Oxford University Press, 1909. 1362 p. H ... A C H PH PT U: © 1917 ... L: [1945] ... C H R: 1967. 1392, 192 p.

231 BIBLE. Luba. Selections. 1913.
Malesona a mu mukanda wa Nzambi. Akufundibua kudi Kuonyi Nxiba. New York, American Tract Society, © 1913. 532 p. Translated by W. M. Morrison. C U

232 BIBLE. O. T. Apocryphal books. Odes of Solomon. English. MarYosip. 1948.
The oldest Christian hymn-book [A.D. 100]. Introduction by Michael MarYosip. [Temple, Tex., Gresham's], © 1948. 92 p. A C L U

233 BIBLE. O. T. Jeremiah. English. Bright. 1964.
Jeremiah. Introduction, translation, and notes by John Bright. [1st ed.] Garden City, N.Y., Doubleday & Co., 1965. 372 p. (The Anchor Bible, 21.) A C L PT R U

234 BIBLE. O. T. Proverbs. English.
The God-centered life; the Proverbs of Solomon, topically arranged and briefly annotated, by Martin A. Hopkins. [Hong Kong, Local Printing Press, 195?]. 92 p. A PT

235 BIBLE. O. T. Proverbs. English. Miller. 1872.
A commentary on the Proverbs: with a new translation by John Miller. New York, Anson D. F. Randolph & Co., © 1872. 651 p. PT R U ... P: 2d ed. Princeton, N.J., Evangelical Reform Publishing Co., 1887.

236 BIBLE. N. T. English. Authorized. 1904.
The harmonized and subject reference New Testament, King James Version, made into a harmonized paragraph, local, topical, textual, and subject reference edition.... Arranged by James W. Shearer. Delaware, N.J., Subject Reference Co., 1904. 649 p. L U

237 BIBLE. N. T. English. Authorized. 1943.
The Testament for fishers of men; offering a simple and practical method for personal work, with selected passages to use in soul-winning. Richmond, John Knox Press, © 1943. 467 p. "Fishers of men, by Wade C. Smith": p. i-xxv. H

238 BIBLE. N. T. Luba-Lulua. Crane.
Dihungila Dihiadihia dia Mukelenge wetu ne Musungidi wetu

Jisu Kilisto. New York, American Bible Society, n.d. 314
p. Translation of the New Testament by Charles L. Crane.
H

239 BIBLE. N. T. Acts of the Apostles. Indian (Keres). 1936.
Jesus Christo ga-umatsityaimishi e-tsaaputyishi. Translation by H. Carroll Whitener. New York, American Bible Society, [1936]. 79 p. PT

240 BIBLE. N. T. I Corinthians. English. Orr-Walther. 1976.
I Corinthians: a new translation. Introduction, with a study
of the life of Paul, notes, and commentary by William F. Orr
and James Arthur Walther. [1st ed.] Garden City, N.Y.,
Doubleday & Co., 1976. 391 p. (The Anchor Bible, 32.)
A C L PT R U

241 BIBLE. N. T. John. Indian (Keres). 1935.
Jesus Christo niya tawa-mani: John Tsidyatrani: the Gos-
pel of John in Keres Indian. Translation by H. Carroll
Whitener. Albuquerque, N.M., n.p., 1935. 72 p. PT

242 BIBLE. N. T. Luke. English. Paraphrases. Taylor.
1955.
St. Luke's life of Jesus, retold in modern language by G.
Aiken Taylor. New York, The Macmillan Co., 1955. 161 p.
A C L R U

243 BIBLE. N. T. Matthew. Indian (Keres). 1933.
Jesus Christo niya tawa-mani: Matthew Tsidyatrani.
Translation by H. Carroll Whitener. New York, American
Bible Society, [1933]. 78 p. PT

244 BIBLE. N. T. Matthew. Selections. Indian (Zuni).
Christmas tewa ton ikyetsan'tu: Merry Christmas: Zuni
Indian. Translation by George Yff, H. Carroll Whitener,
Rex Natewa. n.p., 1940. unpaged. The Gospel of Matthew
I:1-23. PT

245 BIBLICAL studies: essays in honor of William Barclay. Edited by Johnston R. McKay and James F. Miller. Philadelphia, Westminster Press, © 1976. 223 p. A C L PH
R U ... PT U: London, Collins, 1976.

246 BIDDLE, Perry Harvey, 1932-
Abingdon funeral manual. Nashville, Abingdon Press,
© 1976. 254 p. A C H L PT U

247 BIDDLE, Perry Harvey, 1932-
Abingdon marriage manual. Nashville, Abingdon Press,
© 1974. 252 p. A C L PT U

248 *BIELER, André.
The social humanism of Calvin. Translated by Paul T.

Fuhrmann. Foreword by W. A. Visser't Hooft. Richmond, John Knox Press, © 1964. 79 p. Translation of "L'humanisme social de Calvin." A C H L PH PT R U

249 BIGGER, Eber Elam, 1848-1944.
Infant baptism; the Abrahamic covenant and the baptism of infants. Dublin, John T. Drought, n.d. 11 p. Reprinted from Christianity Today, 1938. PT

250 BILLMAN, James Bruce, 1922-1975.
Let's heat up the church. New York, Vantage Press, © 1975. 97 p. L

251 BININGER, Clem Edward, 1910-
The seven last words of Christ. Grand Rapids, Mich., Baker Book House, © 1969. 109 p. PT U

252 BISCEGLIA, John Baptist, 1891-
From Romanism to evangelical Christianity. Kansas City, Mo., n.p., 1945. 16 p. A paper read April 16, 1945, to an organization of Presbyterian ministers in Kansas City. U ... PT: [2d ed. 1949] 23 p.

253 BISCEGLIA, John Baptist, 1891-
Gratitude from the heart of America. Atlanta, Board of Church Extension, Presbyterian Church in the U.S., n.d. unpaged. H

254 BISCEGLIA, John Baptist, 1891-
Home missions, yesterday, today and tomorrow. Atlanta, Executive Committee of Home Missions, Presbyterian Church in the U.S., n.d. 12 p. Address delivered at Sunday morning worship in Montreat in August, 1938. H

255 BISCEGLIA, John Baptist, 1891-
Italian evangelical pioneers. Kansas City, Mo., Brown-White-Lowell Press, 1948. 143 p. A C H L PH PT U

256 BISCEGLIA, John Baptist, 1891-
The Italian mission in the heart of America; now Christ Presbyterian Church and Northeast Community Center. A report in stewardship during Dr. Bisceglia's ministry, June 1, 1918-May 31, 1965. n.p., n.d. 31 p. H

257 BISCEGLIA, John Baptist, 1891-
Italy's contribution to the Reformation. Richmond, Presbyterian Committee of Publication, © 1928. 76 p. A H L U

258 BISCEGLIA, John Baptist, 1891-
Our Protestant heritage: sermon. [Atlanta, Board of Church Extension, Presbyterian Church in the U.S., 1951]. 13 p. Delivered August 19, 1959, during the Conference on Church Extension at Montreat, N.C. H

259 BISCEGLIA, John Baptist, 1891-
A pilgrimage to the Italian mission.... Kansas City, Mo.
Atlanta, Executive Committee of Home Missions, Presbyterian
Church in the U.S., n.d. unpaged. H

260 BISCEGLIA, John Baptist, 1891-
Undiscovered neighbors. Atlanta, Executive Committee of
Home Missions, Presbyterian Church in the U.S., n.d. 12 p.
H

261 BLACK, Hubert Lorraine, 1913-
Good God! Cry or credo? Nashville, Abingdon Press,
© 1966. 144 p. PH

262 BLACKBURN, George Andrew, 1861-1918, ed.
The life work of John L. Girardeau, D.D., LL.D., late
professor in the Presbyterian Theological Seminary, Columbia,
S.C. Columbia, The State Co., 1916. 432 p. A C H L
PT R U

263 BLACKBURN, George Andrew, 1861-1918.
The tithe system: its practical working. n.p., n.d. 295-
300 p. Reprinted from Presbyterian Quarterly, April, 1890.
R

264 BLACKBURN, John Cavitt, 1889-1959.
Marah: bitter waters made sweet. [Atlanta, n.p., 1930].
88 p. C H

265 BLACKWOOD, Andrew Watterson, 1882-
Bible history: Genesis to Esther, popular studies in Old
Testament history. New York, Fleming H. Revell Co., © 1928.
183 p. L PT R U

266 BLACKWOOD, Andrew Watterson, 1882-
Biographical preaching for today: the pulpit use of Bible
cases. Nashville, Abingdon Press, © 1954. 224 p. A C L
PT R U

267 BLACKWOOD, Andrew Watterson, 1882-
Doctrinal preaching for today: case studies of Bible teachings. New York, Abingdon Press, © 1956. 224 p. A C L
PT R U ... PT: Grand Rapids, Mich., Baker Book House,
1975.

268 BLACKWOOD, Andrew Watterson, 1882- ed.
Evangelical sermons of our day; thirty-seven foremost examples of Bible preaching. New York, Harper & Brothers,
© 1959. 383 p. C H L PT R

269 BLACKWOOD, Andrew Watterson, 1882-
Evangelism in the home church. New York, Abingdon-
Cokesbury Press, © 1942. 160 p. A C L PH PT R U

270 BLACKWOOD, Andrew Watterson, 1882-
Expository preaching for today: case studies of Bible passages. Nashville, Abingdon-Cokesbury Press, © 1953. 224 p.
A C L PH PT R U

271 BLACKWOOD, Andrew Watterson, 1882-
The fine art of preaching. New York, The Macmillan Co., 1937. 168 p. A C L PH PT R U

272 BLACKWOOD, Andrew Watterson, 1882-
The fine art of public worship. Nashville, Cokesbury Press, © 1939. 247 p. A C H L PH PT R U

273 BLACKWOOD, Andrew Watterson, 1882-
The funeral, a sourcebook for ministers. Philadelphia, Westminster Press, © 1942. 253 p. A C L PT R U ... C: [1943].

274 BLACKWOOD, Andrew Watterson, 1882-
The growing minister: his opportunities and obstacles. New York, Abingdon Press, © 1960. 192 p. A C H L PT R U

275 BLACKWOOD, Andrew Watterson, 1882-
Leading in public prayer. New York, Abingdon Press, © 1958. 207 p. A C L PT R U

276 BLACKWOOD, Andrew Watterson, 1882-
Meeting God through Bible poets. Nashville, The Upper Room, © 1955. 30 p. C

277 BLACKWOOD, Andrew Watterson, 1882-
The memorial service: our tribute of honor. Philadelphia, Westminster Press, n.d. 8 p. Supplement to "The funeral."
C PT U

278 BLACKWOOD, Andrew Watterson, 1882-
Pastoral leadership. New York, Abingdon-Cokesbury Press, © 1949. 272 p. A C L PT R U

279 BLACKWOOD, Andrew Watterson, 1882-
Pastoral work: a source book for ministers. Philadelphia, Westminster Press, © 1945. 252 p. A C H L PH PT R U

280 BLACKWOOD, Andrew Watterson, 1882-
Planning a year's pulpit work. New York, Abingdon Press, © 1942. 240 p. A C H L PH PT R U

281 BLACKWOOD, Andrew Watterson, 1882-
Preaching from prophetic books. New York, Abingdon-Cokesbury Press, © 1951. 224 p. A L PH PT R U

282 BLACKWOOD, Andrew Watterson, 1882-

Preaching from Samuel. New York, Abingdon-Cokesbury
Press, © 1946. 256 p. A C L PT R U

283 BLACKWOOD, Andrew Watterson, 1882-
Preaching from the Bible. New York, Abingdon-Cokesbury
Press, © 1941. 247 p. A C H L PH PT R U

284 BLACKWOOD, Andrew Watterson, 1882-
Preaching in time of reconstruction. Great Neck, N.Y.,
Pulpit Press, 1945. 63 p. Thirteen biographical and critical
studies of great preachers of the past and present. A C PT
U

285 BLACKWOOD, Andrew Watterson, 1882-
La preparacion de sermones biblicos. El Paso, Casa
Bautista de Publicaciones, 1959. 254 p. A

286 BLACKWOOD, Andrew Watterson, 1882-
The preparation of sermons. New York, Abingdon-Cokesbury
Press, © 1948. 272 p. A C L PT R U ... U: [1st British
ed.] London, Church Book Room Press, [1951]. 298 p.

287 BLACKWOOD, Andrew Watterson, 1882-
The prophets, Elijah to Christ. New York, Fleming H.
Revell Co., © 1917. 232 p. A C H PT R U

288 BLACKWOOD, Andrew Watterson, 1882- comp.
The Protestant pulpit: an anthology of master sermons
from the Reformation to our own day. Nashville, Abingdon
Press, © 1947. 318 p. A C L PH PT R U

289 BLACKWOOD, Andrew Watterson, 1882-
Special-day sermons for evangelicals; thirty-eight represen-
tative examples of Bible preaching on red-letter days of the
Christian year and the calendar year. Great Neck, N.Y.,
Channel Press, © 1961. 448 p. Sermons by Cary N. Weisiger,
III, Ernest L. Stoffel, Wade P. Huie, Jr., William M. Elliott,
Jr., and others. A C L PT R U

290 BLACKWOOD, Andrew Watterson, 1882-
This year of our Lord: sermons for special occasions.
Philadelphia, Westminster Press, © 1943. 244 p. A C L
PT R U

291 BLACKWOOD, Andrew Watterson, 1882-
What does prayer accomplish? Nashville, Tenn., The Upper Room, © 1946. 29 p. U ... C PT U: [Rev. ed.],
© 1950. 31 p.

292 *BLACKWOOD, Carolyn Philips.
How to be an effective church woman. With an introduction
by Andrew W. Blackwood. Philadelphia, Westminster Press,
© 1955. 189 p. A C L PH PT R U

293 *BLACKWOOD, Carolyn Philips.
The pastor's wife. Introduction by Andrew W. Blackwood.
Philadelphia, Westminster Press, © 1951. 187 p.   A C L PH
PT R U

294 BLACKWOOD, James Russell, 1918-
The house on College avenue; the Comptons at Wooster,
1891-1913. Cambridge, Mass., M. I. T. Press, © 1968.
265 p.   H PH

295 BLACKWOOD, James Russell, 1918-
Howard Lowry, a life in education. [Wooster, Ohio], College of Wooster, 1975. 357 p.   PH PT

296 BLACKWOOD, James Russell, 1918-
The soul of Frederick W. Robertson, the Brighton preach-
er ... with an introduction by Andrew Watterson Blackwood,
Sr. New York, Harper & Brothers, © 1947. 201 p.   A C
L PT R U

297 BLAIN, John Mercer, 1869-1932.
Kashing Presbyterian High School (Axson Memorial), Southern Presbyterian mission, Kashing, China. Shanghai, Presbyterian Mission Press, 1904. 17 p.   [In English and Chinese.]
U

298 BLAIN, Robert Waller, 1879-1962.
A real advance in Sunday School extension. Richmond,
Presbyterian Committee of Publication, n.d.   8 p.   U

299 BLAKELY, Hunter Bryson, 1894-1970.
Defending the bulwarks. Richmond, John Knox Press, 1942.
78 p.   A C H L PT R U

300 BLAKELY, Hunter Bryson, 1894-1970.
Facing life's questions. New York, Fleming H. Revell Co.,
© 1938. 192 p.   A C H PT U

301 BLAKELY, Hunter Bryson, 1894-1970.
The glory of clean speech. Richmond, Committee of Religious Education and Publication, n.d.   11 p.   PT U

302 BLAKELY, Hunter Bryson, 1894-1970.
I wager on God. Richmond, John Knox Press, © 1956.
207 p.   A C H L PT R U

303 BLAKELY, Hunter Bryson, 1894-1970.
A plea for abstinence. Richmond, Committee of Religious
Education and Publication, n.d.   12 p.   PT U

304 BLAKELY, Hunter Bryson, 1894-1970.
Religion in shoes; or, Brother Bryan of Birmingham. With
an introduction by Benjamin R. Lacy. Richmond, Presbyterian

Committee of Publication, 1934. 186 p. A C H L PT R
U ... A C H L R U: [Rev. ed.] Richmond, John Knox
Press, © 1953. 188 p. ... L: [1956] ... A C H L PT U:
Prayer point ed. Birmingham, Ala., Birmingham Publishing
Co., © 1967. 190 p.

305 BLAKELY, Hunter Bryson, 1894-1970.
With Christ into tomorrow. Richmond, Presbyterian Committee of Publication, 1936. 160 p. A C H L PT R U

306 BLANTON, Lindsay Hughes, 1832-1914.
Consolidation of Central University and Centre College at
Danville, Ky., under the title of Central University of Ken-
tucky. An address at a public meeting at Richmond, Kentucky,
on April 10, 1901. [Louisville, Ky.], Courier-Journal Job
Printing Co., 1901. 20 p. PT

307 BLANTON, Lindsay Hughes, 1832-1914.
A memorial discourse, preached in the Presbyterian Church,
Paris, Kentucky, January 1st, 1871. Paris, Ky., Western
Citizen, McChesney & Fisher, 1871. 17 p. PH

308 BLANTON, Lindsay Hughes, 1832-1914.
Memorial: Thomas A. Bracken, D.D. Born August 14,
1820. Died April 22, 1902. 2d ed. n.p., [1902]. 52 p.
H PT U

309 BLUFORD, Robert, 1918-
Unwanted pregnancy; the medical and ethical implications
[by] Robert Bluford and Robert E. Petres. [1st ed.] New
York, Harper & Row, © 1973. 116 p. A H L U

310 BOCOCK, John Holmes, 1813-1872.
An address; delivered before the society of alumni of the
Union Theological Seminary, Prince Edward, Virginia, at the
annual commencement, June 13th, 1848. New York, Cady,
Palmer & Co., 1848. 12 p. PH PT

311 BOCOCK, John Holmes, 1813-1872.
The church in the scriptures. A discourse delivered in
the Bridge Street Church, Georgetown, D.C. ... October 30,
1858. Philadelphia, Joseph M. Wilson, 1859. 38 p. U

312 BOCOCK, John Holmes, 1813-1872, comp.
God's word to inquirers. Philadelphia, Presbyterian Board
of Publication, © 1956. 56 p. C PH PT U

313 BOCOCK, John Holmes, 1813-1872.
Response to Bishop Potter, in relation to the designs of
the recent Episcopal memorial papers. Philadelphia, Joseph
M. Wilson, 1858. 16 p. PT

314 BOCOCK, John Holmes, 1813-1872.

Selections from the religious and literary writings ... with
a biographical sketch by C. R. Vaughan. Edited by his widow.
Richmond, Whittet & Shepperson, 1891. 644 p. A C H L
R U

315 BOCOCK, John Holmes, 1813-1872.
Spiritual religion and ceremonial contrasted. Being the substance of a discourse delivered in the Presbyterian Church at
Barboursville, Va., Nov. 13, 1852. Richmond, H. K. Ellyson, 1852. 29 p. PT

316 BOCOCK, John Holmes, 1813-1872.
Why I love my church. [Philadelphia, Presbyterian Board
of Publication and Sabbath-school Work], n.d. 6 p. (Presbyterian Tracts, no. 242.) H PH PT R U

317 BOEHME, Harry, 1889-
Can the Fundamentalists lose? A sermon preached at the
Black Mountain, N.C., Presbyterian Church, July 30th, 1922.
n.p., n.d. 10 p. A

318 BOEHME, Harry, 1889-
The Resurrection. A sermon preached April 1, 1923, at
the Black Mountain, N.C., Presbyterian Church. n.p., n.d.
12 p. A

319 BOEHME, Harry, 1889-
Women of the Bible. Richmond, Presbyterian Committee
of Publication, © 1922. 94 p. A L U

320 BOGGS, Marion A., 1894-
Second Presbyterian Church, Little Rock, Ark., 1882-1957;
a short history covering the 75 years of service. n.p. [1957].
unpaged. A

321 BOGGS, Marion A., 1894-
What does God require--in race relations? Richmond, CLC
Press, © 1964. 48 p. (The Covenant Life Curriculum) C
L U

322 BOGGS, Wade Hamilton, 1883-
Inspiring Christian education in the home. [Louisville, Ky.,
Presbyterian Educational Association of the South], n.d. 4 p.
U

323 BOGGS, Wade Hamilton, 1916-
All ye who labor: a Christian interpretation of daily work.
Richmond, John Knox Press, © 1961. 288 p. A C H L PT
R U ... U: Leader's guide. 42 p.

324 BOGGS, Wade Hamilton, 1916-
Faith healing and the Christian faith. Richmond, John Knox
Press, © 1956. 216 p. A C H L PH PT R U

325 BOGGS, William Ellison, 1838-1920.
   The "elect infant clause" and the overture from the Presbytery of Suwannee. n.p., [1908]. 29 p.   U

326 BOGGS, William Ellison, 1838-1920.
   The New Testament law of marriage and divorce. 2d ed., rev. and enl. [Spartanburg, S.C., Band & White], n.d. 58 p. H PH U

327 BOGGS, William Ellison, 1838-1920.
   Spiritism and the Bible. Columbia, S.C., Presbyterian Publishing House, 1872. 44 p. Republished from the Southern Presbyterian Review, October, 1872.   PH

328 BOLLING, Richard Asa, 1890-1971.
   The Presbyterian Church in Mississippi since 1861. n.p., n.d. 16 p.   C PT

329 BONEY, William Jerry, 1930-1981, ed.
   The new day; Catholic theologians of the renewal. Edited by Wm. Jerry Boney and Lawrence E. Molumby. Richmond, John Knox Press, © 1968. 142 p. Chapters by Wm. Jerry Boney, Ross Mackenzie, Patrick D. Miller, Jr., and others. A C H L PT U

330 BONNER, William Jones, 1882-
   In time of sorrow, a funeral manual. Grand Rapids, Mich., Zondervan Publishing House, © 1942. 140 p.   L

331 BOOKER, James Edward, 1850-1940.
   Home missions! with a few side lights. 2d ed., rev. n.p., n.d. 24 p.   U

332 BOSCH, F. W. Archibald, 1891-1955.
   The Epistle to the Hebrews in outline. Springfield, Mo., Biblia Press, © 1932. 20 p.   U

333 BOSCH, F. W. Archibald, 1891-1955.
   The Gospel of Mark in outline. Springfield, Mo., Biblia Press, © 1934. 32 p.   A

334 BOSCH, F. W. Archibald, 1891-1955.
   Through the book of Acts with a guide. Richmond, Onward Press, 1931. 81 p.   A H R U ... H: Springfield, Mo., Biblia Press.

335 BOTTOMS, Lawrence Wendell, 1908-
   Ecclesiastes speaks to us today. Atlanta, John Knox Press, © 1979. 109 p.   A C L PT R

336 BOTTOMS, Lawrence Wendell, 1908-
   Through conflict to victory; a study in Revelation. Atlanta,

Board of Women's Work, Presbyterian Church in the U.S.,
[1957?]. 46 p. A C U

337 BOWEN, Littleton Purnell, 1833-1933.
The borderland; an idyll of Ridge Park. Kansas City,
Hudson-Kimberly Publishing Co., 1901. 104 p. H U

338 BOWEN, Littleton Purnell, 1833-1933.
A daughter of the covenant: a tale of Louisiana. Rich-
mond, Presbyterian Committee of Publication, © 1901. 281 p.
A H R U

339 BOWEN, Littleton Purnell, 1833-1933.
The days of Makemie; or, The vine planted. A. D. 1680-
1708. Philadelphia, Presbyterian Board of Publication, © 1885.
558 p. A C H L PH R U

340 BOWEN, Littleton Purnell, 1833-1933.
Francis Makemie pageant. n.p., n.d. 19 p. PH U

341 BOWEN, Littleton Purnell, 1833-1933.
Makemieland memorials; with eastern shore wild flowers
and other wild things. Richmond, Whittet & Shepperson,
[1910]. 205 p. PH U

342 BOWEN, Littleton Purnell, 1833-1933.
Makemie's message. Opening sermon of the Presbytery of
New Castle. Preached in the Makemie Memorial Presbyterian
Church, Snow Hill, Md., April 18th, 1911. Wilmington, Del.,
Hubert A. Roop, 1911. 21 p. PH

343 BOWEN, Littleton Purnell, 1833-1933.
Message of the monument. Address ... at the dedication
of the memorial to Colonel John Postley. At Berlin, Maryland, December the third, nineteen hundred and nine. Snow
Hill, Md., Vincent & White, 1909. 12 p. PH

344 BOWEN, Littleton Purnell, 1833-1933.
Mother Rehoboth renewing her youth. n.p., n.d. unpaged.
A poem for the two hundred and fiftieth anniversary celebra-
tion, Rehoboth, Md., October 4, 1933. PH

345 BOWEN, Littleton Purnell, 1833-1933.
The old preacher's story; or, Portraits from life framed
for future use. St. Louis, Presbyterian Publishing Co., 1879.
628 p. A R U ... H: Richmond, Presbyterian Publishing
Co., 1882.

346 BOWEN, Littleton Purnell, 1833-1933.
Souvenir of Makemie Park. Richmond, Whittet & Shepperson, 1916. 18 p. PH

347 BOWEN, Littleton Purnell, 1833-1933.

Trust and do; a sermon that went to rhyme. Richmond, Whittet & Shepperson, 1917. unpaged. PH

348 BOWEN, Littleton Purnell, 1833-1933.
What we believe. Richmond, Presbyterian Publishing Co., 1881. 11 p. U ... U: n.d. 16 p. ... PT U: [Author's rev. ed.] St. Louis, Farris, Smith & Co., 1884. 15 p. ... C: St. Louis, St. Louis Presbyterian, 1894 ... PH U: Richmond, Presbyterian Committee of Publication, n.d.

349 BOWMAN, Benjamin Lowry, 1896-1964.
Transport chaplain; a chronological history of a chaplain in World War II. [Sarasota, Fla., Star Printing Co., 1947]. 145 p. U

350 BOYD, Andrew Hunter Holmes, 1814-1865.
Thanksgiving sermon, delivered in Winchester, Va., on Thursday, 29th November, 1860. [Winchester], Winchester Virginian, 1860. 20 p. PH

351 BOYD, John Hardgrove, 1861-1922.
The Bible, in its relation to education. n.p., n.d. 18 p. PT

352 BOYD, Robert Frederick, 1908-
The Bible and the church. [Richmond, Printed by the author, 1963]. 18 p. C U

353 BOYD, William Joseph, 1908-1977.
A minister speaks. n.p., n.d. 61 p. Appeared in the Saturday issues of the State Gazette, in November, 1957. C

354 BOYER, Elmer Timothy, 1893-
To build him a house: missionary memories. Norfolk, Va., Posung Press, 1976. 206 p. C H L U

355 BOYER, Jonas William, 1890-1947.
God's contact man, a story of pastoral evangelism. Kansas City, Kan., Central Seminary Press, 1945. 165 p. C H L U

356 BOYER, Jonas William, 1890-1947.
The print of the nails: communion meditations. Fulton, Mo., n.p., © 1947. 159 p. L

357 BOYLE, John, 1845-1892.
Foreign evangelists and native ministers. Brazil, Leroy King Bookwalter and Co., 1884. 19 p. U

358 BRACKETT, Gilbert Robbins, 1833-1902.
Charity never faileth: a memorial address ... on the occasion of the laying the cornerstone of the Memorial Hall,

Thornwell Orphanage. Clinton, S.C., Thornwell Orphanage
Press, 1888. 9 p.   U

359   BRACKETT, Gilbert Robbins, 1833-1902.
      The Christian warrior crowned. A discourse commemora-
      tive of the life, character and labors of the Rev. Thos. Smyth.
      Delivered in the Second Presbyterian Church, Charleston,
      S.C., December 14, 1873. [Charleston, Walker, Evans &
      Cogswell, 1874]. 63 p.   C H PT U

360   BRACKETT, Gilbert Robbins, 1833-1902.
      The connection between the laborers of present and past
      generations; and between the labors of earth and the rewards
      of heaven. Two discourses delivered in the Second Presby-
      terian Church, Charleston, So. Ca., on the occasion of its
      sixty-seventh anniversary, May 19, 1878. Charleston, S.C.,
      Lucas & Richardson, 1878. 29 p.   H

361   BRACKETT, Gilbert Robbins, 1833-1902.
      Manual for the use of the members of the Second Presby-
      terian Church, Charleston, S.C. Charleston, Walker, Evans
      & Cogswell, 1894. 128 p.   C H PT R U

362   BRACKETT, Gilbert Robbins, 1833-1902.
      A sermon in memory of the late Caleb N. Averill, de-
      livered in the Second Presbyterian Church, Charleston, S.C.,
      July 22nd, 1900. n.p., n.d. 16 p.   H

363   *BRADFORD, Amory H.
      The life and character of William Finney Junkin, D.D.,
      LL.D. Memorial address ... April 13, 1900. Lynchburg,
      Va., J. P. Bell Co., 1900. 8 p.   H ... H: 12 p.

364   BRADLEY, Samuel Hugh, 1902-1963.
      Thieves in the church. Atlanta, Committee on Steward-
      ship, Presbyterian Church in the U.S., [1945]. unpaged   PH

365   BRANCH, Harold Francis, 1894-
      Christ's ministry and passion in art; inspiring and instruc-
      tive sermons on the world's religious masterpieces. Brief
      biographical sketches of the artists, the technique of the pic-
      tures, how they came to be painted and the great spiritual
      lessons they teach. Philadelphia, Harvey M. Shelley, © 1929.
      176 p.   A H L PH R

366   BRANCH, Harold Francis, 1894-
      Religious picture sermons; the gospel messages of fifteen
      world-famous religious masterpieces. Philadelphia, Harvey
      M. Shelley, © 1934. 233 p.   A H L R U

367   BRANCH, Harold Francis, 1894-
      Sermons on great paintings; the spiritual messages of

fifteen of the world's great religious masterpieces. Philadelphia, Harvey M. Shelley, © 1930. 237 p. A H L PH R

368 BRANCH, Harold Francis, 1894-
The trial of Jesus. Chicago, Bible Institute Colportage Ass'n., © 1924. 31 p. H PH PT U

369 BRANK, Robert Garland, 1824-1895.
The moral law summed up. Bellefonte, Pa., n.p., n.d. 8 p. PT

370 BRANK, Rockwell Smith, 1875-1947.
Bethel, a sermon. Summit, N.J., n.p., 1937. 6 p. PT

371 BRANK, Rockwell Smith, 1875-1947.
Family prayers ... a sermon. Summit, N.J., n.p. [192?]. unpaged. PT

372 BRANK, Rockwell Smith, 1875-1947.
The weapons of Christian warfare. [Summit, N.J., n.p., 1925]. unpaged. PT

373 BRECK, Robert Levi, 1827-1915.
The claims of the English tongue upon the educated men of our country. An address before the Alumni Association of Centre College; delivered at Danville, Ky., June 28, 1862. Cincinnati, Jos. B. Boyd's Job Power-press, 1863. 24 p. PH

374 BRECK, Robert Levi, 1827-1915.
Some objections to the Episcopal Church reconsidered and others stated. Baltimore, Mills & Cox, 1855. 57 p. PT

375 *BRIDGE, Robert T.
"Mr. Standfast." A sermon by the ... assistant minister of the New York Avenue Presbyterian Church, Washington, D.C., on January 30, 1949. In memory of the Reverend Peter Marshall, D.D., minister of the church, who was called to higher service January 25, 1949. n.p., © 1949. 11 p. PH

376 BRIDGES, John Carl, 1895-1961.
Antichrist's coming one world. n.p., © 1955. 136 p. U

377 BRIGHT, John, 1908-
The age of King David: a study in the institutional history of Israel. n.p., n.d. 24 p. Reprinted from Union Seminary Review, February, 1942. U

378 BRIGHT, John, 1908-
Altisrael in der neueren Geschichtsschreibung; eine methodologische Studie. Zurich, Zwingli Verlag, 1961. 139 p. Translation of "Early Israel in recent history writing." L PT U

379 BRIGHT, John, 1908-
The authority of the Old Testament. Nashville, Abingdon
Press, © 1967. 272 p. Lectures on the James A. Gray
Fund of the Divinity School of Duke University, Durham, North
Carolina. A L U ... C PT R: London, SCM Press [1967].

380 BRIGHT, John, 1908-
Biblical authority and Biblical theology. [Chester, Pa.,
Crozer Theological Seminary, 1954]. 24 p. U

381 BRIGHT, John, 1908-
Covenant and promise: the prophetic understanding of the
future in pre-exilic Israel. Philadelphia, Westminster Press,
© 1976. 207 p. A C L PH PT R U

382 BRIGHT, John, 1908-
The date of Ezra's mission to Jerusalem. [Jerusalem,
Magnes Press, 1960]. 70-87 p. Reprinted from Yehezkel
Kaufmann Jubilee volume. U

383 BRIGHT, John, 1908-
The date of the prose sermons of Jeremiah. [Philadelphia,
Society of Biblical Literature and Exegesis, 1951]. 15-35 p.
Reprinted from Journal of Biblical Literature, vol. LXX,
part I, 1951. U

384 BRIGHT, John, 1908-
Early Israel in recent history writing: a study in method.
Chicago, Alec R. Allenson, [1956]. 128 p. A C L ... PT
L R U: London, SCM Press.

385 BRIGHT, John, 1908-
Hananim. [Seoul, Korea, Concordia Press], © 1953.
386 p. Translation into Korean of "The Kingdom of God."
U

386 BRIGHT, John, 1908-
La historia de Israel. Bilbao, Desclee de Brouwer, [1966].
524 p. Translation into Spanish of "A history of Israel."
U ... U: 2. ed. [1970].

387 BRIGHT, John, 1908-
A history of Israel. Philadelphia, Westminster Press,
© 1959. 500 p. A C L PT U ... A C L PT R U: 2d ed.
© 1972. 519 p. ... PH: [1975].

388 BRIGHT, John, 1908-
[Isuraerushi, translated and published from A history of
Israel. Tokyo, Seibunsha, 1968]. 375 p. Title-page and
text in Japanese. U

389 BRIGHT, John, 1908-

The Kingdom of God: the Biblical concept and its meaning for the church. New York, Abingdon-Cokesbury Press, © 1953. 288 p.   A C H L PT R U ... U: The Kingdom of God in Bible and church. London, Lutterworth Press [1955]. 292 p.

390   BRIGHT, John, 1908-
Le royaume de Dieu; la conception biblique et sa significa-tion pour l'Eglise. [Paris, La Société Centrale d'Evangelisa-tion] n.d. 209 p. Translation of "The Kingdom of God."
U

391   BRIMM, Daniel Johnson, 1862-1948.
Evolution versus the Bible: fundamentalist position. [Clin-ton, S.C., Chronicle Publishing Co., 1925]. 16 p.   U

392   BRIMM, Daniel Johnson, 1862-1948.
A syllabus of notes and questions for the study of New Tes-tament history. Ann Arbor, Mich., Edwards Brothers, 1936. 253 p.   C U

393   BRIMM, Daniel Johnson, 1862-1948.
A syllabus of notes and questions for the study of Old Testa-ment history. Ann Arbor, Mich., Edwards Brothers, 1936. 118 ℓ.   U

394   BRIMM, William Waldo, 1837-1915.
Man and the Bible in the light of reason. Atlanta, Frank-lin Printing and Publishing Co., 1894. 251 p.   C H R U

395   BROOKES, James Hall, 1830-1897.
Argument ... delivered before the General Assembly of the Presbyterian Church in the United States, on the 31st of May, 1866, in defence of the Louisville Presbytery. St. Louis, George Knapp & Co., 1866. 19 p.   PT U

396   BROOKES, James Hall, 1830-1897.
Bible reading on the second coming of Christ. n.p., n.d. 10 p.   PT

397   BROOKES, James Hall, 1830-1897.
Chaff and wheat. A defense of verbal inspiration. New York, Fleming H. Revell Co., © 1891. 46 p.   PT R

398   BROOKES, James Hall, 1830-1897.
The Christ. New York, Fleming H. Revell Co., © 1893. 287 p.   H ... R: London, Alfred Holness, [1893].

399   BROOKES, James Hall, 1830-1897.
Did Jesus rise? A fearless facing of the vital fact of Christianity. London, Pickering & Inglis, n.d. 126 p.   L
R ... L: St. Louis, Gospel Book and Tract Depository, n.d. 151 p.

400 BROOKES, James Hall, 1830-1897.
From death unto life; or, The sinner saved. St. Louis,
Gospel Book and Tract Depository, n.d. 132 p. H L R ...
PH: St. Louis, Stephen Paxson ... PT: Chicago, Bible In-
stitute Colportage Ass'n.

401 BROOKES, James Hall, 1830-1897.
God spake all these words. St. Louis, J. T. Smith, © 1895.
152 p. C H U ... L R: Glasgow, Pickering & Inglis, n.d.
154 p.

402 BROOKES, James Hall, 1830-1897, comp.
Gospel hymns. St. Louis, Old School Presbyterian, 1871.
738 p. PH PT

403 BROOKES, James Hall, 1830-1897.
He is not here: the resurrection of Christ. Philadelphia,
Presbyterian Board of Publication and Sabbath-school work,
1896. 170 p. PH PT U

404 BROOKES, James Hall, 1830-1897.
The Holy Spirit. St. Louis, Gospel Book and Tract Depository, n.d. 95 p. H

405 BROOKES, James Hall, 1830-1897.
How far is the Bible inspired? Toronto, Canada, S. R.
Briggs, n.d. 66 p. PT

406 BROOKES, James Hall, 1830-1897.
How to be saved; or, The sinner directed to the Saviour.
Chicago, Fleming H. Revell Co., © 1864. 126 p. PT

407 BROOKES, James Hall, 1830-1897.
How to use the Bible. St. Louis, Edward Bredell, n.d.
46 p. PT U

408 BROOKES, James Hall, 1830-1897.
"I am coming." A setting forth of the second coming of
our Lord Jesus Christ as personal--private--premillennial.
5th ed., rev. London, J. E. Hawkins, [1895]. 175 p.
R ... H L: 7th ed., rev. Glasgow, Pickering & Inglis, n.d.

409 BROOKES, James Hall, 1830-1897.
Is the Bible inspired? Chicago, Gospel Publishing Co.,
n.d. 124 p. R ... PT: St. Louis, Gospel Book and Tract
Depository, n.d. 128 p.

410 BROOKES, James Hall, 1830-1897.
Is the Bible true? Seven addresses. 2d ed. St. Louis,
Chas. B. Cox, [1877]. 237 p. PT R U ... H: 3d ed.

411 BROOKES, James Hall, 1830-1897.

Israel and the church, the terms distinguished as found in the word of God. Chicago, Bible Institute Colportage Ass'n., n.d. 199 p. C H R

412 BROOKES, James Hall, 1830-1897.
Life through the living one. London, Hodder and Stoughton, 1891. 112 p. R

413 BROOKES, James Hall, 1830-1897.
Maranatha: or the Lord cometh. 5th ed. St. Louis, Edward Bredell, [1878]. 545 p. PT ... H: 6th ed. ... R U: New York, Fleming H. Revell Co., [1889]. 554 p.

414 BROOKES, James Hall, 1830-1897.
May Christians dance? Chicago, Fleming H. Revell Co., © 1869. 143 p. H R U ... PH: St. Louis, J. W. McIntyre, 1869. ... PT: 1874.

415 BROOKES, James Hall, 1830-1897.
A memorial sermon, delivered on the twenty-fifth anniversary of the organization of the Second Presbyterian Church, St. Louis, October 11th, 1863. St. Louis, Sherman Spencer, 1864. 23 p. PT

416 BROOKES, James Hall, 1830-1897.
The mystery of suffering. New York, Fleming H. Revell Co., © 1890. 155 p. L ... C H L R: 4th ed. © 1893. 167 p. ... H: © 1923 ... R: Findlay, Ohio, Dunham, n.d. 111 p.

417 BROOKES, James Hall, 1830-1897.
An outline of the books of the Bible. New York, Fleming H. Revell Co., n.d. 179 p. U ... H PH: St. Louis, Gospel Book and Tract Depository, n.d. ... PT: Chicago, Gospel Publishing Co., n.d.

418 BROOKES, James Hall, 1830-1897.
Present truth: being the testimony of the Holy Ghost on the second coming of the Lord, the divinity of Christ and the personality of the Holy Ghost. Springfield, Ill., Edwin A. Wilson, 1877. 236 p. PT

419 BROOKES, James Hall, 1830-1897.
Subjection to civil rulers: the Christian's duty. A fast-day sermon: preached Thursday, April 30th, 1863, in the Second Presbyterian Church, St. Louis. St. Louis, Sherman Spencer, 1863. 16 p. C PT

420 BROOKES, James Hall, 1830-1897.
Till he cometh. Chicago, Gospel Publishing Co., © 1891. 160 p. R ... U: 3d ed., rev. New York, Fleming H. Revell Co., © 1895. 172 p.

421 BROOKES, James Hall, 1830-1897.
Twenty-five years in the Master's service. St. Louis, Bux-
ton & Skinner Stationery Co., 1883. 16 p. U

422 BROOKES, James Hall, 1830-1897.
The way made plain. Philadelphia, American Sunday-school
Union, © 1871. 490 p. H PT ... R U: n.d. 305 p. ...
L R: Grand Rapids, Mich., Baker Book House, [1967].

423 BROOMALL, Wick, 1902-
The anti-Christ: a brief scripture study of the coming satan-
inspired world dictator. n.p., n.d. 15 p. C

424 BROOMALL, Wick, 1902-
The apostasy: a study of the scripture doctrine of apostasy
and the apostasy of the last days. n.p., n.d. 16 p. C

425 BROOMALL, Wick, 1902-
Biblical criticism. Grand Rapids, Mich., Zondervan Publishing House, © 1957. 320 p. C H L PT R U

426 BROOMALL, Wick, 1902-
The Holy Spirit: a scriptural study of his person and work.
New York, American Tract Society, © 1940. 207 p. A R
U ... C H PT R: Grand Rapids, Mich., Baker Book House,
1963. 211 p.

427 *BROWDER, Edward M.
A pioneer Presbyterian preacher in Texas: the Rev. Hugh
Wilson, D.D. Dallas, Tex., Texas Presbyterian, 1916. 8 p.
Reprinted from the Texas Presbyterian, January, 1916. H
PH PT U

428 *BROWDER, Edward M.
Rev. Peter H. Fullinwider, the first Presbyterian minister
to visit and preach in Texas. Dallas, Tex., Texas Presbyterian, 1916. 8 p. Reprinted from the Texas Presbyterian,
August, 1916. H PT PT

429 BROWN, Aubrey Neblett, 1908-
Credible discipleship in a world of affluence and poverty.
[Richmond, Outlook Publishers, 1979]. 11 p. PH

430 BROWN, Frank Augustus, 1876-1967.
Charlotte Brown, a mother in China. The story of the
work of Charlotte Thompson Brown in China from 1909-1949.
[Carville? La., 1953]. 100 p. A C H L PH R U

431 BROWN, Frank Augustus, 1876-1967.
He made it his ambition. The story of William F. Junkin.
[Nashville, Tenn., Executive Committee of Foreign Missions,
Presbyterian Church in the U.S., 1947]. 14 p. PH ... PH:
1949.

432 BROWN, Frank Augustus, 1876-1967.
Heroism on the mission field; lest we forget. n.p., n.d.
11 p. Reprinted from the Christian Observer, October 3,
1956. U

433 BROWN, Frank Augustus, 1876-1967.
The last hundred days: a diary ... Shanghai, 1949. [Nash-
ville, Tenn., Board of World Missions, Presbyterian Church
in the U.S.], n.d. 18 p. C PH U

434 BROWN, Frank Augustus, 1876-1967.
The last of the eight thousand: will the church in China
survive? A look at the church and our former mission work
in Communist China. [Norfolk, Va., F. A. Brown, 1962].
20 p. C PH U

435 BROWN, Frank Augustus, 1876-1967.
Norfolk remembers ... carrying Christ to Africa. The one
hundred and twenty-fifth anniversary celebration of the sailing
of the missionary pioneers, to be commemorated in Norfolk,
March 9-16, 1958. [Norfolk, Va.? 1958]. 31 p. C

436 BROWN, Frank Chilton, 1890-1955.
Lost! A human soul. A handbook for the study of per-
sonal evangelism. Richmond, Presbyterian Committee of
Publication, 1932. 64 p. A C H U

437 BROWN, Frank Chilton, 1890-1955.
Making disciples; a sermon ... delivered at Montreat
Leadership School, July 28, 1940. [Richmond, Executive
Committee of Religious Education and Publication, Presby-
terian Church in the U.S.], n.d. 14 p. C U

438 BROWN, George Thompson, 1921-
Mission to Korea. [Nashville, Tenn.], Board of World
Missions, Presbyterian Church in the U.S., © 1962. 252 p.
"Adapted from ... doctoral thesis to Union Theological Semi-
nary in Richmond." C H PT R U

439 BROWN, Henry, 1804-1881.
Arminian inconsistencies and errors: in which it is shown
that all the distinctive doctrines of the Presbyterian Confession
of Faith are taught by standard writers of the Methodist Episcopal Church. Philadelphia, William S. & Alfred Martien,
1856. 430 p. C H L PH PT R U ... PH: 1857.

440 BROWN, Henry, 1804-1881.
Christian baptism tested by the Scriptures. In two parts:
Part I, The mode of baptism; Part II, Infant baptism. Richmond, Presbyterian Committee of Publication, © 1869. 92,
63 p. Issued also under the title, The mode of baptism tested
by the Scriptures. A C H PT U

441 BROWN, Henry, 1804-1881.
Infant baptism tested by the Scriptures. Richmond, Presbyterian Committee of Publication, © 1868. 63 p. C PH U

442 BROWN, Henry, 1804-1881.
The mode of baptism tested by the Scriptures. In two parts: Part I, The mode of baptism; Part II, Infant baptism tested by the Scriptures. Richmond, Presbyterian Committee of Publication, © 1868. 92, 63 p. Issued also under the title, Christian baptism tested by the Scriptures. C H PT R U ... PH: © 1869.

443 BROWN, James Moore, 1799-1862.
The captives of Abb's valley, a legend of frontier life. Philadelphia, Presbyterian Board of Publication, © 1854. 168 p. H ... A H: Richmond, Presbyterian Committee of Publication, 1927 ... A H L PH U: New ed., with introduction ... by Robert Bell Woodworth. Staunton, Va., McClure Co., 1942. 94, 254 p.

444 BROWN, Milton Perry, 1928-
The authentic writings of Ignatius; a study of linguistic criteria. Durham, N.C., Duke University Press, 1963. 159 p. A C L PT R U

445 BROWNE, Earl Zollicoffer, 1892-
Let's return to the Mosaic authorship of the Pentateuch. [1st ed.] New York, Greenwich Book Publishers, © 1962. 131 p. C R U

446 BROWNE, Fred Zollicoffer, 1878-1975.
An answer to statements made in open letters and published articles by Hay Watson Smith. Texarkana, Lynn-Helms, [1928]. 25 p. U

447 BROWNE, Fred Zollicoffer, 1878-1975.
Feminism, or woman suffrage in the light of Holy Scripture. New York, Charles C. Cook, © 1917. 40 p. C

448 BROWNE, Fred Zollicoffer, 1878-1975.
Visible glory. [1st ed.] New York, Greenwich Book Publishers, © 1957. 133 p. A C L R U

449 BROWNLEE, Edwin Darnall, 1884-1963.
Three-minute morning watches with Jesus. Richmond, Presbyterian Committee of Publication, n.d. 4 p. U

450 BRYAN, William Swan Plumer, 1856-1925.
... Between the death and the resurrection of our Lord: a review of "The glory after the passion" by James S. Stone. n.p., n.d. 10 p. At head of title: "He descended into hell." Reprinted from the Princeton Theological Review, October, 1913. U

451 BRYAN, William Swan Plumer, 1856-1925.
Do we understand Jesus Christ? A sermon preached in
the Church of the Covenant, Chicago. Chicago, Kramer Press,
n.d. 23 p. PH PT

452 BRYAN, William Swan Plumer, 1856-1925.
The General Presbyterian Council. Richmond, Whittet &
Shepperson, 1892. 16 p. PH

453 BRYAN, William Swan Plumer, 1856-1925.
An inquiry into our need of the grace of God. Richmond,
Presbyterian Committee of Publication, 1937. 274 p. (The
Smyth lectures, 1917.) A C R U

454 BRYAN, William Swan Plumer, 1856-1925.
Prayer and the healing of disease. Philadelphia, Westminster Press, 1899. 56 p. H R ... PT: microfilm

455 BRYAN, William Swan Plumer, 1856-1925.
The trial of Rev. Prof. Henry Preserved Smith, D.D., of
Lane Theological Seminary, before the Presbytery of Cincin-
nati. Cincinnati, Robert Clarke & Co., 1893. 51 p. Re-
printed from the Presbyterian Quarterly, April, 1893. PH
PT

456 BRYSON, John Henry, 1831-1897.
Scotch-Irish addresses. The Scotch-Irish people: their
influence in the formation of the government of the United
States of America. Delivered at the Third Congress, held
at Louisville, Ky., May 14, 1891. Inventors of the Scotch-
Irish race of America. Delivered at the Fourth Congress,
held at Atlanta, Ga., on the 28th day of April, 1892. Nashville, Tenn., Publishing House of the Methodist Episcopal
Church, South, 1892. 45 p. PT

457 BRYSON, John Henry, 1831-1897.
The Scotch-Irish people: their influence in the formation
of the government of the United States. An address delivered
at the Third Congress of the Scotch-Irish Society of America,
at Louisville, Ky., May 14, 1891. Nashville, Tenn., Publishing House of the Methodist Episcopal Church, South, 1891.
26 p. PH PT

458 *BUCHANAN, George, 1506-1582.
The powers of the crown in Scotland. Being a translation,
with notes and an introductory essay, of George Buchanan's
"De jure regni apud Scotos" by Charles Flinn Arrowood.
Austin, University of Texas Press, 1949. 150 p. A H PT
U

459 BUCHANAN, Walter McSymon, 1868-1949.
Pilgrimage; or, The development of religious thought and

life. n.p., n.d. 346 p. A C H PT U ... PH: Pomona,
Cal., Progress-Bulletin, n.d.

460 *BUCK, Pearl (Sydenstricker), 1892-1973.
Fighting angel: portrait of a soul. New York, Reynal &
Hitchcock, © 1936. 302 p. The biography of the author's
father, Absalom Sydenstricker. H PT

461 BULLOCK, James Randolph, 1910-
Whatever became of salvation? Atlanta, John Knox Press,
© 1979. 112 p. A H L U

462 BULLOCK, Joseph James, 1812-1892.
Rev. Dr. Bullock's address to his congregation, at the
Franklin Street Presbyterian Church. Baltimore, giving his
reasons for dissolving his connection with the Old School Gen-
eral Assembly of the Presbyterian Church, June 12, 1866.
Baltimore, Innes & Co., 1866. 72 p. C PH PT U

463 BULLOCK, Philip Leslie, 1918-
A leader's guide ... for use with Introduction to the Bible:
vol. 1, The Layman's Bible Commentary. Richmond, John
Knox Press, © 1959. 27 p. R U

464 BULLOCK, Philip Leslie, 1918-
A leader's guide ... for use with Tomorrow's church, to-
morrow's world, by Ernest Trice Thompson. Richmond,
John Knox Press, © 1960. 30 p. U

465 BULLOCK, Robert Haydon, 1913-
Hammer on the rock; the message of the prophet Jeremiah.
Richmond, John Knox Press, © 1962. 64 p. A C H L U

466 BUNTING, Robert Franklin, 1828-1891.
Manual of the First Presbyterian Church, Nashville, Tennes-
see, 1814-1868. Nashville, Southern Methodist Publishing
House, 1868. 102 p. PH PT U

467 BUNTING, Robert Franklin, 1828-1891.
The messiahship of Christ: a discourse, prepared by ap-
pointment and delivered before the Presbytery of Western
Texas, October 24, 1857, and repeated at Oliver's Settlement,
Bexar County, October 16, 1858. San Antonio, Herald Office,
1858. 31 p. PH PT

468 *BUNYAN, John, 1628-1688.
The holy war made by King Shaddai upon Diabolus to regain
the metropolis of the world; or, The losing and taking again of
the town of Mansoul.... With a biographical sketch of the
author, introduction and notes by Wilbur M. Smith. Chicago,
Moody Press, 1948. 378 p. C L R U

469 *BUNYAN, John, 1628-1688.

The Pilgrim's progress, John Bunyan's story rewritten for young people by Wade C. Smith; illustrated by the Little Jetts. New York, Harper & Brothers, © 1932. 104 p. A H ... C U: Boston, W. A. Wilde, © 1950.

470 BURGETT, James Ralston, 1830-1900.
The dead of the Synod of Alabama from 1890 to 1900. A memorial sermon. n.p., n.d. 24 p. H PH

471 BURGETT, James Ralston, 1830-1900.
Historical discourse. Presbyterianism in Mobile. Delivered ... on Sabbath Day, March 6th, 1881, on the occasion of the celebration of the fiftieth anniversary of the organization of the Government Street Presbyterian Church, of Mobile, Ala. Mobile, Henry Farrow & Co., 1881. 20 p. PH

472 BURKHEAD, Jesse DeWitt, 1833-1892.
"Theology for the masses"; or, Bible truths for all men. Atlanta, Jas. P. Harrison & Co., 1888. 343 p. A C H PT R U

473 BURNEY, LeRoy Perry, 1897-1955.
Presbyterian elders and deacons serving Christ in the church. A study course for church officers. [Richmond], Board of Christian Education, Presbyterian Church in the U.S. [1953] 59 p. A C L PT R U

474 *BURNS, James, 1865-1948.
Revivals, their laws and leaders. Two additional chapters by Andrew W. Blackwood, Sr. Grand Rapids, Mich., Baker Book House, 1960. 353 p. C L PT R U

475 BUSCHGEN, Otto William, 1885-1948.
Definitions and decorations. n.p., n.d. 15 p. A sermon from the pulpit of the Memorial Presbyterian Church of Wenonah, N.J., December, 1935. PH

476 BUSCHGEN, Otto William, 1885-1948.
Money for colleges. Philadelphia, Board of Christian Education, Presbyterian Church in the U.S.A., 1924. 158 p. H PH

477 BUSH, Monroe, 1921-
The adventure called death; a quiet conversation with those who grieve, including ten meditations for strength and hope. New York, Bond Wheelwright Co., © 1950. 32 p. U

478 *BUTZER, Martin, 1491-1551.
Instruction in Christian love (1523); translated by Paul Traugott Fuhrmann, with introduction and notes. Richmond, John Knox Press, © 1952. 68 p. A C H L PT R U

479 BYINGTON, Cyrus, 1793-1868.
... A dictionary of the Choctaw language.... Edited by
John R. Swanton and Henry S. Halbert. Washington, Govern-
ment Printing Office, 1915. 611 p. (Smithsonian Institution.
Bureau of American ethnology. Bulletin 46.) H PH PT

480 BYINGTON, Cyrus, 1793-1868.
Holisso anumpa tosholi. An English and Choctaw definer;
for the Choctaw academies and schools. [1st ed.] New York,
S. W. Benedict, 1852. 252 p. H

481 CABANISS, James Allen, 1911-
Agobard of Lyons: churchman and critic. [Syracuse, N.Y.]
Syracuse University Press, © 1953. 137 p. L PT U

482 CABANISS, James Allen, 1911-
Amalarius of Metz. Amsterdam, North-Holland Publishing
Co., 1954. 115 p. PT R U

483 CABANISS, James Allen, 1911-
Cabaniss through four generations: some descendants of
Matthew and George. n.p., © 1971. 38 p. L

484 CABANISS, James Allen, 1911-
Charlemagne. New York, Twayne Publishers, © 1972.
176 p. L R

485 CABANISS, James Allen, 1911-
Freemasonry in Mississippi. [Meridian, Miss.], Published
by Grand Lodge of Mississippi, Free and Accepted Masons,
1976. 56 p. L

486 CABANISS, James Allen, 1911-
A history of the University of Mississippi. University,
Miss., University of Mississippi, 1949. 242 p. L

487 CABANISS, James Allen, 1911-
Judith Augusta, a daughter-in-law of Charlemagne, and
other essays. [1st ed.] New York, Vantage Press, © 1974.
182 p. R

488 CABANISS, James Allen, 1911-
Life and thought of a country preacher, C. W. Grafton.
Richmond, John Knox Press, © 1942. 219 p. A C H L R U

489 CABANISS, James Allen, 1911-
Liturgy and literature; selected essays. University, University of Alabama Press, © 1970. 181 p. A C H L PT U

490 CABANISS, James Allen, 1911-
Liturgy in the Southern Presbyterian Church. Richmond,
n.p., 1942. 18 p. Reprinted from the Union Seminary Review, November, 1942. C PH U

491 CABANISS, James Allen, 1911-
Our Lady of the Apocalypse. Oxford, Miss., n.p., 1954.
unpaged. A L PT

492 CABANISS, James Allen, 1911-
Some neglected features in the early Reformed confessions.
n.p., n.d. 31 p. Reprinted from the Union Seminary Review, August, 1943. H PH

493 CABANISS, James Allen, 1911- ed. and tr.
Sons of Charlemagne; a contemporary life of Louis the
Pious. Translated, with introduction and notes.... [Syracuse,
N.Y.], Syracuse University Press, © 1961. 182 p. Trans-
lation based on the MGH ... and MPL editions of Vita Hludo-
wici imperatoris ... L PT

494 CABANISS, James Allen, 1911-
The University of Mississippi; its first hundred years. 2d
ed. Hattiesburg, Miss., University & College Press of Mississippi, © 1971. 207 p. L R

495 CAIRNS, Fred I., 1907-
Progress is unorthodox. Boston, Beacon Press, 1950.
185 p. L PT

496 CALCOTE, Claude Allen, 1896-1956.
Let's go fishing, the technique of outpost administration.
n.p., 1947. 15 p. U

497 CALDWELL, Andrew Harper, 1814-1899.
Christian baptism, local application not total covering.
New Orleans, E. S. Upton, 1898. 183 p. H

498 CALDWELL, Andrew Harper, 1814-1899.
A sermon, on the revision of the Scriptures. Preached in
Philadelphia Church, Marshall County, Mississippi. Holly
Springs, Miss., Banner Job Office Print., 1853. 26 p. C

499 CALDWELL, Charles Turner, 1865-1965.
Broken purposes, a sermon. Waco, Tex., [Standard], n.d.
unpaged. H

500 CALDWELL, Charles Turner, 1865-1965.
Historical sketch of the First Presbyterian Church, Waco,
Texas. [Waco, Methodist Home Press], 1937. 115 p. A
H R ... PH: [1938].

501 CALDWELL, Charles Turner, 1865-1965, ed.
In the swelling of Jordan: sermons by Texas Presbyterian
preachers. Grand Rapids, Mich., Zondervan Publishing House,
© 1940. 143 p. Sermons by Frank C. Brown, Henry W. Du-
Bose, B. O. Wood, Robert Hill, Conway T. Wharton, Cecil H.

Lang, Samuel L. Joekel, J. M. Lewis, Charles L. King, P. B. Hill, William A. McLeod, James F. Hardie, W. Bristow Gray, Charles T. Caldwell.   A C H R U

502   CALDWELL, Charles Turner, 1865-1965.
The verbal inspiration of the Scriptures.   Weaverville, N.C., Southern Presbyterian Journal Co., [1944].   12 p.   The Fiftieth anniversary sermon.   Reprinted from the Southern Presbyterian Journal, July, 1944.   A

503   CALDWELL, Daniel Templeton, 1892-1952.
Bible teaching in co-operation with public schools.   Richmond, Presbyterian Committee of Publication, © 1936.   29 p. A U

504   CALDWELL, Daniel Templeton, 1892-1952.
They answered the call, by Dan T. Caldwell and B. L. Bowman.   Richmond, John Knox Press, © 1952.   142 p. A C H L R U

505   CALDWELL, Eugene Craighead, 1876-1931.
Chronological outline of the life of Christ.   Richmond, Presbyterian Committee of Publication, n.d.   24 p.   Supplementary help in the Standard Training Course on the Life of Christ.   A

506   CALDWELL, Eugene Craighead, 1876-1931.
The Epistle of James; a book study and brief exposition arranged in twelve lessons.   Richmond, Presbyterian Committee of Publication, © 1931.   125 p.   A H L PT R U

507   CALDWELL, Eugene Craighead, 1876-1931.
The Epistle to the Romans; a book-study and brief exposition ... in twelve lessons.   Richmond, Presbyterian Committee of Publication, © 1930.   63 p.   A C H L R U

508   CALDWELL, Eugene Craighead, 1876-1931.
The fulness of Christ.   n.p., n.d.   557-571 p.   Reprinted from the Princeton Theological Review, October, 1918.   H

509   CALDWELL, Eugene Craighead, 1876-1931.
Life and letters of Paul; twelve studies in outline.   Richmond, Presbyterian Committee of Publication, n.d.   25 p. A U

510   CALDWELL, Eugene Craighead, 1876-1931.
Life in Christ.   Outline of a book study of the Gospel according to John.   n.p., n.d.   22 p.   U

511   CALDWELL, Eugene Craighead, 1876-1931.
Life worthy of the gospel of Christ.   n.p., n.d.   248-261 p.   Reprinted from the Princeton Theological Review, April, 1918.   H

512 CALDWELL, Eugene Craighead, 1876-1931.
The millennium; an exegetical study of Revelation, chapter 20, in the light of the book as a whole. Richmond, Presbyterian Committee of Publication, n.d. 28 p. A C H PT U

513 CALDWELL, Eugene Craighead, 1876-1931.
Outline studies in the New Testament. [Richmond], Union Theological Seminary, n.d. 92 p. H U

514 CALDWELL, Eugene Craighead, 1876-1931.
An outline study of the book of Daniel: "A kingdom that shall stand forever." Richmond, Presbyterian Committee of Publication, n.d. 38 p. Published also under title: "A kingdom that shall stand forever." A U

515 CALDWELL, Eugene Craighead, 1876-1931.
Pauline ideals; outline study of the four prison epistles. n.p., n.d. 4 ℓ. U

516 CALDWELL, Eugene Craighead, 1876-1931.
The purpose of the ages. n.p., n.d. 374-389 p. Reprinted from the Princeton Theological Review, July, 1918. H

517 CALDWELL, Eugene Craighead, 1876-1931.
Supplementary notes on the canon of the New Testament. Printed for the use of students in Union Theological Seminary. Richmond, Union Theological Seminary, n.d. 18 p. U

518 CALDWELL, Eugene Craighead, 1876-1931.
Ultimate triumph of Christ's kingdom. n.p., n.d. 4 ℓ. U

519 CALDWELL, Eugene Craighead, 1876-1931.
Unity in Christ: outline study of the Epistle to the Ephesians. n.p., n.d. 121-143 p. Reprinted from the Union Seminary Review, January, 1924. U

520 CALDWELL, Frank Hill, 1902-
Preaching angles. Nashville, Abingdon Press, © 1954. 126 p. A C H L PT U

521 CALDWELL, William, 1865-1915.
The idea of creation; its origin and its value. Fort Worth, Keystone Printing Co., 1909. 48 p. Diss.-University of Chicago. PT

522 CALHOUN, Lawrence Gibson, 1899-
A igreja local e seu programma de educão religiosa. Lavras, Minas, Imprensa Gammon, 1930. 205 p. U

523 CALHOUN, Malcolm Patterson, 1902- ed.
Christians are citizens: the role of the responsible Christian citizen in an era of crisis.... Illustrated by Ruth S.

Ensign. Richmond, John Knox Press, © 1957. 139 p. Chapters by Edward L. Long, Jr., John D. Moseley, Robert B. McNeill, John H. Marion, Francis Pickens Miller, and others. A C H L R U

524 CALIGAN, James Henley, 1903-1972.
The shadow of heaven; a guide to the creative spiritual appreciation of nature. [1st ed.] New York, Vantage Press, © 1956. 143 p. U

525 *CALVIN, Jean, 1509-1564.
The Epistles of Paul the apostle to the Romans and to the Thessalonians. Translator: Ross Mackenzie. Edinburgh, Oliver and Boyd, [1961]. 433 p. A C L PT U

526 *CALVIN, Jean, 1509-1564.
Instruction in faith (1537); translated with a historical foreword and critical and explanatory notes by Paul T. Fuhrmann. Philadelphia, Westminster Press, © 1949. 96 p. A C H L PH PT R U

527 CALVIN and Calvinism. Addresses delivered before the Presbytery of New Orleans at Slidell, La., April 21, 1909. n.p., n.d. 16 p. Contents.--Calvin the man, by H. W. Burwell.-- Calvin's doctrinal system, by J. W. Caldwell. A U

528 CAMPBELL, Chester McDonald, 1889-1951.
Candles in the breeze. n.p., 1949. 40 p. H U

529 CAMPBELL, Duncan Alexander, 1805-1892.
Atonement, not for the elect only, but for the whole world. Fayetteville, Edward J. Hale, 1843. 14 p. PH

530 CAMPBELL, Henry Fraser, 1824-1891.
Memoir of Rev. Robert Irvine, D.D., M.D., pastor of the First Presbyterian Church, Augusta, Georgia. Prepared for the Committee on Necrology of the Medical Association of Georgia. Augusta, Ga., Joseph Loveday, 1882. 37 p. Reprinted from the Transactions of the Medical Association of Georgia, thirty-second annual session, 1881. C PT

531 CAMPBELL, James Milton, 1932-
Pressure! Richmond, CLC Press, © 1965. 48 p. (The Covenant Life Curriculum.) C L

532 CAMPBELL, Robert Fishburne, 1858-1947.
The church fair and its congeners. Richmond, Presbyterian Committee of Publication, 1894. 29 p. C

533 CAMPBELL, Robert Fishburne, 1858-1947.
Freedom and restraint. New York, Fleming H. Revell Co., © 1930. 207 p. (The Sprunt lectures, 1930.) A C H L PT R U

534 CAMPBELL, Robert Fishburne, 1858-1947.
Mission work among the mountain whites in Asheville Presbytery, North Carolina. Asheville, The Citizen Co., 1899. 24 p.
PH PT U

535 CAMPBELL, Robert Fishburne, 1858-1947.
Some aspects of the race problem in the south. Asheville,
N.C., Asheville Printing Co., 1899. 31 p. H ... H PH PT
U: 2d ed. The Citizen Co. 24 p.

536 CAMPBELL, Robert Fishburne, 1858-1947.
Sunday laws and liberty; a paper read before the Pen and
Plate Club of Asheville, N.C. Asheville, Labor Advocate,
n.d. 17 p. U ... PT U: New York, New York Sabbath
Committee, n.d. 19 p.

537 CAMPBELL, William Addison, 1829-1896.
A commentary on the Gospel according to Mark. Richmond,
Presbyterian Publishing Co., 1881. 348 p. A PT U

538 CAMPBELL, William Addison, 1829-1896.
The power of the people in the government of the church.
n.p., n.d. 404-415 p. A reply to the article, "Representative government in the church," by C. R. Vaughan. Reprinted
from the Presbyterian Quarterly, July, 1894. U

539 CAMPBELL, William Addison, 1829-1896.
The Presbyterian church. [Richmond, Presbyterian Committee of Publication], n.d. 8 p. U

540 CAMPBELL, William Creighton, 1850-1936.
Presbyterianism and its growth! Roanoke, Va., Leader
Printing Co., 1887. 42 p. U

541 CANNON, John Franklin, 1851-1920.
Fiftieth anniversary: Grand Avenue Presbyterian Church,
Grand and Washington Avenues, St. Louis, Missouri. n.p.,
Robertson Printing Co., [1903?]. 44 p. H

542 CANNON, John Franklin, 1851-1920.
Spirituality; an essential qualification for the office of deacon. St. Louis, [C. B. Woodward Co.], 1892. 21 p. U

543 CANNON, Thomas Clarence, 1909-
Pioneer days in the St. Charles Presbyterian Church. n.p.,
n.d. unpaged. PH

544 CARMICHAEL, Patrick Henry, 1889-1977.
A history of the American Association of Schools of Religious Education, 1935-1965. Covina, Calif., American Association of Schools of Religious Education, 1965. 23 p. U

545 CARMICHAEL, Patrick Henry, 1889-1977, ed.

Understanding the books of the New Testament; a guide to Bible study for laymen. Richmond, John Knox Press, © 1952. 205 p. Prepared by Felix B. Gear, Joseph M. Garrison, Patrick D. Miller, Paul Leslie Garber, Henry Wade DuBose, James E. Bear. A C H L U ... C H PT R U: [Rev. ed.], © 1961. 224 p.

546 CARMICHAEL, Patrick Henry, 1889-1977, ed.
Understanding the books of the Old Testament; a guide to Bible study for laymen. Richmond, John Knox Press, © 1950. 173 p. Prepared by W. A. Benfield, Jr., Kenneth J. Foreman, Samuel L. Joekel, E. D. Kerr, John C. Siler. A C H L PT U ... C H R U: [Rev. ed.], © 1961. 188 p.

547 CARR, James McLeod, 1902-
Bright future: a new day for the town and country church. Richmond, John Knox Press, © 1956. 162 p. A C H L R U

548 CARR, James McLeod, 1902-
Glorious ride: the story of Henry Woods McLaughlin. "Little jet" sketches by the author. Atlanta, Church and Community Press, © 1958. 156 p. A C H L PH R U

549 CARR, James McLeod, 1902-
Our church meeting human needs. Birmingham, [Ala.], Progressive Farmer Co., © 1962. 152 p. A C H L R U

550 CARR, James McLeod, 1902-
What is the larger parish? Atlanta, Town and Country Church Department, Presbyterian Church in the U.S., n.d. unpaged. PH

551 CARR, James McLeod, 1902-
Working together in the larger parish. Atlanta, Board of Church Extension, Presbyterian Church in the U.S., © 1960. 105 p. A C H L PH R U

552 CARSE, James Pearce, 1932-
Death and existence: a conceptual history of human mortality. New York, Wiley, © 1980. 473 p. A U

553 CARSON, Charles Clifton, 1870-1944.
The glorious Gospel: sermons. Richmond, Presbyterian Committee of Publication, © 1926. 281 p. H U ... A C R: [2d ed.] Charlotte, N.C., Presbyterian Standard Publishing Co., © 1926. 281 p.

554 CARTER, Hampden C., 1805-1869.
An epitome of the prominent arguments on the design, mode and subjects of Christian baptism: containing the substance of a series of discourses preached in the Presbyterian Church at Lafayette, Walker County, Georgia. Athens, Ga., Christy & Kelsea, 1853. 143 p. C H PT

555 CARTER, Robert Washington, 1858-1903.
The golden opportunity for Christianity and Calvinism; a
reply to Minister Wu Ting Fang. [Davis, W.Va.], n.p., n.d.
8 p.   U

556 CARTLEDGE, Groves Harrison, 1820-1899.
Historical sketches; Presbyterian churches and early set-
tlers in northeast Georgia. Compiled by Jessie Julia Mize
and Virginia Louise Newton. Athens, Ga., n.p., 1960.
208 p.   A C H

557 CARTLEDGE, Groves Harrison, 1820-1899.
The perpetuity of the Abrahamic covenant, and the identity
of the Jewish and Christian church. A sermon. Richmond,
Whittet & Shepperson, 1890. 44 p.   PH

558 CARTLEDGE, Groves Harrison, 1820-1899.
Sermons and discussions, with an autobiography.... Edited
by his sons, Rev. Thomas D. Cartledge, Rev. Samuel J. Cartledge. Richmond, Whittet & Shepperson, 1903. 240 p.   C H
R U

559 CARTLEDGE, Samuel Antoine, 1903-
A basic grammar of the Greek New Testament. Grand Ra-
pids, Mich., Zondervan Publishing House, [1959]. 137 p.
C H PT R U

560 CARTLEDGE, Samuel Antoine, 1903-
The Bible: God's word to man. Philadelphia, Westminster
Press, © 1961. 143 p.   A C L PH PT U

561 CARTLEDGE, Samuel Antoine, 1903-
A conservative introduction to the New Testament. Grand
Rapids, Mich., Zondervan Publishing House, © 1938. 196 p.
C H L R U ... L: 2d ed. [1939] 236 p. ... PT U: 3d ed.
[1941] ... A L: 6th ed. [1951] ... C: 7th ed. 1957.
238 p.

562 CARTLEDGE, Samuel Antoine, 1903-
A conservative introduction to the Old Testament. Grand
Rapids, Mich., Zondervan Publishing House, © 1943. 238 p.
A C H L PT R U ... C H L R: [2d ed.] Athens, Ga., Uni-
versity of Georgia Press, © 1944.

563 CARTLEDGE, Samuel Antoine, 1903-
Fact and fancy about the future life. Richmond, John Knox
Press, © 1943. 69 p.   A C H L PT R U

564 CARTLEDGE, Samuel Antoine, 1903-
Jesus of fact and faith; studies in the life of Christ. Grand
Rapids, Mich., Wm. B. Eerdmans Publishing Co., © 1968.
160 p.   A C PT R U

565 CARTLEDGE, Samuel Jackson, 1864-1940.
The drama of Redemption. Grand Rapids, Mich., Zondervan Publishing House, © 1940. 142 p. Brief biographical
sketch, by Samuel A. Cartledge. A C H R U

566 CARUTHERS, Eli Washington, 1793-1865.
Interesting revolutionary incidents: and sketches of character, chiefly in the "Old North State." 2d series. Philadelphia,
Hayes & Zell, 1856. 448 p. Continuation of his Revolutionary
incidents. H PH

567 CARUTHERS, Eli Washington, 1793-1865.
Revolutionary incidents: and sketches of character, chiefly
in the "Old North State." Philadelphia, Hayes & Zell, 1854.
431 p. H PH U

568 CARUTHERS, Eli Washington, 1793-1865.
A sketch of the life and character of the Rev. David Caldwell, D.D., near sixty years pastor of the churches of Buffalo
and Alamance. Including two of his sermons; some account of
the Regulation, together with the revolutionary ... incidents in
which he was concerned; and a very brief notice of the ecclesiastical and moral condition of North-Carolina while in its
colonial state. Greensborough, N.C., Swaim and Sherwood,
1842. 302 p. A C H L PH R U

569 THE CASE of Dr. E. T. Baird, in the Hustings court, with additional testimony. Richmond, Whittet & Shepperson, 1877.
24 p. PT

570 THE CASE of Professor Mecklin: report of the Committee of
inquiry of the American Philosophical association and the
American Psychological association. n.p., n.d. 69-81 p.
Reprinted from the Journal of Philosophy, Psychology, &
Scient. Meth., Jan., 1914. PT

571 [CASE of the Rev. J. E. White against Purity Presbyterian
Church, Chester, S.C. Columbia, S.C., 1877-78]. 1 v.,
various pagings. Binder's title: "J. E. White vs. Purity
Church." U

572 CASEY, Horace Craig, 1903-
Why I am a Presbyterian. Richmond, Presbyterian Committee of Publication, n.d. 8 p. U

573 CATER, Edwin, 1813-1882.
The appeal of Rev. Edwin Cater ... to the candid judgment
of the people of God against the assaults made upon him on
the floor of the General Assembly at Huntsville, Ala., in May,
1871, and repeated in newspapers, and in the Southern Presbyterian Review, for October, 1871. College Hill [via Oxford],
Miss., Printed for Rev. Edwin Cater, 1871. 31 p. C PH
PT

574 CECIL, Russell, 1853-1925.
The education of the ministry. Prepared and published at
the request of Tuskaloosa Presbytery. Richmond, Presbyterian Committee of Publication, 1894. 27 p. A PT

575 CECIL, Russell, 1853-1925.
The golden rule: a sermon. Richmond, Published as a
memorial by the Executive Committee of Publication, [1925].
unpaged. A C H U

576 CECIL, Russell, 1853-1925.
Hand book of theology. Richmond, Presbyterian Committee
of Publication, © 1923. 114 p. A C H PT R U

577 CECIL, Russell, 1853-1925.
"In trust with the Gospel." Baccalaureate sermon, delivered
at the Theological Seminary at Columbia, S.C., May 9, 1897.
Richmond, Presbyterian Committee of Publication, © 1897.
24 p. C H PT

578 CECIL, Russell, 1853-1925.
Love like the sun. Richmond, Whittett & Shepperson, 1902.
8 p. Reprinted from the Presbyterian Quarterly, October,
1902. PT

579 CECIL, Russell, 1853-1925.
The preacher's message. Richmond, Harvey C. Brown,
[1925]. 16 p. U

580 CECIL, Russell, 1853-1925.
The religion of love. Richmond, Presbyterian Committee
of Publication, © 1924. 68 p. A C H PT R U

581 *CELLERIER, Jacques Elisée, 1785-1862.
Biblical hermeneutics. Chiefly a translation of the Manuel
d'herméneutique biblique, par J. E. Cellerier ... by Charles
Elliott ... and Rev. William Justin Harsha. New York, Anson D. F. Randolph & Co., © 1881. 282 p. PT U

582 CENTER for Hermeneutical Studies in Hellenistic and Modern
Culture.
Jewish Gnostic Nag Hammadi texts: protocol of the third
colloquy, 22 May 1972 ... [by] James M. Robinson. Ber-
keley, CA, The Center, © 1975. 28 p. L PT U

583 CHAFER, Lewis Sperry, 1871-1952.
Analytical questionnaire, based upon and developing the
material presented in lecture form which comprises the course
in systematic theology as given at the Evangelical Theological
College, Dallas, Texas. Dallas, Evangelical College, n.d.
77 p. PT U

584 CHAFER, Lewis Sperry, 1871-1952.

Dispensationalism. [Dallas, Tex., Hicks-Gaston Co.,
1936]. 390-449 p. Reprinted from Bibliotheca Sacra, Oct.-
Dec., 1936. U ... A PT: Rev. ed. Dallas, Tex., Dallas
Seminary Press, © 1951. 108 p.

585 CHAFER, Lewis Sperry, 1871-1952.
The Ephesian letter, doctrinally considered. New York,
Loizeaux Brothers, Bible Truth Depot, © 1935. 176 p.
"First published in the Revelation magazine." A R

586 CHAFER, Lewis Sperry, 1871-1952.
Grace. 2d ed. Philadelphia, Sunday School Times Co.,
1922. 373 p. A L U ... R: Chicago, Moody Press ... H:
3d ed. Bible Institute Colportage Ass'n., 1928 ... R:
1939 ... R: 1947.

587 CHAFER, Lewis Sperry, 1871-1952.
He that is spiritual. n.p., © 1918. 151 p. C PT R
U ... R: Chicago, Moody Press, 1918. 193 p. ... PT H:
Chicago, Bible Institute Colportage Ass'n., 1929 ... A: 1935.

588 CHAFER, Lewis Sperry, 1871-1952.
The Kingdom in history and prophecy. New York, Fleming
H. Revell Co., © 1915. 159 p. A C H PT R U ... L:
Philadelphia, Sunday School Times Co., 1922. 167 p. ... R:
Grand Rapids, Mich., Dunham [1964]. 166 p.

589 CHAFER, Lewis Sperry, 1871-1952.
Major Bible themes, representing forty-nine vital doctrines
of the Scriptures, abbreviated and simplified for popular use,
including suggestive questions on each chapter; with topical
and textual indices. Philadelphia, Sunday School Times Co.,
1926. 329 p. L ... R: Chicago, Moody Press, 1926 ... C:
Chicago, Bible Institute Colportage Ass'n., 1927 ... H:
1930 ... A R: 1937 ... PT: ... 52 vital doctrines.... Revised by John F. Walvoord. Grand Rapids, Mich., Zondervan
Publishing House [1975]. 374 p.

590 CHAFER, Lewis Sperry, 1871-1952.
Must we dismiss the millennium? A critical review of the
pamphlet, "The millennium," by Rev. Eugene C. Caldwell.
Crescent City, Fla., Biblical Testimony League, © 1921.
31 p. A R U

591 CHAFER, Lewis Sperry, 1871-1952.
Salvation. New York, Charles C. Cook, © 1917. 139 p.
A R ... U: Philadelphia, Sunday School Times Co., 1922.
149 p. ... H: 1926 ... C R: Chicago, Moody Press, 1944 ...
C: 1947 ... PT U: Grand Rapids, Mich., Zondervan Publish-
ing House [1972].

592 CHAFER, Lewis Sperry, 1871-1952.
Satan. New York, Gospel Publishing House, © 1909. 162 p.

C U ... R: Montrose, Montrose Christian Literature Society, 1909 ... H L: New and rev. ed. Chicago, Bible Institute Colportage Ass'n., 1927. 180 p. ... A: 1935 ... R: Chicago, Moody Press, 1942 ... R: Grand Rapids, Mich., Dunham Publishing Co. [1964].

593 CHAFER, Lewis Sperry, 1871-1952.
Seven major Biblical signs of the times. An address delivered at the Laymen's Missionary Movement Convention, Atlanta, Ga., June 10-12, 1919. Philadelphia, The Sunday School Times Co., © 1919. 30 p. C R ... H: Seven major signs of the times. Chicago, Bible Institute Colportage Ass'n., 1928.

594 CHAFER, Lewis Sperry, 1871-1952.
Systematic theology. Dallas, Tex., Dallas Seminary Press, © 1947-48. 8 v. A H L PT R U

595 CHAFER, Lewis Sperry, 1871-1952.
True evangelism. New York, Gospel Publishing House [1911]. 159 p. C PT R ... R U: Rev. ed. Philadelphia, Sunday School Times Co., 1919. 143 p. ... L U: 1925 ... A H: Chicago, Bible Institute Colportage Ass'n., 1929.

596 CHAFER, Rollin Thomas, 1868-1940.
The science of Biblical hermeneutics: an outline study of the laws. Dallas, Bibliotheca Sacra, © 1939. 92 p. PT U

597 CHALMERS, Dwight Moody, 1899-1974.
Love in the New Testament. Atlanta, Board of Women's Work, Presbyterian Church in the U.S., [1955?]. 47 p. L R U

598 *CHALMERS, John T.
A reply to Rev. A. J. McKelway, editor of the Presbyterian Standard, on psalmody. n.p., n.d. 22 p. PH

599 CHAMBERLAIN, Hiram, 1797-1866.
Major Sibley's church history cross-examined and put to the test of record. n.p., n.d. 10 p. PH

600 CHAMBERLAIN, Nelson P., 1818-1869.
A sermon [preached in Thibodaux, La., on Sunday, Jan. 1, 1854]. n.p., n.d. 7 p. PH

601 *CHAMBERLIN, Edwin Allan.
Once upon a time: a history of St. Peter's Lutheran-Presbyterian Church, New Columbia, by Edwin Allan Chamberlin and Raymond David Adams. n.p., 1914, 1930. 27 p. PH

602 *CHANDLER, E. Russell.
The Kennedy explosion; the story of Dr. D. James Kennedy.

Elgin, Ill., David C. Cook Publishing Co. [1972]. 125 p.
C ... PT: [1st British ed.] London, Coverdale House.
119 p.

603 CHANEY, James McDonald, 1831-1909.
William the Baptist. Richmond, Presbyterian Committee
of Publication, © 1877. 144 p.   C H L PT R U ... A H L:
5th ed. ... H: 1877. 245 p. ... R: [Wilmington, Del.],
Dept. of Publications, Reformed Presbyterian Evangelical
Synod, n.d. 133 p.

604 *CHANG, Chih-tung, 1835-1909.
China's only hope; an appeal by her greatest viceroy, Chang
Chih-tung, with the sanction of the present emperor, Kwang
Sü; translated from the Chinese edition by Samuel I. Wood-
bridge. New York, Fleming H. Revell Co., © 1900. 151 p.
A H PH

605 CHAPMAN, Robert Hett, 1806-1884.
Christian patriotism; or, The duties which Christians owe
their country. A sermon, delivered on the 4th of July, 1852,
in the Presbyterian Church at Mordisville, Alabama. Philadelphia, Lippincott, Grambo, & Co., 1852. 24 p.   PH

606 CHAPMAN, Robert Hett, 1806-1884.
The importance of knowledge to the soul of man. An educational discourse, delivered by request in the Male Academy
of Mordisville, Alabama, on the afternoon of July 20th, 1852,
preparatory to the annual examination. Philadelphia, Lippincott, Grambo, & Co., 1852. 20 p.   PH PT

607 CHAPMAN, Robert Hett, 1806-1884.
Religion: an indispensable element in true education. An
address delivered before the East Alabama Masonic Female
Institute, at Talladega, Alabama, during its annual examination,
1853. Philadelphia, Lippincott, Grambo, & Co., 1853. 39 p.
PH PT

608 THE CHARGE, the facts, the resolutions. [The charge made
by Mr. B--against Mr. Smith; the facts found by the officers
of Dr. Smith's church; and resolutions adopted by the officers.
Little Rock, Ark., 1927.] 9 p. Concerned with Hay Watson
Smith. A

609 CHARLES, Benjamin Haynes, 1829-1914.
Lectures on prophecy, an exposition of certain Scriptures
with reference to the history and end of the papacy; the restoration of the Jews to Palestine.... Chicago, Fleming H. Revell
Co., © 1897. 320 p.   A C H PT U

610 CHARLESTON, S.C. French Protestant Church.
The French Protestant Church in the city of Charleston,

"The Huguenot Church." A brief history of the church and two addresses delivered on the two hundred and twenty-fifth anniversary of the founding of the church, April fourteenth, nineteen hundred and twelve. Charleston, Walker, Evans & Cogswell Co., 1912. 38 p. Addresses by C. S. Vedder and W. H. S. Demarest. H PH PT

611 THE CHARLESTON Assembly and Rev. J. B. Adger. n.p., n.d. 31 p. C PH

612 CHAUNCEY, George Austin, 1927-
Decisions! Decisions! Richmond, John Knox Press, © 1972. 127 p. A C H L PH PT R U

613 CHAUNCEY, George Austin, 1927-
Evangelism: communicating the Gospel; a leader's guide for a course on evangelism. Atlanta, Board of Church Extension, Presbyterian Church in the U.S. [1960?] 25 p. U

614 CHAUNCEY, George Austin, 1927-
Serving God through worship and work; five Bible studies. [Atlanta, Board of Women's Work, Presbyterian Church in the U.S., 1964]. 49 p. Lectures presented at the Montreat Women's Conference in July, 1963. U

615 CHAUNCEY, George Austin, 1927- ed.
Vietnam and beyond: some alternatives for the United States. [Richmond], Board of Christian Education, Presbyterian Church in the U.S., © 1969. 77 p. L R

616 CHENOBOSKION manuscripts. English. 1977.
The Nag Hammadi library in English. Translated by members of the Coptic Gnostic Library Project of the Institute for Antiquity and Christianity. James M. Robinson, director. New York, Harper & Row, © 1977. 493 p. A C L PT R U

617 CHESTER, Samuel Hall, 1851-1940.
Behind the scenes; an administrative history of the foreign work of the Presbyterian Church in the United States. Austin, Tex., Von Boeckmann-Jones Co., © 1928. 145 p. A C H L PH PT R U

618 CHESTER, Samuel Hall, 1851-1940.
Brazil. [Nashville, Tenn., Executive Committee of Foreign Missions, Presbyterian Church in the U.S.], n.d. 16 p. PH

619 CHESTER, Samuel Hall, 1851-1940.
Hampden Coit DuBose. Nashville, Tenn., Executive Committee of Foreign Missions, Presbyterian Church in the U.S., [1929?]. 8 p. H

620 CHESTER, Samuel Hall, 1851-1940.
Lecture on Japan. n.p., n.d. 16 p. U

621 CHESTER, Samuel Hall, 1851-1940.
Lecture on Korea. n.p., n.d. 16 p. U

622 CHESTER, Samuel Hall, 1851-1940.
Lights and shadows of mission work in the Far East: being
the record of observations made during a visit to the Southern
Presbyterian missions in Japan, China, and Korea in the year
1897. Richmond, Presbyterian Committee of Publication,
© 1899. 133 p. A C H L PT R U

623 CHESTER, Samuel Hall, 1851-1940.
Memories of four-score years; an autobiography. Richmond,
Privately printed for the author by Presbyterian Committee of
Publication, 1934. 235 p. A H L PH PT R U

624 CHESTER, Samuel Hall, 1851-1940.
The missionary crisis in China. Nashville, Tenn., Marshall & Bruce Co., 1901. 24 p. PT U

625 CHESTER, Samuel Hall, 1851-1940.
Pioneer days in Arkansas. Richmond, Published for the
author by the Presbyterian Committee of Publication, © 1927.
68 p. A C H L PH PT R U

626 CHESTER, Samuel Hall, 1851-1940.
The redemption of Mexico. Nashville, Tenn., Executive
Committee of Foreign Missions, Presbyterian Church in the
U.S., n.d. 14 p. PH

627 CHESTER, Samuel Hall, 1851-1940.
Reminiscences of thirty years in a secretary's office. An
address delivered at the General Assembly, Lexington, Kentucky, May, 1925. [Nashville, Tenn.], Executive Board of
Foreign Missions, Presbyterian Church in the U.S., n.d.
31 p. A H PH U

628 CHESTER, Samuel Hall, 1851-1940.
The selection and appointment of missionaries. Nashville,
Executive Committee of Foreign Missions, Presbyterian Church
in the U.S., n.d. 12 p. U

629 CHESTER, Samuel Hall, 1851-1940.
Seventeen years in a secretary's office. n.p., [1917]. 8 ℓ.
PH U

630 *CHIANG, Kai-shek, 1886-1975.
Resistance and reconstruction: messages during China's
six years of war, 1937-1943. New York, Harper & Brothers,
© 1943. 322 p. Dr. Frank Wilson Price, translator of Sun
Yat-sen's San Min Chu I, is responsible for the translation of
the second section. H

631 CHISOLM, James Julius, 1852-1915.

The gambling habit; a growing evil in the American commonwealth. Richmond, Presbyterian Committee of Publication, [1907]. 12 p.   PT U

632   CHISOLM, James Julius, 1852-1915.
The gospel in gold, or the grace of giving. Richmond, Presbyterian Committee of Publication, 1898. 60 p.   PT U

633   CHISOLM, James Julius, 1852-1915.
Mutoto; or, The perfume of the alabaster box. A brief sketch of the life and labors of Bertha Stebbins Morrison, our martyr missionary to Luebo, Africa. Richmond, Presbyterian Committee of Publication, 1914. 107 p.   C H U

634   CHRISTIAN, William Armistead, 1905-
An interpretation of Whitehead's metaphysics. New Haven, Yale University Press, 1959. 419 p.   C L PT U

635   CHRISTIAN, William Armistead, 1905-
Meaning and truth in religion. Princeton, N.J., Princeton University Press, 1964. 273 p.   A C L PT U

636   CHRISTIAN, William Armistead, 1905-
Oppositions of religious doctrines; a study in the logic of dialogue among religions. [New York], Herder and Herder, [1972]. 129 p.   A L U ... PT: [London], Macmillan.

637   CHRISTIAN, William Armistead, 1905-
Person and God in a Spanish valley. New York, Seminar Press, 1972. 215 p.   PT

638   CHRISTIAN, William Armistead, 1905-
Philosophical analysis and philosophy of religion. [Chicago], University of Chicago Press, © 1959. 77-87 p. Reprinted from the Journal of Religion, April, 1959.   U

639   CHUMBLEY, Charles Melvin, 1871-1953.
The man invincible; or, What is it all about--this book we call the Bible? Bridgewater, Va., Cosmos Book Co., 1936. 308 p.   A C L U

640   THE CHURCH and the rural poor, edited by James A. Cogswell. Atlanta, John Knox Press, © 1975. 107 p.   A C H L PT R U

641   CLAGETT, William Hezekiah, 1848-1926.
The mask torn off, or modern spiritualism exposed. 2d ed. St. Louis, Farris, Smith & Co., © 1887. 38 p.   PH PT

642   CLARK, Fred, 1893-
Spiritual treasure in earthen vessels. Dallas, Tex., Mathis, Van Nort & Co., © 1939. 134 p.   A H PT

643 CLARK, Thomas Fetzer, 1928-
History of Myers Park Presbyterian Church, 1926-1966.
[Kingsport, Tenn.], Kingsport Press, © 1966. 237 p. H U

644 CLARK, William Crawford, 1849-1927.
The Christian faith; a handbook of Christian teaching. Boston, Sherman, French & Co., 1915. 347 p. PH R U

645 CLARKE, James Whyte, 1890-1976.
Dynamic preaching. [Westwood, N.J.], Fleming H. Revell
Co., © 1960. 128 p. C L PH PT R U

646 CLARKE, William Robert, 1898-1971.
Pew asks; pulpit answers. Boston, Christopher Publishing
House, © 1967. 161 p. C L PH PT U

647 CLEVELAND, Thomas Parmelee, 1837-1928.
A catechism on baptism. Atlanta, W. C. Dodson, 1886.
23 p. U

648 CLINTON, S. C. Thornwell Orphanage.
Thornwell Orphanage: its principles and product. [Clinton,
S.C., Printing Dept. of Thornwell Orphanage], 1942. 316 p.
Wm. C. Sistar, editorial chairman. A C H PT R

649 CLISBY, Aaron Warner, 1827-1902 or '03.
The relation of church and state. A sermon prepared by
direction of the Presbytery of Florida, and delivered during
its sessions at Micanopy, Fla., November 3, 1866. Columbia, S.C., Southern Presbyterian Review, 1866. 50 p.
H PH

650 CLOSE, Henry Thompson, 1928-
Reasons for our faith. Richmond, John Knox Press, © 1962.
103 p. A C H L R U

651 CLOWER, Joseph Burner, 1907-
The Church in the thought of Jesus. Richmond, John Knox
Press, © 1959. 160 p. A C H L PT R U

652 COATES, Edwin S., 1899-1971.
Presbyterian reunion; have you prayed it through? [Charlottesville, Va., Friends of Presbyterian Union], n.d. 2 ℓ.
U

653 COBB, James Walter, 1872-1961.
The vice of the Sunday paper. Atlanta, Executive Committee of Home Missions, Presbyterian Church in the U.S.,
n.d. unpaged. U

654 COCHRAN, Isaac, 1798-1879.
The light of the world. n.p., n.d. 24 p. (Presbyterian
Tracts, no. 155.) C H L PH PT R U

655 COCKE, Alonzo Rice, 1858-1901.
No immersion in the Bible; or, Baptism as taught and practiced by Christ and the apostles. 4th ed. Richmond, Presbyterian Committee of Publication, © 1896. 80 p. A

656 COCKE, Alonzo Rice, 1858-1901.
Studies in Ephesians. Chicago, Fleming H. Revell Co.,
© 1892. 137 p. H PT U

657 COCKE, Alonzo Rice, 1858-1901.
Studies in the epistles of John; or, The manifested life.
Richmond, Committee of Publication, 1895. 159 p. A C
H R U

658 COCKRUM, Logan Vaud, 1924-
Career & personal counseling service; handbook for local
church leaders. Richmond, Career and Personal Counseling
Service, Presbyterian Church in the U.S., 1972. 35 p.
L U

659 COCKRUM, Logan Vaud, 1924-
Where do I go from here? Work, worship, leisure. By
Logan V. Cockrum and Albert C. Winn. Chicago, Science
Research Associates, © 1972. 76 p. A complete revision of
an earlier work, "You and your lifework," by Albert C. Winn.
C L U ... C L U: Leadership guide. 32 p.

660 COGSWELL, James Arthur, 1922-
Japan. n.p., n.d. 17 p. U

661 COGSWELL, James Arthur, 1922-
Response: the church in mission to a world in crisis.
Richmond, CLC Press, © 1971. 160 p. (The Covenant Life
Curriculum.) A C L PT R U ... C L R U: Sue Nichols
and James A. Cogswell. Teacher's book. 110 p.

662 COGSWELL, James Arthur, 1922-
Until the day dawn. Cover and design by Claire Randall.
[Nashville, Tenn.], Board of World Missions, Presbyterian
Church in the U.S., © 1957. 226 p. A C H L PT R U

663 COGSWELL, Robert Eugene, 1921-
Written on many hearts: the history of the First Presbyterian Church, Shelbyville, Bedford County, Tennessee, 1815-
1965. Nashville, Tenn., Parthenon Press, [1965]. 279 p.
C L U

664 COLUMBIA Theological Seminary, Decatur, Ga.
Memorial volume of the semi-centennial of the Theological
Seminary at Columbia, South Carolina. Columbia, Presbyterian
Publishing House, 1884. 440 p. Addresses: B. M. Palmer,
James H. Saye. Discourses: T. E. Peck, Henry M. Smith,

C. A. Stillman, John L. Girardeau. Historical sketches: George Howe, J. Leighton Wilson. Memorial sketches of deceased professors and students: Thomas Goulding by F. R. Goulding, James Henley Thornwell by John B. Adger, Charles Colcock Jones by John Jones, Aaron Whitney Leland by Joseph Bardwell, William Swan Plumer by Moses D. Hoge. Eulogy on George Howe by John L. Girardeau. Sketches of 135 deceased students. A C H L PH PT R U

665 COMFORT, Eugene Chambliss, 1883-
The partiality of Jesus; or, Meditations on eight of our Lord's favorites. Grand Rapids, Mich., Reformed Press, © 1932. 154 p. C H PT R U

666 COMMEMORATIVE exercises [Dec. 30, 1883] on the fortieth anniversary of the installation of the Rev. Joseph B. Stratton, D.D., pastor of the Presbyterian Church at Natchez, Miss. Philadelphia, J. B. Lippincott & Co., 1884. 85 p. Sermons, addresses by the Revs. Thomas R. Markham, John W. Henderson, Joseph B. Stratton. PH

667 THE COMPLETE correspondence between Union members of Pine Street Presbyterian Church and their pastor, Rev. S. B. McPheeters, D.D., upon the subject of loyalty to the government. St. Louis, n.p., [1862]. 18 p. PH

668 THE CONCEPT of willing: outdated idea or essential key to man's future? Edited by James N. Lapsley. Foreword by Seward Hiltner. New York, Abingdon Press, © 1967. 222 p. A C L PT

669 CONNELLY, J. M., 1811-1895.
"Revelation explained": "Breve et punctatim." "Et multum in parvo." "Et simpliciter." Houston, Tex., E. H. Cushing, 1876. 217 p. A C H PT U

670 CONNING, Gordon Russell, 1904-
The new shape of life. Wilmington, Del., Mercantile Press, © 1968. 157 p. PT

671 THE CONTEXT of contemporary theology; essays in honor of Paul Lehmann. Edited by Alexander J. McKelway and E. David Willis. Atlanta, John Knox Press, © 1974. 270 p. A C H L PT U

672 CONVERSE, Amasa, 1795-1872.
A discourse, delivered before the Amelia Washington Lodge, of Free and Accepted Masons, on the anniversary of St. John, Sunday, June 24, A.L. 5827. Richmond, n.p., 1827. 16 p. PH

673 CONVERSE, Amasa, 1795-1872.

Scriptural view of the mode of baptism. In a letter to an inquirer. Richmond, J. Macfarlan, 1832. 38 p.   PT

674   CONVERSE, James Booth, 1844-1914.
The Bible and land. Morristown, Tenn., James B. Converse, 1889. 251 p.   H R U

675   CONVERSE, James Booth, 1844-1914.
A summer vacation; sketches and thoughts abroad, in the summer of 1877. Louisville, Ky., Converse & Co., 1878. 201 p.   H

676   CONVERSE, James Booth, 1844-1914.
There shall be no poor. Richmond, Onward Press, © 1913. 182 p.   A C H U

677   CONVERSE, James Booth, 1844-1914.
Uncle Sam's Bible; or, Bible teaching about politics. Chicago, Schulte Publishing Co., © 1898. 230 p.   A

678   COOPER, Williamson Lee, 1889-1972.
Stuart Robinson School and its work; a study in meeting the needs of our school community and plans for future service. Nashville, Tenn., Parthenon Press, © 1936. 124 p.   H L U

679   CORKEY, William Barnet Harold, 1908-
Education for Christian citizenship. n.p., n.d. 16 p. Carey lecture.   PT

680   A CORRESPONDENCE between some of the members of the Pine Street Presbyterian Church and its pastor [Dr. S. B. McPheeters]. St. Louis, n.p., 1862. 29 p.   A C PH PT U

681   CORRESPONDENCE between the Presbytery of Baltimore and the Rev. J. G. Hamner: accompanied with documentary proof of the unfounded allegations of said Presbytery, against said Hamner; together with such remarks, as seem necessary in the premises. Baltimore, Publication Rooms, 1840. 30 p. PH PT

682   COULTER, David, 1808-1878.
Memoir ... with reminiscences, letters, lectures and sermons. St. Louis, Presbyterian Publishing Co., n.d. 551 p. A H PH PT U

683   COURTENAY, Walter Rowe, 1902-
"I believe, but ...?" A reaffirmation of faith. Richmond, John Knox Press, © 1950. 182 p.   A C H L U

684   COURTENAY, Walter Rowe, 1902-
The road ahead (II Chronicles 10:1-16). [A sermon delivered on Lincoln's birthday, February 12, 1950, in the First

Presbyterian Church, Nashville, Tenn.]. n.p., n.d. unpaged.
PH

685 COURTNEY, Lloyd McFarland, 1889-1979.
The church on the Western waters; an history of Green-
brier Presbytery and its churches. Richmond, Whittet &
Shepperson, 1940. 123 p. H PH PT U

686 COUSAR, James English, 1893-
The history of the First Presbyterian Church, Florence,
South Carolina. Centennial ed., 1861-1961. n.p., [1962].
46 p. C

687 *COVERT, William Chalmers.
The spirit and message of Dr. W. Beatty Jennings in the
First Presbyterian Church of Germantown. A sermon ...
Sunday, September 15, 1935. Germantown, Penn., n.p.,
1935. 7 p. H PH

688 COWAN, Alexander M., 1792-1875.
The Oberlin theology, contrasted with that of the Confes-
sion of Faith of the Presbyterian Church. Mansfield, Ohio,
J. C. Gilkison & Son, 1841. 36 p. PH

689 COX, Robert Henry, 1911-
Thru the Word with chart and compass. [Concord, N.C.,
The author, 1939]. 32 p. U

690 CRABB, Cecil Van Meter, 1889-1972.
The individual in our present-day world, making the grade
today. New York, Fleming H. Revell Co., © 1938. 93 p.
A H L PT R U

691 CRABB, Cecil Van Meter, 1889-1972.
Personality prevails; or, The human equation in a machine
age. Richmond, Published for the author by Presbyterian
Committee of Publication, © 1929. 158 p. A H L PT R U

692 CRABB, Cecil Van Meter, 1889-1972.
Psychology's challenge to Christianity. Richmond, Pres-
byterian Committee of Publication, © 1923. 210 p. A C H
L PT R U

693 CRAIG, David Irvin, 1849-1925.
A historical sketch of New Hope Church, in Orange County,
N.C. Reidsville, N.C., S. W. Paisley, 1886. 47 p. PH ...
PH: Rev. ed. n.p., 1891. 54 p.

694 CRAIG, David Irvin, 1849-1925.
A history of the development of the Presbyterian Church in
North Carolina, and of the synodical home missions, together
with evangelistic addresses. Richmond, Whittet & Shepperson,

© 1907. 192 p. Addresses by James I. Vance, J. Wilbur Chapman, S. L. Morris, Wm. Black.   A C H L PH PT R U

695 CRAIG, Edward Marshall, 1867-1928, ed.
Highways and byways of Appalachia; a study of the work of the Synod of Appalachia of the Presbyterian Church in the U.S. [Kingsport, Tenn., Kingsport Press], 1927. 183 p.   A H L R U

696 CRAIG, John Newton, 1831-1900.
A brief history of the General Assembly's home missions, Presbyterian Church in the United States ... 1861-1898. Atlanta, Franklin Printing and Publishing Co., 1898. 38 p. C U

697 CRANE, Charles LaCoste, 1884-1953.
Dikuatshisha dia kuyila dia dihungila dikulukulu. Mikanda ya 1 Bakelenge-Esete. Luebo, Congo Belge, 1930. 304 p. Commentary, Kings through Esther, in Baluba.   H

698 CRANE, Charles LaCoste, 1884-1953.
Facts about Africa and our Congo mission, in question and answer form. Nashville, Executive Committee of Foreign Missions, Presbyterian Church in the U.S., 1917. 47 p. A R U

699 CRANE, Charles LaCoste, 1884-1953.
Kudiunda kua ekelesia wa Jiso Kilisto. Luebo, Congo Belge, Afrique, 1930. 232 p. Church history, in Baluba. H

700 CRANE, John Curtis, 1888-1964.
Creation. n.p., n.d. 22 p. "From a compilation systematic theology translated into Korean and being translated into Chinese. "   C PT U

701 CRANE, John Curtis, 1888-1964, tr.
The influence of the weekly rest-day on human welfare. Translated into Korean by J. C. Crane and H. C. Kim. Seoul, Korea, Christian Literature Society of Korea, 1931. unpaged.   U

702 CRANE, John Curtis, 1888-1964.
The sacerdotal prayer of our Lord: studies in the 17th chapter of John. Pyengyang, Korea, n.p., 1940. 109 p. R PT U

703 CRANE, John Curtis, 1888-1964.
Systematic theology; a compilation from the works of R. L. Dabney, R. A. Webb, Louis Berkhof and many modern theologians. Gulfport, Miss., Specialized Printing Co., 1953. 3 v. C H L PT R U ... PT U: Indices. [1963]. 102 p. ... A: Vol. I.

704 CRANE, John Curtis, 1888-1964, tr.
Systematic theology. [Seoul, Department of Christian Edu-
cation, Presbyterian Church in the U.S., 1955]. unpaged. In
Korean. A C U

705 CRANE, William Earl, 1899-
Where God comes in; the divine "plus" in counseling. Waco,
Tex., Word Books, © 1970. 147. A H PT U

706 CRAWFORD, Alexander Warwick, 1857-1924.
North Carolina: the great opportunity. Greensboro, N.C.,
Jos. J. Stone & Co., 1923. 41 p. U

707 CRAWFORD, John Richard, 1932-
A Christian and his money. Nashville, Abingdon Press,
© 1967. 176 p. A C L PT R U

708 CRAWFORD, John Richard, 1932-
Only by thumb, by J. Walker [pseud.]. New York, Vantage
Press, © 1964. 141 p. U

709 CRAWFORD, John Richard, 1932-
Protestant missions in Congo, 1878-1969. n.p., [1969?].
26 p. A C H R U

710 CRIM, Keith Renn, 1924-
Limericks, lay and clerical [by] Casey Renn [pseud.].
Richmond, John Knox Press, © 1969. 55 p. U

711 CRIM, Keith Renn, 1924-
The royal Psalms. Richmond, John Knox Press, © 1962.
127 p. A C H L PT U

712 *CROFTS, Alfred, 1903-
A history of the Far East, by Alfred Crofts [and] Percy
Buchanan. New York, David McKay Co., [1961]. 626 p. C

713 *CROW, Paul Abernathy, 1931-
Church union at midpoint. Edited by Paul A. Crow, Jr.,
and William Jerry Boney. New York, Association Press,
© 1972. 253 p. A C L PT R U

714 CROWE, William, 1871-1962.
Is organic union of the Presbyterian churches to be de-
sired? [Weaverville, N.C., Southern Presbyterian Journal],
n.d. 8 p. U

715 CROWE, William, 1871-1962.
Those fifty days. An examination of some important incidents of an important period. St. Louis, Frederick Co.,
1938. 122 p. A C H L R U

716 CROWE, William, 1871-1962.

The romance of Westminster: an address delivered on the
seventy-seventh anniversary of Westminster Presbyterian
Church, St. Louis, November 23, 1930. St. Louis, n.p.,
1930. 16 p. A

717 CROWE, William, 1871-1962.
Under the study lamp: a melange of meditations. Talladega, Ala., Brannon Printing Co., n.d. unpaged. H L R

718 CROWE, William, 1899-1969.
A church and a minister during a significant decade. A
report to the session and diaconate, First Presbyterian Church,
Wilmington, N.C. Wilmington, n.p., 1952. 13 p. U

719 CROZIER, Robert Hoskins, 1836-1913.
Araphel; or, The falling stars of 1833: a story of evolution.
Richmond, Presbyterian Publishing Co., 1884. 527 p. H

720 CROZIER, Robert Hoskins, 1836-1913.
Call of Christ: a story of foreign missions. Richmond,
Whittet & Shepperson, [190?]. 220 p. A H R U

721 CROZIER, Robert Hoskins, 1836-1913.
The cave of Hegobar; or, The fiend of 1878. A story. As-
bury Park, N.J., Presbyterian Publishing Co., 1885. 675 p.
H

722 CROZIER, Robert Hoskins, 1836-1913.
Deep waters; or, A strange story. St. Louis, Farris,
Smith & Co., n.d. 367 p. A C ... A H R U: Deep
waters: a story of predestination. 2d ed. Richmond, Richmond Press, n.d. 288 p.

723 CROZIER, Robert Hoskins, 1836-1913.
Fiery trials; or, A story of an infidel's family. Memphis,
Rogers & Co., 1882. 527 p. R

724 CROZIER, Robert Hoskins, 1836-1913.
Golden rule; a tale of Texas. Richmond, Whittet & Shepperson, 1900. 179 p. A H U

725 CROZIER, Robert Hoskins, 1836-1913.
Kirk Ward's ghost; or, A modern miracle. Palestine, Tex.,
Palestine Printing Co., 1909. 139 p. U

726 *CULLMANN, Oscar.
The Christology of the New Testament. Translated by
Shirley Guthrie and Charles A. M. Hall. Philadelphia, West-
minster Press, © 1959. 342 p. A C L PT R U ... C U:
London, SCM Press, [1963]. 346 p.

727 CULVERHOUSE, Cecil Griffith, 1924-
Confronted by Christ, a study of selected incidents from

the Gospel of John. Richmond, CLC Press, © 1967. 80 p.
(The Covenant Life Curriculum.) C L U

728 CUNNINGHAM, Thomas McHutchin, 1887-
God so loved the world and other songs. n.p., n.d. 23 p.
U

729 CUNNINGHAM, Thomas McHutchin, 1887-
Hugh Wilson, a pioneer saint, missionary to the Chickasaw
Indians and pioneer minister in Texas; with a genealogy of the
Wilson family, including 422 descendants of Rev. Lewis Feuil-
leteau Wilson. [Dallas, Wilkinson Printing Co.], © 1938.
150 p. A H L U

730 *CURRIE, Anne Alison (Harrison).
Great Protestant leaders; biographical sketches of nine great
leaders. Studies for 1952-53 ... prepared by Alison H. and
Thomas W. Currie. [Atlanta, Board of Women's Work, Presbyterian Church in the U.S., 1952?]. 86 p. A H U

731 CURRIE, Armand London, 1899-
The man who owned the stable. Richmond, John Knox
Press, © 1943. 30 p. H L U

732 CURRIE, Armand London, 1899-
My son. Richmond, John Knox Press, © 1945. 29 p.
"A Christmas story told ... at the midnight service on Christ-
mas eve, 1944, in the Second Presbyterian Church, Richmond,
Virginia." L U

733 CURRIE, David Mitchell, 1918-
Come, let us worship God: a handbook of prayers for
leaders of worship. [1st ed.] Philadelphia, Westminster Press,
© 1977. 132 p. A C L PH PT U

734 CURRIE, Stuart Dickson, 1922-1975.
The beginnings of the church. Illustrated by Kathleen Elgin.
Richmond, CLC Press, © 1966. 143 p. (The Covenant Life
Curriculum.) C U ... L: [1967].

735 CURRIE, Thomas White, 1879-1943.
The Christian ministry. [Louisville, Ky., Committee of
Christian Education, Presbyterian Church in the U.S.], n.d.
7 p. PH

736 CURRIE, Thomas White, 1879-1943.
El contenido de la Biblia; temas y bosquejos de los libros
del Antiquo y Nuevo testamento. Kingsville, Tex., Texas-
Mexican Industrial Institute, [1940]. 119 p. A

737 CURRIE, Thomas White, 1879-1943.
Estudios sobre los Salmos. Version Castellana de Santiago

O. Shelby. Mexico, D. F., Casa de Publicaciones "El Faro,"
1949. 186 p. A

738 CURRIE, Thomas White, 1879-1943.
Studies in the Psalms. Kingsville, Tex., Tex.-Mex. Printery, 1941. 107 p. A C

739 CURRIE, Thomas White, 1914-
Austin Presbyterian Theological Seminary: a seventy-fifth
anniversary history. San Antonio, Trinity University Press,
© 1978. 285 p. Based on the author's thesis (Th.D.).
A C PT R U

740 CURRIE, Thomas White, 1914-
Our cities for Christ. Atlanta, Board of Church Extension,
Presbyterian Church in the U.S., © 1954. 49 p. A U

741 CURRY, Albert Bruce, 1852-1939.
Historic churches of West Tennessee. Written for the
Presbyterian Pastors' Association, Memphis, Tennessee,
March 19, 1923. Read before Memphis Presbytery, April,
1923, in session at Purdy, Tennessee. n.p., n.d. 16 p.
A

742 CURRY, Albert Bruce, 1852-1939.
History of the Second Presbyterian Church of Memphis,
Tennessee. [Memphis, Adams Printing and Stationery Co.,
1936?]. 128 p. A C H U

743 CURRY, Albert Bruce, 1852-1939.
Peter's vision. [Tuscaloosa, Ala., Presbyterian General
Assembly's Committee on Colored Evangelization], n.d. 16 p.
U

744 CURRY, Albert Bruce, 1852-1939.
The poor man at the gate. Atlanta, Executive Committee
of Home Missions of the Presbyterian Church in the U.S.,
n.d. 16 p. U

745 CURRY, Albert Bruce, 1852-1939.
Practical lessons from the early ministry of Jesus. Rich-
mond, Published for the author by Presbyterian Committee of
Publication, 1935. 214 p. A C H R U

746 CURRY, Albert Bruce, 1852-1939.
Practical lessons from the later ministry of Jesus. Rich-
mond, Published for the author by Presbyterian Committee of
Publication, 1938. 247 p. A C H L R U

747 CURRY, Albert Bruce, 1852-1939.
The responsibility of the church for an adequate ministerial
supply and how it may be met. Louisville, Ky., Executive

Committee of Christian Education and Ministerial Relief of the
Presbyterian Church in the U.S., 1911. 16 p.   U

748 DABNEY, Robert Lewis, 1820-1898.
The believer born of Almighty Grace: a sermon on Ephesians 1:19, 20. Richmond, Presbyterian Committee of Publication, 1871. 40 p.   PH U

749 DABNEY, Robert Lewis, 1820-1898.
The Bible its own witness. A sermon delivered ... in the
Presbyterian Church at Farmville, Va. Richmond, Shepper-
son & Graves, 1871. 20 p.   A

750 DABNEY, Robert Lewis, 1820-1898.
A caution against anti-Christian science. A sermon on
Colossians II.8. Preached in the Synod of Virginia, October
20, 1871. Richmond, James E. Goode, 1871. 19 p.   C
PH U

751 DABNEY, Robert Lewis, 1820-1898.
Christ our penal substitute. Richmond, Presbyterian Com-
mittee of Publication, © 1898. 115 p. Davidson College
Divinity lectures, 1897.   A C H L PT R U

752 DABNEY, Robert Lewis, 1820-1898.
Christ our substitute. [Richmond, Presbyterian Committee
of Publication], n.d. 4 p.   U

753 DABNEY, Robert Lewis, 1820-1898.
The Christian Sabbath: its nature, design, and proper observance. Philadelphia, Presbyterian Board of Publication,
© 1882. 93 p.   A C PH PT R U

754 DABNEY, Robert Lewis, 1820-1898.
The Christian's best motive for patriotism. A sermon:
preached in the College Church, Hampden Sidney, Va., on the
1st of November, 1860. A general fast-day, appointed by the
Synod of Virginia, to pray for escape from national convul-
sions. Richmond, Chas. H. Wynne, 1860. 14 p.   C PH
PT U

755 DABNEY, Robert Lewis, 1820-1898.
A defence of Virginia (and through her, of the South) in
recent and pending contests against the sectional party. New
York, E. J. Hale & Son, 1867. 356 p.   C H L PH PT U ...
C P: New York, Negro Universities Press, [1969] ... R:
Harrisonburg, Va., Sprinkle Publications, 1977.

756 DABNEY, Robert Lewis, 1820-1898.
A discourse on the uses and results of church history, delivered ... at his induction into the Professorship of Ecclesiastical History and Polity in Union Theological Seminary,

Virginia. Richmond, Ritchies and Dunnavant, 1854. 23 p.
C H PH PT U

757 DABNEY, Robert Lewis, 1820-1898.
A discussion of some of the changes proposed by the Committee of the General Assembly, in their revised book of discipline. n.p., n.d. 48 p. From the Southern Presbyterian
Review, April, 1859. PH

758 DABNEY, Robert Lewis, 1820-1898.
Discussions. Edited by C. R. Vaughan. Richmond, Pres-
byterian Committee of Publication, 1890-1897. 4 v. Vol. 4:
Mexico, Mo., Crescent Book House, 1897. A C H L PT
R U ... C L R U: London, Banner of Truth Trust, [1967].
2 v.

759 DABNEY, Robert Lewis, 1820-1898.
Dr. Girardeau's "Instrumental music in public worship":
a review. Richmond, Whittet & Shepperson, 1889. 9 p. U

760 DABNEY, Robert Lewis, 1820-1898.
Ecclesiastical relations of Negroes; speech ... in the Synod
of Virginia, Nov. 9, 1867, against the ecclesiastical equality
of Negro preachers in our church and their right to rule over
white Christians. Richmond, Office of Boys and Girls Monthly, 1868. 16 p. H PH PT U

761 DABNEY, Robert Lewis, 1820-1898.
Fiction, no defence of truth; or, A review of Theodosia
Earnest. Richmond, William H. Clemmitt, 1859. 154 p.
Reprinted from the Central Presbyterian. PT

762 DABNEY, Robert Lewis, 1820-1898.
The five points of Calvinism. Richmond, Presbyterian
Committee of Publication, 1895. 80 p. A H L PT R U

763 DABNEY, Robert Lewis, 1820-1898.
The immortality of the soul. Richmond, Presbyterian Committee of Publication, 1892. 37 p. Reprinted from the Presbyterian Quarterly, October, 1892. A H R U

764 DABNEY, Robert Lewis, 1820-1898.
The inductive logic. London, E. Stanford, n.d. 34 p.
U

765 DABNEY, Robert Lewis, 1820-1898.
Jackson; an elegy. [Richmond], n.p., n.d. 11 p. U

766 DABNEY, Robert Lewis, 1820-1898.
The latest infidelity: a reply to Ingersoll's positions.
Richmond, Presbyterian Committee of Publication, 1890.
68 p. C H

767 DABNEY, Robert Lewis, 1820-1898.
　　　Letter ... to the Rev. S. J. Prime, D.D., one of the edit-
ors of the New York Observer, on the state of the country.
Richmond, MacFarlane & Fergusson, 1861. 12 p.　U

768 DABNEY, Robert Lewis, 1820-1898.
　　　Life and campaigns of Lieut.-Gen. Thomas J. Jackson
[Stonewall Jackson].　New York, Blelock & Co., 1866. 742 p.
Appendix: The religious character of Stonewall Jackson, by
James Power Smith; and Stonewall Jackson's colored Sunday
School, by Margaret J. Preston. unpaged.　A C H L R U ...
H R: Harrisonburg, Va., Sprinkle Publications, 1976 ... H:
1977.

769 DABNEY, Robert Lewis, 1820-1898.
　　　Life of Lieut.-Gen. Thomas J. Jackson [Stonewall Jackson].
Abridged from the larger work.　London, James Nisbet & Co.,
1868. 278 p.　H

770 DABNEY, Robert Lewis, 1820-1898.
　　　Life of Lieut.-Gen. Thomas J. Jackson [Stonewall Jackson].
Edited by Rev. W. Chalmers.　London, James Nisbet & Co.,
1864-1866. 2 v.　A PH

771 DABNEY, Robert Lewis, 1820-1898.
　　　A memorial of the Christian life and character of Francis
S. Sampson.　Richmond, Enquirer Book and Job Press, 1855.
122 p.　A C H PH PT U

772 DABNEY, Robert Lewis, 1820-1898.
　　　The new South.　A discourse delivered at the annual commencement of Hampden Sidney College, June 15th, 1882, before
the Philanthropic and Union literary societies.　Raleigh, N.C.,
Edwards, Broughton & Co., 1883. 16 p.　H U

773 DABNEY, Robert Lewis, 1820-1898.
　　　On final cause, being a paper read before the Victoria Institute, or Philosophical Society of Great Britain.　To which
is added a paper, Structure and structureless, by Lionel S.
Beale. n.p., n.d. 25 p.　U

774 DABNEY, Robert Lewis, 1820-1898.
　　　Parental obligation.　A tract.　St. Louis, Presbyterian Publishing Co., n.d. 27 p.　C U

775 DABNEY, Robert Lewis, 1820-1898.
　　　The practical philosophy.　Being the philosophy of the feel-
ings, of the will, and of the conscience, with the ascertain-
ment of particular rights and duties.　Kansas City, Mo., Hudson, Kimberly Publishing Co., 1897. 521 p.　Imprint covered
by label: "Mexico, Mo., Crescent Book House."　A H R U ...
C L PT R U: Mexico, Mo., Crescent Book House, 1897.
530 p.

776 DABNEY, Robert Lewis, 1820-1898.
Presbyterianism, with the modern improvements. As illustrated by the sayings and doings of the broad church General
Assembly, recently convened in Baltimore, Md. n.p., 1873.
12 p.   U

777 DABNEY, Robert Lewis, 1820-1898.
A review of "Theodosia Earnest; or, The heroine of faith."
3d ed. Richmond, Shepperson & Graves, 1869. 147 p. Formerly, "Fiction, no defence of truth."   A C H L PT R U

778 DABNEY, Robert Lewis, 1820-1898.
Sacred rhetoric; or, A course of lectures on preaching.
Delivered in the Union Theological Seminary of the General
Assembly of the Presbyterian Church in the U.S., in Prince
Edward, Va.... Printed for the use of his students. Rich-
mond, Presbyterian Committee of Publication, 1870. 361 p.
A C PH PT R ... H U: 2d ed., rev. 1881 ... L R U:
3d ed., rev. 1902.

779 DABNEY, Robert Lewis, 1820-1898.
The sensualistic philosophy of the nineteenth century, considered. New York, Anson D. F. Randolph & Co., © 1875.
369 p.   A C H PT R U ... R: New and enl. ed. © 1887.
415 p.

780 DABNEY, Robert Lewis, 1820-1898.
The sin of the tempter; a sermon on Habakkuk, ii chap.,
xv verse. Lynchburg, Va., Published at the request of the
young men in his charge, 1860. 14 p.   PH U

781 DABNEY, Robert Lewis, 1820-1898.
Syllabus and notes of the course of systematic and polemic
theology taught in Union Theological Seminary, Virginia....
Published by the students. Richmond, Shepperson & Graves,
1871. 323 p.   A C L R U ... C H U: 2d ed. St. Louis,
Presbyterian Publishing Co., 1878. 903 p. ... PH U: 3d
ed. Asbury Park, N.J., n.p., 1885 ... C U: 4th ed.
Richmond, Presbyterian Committee of Publication, 1890 ...
C H L: 5th ed. (1871) ... C H L U: 6th ed. 1927 ...
C R: Lectures in systematic theology. Grand Rapids, Mich.,
Zondervan Publishing House, [1972] [reprint of 1878 ed].

782 DABNEY, Robert Lewis, 1820-1898.
What is a call to the gospel ministry? Richmond, Pres-
byterian Committee of Publication, n.d. 32 p.   A C H L
PH U

783 DABNEY, Robert Lewis, 1820-1898.
What is a call to the ministry? n.p., n.d. 16 p. Reprinted from the Central Presbyterian.   PH

784 DABNEY, Robert Lewis, 1820-1898.

The world white to harvest: reap; or it perishes. A sermon preached for the Board of Foreign Missions of the Presbyterian Church, in New York, May 2, 1858. New York, Printed for the Board of Foreign Missions by Edward O. Jenkins, 1858. 19 p. C PH U

785 DALLAS, James Maxwell, 1861-1942.
Historic Greenvale, "Old Greenville Church." From the organization of the church until the close of 1923. [Abbeville, S.C., Banner Publishing Co.], 1925. 55 p.

786 DANA, William Coombs, 1810-1880, ed.
A collection of hymns: supplementary to the Psalms and Hymns of Dr. Watts. New York, Daniel Dana, Jr., 1859. 396 p. C PH PT

787 DANA, William Coombs, 1810-1880.
Comprehensive scripture catechism for all evangelical Christians. Philadelphia, Presbyterian Board of Publication, © 1872. 24 p. PH PT

788 DANA, William Coombs, 1810-1880.
Correspondence between the Rev. Messrs. Dana and Smyth, through the mediation of the Hon. R. B. Gilchrist and the Rev. Dr. Bachman. Charleston, T. W. Haynes, 1847. 10 p. C H PH PT U

789 DANA, William Coombs, 1810-1880.
A discourse delivered February 3, 1850, at the dedication of the Central Church, erected by the Third Presbyterian congregation of Charleston. Charleston, S.C., John Russell, 1850. 20 p. PH

790 DANA, William Coombs, 1810-1880.
A discourse, delivered on the seventh anniversary of the dedication of the Central Presbyterian Church, Charleston, February 1, 1857. Charleston, Walker, Evans & Co., 1857. 24 p. C PH

791 DANA, William Coombs, 1810-1880.
Follow after charity. A sermon delivered in the Central Presbyterian Church, Charleston, S.C., December 6th, 1874. Charleston, News and Courier Job Presses, 1874. 10 p. C

792 DANA, William Coombs, 1810-1880.
The life of Daniel Dana, D.D. By members of his family. With a sketch of his character, by W. B. Sprague, D.D. Boston, J. E. Tilton and Co., 1866. 279 p. C L PH PT

793 DANA, William Coombs, 1810-1880.
Presbyterian Church government. A sermon, delivered before the Charleston Union Presbytery, March 22, 1870 ... with

A report to Presbytery, by John Forrest, D.D., pastor of the First Presbyterian Church. Charleston, Walker, Evans & Cogswell, 1870. PH

794 DANA, William Coombs, 1810-1880.
The sense of honor: a discourse delivered in the Central Presbyterian Church, Charleston, S.C., January 25, 1857. Charleston, Walker, Evans & Co., 1857. 19 p. PH

795 DANA, William Coombs, 1810-1880.
A sermon commemorative of Rev. John Forrest, D.D., delivered in the First Presbyterian Church, Charleston, October 19th, 1879. Charleston, S.C., H. P. Cooke & Co., 1879. 11 p. PH

796 DANA, William Coombs, 1810-1880.
A sermon delivered in the Central Presbyterian Church, Charleston, S.C., Nov. 21, 1860, being the day appointed by state authority for fasting, humiliation and prayer. Charleston, Evans & Cogswell, 1860. 12 p. H PT

797 DANA, William Coombs, 1810-1880.
A sermon delivered in the Central Presbyterian Church, Charleston, S.C., on the second Sunday in February, 1876, being the fortieth anniversary of his ordination. Charleston, S.C., Walker, Evans & Cogswell, 1876. 18 p. PH

798 DANA, William Coombs, 1810-1880.
A transatlantic tour: comprising travels in Great Britain, France, Holland, Belgium, Germany, Switzerland, and Italy. Philadelphia, Perkins & Purves, 1845. 391 p. C PH R

799 DANA, William Coombs, 1810-1880.
Two discourses on the moral state of man. Delivered in the Central Church, Charleston, April 13 and 20, 1851. Charleston, Edward C. Councell, 1851. 28 p. C

800 DANIEL, Emmett Randolph, 1935-
The Franciscan concept of mission in the High Middle Ages. [Lexington], University Press of Kentucky, © 1975. 168 p. L PT U

801 DAVID Howard Scanlon: thirty-eight years in the King's service. Resignation of Rev. David H. Scanlon, pastor of the First Presbyterian Church, Durham, North Carolina, October 10, 1937. n.p., [1938]. 23 p. PT

802 *DAVIDS, Richard C.
The man who moved a mountain. Philadelphia, Fortress Press, [1970]. 253 p. The story of Bob (Robert W.) Childress. C H PT U

803 DAVIDSON, Robert Franklin, 1902-

Philosophies men live by. New York, Dryden Press, [1953]. 486 p. A ... U: 2d ed. New York, Holt, Rinehart and Winston, [1974]. 442 p.

804 DAVIDSON, Robert Franklin, 1902-
Rudolf Otto's interpretation of religion. Princeton, N.J., Princeton University Press, 1947. 213 p. A C H L PT U

805 DAVIDSON, Robert Franklin, 1902-   ed.
The search for meaning in life; readings in philosophy. New York, Holt, Rinehart and Winston, © 1962. 415 p.   L

806 DAVIDSON College, Davidson, N.C.
Alumni catalogue of Davidson College ... 1837-1924. Edited by Thomas Wilson Lingle. Charlotte, N.C., Presbyterian Standard Publishing Co., 1924. 315 p.   H R U

807 DAVIDSON College, Davidson, N.C.
First semi-centenary celebration of Davidson College. Addresses, historical and commemorative, delivered at the annual commencement, Wednesday, June 13,, 1887. Raleigh, N.C., E. M. Uzzell, 1888. 165 p. Participants included Jethro Rumple, R. Z. Johnston. Biographical sketches of Samuel Williamson, Drury Lacy, J. L. Kirkpatrick, G. Wilson McPhail, A. D. Hepburn. A C H L PH R U

808 DAVIDSON College, Davidson, N.C.
Inauguration exercises, John Rood Cunningham, A.B., B.D., D.D., LL.D., Saturday, October 18, 1941, 10:30 A.M., auditorium, Chambers Building. Davidson, N.C., Davidson College, [1942]. 48 p. Davidson College Bulletin, vol. XLII, July, 1942. Participants included Daniel S. Gage, Walter L. Lingle, Henry H. Sweets, Theodore Meyer Greene, and John R. Cunningham. C H U

809 DAVIDSON College, Davidson, N.C.
The semi-centennial catalogue ... 1837-1887. Under the auspices of the Alumni Association. Edited by W. A. Withers, with the assistance of W. S. Lacy ... W. W. Moore ... Raleigh, E. M. Uzzell, 1891. 194 p. A H PH U

810 DAVIS, Augustus Lee, 1888-1968.
Present day Catholicism in Brazil. n.p., n.d. unpaged. PH

811 DAVIS, Robert Pickens, 1911-
Church camping; administrative manual for sponsoring units, planning committees, and directories. Art by Ruth Ensign. Richmond, John Knox Press, © 1969. 140 p. A C H L PH PT R U

812 DAVIS, Robert Pickens, 1911-

Senior high conference, manual. Richmond, CLC Press,
© 1967. 44 p. (The Covenant Life Curriculum.) C L U

813 DEMAREST, Gary William, 1926-
Christian alternatives within marriage. Waco, Tex., Word
Books, © 1977. 126 p. A PT U

814 DEMAREST, Gary William, 1926-
Colossians: the mystery of Christ in us. Waco, Tex.,
Word Books, © 1979. 191 p. PT

815 DENDY, Marshall Coleman, 1902-
Changing patterns in Christian education. Richmond, John
Knox Press, © 1964. 96 p. A C H L PT U

816 DENDY, Marshall Coleman, 1902-
A study of the catechism; the Westminster Shorter Cate-
chism for families. Richmond, CLC Press, © 1966. 191 p.
(The Covenant Life Curriculum.) C L PH U

817 DE SANTO, Charles P., 1923-
The book of Revelation, a study manual. Grand Rapids,
Mich., Baker Book House, © 1967. 112 p. R U ... L:
[1974].

818 DE SANTO, Charles P., 1923-
Love and sex are not enough. Scottdale, Pa., Herald
Press, © 1977. 157 p. A L U

819 *DESCHAMPS, Margaret Burr.
Benjamin Morgan Palmer: orator-preacher. n.p., n.d.
22 p. Reprinted from the Southern Speech Journal, September,
1953. A PH U

820 DEWITZ, Ludwig Richard Max, 1916-
The concept of balance in the Old Testament ... inaugural
address as Professor of Old Testament Languages, Literature
and Exegesis, delivered in the Columbia Presbyterian Church
on March 18, 1964. Columbia Theological Seminary Bulletin,
July, 1964. 1-18 p. A C H PT R U

821 DEWITZ, Ludwig Richard Max, 1916-
Messianic concepts in the Old Testament. Jackson, Miss.,
Belhaven College, 1957. 24 p. Bulletin, Belhaven College,
March, 1957. C U

822 DEWITZ, Ludwig Richard Max, 1916-
What makes a Jew? Richmond, CLC Press, © 1964.
48 p. (The Covenant Life Curriculum.) C R U ... L:
(1966).

823 DICKSON, Andrew Flinn, 1825-1879.

Christ in front. Philadelphia, Presbyterian Board of Publication, © 1879. 12 p.   PH

824   DICKSON, Andrew Flinn, 1825-1879.
Hazael; or, Know thyself. Philadelphia, American Sunday-school Union, © 1857. 106 p.   C R

825   DICKSON, Andrew Flinn, 1825-1879.
Lessons about salvation; from the life and words of the Lord Jesus. Being a second series of plantation sermons. Philadelphia, Presbyterian Board of Publication, © 1860. 264 p.   C PH U

826   DICKSON, Andrew Flinn, 1825-1879.
The light: is it waning? Why? How much? And what shall we do? Boston, Congregational Publishing Society, 1879. 156 p.   U

827   DICKSON, Andrew Flinn, 1825-1879.
Plantation sermons, or Plain and familiar discourses for the instruction of the unlearned. Philadelphia, Presbyterian Board of Publication, © 1856. 170 p.   " ... first appeared as a monthly series in the Southern Presbyterian."   A C L PH R U

828   DICKSON, Andrew Flinn, 1825-1879.
The temptation in the desert: lessons from Christ's conflict and victory. New York, American Tract Society, © 1872. 144 p.   A U

829   DIEHL, Charles Edward, 1875-1964, comp.
The story of a vineyard. The work of the Presbyterian Church U.S. in the Synod of Tennessee. Memphis, Tenn., Davis Printing Co., [1927]. 96 p.   A H L U

830   DIEHL, George West, 1887-1975.
The brick church on Timber Ridge. [Verona, Va., McClure Printing Co.], © 1975. 279 p.   H PT U

831   DIEHL, George West, 1887-1975.
"Heritage of Lexington Presbytery." n.p., n.d. 17 p.   U

832   DIEHL, George West, 1887-1975.
A history of the Collierstown Presbyterian Church. Exxington, Va., Harlow's Printing Shop, 1951. 24 p.   H

833   DIEHL, George West, 1887-1975.
Old Oxford and her families. [Verona, Va.], McClure Press, © 1971. 217 p.   H PH U

834   DIEHL, George West, 1887-1975.

The Rev. Samuel Houston, V.D.M. [Verona, Va.], Mc-
Clure Press, © 1970. 123 p. H PH U

835 DIEHL, George West, 1887-1975.
The triangle of life. Athens, W.Va., College Press, n.d.
90 p. U

836 DIEHL, George West, 1887-1975.
We Presbyterians. Corpus Christi, Tex., The author,
[1947]. 44 p. H R U

837 DISCOURSES at the inauguration of the Rev. William Henry
Green, as Professor of Biblical and Oriental Literature in
the Theological Seminary at Princeton, N.J., delivered at
Princeton, September 30, 1851, before the directors of the
seminary. I. The charge; by the Rev. Samuel Beach Jones,
D.D., of Bridgeton, N.J. II. The inaugural discourse.
Philadelphia, C. Sherman, 1851. 71 p. PH PT

838 DOAK, John Keith Whitfield, 1814-1891.
Letter to D. L. Moody: being a declaration of the only
true church polity, for every person, Jew or Gentile. Tunnel
Hill, Ga., n.p., 1876. 13 p. PT

839 DOAK, Samuel Witherspoon, 1785-1864.
A sermon delivered at the instalment of the Rev. John W.
Doak, D.D., pastor of Salem and Leesburg ... Salem, April
28, 1820. Knoxville, Tenn., Heiskell and Brown, 1820.
23 p. PH

840 DOAK, Samuel Witherspoon, 1785-1864.
A sermon, delivered on the 13th of April, 1815. It being
the day of public thanksgiving, recommended by the President
of the United States of America. Philadelphia, Joseph M.
Sanderson, 1815. 17 p. PH

841 DOBYNS, William Ray, 1861-1932.
As--So. Addresses on personal evangelism ... delivered
at Memphis convention, Laymen's Missionary Movement,
Presbyterian Church in the U.S. [Athens, Ga., Laymen's
Missionary Movement, Presbyterian Church in the U.S.],
n.d. 54 p. H

842 DOBYNS, William Ray, 1861-1932.
The Book in the light of its books; an introduction to a
comprehensive knowledge of the Bible.... With introduction
by Henry H. Sweets. New York, Fleming H. Revell Co.,
© 1929. 188 p. A C H L R U

843 DOBYNS, William Ray, 1861-1932.
In memoriam. Rev. Joshua Barbee. Born December 4,
1835. Died October 10, 1900. n.p., [1901]. 33 p. H

844 DR. ROBERT F. Boyd, minister. Richmond, Va., Published by Friends; printed by W. M. Brown and Son, [1976?]. 62 p.   U

845 DR. ROBERT Lee Bell Day celebration. Seventy-sixth birthday anniversary, Tuskegee, Alabama, Tuesday, July 2, 1946. n.p., n.d. 4 p.   U

846 DODGE, David Witherspoon, 1887-
Southern rebel in reverse; the autobiography of an idolshaker ... in cooperation with Clair M. Cook. [1st ed.] New York, American Press, © 1961. 178 p.   C L PT U

847 DODGE, Richard Daniel, 1889-1971.
Our rational faith. Richmond, Presbyterian Committee of Publication, © 1923. 172 p.   A C H L PT R U

848 DODSON, Samuel Kendrick, 1884-1977.
From darkness to light; a study of the spiritual meanings of light and darkness as revealed in God's Word to mankind. [1st ed.] New York, Greenwich Book Publishers, © 1959. 110 p.   A H R U

849 DOGGETT, Marshall Wellington, 1855-1941.
The tragedy of sin. Kingsport, Tenn., Southern Publishers, © 1935. 175 p.   A C L U

850 DONALDSON, Newton, ca. 1852-1924.
History of the class of 1879, W. & J. C. Lorain, Ohio, DeVeny & McCahon [1920?]. 113 p.   PH

851 DONALDSON, Newton, ca. 1852-1924.
"I promise Him." Huntington, W.Va., n.p., n.d. 56 p. Pamphlet of sermons, addressed especially to the young.   U

852 DOOM, Robert Isaac, 1930-
Faith that matters. Pine Bluff, Ark., Perdue Co., 1975. 74 p.   C L

853 DOOM, Robert Isaac, 1930-
Hope for renewal. Ste. Genevieve, Mo., Wehmeyer Printing Co., 1977. 100 p.   C

854 DOUGLAS, John, 1809-1879.
Dedication sermon, preached at the opening of the New Presbyterian Church, in Chesterville, S.C. ... January 21st, 1855. Charleston, A. J. Burke, 1855. 16 p.   C PH

855 DOUGLAS, John, 1809-1879.
Divine approbation, the great object of all study. A discourse delivered before the religious societies of Jefferson College, at the annual Commencement, August, 1857. Pittsburgh, W. S. Haven, 1857. 26 p.   PH

856 DOUGLAS, John, 1809-1879.
   The history of Purity Church ... 1865. Columbia, S.C.,
   Presbyterian Publishing House, 1870. 30 p.   PH

857 DOUGLAS, John, 1809-1879.
   The history of Steele Creek Church, Mecklenburg, N.C.
   Columbia, S.C., Presbyterian Publishing House, 1872. 81 p.
   H PH

858 DOUGLAS, John, 1809-1879.
   The rise and progress of Sabbath-schools. Pittsburgh,
   "United Presbyterian" Office, 1861. 64 p.   PH

859 DOUGLAS, John, 1809-1879.
   The Scottish Reformation: its necessity, causes, and results; being a sermon preached at the celebration of its Ter-
   centenary anniversary, in the First Reformed Presbyterian
   Church, Pittsburgh, on Sabbath, December 23d, 1860. Pittsburgh, "United Presbyterian" Office, 1861. 48 p.   PH

860 DOUGLASS, John Jordan, 1875-1940.
   The bells. Illustrated by Lieut. John B. Mallard. [Char-
   lotte, N.C., Presbyterian Standard Publishing Co.], 1919.
   126 p.   U

861 DOWNEY, William Walton, 1849-1889.
   History of Paxton Church. Harrisburg, Pa., Independent
   Steam Book and Job Print., 1877. 46 p.   PT

862 Doyle, William Bruce, 1877-1952.
   The Holy Family as viewed in our Lord's unfolding minis-
   try. New York, Fleming H. Revell Co., © 1916. 120 p.
   H

863 DRUMMOND, James, 1856-1927.
   Mary searching for Jesus. Philadelphia, Presbyterian
   Board of Publication, n.d. 32 p.   PH

864 DUBOSE, Hampden Coit, 1845-1910.
   ... The dragon, image, and demon; or, The three religions
   of China: Confucianism, Buddhism, and Taoism. Giving an
   account of the mythology, idolatry, and demonolatry of the
   Chinese. New York, A. C. Armstrong & Son, 1887. 468 p.
   Alternative title in Chinese characters at head of title-page.
   C H PT R U ... A H: Richmond, Presbyterian Committee
   of Publication, © 1899.

865 DUBOSE, Hampden Coit, 1845-1910.
   Memoirs of Rev. John Leighton Wilson, D.D., missionary
   to Africa, and secretary of foreign missions. Richmond,
   Presbyterian Committee of Publication, 1895. 336 p.   A C
   H PH PT R U

866 DUBOSE, Hampden Coit, 1845-1910.
Natural & apologetic theology; or, The fundamental evidences of Christianity. n.p., 1906. In Chinese. H PT

867 DUBOSE, Hampden Coit, 1845-1910.
Preaching in Sinim; or, The gospel to the Gentiles, with hints and helps for addressing a heathen audience. Richmond, Presbyterian Committee of Publication, 1893. 241 p. A C H L PT R U

868 DUBOSE, Hampden Coit, 1845-1910.
The school of Tyrannus, or reaching the masses by preaching and colportage. Shanghai, American Presbyterian Mission Press, 1897. 14 p. PH

869 DUBOSE, Henry Wade, 1884-1960.
About Thy table. Richmond, Presbyterian Committee of Publication, n.d. 16 p. U

870 DUBOSE, Henry Wade, 1884-1960.
We believe: a study of the Apostles' Creed. Atlanta, Committee of Woman's Work, Presbyterian Church in the U.S., [1949?]. 56 p. A C H L PT R U ... A H U: Richmond, John Knox Press, © 1960. 79 p.

871 DUCKWALL, John McCarty, 1855-1940.
The old parson and the barking dog. Richmond, Onward Press, n.d. 11 p. U

872 DUCKWALL, John McCarty, 1855-1940.
What is Freemasonry? A chip off the old block, and other sketches. n.p., n.d. 24 p. U

873 DUDLEY, Harold James, 1902-
Our mission to the Jews. [Weaverville, N.C., Southern Presbyterian Journal Co.], n.d. 6 p. Reprinted from the Southern Presbyterian Journal, February, 1943. U

874 DUHS, Robert Carl, 1924-
Abiding in Christ, a study in First John. n.p., n.d. 64 p. C R

875 DUHS, Robert Carl, 1924-
Jesus Christ: Alpha and Omega. Butler, Ind., Higley Press, © 1955. 120 p. C H R

876 DUHS, Robert Carl, 1924-
Kings and priests; a study of the priesthood of the believer. n.p., Adams Press, n.d. 84 p. H R

877 DUPUY, Benjamin Hunter, 1845-1926.
The Huguenot Bartholomew Dupuy and his descendants.

Louisville, Ky., Courier-Journal Job Printing Co., 1908. 439 p.   U

878 *EAGLETON, Davis Foute, comp.
A memorial sketch of Rev. George Ewing Eagleton: the record of a busy life. Compiled from his diary by his son. Richmond, Whittet & Shepperson, [1900?]. 81 p.   A H R U

879 *EAGLETON, Davis Foute.
A prince in Israel; a review of the life of the Rev. A. W. Wilson, 1833-1912. n.p., n.d. 26 p.   A

880 *EAGLETON, Davis Foute.
A tribute to the memory of Rev. W. J. B. Lloyd, missionary to the Choctaw Indians, 1870-1916. Richmond, Presbyterian Committee of Publication, 1916. 50 p.   H

881 EAGLETON, William, 1796-1866.
Essays on baptism. Philadelphia, Henry Perkins, 1847. 151 p.   PT

882 EAGLETON, William, 1796-1866.
Reply ... to the strictures on his essays by the Rev. J. L. Walker. Murfreesborough, Tenn., D. W. Taylor, 1849. 50 p.   PH

883 EAGLETON, William, 1796-1866.
A sermon on final perserverance delivered at Washington, Rhea County. [Knoxville], Heiskell & Brown, 1825. 64 p. PT

884 EAGLETON, William, 1796-1866.
A sermon preached at the funeral of Mr. John Eakin, Shelbyville, Tennessee, about the year 1849. n.p., n.d. 14 p. Typed title-page.   H

885 *EARLE, John R., 1935-
Spindles and spires: a re-study of religion and social change in Gastonia, by John R. Earle, Dean D. Knudsen, and Donald W. Shriver, Jr. Atlanta, John Knox Press, © 1976. 382 p.   A C H L PT U

886 EARLY Western Pennsylvania hymns & hymn-tunes, 1816-1846. Collected and edited by Jacob A. Evanson and George Swetnam. Coraopolis, Penna., Yahres Publications, 1958. 28 p.   PH

887 *EBY, Frederick, 1874-
The history and philosophy of education, ancient and medieval, by Frederick Eby and Charles Flinn Arrowood. New York, Prentice-Hall, 1940. 966 p.   A ... C PT: [1960].

888 EDDINS, James Franklin, 1876-1942.

Finding and filing Bible facts and features. Boston, Chapman & Grimes, © 1936. 115 p. H

889 EDMISTON, Alonzo Lmore, 1879-1954.
Mukanda muibidi wa agalonomie. Wakafundibua kudi luongoso. [Luebo], American Presbyterian Congo Mission, 1931. 203 p. Practical guide to agriculture. H

890 EDMONDS, Henry Morris, 1878-1960.
Beginning the day. New York, Abingdon-Cokesbury Press, n.d. unpaged. A prayer for each day of the year. H

891 EDMONDS, Henry Morris, 1878-1960.
The foundations of our liberties. n.p., n.d. 15 p. C

892 EDMONDS, Henry Morris, 1878-1960.
A parson's notebook. Birmingham, Ala., Elizabeth Agee's Bookshelf, 1961. 310 p. A L

893 EDMONDS, Henry Morris, 1878-1960.
Studies in power. Nashville, Cokesbury Press, 1931. 216 p. L R

894 EDMONDS, Henry Morris, 1878-1960.
The way, the truth, and the life. Nashville, Cokesbury Press, © 1936. 216 p. A H

895 EDWARDS, George Riley, 1920-
Jesus and the politics of violence. [1st ed.] New York, Harper & Row, © 1972. 186 p. C L PT U

896 EFIRD, James Michael, 1932-
Christ, the church, and the end: studies in Colossians and Ephesians. Valley Forge, Judson Press, © 1980. 110 p. U

897 EFIRD, James Michael, 1932-
Daniel and Revelation: a study of two extraordinary visions. Valley Forge, Judson Press, © 1978. 144 p. L PT R

898 EFIRD, James Michael, 1932-
Jeremiah, prophet under siege. Valley Forge, Judson Press, © 1979. 136 p. A L PT R U

899 EFIRD, James Michael, 1932-
The New Testament writings: history, literature and interpretation. [Atlanta: John Knox Press], © 1980. 223 p. A C H L U

900 EFIRD, James Michael, 1932-
These things are written; an introduction to the religious ideas of the Bible. Atlanta, John Knox Press, © 1978. 169 p. A C L PT R U

901 EGGLESTON, Richard Beverly, 1867-1927.
     Kitty Knight, by Ralph Conkley, [pseud.]. Richmond,
     Whittet & Shepperson, 1913. 313 p. U

902 ELLA DAVIDSON LITTLE: in memoriam. n.p., n.d. 40 p.
     Participating were Lacy L. Little, E. W. Smith, P. F. Price,
     and others. A H PT U

903 ELLIOTT, William Marion, 1903-
     Coming to terms with life. Richmond, John Knox Press,
     © 1944. 142 p. Sermons. H L R U

904 ELLIOTT, William Marion, 1903-
     The cure for anxiety. Richmond, John Knox Press, © 1964.
     92 p. "The substance of these nine chapters appeared in ...
     'For the living of these days.'" A C H L R U

905 ELLIOTT, William Marion, 1903-
     Every man in his place. Atlanta, Committee on Steward-
     ship and Finance, Presbyterian Church in the U.S., n.d.
     unpaged. PH

906 ELLIOTT, William Marion, 1903-
     For the living of these days. Richmond, John Knox Press,
     © 1946. 154 p. A C H L PT R U

907 ELLIOTT, William Marion, 1903-
     Lift high that banner! Richmond, John Knox Press, 1950.
     153 p. A C H L PH PT R U

908 ELLIOTT, William Marion, 1903-
     Power to master life; the message of Philippians for today.
     New York, Abingdon Press, © 1964. 143 p. A C H L R U

909 ELLIOTT, William Marion, 1903-
     Some impressions of the Far East. Nashville, Tenn.,
     Executive Committee of Foreign Missions, Presbyterian Church
     in the U.S., n.d. 9 p. U

910 ELLIOTT, William Marion, 1903-
     Two sons. Richmond, John Knox Press, © 1955. 62 p.
     A C H L R U

911 ELLIOTT, William Marion, 1903-
     What about the National Council of Churches? An address.
     Dallas, Tex., Highland Park Presbyterian Church, [1960].
     unpaged. U

912 *EMPIE, Paul C., ed.
     Marburg revisited; a reexamination of Lutheran and Re-
     formed traditions. Editors: Paul C. Empie & James I. Mc-
     Cord. Minneapolis, Augsburg Publishing House, © 1966.

193 p. Papers and summaries prepared in connection with a series of annual meetings held from Feb. 1962 through Feb. 1966. A C H L PH PT R U

913 EMURIAN, Sisag Krikor, 1874-1968, comp.
The Westminster Shorter Catechism; an original musical setting for solo voices and mixed quartet or chorus.... Arranged by Henri Emurian. Richmond, Presbyterian Committee of Publication, [1936]. 52 p. Introduction by Ernest Trice Thompson. H PH U

914 ENGLISH, Thomas Reese, 1806-1869.
A sermon, preached in Salem Church, February 6th, 1842, in commemoration of its late pastor Rev. Robert Wilson James. Charleston, A. E. Miller, 1842. 23 p. C

915 ENGLISH, Thomas Reese, 1850-1915.
Studies in the minor prophets. For the use of the middle class in Union Theological Seminary, Richmond, Va. Richmond, Whittet & Shepperson, 1898. 70 p. U

916 ENGSTROM, Winfred Andrew, 1925-
Multi-media in the church: a beginner's guide for putting it all together. Richmond, John Knox Press, © 1973. 128 p. A C H L PH PT R U

917 ENSIGN, John Edward, 1923-
Camping together as Christians: a guide for junior high camp leaders, by John and Ruth Ensign. Illustrated by Ruth Singley Ensign. Richmond, John Knox Press, © 1958. 148 p. A C H L R U

918 ENSIGN, John Edward, 1923-
Stewards in God's world; a guide for junior high camp leaders, by John and Ruth Ensign. Illustrated by Ruth Singley Ensign. Richmond, John Knox Press, © 1953. 144 p. H U ... U: My camp book; stewards in God's world [camper's book]. 63 p.

919 ERDMAN, William Jacob, 1834-1923.
Ecclesiastes. A study. Philadelphia, Avil Printing Co., 1895. 88 p. PH ... R: Ecclesiastes; the book of the natural man. Chicago, Bible Institute Colportage Ass'n., n.d. ... U: New York, Gospel Publishing House, n.d.

920 ERDMAN, William Jacob, 1834-1923.
The Holy Spirit and Christian experience. 3d ed., rev. New York, Gospel Publishing House, © 1909. 51 p. L

921 ERDMAN, William Jacob, 1834-1923.
Notes on the Revelation.... Edited by Charles R. Erdman. New York, Fleming H. Revell Co., © 1930. 102 p. A R U

922 ERDMAN, William Jacob, 1834-1923.
An outline study of the Gospel according to John. n.p.,
n.d. 74 p. PT

923 ERDMAN, William Jacob, 1834-1923.
The parousia of Christ a period of time; or, When will the
church be translated? Chicago, Gospel Publishing Co., n.d.
146 p. C PH PT

924 ERDMAN, William Jacob, 1834-1923.
Sanctification and the second coming of Christ. Two Bible
readings by Rev. W. J. Erdman and J. H. Brooks. Given
at the Swampscott conference, 1876. Rochester, N.Y., Ar-
mour Bearer, 1876. 8 p. U

925 ERDMAN, William Jacob, 1834-1923.
The unseen world: a concordance with notes. 2d ed., rev.
Chicago, Fleming H. Revell Co., n.d. 41 p. PT

926 ESTES, Frank Bigham, 1896-
History of Orangeburg Presbyterian Church, 1835-1935.
[Orangeburg, S.C., Observer Publishing Co.], n.d. 14 p.
C H

927 ESTES, Frank Bigham, 1896-
History of the 1st. Presbyterian Church of Orangeburg,
1835-1950. Orangeburg, S.C., Walter D. Berry, 1950. 11 p.
H

928 EVANGELICAL roots; a tribute to Wilbur Smith, edited by
Kenneth S. Kantzer. Nashville, Thomas Nelson, © 1978.
250 p. A PT U

929 EVANGELICAL Theological Society.
New perspectives on the Old Testament. J. Barton Payne,
editor. Waco, Tex., Word Books, © 1970. 305 p. Papers
presented at the 20th annual meeting, Dec. 26-28, 1968.
C L PT R U

930 EVANGELISTIC preaching. A symposium by Wade P. Huie,
Jr., Kenneth G. Phifer, Ben Lacy Rose, David L. Stitt. At-
lanta, Board of Church Extension, Presbyterian Church in the
U.S., n.d. 16 p. C

931 EVANS, Benjamin Hoyt, 1923-1977.
Programs for young people. Grand Rapids, Mich., Baker
Book House, 1963. 106 p. Cover-title: 30 programs for
young people. R

932 EVANS, Benjamin Hoyt, 1923-1977.
Youth programs about Bible people. Grand Rapids, Mich.,
Baker Book House, 1964. 107 p. Cover-title: 24 programs
about Bible people. R

933 EXEGESIS: problems of method and exercises in reading
(Genesis 22 and Luke 15). Gerald Antoine [and others] ...
translated by Donald G. Miller. Pittsburgh, Pickwick Press,
1978. 469 p.   L PT U

934 EXPLORATIONS in public policy; essays in celebration of the
life of John Osman.... Editors: May Maury Harding and
Mary E. Osman. Memphis, Southwestern at Memphis, 1980.
91 p.   L

935 FACKLER, John G.,   -ca. 1891.
A sermon preached on the occasion of the dedication of the
Central Presbyterian Church, San Francisco, California, No-
vember 26th, 1865. San Francisco, George W. Stevens and
Co., 1865. 16 p.   PH

936 FAIR, Robert Anderson, 1820-1899.
Our slaves should have the Bible. An address delivered
before the Abbeville Bible Society, at its anniversary, July,
1854. Due West, S.C., Telescope Press, 1854. 24 p.
PH PT

937 FAIRLY, John L., 1888-1964.
Children of believing parents. Richmond, Board of Chris-
tian Education, Presbyterian Church in the U.S., n.d. 6 p.
U

938 FAIRLY, John L., 1888-1964.
Kinder fragen--Christen antworten. Kassel, J. G. Oncken
Verlag, [1959]. 91 p. Übertragung ... von Helmut Pohl;
Titel der Originalausgabe: Using the Bible to answer ques-
tions children ask.   U

939 FAIRLY, John L., 1888-1964.
Our curriculum materials. [Richmond, Presbyterian Committee of Publication], n.d. 23 p.   U

940 FAIRLY, John L., 1888-1964.
Using the Bible to answer questions children ask [by] John
L. & Arleene Gilmer Fairly. Richmond, John Knox Press,
© 1958. 99 p.   A C H L U

941 FAITH on the frontier: religion in Colorado before August
1876, edited by Louisa Ward Arps. Religion in Colorado:
a bibliography, compiled by Harold M. Parker, Jr. Den-
ver, Colo., Colorado Council of Churches, 1976. 155 p.
L H PH PT

942 FARLEY, William Edward, 1929-
Ecclesial man: a social phenomenology of faith and reality.
Philadelphia, Fortress Press, © 1975. 282 p.   A C L PT U

943 FARLEY, William Edward, 1929-

Requiem for a lost piety; the contemporary search for the Christian life. Philadelphia, Westminster Press, © 1966. 139 p.   A C L PT R U

944   FARLEY, William Edward, 1929-
The transcendence of God, a study in contemporary philosophical theology. Philadelphia, Westminster Press, © 1960. 255 p.   A C L PT R U

945   FARRIS, Robert Perry, 1826-1903.
Mariolatry; or, The worship of the virgin Mary and its support from Scripture. [St. Louis, Buschart Brothers Printing], n.d. 16 p.   U

946   FAST-DAY sermons; or, The pulpit on the state of the country. New York, Rudd & Carleton, 1861. 336 p. Sermons by J. H. Thornwell, B. M. Palmer, Robert L. Dabney, and others. A C H L PH R U

947   *FAUSSET, Andrew Robert, 1821-1910.
The poetical books of the Holy Scriptures. With a critical and explanatory commentary by the Rev. A. R. Fausset ... and Rev. B. M. Smith ... Philadelphia, James S. Claxton, 1867. unpaged. H PT U

948   FICKLEN, James Burwell, 1875-1932.
The brown eyed lady with the alabaster skin. Atlanta, Hubbard & Hancock Co., 1928. 71 p.   H

949   FICKLEN, James Burwell, 1875-1932.
Is prayer worth while? Prayer in the light of science, revelation, and experience. Richmond, Presbyterian Committee of Publication, n.d. 15 p.   U

950   FINLEY, George Williamson, 1838-1909.
The sphere and rights of woman in the church. Richmond, Presbyterian Committee of Publication, [1899]. 16 p.   U

951   FISHER, Michael Montgomery, 1834-1891.
History of Westminster College, 1851-1903; from 1851 to 1887, by M. M. Fisher; edited and continued to 1903 by John J. Rice. Columbia, Mo., E. W. Stephens, 1903. 380 p. H L PH PT

952   FISHER, Michael Montgomery, 1834-1891.
The three pronunciations of Latin. 2d ed. Boston, New England Publishing Co., 1879. 152 p.   C

953   FISK, Pliny,   -1866.
The Holy land an interesting field of missionary enterprise. A sermon, preached ... just before the departure of the Palestine mission. Boston, n.p., 1819. 21-52 p.   PT

954 FLEMING, John Kerr, 1892-
A Cowan lineage of 400 years, by John K. Fleming and Luther French Cowan, Sr. Mount Airy, N.C., Cockerham Printing, 1976. 66 p. U

955 FLEMING, John Kerr, 1892-
The Cowans from County Down. Raleigh, N.C., Derreth Printing Co., © 1971. 440 p. U

956 FLEMING, John Kerr, 1892-
History of the Third Creek Presbyterian Church, Cleveland, North Carolina, 1787-1966, Concord Presbytery. Raleigh, N.C., Synod of North Carolina, 1967. 199 p. C H PH R U

957 FLEMING, John Kerr, 1892-
In freedom's cause: Samuel Young of Rowan County, N.C. Salisbury, N.C., Rowan Publishing Co., 1958. 44 p. PH

958 FLEMING, Robert Hanson, 1846-1919.
The catholicity of Presbyterianism. An address delivered in Aberdeen, Scotland, June 20, 1913, to the Council of Presbyterian and Reformed Churches. Pulaski, Va., B. D. Smith & Brothers, n.d. 10 p. C PT U

959 FLETCHER, Donald Rodgers, 1919-
Gates of brass; a narrative poem on the passion and triumph of the Son of God. Philadelphia, Presbyterian Press, 1942. 44 p. PT

960 FLINN, John William, 1847-1907.
Centennial sermon: relations between education and religion. South Carolina centennial, Columbia, S.C., January 8, 1905. Columbia, R. L. Bryan Co., 1905. 16 p. U

961 FLINN, John William, 1847-1907.
Evolution and theology. Columbia, S.C., Presbyterian Publishing House, 1885. 507-589 p. "The consensus of science against Dr. Woodrow's opponents." Reprinted from the Southern Presbyterian Review, July, 1885. C

962 *FLOURNOY, Francis Rosebro.
Benjamin Mosby Smith, 1811-1893. Richmond, Richmond Press, 1947. 153 p. A C H L PH R U

963 FLOURNOY, Parke Poindexter, 1839-1935.
... The bearing of archaeological and historical research upon the New Testament. [London], Morgan & Scott, n.d. 16 p. At head of title: Tracts for new times, no. 5. H PT U

964 FLOURNOY, Parke Poindexter, 1839-1935.
Byla evangelia napsána v prvém století? Několik dokladu

pro hodnovĕrnost novozákonnich spisu.... Cesky upravil J. A. Kohout. Praha, Tiskem knihtiskarny "Gutenburg" Jaroslava Hencla, n.d. 23 p. Slavonic translation of "Were the Gospels written in the first century?" PT

965 FLOURNOY, Parke Poindexter, 1839-1935.
The diatessaron of Tatian and its evidential value. n.p., n.d. 37 p. PT

966 FLOURNOY, Parke Poindexter, 1839-1935.
The Earl of Rochester; his career as a courtier and its end [a soul clinic]. Richmond, Presbyterian Committee of Publication, © 1927. 38 p. U

967 FLOURNOY, Parke Poindexter, 1839-1935.
Ferris's "Formation of the New Testament." n.p., n.d. 26 p. Reprinted from Bibliotheca Sacra, July and October, 1909. U

968 FLOURNOY, Parke Poindexter, 1839-1935.
The Gospel according to the Hebrews. n.p., n.d. 23 p. Reprinted from the Presbyterian Quarterly, July, 1903. PT

969 FLOURNOY, Parke Poindexter, 1839-1935.
A historical discourse, delivered at Rockville & Bethesda churches, on the first Sabbath of April, 1880, by the pastor. Baltimore, Messenger Publishing Co., [1881]. 18 p. H PH PT

970 FLOURNOY, Parke Poindexter, 1839-1935.
New light on the New Testament; an account of some interesting discoveries which bear important testimony as to the time when the Gospels and other books of the New Testament were written. Philadelphia, Westminster Press, 1903. 193 p. A C H L PH PT U

971 FLOURNOY, Parke Poindexter, 1839-1935.
The original facts of Christianity. [Bethesda, Md.], n.p., n.d. 234-254 p. Reprinted from the Presbyterian Quarterly, April, 1900. PT

972 FLOURNOY, Parke Poindexter, 1839-1935.
The search-light of St. Hippolytus: the papacy and the New Testament in the light of discovery.... With an introduction by Prof. Walter W. Moore. New York, Fleming H. Revell Co., 1896. 250 p. A C H L PT R U

973 FLOURNOY, Parke Poindexter, 1839-1935.
Who was "Darius the Median?"--New light from Babylonian tablets. n.p., n.d. 602-612 p. Reprinted from the Presbyterian Quarterly, October, 1900. PT

974 FLOW, John Eldred, 1874-1954.

Evangelistic sermons. Concord, N.C., n.p., n.d. 96 p.
U

975   FLOW, John Eldred, 1874-1954.
      Some Southern Presbyterian sermons. Concord, N.C., n.p.,
      n.d. 88 p.   A C H R U

976   FOGARTIE, James Eugene, 1924-
      In search of Christmas. Richmond, John Knox Press,
      [1957]. 15 p.   U

977   FOGLEMAN, William Jethro, 1928-
      I live in the world. Richmond, CLC Press, © 1966.
      223 p. (The Covenant Life Curriculum.)   C U ... L:
      [1969] ... C L U: Leaders' guide. 95 p.

978   FOOTE, William Henry, 1794-1869.
      The example of Christ. [A sermon]. n.p., n.d. 16 p.
      PH

979   FOOTE, William Henry, 1794-1869.
      The Huguenots; or, Reformed French Church. Their prin-
      ciples delineated; their character illustrated; their sufferings
      and successes recorded. Richmond, Presbyterian Committee
      of Publication, [1870]. 627 p.   A C H PH PT R U

980   FOOTE, William Henry, 1794-1869.
      The righteous shall be in everlasting remembrance. A
      sermon, delivered Sabbath a.m., February 8, 1857, in the
      Presbyterian Church, Moorefield, Hardy County, Va., on the
      occasion of the death of Rev. William N. Scott, on the morn-
      ing of January 24, 1857. Philadelphia, Joseph M. Wilson,
      1857. 29 p.   PT

981   FOOTE, William Henry, 1794-1869.
      The services at the funeral of Mrs. Hannah A. Armstrong,
      who departed this life Thursday, August 3, 1854, and was
      buried Friday, August 4, 1854. Romney, Va., John W. Woods,
      1854. 16 p.   PH

982   FOOTE, William Henry, 1794-1869.
      Sketches of North Carolina, historical and biographical,
      illustrative of the principles of a portion of her early settlers.
      New York, Robert Carter & Brothers, 1846. 557 p.   A C
      H L PH PT R U ... C U: [2d ed.] Dunn, N.C., Reprint
      Co., 1912 ... C H L PH PT R U: 3d ed. Raleigh, N.C.,
      Committee on Historical Matters of the Synod of North Caro-
      lina and the North Carolina Presbyterian Historical Society,
      © 1965. 593 p.

983   FOOTE, William Henry, 1794-1869.
      Sketches of Virginia, historical and biographical. [1st]-
      2d series. Philadelphia, W. S. Martien [etc.], 1850-55. 2 v.

Vol. 2 published by J. B. Lippincott & Co. A H L PH PT
R U ... L PH PT: v. 2, 2d series, 2d ed., rev., 1856.
568 p. ... A C H L PH R U: [New ed.] Richmond, John
Knox Press, [1966]. 616 p.

984 FORD, Leighton Frederick Sandys, 1931-
     The Christian persuader. New York, Harper & Row,
     © 1966. 159 p. A L PT R U ... L: [1976].

985 FORD, Leighton Frederick Sandys, 1931-
     Good news is for sharing. Elgin, Ill., David C. Cook
     Publishing Co., © 1977. 203 p. Spine title: Good news.
     C PT U

986 FORD, Leighton Frederick Sandys, 1931-
     Letters to a new Christian. [Minneapolis, Minn.], Billy
     Graham Evangelistic Association, © 1967. 64 p. R

987 FORD, Leighton Frederick Sandys, 1931-
     New man ... new world. Waco, Tex., Word Books,
     © 1972. 119 p. C PT R

988 FORD, Leighton Frederick Sandys, 1931-
     One way to change the world. [1st ed.] New York, Har-
     per & Row, © 1970. 119 p. C L PT R U

989 FOREMAN, Kenneth Joseph, 1891-1967.
     Adults in the school: manual. Richmond, CLC Press,
     © 1963. 55 p. (The Covenant Life Curriculum.) C L U

990 FOREMAN, Kenneth Joseph, 1891-1967.
     Candles on the glacier: warm thoughts for a cold world:
     being fables and fantasies about faith for the modern mind.
     New York, Association Press, © 1956. 184 p. C H L PT
     U

991 FOREMAN, Kenneth Joseph, 1891-1967.
     Christian patterns of life; programs for the general meet-
     ings of the Women of the Church, 1951-1952. Atlanta, Board
     of Women's Work, Presbyterian Church in the U.S., [1951].
     108 p. U

992 FOREMAN, Kenneth Joseph, 1891-1967.
     Do they need us anymore? [Nashville, Tenn., Board of
     World Missions, Presbyterian Church in the U.S., 1957?).
     15 p. U

993 FOREMAN, Kenneth Joseph, 1891-1967.
     From this day forward: thoughts about a Christian marriage.
     Richmond, Outlook Publishers, 1950. 71 p. A C L PT R U

994 FOREMAN, Kenneth Joseph, 1891-1967.
     God's will and ours; an introduction to the problem of

freedom, foreordination and faith. [1st ed.] Richmond, Outlook Publishers, © 1954. 63 p. A H L PH R U

995 FOREMAN, Kenneth Joseph, 1891-1967.
How to learn the will of God. [Richmond, Presbyterian
Outlook], n.d. 8 p. U

996 FOREMAN, Kenneth Joseph, 1891-1967.
How to prepare for communion. [Richmond, Presbyterian
Outlook], n.d. 4 p. U

997 FOREMAN, Kenneth Joseph, 1891-1967.
Identification: human and divine. Richmond, John Knox
Press, © 1963. 160 p. A C H L PH PT R U

998 FOREMAN, Kenneth Joseph, 1891-1967.
Introduction to the Bible [by] Kenneth J. Foreman, Balmer
H. Kelly, Arnold B. Rhodes, Bruce M. Metzger [and] Donald
G. Miller. Richmond, John Knox Press, © 1959. 171 p.
(The Layman's Bible Commentary, v. 1.) A C H L PT R
U ... U: "Large print edition."

999 FOREMAN, Kenneth Joseph, 1891-1967.
The letter of Paul to the Romans. The first letter of
Paul to the Corinthians. The second letter of Paul to the
Corinthians. Richmond, John Knox Press, © 1961. 152 p.
(The Layman's Bible Commentary, v. 21). A C H L PT
R U ... L: Japanese translation by Haruyosi Huzimoto.
Tokyo, Board of Publications, United Church of Christ in
Japan, © 1961. 281 p.

1000 FOREMAN, Kenneth Joseph, 1891-1967.
Methuselah; fantasy on a moral theme. With 12 line
drawings by Doyle Robinson. Richmond, John Knox Press,
© 1968. 125 p. A C H L PT R U

1001 FOREMAN, Kenneth Joseph, 1891-1967.
Modern messages from ancient prophets. Philadelphia,
Westminster Press, © 1943. 47 p. U

1002 FOREMAN, Kenneth Joseph, 1891-1967.
The saint in the window and the saint in the house: a
fantasy. [Richmond, Outlook Publishers], © 1954. unpaged.
U

1003 FOUR PRESBYTERIAN pioneers in Congo. [This book is of-
fered by the First Presbyterian Church of Anniston, Alabama,
in observance of the birth of Samuel Norvell Lapsley ...
April 14, 1866. Anniston, Ala., First Presbyterian Church,
1965]. 124, 153, 32, 28 p. Cover-title. Contents.--Life
and letters of Samuel Norvell Lapsley, by Samuel Norvell
Lapsley.--Presbyterian pioneers in Congo, by William H.
Sheppard.--Maria Fearing: a mother to African girls, by

Althea Brown Edmiston.--Lucy Gantt Sheppard: shepherdess of His sheep on two continents, by Julia Lake Kellersberger. C H R U

1004 FOUSHEE, Clyde C., 1900-1973.
Animated object talks. Grand Rapids, Mich., Baker Book House, © 1973. 159 p.   R

1005 FOWLE, James Luther, 1897-1978.
Planned services for church groups. Richmond, John Knox Press, © 1946. 212 p.   A C H L R U

1006 FOWLE, James Luther, 1897-1978.
So many people. Richmond, John Knox Press, © 1944. 159 p.   A H L PT R U

1007 FOWLE, James Luther, 1897-1978.
So many people. Richmond, John Knox Press, © 1944. 159 p.   A H L PT R U

1008 *FOX, Vernelle.
Pilot project for clinical training of clergymen in the field of alcoholism, by Vernelle Fox, John M. Crow [and others]. Atlanta, Georgia Department of Public Health, [1976?]. 83 p. "In consultation with ... Thomas H. McDill [and others]." C

1009 *FRANCIS, Fred O., comp.
Conflict at Colossae; a problem in the interpretation of early Christianity, illustrated by selected modern studies. Edited and translated with an introduction and epilogue by Fred O. Francis and Wayne A. Meeks. [Missoula, Mont.], Society of Biblical Literature, 1973. 222 p.   U ... A C L PT: Rev. ed. [Cambridge, Mass.], Society of Biblical Literature, © 1975.

1010 FRANK HENRY GAINES, D.D., LL.D. Minister of the Gospel, founder and President of Agnes Scott College: July 25, 1852--April 14, 1923. n.p., n.d. unpaged.   H PT

1011 FRASER, Abel McIver, 1856-1933.
Doctor Fraser and his sermons. Edited by Rev. William E. Hudson. New York, Fleming H. Revell Co., © 1920. 159 p.   A H PH R U

1012 FRASER, Abel McIver, 1856-1933.
The sphere and rights of woman in the church, by Abel M. Fraser [and others]. Richmond, Presbyterian Committee of Publication, [1899]. 16 p.   U

1013 FRASER, Abel McIver, 1856-1933.
Suppose the tithe law is repealed, what then? Chattanooga,

Tenn., General Assembly's Stewardship Committee, Presbyterian Church in the U.S., n.d. 15 p. PH

1014 FRASER, Abel McIver, 1856-1933.
What is to be your life work? Why not the ministry?
Louisville, Ky., Executive Committee of Christian Education
and Ministerial Relief of the Presbyterian Church in the U.S.,
n.d. 8 p. U ... U: Richmond, Presbyterian Committee
of Publication.

1015 FRASER, Thomas Layton, 1899-1977.
Back when: a biography of Joseph Bacon Fraser and
Maria Boulineau Fraser of Hinesville, Georgia, and their
children. [Clinton, S.C., Thomas Layton Fraser], © 1976.
179 p.

1016 FRASER, Thomas Layton, 1899-1977.
The life and philosophy of Christ. [3d ed., rev.] Grand
Rapids, Mich., Wm. B. Eerdmans Publishing Co., © 1961.
308 p. R U

1017 FRASER, Thomas Layton, 1899-1977.
A survey of the Old Testament. 3d ed., rev. n.p.,
© 1955. 184 p. U ... A C R: 6th ed., rev. Grand
Rapids, Mich., Wm. B. Eerdmans Publishing Co., [1965]
© 1962.

1018 FRAZER, George Stanley.
Christianity and the man of to-day. Nashville, Tenn.,
Publishing House of the Methodist Episcopal Church, South,
1917. 163 p. U

1019 FRAZER, William Henry, 1873-1953.
Bible notes. Charlotte, N.C., Presbyterian Standard,
1924. 158 p. H R U

1020 FRAZER, William Henry, 1873-1953.
Challenging mantles; a series of chapel talks. [Charlotte,
N.C., Queen City Printing Co., 1926]. 180 p. H U

1021 FRAZER, William Henry, 1873-1953.
Fireside musings of "Uncle" Rastus and "Aunt" Randy.
Charlotte, N.C., Murrill Press, 1925. 101 p. H

1022 FRAZER, William Henry, 1873-1953.
The Possumist, and other stories. Charlotte, N.C.,
Murrill Press, 1924. 68 p. A H

1023 FRAZER, William Henry, 1873-1953.
Why I favor preserving the Southern Church. [Weaverville,
N.C., Southern Presbyterian Journal], n.d. 6 ℓ. U

1024 FREELAND, Paul Butterfield, 1904-1977.

The First Presbyterian Church of Crowley, Louisiana: a brief history, 1890-1965. Crowley, n.p., 1965. 54 p.   H

1025   FRIERSON, Edward Ogelvie, 1832-1889.
The Lord's Prayer. Norfolk, Va., Pollock & Barcroft, n.d.   82 p.   A C R

1026   FROM BONDAGE to Freedom; God's varied voices. The Narrative: Exodus; a drama of redemption [by] James Sprunt; Prophecy: Isaiah 40-66; the freedom of servanthood [by] Robert H. Bullock; Gospel: John; the way to life [by] Vernon H. Kooy; Epistle: Galatians; the life of freedom [by] Bernard J. Mulder. Richmond, CLC Press, © 1967. 441 p. (The Covenant Life Curriculum.)   C L R U ... C L R U: Teacher's book. 350 p.

1027   FROM FAITH to faith: essays to honor of Donald G. Miller on his seventieth birthday. Edited by Dikran Y. Hadidian. Pittsburgh, Pickwick Press, 1979. 446 p. Essays by Donald G. Miller, F. Wellford Hobbie, James L. Mays, John Bright, Dietrich Ritschl, and others.   A C H L PT U

1028   FRONTIS, Stephen, 1792-1867.
The duty of Christians to support missionaries to the heathen. Boston, n.p., 1834. 16 p.   PT

1029   *FRY, Rose W.
Collections of the Rev. John McElhenny, D.D., by his granddaughter. Richmond, Whittet & Shepperson, 1893. 291 p. Contains Dr. M. L. Lacy's funeral discourse. A H L PH U

1030   FRY, Thomas Albert, 1919-
Change, chaos, and Christianity. Westwood, N.J., Fleming H. Revell Co., © 1967. 124 p.   A L PT U

1031   FRY, Thomas Albert, 1919-
Doing what comes supernaturally. Westwood, N.J., Fleming H. Revell Co., © 1966. 126 p.   A H L U

1032   FRY, Thomas Albert, 1919-
Get off the fence! Morals for moderns. [Westwood, N.J.], Fleming H. Revell Co., © 1963. 127 p.   C H L PT U

1033   FRY, Thomas Albert, 1919-
They dared to dream. Waco, Tex., Word Books, © 1972. 170 p.   U

1034   FRYE, James Bruce, 1930-
The Mills River Presbyterian Church, Horse Shoe, N.C., Horse Shoe, Mills River Presbyterian Church, 1959. 35 p. U

1035 FUDGE, Samuel Royal, 1922-
Living with today's teenagers. Durham, N.C., Moore
Publishing Co., © 1970. 109 p.   L U

1036 FUHRMANN, Paul Traugott, 1903-1968.
Extraordinary Christianity; the life and thought of Alexander Vinet. With a preface by John T. McNeill. Philadelphia, Westminster Press, © 1964. 125 p.   A C H L PH
PT R U

1037 FUHRMANN, Paul Traugott, 1903-1968.
God-centered religion, an essay inspired by some French
and Swiss Protestant writers. Grand Rapids, Mich., Zondervan Publishing House, © 1942. 237 p.   C L PT U

1038 FUHRMANN, Paul Traugott, 1903-1968.
An introduction to the great creeds of the church. Phila-
delphia, Westminster Press, © 1960. 144 p.   A C H L
PT R U

1039 FUHRMANN, Paul Traugott, 1903-1968.
Luther's vision of the Kingdom of God [or, The three
kingdoms according to Luther]. Westminster, Md., The
Times, 1951. 16-24 p. Reprinted from the Drew Gateway,
Spring, 1951.   C PT U

1040 FUHRMANN, Paul Traugott, 1903-1968.
Philosophical elements in the early Reformed tradition.
n.p., n.d. 16 p.   H U

1041 FUHRMANN, Paul Traugott, 1903-1968.
"The theology of conscience" in Pascal and his Swiss
Protestant successors. Madison, N.J., n.p., 1933. 13 p.
Abstract of thesis (Ph.D.)--Drew University, 1933.   U

1042 FUHRMANN, Paul Traugott, 1903-1968.
Why Calvin? [Inaugural address as Professor of Church
History at Columbia Theological Seminary, Decatur, Ga.
Delivered May 7, 1962]. 13 p. Columbia Seminary Bulle-
tin, July, 1962.   C H R U

1043 FULTON, Charles Darby, 1892-1977.
The church in a revolutionary world. [Nashville, Tenn.,
Board of World Missions, Presbyterian Church in the U.S.,
1956]. 11 p.   U

1044 FULTON, Charles Darby, 1892-1977.
Now is the time ... published for Executive Committee of
Foreign Missions, Presbyterian Church in the U.S. Rich-
mond, John Knox Press, © 1946. 188 p.   A C H L PT
R U

1045 FULTON, Charles Darby, 1892-1977.

Our philosophy of missions. Our program of missions.
Contemporary problems in missions. A series of three lec-
tures delivered before the Synod of Virginia at Massanetta
Springs, June 29-30, 1959. Nashville, Board of World Mis-
sions, Presbyterian Church in the U.S. [1959]. 3 pamphlets.
A C

1046 FULTON, Charles Darby, 1892-1977.
Star in the East. Richmond, Presbyterian Committee of
Publication, © 1938. 264 p. A C H PH R U

1047 FULTON, Robert Edwin, 1877-1957.
Historical sketch of Tuscaloosa Presbytery, organized
February 25, 1835. n.p., n.d. 23 p. A PH U

1048 FUNERAL discourses on the death of Mrs. Henrietta M. Dawson, wife of the Hon. Wm. C. Dawson, of Georgia, who died
at Washington City, April 7, 1850. Washington, Jno. T.
Towers, 1850. 30 p. Discourses by Rev. Francis Bowman
and others. PH

1049 THE FUTURE of our religious past; essays in honour of Ru-
dolf Bultmann. Edited by James M. Robinson; translated by
Charles E. Carlston and Robert P. Scharlemann. [London],
SCM Press, [1971]. 372 p. A C L PT R U

1050 GABBARD, Elmer Everett, 1890-
"Digging the old wells again." An Easter message, 1940.
[Buckhorn, Ky., The author], 1940. unpaged. PH

1051 *GAEBELEIN, Arno Clemens, 1861-1945.
The Jewish question ... [and] The messianic question, by
C. I. Scofield. New York, Publication Office "Our Hope,"
© 1912. 137 p. A L R U

1052 GAGE, Daniel Shaw, 1863-1951.
The voice by Galilee: a study of John XXI. Richmond,
Presbyterian Committee of Publication, © 1917. 46 p.
C H

1053 GAILEY, James Herbert, 1916-
The beginning of wisdom. Inaugural address ... upon being inducted into the chair of Old Testament Language, Literature, and Exegesis at Columbia Theological Seminary. Delivered in the chapel of the seminary, Nov. 1, 1955. 9 p.
Bulletin of Columbia Theological Seminary, April, 1956.
A C H

1054 GAILEY, James Herbert, 1916-
The book of Micah. The book of Nahum. The book of
Habakkuk. The book of Zephaniah. The book of Haggai. The
book of Zechariah. The book of Malachi. Richmond, John

Knox Press, © 1962. 144 p. (The Layman's Bible Commentary, v. 15.)   A C H L PT R U

1055   GAILEY, James Herbert, 1916-
Jerome's Latin version of Job from the Greek, chapters 1-26; its text, character, and provenance. [Princeton Theological Seminary, 1948.] 11 p. Abstract of thesis--Princeton Theological Seminary. Contains biographical sketch.   C PT U

1056   GAINES, Frank Henry, 1852-1923.
Bible course: outline and notes. Atlanta, Franklin Printing and Publishing Co., 1895-98. 3 v.   H R U

1057   GAINES, Frank Henry, 1852-1923.
The college and the kingdom. Louisville, Ky., Executive Committee of Christian Education and Ministerial Relief, Presbyterian Church in the U.S., n.d. 15 p.   U

1058   GAINES, Frank Henry, 1852-1923.
The story of Agnes Scott College (1889-1921). n.p., n.d. 68 p.   A C PT

1059   GAINES, Frank Henry, 1852-1923.
The type of Christianity of college women. Louisville, Ky., Executive Committee of Christian Education and Ministerial Relief, Presbyterian Church in the U.S., n.d. 16 p. U

1060   GAINES, Frank Henry, 1852-1923.
The woman crisis and the woman's college. Louisville, Ky., Executive Committee of Christian Education and Ministerial Relief, Presbyterian Church in the U.S., n.d. 14 p. U

1061   GALLAHER, Thomas, 1832-1909.
Infant salvation; or, The future state of children dying in infancy: a discourse. [Rensselaer, Mo.], n.p., 1899. 60 p.   A PH PT

1062   GALLAHER, Thomas, 1832-1909.
A short method with the dipping anti-pedobaptsts (!). St. Louis, Presbyterian Publishing Co., 1878. 340 p.   A C H L R

1063   GAMBLE, Connolly Currie, 1921-
The seminary library and the continuing education of the minister. [Urbana, Ill.], University of Illinois, 1960. 270-280 p. Reprinted from Library Trends, vol. 9, no. 2. A PT U

1064   GAMBLE, William Arnett, 1894-1973.

Ten sermons for ten years. [Raymond, Miss., Keith Press, 1940]. 99 p.   C R U

1065   GAMBLE, William Arnett, 1894-1973.
Trumpets of the Lord: proclaiming God's wonderful words of life. [1st ed.] New York, Vantage Press, © 1971. 163 p.   C H U

1066   GAMMON, Samuel Rhea, 1865-1928.
The evangelical invasion of Brazil: or a half century of evangelical missions in the land of the southern cross.   Richmond, Presbyterian Committee of Publication, © 1910.   179 p. A C H PT U

1067   GAMMON, William Jefferson, 1876-1967.
Old Gammon families and their descendants.   Montreat, N.C., n.p., 1965.   176 p.   H

1068   GARBER, Paul Leslie, 1911-
James Henley Thornwell, Presbyterian defender of the Old South. n.p., n.d.   23 p.   Reprinted from Union Seminary Review, February, 1943.   PH

1069   GARBER, Paul Leslie, 1911-
A reconstruction of Solomon's temple. Rev. [New York, Archaeology, 1960].   165-172 p.   Reprinted from Archaeology, Autumn, 1952.   H

1070   GARBER, Paul Leslie, 1911-
Solomon's temple: a reconstruction based on the Howland-Garber model by E. G. Howland, Paul L. Garber. n.p., n.d.   48 p.   H

1071   GARBER, Paul Leslie, 1911-
Solomon's temple, by Paul L. Garber and E. G. Howland. [Troy, Ohio], n.p., © 1950.   31 p.   U

1072   GARBER, Paul Leslie, 1911-
Victor of the dark domain. Atlanta, Presbytery of Atlanta [Presbyterian Church in the U.S.], 1963.   8 p.   Moderator's sermon, January 22, 1963.   C H

1073   GARRETT, Willis Edward, 1914-
The life that wins; salvation sermonettes. [1st ed.] New York, Exposition Press, © 1954.   56 p.   U

1074   GARRISON, Joseph Marion, 1904-
Heads up for college. Richmond, John Knox Press, © 1944. 60 p.   H U

1075   GARRISON, Joseph Marion, 1904-
"Here comes ... Murphy": an appreciation for the Rev.

Murphy Williams, pastor emeritus 1946-1955, in the Presbyterian Church of the Covenant, Greensboro, N.C., n.p., [1956]. 40 p.   A U

1076   GARRISON, Joseph Marion, 1904-
       The Missouri Presbytery, 1817-1937. n.p., n.d.   35 p.
       PH

1077   GARRISON, Pinkney Jefferson, 1906-
       Presbyterian polity and procedures: the Presbyterian Church, U.S. Richmond, John Knox Press, © 1953. 190 p.
       A C H L PT R U

1078   GARTH, John Goodall, 1871-1952.
       The idyll of the Shepherd. New York, George H. Doran Co., © 1911. 58 p.   H L ... H: 2d ed. Charlotte, N.C., Standard Printing Co., 1932. 64 p. ... U: [3d ed.] 1934.

1079   GARTH, John Goodall, 1871-1952.
       The little Gospel: a popular study of John 3:16. [Charlotte, N.C., Observer Printing House], © 1952. 158 p.
       A C H R U

1080   GARTH, John Goodall, 1871-1952.
       The mission of the Presbyterian Church. Richmond, Presbyterian Committee of Publication, © 1900. 11 p.   PT

1081   GARTH, John Goodall, 1871-1952.
       Sixty years of home missions in the Presbyterian Synod of North Carolina. [Charlotte? n.p., 1948?]. 86 p.   H PT R U

1082   GARTH, James Goodall, 1871-1952, comp.
       World wide revival songs, no. 2, for the church, Sunday School, and evangelistic campaigns. Siloam Springs, Ark., © 1921. 277 p.   PH

1083   GAUSS, Joseph Henry, 1855-
       The Bible's authority supported by the Bible's history. [St. Louis, Buxton & Skinner, 1896]. 64 p.   PH PT

1084   GAUSS, Joseph Henry, 1855-
       God's truth versus man's theories: Bible deliverance from Satan's deceits. St. Louis, Mo., Frederick Printing Co., n.d. 314 p.   R

1085   GAUSS, Oscar William, 1842-1918.
       An historical sermon delivered in the Presbyterian Church, at Booneville, Missouri ... August 27, 1876. St. Louis, C. R. Barns, 1876. 30 p.   H PH

1086   GEAR, Felix Bayard, 1899-1982.

Basic beliefs of the Reformed faith; a Biblical study of Presbyterian doctrine. Richmond, John Knox Press, © 1960. 80 p.　A C H L PH PT R U

1087　GEAR, Felix Bayard, 1899-1982.
　　　Can Calvinism live again?　n.p., n.d.　12 p.　U

1088　GEAR, Felix Bayard, 1899-1982.
　　　Our Presbyterian belief.　Atlanta, John Knox Press, © 1980.　90 p.　C H L U

1089　*GEORGE, James Zachariah, 1826-1897.
　　　The political history of slavery in the United States ... with a foreword and a sketch of the author's life by William Hayne Leavell....　New York, The Neale Publishing Co., 1915.　342 p.　PT U

1090　GEORGE, William, 1828-1897 or '98.
　　　A memorial sermon, delivered on the fiftieth anniversary of the organization of Mount Horeb Church, in Fayette County, Kentucky, April 22, 1877.　Cincinnati, Robert Clarke & Co., 1877.　30 p.　PH PT

1091　GEORGE, William, 1828-1897 or '98.
　　　A memorial sermon, delivered on the ninetieth anniversary of the organization of Bethel Church, in Fayette County, Kentucky.　Paris, Ky., F. L. & J. R. McChesney, 1880.　36 p. H PT U

1092　GEORGE, William, 1828-1897 or '98.
　　　Presbyterianism contrasted with prelacy and independency: a sermon delivered before West-Lexington Presbytery at its fall meeting in Bethel Church, September, 1879.　Louisville, Ky., Courier-Journal Job Rooms, 1880.　27 p.　C U

1093　GETTY, Walter, 1882-1969.
　　　Home-coming of the service man.　Philadelphia, Penna., Committee on Camp and Church Activities, Presbyterian Wartime Service Commission, n.d.　15 p.　PH

1094　GETTYS, Joseph Miller, 1907-
　　　Christ in you: your hope of glory, your power for service!　Atlanta, Board of Women's Work, Presbyterian Church in the U.S., [1952].　48 p.　"For Circle Bible leader." PH PT U

1095　GETTYS, Joseph Miller, 1907-
　　　Hark to the trumpet: the message of the prophets for the world of today.　Richmond, John Knox Press, 1948.　191 p. A C H L R U

1096　GETTYS, Joseph Miller, 1907-
　　　How to enjoy studying the Bible.　Rev. ed.　Richmond,

[The author], © 1945. 37 p.   U ... U: Richmond, John
Knox Press, [1950]. 52 p. ... A: 1953 ... C L R U:
[Rev. ed., enl.], © 1956. 72 p. ... U: [1967] ... U:
Teacher's guide [for rev. ed.].

1097 GETTYS, Joseph Miller, 1907-
How to study Acts. Richmond, John Knox Press, © 1959.
219 p.   A C H L R U

1098 GETTYS, Joseph Miller, 1907-
How to study Ephesians. Richmond, John Knox Press,
© 1954. 64 p.   A C H L R U ... U: [1955] ... A:
Leader's guide. 24 p.

1099 GETTYS, Joseph Miller, 1907-
How to study I Corinthians. Richmond, John Knox Press,
© 1951. 128 p.   A C H L PT R U

1100 GETTYS, Joseph Miller, 1907-
How to study John. Richmond, John Knox Press, © 1960.
153 p.   C H L R U ... C: [Joseph M. Gettys, reprinted,
1977].

1101 GETTYS, Joseph Miller, 1907-
How to study Luke. Richmond, John Knox Press, © 1947.
144 p.   A C H L R U ... U: Rev. ed. Clinton, S.C.,
Joseph M. Gettys, [1975] © 1962. 153 p.

1102 GETTYS, Joseph Miller, 1907-
How to study Philippians, Colossians, and Philemon.
Richmond, John Knox Press, © 1964. 87 p.   A C H L R U

1103 GETTYS, Joseph Miller, 1907-
How to study the Revelation. Richmond, John Knox Press,
© 1946. 131 p.   A L R U ... A L PT: [1947] ... A H
L R: [Rev. ed. 1963]. 117 p. ... C: Clinton, S.C.
Joseph M. Gettys, 1973.

1104 GETTYS, Joseph Miller, 1907-
How to teach Acts. Richmond, John Knox Press, © 1959.
61 p.   A C L R U

1105 GETTYS, Joseph Miller, 1907-
How to teach I Corinthians. Richmond, John Knox Press,
© 1951. 107 p.   A C L R U

1106 GETTYS, Joseph Miller, 1907-
How to teach John. Richmond, John Knox Press, © 1960.
80 p.   L R

1107 GETTYS, Joseph Miller, 1907-
How to teach Luke. A leader's guide for How to study

Luke. Richmond, John Knox Press, © 1958. 64 p. A C H L R U

1108 GETTYS, Joseph Miller, 1907-
How to teach Philippians, Colossians, and Philemon. Richmond, John Knox Press, © 1964. 45 p. A C L R U

1109 GETTYS, Joseph Miller, 1907-
How to teach the Bible. Richmond, John Knox Press, © 1949. 163 p. A H L PT U ... C: [Rev. and enl., 1955]. 175 p. ... A C H L R U: [Rev. ed.], © 1961. 112 p.

1110 GETTYS, Joseph Miller, 1907-
How to teach the Revelation. Richmond, John Knox Press, © 1955. 56 p. A C L U ... C L R: Rev. ed. [1964] © 1963.

1111 GETTYS, Joseph Miller, 1907-
Living the gospel: a study of I Peter. Richmond, CLC Press, © 1970. 78 p. (The Covenant Life Curriculum.) C L U ... C L U: Teacher's book. 63 p.

1112 GETTYS, Joseph Miller, 1907-
Meet your church; how Presbyterians think and live. Richmond, John Knox Press, © 1955. 62 p. A C H L U ... H: [1967] ... A C H U: Leader's guide. 35 p.

1113 GETTYS, Joseph Miller, 1907-
The signs of the times; an interpretation of Mark 13. [Columbia, S.C., R. L. Bryan Co.], 1939. 15 p. U

1114 GETTYS, Joseph Miller, 1907-
Surveying the historical books. Richmond, John Knox Press, © 1963. 163 p. A C H L R U

1115 GETTYS, Joseph Miller, 1907-
Surveying the Pentateuch. Greenwood, S.C., Attic Press, © 1962. 147 p. C R ... A L U: Richmond, John Knox Press, © 1962.

1116 GETTYS, Joseph Miller, 1907-
Teaching others how to teach the Bible. Richmond, John Knox Press, © 1961. 37 p. A C L R U

1117 GETTYS, Joseph Miller, 1907-
Teaching pupils how to study the Bible, a teacher's guide for How to enjoy studying the Bible. Richmond, John Knox Press, © 1950. 60 p. A C R U ... C H L U: Rev. ed. © 1951.

1118 GETTYS, Joseph Miller, 1907-

Teaching the historical books. Richmond, John Knox
Press, © 1963. 63 p. A C H L U

1119 GETTYS, Joseph Miller, 1907-
Teaching the Pentateuch. Richmond, John Knox Press,
© 1962. 59 p. A C L R U

1120 GETTYS, Joseph Miller, 1907-
These things abide: the Ten Commandments in the light
of the teachings of Jesus ... for Circle Bible leader. Atlanta, Board of Women's Work, Presbyterian Church in the
U.S., [1951]. 60 p. A C U

1121 GETTYS, Joseph Miller, 1907-
What Presbyterians believe: an interpretation of the Westminster standards. Dallas, Tex., First Presbyterian Church,
© 1953. 128 p. A C PH U ... A: [1955] ... H: n.p.,
Joseph M. Gettys, 1958 ... R: [1966] ... A R U: Leader's
guide. © 1955. 48 p.

1122 GETTYS, Joseph Miller, 1907-
Your church and your home.... Suggestions for the study
of "Beside the hearthstone," by Robert A. Lapsley, Jr.;
with additional resource material suggested by Harvey W.
Walters and William H. Ramkey. Richmond, John Knox
Press, n.d. 32 p. A U

1123 GHISELIN, Charles, 1853-1943.
A prize essay on the character of Jesus Christ. Norfolk,
Va., J. D. Ghiselin, n.d. 13 p. U

1124 GIBBONEY, Charles Haller, 1914- ed.
By faith: pioneering in home missions. Atlanta, Board
of Church Extension, Presbyterian Church in the U.S.,
© 1951. 188 p. Chapters by Cary R. Blain, Walter B.
Passiglia, Arthur V. Boand, Oscar Gardner, Lawrence W.
Bottoms, Goodridge A. Wilson, Cecil Lang, William E.
Crane, Leslie H. Patterson, and others. A C H L R U

1125 GIBBONEY, Charles Haller, 1914-
Frontiers of hope: widening horizons in church extension.
Atlanta, Board of Church Extension, Presbyterian Church in
the U.S., © 1952. 214 p. A C H L U

1126 GIBBS, John Gamble, 1930-
Creation and redemption, a study in Pauline theology.
Leiden, E. J. Brill, 1971. 194 p. (Supplements to Novum
Testamentum, vol. XXVI.) A revision of the author's thesis,
Princeton Theological Seminary, 1966. A C L PT U

1127 *GIBONEY, Ezra P.
The life of Mark A. Matthews, "Tall pine of the Sierras."

By Ezra P. Giboney and Agnes M. Potter. Grand Rapids, Mich., Wm. B. Eerdmans Publishing Co., 1948. 134 p. C PH PT R

1128 *GILBERT, John L.
Review of Rev. Henry H. Paine's sermon, preached by the appointment of the Presbytery of Montgomery at Wytheville, Va., September 13, 1845. Fincastle, n.p., 1850. 69 p. PH

1129 GILDERSLEEVE, Benjamin, 1791-1875.
The mediatorial probation. A review of a sermon delivered at the installation of Rev. Charles Rich, as pastor of the North Presbyterian Church, Buffalo, New York, by Rev. G. W. Heacock, pastor of La Fayette Street Church; Buffalo, Faxon's Press, 1848. PP. 20. By the Rev. B. Gildersleeve, of Richmond, Va. Buffalo, Seaver and Foy, 1848. 16 p. PH

1130 GILDERSLEEVE, Benjamin, 1791-1875.
A sermon, preached in the Second Presbyterian Church, Charleston, October 6, 1827, at the funeral of the Rev. T. Charlton Henry, D.D., late pastor of said church. Charleston, Observer Office Press, 1827. 32 p. PH

1131 GILLESPIE, Richard Thomas, 1909-1977.
God making his appeal through us. Inaugural address ... upon being inducted into the chair of homiletics at Columbia Theological Seminary. Delivered in the chapel of the seminary, Nov. 2, 1955. 11-23 p. Bulletin of Columbia Theological Seminary, April, 1956. A C H

1132 GILMER, George Hudson, 1866-1947.
Creation; an exposition of the first and second chapters of Genesis. [Pulaski, Va., B. D. Smith & Brothers], n.d. 22 p. U

1133 GILMOUR, Abram David Pollock, 1876-1948.
The denominational college: a denominational necessity. Delivered at the General Assembly ... May 18, 1912. Louisville, Ky., Executive Committee of Christian Education and Ministerial Relief, Presbyterian Church in the U.S., n.d. 16 p. U

1134 GIRARDEAU, John Lafayette, 1825-1898.
An address on behalf of the Society for the relief of superannuated ministers and the indigent families of deceased ministers of the Synod of South Carolina.... Delivered at Sumterville, S.C., October 29, 1858. Columbia, S.C., R. W. Gibbes, 1858. 19 p. C H PH

1135 GIRARDEAU, John Lafayette, 1825-1898.

Calvinism and evangelical Arminianism: compared as to
election, reprobation, justification, and related doctrines.
Columbia, S.C., W. J. Duffie, 1890. 574 p.   A C H L
PH PT R U

1136   GIRARDEAU, John Lafayette, 1825-1898.
A catechism for the oral instruction of coloured persons
who are inquirers concerning religion, or candidates for
admission to the church.   Charleston, Evans & Cogswell,
1860.   88 p.   H

1137   GIRARDEAU, John Lafayette, 1825-1898.
Christ's pastoral presence with his dying people.   A ser-
mon delivered January 7th, 1872, in Zion Church, Glebe
Street, Charleston, S.C.   Charleston, Walker, Evans &
Cogswell, 1872.   16 p.   C

1138   GIRARDEAU, John Lafayette, 1825-1898.
Conscience and civil government.   An oration delivered
before the Society of Alumni of the College of Charleston,
on Commencement Day, March 27th, 1860.   Charleston,
Evans & Cogswell, 1860.   20 p.   PH PT

1139   GIRARDEAU, John Lafayette, 1825-1898.
Discussions of philosophical questions....   Edited by Rev.
George A. Blackburn.   Richmond, Presbyterian Committee
of Publication, © 1900.   515 p.   A C H L PT R U

1140   GIRARDEAU, John Lafayette, 1825-1898.
Discussions of theological questions....   Edited by Rev.
George A. Blackburn.   Richmond, Presbyterian Committee
of Publication, © 1905.   534 p.   A C H L PT R U

1141   GIRARDEAU, John Lafayette, 1825-1898.
Individual liberty and church authority.   A sermon preached
at Westminster Church, Charleston, Thursday night, April 11,
1889, during the sessions of Charleston Presbytery.   Columbia, S.C., William Sloane, 1889.   18 p.   C PH

1142   GIRARDEAU, John Lafayette, 1825-1898.
Instrumental music in the public worship of the church.
Richmond, Whittet & Shepperson, 1888.   208 p.   A C H L
PH PT R U

1143   GIRARDEAU, John Lafayette, 1825-1898.
The remembrance of the righteous.   A memorial sermon,
occasioned by the death of the Rev. David H. Porter, D.D.,
and preached in the First Presbyterian Church, Savannah,
Ga., Feb. 8th, 1874.   Columbia, S.C., Presbyterian Publishing House, 1874.   27 p.   C PH

1144   GIRARDEAU, John Lafayette, 1825-1898.

Sermons.... Edited by Rev. George A. Blackburn, under the auspices of the synods of South Carolina, Georgia, Alabama and Florida. Columbia, S.C., The State Co., 1907. 412 p.   A C H L PT R U

1145 GIRARDEAU, John Lafayette, 1825-1898.
The substance of two speeches on the teaching of evolution in Columbia Theological Seminary, delivered in the Synod of South Carolina, at Greenwood, S.C., Oct., 1884. Columbia, S.C., William Sloane, 1885. 35 p.   C H U

1146 GIRARDEAU, John Lafayette, 1825-1898.
Theology as a science, involving an infinite element. Inaugural address delivered before the General Assembly at Savannah, Ga., May 23d, 1876. Columbia, S.C., Presbyterian Publishing House, 1876. 34 p.   C PH U

1147 GIRARDEAU, John Lafayette, 1825-1898.
The will in its theological relations. Columbia, S.C., W. J. Duffie, 1891. 497 p.   A C H L PH PT R U

1148 GLASGOW, Samuel McPheeters, 1883-1963.
Applied Christianity: a study in the Epistle of James. Atlanta, Board of Women's Work, Presbyterian Church in the U.S., © 1950. 51 p.   L U

1149 GLASGOW, Samuel McPheeters, 1883-1963.
Border trails. n.p., n.d. 47 p.   U

1150 GLASGOW, Samuel McPheeters, 1883-1963.
Chapels: today's evangelistic frontier. Richmond, Presbyterian Committee of Publication, © 1939. 111 p.   A C H L R U

1151 GLASGOW, Samuel McPheeters, 1883-1963.
Daily communion. Grand Rapids, Mich., Wm. B. Eerdmans Publishing Co., 1933. 399 p.   A H L ... H: 3d ed. 1936. 366 p. ... R U: 4th ed., 1951.

1152 GLASGOW, Samuel McPheeters, 1883-1963.
The General epistles; studies in the letters of James, Peter, John and Jude. New York, Fleming H. Revell Co., © 1928. 169 p.   A C H PT R U

1153 GLASGOW, Samuel McPheeters, 1883-1963.
A most successful mission of the church. [Atlanta, Executive Committee of Home Missions, Presbyterian Church in the U.S.], n.d. 2 ℓ.   U

1154 GLASGOW, Samuel McPheeters, 1883-1963.
My tomorrow's self. New York, Richard R. Smith, 1931. 152 p.   H PT R U

1155 GLASGOW, Samuel McPheeters, 1883-1963.
Needed counsel for new Christians, by Samuel McPheeters
Glasgow, Cecil Herbert Lang, Julia Lake Skinner. Richmond,
Presbyterian Committee of Publication, © 1923. 72 p. A
C L U ... H R: 47 p.

1156 GLASGOW, Samuel McPheeters, 1883-1963.
The Son of Man seeking men in the Gospel of Mark. A
series of studies in Christ's methods of evangelism based on
Mark's Gospel. Delivered at Montreat, N.C., to the Auxiliary Training School, July 6-13, 1933. Richmond, Presbyterian Committee of Publication, © 1933. 24 p. U

1157 GLASGOW, Samuel McPheeters, 1883-1963.
The splendor of Grace: devotional studies in Ephesians.
[Atlanta], Committee on Woman's Work, Presbyterian Church
in the U.S., © 1937. 63 p. C

1158 GLASGOW, Samuel McPheeters, 1883-1963.
Un consejo opportuno a los recien convertidos. Mexico,
Casa de Publicaciones "El Faro, " 1949. 60 p. Translation
into Spanish of "Needed counsel for new Christians. " U

1159 *GLASGOW, Tom.
Shall the Southern Presbyterian Church abandon its historic
position; a plea for common honesty exposing the attack of
Dr. Ernest Trice Thompson, of Union Theological Seminary,
upon the standards of the Presbyterian Church in the United
States. [Charlotte, N.C.], n.p., n.d. 20 p. H U

1160 GLASS, Gilbert, 1875-1934.
What is a Christian home? Richmond, Presbyterian Committee of Publication, n.d. 6 p. U

1161 *GLASSCOCK, Elizabeth H.
Teacher's course guide: The beginnings of the church [by
Stuart D. Currie]. Richmond, CLC Press, © 1966. (The
Covenant Life Curriculum.) C ... L: [1967].

1162 *GLASSCOCK, Elizabeth H.
Supplement [for] The beginnings of the church [by] Eliza-
beth H. Glasscock [and] Stuart D. Currie. [Richmond, CLC
Press], n.d. 14 p. (The Covenant Life Curriculum.) L

1163 GOD glorified in the fire: the last days of Rev. William S.
Plumer, D.D. New York, American Tract Society,
n.d. 29 p. PH

1164 GOD'S CHRIST and his people: studies in honour of Nils Al-
strup Dahl; edited by Jacob Jervell, Wayne A. Meeks.
Oslo, Universitetsforlaget, © 1977. 295 p. A C PT U

1165 GOFF, John, 1863-1938.
The baptism of Jesus, a sermon. n.p., n.d. 23 p. U

1166 GOFF, John, 1863-1938.
Bible baptism vs. baptism of inference. Richmond, Presbyterian Committee of Publication, 1914. 48 p. U

1167 GOFF, John, 1863-1938.
How was Jesus baptized and why? By questions and answers; a tract for young people. Union Springs, Ala., n.p., [1926]. 22 p. A ... U: Richmond, Presbyterian Committee of Publication, n.d. 24 p.

1168 GOFF, John, 1863-1938.
Pith and point of baptism by questions and answers. A tract for young people. Richmond, Presbyterian Committee of Publication, n.d. 64 p. H U

1169 GOFF, John, 1863-1938, comp.
Sermons for mothers as delivered on Mothers' Day by representative ministers of the southland. Atlanta, John Goff, n.d. 76 p. Sermons by J. E. Hannah, Robert Ivey, D. M. McIver, W. O. Shewmaker, John Goff. H

1170 GOOD, John Walter, 1879-1971.
The Jesus of our fathers. New York, The Macmillan Co., 1923. 842 p. A C H L PT R U

1171 GOODMAN, Frank Leroy, 1900-1968.
The Union Church story; a historical sketch of Union Presbyterian Church, Churchville, Augusta County, Virginia. n.p., n.d. 15 p. U

1172 GOODPASTURE, Henry McKennie, 1929-
The Latin American soul of John A. Mackay. [Lancaster, Pa., n.p., 1970]. 265-292 p. PT

1173 GOODYKOONTZ, Harry Gordon, 1906-
Baptism in a Presbyterian congregation. [Richmond, Board of Christian Education, Presbyterian Church in the U.S.], n.d. unpaged. H

1174 GOODYKOONTZ, Harry Gordon, 1906-
Christian ways for college days. Richmond, John Knox Press, © 1949. 78 p. H L R U ... A: [1954].

1175 GOODYKOONTZ, Harry Gordon, 1906-
"The minister and the layman"; an address ... given before Memphis Presbytery. In session at Brooks Road Presbyterian Church, Memphis, Tenn., Jan. 28, 1958. Memphis, Tenn., n.p., 1958. 11 p. A U

1176 GOODYKOONTZ, Harry Gordon, 1906-

The minister in the Reformed tradition. Richmond, John Knox Press, © 1963. 176 p. A C H L PH PT R U

1177 GOODYKOONTZ, Harry Gordon, 1906-
The persons we teach. Philadelphia, Westminster Press, © 1965. 187 p. A C L PH PT R U

1178 GOODYKOONTZ, Harry Gordon, 1906-
Program materials and methods for student groups. Louisville, Ky., Joint Committee on Student Work, Presbyterian Church in the U.S., n.d. 27 p. U

1179 GOODYKOONTZ, Harry Gordon, 1906-
Training to teach: a basic course in Christian education [by] Harry G. and Betty L. Goodykoontz. Philadelphia, Westminster Press, © 1961. 141 p. A C H L PT R U

1180 GOODYKOONTZ, Harry Gordon, 1906-
Why do Presbyterians baptize infants? n.p., n.d. 8 p. U

1181 GORDON, Edward Clifford, 1842-1922.
Obstacles to the union between northern and southern Presbyterian churches ... September 1906. n.p., n.d. 34 p. U

1182 GORDON, Edward Clifford, 1842-1922.
An open letter. n.p., n.d. 5 p. Reprinted from Presbyterian Standard, Dec. 8, 1915. U

1183 GORDON, Edward Clifford, 1842-1922.
The Sunday School teachers' work; what it is, and how to do it. Richmond, Presbyterian Committee of Publication, © 1887. 89 p. A H U

1184 GOULDING, Francis Robert, 1810-1881.
The young marooners on the Florida coast.... With introduction by Joel Chandler Harris. 5th ed. Philadelphia, William S. and Alfred Martien, 1856. 422 p. PH ... C: New York, Dodd, Mead and Co., © 1887. 452 p. ... H: 1927. 345 p.

1185 GOUWENS, Teunis Earl, 1886-1960.
Are we responsible? Sermon ... delivered November 1, 1931, at Second Presbyterian Church, Louisville, Kentucky. n.p., n.d. 12 p. H

1186 GOUWENS, Teunis Earl, 1886-1960.
Barriers to God. Sermon ... delivered Sunday, April 15, 1934, Second Presbyterian Church, Louisville, Kentucky. n.p., n.d. 14 p. H

1187 GOUWENS, Teunis Earl, 1886-1960.

Beyond our senses.... Sermon delivered Sunday, Nov. 10, 1946, in the Second Presbyterian Church, Louisville, Ky. n.p., n.d. 13 p.   H

1188   GOUWENS, Teunis Earl, 1886-1960.
Can we repeat the creed? An interpretation of difficult phrases in the Apostles' Creed. Nashville, Cokesbury Press, © 1936. 144 p.   C H L PT R U

1189   GOUWENS, Teunis Earl, 1886-1960.
The far horizons of Scripture. New York, Fleming H. Revell Co., © 1942. 160 p.   A C H L R U

1190   GOUWENS, Teunis Earl, 1886-1960.
He opened The Book. New York, Fleming H. Revell Co., © 1940. 187 p.   A L PT R U

1191   GOUWENS, Teunis Earl, 1886-1960.
Keep your faith. New York, Fleming H. Revell Co., © 1943. 142 p.   L PT R U

1192   GOUWENS, Teunis Earl, 1886-1960.
The law of increasing return. A sermon ... delivered Sunday, September 12, 1943, in the Second Presbyterian Church, Louisville, Kentucky. n.p., n.d. 12 p.   H

1193   GOUWENS, Teunis Earl, 1886-1960.
The rock that is higher, and other addresses. New York, Fleming H. Revell Co., © 1922. 160 p.   H L R

1194   GOUWENS, Teunis Earl, 1886-1960.
The stirred nest. Nashville, Cokesbury Press, © 1933. 174 p.   C H L R U

1195   GOUWENS, Teunis Earl, 1886-1960.
This uncertain world. Sermon ... delivered Sunday, December 10, 1933, Second Presbyterian Church, Louisville, Kentucky. n.p., n.d. 14 p.   H

1196   GOUWENS, Teunis Earl, 1886-1960.
Why I believe. Nashville, Tenn., Cokesbury Press, 1930. 147 p. Sermons.   A C H L R

1197   GOUWENS, Teunis Earl, 1886-1960.
Will God do nothing? Sermon ... delivered Sunday, November 24, 1935.   H

1198   GRAFTON, Thomas Hancock, 1905-
Religious origins and sociological theory. n.p., n.d. 726-739 p. Reprinted from American Sociological Review, December, 1945.   U

1199   GRAFTON, Thomas Hancock, 1905-

The sociology of right and wrong. n.p., n.d. 86-95 p.
Reprinted from American Sociological Review, February,
1947. U

1200 GRAHAM, Alfred Thurston, 1858-1917.
A call to the ministry; an appeal to the young men of the
Southern Presbyterian Church. Richmond, Presbyterian
Committee of Publication, [1904?]. 35 p. A U

1201 GRAHAM, Alfred Thurston, 1858-1917.
Gambling; a letter to college men and a few others. Rich-
mond, Presbyterian Committee of Publication, 1911. 22 p.
U

1202 GRAHAM, Alfred Thurston, 1858-1917.
Memorial. Rev. Henry Miller. [Lexington, Va., County
News Print], n.d. 22 p. H

1203 GRAHAM, Bothwell, 1853-1931.
The philosophy of Christianity. Columbia, S.C., R. L.
Bryan Co., 1917. 144 p. A C PT R U

1204 GRAHAM, Bothwell, 1853-1931.
The self-evolution of God and his creation of nature.
Greenville, S.C., Houston Book Store, 1923. 96 p. R

1205 GRAHAM, Donald Carson, 1910-
The common evils of modernism as seen in both the National Council and the Northern Presbyterian Church. Weaverville, N.C., Southern Presbyterian Journal, n.d. 8 ℓ. Reprinted from the Southern Presbyterian Journal, Oct. 29,
1952. U

1206 GRAHAM, Henry Tucker, 1865-1951.
Exchange for the soul. Red Springs, N.C., The author,
n.d. 9 p. U

1207 GRAHAM, Henry Tucker, 1865-1951.
Infallible proof of the resurrection of Christ. Richmond,
Presbyterian Committee of Publication, n.d. 19 p. U

1208 GRAHAM, Henry Tucker, 1865-1951.
Jesus Christ, the same yesterday, and to-day, and forever.
Richmond, Presbyterian Committee of Publication, n.d. 12 p.
U

1209 GRAHAM, Henry Tucker, 1865-1951.
Men of might. Philadelphia, Historical Publication Society,
© 1947. 54 p. H R U

1210 GRAHAM, Henry Tucker, 1865-1951.
An old manse and other sermons. Philadelphia, Historical
Publication Society, 1948. 112 p. A C H R U

1211 GRAHAM, Henry Tucker, 1865-1951.
       Some things for which the South did not fight in the War
       Between the States. [Wadesboro, N.C., n.p., 1946]. 12 p.
       U

1212 GRAHAM, Henry Tucker, 1865-1951.
       Stonewall Jackson, the man, the soldier, the Christian.
       Florence, S.C., n.p., n.d. 14 p.   U

1213 GRAHAM, James Robert, 1824-1914.
       The divine unfolding of God's plan of redemption. Grand
       Rapids, Mich., Zondervan Publishing House, © 1938. 128 p.
       H R U

1214 GRAHAM, James Robert, 1824-1914.
       The planting of the Presbyterian Church in northern Vir-
       ginia, prior to the organization of Winchester Presbytery,
       December 4, 1794. Winchester, Va., Geo. F. Norton Pub-
       lishing Co., 1904. 168 p.   A C H PH PT R U

1215 GRAHAM, James Robert, 1824-1914.
       Semi-centennial sermon ... and anniversary exercises at
       the Presbyterian Church of Winchester, Sunday, October 13,
       1901. Winchester, Va., Evening News-Item Job Print.,
       1901. 32 p.   U

1216 GRAHAM, Randolph Watson, 1924-
       The Covenant Life core guide; introduction, index and
       suggestions for surveying the Covenant Life Curriculum core
       books for adults, by Randolph Graham, Jr., and William M.
       Ramsey. Richmond, CLC Press, n.d. 32 p. (The Cove-
       nant Life Curriculum.)   L

1217 GRASTY, John Sharshall, 1825-1883.
       Death and life. An exposition of Romans VI, 23. Shelby-
       ville, Ky., Logan & Scearce, 1873. 21 p.   U

1218 GRASTY, John Sharshall, 1825-1883.
       Faith's battles and victories; or, Thoughts for troublous
       times. New York, Anson D. F. Randolph & Co., 1870.
       285 p.   U ... H: Richmond, Presbyterian Committee of
       Publication, 1872 ... A R: 1889.

1219 GRASTY, John Sharshall, 1825-1883.
       Memoir of Rev. Samuel B. McPheeters.... With an intro-
       duction, by Rev. Stuart Robinson. St. Louis, Southwestern
       Book and Publishing Co., 1871. 384 p.   A C H PH PT R
       U

1220 GRASTY, John Sharshall, 1825-1883.
       Sin and its wages. [Richmond, Presbyterian Committee
       of Publication], n.d. 8 p.   U

1221 GRASTY, John Sharshall, 1825-1883.
The way to Zion. Richmond, Presbyterian Committee of
Publication, n.d. 12 p. U

1222 GRAVES, Frederick Roscoe, 1868-1943, comp.
North Mississippi Presbytery. A chronological list of the
churches, ministers, candidates, moderators, stated clerks,
and commissioners to the General Assembly from the organization of the Presbytery in 1856 through the church year
1941-42. Sardis, Southern Reporter, 1942. 48 p. H

1223 GRAVES, Frederick Roscoe, 1868-1943, comp.
The Presbyterian work in Mississippi. Sumner, Sentinel
Press, 1927. 142 p. C H R U

1224 GRAVES, Joseph Armstrong, 1846-1915.
The history of the Bethesda Presbyterian Church in Hinds
County, Mississippi. A discourse ... delivered before the
congregation on Sabbath, December 22, 1878, Synod of Mississippi, Presbytery of Central Mississippi. Richmond, Whittet & Shepperson, 1879. 21 p. H PH U

1225 GRAY, John Hannah, 1805-1878.
Inaugural address, delivered on the 7th July, 1858, before
the trustees of the La Grange Synodical College. Memphis,
Avalanche Job Printing and Publishing House, 1858. 23 p.
H

1226 GRAY, William Bristow, 1873-1959.
Poems to radiate the lessons of fifty-eight; a devotional
thought in verse for each Sunday School lesson of the year.
[1st ed.] New York, Pageant Press, © 1957. 56 p. A L

1227 GRAY, William Bristow, 1873-1959.
Prayer and purpose; sixty-four meditations for personal
workers. [Kingsville, Tex., Tex.-Mex. Printery], n.d.
36 p. A

1228 GREEN, James Benjamin, 1871-1967.
The distinctive teachings of Presbyterianism. [Weaverville,
N.C., Southern Presbyterian Journal], n.d. 16 p. Originally
delivered to the Jubilee Assembly in Augusta, Ga. Reprinted
from the Southern Presbyterian Journal, April 29, 1959.
H U

1229 GREEN, James Benjamin, 1871-1967.
Studies in the Holy Spirit. New York, Fleming H. Revell
Co., © 1936. 126 p. A C H L PT R U ... C H PT U:
Weaverville, N.C., Southern Presbyterian Journal, © 1957.
130 p.

1230 GREEN, James Benjamin, 1871-1967.

Why we baptize by sprinkling. [Weaverville, N.C., Southern Presbyterian Journal], n.d. 12 p.   U

1231   GREENSBORO, N.C. First Presbyterian Church.
The action taken by the First Presbyterian Church of Greensboro, North Carolina, upon the resignation of their pastor, Rev. Egbert W. Smith, D.D. Greensboro, Jos. J. Stone & Co., n.d. 18 p.   PH

1232   GREGORY, Andrew Painter, 1867-1955.
The Bible and prayer. n.p., n.d. 24 p.   U

1233   GREGORY, Andrew Painter, 1867-1955.
The Bible on hell. n.p., n.d. 11 p.   U

1234   GREGORY, Andrew Painter, 1867-1955.
Children and the kingdom. n.p., n.d. 4 p.   U

1235   GREGORY, Andrew Painter, 1867-1955.
For personal workers; pray! go! speak! n.p., n.d. 4 p.
U

1236   GREGORY, Andrew Painter, 1867-1955.
For young Christians. n.p., n.d. 12 p.   U

1237   GREGORY, Andrew Painter, 1867-1955.
The gospel of love. n.p., n.d. 16 p.   U

1238   GREY, John Hunter, 1872-1957.
Sketch of Montgomery Presbytery, 1843-1943 ... presented at the centennial meeting of Montgomery Presbytery held in the Quaker Memorial Presbyterian Church of Lynchburg, Virginia, on Tuesday, September 21, 1943. n.p., n.d.
16 p.   PH PT

1239   GRIBBLE, Robert Francis, 1890-1970.
Calvinistic complexion. n.p., n.d. 7 p. Reprinted from the Southern Presbyterian Journal, August, 1944.   U

1240   GRIDER, Edgar McLean, 1934-
Can I make it one more year?: overcoming the hazards of ministry. Atlanta, John Knox Press, © 1980. 144 p.
A C H L PT U

1241   GRINNAN, Randolph Bryan, 1860-1942.
Commentary on Ephesians. Tokyo, Japan, Methodist Publishing House, 1898. In Japanese.   H

1242   GRISSETT, Finley McCorvey, 1889-
Lights and shadows in the African forest. New York, Board of Foreign Missions, Presbyterian Church in the U.S.A., 1925. unpaged.   PH

1243 GROVES, William Henry, 1846-1916.
The rational memory. Gloucester, Va., W. H. Groves,
1901. 115 p. U ... U: 2d ed. New York, Cosmopolitan
Press, 1912. 172 p.

1244 GRUNDY, Robert Caldwell, 1807-1865.
A discussion of the mode and subjects of Christian bap-
tism: in a series of letters first published in the Maysville
"Post-Boy," during the months of April, May, and June, of
the year 1851. By Rev. R. C. Grundy, D.D., of the Pres-
byterian Church, and Elder John Young, of the Christian
Church. Maysville, Ky., Post-Boy Office, 1851. 166 p.
PH PT

1245 GRUNDY, Robert Caldwell, 1807-1865.
The doctrine of divine providence; as taught by reason and
revelation. A sermon, preached in the Presbyterian Church,
Maysville, Ky., on Sabbath morning, August 20th, 1854.
Maysville, Maysville Eagle Office, 1854. 27 p. PHS

1246 GRUNDY, Robert Caldwell, 1807-1865.
The reply ... to a pamphlet by a Catholic layman, in
answer to three discourses of his on Roman Catholicism, delivered in the town of Springfield, Kentucky, August 13th,
1843. Maysville, Ky., Collins & Brown, 1843. 23 p. PH

1247 GRUNDY, Robert Caldwell, 1807-1865.
A sermon, delivered in the Central Presbyterian Church,
Cincinnati, Ohio, showing the reasons why the rebellion has
not been suppressed--the great results thus far of the war,
and the encouragements to go forward in the assurance of
triumphant success--the true origin and nature, historically,
of secession as a political principle--how God regards it,
and what use he has for it, by the pastor, August 4, 1864,
the day appointed by the congress and President of the United
States for national fasting, humiliation, and prayer. Cincinnati, Moore, Wilstach & Baldwin, 1864. 29 p. PH

1248 GRUNDY, Robert Caldwell, 1807-1865.
The temporal power of the Pope dangerous to the religious
and civil liberties of the American republic: a review of the
speech of the Hon. Joseph R. Chandler, delivered in the
House of Representatives of the United States, January 10th,
1855. Delivered in the Presbyterian Church, Maysville, Ky.,
on Sunday evening, February 11, 1855. Maysville, Maysville
Eagle Office, 1855. 13 p. PH

1249 GRUNDY, Robert Caldwell, 1807-1865.
Total abstinence a Christian duty, or the Bible disabused.
A sermon, preached on Sabbath morning, in the Presbyterian
Church, Maysville, Ky., January 31, 1841. Maysville, Eagle
Office, 1841. 24 p. PH PT

1250   GUERRANT, Edward Owings, 1838-1916.
       Forty years among the American highlanders. [Atlanta,
Executive Committee of Home Missions, Presbyterian Church
in the U.S.], n.d.   4 p.   U

1251   GUERRANT, Edward Owings, 1838-1916.
       The galax gatherers: the Gospel among the Highlanders....
Edited by his daughter, Grace. Richmond, Onward Press,
© 1910.   220 p.   A C H PH U

1252   GUERRANT, Edward Owings, 1838-1916.
       The gospel of the lilies. Boston, Sherman, French & Co.,
1912.   224 p.

1253   GUERRANT, Edward Owings, 1838-1916.
       The Mormons. Richmond, Presbyterian Committee of
Publication, 1899.   12 p.   PT U

1254   GUERRANT, Edward Owings, 1838-1916.
       The soul winner. Lexington, Ky., John B. Morton & Co.,
© 1896.   252 p.   A C H L R U

1255   GUICE, Charles Edwin, 1896-1946.
       The first friends of the Finest Friend; studies of "The
Twelve." Morrilton, Ark., Morrilton Democrat, [1932].
122 p.   A L R U

1256   GUILLE, George E., 1873-1931.
       Isaac and Rebekah. Chicago, Bible Institute Colportage
Ass'n., © 1914.   31 p.   H

1257   GUILLE, George E., 1873-1931.
       The judgment seat of Christ. Who stands there? When?
What for? Chicago, Bible Institute Colportage Ass'n.,
© 1916.   38 p.   H

1258   GUILLE, George E., 1873-1931.
       Soiled feet in the Master's hands. New York, Charles C.
Cook, n.d.   32 p.   U

1259   GUILLE, George E., 1873-1931.
       Sonship; its present privileges and future manifestations.
Chicago, Bible Institute Colportage Ass'n. [Moody Press].
29 p.   H

1260   GUNN, George Wilson, 1926-
       For adults only; a study guide for high school seniors and
graduates. Richmond, CLC Press, © 1966.   64 p.   (The
Covenant Life Curriculum.)   C L U

1261   GUNN, James Woodside, 1928-
       A time, and times, and half a time: Christian affirmations

in the book of Revelation. Richmond, CLC Press, © 1966.
48 p. (The Covenant Life Curriculum.)   C L U

1262 GUTHRIE, Shirley Caperton, 1927-
      Christian doctrine, teachings of the Christian church. Rich-
      mond, CLC Press, © 1968. 413 p. (The Covenant Life
      Curriculum.)   A C L PT R U ... C L R U: Teacher's
      book. 268 p.

1263 GUTHRIE, Shirley Caperton, 1927-
      Freedom to be human. St. Petersburg, Fla., Florida
      Presbyterian College [1966]. 28 p. Delivered at Florida
      Presbyterian College during "Faith in Dialogue Week," Feb-
      ruary 14-18, 1966.   C PT U

1264 GUTHRIE, Shirley Caperton, 1927-
      Priests without robes, the priesthood of believers. Rich-
      mond, CLC Press, © 1964. 48 p. (The Covenant Life Cur-
      riculum.)   C L U

1265 GUTHRIE, Shirley Caperton, 1927-
      The theological character of Reinhold Niebuhr's social
      ethic. Winterthur, P. G. Keller, 1959. 191 p.   A C PT
      R U

1266 GUTIÉRREZ, Fernando, 1918-
      Curas represaliados en la franquismo. Madrid: Akal,
      1977. 195 p.   PT

1267 GUTZKE, Manford George, 1896-
      Born to serve: the Christian--God's servant. Glendale,
      Calif., G/L Regal Books, © 1972. 137 p.   C R

1268 GUTZKE, Manford George, 1896-
      Division, despair, & hope; daily devotions and Bible studies.
      Glendale, Calif., G/L Regal Books, © 1969. 167 p.   C

1269 GUTZKE, Manford George, 1896-
      Fear not: a Christian view of death. Grand Rapids, Mich.,
      Baker Book House, © 1974.   L PT

1270 GUTZKE, Manford George, 1896-
      Go Gospel; daily devotions and Bible studies in the Gospel
      of Mark. Glendale, Calif., G/L Regal Books, © 1968.
      183 p.   C R

1271 GUTZKE, Manford George, 1896-
      Help thou my unbelief. Nashville, Thomas Nelson, © 1974.
      124 p.   A C H PT R

1272 GUTZKE, Manford George, 1896-
      John Dewey's thought and its implications for Christian

education. New York, King's Crown Press, 1956. 270 p.
A C L PT R U

1273 GUTZKE, Manford George, 1896-
Living in the Spirit--is it real? Grand Rapids, Mich.,
Baker Book House, © 1972. 238 p. C R

1274 GUTZKE, Manford George, 1896-
A look at the book; daily devotions and studies in the
Bible and what it says about itself. Glendale, Calif., G/L
Regal Books, © 1969. 148 p. R

1275 GUTZKE, Manford George, 1896-
Plain talk about Christian words. Johnson City, Tenn.,
Royal Publishers, © 1964. 222 p. U ... A C R: Grand
Rapids, Mich., Zondervan Publishing House, [1965]. 234 p.

1276 GUTZKE, Manford George, 1896-
Plain talk about real Christians. Grand Rapids, Mich.,
Baker Book House, © 1972. 118 p. C

1277 GUTZKE, Manford George, 1896-
Plain talk about the books of the Bible. n.p., n.d. 76 p.
H R

1278 GUTZKE, Manford George, 1896-
Plain talk about the Holy Spirit. Grand Rapids, Mich.,
Baker Book House, © 1974. 178 p. C PT U

1279 GUTZKE, Manford George, 1896-
Plain talk on Acts. Grand Rapids, Mich., Zondervan Publishing House, © 1966. 221 p. A C L R U

1280 GUTZKE, Manford George, 1896-
Plain talk on Colossians. Grand Rapids, Mich., Zondervan Publishing House, © 1981. 96 p. C

1281 GUTZKE, Manford George, 1896-
Plain talk on Deuteronomy. Grand Rapids, Mich., Zondervan Publishing House, © 1979. 127 p. C

1282 GUTZKE, Manford George, 1896-
Plain talk on Ephesians. Grand Rapids, Mich., Zondervan
Publishing House, © 1973. 191 p. C PT R U

1283 GUTZKE, Manford George, 1896-
Plain talk on Exodus. Grand Rapids, Mich., Zondervan
Publishing House, © 1974. 244 p. C PT R U

1284 GUTZKE, Manford George, 1896-
Plain talk on First and Second Corinthians. Grand Rapids,
Mich., Zondervan Publishing House, © 1978. 283 p. C PT
U

1285 GUTZKE, Manford George, 1896-
Plain talk on Galatians. Grand Rapids, Mich., Baker
Book House, © 1972. 175 p. C PT R U

1286 GUTZKE, Manford George, 1896-
Plain talk on Genesis. Grand Rapids, Mich., Zondervan
Publishing House, © 1975. 143 p. C PT U

1287 GUTZKE, Manford George, 1896-
Plain talk on Hebrews. Grand Rapids, Mich., Zondervan
Publishing House, © 1976. 122 p. C PT U

1288 GUTZKE, Manford George, 1896-
Plain talk on Isaiah. Grand Rapids, Mich., Zondervan
Publishing House, © 1977. 256 p. C PT R U

1289 GUTZKE, Manford George, 1896-
Plain talk on James. Grand Rapids, Mich., Zondervan
Publishing House, © 1969. 189 p. C PT R

1290 GUTZKE, Manford George, 1896-
Plain talk on John. Grand Rapids, Mich., Zondervan
Publishing House, © 1968. 213 p. A C PT R ... U:
[1971]. 212 p.

1291 GUTZKE, Manford George, 1896-
Plain talk on Leviticus and Numbers. Grand Rapids,
Mich., Zondervan Publishing House, © 1981. 128 p. C

1292 GUTZKE, Manford George, 1896-
Plain talk on Luke. Grand Rapids, Mich., Zondervan
Publishing House, © 1966. 180 p. C R

1293 GUTZKE, Manford George, 1896-
Plain talk on Mark. Grand Rapids, Mich., Zondervan
Publishing House, © 1975. 192 p. C PT U

1294 GUTZKE, Manford George, 1896-
Plain talk on Matthew. Grand Rapids, Mich., Zondervan
Publishing House, © 1966. 245 p. C PT R U

1295 GUTZKE, Manford George, 1896-
Plain talk on Peter and Jude. Grand Rapids, Mich., Zondervan Publishing House, © 1979. 203 p. C PT

1296 GUTZKE, Manford George, 1896-
Plain talk on Philippians. Grand Rapids, Mich., Zondervan Publishing House, © 1973. 281 p. C PT U

1297 GUTZKE, Manford George, 1896-
Plain talk on prayer. Grand Rapids, Mich., Baker Book
House, © 1973. 182 p. C R U

1298 GUTZKE, Manford George, 1896-
Plain talk on Revelation. Grand Rapids, Mich., Zondervan
Publishing House, © 1979. 176 p. C PT R U

1299 GUTZKE, Manford George, 1896-
Plain talk on Romans. Grand Rapids, Mich., Zondervan
Publishing House, © 1976. 185 p. C PT U

1300 GUTZKE, Manford George, 1896-
Plain talk on the Epistles of John. Grand Rapids, Mich.,
Zondervan Publishing House, © 1977. 122 p. C R U

1301 GUTZKE, Manford George, 1896-
Plain talk on the Minor Prophets. Grand Rapids, Mich.,
Zondervan Publishing House, © 1980. 140 p. C U

1302 GUTZKE, Manford George, 1896-
Plain talk on the Resurrection. Grand Rapids, Mich.,
Baker Book House, © 1974. 73 p. C PT R

1303 GUTZKE, Manford George, 1896-
Plain talk on Thessalonians. Grand Rapids, Mich., Zondervan Publishing House, © 1980. 105 p. C

1304 GUTZKE, Manford George, 1896-
Plain talk on Timothy, Titus & Philemon. Grand Rapids,
Mich., Zondervan Publishing House, © 1978. 235 p. C
PT

1305 GUTZKE, Manford George, 1896-
Saved to serve; studies in Second Corinthians. Atlanta,
Committee on Woman's Work, Presbyterian Church in the
U.S., © 1944. 52 p. A C R

1306 GUTZKE, Manford George, 1896-
Sent from God. Richmond, Published for the Executive
Committee of Home and Foreign Missions by John Knox
Press, © 1940. 138 p. A C H R U

1307 GUTZKE, Manford George, 1896-
Souls in prison. Nashville, Tenn., Thomas Nelson,
© 1975. 157 p. C PT U

1308 GUTZKE, Manford George, 1896-
Wanderers, slaves & kings; daily devotions and Bible
studies. Glendale, Calif., G/L Regal Books, © 1969.
168 p. C

1309 GWYNN, Price Henderson, 1892-1967.
Acts ... words about deeds. A study in the book of
Acts. Leader's guide for Circle Bible Leader. Atlanta,
Board of Women's Work, Presbyterian Church in the U.S.,
[1956?]. 76 p. U

1310 GWYNN, Price Henderson, 1892-1967.
God in higher education. A reprint of an address delivered at Presbyterian Junior College, Maxton, N.C., Synod
of North Carolina, September 12, 1951. n.p., n.d. unpaged.
H U

1311 GWYNN, Price Henderson, 1892-1967.
Leader's guide for use with The church in Christian faith
and life. [Philadelphia], Board of Christian Education of the
Presbyterian Church in the U.S.A., © 1950. 13 p.   PH

1312 GWYNN, Price Henderson, 1892-1967.
Leadership education in the local church. Philadelphia,
Published for the Cooperative Association by Westminster
Press, © 1952. 157 p.   A C H L PH PT R U

1313 GWYNN, Price Henderson, 1892-1967.
Tackling the problem of Christian higher education. n.p.,
n.d. 20 p.   U

1314 *HAENCHEN, Ernst, 1894-
Das Johannesevangelium: ein Kommentar ... mit einem
Vorwort von James M. Robinson. Tübingen, J. C. B. Mohr
(Paul Siebeck), 1980. 614 p.   A U

1315 HALL, Benjamin Franklin, 1908-
... This company of new men; a study of the Thessalonian
church. Richmond, CLC Press, © 1965. 80 p. (The Covenant Life Curriculum.) At head of title: Leaders' booklet
for senior high conference.   C L U

1316 HALL, Benjamin Franklin, 1908-
The word of B. Frank Hall: articles 1954-1974.... Wilmington, N.C., Privately published by friends of the author,
1978. 271 p. All articles in this collection appeared originally in the Wilmington Star-News.   U

1317 HALL, Joseph Kirkland, 1865-1949.
History of Goshen Church ... presented ... at the celebration of the 175th anniversary of Goshen Presbyterian
Church, observed Sunday, October 15th, 1939. n.p., n.d.
13 p.   PH PT

1318 HALL, Joseph Kirkland, 1865-1949, comp.
The Reverend James Davidson Hall and his descendants.
1806-1946. [Rev.] Belmont, N.C., n.p., [1946]. 21 p.
U ... PH: 15 p.

1319 HALL, Joseph Kirkland, 1865-1949.
Sardis Church, a historical sketch at the centennial of the
church. n.p., n.d. 14 p.   PH

1320 HALL, Ralph J., 1891-1981.

The main trail. Edited by Vic Jameson. San Antonio, Tex., The Naylor Co., © 1971. 193 p. A C PT

1321 HALL, Ralph J., 1891-1957.
A Sunday School missionary's dream that came true.
[New York, Board of National Missions, Presbyterian Church in the U.S.A., 1940]. unpaged. PH

1322 HALL, Robert McAlpine, 1863-1941.
The modern siren. New York, Publication Office "Our Hope," © 1916. 164 p. A C H R U

1323 HALL, Warner Leander, 1907-
Biblical & Reformed basis for reunion. [Charlottesville, Va., Friends of Presbyterian Union], n.d. 2 ℓ. U

1324 HALL, Warner Leander, 1907-
Symbols of the faith. Richmond, CLC Press, © 1965.
47 p. (The Covenant Life Curriculum.) C L U

1325 HALL, Warner Leander, 1907-
To the greater glory of God. The sermon delivered as part of the first service of worship in the new church [Covenant Presbyterian Church]. n.p., n.d. 12 p. PH

1326 HALL-QUEST, Alfred Lawrence, 1879-
The textbook; who to use and judge it. New York, The Macmillan Co., 1920. 265 p. U

1327 HALL-QUEST, Alfred Lawrence, 1879-
The university afield. New York, The Macmillan Co., 1926. 292 p. L

1328 HAMAN, Thomas Luther, 1846-1918.
Beginnings of Presbyterianism in Mississippi. n.p., n.d. 203-221 p. Reprinted from Publications of the Mississippi Historical Society, vol. X. C H

1329 HAMILTON, Charles Granville, 1905-
The flag was flame above a sea of gray. n.p., [1975?]. 189 p. C

1330 HAMILTON, Charles Granville, 1905-
Mississippi, I love you still; collected poems. Fulton, Miss., Itawamba County Times, 1974. 130 p. PT

1331 HAMILTON, Charles Granville, 1905-
Old Testament introduction. n.p., n.d. 3 p. PT

1332 HAMILTON, Charles Granville, 1905-
Our brother Augustus: July 20, 1908-March 19, 1935; [poems by] George Gordon Hamilton and Charles Granville Hamilton. n.p., [1936]. PT

1333 HAMILTON, Charles Granville, 1905-
You can't steal first base. New York, Philosophical Library, © 1971. 137 p.   C PT U

1334 HAMILTON, Evelyn Harrison, 1895-
Afraid? Of what? And other poems and sketches. [Hong Kong, Cathay Press], © 1960. 97 p.   C H ... H: © 1963. 113 p. ... H: 3d ed., enl. © 1968. 121 p.

1335 HAMILTON, Evelyn Harrison, 1895-
"I am not afraid!" The story of John W. Vinson, Christian martyr in China. [Nashville, Tenn., Board of World Missions, Presbyterian Church in the U.S.], n.d. 20 p.
C U

1336 HAMILTON, Evelyn Harrison, 1895-
"Not worthy to be compared," the story of John and Betty Stam, and "the Miracle baby," Helen Priscilla Stam. [Shanghai, The Missionary Supplier, 1935]. 22 p.   C ... PH: Rev. ed. 1935. 33 p.

1337 HAMILTON, Floyd Eugene, 1890-1969.
Basic principles in educational and medical mission work, by Floyd E. Hamilton and Thomas Cochrane. London, World Dominion Press, 1928. 17 p.   PH PT

1338 HAMILTON, Floyd Eugene, 1890-1969.
The basis of Christian faith; a modern defense of the Christian religion. New York, George H. Doran Co., © 1927. 335 p.   C PT U ... C PT: Rev. ed. New York, Harper & Brothers, © 1933. 348 p.   A C: 3d rev. ed. New York, Harper & Brothers, © 1946. 354 p. ... A: Rev. and enl. ed. New York, Harper & Row, © 1964. 364 p.

1339 HAMILTON, Floyd Eugene, 1890-1969.
The basis of evolutionary faith; a critique of the theory of evolution. London, James Clarke & Co., [1931]. 223 p.
H PT R

1340 HAMILTON, Floyd Eugene, 1890-1969.
The basis of millennial faith. Grand Rapids, Mich., Wm. B. Eerdmans Publishing Co., 1942. 160 p.   A C L PT U ... C R: 1952 ... R: 1955.

1341 HAMILTON, Floyd Eugene, 1890-1969.
The Epistle to the Galatians; a study manual. Grand Rapids, Mich., Baker Book House, 1959. 66 p.   PT R U

1342 HAMILTON, Floyd Eugene, 1890-1969.
The Epistle to the Romans; an exegetical and devotional commentary. Grand Rapids, Mich., Baker Book House, 1958. 235 p.   A C PT R U

1343 HAMILTON, Floyd Eugene, 1890-1969.
The Reformed faith in the modern world. [Philadelphia, Committee on Christian Education, Orthodox Presbyterian Church], n.d. 32 p. C

1344 HAMNER, James Garland, 1798-1887.
Child-membership. Philadelphia, Presbyterian Publication Committee, n.d. 18 p. PH PT

1345 HAMNER, James Garland, 1798-1887.
A pastor's parting sermon. Baltimore, n.p., 1855. 43 p. PH

1346 HAMNER, James Garland, 1798-1887.
Spiritualism versus formalism and ritualism; a sermon. Baltimore, Sherwood & Co., 1850. 24 p. PH

1347 HANDY, Isaac William Ker, 1815-1878.
The folly of avarice: a sermon delivered in Buckingham Presbyterian Church, Berlin, Md., August 15, 1841. Philadelphia, Office of the Christian Observer, 1841. 27 p. PH

1348 HANDY, Isaac William Ker, 1815-1878.
Our national sins. A sermon, delivered in the First Presbyterian Church, Portsmouth, Va., on the day of fasting, humiliation and prayer, January 4, 1861. Portsmouth, Office of the Daily and Weekly Transcript, 1861. 20 p. PH

1349 HANDY, Isaac William Ker, 1815-1878.
The terrible doings of God. A sermon delivered in the Court St. Baptist Church, Portsmouth, Va. On Sabbath morning, Dec. 30, 1855, commemorative of twenty-eight members of Old Dominion Lodge, no. V, who died during the late epidemic. Portsmouth, Daily Transcript Office, 1856. 24 p. PH

1350 HANDY, Isaac William Ker, 1815-1878.
United States bonds; or, Duress by federal authority: a journal of current events during an imprisonment of fifteen months, at Fort Delaware. Baltimore, Turnbull Brothers, 1874. 670 p. H U

1351 *HARDIE, Katherine E. (Hall), 1879-
On eagles' wings: Brazilian mission, 1900-1945. Richmond, William Byrd Press, [1964?]. 292 p. Biography of Alva Hardie, 1873-1955. C H L U

1352 HARDIN, Robert, 1789-1867.
The evangelical scheme. A sermon, preached before the Synod of Memphis, at its sessions in Jackson, Tenn., October, 1852. Louisville, Hull and Brother, 1853. 26 p. PH

1353 HARLAN, George William, 1824-1922.
Farmington Church semi-centennial. A discourse. Farmington, Mo., Barroll & Co., 1882. 20 p. PH

1354 *HARRIS, Eva.
Biblical teachings on the Kingdom of God; a teaching guide for His kingdom is forever [by Ernest Lee Stoffel]. By Eva Harris and Brevard Alexander Howell. [Richmond], John Knox Press, © 1957. 32 p. U

1355 HARRIS, John Stitt, 1832-1864.
An expository critique, being a vindication of an article, entitled "Old errors revived and rejuvenated in South Carolina" by "Reuchlin," [pseud.]. Yorkville, S.C., Enquirer Office, 1860. 47 p. PH

1356 HARRIS, John Stitt, 1832-1864.
A life devoted to Christ, a memorial sermon occasioned by the death of Rev. Pierpont E. Bishop, preached by request of session of Bethesda, March 20th, 1859. Charleston, S.C., Walker, Evans & Co., 1859. 35 p. U

1357 HARRISON, Peyton, 1800-1887.
A pastoral letter from the Synod of Virginia to the young men of the Presbyterian Church. Philadelphia, Presbyterian Board of Publication, n.d. 18 p. PH U

1358 HARSHA, William Justin.
Memorial sermon, preached Sabbath morning, December 21, 1890.... Upon the occasion of the thirtieth anniversary of the organization of the First Presbyterian Church of Omaha, Nebraska, December 23, 1860. [Omaha, Neb.], n.p., n.d. 24 p. PH

1359 HARSHA, William Justin.
Sabbath-day journeys; a study of the thirty-third chapter of Numbers. New York, Fleming H. Revell Co., © 1896. 275 p. H PH PT

1360 HARSHA, William Justin.
The story of Iowa. Omaha, Neb., Central West Co., 1890. 341 p. H PH

1361 HARWELL, Robert Ritchie, 1871-1959.
The principal versions of Baruch. n.p., [1915]. 66 p. Diss.-Yale University. PT

1362 HASSELL, Andrew Pierson, 1881-1941.
"Whom the Lord loveth"; or, The meaning of trials in the Christian's experience. Richmond, Presbyterian Committee of Publication, n.d. 15 p. U

1363 HASSELL, James Woodrow, 1886-1979.

The truth about Jehovah's witnesses. [Weaverville, N.C., Southern Presbyterian Journal], n.d. 8 p. Reprinted from the Southern Presbyterian Journal, May 2, 1951. U

1364 HAWES, Herbert Henry, 1834-1906.
The Abrahamic covenant. St. Louis, Presbyterian Publishing Co., [1879]. 94 p. A H

1365 HAWES, Herbert Henry, 1834-1906.
Baptism mode-studies. Richmond, Whittet & Shepperson, 1887. 109 p. A H L R U

1366 HAWES, Herbert Henry, 1834-1906.
Bible church studies.... An independent course of Bible study, apart from former studies and beliefs and exclusive of all sources of information save the Word of God. [Roanoke, Va., Stone Printing and Manufacturing Co.], © 1897. 398 p. C H R U

1367 HAWES, Herbert Henry, 1834-1906.
Doubts. Richmond, Whittet & Shepperson, 1889. 70 p. A H U

1368 HAWES, Herbert Henry, 1834-1906.
Is my heart changed? Richmond, Whittet & Shepperson, 1887. 43 p. U

1369 HAWES, Herbert Henry, 1834-1906.
Letters addressed to an inquirer. Richmond, Presbyterian Committee of Publication, n.d. 31 p. U

1370 HAWES, Herbert Henry, 1834-1906.
The ordinance of baptism: what is it? Staunton, Va., n.p., 1887. 4 p. U

1371 HAY, Samuel Hutson, 1883-1972.
How to become a Christian. [Morristown, Tenn., Session of First Presbyterian Church], n.d. 3 p. U ... U: Richmond, Presbyterian Committee of Religious Education and Publication, n.d. 4 p.

1372 HAY, Samuel Hutson, 1883-1972.
Why be a Christian? [Morristown, Tenn., Session of First Presbyterian Church], n.d. 3 p. U

1373 HAY, Thomas Park, 1854-1921.
Take my yoke upon you. Richmond, Presbyterian Committee of Publication, 1895. 13 p. U

1374 HAYES, John Alexander, 1898-1978.
How red this dust. [1st ed.] New York, Pageant Press, 1955. 250 p. L

1375 HAYES, John Alexander, 1898-1978.
      An old rusty bayonet. McDonough, Ga., Press of the
      Deep South, 1951. 29 p. L U

1376 HAYES, John Alexander, 1898-1978.
      The Ten Commandments, a present-day interpretation.
      New York, Fleming H. Revell Co., © 1931. 191 p. A L
      PT

1377 HAYNER, Paul Collins, 1918-
      Reason and existence; Schelling's philosophy of history.
      Leiden, E. J. Brill, 1967. 176 p. A PT U

1378 HAYNES, Robert Talmadge, 1926-
      Christ's eternal invitation. Richmond, John Knox Press,
      © 1963. 62 p. A C H L PT R U

1379 HEDLESTON, Winn David, 1862-1936.
      Lamp oil. An essay to help some understand the plan of
      salvation. Richmond, Whittet & Shepperson, 1898. 147 p.
      R

1380 HELM, Ben, 1844-1928.
      The abiding life (John XV). Louisville, Ky., Pentecostal
      Publishing Co., n.d. 106 p. H

1381 HELM, Ben, 1844-1928.
      Allie in Beulah land, or Swannanoa camp-meeting. A Ken-
      tucky story. Louisville, Ky., Pentecostal Publishing Co.,
      © 1901. 284 p. H

1382 HELM, Ben, 1844-1928.
      A commentary on St. Paul's Epistle to the Romans.
      Louisville, Ky., Pentecostal Publishing Co., 1907. 467 p.
      H U

1383 HELTZEL, Massey Mott, 1915-1980.
      The invincible Christ. New York, Abingdon Press,
      © 1957. 142 p. A C L PT U

1384 HEMPHILL, Charles Robert, 1852-1932.
      Christ's testimony to the Mosaic authorship of the Penta-
      teuch. Inaugural address delivered September 19, 1883 ...
      [as] Professor of Biblical Literature in the Theological Semi-
      nary at Columbia, S.C. Columbia, Presbyterian Publishing
      House, 1884. 17 p. Reprinted from the Southern Presby-
      terian Review, January, 1884. C PT U

1385 HENDERLITE, George Edward, 1863-1946.
      The gospel of salvation as Paul taught and preached it.
      n.p., n.d. 48 p. U

1386 HENDERLITE, George Edward, 1863-1946.

How to do all things and always be content ... notes on
Philippians. Richmond, Presbyterian Committee of Publication, 1920. 22 p. H

1387 HENDERLITE, George Edward, 1863-1946.
Notes on the First Epistle of John. n.p., n.d. 72 p.
U

1388 HENDERLITE, George Edward, 1863-1946.
Notes on three petitions in Paul's prayer in Eph. I. n.p.,
n.d. 14 p. U

1389 HENDERSON, John W., 1832-1916.
A competitive essay on the Sabbath.... With an intro-
duction by Rev. Jos. B. Stratton, D.D. New Orleans,
"Franklin" Print., 1877. 43 p. PH

1390 HENDERSON, Robert Thornton, 1928-
The disciplines of preaching evangelism. Atlanta, Office
of Evangelism and Church Development, Presbyterian Church
in the U.S., [1979]. unpaged. C

1391 HENDERSON, Robert Thornton, 1928-
Joy to the world: an introduction to Kingdom evangelism.
Atlanta, John Knox Press, © 1980. 207 p. A C H L U

1392 HENDERSON, Robert Thornton, 1928-
A layperson's guide to practical evangelism. Atlanta,
Office of Evangelism and Church Development, Presbyterian
Church in the U.S., [1979]. unpaged. C

1393 HENDERSON, Robert Thornton, 1928-
Of beans and Philistines; a handbook on evangelism for
plain Presbyterians. [Atlanta, Materials Distribution Center,
1976]. 1 v. (various pagings) A L

1394 HENDERSON, Thomas Chalmers, 1924-1974.
Sermons and prayers, 1970-1974. [Prairie Village, Kansas, n.p., 1974?]. 78 p. L

1395 HENDERSON, William Rossman, 1845-1933.
Infant church membership. Richmond, Presbyterian Committee of Publication, [1914]. 40 p. U

1396 HENDERSON, William Rossman, 1845-1933.
The Presbyterian-Cumberland union (1906). n.p., n.d.
14 p. Reprinted from the Union Seminary Magazine, Oct.-
Nov., 1906. A

1397 HENDRICK, John Robert, 1927-
Guide for Presbytery working groups in evangelism. Atlanta, Office of Evangelism and Church Development, Presbyterian Church in the U.S., [1978]. unpaged. C

1398 HENDRICK, John Robert, 1927-
Opening the door of faith: the why, when, and where of
evangelism. Atlanta, John Knox Press, © 1977. 112 p.
A C H L PT R U

1399 HENDRICK, John Thilman, 1815-1897 or '98.
Letters to the self-styled reformers. Cynthiana, Ky.,
Visitor Office, 1838. 120 p. PH

1400 HENEGAR, Edward, 1936-
Structuring the whole church for evangelism. Atlanta,
Office of Evangelism and Church Development, Presbyterian
Church in the U.S., [1979]. C

1401 *HENRY, Robert H.
Let's not forget McGuffey. Darlington, Penna., Little
Beaver Historical Society, 1964. 14 p. A poem on William
Holmes McGuffey. PH

1402 HENRY, Stuart Clark, 1914-
George Whitefield: wayfaring witness. New York, Abingdon Press, © 1957. 224 p. A C H L PH PT R U

1403 HENRY, Stuart Clark, 1914- ed.
A miscellany of American Christianity; essays in honor of
H. Shelton Smith. Durham, N.C., Duke University Press,
1963. 390 p. Essays by P. L. Garber, S. C. Henry, and
others. A C H L PT U

1404 HENRY, Stuart Clark, 1914-
Unvanquished Puritan; a portrait of Lyman Beecher.
Grand Rapids, Mich., Wm. B. Eerdmans Publishing Co.,
© 1973. 299 p. A C H L PH PT U

1405 HENSLEY, Philip Henry, Jr.
Our Spanish work in Tampa, Florida. [Atlanta, Executive
Committee of Home Missions, Presbyterian Church in the
U.S.], n.d. 2ℓ. U

1406 HEPBURN, Andrew Dousa, 1830-1921.
Manual of English rhetoric. Cincinnati, Van Antwerp,
Bragg & Co., © 1875. 280, 30 p. R

1407 HERNDON, John Rankin, 1862-1920.
Bible studies on Christian baptism. Richmond, Whittet &
Shepperson, 1902. 116 p. A C H U

1408 HERRON, Charles, 1863-1942.
The desert seminary, or Paul's training for the ministry
in Arabia: an address, delivered at the opening of ... the
Presbyterian Theological Seminary at Omaha, Neb., Sept. 16,
1915. n.p., n.d. 23 p. PT

1409 HERRON, Charles, 1863-1942.
    Watchman, what of the night? Thanksgiving sermon, delivered ... at the Presbyterian Church, Troy, November, 1895. n.p., n.d. 26 p. PT

1410 HEYER, George Stuart, 1930-
    Signs of our times: theological essays on art in the twentieth century. Grand Rapids, Mich., Wm. B. Eerdmans Publishing Co., © 1980. 70 p. The Gunning Lectures, University of Edinburgh, 1975. A L U

1411 HIEMSTRA, William Louis, 1915-
    Devotional monologs: brief essays on Bible characters. Grand Rapids, Mich., Baker Book House, © 1967. 82 p. R

1412 HILL, Halbert Green, 1831-1924.
    An address on the character and influence of John Knox ... Florence, S.C., September 27, 1905. n.p., n.d. 15 p. U

1413 HILL, Halbert Green, 1831-1924.
    A prize essay on the difficulties and practical duties of life. Baltimore, T. Newton Kurtz, 1858. 22 p. PH

1414 HILL, Pierre Bernard, 1877-1958.
    Don't worry. Hunt, Tex., P. B. Hill, n.d. unpaged. U

1415 HILL, Pierre Bernard, 1877-1958.
    Making a home. 3d ed. Victoria, Tex., P. B. Hill, © 1944. unpaged. R U

1416 HILL, Pierre Bernard, 1877-1958.
    The meaning of death. Victoria, Tex., P. B. Hill, © 1945. unpaged. R U

1417 HILL, Pierre Bernard, 1877-1958.
    Poems. San Antonio, Tex., Dullnig Printing Co., © 1954. 18 p. U

1418 HILL, Pierre Bernard, 1877-1958.
    Preparation for church membership. 2d ed. n.p., 1930. unpaged. A ... U: 5th ed. n.p., 1940 ... C: 9th ed. 1946 ... A: 11th ed. [San Antonio, Tex., P. B. Hill], 1951 ... R: 13th ed. 1958.

1419 HILL, Pierre Bernard, 1877-1958.
    The truth about evolution. San Antonio, Tex., Dullnig Printing Co., © 1925. 36 p. A U

1420 HILL, Pierre Bernard, 1877-1958.

What have you done? A manual for new Christians. Hunt,
Tex., P. B. Hill, n.d. unpaged. U

1421 HILL, Pierre Bernard, 1877-1958.
      What Presbyterians believe. Rev. ed. [Compiled by
      daughter, Martha]. Hunt, Tex., P. B. Hill, © 1940. un-
      paged. A C R U

1422 HILL, Robert, 1868-1962.
      Do we need the Sabbath? Richmond, Presbyterian Com-
      mittee of Publication, [1915]. 15 p. U

1423 HILL, Robert, 1868-1962.
      Sunday amusements. Richmond, Presbyterian Committee
      of Publication, n.d. 16 p. U

1424 HILL, Thomas English, 1909-
      Contemporary ethical theories. New York, The Macmillan
      Co., 1950. 368 p. A L ... C U: 1959.

1425 HILL, Thomas English, 1909-
      Contemporary theories of knowledge. New York, Ronald
      Press Co., © 1961. 583 p. A L R U

1426 HILL, Thomas English, 1909-
      Ethics in theory and practice. New York, Thomas Y.
      Crowell, 1956. 431 p. L U

1427 *HILL, William Lauriston, 1835-
      Bluebird songs of hope and joy, by Wm. Laurie Hill ...
      and Rev. Halbert G. Hill ... Boston, Richard G. Badger,
      © 1916. 192 p. H R

1428 HILL, William Wallace, 1815-1878.
      Twyman Hogue, or early piety illustrated. Philadelphia,
      Presbyterian Board of Publication, © 1859. 186 p. Bio-
      graphical sketch. H PH U

1429 *HILLDRUP, Robert Leroy.
      An American missionary to Meiji Japan. Privately printed,
      1970. 138 p. Biography of R. Bryan Grinnan. H

1430 HILLS, Edward Freer, 1912-
      Believing Bible study. Des Moines, Iowa, Christian Re-
      search Press, © 1967. 223 p. R

1431 HILLS, Edward Freer, 1912-
      Evolution in the space age. Des Moines, Iowa, Christian
      Research Press, © 1967. 40 p. R

1432 HILLS, Edward Freer, 1912-
      The King James version defended! A Christian view of

the New Testament manuscripts. Des Moines, Iowa, Christian Research Press, 1956. 158 p.   C PT R U

1433 HILLS, Edward Freer, 1912-
Space age science. Des Moines, Iowa, Christian Research Press, © 1964. 84 p.   R

1434 HOBSON, Benjamin Lewis, 1859-1918.
The task of the apologetic of today. Inaugural address ... as Professor of Apologetics and Missions, McCormick Theological Seminary, Chicago, Ill. (May 2, 1894). n.p., 1895. 34 p.   PH

1435 HODGE, Richard Morse, 1864-1928.
Historical atlas and chronology of the life of Jesus Christ; a text book and companion to a harmony of the gospels. Wytheville, Va., D. A. St. Clair Press, 1899. 39 p. A C H PT U

1436 HODGE, Richard Morse, 1864-1928.
Historical geography of Bible lands: a manual for teachers. New York, Charles Scribner's Sons, © 1915. 84 p. PT

1437 HODGE, Richard Morse, 1864-1928.
Manual methods of Sunday-school teaching, with full directions and photographs of work executed by Sunday-school pupils. New York, Union Theological Seminary, 1905. 39 p. U

1438 HODGE, Richard Morse, 1864-1928.
Questions on the life of Christ. Nashville, Tenn., n.p., 1898. 20 p.   PT

1439 HODGE, Richard Morse, 1864-1928.
Sunday school curriculum, a standard of excellence and a graded course of instruction, prepared by Richard Morse Hodge and Alexander L. Phillips. Nashville, Tenn., Bible Institute, 1900. 18 p.   PT

1440 HODGE, Samuel, 1829-1892.
The New Bethel centennial, comprising an account of the centennial exercises of the New Bethel Presbyterian Church, Sullivan County, Tennessee, and the historical sermon. Bristol, Tenn., J. L. King's Job Printing, 1882. 41 p. A

1441 HODGMAN, Stephen Alexander, ca. 1808-1887.
Moses and the philosophers, in three parts: The physical system; The moral problem; The mercy seat. The whole together giving a view of the universe, as written by Moses, the servant of God. Philadelphia, [Ferguson Brothers & Co.], 1882. 3 pts. in 1 v.   PT ... U: 1884.

1442 HOFFMAN, Fred Wakefield, 1889-1979.
Revival times in America. Boston, W. A. Wilde Co.,
© 1956. 189 p. A C L PT R U

1443 HOGE, Moses Drury, 1818-1899.
Addresses at the sixty-second anniversary of the American
Bible Society, 1878. n.p., n.d. 8 p. U

1444 HOGE, Moses Drury, 1818-1899.
Cause and cure of despondency; a sermon delivered ... at
Second Presbyterian Church, Sunday morning, October 2,
1898. Richmond, James E. Goode Printing Co., 1898. 15 p.
PH U

1445 HOGE, Moses Drury, 1818-1899.
... Commemoration of forty-five years of service by the
Rev. Moses Drury Hoge, D.D., LL.D., as pastor of the
Second Presbyterian Church of the city of Richmond, Virginia.
Richmond, Whittet & Shepperson, [1891?]. 243 p. At head
of title: 1845-1890. PH

1446 HOGE, Moses Drury, 1818-1899.
Forgiveness of injuries. A sermon delivered in the Second
Presbyterian Church ... on Sunday, March 3, 1889. Rich-
mond, n.p., 1889. 14 p. PT

1447 HOGE, Moses Drury, 1818-1899.
Honorable old age. A sermon preached at the funeral of
Capt. Benjamin Sheppard in the Second Presbyterian Church,
Richmond, Virginia. Richmond, H. K. Ellyson, 1855. 19 p.
H U

1448 HOGE, Moses Drury, 1818-1899.
Memorial discourse on the planting of Presbyterianism in
Kentucky one hundred years ago. Louisville, Ky., Courier-
Journal Job Printing Co., n.d. 19 p. H PH U

1449 HOGE, Moses Drury, 1818-1899.
The memories, hopes and duties of the hour: a historic
discourse, delivered at Washington and Lee University, Lexington, Virginia, June 15, 1886. Richmond, Whittet &
Shepperson, 1886. 28 p. C U

1450 HOGE, Moses Drury, 1818-1899.
Mission field of the South, a sermon delivered on Friday,
Oct. 10, 1873, at the meeting of the Evangelical Alliance in
the city of New York. Richmond, The Whig, 1873. 11 p.
U

1451 HOGE, Moses Drury, 1818-1899.
The perfection of beauty, and other sermons.... With a
lecture on "The success of Christianity and evidence of its

divine origin," delivered at the University of Virginia. Richmond, Presbyterian Committee of Publication, 1904. 335 p. A C H R U

1452 HOGE, Moses Drury, 1818-1899.
Portraitures of four pastors. Richmond, Presbyterian Committee of Publication, 1892. 16 p. Sketches of John H. Rice, William J. Armstrong, William S. Plumer, Thomas V. Moore. A PH U

1453 HOGE, Moses Drury, 1818-1899.
The victory won: a memorial of the Rev. Wm. J. Hoge, D.D., late pastor of the Tabb Street Presbyterian Church, Petersburg, Va. Richmond, Presbyterian Committee of Publication, 1864. 16 p. U

1454 HOGE, Peyton Harrison, 1858-1940.
The divine tragedy; a drama of the Christ. New York, Fleming H. Revell Co., © 1905. 146 p. A C H L R U

1455 HOGE, Peyton Harrison, 1858-1940.
Moses Drury Hoge: life and letters. By his nephew. Richmond, Presbyterian Committee of Publication, © 1899. 518 p. A C H L PH PT R U

1456 HOGE, Peyton Harrison, 1858-1940.
The officers of a Presbyterian congregation. Three sermons preached in the First Presbyterian Church of Wilmington, N.C. n.p., [1885]. 72 p. U

1457 HOGE, William James, 1825-1864.
Blind Bartimeus; or, The story of a sightless sinner, and his Great Physician. New York, American Tract Society, © 1858. 257 p. A C H PH PT U ... C PH: New York, Sheldon, Blakeman & Co., 1859 ... PH PT: 1860 ... H: New ed. London, James Nisbet and Co., 1863. 162 p.

1458 HOGE, William James, 1825-1864.
A discourse, delivered by the ... collegiate pastor of the Brick Presbyterian Church, New York, on the resignation of his charge, July 21, 1861. New York, Baker & Godwin, 1861. 26 p. PH PT U

1459 HOGE, William James, 1825-1864.
Sketch of Dabney Carr Harrison, minister of the gospel and captain in the army of the Confederate States of America. Richmond, Presbyterian Committee of Publication, 1862. 55 p. H ... A PH: 1863. 48 p.

1460 HOGSHEAD, Alexander Lewis, 1816-1880.
The gospel self-supporting. Wytheville, D. A. St. Clair, 1873. 258 p. Appendix: Will a Christian rob God? or,

The tithe the minimum of the Christian's oblations, by John
W. Pratt. 201-258 p. A C H R U

1461 HOLDERBY, Andrew Roberdeau, 1839-1924.
      The pastor and his elders. Richmond, Presbyterian Com-
mittee of Publication, © 1899. 18 p.   PT U

1462 HOLLADAY, James Minor, 1866-1937, comp.
      A partial history of Fincastle Presbyterian Church. Rich-
mond, Whittet & Shepperson, 1902. 83 p.   PH

1463 HOLLIFIELD, Ambrose Nelson, ca. 1851-1901.
      Christian science, or mind cure. A sermon ... preached
in the Grand Avenue and the First Presbyterian churches,
St. Louis, Mo., the Alexander Presbyterian Church, Philadelphia, Pa., and the Third Presbyterian Church, Newark,
N.J. Newark, Advertiser Printing House, 1889. 22 p.   PH

1464 HOLLIFIELD, Ambrose Nelson, ca. 1851-1901.
      Remembering the days of old: 1824-1899; or, The Puri-
tans and their descendants. A discourse, delivered June
11th, 1899, in commemoration of the seventy-fifth anniversary
of the organization of the Third Presbyterian Church of Newark, New Jersey. n.p., n.d. 99 p.   H

1465 HOLLIFIELD, Ambrose Nelson, ca. 1851-1901.
      "Shall we legalize Sabbath desecration, and races?" A
sermon preached in the Third Presbyterian Church, Newark,
N.J. Newark, Advertiser Printing House, 1891. 16 p.
PH PT

1466 HOLLINGSWORTH, Aaron Hayden, 1903-
      Marriage and family living today. Roanoke, Va., Second
Presbyterian Church, n.d. 49 p.   H U

1467 HOLLINGSWORTH, William Franklin, 1867-1946.
      The church school and our young women. Louisville, Ky.,
Executive Committee of Christian Education and Ministerial
Relief, Presbyterian Church in the U.S., [1916]. 15 p.   U

1468 HOLT, David Rice, 1925-
      Handbook of church finance. New York, The Macmillan
Co., 1960. 201 p.   A C H L PH PT U

1469 HOOPER, Thomas Williamson, 1832-1915.
      "Lead me to the rock." Philadelphia, Presbyterian Board
of Publication and Sabbath-school Work, © 1892. 174 p.
A C PT U

1470 HOOPER, Thomas Williamson, 1832-1915.
      Mose the sexton; or, A talk about popery. Philadelphia,
Presbyterian Board of Publication, © 1879. 34 p.   PH

1471 HOPKINS, Henry Harvey, 1804-1877.
Man and his enemy; man and his friend. Two dis-
courses. Louisville, Hull & Brother, 1849. 27 p. PH
PT

1472 HOPKINS, Martin Armstrong, 1889-1964, tr.
Biblical theology of the Old Testament ... based on the
class room notes of Geerhardus Vos. Shanghai, Christian
Book Room, [1935]. 340 p. In Chinese. PT

1473 HOPKINS, Martin Armstrong, 1889-1964.
The open door in China; a scriptural interpretation of
missions by a missionary. Hankow, China, Religious Tract
Society Press, [1937]. 189 p. A H PT R U

1474 HOPKINS, Martin Armstrong, 1889-1964.
The philosophy of Biblical prophecy. n.p., n.d. 23 p.
Reprinted from the China Fundamentalist, January-March,
1931. PT

1475 HOPKINS, Martin Armstrong, 1889-1964.
Practical Kouyü commentary on First Corinthians: exege-
tical, analytical, expository. 4th ed., rev. Hong Kong,
Alliance Press, n.d. 259 p. In Chinese. PT

1476 HOPKINS, Martin Armstrong, 1889-1964.
A practical Mandarin commentary on First Corinthians;
exegetical, analytical, expository. Hankow, Religious Tract
Society, n.d. 358 p. In Chinese. PT

1477 HOPKINS, Martin Armstrong, 1889-1964.
Premillennialism, dispensationalism and the Westminster
standards. [Athens, Ga.], n.p., n.d. 12 p. C

1478 HOPKINS, Martin Armstrong, 1889-1964.
The Revelation of Jesus Christ: a practical Kuoyü com-
mentary: exegetical, analytical, expository. Hong Kong,
Christian Witness Press, n.d. 363 p. In Chinese. PT

1479 HOPKINS, Martin Armstrong, 1889-1964.
The Revelation of Jesus Christ analyzed. [Tenghsien,
Shantung, China, North China Theological Seminary], n.d.
9 p. PT

1480 HOPPER, Joseph, 1892-1971.
Concurring witnesses looking unto Jesus. Atlanta, Committee on Woman's Work, Presbyterian Church in the U.S.,
© 1945. 48 p. U

1481 HOPPER, Joseph Barron, 1921-
The case for Korea: nail up the windows? Nashville,
Tenn., Board of World Missions, Presbyterian Church in the
U.S., [1949?]. 4 p. U

1482 HORTON, Thomas Corwin, ca. 1849-1932, comp.
      The wonderful names of our wonderful Lord; three hundred
and sixty five names and titles of the Lord Jesus Christ as
found in the Old and New Testament, one for every day in
the year. Los Angeles, Calif., Grant Publishing House,
1925. 191 p. U ... R: 4th ed., rev. © 1928. 191 p.

1483 HOUGH, Robert Ervin, 1874-1965.
      The Christian after death. Chicago, Moody Press, © 1947.
169 p. C H L R U

1484 HOUGH, Robert Ervin, 1874-1965.
      The ministry of the Glory Cloud. New York, Philosophical
Library, © 1955. 145 p. H PT R U

1485 HOUSTON, Matthew Hale, 1841-1905.
      By his life. Richmond, Whittet & Shepperson, 1899.
105 p. A C PT U

1486 HOUSTON, Matthew Hale, 1841-1905.
      Dr. Strickler on perfectionism; a review. Atlanta, E. W.
Allen & Co., 1904. 21 p. A review of Dr. Strickler's ar-
ticle "Perfectionism" which appeared in the Union Seminary
Magazine, April-May, 1903. PT U

1487 HOUSTON, Matthew Hale, 1841-1905.
      How is your minister supported? St. Louis, Presbyterian
Publishing Co., n.d. 54 p. R

1488 HOUSTON, Matthew Hale, 1841-1905.
      How was Jesus baptized? Richmond, Whittet & Shepper-
son, 1881. 45 p. PT ... U: Richmond, Presbyterian Committee of Publication, 1889. 41 p. ... R: © 1894.

1489 HOUSTON, Samuel Rutherford, 1806-1887, comp.
      Brief biographical accounts of many members of the Hous-
ton family accompanied by a genealogical table. Cincinnati,
Elm Street Printing Co., 1882. 420 p. H

1490 HOUSTON, Samuel Rutherford, 1806-1887.
      A historical address ... at a centennial celebration of the
organization of the Presbyterian Church, at Union, West
Virginia, August 1st, 1883. Richmond, E. B. Marquess &
Co., 1883. 23 p. U

1491 HOW MUCH shall I give? A series of tracts on the subject
      of systematic benevolence. Philadelphia, Presbyterian Board
of Publication, [1857]. Variously paged. Includes: Address
on systematic benevolence, by the General Assembly to the
ministers and churches under its care. --The great giver, by
the Rev. W. S. Plumer, D.D. C H PH PT U

1492 HOWARD, Charles Morse,   -1908.

Book of instruction for the unconverted, the anxious inquirer, the young convert, and for Christians, children and parents. What to do in prayer meeting; also sixteen reasons why I should believe the Bible. n.p., © 1895. 28 p.   H

1493   HOWARD, Charles Morse,   -1908.
Reviving hymns for the new life. 4th ed. enl. Lynchburg, J. P. Bell & Co., 1878. 128 p.   H ... A: 5th ed. enl. 1886. 154 p.

1494   HOWARD, George Parkinson, 1882-
¡Creo en la Iglesia! Buenos Aires, Editorial "La Aurora, " 1942. 96 p.   A

1495   HOWARD, George Parkinson, 1882-
¿Libertad religiosa en la América Latina? 2d ed.   Buenos Aires, Editorial "La Aurora, " [1945]. 249 p.   A

1496   HOWARD, George Parkinson, 1882-
Nuestra civilización apostata; diagnosis de la enfermedad espiritual de nuestro siglo. Santiago de Chile, Imprenta Universitaria, 1939. 125 p.   C

1497   HOWARD, George Parkinson, 1882-
Pan y estrellas, orientaciones para la juventud en el siglo de la fuerza atómica. Buenos Aires, Editorial "La Aurora, " [1946]. 181 p.   A

1498   HOWARD, George Parkinson, 1882-
Religious liberty in Latin America? Foreword by John A. Mackay. Philadelphia, Westminster Press, © 1944. 170 p. A C H L PH PT R U

1499   HOWARD, George Parkinson, 1882-
Rivales del Cristianismo. Buenos Aires, Editorial "La Aurora, " 1940. 124 p.   A

1500   HOWARD, George Parkinson, 1882-
A spiritual adventure in South America. New York, Committee on Cooperation in Latin America, 1943. 68 p.   PH

1501   HOWARD, George Parkinson, 1882-
We Americans: North and South. New York, Friendship Press, © 1951. 148 p.   A C H L PT U

1502   HOWE, George, 1802-1883.
An address delivered at Columbia (S.C.), March 28, 1832, at the inauguration of the author, as Professor of Biblical Literature, in the Theological Seminary of the Synod of South Carolina and Georgia. Charleston, Observer Office Press, 1832. 27 p.   PH

1503   HOWE, George, 1802-1833.

An appeal to the young men of the Presbyterian Church in the Synod of South Carolina and Georgia. n.p., 1836. 48 p. A C H PH R U

1504 HOWE, George, 1802-1883.
Discourse in commemoration of the life and labors of Rev. George Cooper Gregg, pastor of Salem Church, Sumter District, S.C., delivered in said church on Sabbath, Jan. 19, 1862. Columbia, S.C., R. W. Gibbes, 1862. 21 p. H PH

1505 HOWE, George, 1802-1883.
A discourse on theological education; delivered on the bicentenary of the Westminster Assembly of Divines, July, 1843. To which is added, advice to a student preparing for the ministry. New York, Leavitt, Trow & Co., 1844. 243 p. A C H PH R U

1506 HOWE, George, 1802-1833.
Early history of Presbyterianism in South Carolina: a sermon preached at the opening of the Synod of South Carolina, in Charleston, S.C., November 15, 1854. Columbia, S.C., I. C. Morgan, 1855. 22 p. PH

1507 HOWE, George, 1802-1883.
The early Presbyterian immigration into South Carolina: a discourse delivered before the General Assembly in New Orleans, May 7th, 1858, by appointment of the Presbyterian Historical Society. Columbia, S.C., R. W. Gibbes, 1858. 41 p. PH PT

1508 HOWE, George, 1802-1883.
The endowments, position and education of woman. An address delivered before the Hemans and Sigourney societies of the Female High School at Limestone Springs, July 23, 1850. Columbia, S.C., I. C. Morgan, 1850. 22 p. C PH

1509 HOWE, George, 1802-1883.
Eulogy on the Rev. Joshua Bates.... Delivered on Commencement Day, August 9, 1854. Boston, T. R. Marvin, 1885. 40 p. C PT

1510 HOWE, George, 1802-1883.
History of the Presbyterian Church in South Carolina.... Prepared by order of the Synod of South Carolina. Columbia, Duffie & Chapman, 1870-1883. 2 v. Vol. 2 published by W. J. Duffie. A C H L PH PT R U ... C H L: [Synod of South Carolina, Presbyterian Church in the U.S.], © 1965, © 1966.

1511 HOWE, George, 1802-1883.
The Scotch-Irish, and their first settlements on the Tyger

River and other neighboring precincts in South Carolina. A centennial discourse delivered at Nazareth Church, Spartanburg District, S.C., September 14, 1861. Columbia, S.C., Southern Guardian Steam-power Press, 1861. 31 p. C H

1512 HOWE, George, 1802-1883.
The secondary and collateral influences of the sacred scriptures. Columbia, S.C., I. Chanler Morgan, 1853. 27 p. PH

1513 HOWE, George, 1802-1883.
"Thy kingdom come." A missionary sermon, preached before the Presbytery of Harmony, at the Brick Church in Salem, South Carolina. Columbia, Abner Landrum, 1833. 20 p. C PH

1514 HOWE, George, 1802-1883.
The value and influence of literary pursuits: an oration delivered before the Eumenean and Philanthropic societies of Davidson College, N.C., on Commencement Day, August 13th, 1846. Columbia, S.C., I. C. Morgan, 1846. 27 p. C PH PT

1515 HOWELL, Andrew Jackson, 1869-1947.
The book of Wilmington. [Wilmington, N.C., Wil-Stamp and Printing Co., 1930]. 206 p. H

1516 HOWELL, Andrew Jackson, 1869-1947.
A history of First Presbyterian Church, Wilmington, North Carolina. [Wilmington, N.C., n.p., 1951]. 16 p. PH U

1517 HOWERTON, James Robert, 1861-1924.
The church and social reforms. New York, Fleming H. Revell Co., © 1913. 127 p. A C H L PH PT R U

1518 HOWERTON, James Robert, 1861-1924.
Freedom and causality in their ethical aspects. Being the lectures delivered on the Reineicker Foundation at the Protestant Episcopal Theological Seminary of Virginia, December, 1914. [Richmond, Presbyterian Committee of Publication], © 1915. 86 p. A C H R U

1519 HOWIE, Carl Gordon, 1920-
Being and becoming (The Christian life). Philadelphia, Department of Chaplains and Service Personnel, United Presbyterian Church in the U.S.A., n.d. 12 p. PH

1520 HOWIE, Carl Gordon, 1920-
The book of Ezekiel. The book of Daniel. Richmond, John Knox Press, © 1961. 142 p. (The Layman's Bible Commentary, v. 13.) A C H L PT R U

1521 HOWIE, Carl Gordon, 1920-
The creative era between the Testaments. Richmond,
John Knox Press, © 1965. 96 p.   A C H L PT R U

1522 HOWIE, Carl Gordon, 1920-
The date and composition of Ezekiel. Philadelphia, So-
ciety of Biblical Literature, 1950. 121 p. Thesis--Johns
Hopkins University.   A C L PT R U

1523 HOWIE, Carl Gordon, 1920-
The Dead Sea Scrolls and the living church. Richmond,
John Knox Press, © 1958. 128 p.   A C H L PT R U

1524 HOWIE, Carl Gordon, 1920-
God in the eternal present. Richmond, John Knox Press,
© 1959. 128 p.   A C H L PT R U

1525 HOWIE, Carl Gordon, 1920-
Man, woman and God. [Royal Oak, Mich., Cathedral
Publishers], © 1974. 72 p. Cover-title.   U

1526 HOWIE, Carl Gordon, 1920-
The Old Testament story. [1st ed.] New York, Harper
& Row, © 1965. 183 p.   A L U ... L: London, Universi-
ties Press, [1967].

1527 HOWIE, Carl Gordon, 1920-
Presbyterianism: a restatement in question and answer
form. [Royal Oak, Mich., Cathedral Publishers], © 1975.
60 p.   PH

1528 HOWIE, Carl Gordon, 1920-   , comp.
Sermons for all seasons. Royal Oak, Mich., Cathedral
Publishers, 1975. 72 p.   R

1529 HOWIE, Carl Gordon, 1920-
The Ten Commandments in contemporary life. [Royal
Oak, Mich., Cathedral Publishers], © 1978. 84 p.   L

1530 HOWIE, Carl Gordon, 1920-
You too may be a Presbyterian. [Royal Oak, Mich., Cathedral Publishers, 1971]. 24 p. Cover-title.   PH U

1531 HOWISON, Robert Reid, 1820-1906.
God and creation. Richmond, West, Johnston & Co.,
1883. 578 p.   A C H L PT U

1532 HOWISON, Robert Reid, 1820-1906.
A history of the United States of America. Intended for
students in schools, academies, colleges, universities and at
home, and for general readers. Richmond, Everett Waddey
Co., 1892. 936 p.   U

1533 HOWISON, Robert Reid, 1820-1906.
      A history of Virginia, from its discovery and settlement
      by Europeans to the present time. Philadelphia, Carey &
      Hart, 1846-48. Vol. 2: Richmond, Drinker and Morris,
      1848. H PT U ... PH: v. 1.

1534 HOYT, Nathan, 1793-1866.
      Confirmation without laying on of hands. Philadelphia,
      Presbyterian Board of Publication, © 1860. 47 p.   PH PT

1535 HOYT, Nathan, 1793-1866.
      History of a church in the South. Philadelphia Presby-
      terian Board of Publication, n.d. 11 p. (Presbyterian
      Tracts.)   C H L PH PT R U

1536 HOYT, Nathan, 1793-1866.
      Infant membership secured by the Abrahamic covenant.
      Philadelphia, Presbyterian Board of Publication, n.d. 20 p.
      (Presbyterian Tracts, no. 163.)   C H L PH PT R U

1537 HOYT, Thomas Alexander, 1828-1903.
      A plea for the higher culture of woman. An address, de-
      livered on Commencement Day of the Laurensville Female
      College, July 1, 1858. Laurensville, S.C., Robert M.
      Stokes, 1858. 23 p. PH

1538 HOYT, Thomas Alexander, 1828-1903.
      Reopening of the Chambers Presbyterian Church, Phila-
      delphia. Sermon and address of rededication ... October 12,
      1884. Philadelphia, George H. Buchanan & Co., 1884. 29 p.
      PH

1539 HOYT, Thomas Alexander, 1828-1903.
      Theology as a popular science. Philadelphia, Presbyterian
      Board of Publication and Sabbath-school work, 1902. 22 p.
      PH PT

1540 HUDSON, George, 1866-1916.
      The New Testament teaching on the Atonement. Richmond,
      Presbyterian Committee of Publication, [1913]. 50 p.   C U

1541 HUDSON, George Alexander, 1894-
      Campaigning for Christ in China (a presentation of the
      Christian message to a non-Christian audience). Shanghai,
      China, Christian Literature Society, 1939. 103 p.   A C
      H U

1542 HUDSON, George Alexander, 1894-
      Communism in China and its challenge. Decatur, Ga.,
      Decatur Presbyterian Church, [1951]. 15 p.   C U

1543 HUDSON, Waddy Hampton, 1867-1960.
      The outlook for Christianity in China. [Nashville, Board

of World Missions, Presbyterian Church in the U.S.], n.d.
unpaged. Address delivered at the General Assembly, Meridian, Mississippi, May, 1938. PT

1544 HUDSON, William Emmitt, 1873-1954.
The adventures of a dreamer; an autobiography. Staunton,
Va., McClure Printing Co., n.d. 76 p. U

1545 HUIE, Wade Prichard, 1923-
"Ears to hear." The address given ... on the occasion
of his inauguration as Peter Marshall Professor of Homile-
tics, Columbia Theological Seminary, May 10, 1963. 11-24 p.
Bulletin of Columbia Theological Seminary, August, 1963.
C H PT R U

1546 HUIE, Wade Prichard, 1923-
The poverty of abundance; from text to sermon on Luke
16:19-31. n.p., n.d. 403-420 p. Reprinted from Interpretation, October, 1968. C

1547 *HUMPHREY, Edward Porter, 1809-1887.
Memoirs of the Rev. Thomas Cleland, D.D., compiled
from his private papers. By Edward P. Humphrey and
Thomas H. Cleland. Cincinnati, Moore, Wilstach, Keys &
Co., 1859. 199 p. L PH

1548 HUNT, Isaac Cochrane, 1876-1936, ed.
A class book on home missions. Issued under the authority of the Executive Committee of Home Missions of the Synod
of Kentucky, Presbyterian Church in the United States, March,
1914. Lexington, Ky., Transylvania Printing Co., 1914.
263 p. L

1549 HUNT, Isaac Cochrane, 1876-1936, ed.
Presbyterian home missions in Kentucky. Lexington, Ky.,
Transylvania Printing Co., 1914. 263 p. H

1550 HUSKE, Marion Strange, 1889-1977.
The centennial history of the First Presbyterian Church,
Reidsville, North Carolina. Approved by the session. n.p.,
1975. 54 p. U

1551 HUTCHESON, Richard Gordon, 1921-
The chaplain and the structures of the military society.
n.p., n.d. 12 p. Reprinted from The Chaplain. PH

1552 HUTCHESON, Richard Gordon, 1921-
The churches and the chaplaincy. Atlanta, John Knox
Press, © 1975. 223 p. A C L PT R U

1553 HUTCHESON, Richard Gordon, 1921-
Wheel within the wheel: confronting the management crisis

of the pluralistic church. Atlanta, John Knox Press, © 1979.
272 p.   A L PT U

1554   HUTCHISON, John Russell, 1807-1878.
       Reminiscences, sketches and addresses, selected from my
       papers during a ministry of forty-five years in Mississippi,
       Louisiana and Texas. Houston, Tex., E. H. Cushing, 1874.
       262 p.   A H PT R

1555   HUTCHISON, Stuart Nye, 1877-
       Bible boys and girls. New York, Fleming H. Revell Co.,
       © 1922. 189 p.   PT

1556   HUTCHISON, Stuart Nye, 1877-
       The children's hour; more five-minute sermons. New
       York, Fleming H. Revell Co., © 1918. 192 p.   H PT
       U ... R: For the children's hour.

1557   HUTCHISON, Stuart Nye, 1877-
       A message from the moderator. New York, Presbyterian
       War-time Service Commissioned Officers, 1941. unpaged.
       PH

1558   HUTCHISON, Stuart Nye, 1877-
       The soul of a child: five-minute sermons to children.
       New York, Fleming H. Revell Co., © 1916. 191 p.   Re-
       printed in part from the Presbyterian of the South.   A C
       PT U

1559   HUTCHISON, Stuart Nye, 1877-
       An unfrequented path to immortality. n.p., [1925]. 10 p.
       PH

1560   HUTTON, Cornelius Marion, 1835-1922.
       The analytical Shorter Catechism, arranged also with em-
       phasis and designed thus to render it easier to understand
       and memorize. Richmond, Presbyterian Committee of Pub-
       lication, 1893. 37 p.   A U

1561   HUTTON, Milton Calhoun, 1843-1926.
       Early dew, a collection of short sermons for children.
       Richmond, Presbyterian Publishing Co., 1882. 139 p.
       A C ... U: 2d ed. Richmond, Presbyterian Committee of
       Publication, 1886. 136 p. ... H: 3d ed.

1562   HUTTON, Milton Calhoun, 1843-1926.
       The final perseverance of the saints. Georgetown, Tex.,
       People's Sentinel Press, 1897. 60 p.   A C H

1563   HUTTON, Milton Calhoun, 1843-1926.
       Revised manual of the Presbytery of Central Texas. n.p.,
       Von Boeckmann & Co., 1901. 91 p.   PH

1564 HYMES, Hamilton Andrew, 1863-1939.
The preacher's message for the twentieth century: an anniversary sermon preached in the Second Presbyterian Church, New Albany, Ind., Dec. 13, 1903. n.p., n.d. 24 p. PT

1565 IN MEMORIAM Alexander Doak McClure. [Raleigh, N.C., Edwards & Broughton Printing Co., 1920]. 71 p. Resolutions, tributes. A sketch of his life. C

1566 IN MEMORIAM. [Charleston, S.C., Walker, Evans & Cogswell, 1874]. 76, 63, 24, 23 p. Lettered on cover: In memoriam. Thomas Smyth, D.D. C PH PT

1567 IN MEMORIAM, Joseph Charless. Being a compendium of the action of the several public institutions and corporations with which the deceased was connected at the time of his death; eulogies of the press; and funeral sermon, preached at the Second Presbyterian Church, June 6, 1859, by S. B. McPheeters. St. Louis, George Knapp & Co., 1868. 63 p. C

1568 IN MEMORIAM, Rev. Gilbert Glass, D.D., 1875-1934. By Henry H. Sweets, R. E. Magill [and others]. n.p., n.d. 14 p. H U

1569 IN MEMORIAM: Rev. Gilbert R. Brackett, D.D. Abbeville, S.C., Press and Banner Print., 1905. 53 p. H PH

1570 IN MEMORIAM: Rev. Henry Alexander White, A.M., Ph.D., D.D., LL.D. Decatur, Ga., 1927. 26 p. Columbia Theological Seminary Bulletin, October, 1927. Contributors are Rev. W. M. McPheeters, Rev. Chas. P. Coble, Rev. Neal L. Anderson, Rev. R. T. Gillespie. C PH PT

1571 IN MEMORIAM. Rev. J. Henry Smith, D.D. Born in Lexington, Va., August 13, 1820. Died in Greensboro, N.C., November 22, 1897. [Baltimore, John Murphy Co., 1900]. 110 p. A C R U

1572 IN MEMORIAM. Rev. Joseph Hamilton Martin. Born August 11, 1825. Died February 7, 1887. [Atlanta, Jas. P. Harrison & Co.], n.d. 35 p. Sermon by Rev. J. G. Hunter (Georgetown, Ky.). C

1573 IN MEMORIAM. Rev. Robert Ernest Caldwell, D.D., born October 18, 1858, died January 3, 1904. [Baltimore, John Murphy Co., 1905]. 100 p. C U

1574 IN MEMORIAM. [Rev. William S. Plumer] by E. Douglas Plumer, Kate P. Bryan. n.p., n.d. 24 p. H PH

1575 IN MEMORIAM, Richard Clark Reed, D.D., LL.D., 1851-1925. Columbia, S.C., Columbia Theological Seminary, 1926.

33 p. Bulletin of Columbia Theological Seminary, January, 1926. Participating were Richard T. Gillespie, Wm. M. McPheeters, J. R. Bridges, John McSween.   C H PT

1576   IN MEMORIAM Robert Lewis Dabney, born, March 5th, 1820, died, January 3rd, 1898. Knoxville, Tenn., University of Tennessee Press, 1899. 41 p. Robert Lewis Dabney--a sketch, by Thomas C. Johnson. Tributes by James [John] B. Shearer, Benjamin M. Palmer, G. B. Strickler, Moses D. Hoge, Thornton R. Sampson, S. Taylor Martin.   C H PT U

1577   IN MEMORIA M. [Wm. Francis Robertson, 1834-1875. Charleston, S.C., Walker, Evans, & Cogswell, 1875]. 13 p. "... tribute to his memory was delivered by the Rev. John L. Girardeau ... " Other participants were R. H. Kinnaird, J. G. Hunter, J. J. Robinson.   C

1578   IN MEMORIAM. William Marcellus McPheeters. Born April 8, 1854; died August 14, 1935. Professor of Old Testament Literature and Exegesis, Columbia Theological Seminary, 1888-1935. 26 p. Bulletin, Columbia Theological Seminary, July, 1936. Funeral service and addresses by Dr. S. C. Byrd, Dr. J. McDowell Richards, Dr. John McSween.   A C H PT R U

1579   IN MEMORY of Rev. Benjamin Morgan Palmer, D.D., pastor of the First Presbyterian Church, New Orleans, La., December 1856 to May 1902. Memorial address by Rev. Eugene Daniel, D.D., Lewisburg, W.Va. Tribute by Dr. I. L. Leucht, Touro Synagogue. n.p., n.d. 22 p.   A H PH

1580   IN MEMORY of Rev. Thomas A. Hoyt, D.D., former pastor, First Presbyterian Church, Nashville, Tenn. Sermon delivered by Rev. J. H. McNeilly, D.D. ... funeral services held at the First Presbyterian Church, Nashville, Tenn., July 5, 1903, and resolutions of the officers. Nashville, First Presbyterian Church, n.d. 27 p.   H

1581   IN THE GENERAL ASSEMBLY of the Presbyterian Church in the United States. Complaint of James Woodrow versus the Synod of Georgia; in case of the Presbyterian Church in the United States [Rev. Dr. Wm. Adams, voluntary prosecutor] versus James Woodrow. Argument of the complainant, James Woodrow. Columbia, S.C., Presbyterian Publishing House, 1888. 41 p.   PT

1582   THE INAUGURATION of Marshall Scott Woodson as President of Flora Macdonald College. Red Springs, N.C., Flora Macdonald College, 1951. unpaged.   PT

1583   INAUGURATION of the Jackson statue. Introductory address

of Governor Kemper and oration by Rev. Moses D. Hoge,
D.D., on Tuesday, October 26, 1876. Richmond, Wm. Ellis
Jones, 1885. 30 p.   C H PH U

1584   THE INAUGURATION of Walter Lee Lingle as the eleventh
President of Davidson College, June 3, 1930. Davidson,
N.C., Davidson College Bulletin, September, 1930. 44 p.
Participants included David H. Scanlon, Davidson M. Douglas,
Benjamin Rice Lacy, Henry H. Sweets, C. M. Richards, and
Walter Lee Lingle.   R U

1585   INMAN, Samuel Martin, 1905-1978.
The roots of a banyan tree: the story of one Christian's
ministry, 1928-1970. [Franklin Springs, Ga., Advocate
Press], © 1978. 122 p.   C L

1586   INSTALLATION services of the Rev. William J. Hoge, as
associate pastor of the Brick Presbyterian Church, in the
city of New York, May 22, 1859. New York, M. W. Dodd,
1859. 46 p.   U

1587   International Congress of Learned Societies in the Field of
Religion, Los Angeles, 1972.
Religion and the humanizing of man: plenary addresses.
Edited by James M. Robinson. 2d rev. ed. [Waterloo, Ont.],
Council on the Study of Religion, 1973. 226 p.   C PT U

1588   Interpretation.
Tools for Bible study, edited by Balmer H. Kelly [and]
Donald G. Miller. Richmond, John Knox Press, © 1956.
159 p.   A C H L PT R U

1589   THE INTERPRETER'S dictionary of the Bible; an illustrated
encyclopedia identifying and explaining all proper names and
significant terms and subjects in the Holy Scriptures, including the Apocrypha, with attention to archaeological discoveries
and researches into the life and faith of ancient times. Supplementary volume. [Editorial Board: Keith Crim, general
editor, and others]. Nashville, Abingdon, © 1976. 998 p.
A C L PH PT R U

1590   INTERPRETING the Gospels. Edited by James Luther Mays.
Philadelphia, Fortress Press, © 1981. 307 p.   C L R U

1591   IRVINE, Robert, 1814-1881.
The certainty of death, and the preparation necessary for
meeting it: a sermon preached in the St. John Presbyterian
Church, on the last Sabbath of 1847. Saint John, N.B., Henry Chubb & Co., 1848. 16 p.   PH

1592   IRVINE, William, 1848-1911.
Memorial: Mrs. Elizabeth Irvine Blanton, wife of Rev.

L. H. Blanton, Richmond, Ky. [Danville, Ky., n.p., 1902].
49 p. H

1593 IRWIN, David Hanson, ca. 1866-1895, ed.
The Pacific Coast pulpit. New York, Fleming H. Revell
Co., © 1893. 247 p. PH

1594 IRWIN, John Chandler.
A sermon: preached in the First Presbyterian Church,
Logansport, Indiana ... on the death of Capt. N. Palmer
Dunn ... who was killed in the battle of Chicamauga, Ten-
nessee, September 19th, 1863. Washington, H. Polkinhorn,
1863. 23 p. PH

1595 IRWIN, Leonidas Willson, 1862-1937, comp.
A manual for the Presbyterian Church in the United States
for 1899. Richmond, Presbyterian Committee of Publication,
n.d. 69 p. U

1596 IRWIN, Leonidas Willson, 1862-1937.
Rev. William MacCutchan Morrison, D.D.; an address
delivered ... in Lee Chapel, Washington and Lee University,
June 7, 1926. Lexington, Va., Washington and Lee Univer-
sity, 1927. 20 p. Washington and Lee University. Bulletin,
Jan. 5, 1927. H U

1597 IRWIN, Leonidas Willson, 1862-1937, comp.
A year book of the Presbyterian Church in the United
States for 1896-97, containing a statement of principles, history, and a summary of work of the church during the past
year. Richmond, Presbyterian Committee of Publication,
[1897]. 55 p. U ... U: 1897 ed. 65 p.

1598 *JACKSON, Gladys.
Study guide: the worship and work of the congregation, by
Gladys Jackson and John H. McKinnon. [Atlanta], General
Council, Presbyterian Church in the U.S., © 1964. 72 p.
C U

1599 JACKSON, Matthew White, 1795-1880.
Water baptism, as taught in the sacred scriptures, and
not by profane authors: a sermon. Petersburg, n.p.,
1856. 31 p. PT

1600 JACOBS, Allen Cleveland, 1918-1971.
Presbyterian home for children, Talladega, Alabama,
1864-1964; an historical collection. n.p., [1964?]. 321 p.
C H L

1601 JACOBS, Ferdinand, 1808-1894.
The committing of our cause to God. A sermon preached
in the Second Presbyterian Church, Charleston, South-Carolina,

on Friday, the 6th of December, a day of fasting, humiliation and prayer, appointed by the legislature of South-Carolina,
in view of the state of our federal relations. Charleston,
S.C., A. J. Burke, 1850. 24 p. PH ... U: Charleston,
S.C., Edward C. Councell, 1851.

1602 JACOBS, Thornwell, 1877-1956.
Drums of doomsday. New York, E. P. Dutton & Co.,
1942. 501 p. A H R

1603 JACOBS, Thornwell, 1877-1956.
For heretics only. Atlanta, Westminster Publishers,
© 1954. 293 p. H PT U

1604 JACOBS, Thornwell, 1877-1956.
The generation of the silver bell. The address of dedication of the carillonic bells, First Presbyterian Church, Clinton, S.C. n.p., n.d. 23 p. PT

1605 JACOBS, Thornwell, 1877-1956.
Islands of the blest and other poems. Oglethorpe Univer-
sity, Ga., Oglethorpe University Press, 1928. 335 p. H
PT

1606 JACOBS, Thornwell, 1877-1956.
The life of William Plumer Jacobs. New York, Fleming
H. Revell Co., © 1918. 277 p. A C H L PT R U

1607 JACOBS, Thornwell, 1877-1956.
Neath the shadow of his wing. By Lonnie Loyle [pseud.].
Clinton, S.C., Thornwell Orphanage Press, © 1900. 242 p.
H

1608 JACOBS, Thornwell, 1877-1956.
The new science and the old religion. Oglethorpe Uni-
versity, Ga., Oglethorpe University Press, © 1927. 463 p.
H PT R ... A U: [2d ed., rev. and enl.] © 1935. 526 p.

1609 JACOBS, Thornwell, 1877-1956.
Not knowing whither he went. Oglethorpe University, Ga.,
Oglethorpe University Press, 1933. 257 p. C PT R U

1610 JACOBS, Thornwell, 1877-1956.
The Oglethorpe story. Atlanta, Oglethorpe University,
1916. 154 p. Oglethorpe University Bulletin, July, 1916.
A C H PT

1611 JACOBS, Thornwell, 1877-1956.
Red lanterns on St. Michael's. [1st ed.] New York, E.
P. Dutton & Co., 1940. 670 p. H U

1612 JACOBS, Thornwell, 1877-1956.

Sequel and supplement to Not knowing whither he went; consisting of four letters revealed after the publication of the story of John and Mary Roderick, with a short introduction by Thornwell Jacobs. Oglethorpe University, Ga., Oglethorpe University Press, © 1935. 32 p. U

1613 JACOBS, Thornwell, 1877-1956.
Sinful Sadday, son of a cotton mill: a story of a little orphan boy who lived to triumph. Nashville, Tenn., Smith & Lamar, 1907. 131 p. PT

1614 JACOBS, Thornwell, 1877-1956.
Step down, Dr. Jacobs; the autobiography of an autocrat. 1st ed. Atlanta, Westminster Publishers, © 1945. 1091 p. H PT R U

1615 JACOBS, Thornwell, 1877-1956.
The story of Christmas; sun, Saviour and Santa Claus. [Oglethorpe University, Ga., Oglethorpe University Press], © 1941. unpaged. Cover-title. PT

1616 JACOBS, Thornwell, 1877-1956.
Story of "the silk of the trade." Rion, S.C., Winnsboro Blue Granite, © 1952. 30 p. H

1617 JACOBS, Thornwell, 1877-1956.
When for the truth. [1st ed.] Charleston, S.C., Walker, Evans & Cogswell, 1950. 587 p. A novel of reconstruction days in South Carolina. H

1618 JACOBS, Thornwell, 1877-1956, ed.
William Plumer Jacobs; literary and biographical. Oglethorpe University, Ga., Oglethorpe University Press, © 1942. 631 p. A H R

1619 JACOBS, William Plumer, 1842-1917.
Almighty God careth for me. A history of God's work through his people for the Thornwell Orphanage, being the testimony of a grateful heart. Clinton, S.C., Thornwell Orphanage Press, 1888. 75 p. C U

1620 JACOBS, William Plumer, 1842-1917.
Diary of William Plumer Jacobs. Edited by Thornwell Jacobs. Oglethorpe University, Ga., Oglethorpe University Press, © 1937. 484 p. A C H PT R

1621 JACOBS, William Plumer, 1842-1917.
The history of the Clinton Presbyterian Church. Clinton, S.C., Clinton Printing House, 1880. 14 p. PH

1622 JACOBS, William Plumer, 1842-1917.
The pioneer. Clinton, S.C., Jacobs Press, n.d. 126 p. R

1623 JACOBS, William Plumer, 1842-1917.
To Jerusalem and "the regions beyond." On the steamer
Friesland. Clinton, S.C., Thornwell Orphanage Press,
1897. 155 p. A H

1624 JACOBS, William States, 1871-1951.
Presbyterianism in Nashville. A compilation of historic
data. Nashville, Tenn., Cumberland Press, 1904. 76 p.
A C L PH

1625 JAMES, Harrell Grady, 1909-
Fiery little Indian apostle: a review ... of "Life and
letters of Oscar Gardner" by Walter A. Bennett. Spiro,
Okla., Spiro Graphic Printers, n.d. 32 p. PH

1626 *JAMIESON, Robert, 1802-1880.
A commentary, critical, experimental and practical, on the
Old and New Testaments, by the Rev. Robert Jamieson ...
Rev. A. R. Fausset ... and the Rev. David Brown ... Grand
Rapids, Mich., Wm. B. Eerdmans Publishing Co., 1948.
6 v. "American edition, with a biographical sketch of the
authors, by Dr. Wilbur M. Smith." L PT

1627 JAMISON, Albert Leland, 1911-
Light for the Gentiles; Paul and the growing church.
Philadelphia, Westminster Press, © 1961. 91 p. A L PT

1628 JEFFRIES, John Campbell, 1910-
The law in the Prayer; the Ten Commandments in the
Lord's Prayer. New York, Exposition Press, © 1952. 97 p.
L PT

1629 JEFFRIES, John Campbell, 1910-
This same Jesus; the doctrine of the Holy Spirit. New
York, Exposition Press, © 1950. 100 p. L PT U

1630 JENNINGS, William Beatty, 1859-1935.
The social teachings of Christ Jesus; a manual for Bible
classes, Christian associations, social study groups, etc.
New York, Fleming H. Revell Co., © 1915. 111 p. C L
PT U

1631 JOEKEL, Samuel Levinson, 1893-1954.
"Compaginado todo"; guia para promover el estudio indi-
vidual de los libros de la Biblia. Mexico, D.F., Casa de
Publicaciones "El Faro," 1952. 104 p. Translation of
"Fitly framed together." A

1632 JOEKEL, Samuel Levinson, 1893-1954.
"Fitly framed together": a guide to further study of the
individual books of the Bible. Atlanta, Committee on Woman's
Work, Presbyterian Church in the U.S. [1948] 64 p.

H U ... A C L U: Richmond, John Knox Press, [1953] ...
R: [1962].

1633 JOEKEL, Samuel Levinson, 1893-1954.
While it is day. Richmond, John Knox Press, © 1942.
135 p.   A C H R U

1634 JOHN LEIGHTON WILSON, apostle to Africa, liberator of slaves,
friend of mankind. Columbia, S.C., The State Co., [1909?].
46 p. Reprinted from the "Wilson centenary" edition of The
State, March 25, 1909.   C

1635 JOHNSON, Charles Earl, 1921-
London bridge in Arizona; a novel. |Cambridge, Eng.,
Cambridge Aids to Learning], 1973. 55 p.   U

1636 JOHNSON, Clifford Ross, 1916-1970.
Every moment an Easter. [1st ed. Alexandria? Va.,
Privately published for the members and friends of Westminster Presbyterian Church, Alexandria, Virginia], © 1962.
125 p.   U

1637 JOHNSON, Clifford Ross, 1916-1970.
Jesus' financial troubles, and other sermons; a collection
of homilies from the pulpit of Westminster Presbyterian
Church, Alexandria, Virginia. |Alexandria? National Publish-
ing Co., 1953]. 45 p.   U

1638 JOHNSON, Early Ashby, 1917-
Communion with young saints. Richmond, John Knox Press,
© 1959. 111 p.   A C H L R U

1639 JOHNSON, Early Ashby, 1917-
The crucial task of theology. Richmond, John Knox Press,
© 1958. 222 p.   A C H L PT R U

1640 JOHNSON, Early Ashby, 1917-
Saved--from what? Richmond, John Knox Press, © 1966.
79 p.   A C H L PH U

1641 JOHNSON, George Franklin, 1896-
Until the day dawn. [Atlanta, Board of Annuities and Relief, Presbyterian Church in the U.S.], n.d. unpaged. A
play.   U

1642 JOHNSON, John Scott, 1871-1958.
Baptism. n.p., n.d. 40 p.   U

1643 JOHNSON, Thomas Cary, 1859-1936.
Baptism in the Apostolic age. Richmond, Presbyterian
Committee of Publication, 1912. 94 p.   A C H L R U

1644 JOHNSON, Thomas Cary, 1859-1936.

A brief sketch of the United Synod of the Presbyterian Church in the United States of America. n.p., Knickerbocker Press, 1897. 38 p. Reprinted from vol. 8, American Society of Church History. Papers. A C U

1645 JOHNSON, Thomas Cary, 1859-1936.
Burney's soteriology and the Cumberland theology. n.p., n.d. 157-176 p. Reprinted from the Presbyterian Quarterly, April, 1891. PT

1646 JOHNSON, Thomas Cary, 1859-1936.
Christian science. Richmond, Presbyterian Committee of Publication, n.d. 48 p. A C U

1647 JOHNSON, Thomas Cary, 1859-1936.
The duty of the church to quit robbing the masses of the Gospel. n.p., n.d. 74-89 p. U

1648 JOHNSON, Thomas Cary, 1859-1936.
Effectual calling. n.p., n.d. 401-425 p. Reprinted from the Evangelical Quarterly, Oct. 15, 1930. U

1649 JOHNSON, Thomas Cary, 1859-1936.
The existence of God. n.p., n.d. 23 p. U

1650 JOHNSON, Thomas Cary, 1859-1936.
God's answer to evolution.... Being some account of the origin, nature, and relationships of man, according to the Bible. Richmond, Presbyterian Committee of Publication, © 1924. 110 p. A C H PT R U

1651 JOHNSON, Thomas Cary, 1859-1936.
History of the Southern Presbyterian Church. In the American Church History series. vol. XI. New York, Christian Literature Co. |1894] 311-479 p. A C H L PH PT R U ... H R U: 1894. 311-487 p. ... C: Charles Scribner's Sons, 1900 ... R: 1911.

1652 JOHNSON, Thomas Cary, 1859-1936.
The Hon. Thomas S. Bocock. Lynchburg, Va., J. P. Bell Co., n.d. 8 p. U

1653 JOHNSON, Thomas Cary, 1859-1936.
Inspiration, synopsis of lectures on. n.p., n.d. 32 p. C PH U

1654 JOHNSON, Thomas Cary, 1859-1936.
Introduction to Christian missions. Richmond, Presbyterian Committee of Publication, © 1909. 220 p. C L PT R U ... A C H PH: 2d ed. © 1910.

1655 JOHNSON, Thomas Cary, 1859-1936.

John Calvin and the Genevan reformation: a sketch. Richmond, Presbyterian Committee of Publication, © 1900. 94 p. A C H L PH PT R U

1656 JOHNSON, Thomas Cary, 1859-1936.
John Calvin: Who was he? Of what sort was he? What did he do for the world? [Richmond], Richmond Press, [1909?]. 31 p. An address delivered October 7, 1909, before the Presbytery of Roanoke, meeting at Hat Creek. A C L PH U

1657 JOHNSON, Thomas Cary, 1859-1936.
Junior church history notes. n.p., n.d. 46 p. U

1658 JOHNSON, Thomas Cary, 1859-1936.
Lectures on repentance, sanctification, and good works [a revision of the lectures LV.-LVII. of Dabney's Theology]. n.p., n.d. 70 p. A C PH U

1659 JOHNSON, Thomas Cary, 1859-1936.
The life and letters of Benjamin Morgan Palmer. Richmond, Presbyterian Committee of Publication, © 1906. 688 p. A C H L PH PT R U

1660 JOHNSON, Thomas Cary, 1859-1936.
The life and letters of Robert Lewis Dabney. Richmond, Presbyterian Committee of Publication, © 1903. 585 p. A C H L PH PT R U ... A R: [Edinburgh], Banner of Truth Trust, [1977].

1661 JOHNSON, Thomas Cary, 1859-1936.
The membership of the churches of apostolic times according to New Testament teaching. n.p., n.d. 22-37 p. Reprinted from the Union Seminary Magazine. U

1662 JOHNSON, Thomas Cary, 1859-1936.
The mode of baptism in the Apostolic age; or, Some strictures on Philip Schaff's account of baptism in the age of the apostles. Petersburg, Va., Fenn & Owen, [187?]. 47 p. U

1663 JOHNSON, Thomas Cary, 1859-1936.
Mormonism. Richmond, Whittet & Shepperson, n.d. 34 p. A L U

1664 JOHNSON, Thomas Cary, 1859-1936.
Outlines of the history of the Presbyterian Church in the United States of America. [Richmond], Richmond Press, n.d. U

1665 JOHNSON, Thomas Cary, 1859-1936.
Paul's obligation to missionary effort, and the way he met

them. Richmond, Whittet & Shepperson, 1904. 14 p. Reprinted from the Union Seminary Magazine, Dec. 1903-Jan. 1904. C PH U

1666 JOHNSON, Thomas Cary, 1859-1936.
Questions and notes on church history, medieval and modern church. [Richmond], Richmond Press, n.d. 70 p.   A U

1667 JOHNSON, Thomas Cary, 1859-1936.
Repentance unto life. London, James Clarke & Co., n.d. 21 p. Reprinted from the Evangelical Quarterly, January, 1933. U

1668 JOHNSON, Thomas Cary, 1859-1936.
Russellism. Richmond, Presbyterian Committee of Publication, n.d. 64 p. A R U

1669 JOHNSON, Thomas Cary, 1859-1936.
Saving faith. London, James Clarke & Co., n.d. 257-277 p. Reprinted from the Evangelical Quarterly, July, 1931. U

1670 JOHNSON, Thomas Cary, 1859-1936.
Some modern isms. Richmond, Presbyterian Committee of Publication, © 1919. 192 p. Lectures delivered to senior class in Union Theological Seminary in Virginia, in January, 1918. A C H L PT R U

1671 JOHNSON, Thomas Cary, 1859-1936.
Virginia Presbyterianism and religious liberty in colonial and revolutionary times. Richmond, Presbyterian Committee of Publication, 1907. 128 p. A C H L PH PT R U

1672 JOHNSON, Thomas Cary, 1859-1936.
Wilhelm Herrmann's systematic theology. n.p., n.d. 373-393 p. Reprinted from the Princeton Theological Review, July, 1928. U

1673 JOHNSON, Wilfred Roland, 1886-1964.
Magnetism of the manger. Grand Rapids, Mich., Wm. B. Eerdmans Publishing Co., 1938. 131 p. A C U

1674 JOHNSON, Wilfred Roland, 1886-1964.
Why believe? Sermons to establish faith.... Foreword by Conway T. Wharton. Grand Rapids, Mich., Zondervan Publishing House, © 1942. 141 p. A H R

1675 JOHNSTON, Thomas Pinckney, 1808-1883.
Experience of a missionary family in Turkey. Charlotte, N.C., Observer Steam Job Print., 1879. 32 p. U

1676 JONES, Arthur Gray, 1868-1929.

Calvin: the times: the man: the historic significance. [Address delivered before the Synod of Texas of the Presbyterian Church in the United States, at San Angelo, Texas, November 18, 1909. Fort Worth, Tex., Keystone Printing Co., 1909]. 16 p. A H

1677 JONES, Arthur Gray, 1868-1929.
The evangelistic preacher. An address to the pre-Assembly evangelistic conference in the Westminster Presbyterian Church, St. Louis, Missouri, May 18, 1921. n.p., n.d. unpaged. PH

1678 JONES, Arthur Gray, 1868-1929.
Presbyterianism. An address delivered at Victoria, Texas, September 27th, 1901, on the fiftieth anniversary of the Presbytery of Western Texas. n.p., n.d. 11 p. A PH U

1679 JONES, Arthur Gray, 1868-1929.
Temple builders, and other sermons. New York, Fleming H. Revell Co., © 1929. 192 p. A C H R U

1680 JONES, Arthur Gray, 1868-1929.
Thornton Rogers Sampson, D.D., LL.D., 1852-1915; a biographical sketch. [Richmond], Richmond Press, © 1917. 136 p. A C H R U

1681 JONES, Charles Colcock, 1804-1863.
Address to the senior class in the Theological Seminary of the Synod of South Carolina and Georgia, on the evening of the anniversary, Columbia, July 10th, 1837. Savannah, Thomas Purse & Co., 1837. 18 p. PH PT

1682 JONES, Charles Colcock, 1804-1863.
A catechism for colored persons. Charleston, Observer Office Press, 1834. 108 p. U ... C: xerox copy ... A: microfilm.

1683 JONES, Charles Colcock, 1804-1863.
A catechism of Scripture doctrine and practice for families and Sabbath-schools, designed also for the oral instruction of colored persons. 3d ed. Savannah, Thomas Purse & Co., 1844. 154 p. L ... C: 1845 ... A: microfilm ... H R: 6th ed. Savannah, John M. Cooper & Co., © 1837 ... H PH PT: Philadelphia, Presbyterian Board of Publication, © 1852.

1684 JONES, Charles Colcock, 1804-1863.
The glory of woman is the fear of the Lord. A sermon. Philadelphia, William S. Martien, 1847. 60 p. PH PT U ... C H L PH PT R U: Philadelphia, Presbyterian Board of Publication, n.d. 32 p. (Presbyterian Tracts, no. 174.)

1685 JONES, Charles Colcock, 1804-1863.

Historical address, delivered to the Liberty Independent
Troop, upon its anniversary, February 22, 1856. Savannah,
John M. Cooper & Co., 1856. 63 p. PH

1686 JONES, Charles Colcock, 1804-1863.
The history of the church of God during the period of rev-
elation. New York, Charles Scribner & Co., 1867. 558 p.
A C PH R U ... PT: Pt. I, The church during the Old
Testament dispensation.

1687 JONES, Charles Colcock, 1804-1863.
Indian remains in southern Georgia. Address delivered
before the Georgia Historical Society, on its twentieth anniversary, February 12th, 1859. Savannah, John M. Cooper
& Co., 1859. 25 p. PT

1688 JONES, Charles Colcock, 1804-1863.
The religious instruction of the negroes. A sermon, delivered before associations of planters in Liberty and M'Intosh
counties, Georgia. 4th ed. Princeton, N.J., D'Hart &
Connolly, 1832. 38 p. PH PT U

1689 JONES, Charles Colcock, 1804-1863.
Religious instruction of the negroes. An address delivered
before the General Assembly of the Presbyterian Church, at
Augusta, Ga., December 10, 1861. Richmond, Presbyterian
Committee of Publication, [1862?]. 25 p. H ... C: xeroxed
copy.

1690 JONES, Charles Colcock, 1804-1863.
The religious instruction of the negroes. In the United
States. Savannah, Ga., Thomas Purse, 1842. 277 p.
A C H L PH PT R U ... H PH R: New York, Negro Uni-
versities Press, [1969] ... L: Freeport, N.Y., Books for
Libraries Press, 1971.

1691 JONES, Charles Colcock, 1804-1863.
Sketch of the life and character of Miss Anne Clay: delivered at her funeral service, in Bryan Church, Georgia,
the second Sabbath in January, 1843. Boston, Crocker and
Brewster, 1844. 23 p. C

1692 JONES, Charles Colcock, 1804-1863.
Suggestions on the religious instruction of the negroes in
the Southern states: together with an appendix containing
forms of church registers, form of a constitution, and plans
of different denominations of Christians. Philadelphia, n.p.,
1847. 56 p. PT ... PH U: Philadelphia, Presbyterian
Board of Publication, n.d. 132 p.

1693 JONES, Charles Colcock, 1804-1863.
Third annual report of the missionary to the negroes, in

Liberty County, Ga., presented to the association. Riceborough, Jan., 1836. Charleston, n.p., 1836. 21 p. PT

1694 JONES, Frank Dudley, 1874-1946.
History of Purity Presbyterian Church of Chester, South Carolina, 1787-1937. [Charlotte, N.C., Standard Printing Co., 1938]. 186 p. H PT U

1695 JONES, Frank Dudley, 1874-1946, ed.
History of the Presbyterian Church in South Carolina since 1850. Edited by F. D. Jones, D.D., and W. H. Mills, D.D.; published by the Synod of South Carolina. Columbia, S.C., R. L. Bryan Co., 1926. 1094 p. A C H L PH PT R U

1696 JONES, James Archibald, 1911-1966.
The church and its ministry. Inaugural address [as President] delivered April 4, 1956, in Schauffler Hall, Union Theological Seminary, Richmond, Virginia. Richmond, Union Theological Seminary, 1956. 20 p. A PT U

1697 JONES, James Archibald, 1911-1966.
The Holy Spirit and today: a devotional study in the ministry of the Spirit. Atlanta, Board of Women's Work, Presbyterian Church in the U.S., [1952]. 71 p. C U

1698 JONES, James Archibald, 1911-1966.
Prayers for the people; a memorial collection of pulpit prayers. Richmond, John Knox Press, © 1967. 127 p. C H L R U ... A: [1968] ... H: [Richmond], Union Theological Seminary in Virginia, © 1967.

1699 JONES, James Archibald, 1936-
Take heed! Take heart! Sermons preached at First Presbyterian Church, Richmond, Virginia. [Richmond, First Presbyterian Church, 1973?]. 79 p. U

1700 JONES, Robert Franklin, 1911-1980.
Seven words to the cross. Richmond, John Knox Press, © 1961. 92 p. A C H L U

1701 JONES, Samuel Beach, 1811-1883.
Dr. S. B. Jones' address on the responsibilities and duties of teachers. n.p., [1854?]. 16 p. PH

1702 JONES, Thomas Laird, 1930-
When leisure is the Lord's. Richmond, CLC Press, © 1964. 48 p. (The Covenant Life Curriculum.) C L U

1703 JOPLING, Robert Ware, 1865-1944.
Studies in the Confession of Faith; or, The five points of Calvinism examined. [Clinton, S.C., Jacobs Press], © 1942. 90 p. A C H L PT U

1704 JUMPER, Andrew Albert, 1927-
Chosen to serve: the deacon. A practical manual for the operation of the board of deacons in the Presbyterian Church in the United States. Richmond, John Knox Press, © 1961. 128 p.   A C H L PT R U ... L: [1962].

1705 JUMPER, Andrew Albert, 1927-
The noble task: the elder. A practical manual for the operation of the church session in the Presbyterian Church in the United States. Richmond, John Knox Press, © 1961. 143 p.   A C H L R U ... L: [1962] ... C H L R: Rev. ed. [1965] 158 p. ... C: 1970.

1706 JUNKIN, Ebenezer Dickey, 1829-1891.
A history of the church and congregation of New Providence, Lexington Presbytery, Virginia. n.p., Published by request of the congregation, 1871. 34 p.   PT

1707 *JUNKIN, Mary L.
Rev. William McCleery Junkin. n.p., [1931?]. 4 p.   U

1708 *JUNKIN, Nettie (DuBose), comp.
For the glory of God. Memoirs of Dr. and Mrs. H. C. DuBose of Soochow, China.... Published by the children of Dr. and Mrs. DuBose. Lewisburg, W.Va., For sale by Rev. W. H. DuBose, n.d. 76 p.   A C H U

1709 JUNKIN, William Finney, 1831-1900.
A sermon preached in Glebe Street Church, Charleston, S.C., on the morning of Sabbath, Oct. 15, 1882. Charleston, S.C., Walker, Evans & Cogswell, 1883. 14 p.   C H

1710 KADEL, William Howard, 1913-
Prayers for every need. Richmond, John Knox Press, © 1957. 167 p.   A C H L U

1711 *KAGAWA, Toyohiko, 1888-1960.
Meditations on the Holy Spirit; translated by Charles A. Logan. Nashville, Cokesbury Press, © 1939. 167 p.   C L PT U

1712 KALOPOTHAKES, Michael Demetrius, 1825-1911.
An essay on Hippocrates. Philadelphia, King & Baird, 1857. 15 p.   H

1713 KELLER, William Chester, 1911-
Save the nails: reflections from my life and ministry. [Clinton, S.C., W. Chester Keller], 1977. 67 p.   C

1714 KELLERSBERGER, Eugene Roland, 1888-1966.
Twelve questions about leprosy [Hansen's disease]. New York, American Leprosy Missions, n.d. 6 p.   U

1715 *KELLERSBERGER, Julia Lake (Skinner), 1897-
Doctor of the happy landings, by Julia Lake and Eugene
Kellersberger. Richmond, John Knox Press, © 1949. 265 p.
A C H L PH PT R U ... A: [1951].

1716 *KELLERSBERGER, Julia Lake (Skinner) 1897-
The mission of the mission to lepers, by Julia Lake and
Eugene Kellersberger. [New York, American Mission to
Lepers], n.d. 4 p. PH U

1717 KELLY, Balmer Hancock, 1914-
The book of Ezra. The book of Nehemiah. The book of
Esther. The book of Job. Richmond, John Knox Press,
© 1962. 152 p. (The Layman's Bible Commentary, v. 8.)
A C H L PT R U

1718 KELLY, Balmer Hancock, 1914-
A theology for proclamation.... Inaugural address [as
Professor of Biblical Theology] delivered March 2, 1954, in
Schauffler Hall, Union Theological Seminary, Richmond,
Virginia. Richmond, Union Theological Seminary, 1954.
23 p. A C H R U

1719 KELLY, Balmer Hancock, 1914-
Thus saith the Lord; the minor prophets speak for our
day: Amos, Hosea, Micah, Habakkuk, Zechariah, Malachi.
Atlanta, Board of Women's Work, Presbyterian Church in
the U.S., [1956]. 107 p. C L R U

1720 KENNEDY, Dennis James, 1930-
Evangelism explosion.... Foreword by Billy Graham.
[3d ed.] Wheaton, Ill., Tyndale House Publishers, [1970].
187 p. A C ... PT: 5th ed. [1971] ... C L R: [Rev.
ed.] © 1977. 234 p.

1721 KENNEDY, Dennis James, 1930-
The God of great surprises. Wheaton, Ill., Tyndale House
Publishers, © 1973. 102 p. C PH PT R

1722 KENNEDY, Dennis James, 1930-
Spiritual renewal! Glendale, Calif., G/L Regal Books,
© 1973. 92 p. A PT U

1723 KENNEDY, Dennis James, 1930-
This is the life: guidelines for Christian growth. Glendale, Calif., G/L Regal Books, © 1973. 102 p. R

1724 KENNEDY, Dennis James, 1930-
Truths that transform. Old Tappan, N.J., Fleming H.
Revell Co., © 1974. 160 p. C PT

1725 KENNEDY, William Bean, 1926-
Into covenant life. Richmond, CLC Press, © 1963.

221 p. (The Covenant Life Curriculum.) C H L U ...
C H L U: Teacher's book. 376 p.

1726 KENNEDY, William Bean, 1926-
The shaping of Protestant education; an interpretation of
the Sunday School and the development of Protestant educational strategy in the United States, 1789-1860. New York,
Association Press, © 1966. 93 p. A C H L PT R U

1727 KERR, James Witherspoon, 1820-1901.
The covenants and the Covenanters. Covenants, sermons,
and documents of the Covenanted Reformation. Edinburgh,
R. W. Hunter, [1895]. 442 p. H

1728 KERR, James Witherspoon, 1820-1901.
The discipline of dancing; a review of the Block case and
of the sermons of Rev. J. T. Leftwich, D.D. Atlanta,
James P. Harrison & Co., 1878. 23 p. U

1729 KERR, Robert Pollok, 1850-1923.
Bible baptism. Richmond, Presbyterian Committee of
Publication, 1892. 56 p. U

1730 KERR, Robert Pollok, 1850-1923.
The blue flag; or, The Covenanters who contended for
"Christ's crown and covenant." Richmond, Presbyterian
Committee of Publication, 1905. 146 p. A H L PH PT
R U

1731 KERR, Robert Pollok, 1850-1923.
The dance, the card table, the theatre, and the wine cup.
Richmond, Presbyterian Committee of Publication, [1898].
24 p. PT

1732 KERR, Robert Pollok, 1850-1923, comp.
Hymns of the ages for public and social worship. New
York, Anson D. F. Randolph & Co., 1891. 306 p. H
PT ... C H: 2d ed. 1891 ... U: Richmond, Presbyterian
Committee of Publication, [1893] ... A PT: Richmond, B.
F. Johnson, 1902. 316 p.

1733 KERR, Robert Pollok, 1850-1923.
The land of holy light: a book of travel through Bible
countries. Richmond, Presbyterian Committee of Publication, 1891. 346 p. A C H L PH R U

1734 KERR, Robert Pollok, 1850-1923.
Northminster Presbyterian Church, Baltimore City, Maryland; historical memorial of the twenty-fifth anniversary of
the organization, March fifth, nineteen-five. n.p., n.d.
72 p. U

1735 KERR, Robert Pollok, 1850-1923.

The people's history of Presbyterianism in all ages.
Richmond, Presbyterian Committee of Publication, 1888.
284 p.   A C H L PH PT R U ... A: 3d ed. ... H PH:
4th ed. 1894 ... A R U: 5th ed. © 1888.

1736   KERR, Robert Pollok, 1850-1923.
Predestination and free agency, a sermon delivered in the
First Presbyterian Church of Richmond, Va. Richmond,
Whittet & Shepperson, 1897. 19 p.   A

1737   KERR, Robert Pollok, 1850-1923.
A Presbyterian communion-class catechism: a book of
questions for use in the special instruction of persons about
to make a public confession of Christ. Richmond, Whittet
& Shepperson, n.d. 31 p.   U ... U: Richmond, Presbyterian Committee of Publication, © 1896. 58 p.

1738   KERR, Robert Pollok, 1850-1923.
Presbyterianism for the people. Philadelphia, Presby-
terian Board of Publication, © 1883. 80 p.   A C H L PH
PT U ... H: [1884].

1739   KERR, Robert Pollok, 1850-1923.
Questions on "The history of the Presbyterian Church in
all ages." Richmond, Presbyterian Committee of Publication,
© 1897. 23 p.   U

1740   KERR, Robert Pollok, 1850-1923.
The voice of God in history. Richmond, Presbyterian
Committee of Publication, 1890. 283 p.   A C H L R U

1741   KERR, Robert Pollok, 1850-1923.
Will the world outgrow Christianity, and other interroga-
tions on vital themes. New York, Fleming H. Revell Co.,
© 1901. 148 p.   A PT R U

1742   KING, Charles Leonidas, 1892-
The Holy Spirit in the Bible. A transcription; lecture
series presented at the School of Christian Living, 1977-
1978. n.p., [1978?]. 63 p.   H

1743   KING, Charles Leonidas, 1892-
Wednesday evening Bible studies. Richmond, Grace Covenant Presbyterian Church, 1922-24. unpaged. A series of
leaflets ... on selected books of the Bible.   U

1744   KING, Samuel Alexander, 1834-1918.
How far has original Calvinism been modified by time?
Richmond, Whittet & Shepperson, n.d. 29 p.   A H PT
R ... PH: [1909].

1745   KING, Samuel Alexander, 1834-1918.

Presbyterian doctrines, as contained in the five points of
Calvinism. Richmond, Presbyterian Committee of Publication,
[1909]. 45 p. PH PT U

1746 KING, Samuel Alexander, 1834-1918.
Presbyterianism; an address delivered in the First Presbyterian Church, San Antonio, Texas, Nov. 3d, 1901, upon
the occasion of the fiftieth anniversary of the organization of
the church. n.p., 1901. 31 p. PH U

1747 KING, Samuel Alexander, 1834-1918.
A sermon, delivered in the First Presbyterian Church,
Waco, Texas. On Thanksgiving day, November 29, 1894.
Columbia, Mo., E. W. Stephens, 1895. 24 p. A

1748 KING, Samuel Alexander, 1834-1918.
A sermon, delivered in the Presbyterian Church at Milford, Texas. Confederate Fast day, Friday, April 8th, 1864.
Being the day set apart by the Confederate Congress as a
day of fasting and prayer. Houston, E. H. Cushing & Co.,
1864. 14 p. H PH

1749 KING, Samuel Alexander, 1834-1918.
The system of theology of the Westminster standards. A
sermon delivered at the 50th session of the Synod of Texas:
at Houston, Texas, November 26th, 1905. Richmond, Presbyterian Committee of Publication, n.d. 27 p. PT

1750 KINNEY, Laurence Forman, 1902-1966.
Not like ordinary men: a study of First Corinthians.
Richmond, John Knox Press, © 1961. 76 p. A C H L
R U

1751 KIRK, Harris Elliott, 1872-1953.
The consuming fire. New York, The Macmillan Co.,
1919. 183 p. A C H L PT R U

1752 KIRK, Harris Elliott, 1872-1953.
A design for living. New York, Fleming H. Revell Co.,
© 1943. 93 p. The Rockwell Lectures, Rice Institute,
Houston, Texas. L PT R U

1753 KIRK, Harris Elliott, 1872-1953.
The glory of common things. London, Westminster Publishing Co., © 1930. 160 p. PT

1754 KIRK, Harris Elliott, 1872-1953.
A man of property; or, The Jacob saga. [1st ed.] New
York, Harper & Brothers, 1935. 109 p. C H L PT R U

1755 KIRK, Harris Elliott, 1872-1953.
The old minister. n.p., [1901?]. unpaged. Sermon

preached at the First Presbyterian Church, Florence, Alabama, on Sunday, July 8th, 1901.   U

1756   KIRK, Harris Elliott, 1872-1953.
       One generation to another. New York, Fleming H. Revell Co., © 1924. 225 p.   A C L PT R U

1757   KIRK, Harris Elliott, 1872-1953.
       Our Presbyterian heritage; an address ... at the tercentenary celebration of the Westminster Assembly ... in the First Presbyterian Church, Baltimore, Maryland, Sunday, October 31, 1943. n.p., n.d. 16 p.   PH U

1758   KIRK, Harris Elliott, 1872-1953.
       The religion of power; a study of Christianity in relation to the quest for salvation in the Graeco-Roman world, and its significance for the present age. [London], Hodder and Stoughton; New York, George H. Doran Co., © 1916. 317 p. The Sprunt Lectures, 1916.   A C H L PT R U

1759   KIRK, Harris Elliott, 1872-1953.
       The spirit of Protestantism. Nashville, Tenn., Cokesbury Press, 1930. 233 p. The Cole Lectures, Vanderbilt University, 1930.   A C H L PH PT R U

1760   KIRK, Harris Elliott, 1872-1953.
       Stars, atoms, and God. Chapel Hill, University of North Carolina Press, 1932. 100 p.   A C H L PT R U ... PH: London, Hodder and Stoughton, 1932. 111 p.

1761   KIRKPATRICK, John Lycan, 1813-1885.
       A funeral discourse, delivered on Sunday morning, April 10, 1859, in the Independent or Congregational (Circular) Church of Charleston, on the death of Rev. Reuben Post, D.D., late pastor of that church. Charleston, Walker, Evans & Co., 1859. 32 p.   H PH

1762   KIRKPATRICK, John Lycan, 1813-1885.
       The moral tendency of the doctrine of falling from grace examined. A sermon preached before the Synod of Alabama at the opening of its sessions in Gainesville, October 24th, 1844. Mobile, Register and Journal Office, 1845. 28 p.   PH

1763   KIRKPATRICK, John Lycan, 1813-1885.
       A sermon, preached on the occasion of the death of Mrs. Mary Chamberlin Brackett, in the Presbyterian Church, Gainesville, Ala., March 2, 1851. St. Louis, Hill & M'Kee, 1851. 24 p.   PH

1764   KIRKPATRICK, Robert White, 1908-
       The creative delivery of sermons.... With a foreword by

Dr. Ralph W. Sockman. New York, The Macmillan Co., 1944. 235 p. A C H L PH R U ... PT: 1954.

1765 KIRKPATRICK, Robert White, 1908-
Preaching as experience.... Inaugural address [as Professor of Preaching] delivered March 3, 1954, in Schauffler Hall, Union Theology Seminary, Richmond, Virginia. [Richmond, Union Theological Seminary], © 1955. 18 p. A C U

1766 *KLAUSNER, Joseph, 1874-1958.
From Jesus to Paul.... Translated from the Hebrew by William F. Stinespring. New York, The Macmillan Co., 1943. 624 p. A C L PT U ... L: 1944 ... PT R: London, George Allen & Unwin [1946] ... R: Boston, Beacon Press, [1961].

1767 *KLAUSNER, Joseph, 1874-1958.
The messianic idea in Israel, from its beginning to the completion of the Mishnah.... Translated from the 3d Hebrew ed. by William F. Stinespring. New York, The Macmillan Co., 1955. 543 p. A C L PT U ... L: London, George Allen and Unwin, [1956].

1768 KNIGHT, Lucian Lamar, 1868-1933.
Alexander H. Stephens, the sage of Liberty Hall, Georgia's great commoner. [Athens, Ga., The McGregor Co., 1930]. 169 p. Part I by Lucian Lamar Knight. Parts II and III, "Extracts from writings of Mr. Stephens and tributes to his memory compiled by Mrs. Horace M. Holden." H

1769 KNIGHT, Lucian Lamar, 1868-1933.
Georgia's landmarks, memorials and legends. Atlanta, Byrd Printing Co., 1913-14. 2 v. PT

1770 KNIGHT, Lucian Lamar, 1868-1933.
Memorials of Dixie-land: orations, essays, sketches and poems on topics historical, commemorative, literary and patriotic. Atlanta, Byrd Printing Co., 1919. 604 p. R

1771 KNIGHT, Lucian Lamar, 1868-1933.
Reminiscences of famous Georgians, embracing episodes and incidents in the lives of great men of the state; also an appendix devoted to extracts from speeches and addresses. 2d ed., v. 1; 1st ed., v. 2. Atlanta, Franklin-Turner Co., 1907-1908. 2 v. PT

1772 KNIGHT, Lucian Lamar, 1868-1933.
Stone mountain; or, The lay of the gray minstrel. An epic poem in twenty-four parts. Atlanta, Johnson-Dallis Co., 1923. 277 p. R

1773 KNIGHT, Lucian Lamar, 1868-1933.

Tracking the sunset; or, The shrines of history around the world. Atlanta, Stein Printing Co., 1925. 628 p.   R

1774   KNIGHT, Lucian Lamar, 1868-1933.
Woodrow Wilson, the dreamer and the dream. Atlanta, Johnson-Dallis Co., © 1924. 135 p.   A C H PH PT R U

1775   *KÖSTER, Helmut, 1926-
Entwicklungslinien durch die Welt des frühen Christentums. Von Helmut Köster und James M. Robinson. Tübingen, J. C. B. Mohr (Paul Siebeck), 1971. 276 p. German ed. of "Trajectories through Early Christianity."   U

1776   KRAEMER, Charles Edgar Stanberry, 1909-
Planning for the Covenant Life Curriculum in a local church; a guide. [Richmond], Board of Christian Education, Presbyterian Church in the U.S., © 1962. 47 p. (The Covenant Life Curriculum.)   L U

1777   KUIST, Howard Tillman, 1895-
The book of Jeremiah. [Chicago, Lutheran Student Association of America, 1953]. unpaged. Reprinted from Interpretation, July, 1950.   PT

1778   KUIST, Howard Tillman, 1895-
The book of Jeremiah. The Lamentations of Jeremiah. Richmond, John Knox Press, © 1960. 148 p. (The Layman's Bible Commentary, v. 12.)   A C H L PT R U ... U: Japanese edition. Translated by Michiharu Shinya. Tokyo, Japan, © 1964.

1779   KUIST, Howard Tillman, 1895-
Exegetical footnotes to the Epistle to the Hebrews. New York, Biblical Seminary in New York, (1932?). 18 p. Including reprints from the Biblical Review, 1931-1932.   PT R U

1780   KUIST, Howard Tillman, 1895-
How to enjoy Nehemiah. [Richmond, The author], © 1941. 14 p.   U

1781   KUIST, Howard Tillman, 1895-
How to enjoy the Bible. Richmond, John Knox Press, © 1939. 16 p. Reprinted from the Presbyterian of the South.   PT U

1782   KUIST, Howard Tillman, 1895-
Is a history of the philosophy of history worthwhile? A review of Flint's History of the philosophy of history. [New York], New York University Philosophical Society, 1921-22. 8 p.   U

1783   KUIST, Howard Tillman, 1895-

New Testament book studies. n.p., [The author], © 1957. unpaged. R

1784 KUIST, Howard Tillman, 1895-
Old Testament book studies. n.p., [The author], © 1958. unpaged. R

1785 KUIST, Howard Tillman, 1895-
The pedagogy of St. Paul. New York, George H. Doran Co., © 1925. 169 p. Published also as thesis (Ph.D.), New York University, 1924. A C L PT U

1786 KUIST, Howard Tillman, 1895-
Reflections of theology from Gone with the wind. n.p., © 1939. 15 p. Reprinted from Union Seminary Review, October, 1939. PT U

1787 KUIST, Howard Tillman, 1895-
Scripture and the Christian response. Richmond, John Knox Press, [1964]. 189 p. First published under title: These words upon thy heart. A C H L PT R U

1788 KUIST, Howard Tillman, 1895-
These words upon thy heart; Scripture and the Christian response. Richmond, John Knox Press, 1947. 189 p. The Sprunt Lectures, 1946. A C H L PT U

1789 KUIST, Howard Tillman, 1895-
The training of men in the Christian tradition.... Inaugural address [as Walter H. Robertson Professor of New Testament] delivered during Sprunt Lecture week, Friday, February 7, 1941. [Richmond, Union Theological Seminary, 1941]. 24 p. Reprinted from the Union Seminary Review, April, 1941. PH PT U

1790 KUIST, Howard Tillman, 1895-
The use of the Bible in the forming of men. n.p., n.d. 14 p. Reprinted from the Princeton Seminary Bulletin, June, 1944. PT U

1791 KUIST, Howard Tillman, 1895-
The world God wants: studies in Jeremiah. [Chicago, National Lutheran Council, 1953]. unpaged. PT

1792 LACY, Benjamin Rice, 1886-1981.
George W. Watts; the seminary's great benefactor. A memorial address ... at the First Presbyterian Church, Durham, North Carolina, November 21, 1937. n.p., n.d. 28 p. H PH PT R U

1793 LACY, Benjamin Rice, 1886-1981.
Jessie Scott Armistead, D.D. Richmond, Union Seminary

Bulletin, 1935. 7 p. Union Seminary Bulletin, v. 13, ser. 2, no. 2. H PT U

1794 LACY, Benjamin Rice, 1886-1981.
The priesthood of all believers; sermon of the retiring moderator at the opening of the 91st General Assembly of the Presbyterian Church, U.S., Orlando, Fla., 1951. [Richmond, Outlook Publishers], n.d. unpaged. U

1795 LACY, Benjamin Rice, 1886-1981.
Revivals in the midst of the years. Richmond, John Knox Press, 1943. 167 p. The Smyth Lectures, 1942. A C H L PT R U ... A C H L U: [Nashville, Tenn.], Royal Publishers, 1968. 193 p. ... A: [Hopewell, Va., Presbyterian Evangelical Fellowship], 1968. "Reprinted with corrections and additional material."

1796 LACY, Benjamin Rice, 1886-1981.
A series of letters from the President of Union Theological Seminary to the Christian students of Davidson College. n.p., n.d. 8 p. U

1797 LACY, Beverly Tucker, 1819-1900.
A sermon, on the death of the Rev. Wm. M. Atkinson, D.D. Winchester, [Va.], Republican Office,' 1849. 13 p. H PH U

1798 LACY, Drury, 1802-1884.
A Thanksgiving discourse. Raleigh, N.C., n.p., 1851. 18 p. PT

1799 LACY, Matthew Lyle, 1833-1912.
Resolutions of respect to the character and memory of Rev. Jno. McElhenney, D.D., and the funeral sermon. Lewisburg, W.Va., "Independent" Job Office Print., 1871. 15 p. PT

1800 LACY, William Sterling, 1842-1899.
Funeral sermon preached at Buffalo Church on the death of Roderick Newton Bryan. n.p., n.d. 8 p. U

1801 LACY, William Sterling, 1842-1899.
William Sterling Lacy: memorial, addresses, sermons. Richmond, Presbyterian Committee of Publication, © 1900. 198 p. Memorial, by Rev. James P. Smith. A C H L R U

1802 LAFFERTY, John Wilson, 1862-1941.
Baptism: Presbyterial sermon. n.p., n.d. 11 p. PT

1803 LAMBDIN, Milton Bennett, 1850-1940.
The higher criticism: its rationalistic type. Richmond,

Whittet & Shepperson, n.d. 13 p. Reprinted from the Union
Seminary Magazine, Dec. 1907-Jan. 1908. U

1804 LAMOTTE, Louis Cossitt, 1902-
Colored light: the story of the influence of Columbia Theological Seminary, 1828-1936. Richmond, Presbyterian Committee of Publication, 1937. 356 p. A C H L PH PT R U

1805 LANCASTER, Richard Venable, 1863-1938.
The creed of Christ; a study in the Gospels. Richmond,
Presbyterian Committee of Publication, © 1905. 206 p.
A H L U ... C R U: Chicago, Winona Publishing Co.,
[1905].

1806 LANDRUM, Charles Logan, 1900-
Our delinquent children; a study of juvenile delinquency.
Minneapolis, Institute of Crime Prevention, © 1946. 26 p.
U

1807 LANG, Arthur, 1886-1923.
The early history of the family. n.p., n.d. 406-422 p.
From the Contemporary Review, v. 44. PT

1808 LANG, George, 1879-1971.
The south in the national economic setting. [Tuscaloosa?
1928?]. 62 p. "Address ... delivered before the Alabama
Bankers Association, in convention at Mobile, Ala., May 18,
1928." H

1809 LAPSLEY, James Norvell, 1930-
... A conceptualization of health in psychiatry. [Topeka,
Kan., Menninger Clinic, 1962]. 161-177 p. Reprinted from
the Bulletin of the Menninger Clinic, July, 1962. PT

1810 LAPSLEY, James Norvell, 1930-
Salvation and health; the interlocking processes of life.
Philadelphia, Westminster Press, © 1972. 174 p. A C
L PH PT U

1811 LAPSLEY, Robert Alberti, 1858-1934.
No sudden sanctification. Richmond, Presbyterian Committee of Publication, n.d. 16 p. U

1812 LAPSLEY, Robert Alberti, 1858-1934.
Practical Calvinism, or Scripture doctrine, of the final
perseverance of the saints. Nashville, Bang, Walker & Co.,
n.d. 40 p. PH

1813 LAPSLEY, Robert Alberti, 1858-1934.
Scriptural holiness. Richmond, Presbyterian Committee
of Publication, © 1900. 55 p. U

1814 LAPSLEY, Robert Alberti, 1858-1934.

The songs of Zion: a brief study of our hymns--their
history, excellence, authorship, and place in the affection
and experiences of the people of God. Richmond, Presbyterian Committee of Publication, © 1925. 125 p. A C H
PT R U ... H L: 146 p.

1815 LAPSLEY, Robert Alberti, 1884-1953.
Beside the hearthstone. Richmond, John Knox Press,
© 1950. 159 p. A C H L PH R U

1816 LAPSLEY, Robert Alberti, 1884-1953.
The book of the witnesses for Jesus; studies in the book
of Acts. Richmond, Presbyterian Committee of Publication,
1931. 88 p. A H L R U

1817 LAPSLEY, Robert Alberti, 1884-1953.
The Bridge of God: a spiritual interpretation of the Natural Bridge of Virginia. Richmond, John Knox Press,
© 1951. 61 p. A H U

1818 LAPSLEY, Robert Alberti, 1884-1953.
Home mission investments. Richmond, John Knox Press,
© 1946. 144 p. A C H L R U

1819 LAPSLEY, Robert Alberti, 1884-1953.
Like as we are. Richmond, John Knox Press, © 1939.
117 p. A C H L PH R U

1820 LAPSLEY, Robert Alberti, 1884-1953.
On Vesper Hill: talks to teen-agers. Richmond, John
Knox Press, © 1953. 144 p. A H L U

1821 LAPSLEY, Robert Alberti, 1884-1953.
Portraits of the Master (a study in the Gospel of Mark).
For Circle Bible leader. Atlanta, Board of Women's Work,
Presbyterian Church in the U.S., n.d. 59 p. R U

1822 LAPSLEY, Robert Alberti, 1884-1953.
William Almon Hart, 1860-1926: "In memoriam." n.p.,
n.d. 17 p. U

1823 LAPSLEY, Samuel Baxter, 1889-1956.
From the past to the present: a handbook on Assembly's
home missions. Richmond, John Knox Press, 1947. 77 p.
A C R U

1824 LAPSLEY, Samuel Baxter, 1889-1956.
It is time to speak. An address given at the meeting of
the Association for the Preservation and Continuation of the
Southern Presbyterian Church ... August 20, 1952. Weaverville, N.C., Southern Presbyterian Journal, n.d. 6 ℓ. U

1825 LAPSLEY, Samuel Norvell, 1866-1892.

Life and letters of Samuel Norvell Lapsley, missionary to the Congo Valley, West Africa, 1866-1892. Richmond, Whittet & Shepperson, 1893. 242 p. Compiled and edited by his father, James W. Lapsley. A C L PT U

1826 LATIMER, James Fair, 1845-1892.
The Lollards. n.p., n.d. 27 p. Reprinted from the Presbyterian Quarterly, April, 1888. U

1827 LATIMER, Robert Milton, 1857-1918.
Things to think on. 5th ed. Nashville, Tenn., Robert M. Latimer, 1913. 60 p. U

1828 LAW, Patrick Redd, 1849-1912.
Address on the influence of Presbyterianism on our national life ... delivered at the dedication of the Monroe Presbyterian Church, April 5, 1906. n.p., [1906?]. 17 p. PH

1829 LAW, Thomas Hart, 1838-1923.
Citadel cadets: the journal of Cadet Tom Law, published from the original manuscript. [1st ed.] Clinton, S.C., P C Press, © 1941. 346 p. A H R

1830 LAWRENCE, A. B., ca. 1787-1862.
Notes and observations, suggested by reading a pamphlet entitled "The unity of the church; The ministry; The apostolical succession: Three discourses, by the Rt. Rev. James Hervey Otey, Bishop of Tennessee." Vicksburg, M. Shannon, 1844. 47 p. U

1831 LAWS, Samuel Spahr, 1824-1921.
An address ... in behalf of Westminster College, founded and sustained by the Old School Presbyterian Church of Missouri, at Fulton, Mo. St. Louis, Sherman Spencer, 1857. 40 p. PH

1832 LAWS, Samuel Spahr, 1824-1921.
Anticipations of science and philosophy. [Columbia, S.C., n.p., 1894]. 32 p. Inaugural address as "Perkins Professor of Natural Science in Connection with Revelation and Christian Apologetics," in the Presbyterian Theological Seminary, at Columbia, S.C., May 10, 1894. C PH

1833 LAWS, Samuel Spahr, 1824-1921.
The at-onement by the Christian Trinity: or, The legal and spiritual salvation of man from sin makes manifest the dual philosophy of the Gospel. [Washington, D.C., The author], 1919. 181 p. A C H L PT R U

1834 LAWS, Samuel Spahr, 1824-1921.
A Bible study of the two obstacles between man and

heaven. Washington, D.C. [Judd & Detweiler, 1903].
Read before the Presbyterian Ministers' Association of
Washington, D.C., 1902. H PT U

1835 LAWS, Samuel Spahr, 1824-1921.
Christianity, its true nature. Washington, D.C., Judd
& Detweiler, 1903. 30 p. C H PT U

1836 LAWS, Samuel Spahr, 1824-1921.
Does might make right? n.p., n.d. unpaged. Reprinted from the Presbyterian, Feb. 11, 18, 25, 1915. PT

1837 LAWS, Samuel Spahr, 1824-1921.
Foreign missions: Dr. Chester's official criticism and
spurious doctrine of missions. [Washington, D.C., n.p.,
1907]. 24 p. PT U

1838 LAWS, Samuel Spahr, 1824-1921.
... A letter ... to the Synod of Missouri (O. S.), which
met at Columbia, Missouri, October 8, 1872. St. Louis,
Southwestern Book & Publishing Co., 1872. 166 p. At
head of title: [For the Old School Presbyterian]. Appendix:
103-166 p. PH PT ... H PH PT U: 2d ed. New York,
S. Angell, 1873.

1839 LAWS, Samuel Spahr, 1824-1921.
Life and labors of Louis Pasteur. A paper read before
the American Medical Association at St. Louis, Mo., May,
1886. Columbia, Mo., Herald Publishing House, 1886. 28 p.
PT

1840 LAWS, Samuel Spahr, 1824-1921.
"Nascetur ridiculus mus, " or, Polygamy in the Greensboro
assembly of the Presbyterian Church in the United States,
1908. New Orleans, American Printing Co., 1908. 27 p.
PT

1841 LAWS, Samuel Spahr, 1824-1921.
An overture by a presbyter: to the Synods of South Carolina, Georgia, Alabama, and Florida, concerning changes in
the constitution of Columbia Theological Seminary relative to
the retirement of professors. [Columbia, S.C., Bryan Printing Co., 1897]. 16 p. C PH

1842 LAWS, Samuel Spahr, 1824-1921.
Polygamy and citizenship in church and state. Washington,
D.C., Judd & Detweiler, 1906. 227 p. H PH PT R ...
U: 212 p.

1843 LAWS, Samuel Spahr, 1834-1921.
Reasons for the organization and for the perpetuation of
the Southern Presbyterian Church. A Washington city church
declared vacant. n.p., n.d. 32 p. PT

1844   LAWS, Samuel Spahr, 1824-1921.
       Seminary students' temptations. Extracts from the open-
ing address delivered before the faculty and students of Columbia Seminary, September, 1895. Richmond, Whittet &
Shepperson, 1896. 8 p. Reprinted from the Presbyterian
Quarterly, January, 1896. PT

1845   LAWS, Samuel Spahr, 1824-1921.
       A thesis on the dual constitution of man, or neuro-
psychology. New York, S. Angell, 1875. 35 p. Inaugural
thesis, Bellevue Hospital Medical College. Republished
from Archives of Electrology and Neurology, November,
1875. PT

1846   LAWS, Samuel Spahr, 1824-1921.
       The virgin birth of our Saviour Christ. [Washington, D.C.,
n.p., 1916]. 15 p. PT

1847   LEAVELL, William Hayne, 1850-1930.
       After fifty years of public service. Houston, Tex.,
William H. Leavell, n.d. 15 p. H U

1848   LEAVELL, William Hayne, 1850-1930.
       Shall we test the validity of the fifteenth amendment? A
discussion. n.p., n.d. 54 p. A revised and enlarged edition of "The annulment of the fifteenth amendment: a discussion." U

1849   LEAVENWORTH, Abner Johnson, 1803-1869.
       Reasons for not being a Baptist: by a lover of Scripture
and truth. Charlotte, N.C., n.p., 1834. 62 p. PT

1850   LEE, William States, 1793-1875.
       A sermon, on the death of the late Rev. William Hollins-
head, D.D. Charleston, Times Office, 1818. 21 p. PH
PT

1851   LEE, William States, 1793-1875.
       A sermon, preached before the Charleston Union Presby-
tery, at the opening of their session in Charleston, November 17th, 1840. Charleston, S.C., B. B. Hussey, 1840.
16 p. PH ... U: Xeroxed copy.

1852   *LEGERTON, Clifford L., comp.
       Historic churches of Charleston, South Carolina. Edited
by Edward G. Lilly. Charleston, Legerton and Co., 1966.
171 p. H PH

1853   LEGTERS, Leonard Livingston, 1873-
       Partakers. Philadelphia, Pioneer Mission Agency, © 1936.
95 p. A

1854   LEGTERS, Leonard Livingston, 1873-

The simplicity of the Spirit-filled life. [5th ed.] Philadelphia, Christian Life Literature Fund, [1936]. 63 p. A

1855 LEGTERS, Leonard Livingston, 1873-
Union with Christ; a victory. 2d ed., rev. Philadelphia,
Christian Life Literature Fund, [1935]. 96 p. A

1856 LEITH, John Haddon, 1919-
Assembly at Westminster; Reformed theology in the mak-
ing. Richmond, John Knox Press, © 1973. 127 p. A C
H L PT R U

1857 LEITH, John Haddon, 1919- ed.
Creeds of the churches; a reader in Christian doctrine
from the Bible to the present. Chicago, Aldine Publishing
Co., © 1963. 589 p. C L PT R U ... A H U: [1st ed.]
Garden City, N.Y., Doubleday and Co., 1963 ... A C H L
PH PT R U: Rev. ed. Richmond, John Knox Press, [1973].
597 p.

1858 LEITH, John Haddon, 1919-
Greenville Presbyterian Church: the story of a people,
1765-1973. Greenwood County, S.C., Published by authority
of the session of Greenville Presbyterian Church, 1973.
155 p. C U

1859 LEITH, John Haddon, 1919-
An introduction to the Reformed tradition: a way of being
the Christian community. Atlanta, John Knox Press, © 1977.
253 p. A C H L PH PT R U

1860 LEITH, John Haddon, 1919-
John Calvin and social responsibility. n.p., n.d. 2 p.
Reprinted from the Presbyterian Outlook. U

1861 LELAND, Aaron Whitney, 1787-1871.
Christian mourning. A funeral discourse, occasioned by
the death of Mrs. Sarah Hibben. Charleston, n.p., 1827.
31 p. PT

1862 LELAND, Aaron Whitney, 1787-1871.
Discourse delivered ... on the 27th December, 1815, before the Grand Lodge of South-Carolina. Charleston, S.C.,
n.p., 1816. 19 p. PT

1863 LELAND, Aaron Whitney, 1787-1871.
A funeral discourse commemorative of William Swinton
Bennett, delivered ... on the 21st of December, 1823.
Charleston, n.p., 1824. 28 p. PT

1864 LELAND, Aaron Whitney, 1787-1871.
Sermon delivered ... at the organization of the Third

Presbyterian Church ... Charleston, S.C. Charleston, n.p., 1823. 32 p. PT

1865 LELAND, Aaron Whitney, 1787-1871.
A sermon, delivered on the 29th Dec., 1814, at the dedication of the new Scotch Presbyterian Church, in Charleston, S.C. Charleston, n.p., 1815. 25 p. PT

1866 LESLIE, John Douglass, 1860-1935.
Presbyterian law and procedure in the Presbyterian Church in the United States. Richmond, Presbyterian Committee of Publication, 1930. 411 p. A C H L PH PT R U

1867 LESLIE, John Douglass, 1860-1935.
A ready reference manual for church officers and courts of the Presbyterian Church in the United States. Richmond, Presbyterian Committee of Publication, 1923. 60 p. H U ... A H L PH R U: [Rev. ed.] 1930. 61 p.

1868 LEWIS, Frank Bell, 1911-1967.
Reformed faith and today's ethical tensions.... Inaugural address [as Professor of Christian Ethics] delivered March 1, 1955, in Schauffler Hall, Union Theological Seminary. [Richmond, Union Theological Seminary, 1955]. 13 p. A C U

1869 LEWIS, Frederick Wheeler, 1873-1968.
Prayers that are different. Grand Rapids, Mich., Wm. B. Eerdmans Publishing Co., © 1964. 166 p. PH

1870 LEWIS, James N., 1809-1887.
A sermon on election. Wytheville, Va., D. A. St. Clair, 1860. 12 p. PH

1871 LEWIS, James N., 1809-1887.
What is Bible baptism? Wytheville, Va., D. A. St. Clair, n.d. 8 p. PH PT

1872 LEWIS, James N., 1809-1887.
Why are you not a Christian? Philadelphia, Presbyterian Board of Publication, n.d. 16 p. PH

1873 LEWIS, James N., 1809-1887.
Why do you do it? Richmond, Presbyterian Committee of Publication, n.d. 8 p. U

1874 LEYBURN, Edward Riley, 1865-1958.
The world's debt to the Jew. n.p., n.d. 22 p. U

1875 LEYBURN, George William, 1809-1975.
God's message to the young; or, The obligations and the advantages of early piety, seriously urged upon young persons,

in connexion with Eccles. xii.1. New York, M. W. Dodd, 1857. 179 p. U

1876 LEYBURN, John, 1814-1893.
Christian activity: a sermon preached in the First Reformed Presbyterian Church, Philadelphia, on Sabbath morning, January 2, 1859. Philadelphia, William S. & Alfred
Martien, 1859. 30 p. PH

1877 LEYBURN, John, 1814-1893.
Dead, yet speaking. A memorial sermon on the life and
character of the late Mr. James M. Horton. Baltimore,
Young Men's Christian Association, 1873. 25 p. PH

1878 LEYBURN, John, 1814-1893.
A discourse in commemoration of the bicentenary of the
Westminster Assembly. Preached to the congregation of the
Presbyterian Church, Petersburg, Virginia, on Sabbath morn-
ing, July 2, 1843. Together with a discourse on predestina-
tion, preached to the same congregation, Sabbath morning,
June 18, 1843. [Petersburg], n.p., 1843. 40 p. PH

1879 LEYBURN, John, 1814-1893.
Hints to young men from the parable of the prodigal son.
Philadelphia, Presbyterian Board of Publication and Sabbath-
school Work, © 1888. 183 p. PH PT

1880 LEYBURN, John, 1814-1893.
Individual responsibility, or, work enough for every church-
member. Philadelphia, Presbyterian Board of Publication,
n.d. 16 p. (Presbyterian Tracts, no. 164.) C H L PH
PT R U

1881 LEYBURN, John, 1814-1893.
Memorial sermon on Telfair Marriott ... Sunday, May 14,
1882. Baltimore, Sun Book and Job Printing Office, 1882.
12 p. PH

1882 LEYBURN, John, 1814-1893.
National mercies, sins, and duties. A discourse, preached
to the congregation of the Presbyterian Church, Petersburg,
Virginia, on Sabbath morning, July 5th, 1846. n.p., 1846.
23 p. PH

1883 LEYBURN, John, 1814-1893.
Scriptural baptism explained and defended; being the sub-
stance of two discourses preached in the Presbyterian Church,
Petersburg, Virginia. n.p., 1847. 42 p. PH PT U

1884 LEYBURN, John, 1814-1893.
The soldier of the cross; a practical exposition of Ephesians VI.10-18. New York, Robert Carter & Brothers, 1851.
339 p. R U ... PH PT: 2d ed. 1851.

1885 LILLY, David Clay, 1870-1939.
Faith of our fathers. Richmond, Presbyterian Committee
of Publication, 1935. 143 p. A C H L PH PT R U

1886 LILLY, David Clay, 1870-1939.
A man and his money. [Chattanooga, Tenn., General
Assembly's Stewardship Committee, Presbyterian Church in
the U.S.], n.d. 15 p. U

1887 LILLY, David Clay, 1870-1939.
A partnership in living; a course of four Bible studies on
stewardship. Chattanooga, Tenn., General Assembly's
Stewardship Committee, Presbyterian Church in the U.S.,
n.d. 63 p. A H L PH R U

1888 LILLY, David Clay, 1870-1939.
Some teachings of Jesus. St. Louis, Woman's Auxiliary,
Presbyterian Church in the U.S., [1926?]. unpaged. A H

1889 LILLY, Edward Owings Guerrant, 1898-1981.
Beyond the burning bush: First (Scots) Presbyterian
Church, Charleston, S.C. Charleston, Garnier & Co.,
1971. 73 p. C H U

1890 LINCOLNTON, N.C. Presbyterian Church.
Rev. Robert Zenas Johnston, 1834-1908: memorial tributes. Durham, N.C., Seeman Printery, 1908. 32 p. H

1891 LINDSAY, John Oliver, 1823-1900.
The eldership. A sermon preached by appointment before
the Presbytery of South Carolina. Due West, S.C., Due
West Telescope Press, 1859. 22 p. PH

1892 *LINDSELL, Harold, 1913-
A handbook of Christian truth, by Harold Lindsell and
Charles J. Woodbridge. Westwood, N.J., Fleming H. Revell
Co., © 1953. 351 p. PT R U

1893 LINGLE, Thomas Wilson, 1871-1937.
Die Bedeutung der Entwickelungsgeschichte für die Ethik,
mit besonderer Rücksicht auf Huxley. Leipzig, Druck von
Sellman & Henne, 1899. 58 p. Inaug.-diss.--Leipzig.
PT U

1894 LINGLE, Thomas Wilson, 1871-1937.
History of Thyatira Church, 1753 to 1925; including address delivered by Rev. S. C. Alexander at the centennial
celebration held on October 17, 1885. Statesville, N.C.,
Brady Printing Co., 1925. 61 p. H PH U

1895 LINGLE, Walter Lee, 1868-1956.
The Bible and social problems. New York, Fleming H.

Revell Co., © 1929. 192 p. The Sprunt Lectures, 1929.
A C H L PH PT R U

1896 LINGLE, Walter Lee, 1868-1956.
The burning of Servetus: (the substance of an address de-
livered before the Synod of Georgia). n.p., n.d. 14 p.
PT

1897 LINGLE, Walter Lee, 1868-1956.
Cub Creek Church; its place in history; an address made
at Cub Creek Church, June 26, 1838. Hampden-Sydney, Va.,
Hampden-Sydney College, [1938]. 24 p. Bulletin of Hampden-
Sydney College, August, 1938. U

1898 LINGLE, Walter Lee, 1868-1956.
The first General Assembly and the events leading up to
it. An address delivered before the Western Section, Alliance of the Reformed Churches Throughout the World Holding
the Presbyterian System, Princeton, N.J., February 24,
1938. Philadelphia, Publicity Department of the General Assembly, n.d. 22 p. PH PT

1899 LINGLE, Walter Lee, 1868-1956.
In memoriam: Union Seminary cemetery at Hampden-
Sidney. [Richmond, Richmond Press], n.d. 16 p. Lists
professors of Union Theological Seminary buried at Hampden-
Sidney: John Holt Rice, George A. Baxter, Samuel L.
Graham, Francis S. Sampson, Samuel B. Wilson, Benjamin
M. Smith, James F. Latimer, Thomas E. Peck, Robert L.
Dabney. R

1900 LINGLE, Walter Lee, 1868-1956.
Memories of Davidson College. Richmond, John Knox
Press, © 1947. 157 p. C H L PH PT R U

1901 LINGLE, Walter Lee, 1868-1956.
Preparing for the ministry. Louisville, Ky., Committee
on Christian Education, Presbyterian Church in the U.S.,
n.d. 12 p. PH

1902 LINGLE, Walter Lee, 1868-1956.
Presbyterianism: a heritage and a challenge; a textbook
on Presbyterianism. Richmond, Presbyterian Committee of
Publication, n.d. 32 p. A C L PH PT R U

1903 LINGLE, Walter Lee, 1868-1956.
Presbyterians, their history and beliefs. Richmond, Presbyterian Committee of Publication, © 1928. 199 p. A C
H PH PT R U ... H R U: Richmond, John Knox Press,
© 1944. 127 p. ... A C U: [1948] ... H U: Rev. ed.
[1950] ... A L: [1951] ... U: [1953] ... PH: [1954] ...
U: [1959] 128 p. ... H R U: Rev. ed. Revised by T.

Watson Street. © 1960 ... A C H L PH PT R U: [4th rev. ed.] By Walter L. Lingle and John W. Kuykendall. © 1978. 110 p.

1904 LINGLE, Walter Lee, 1868-1956.
Thyatira Presbyterian Church, Rowan County, North Carolina (1753-1948). Statesville, N.C., Brady Printing Co., n.d. 71 p.   H U

1905 LINGLE, Walter Lee, 1868-1956.
Tolerance and intolerance. Richmond, Presbyterian of the South, [1928]. 11 p.   U

1906 LINGLE, Walter Lee, 1868-1956.
What kind of education? n.p., n.d.   12 p.   Reprinted from the Christian Observer, January 30, 1946.   U

1907 LINGLE, Walter Lee, 1868-1956.
Why I believe in the deity of Jesus Christ.... A lecture delivered on the Macartney Foundation in the Arch Street Presbyterian Church, Philadelphia, January 28, 1936. Richmond, Presbyterian Committee of Publication, 1936.   34 p.
A C U

1908 LINK, Luther, 1859-1915.
Infant salvation and confessional revision. Richmond, Onward Press, 1912.   101 p.   A C H L PT U

1909 LINK, Luther, 1859-1915.
Is baptism initiatory? Richmond, Whittet & Shepperson, 1903.   22 p.   Reprinted from the Presbyterian Quarterly, January, 1903.   PT

1910 LINN, Samuel Pollock, 1842-1887, comp.
Words that burn; or, Truth and life. A compilation of the brightest thoughts and choicest selections from the world's best authors.   Philadelphia, J. H. Chambers & Co., 1883.   728 p.   U

1911 LISTON, Robert Todd Lapsley, 1898-
Minority report from committee on a new Confession of Faith. [Mountain City, Tenn., The author, 1974).   7 p.
PT

1912 LISTON, Robert Todd Lapsley, 1898-
The neglected educational heritage of Southern Presbyterians. Bristol, Tenn., Privately printed, [1956].   73 p.   C
H L R U

1913 LITTLE, Archibald Alexander, 1860-1939.
The highway to happiness: sermons. Grand Rapids, Mich., Zondervan Publishing House, 1935.   204 p.   A C
H R U

1914 LITTLE, Daniel Doak, 1873-1933.
      Faith or works? By one who has tried both ways. Rich-
      mond, Presbyterian Committee of Publication, n.d. 12 p.
      U

1915 LITTLE, Daniel Doak, 1873-1933.
      History of the Presbytery of Columbia, Tennessee. Colum-
      bia, Tenn., Maury Democrat, 1928. 45 p. A PH R

1916 LITTLE, Daniel Doak, 1873-1933.
      Mr. Paxton's solution; or, How one minister solved the
      financial problem. Richmond, Texarkana, Presbyterian Com-
      mittee of Publication, n.d. 22 p. U

1917 LITTLE, James.
      The cross in Holy Scripture; a study of the nature and
      significance of Christ's redemptive work. London, Robert
      Scott, 1911. 147 p. A

1918 LITTLE, James.
      The day-spring and other sermons. Edinburgh, Oliphant,
      Anderson & Ferrier, 1907. 312 p. PT R U

1919 LITTLE, James.
      Glorying in the Lord. Edinburgh, Oliphant, Anderson &
      Ferrier, 1912. 254 p. U

1920 LITTLE, James.
      Good tidings for Christmas and the New Year, 1901-1902.
      Belfast (Ireland), Wm. Strain and Sons, 1901. 28 p. PT

1921 LITTLE, James.
      New Year's sermon, delivered ... [in] the Presbyterian
      Church, Quincy, Florida, January 1st., 1873. Quincy, M. B.
      Owens, n.d. 8 p. C

1922 LITTLE, Lacy LeGrand, 1868-1946.
      'Rivershade''; a historical sketch of Kiangyin Station, China.
      n.p., [1928?]. 63 p. C H R U

1923 LOFQUIST, Henry Victor, 1897-
      An uncommon commonplace: a collection of sermons and
      articles. n.p., 1942. 140 p. A C H PT U

1924 LOGAN, Charles Alexander, 1874-1955.
      Devotional commentary on Exodus. Tokyo, Ginza, n.d.
      In Japanese. H

1925 LOGAN, Charles Alexander, 1874-1955.
      Devotional commentary on Genesis. [Tokyo, Christian
      Literature Society], n.d. 7, 16, 233 p. In Japanese.
      H PT

1926 LOGAN, Charles Alexander, 1874-1955.
Jesus introduces himself. Tokyo, Methodist Publishing
House, 1934. 118 p. In Japanese. H

1927 LOGAN, Charles Alexander, 1874-1955.
Jesus of Nazareth. Tokyo, Alpha Press, 1935. unpaged.
In Japanese. H

1928 LOGAN, Charles Alexander, 1874-1955.
The Psalms as spiritual songs; a devotional commentary.
Tokyo, Methodist Publishing House, 1938. 2 v. In Japanese.
H

1929 *LOGAN, Samuel Crothers, 1823-1907.
Correspondence between the Rev. S. C. Logan, Pittsburgh,
Pa., and the Rev. Dr. J. Leighton Wilson, Columbia, S.C.
[Columbia, Southern Presbyterian, 1868]. 15 p. PH

1930 LOGAN, William Malcom, 1912-
In the beginning God. Richmond, John Knox Press, © 1957.
90 p. A C L PT R U ... C H: [1961].

1931 LONG, Isaac Jasper, 1834-1891.
A discourse commemorative of the life, character and services of the Rev. Thomas Rice Welch, D.D., delivered before the Synod of Arkansas at Camden, Ark., November 17,
1886. St. Louis, Farris, Smith & Co., 1886. 17 p. H

1932 LONG, Isaac Jasper, 1834-1891.
Outline of ecclesiastical history. For the use of colleges,
high schools and theological classes. St. Louis, Farris,
Smith & Co., © 1888. 125 p. A C R U

1933 LONG, Isaac Jasper, 1834-1891.
Sketch of Arkansas College; origin and early history.
n.p., n.d. 18 p. A

1934 LONG, Roswell Curtis, 1892-1960.
More stewardship parables of Jesus. New York, Abingdon-
Cokesbury Press, © 1947. 140 p. U

1935 LONG, Roswell Curtis, 1892-1960.
Stewardship parables of Jesus. Nashville, Cokesbury
Press, © 1931. 230 p. A C H L R U

1936 LONG, Roswell Curtus, 1892-1960.
The story of our church. Richmond, Presbyterian Committee of Publication, 1932. 188 p. A C H L PH R U

1937 LONGENECKER, Jay Hershey, 1889-
Centuries of progress in forty-five years. n.p., n.d.
4 p. U

1938 LONGENECKER, Jay Hershey, 1889-
Memories of Congo; tales of adventure and work in the
heart of Africa. Johnson City, Tenn., Royal Publishers,
© 1964. 159 p. C H L R U

1939 LOUGHRIDGE, Robert McGill, 1809-1900.
English and Muskokee dictionary. Collected from various
sources and revised, by Rev. R. M. Loughridge, D.D.,
missionary to the Creek Indians, and Elder David M. Hodge,
interpreter. Creek Mission. Indian Territory. St. Louis,
J. T. Smith, 1890. 236 p. H PH ... PH: Philadelphia,
Westminster Press, 1914.

1940 LOUGHRIDGE, Robert McGill, 1809-1900.
The mode of baptism taught and practiced by Jesus Christ.
Eufaula, Wealaka, Indian Territory, Printed for the author,
1882. 16 p. PT

1941 LOUGHRIDGE, Robert McGill, 1809-1900, tr.
Mvskoke Setempohetv. Translation of the introduction to
the Shorter Catechism into the Creek language. Park Hill,
Mission Press, J. Candy & E. Archer, 1846. 31 p.
PH ... PH: Nakcokv Setempohetv. 2d ed., rev. and improved. Philadelphia, Presbyterian Board of Publication,
1858. 34 p. ... PH PT: 4th ed., rev. and improved.
1918. 31 p.

1942 LOUGHRIDGE, Robert McGill, 1809-1900, comp.
Nakcokv esyvhiketv. Muskokee hymns. Collected and re-
vised by Rev. R. M. Loughridge, A. M., and David Winslett,
interpreter. Park Hill, Mission Press, 1851. 144 p.
PT ... PH: New York, Mission House, 1859. 216 p. ...
PH: 4th ed., rev. and enl. 220 p. ... PH PT: 5th ed.,
rev. Philadelphia, Presbyterian Board of Publication and
Sabbath-school Work, [1907]. 221 p.

1943 LOUGHRIDGE, Robert McGill, 1809-1900.
Sprinkling; the mode of baptism taught and practiced by
Jesus Christ and his apostles: the proofs presented. 3d ed.
Richmond, Presbyterian Committee of Publication, n.d.
77 p. PT R

1944 LOUISVILLE, KY. Louisville Presbyterian Theological Seminary.
A new president [Dr. Albert Curry Winn]. n.p., n.d.
unpaged. L PH

1945 LOVE, Herbert Alexander, 1878-1945, comp.
Opportunities=responsibilities; the work of the Presbyterian Church U.S. in Florida. n.p., 1927. 163 p. H U

1946 LOWRANCE, William Bellinger, 1911-1956.

The story of the Old Rodney Presbyterian Church. 1st
ed. Port Gibson, Miss., Reveille Press, 1955. 15 p.
A R

1947 *LOWRY, Howard Foster, 1901-1967.
College talks. Edited by James R. Blackwood. New York,
Oxford University Press, 1969. 177 p. H L PH PT

1948 LUCK, George Coleman, 1913-
Daniel. Chicago, Moody Press, © 1958. 127 p. U

1949 LUCK, George Coleman, 1913-
Ezra and Nehemiah: a commentary. Chicago, Moody
Press, © 1961. 127 p. U

1950 LUCK, George Coleman, 1913-
First Corinthians. Chicago, Moody Press, © 1958.
128 p. U

1951 LUCK, George Coleman, 1913-
James: faith in action. Chicago, Moody Press, © 1954.
124 p. L

1952 LUCK, George Coleman, 1913-
Luke: the gospel of the son of man. Chicago, Moody
Press, © 1960. 127 p. PT

1953 LUCK, George Coleman, 1913-
Zechariah: a study of the prophetic visions. Chicago,
Moody Press, © 1957. 125 p. A

1954 LYLE, George Tate, 1836-1913.
The Christian Church. Its republicanism. A new view
of baptism. Charleston, W. Va., Donnally Publishing Co.,
1902. 104 p. A H PT R U

1955 LYLES, John Steedman, 1926-
Youth and alcoholic beverages. Richmond, CLC Press,
© 1966. 48 p. (The Covenant Life Curriculum.) C L U

1956 LYNCH, Ernest Carlyle, 1878-1946.
Manual of the Presbyterian Church, Versailles, Kentucky.
n.p., n.d. unpaged. H

1957 LYNN, Lucius Ross, 1875-1966.
Hanging 'round an orphanage. [Clinton, S.C., Thornwell
Orphanage Press], 1928. 125 p. A C H PH U ... PT:
2d ed. 1933. 124 p.

1958 LYNN, Lucius Ross, 1875-1966.
The place of the church in a child welfare program....
Delivered at Columbia Theological Seminary ... February

25-27, 1936, and Louisville Presbyterian Seminary ...
March 4, 5, 1936. [Clinton, S.C., Thornwell Orphanage
Press, 1936]. 21 p.   H U

1959   LYNN, Lucius Ross, 1875-1966.
The story of Thornwell Orphanage, Clinton, South Carolina, 1875-1925. Richmond, Presbyterian Committee of Publication, © 1924.   239 p.   A C H L PH R U

1960   LYON, James Adair, 1814-1882.
An address on the missionary aspect of African colonization.   St. Louis, T. W. Ustick, 1850.   21 p.   C PH

1961   LYON, James Adair, 1814-1882.
The certainty of the final triumph of the Gospel: a ser-
mon preached by appointment before the Synod of Mississippi.
Natchez, Daily Courier Office, 1857.   21 p.   PH

1962   LYON, James Adair, 1814-1882.
A lecture on Christianity and the civil laws.   Columbus,
"Mississippi Democrat" Print., 1859.   32 p.   C PH PT

1963   LYON, James Adair, 1814-1882.
The reiterated charges made by Rev. J. W. Cunningham,
answered and refuted. Jonesborough, Ten., The "Sentinel"
Office, 1840.   30 p.   PH

1964   LYON, James Adair, 1814-1882.
Slavery and the duties growing out of the relation.   n.p.,
n.d.   37 p.   Reprinted from the Southern Presbyterian Review, July, 1863.   PT

1965   LYON, Milford Hall, 1868-1953.
For the life that now is; the present worth of Christian
faith.   New York, Fleming H. Revell Co., © 1909.   151 p.
A PT

1966   LYON, Milford Hall, 1868-1953.
The lordship of Jesus.   Chicago, Fleming H. Revell Co.,
1909.   130 p.   A PT

1967   LYTCH, William Elbert, 1928-
History of Bethesda Presbyterian Church, 1765-1965, Cas-
well County, N.C. [Yanceyville, N.C., n.p., 1965].   87 p.
U

1968   McALLISTER, James Gray, 1872-1970.
The book pre-eminent. [An address delivered ... at his
inauguration as Adjunct Professor of Hebrew, Union Theological Seminary, Richmond, Va., Monday evening, May 8,
1905].   n.p., n.d.   11 p.   U

1969   McALLISTER, James Gray, 1872-1970.

Borderlands of the Mediterranean.... With an introduction by Rev. Walter W. Moore. Richmond, Presbyterian Committee of Publication, © 1925. 294 p. A C H L R U

1970 McALLISTER, James Gray, 1872-1970.
Edward O. Guerrant: apostle to the southern highlanders, by J. Gray McAllister and Grace Owings Guerrant. Richmond, Richmond Press, 1950. 238 p. A C H L R U

1971 McALLISTER, James Gray, 1872-1970.
Family records, compiled for the descendants of Abraham Addams McAllister and his wife Julia Ellen (Stratton) McAllister, of Covington, Virginia, containing a sketch of A. A. McAllister. [Easton, Pa., Chemical Publishing Co.], 1912. 88 p. H PH U

1972 McALLISTER, James Gray, 1872-1970, comp.
A rapid survey of the Bible, issued by the Department of the English Bible, Union Theological Seminary, Richmond, Virginia. Richmond, Richmond Press, 1935. 31 p. U

1973 McALLISTER, James Gray, 1872-1970.
Recognition in heaven: a sermon. Richmond, Whittet & Shepperson, 1902. 16 p. U

1974 McALLISTER, James Gray, 1872-1970.
Sketch of Captain Thompson McAllister, Co. A., 27th Virginia Regiment. Petersburg, Va., Fenn & Owen, 1896. 39 p. H PH U

1975 McALLISTER, James Gray, 1872-1970.
Studies in Old Testament history. Richmond, Richmond Press, 1925. 126 p. A C H L R U

1976 McALLISTER, Robert Samuel, 1830-1892.
A talk on a Sunday train. Richmond, Whittet & Shepperson, 1886. 64 p. A U

1977 McALPINE, Robert Eugenius, 1862-1950.
A great educator. Nashville, Tenn., Executive Committee of Foreign Missions, Presbyterian Church in the U.S., [1930?]. 8 p. U

1978 McCARTER, Neely Dixon, 1929-
Designing theological curriculum. n.p., © 1979. 151 p. A C R U

1979 McCARTER, Neely Dixon, 1929-
Hear the word of the Lord. Richmond, CLC Press, © 1964. 223 p. (The Covenant Life Curriculum.) C L R U ... C L R U: Leader's guide. 96 p.

1980 McCARTER, Neely Dixon, 1929-

Help me understand, Lord: prayer responses to the Gospel of Mark. [1st ed.] Philadelphia, Westminster Press, © 1978. 121 p. A C L PH U

1981 McCASLIN, Robert Horace, 1884-1958.
Presbyterianism in Memphis, Tennessee. Memphis, Adams Printing & Stationery Co., n.d. 141 p. H

1982 McCASLIN, Robert Horace, 1884-1958.
Things worth while. [Jacksonville, Fla.], J. Ben Wand, 1928. 135 p. H U

1983 McCHAIN, James, 1819-1869.
Address delivered at the funeral of Mrs. Cynthia A. Henritze, wife of P. E. B. C. Henritze, Esq., in the Presbyterian Church of Abingdon, Va., August 28, 1853. Baltimore, John D. Toy, 1853. 16 p. PH

1984 McCLELLAND, Brainard Taylor, 1845-1901.
The system of doctrine formulated by the Westminster Assembly. An address delivered before the Synod of Texas, December, 1897. Richmond, Presbyterian Committee of Publication, © 1899. 18 p. PT U

1985 McCLOY, Shelby Thomas, 1898-
Gibbon's antagonism to Christianity. Chapel Hill, University of North Carolina Press, 1933. 400 p. Issued also as thesis (Ph.D.), Columbia University. A PT U ... A: London, Williams & Norgate, 1933.

1986 McCLOY, Shelby Thomas, 1898-
Government aid to large families in Normandy, 1764-1786. n.p., n.d. Reprinted from Social Forces, March 1940. U

1987 McCLOY, Shelby Thomas, 1898-
The Humanitarian movement in eighteenth-century France. [Lexington, Ky.], University of Kentucky Press, © 1957. 274 p. H PT

1988 McCLOY, Shelby Thomas, 1898-
The Negro in the French West Indies. [Lexington, Ky.], University of Kentucky Press, © 1966. 278 p. H

1989 McCLOY, Shelby Thomas, 1898-
Rationalists and religion in the eighteenth century. n.p., n.d. 467-482 p. Reprinted from the South Atlantic Quarterly, October, 1947. U

1990 McCLURE, Alexander Doak, 1850-1920.
"Another Comforter"; a study of the mission of the Holy Ghost. New York, Fleming H. Revell Co., © 1897. 127 p. A C H L PH PT

1991 McCLURE, James Alexander, 1872-1965.
The McClure family. Limited ed. Petersburg, Va.,
Frank A. Owen, 1914. 232 p. U

1992 McCLURE, Robert Edwin, 1897-1974.
What is man to believe. The Westminster Shorter Catechism; an arrangement of the answers only--outlined for discussion and study. Asheville, N.C., R. E. McClure, n.d.
23 p. R U

1993 McCLURE, Robert Edwin, 1897-1974.
When Christmas comes, and other poems. Asheville,
N.C., R. E. McClure, © 1963. 48 p. U

1994 McCONNELL, Thomas Maxwell, 1851-1927.
Claims of the ministry. [Richmond, Presbyterian Com-
mittee of Publication], n.d. 12 p. Reprinted from the
Christian Observer. U

1995 McCONNELL, Thomas Maxwell, 1851-1927.
Day-dawn of Christianity; or, The Gospel in the Apostolic
age. Nashville, Tenn., Publishing House of the M. E.
Church, South, 1888. 448 p. H U

1996 McCONNELL, Thomas Maxwell, 1851-1927.
Eve and her daughters; or, Heroines of home. Phila-
delphia, Westminster Press, 1900. 295 p. C PH R ...
H: 1905.

1997 McCONNELL, Thomas Maxwell, 1851-1927.
Hand-book of history of the Presbyterian Church of Greenville, S.C. Compiled ... as a souvenir of the "Semi-
centennial" or "Golden Anniversary" of the church's organization, held in the "Washington Street" or First Presbyterian
Church, February 23-27, 1898. n.p., n.d. 60 p. PH

1998 McCONNELL, Thomas Maxwell, 1851-1927.
The last week with Jesus. Nashville, Southern Methodist
Publishing House, 1886. 219 p. C H U

1999 McCONNELL, Thomas Maxwell, 1851-1927.
Messages for men. Bristol, Tenn., King Printing Co.,
1921. 157 p. H

2000 McCONNELL, Thomas Maxwell, 1851-1927.
Repentance. Richmond, Presbyterian Committee of Publication, n.d. 14 p. PT

2001 McCORD, James Iley, 1919-
From a thread even to a shoelatchet. Sermon. New York,
Division of Radio and Television, United Presbyterian Church,
U.S.A., 1965. unpaged. PH

2002   McCORD, James Iley, 1919-
       The Heidelberg Catechism: an ecumenical confession.
[Sea Cliff, N.Y., Christ's Mission], 1963. unpaged. Ur-
sinus College Founders' Day address, November 4, 1962.
PT

2003   McCORD, James Iley, 1919-
       The quest for the human. Sweet Briar College, Sweet
Briar, Virginia, April 21, 1969. n.p., n.d. 12 p. The
Eugene William and Mary Ely Lyman lecture. PT

2004   McCORD, James Iley, 1919-
       "Religion behind the Iron Curtain." A sermon preached
in the Myers Park Presbyterian Church, Charlotte, North
Carolina, December 9, 1956. n.p., n.d. 10 p. A

2005   McCORD, James Iley, 1919- ed.
       Service in Christ: essays presented to Karl Barth on his
80th birthday, edited by James I. McCord and T. H. L.
Parker. London, Epworth Press, [1966]. 223 p. A C L
PT R U

2006   McCORD, James Iley, 1919-
       ... Wanted--prophets! Sermon [in the] Westminster Pres-
byterian Church, Minneapolis, Minn. [Minneapolis, n.p.,
1975]. unpaged. PT

2007   McCORKLE, Francis Allison,   -1869.
       A treatise on church government. Being the substance of
a sermon delivered in the Presbyterian Church, Greeneville,
preparatory to the ordination of an elder, and two deacons
on the 27th January, 1850. Greeneville, Tenn., "Spy" Office,
1850. 76 p. PH

2008   McCORKLE, William Hart, 1900-1981.
       You can witness. Atlanta, Board of Church Extension,
Presbyterian Church in the U.S., © 1955. 141 p. A C H
L R U

2009   McCORKLE, William Parsons, 1855-1933.
       Anti-Christian sociology as taught in the Journal of Social
Forces; presenting a question for North Carolina Christians.
Rev. ed. Burlington, N.C., A. D. Pate & Co., [192?].
32 p. U

2010   McCORKLE, William Parsons, 1855-1933.
       Christian science, or the false christ of 1866: an exami-
nation of the origin, animus, claims, philosophical absurdi-
ties, medical fallacies and doctrinal contents of the new
gospel of mental healing. Richmond, Presbyterian Committee
of Publication, © 1899. 321 p. A C H L PT R U

2011   MacCORMAC, Earl Ronald, 1935-

Metaphor and myth in science and religion. Durham, N.C., Duke University Press, 1976. 167 p.   A L PT U

2012 McCORMICK, Scott, 1929-
The Lord's Supper, a Biblical interpretation. Philadelphia, Westminster Press, © 1966. 126 p.   A C H L PH PT R U

2013 *McCOY, Charles S.
The Gospel on campus: rediscovering evangelism in the academic community, [by] Charles S. McCoy [and] Neely D. McCarter. Richmond, John Knox Press, © 1959. 123 p. A C H L PT R U

2014 *McCRACKEN, George Englert, 1904-   ed.
Early medieval theology. Newly translated and edited by George E. McCracken in collaboration with Allen Cabaniss. Philadelphia, Westminster Press, [1957]. 430 p. (The Library of Christian Classics, v. 9.)   A C L PT R U

2015 McCULLAGH, Joseph Hamilton, 1855-1927.
"The Sunday-school man of the South." A sketch of the life and labors of the Rev. John McCullagh, Philadelphia, American Sunday-school Union, © 1889. 189 p.   A H PT R U

2016 McDILL, Joseph Moody, 1911-1981.
Milton and the pattern of Calvinism. Nashville, Tenn., n.p., 1942. 432 p. Thesis--Vanderbilt University, 1938. PT ... H L U: Folcroft, Pa., Folcroft Press, [1969].

2017 McDILL, Thomas Haldane, 1917-
Calvinism and the cure of souls. Inaugural address ... upon being inducted into the chair of Pastoral Theology and Pastoral Counseling at Columbia Theological Seminary ... delivered in the chapel of the seminary, Nov. 4, 1955. [Decatur, Ga., Columbia Theological Seminary, 1956]. 39-56 p. Bulletin of Columbia Theological Seminary, April, 1956.   C H U

2018 McDILL, Thomas Haldane, 1917-
Released power for today. [Twelve programs centered in people.] Atlanta, Board of Women's Work, Presbyterian Church in the U.S., [1954?]. 96 p.   C U

2019 McDONALD, Angus, 1846-1909.
The old paths; questions and answers about the good old way. Nashville, Tenn., University Press, 1894. 176 p. C H R U

2020 McELHENNY, John, 1781-1871
... Deuteronomy VIII.2. Semi-centenary sermon, delivered ... [at] the Presbyterian Church at Lewisburg, Va. Lewisburg, Crane & Harlow, 1858. 16 p.   PH PT

2021 McELROY, Isaac Stuart, 1853-1931.
      Infant baptism: a discourse, delivered in the First Pres-
byterian Church, Lexington, Ky. Richmond, Presbyterian
Committee of Publication, 1889. 40 p. C U

2022 McELROY, Isaac Stuart, 1853-1931.
      The Louisville Presbyterian Theological Seminary. Char-
lotte, N.C., Presbyterian Standard Publishing Co., 1929.
149 p. A C L PH PT R U

2023 McELROY, Isaac Stuart, 1853-1931.
      Some pioneer Presbyterian preachers of the Piedmont
North Carolina. [Gastonia, N.C., Loftin & Co., 1928].
50 p. Sketches of Robert Hall Morrison, John Joseph Kennedy, Robert Zenas Johnston, Robert Newton Davis, James
Davidson Hall, R. P. Smith, and others. A H PH PT U

2024 McELROY, Samuel Addison, 1860-1935.
      Poems. Idabel, Gazette Print., n.d. 8 p. PT ...
PT: 16 p.

2025 McELROY, Samuel Addison, 1860-1935.
      Shall Southwestern Presbyterian Home and School for Or-
phans be moved from Files Valley? Facts that must be considered for an intelligent action. (Itasca, Tex., n.p., 1919].
31 p. PT

2026 McELROY, Samuel Addison, 1860-1935.
      Shall we know our friends in heaven? n.p., n.d. 12 p.
PT

2027 McFADYEN, Henry Richard, 1877-1964.
      Jesus of Nazareth: an outline study of the life of Christ.
[New Rochelle, N.Y.], n.p., © 1958. 27 p. H

2028 *McGAUGHEY, Janie W.
      Hallie Paxson Winsborough; a sketch of her life. [Atlanta,
Committee on Woman's Work, Presbyterian Church in the
U.S.], n.d. unpaged. Contents.--A woman called of God,
by Janie W. McGaughey.--A woman of faith and works, by
Henry H. Sweets.--A woman of wisdom and ability, by Eg-
bert W. Smith. C

2029 McGEACHY, Archibald Alexander, 1869-1928.
      Why I am a Presbyterian. Sunday, May 18, 1901. [Ful-
ton, Mo., W. D. Thomas], n.d. 16 p. U

2030 McGEACHY, Daniel Patrick, 1929-
      Beyond the facts ... acts: a process guide for groups
doing further learning in justice, liberation and development.
New York, Friendship Press, © 1973. 63 p. C U

2031 McGEACHY, Daniel Patrick, 1929-

Common sense and the Gospel: a study of the Wisdom
books. Richmond, CLC Press, © 1970. 126 p. (The Covenant Life Curriculum.) C L U ... C L U: Teacher's
book. 96 p.

2032 McGEACHY, Daniel Patrick, 1929-
       The dry ground; a poem of wisdom illustrated by six in-
       ventions. n.p., [1967?]. unpaged. U

2033 McGEACHY, Daniel Patrick, 1929-
       The Gospel according to Andy Capp. Richmond, John
       Knox Press, © 1973. 132 p. A C H L PT R U

2034 McGEACHY, Daniel Patrick, 1929-
       Help, Lord! A guide to public and private prayer. At-
       lanta, John Knox Press, © 1978. 120 p. A C L PT U

2035 McGEACHY, Daniel Patrick, 1929-
       A matter of life and death. Richmond, John Knox Press,
       © 1966. 80 p. A C H L PH U

2036 McGEACHY, Daniel Patrick, 1929-
       A new song. Nashville, n.p., © 1973. 16 ℓ. C U

2037 McGEACHY, Daniel Patrick, 1929-
       A new new song. Nashville, Tenn., A New Song,
       © 1976. 32 p. U

2038 McGEACHY, Daniel Patrick, 1929-
       Table talk. Nashville, Tenn., Pat McGeachy, © 1976.
       21 p. U

2039 McGEACHY, Daniel Patrick, 1929-
       Traveling light. Nashville, Abingdon Press, © 1975.
       112 p. C U

2040 McGEACHY, Neill Roderick, 1909-1979.
       A history of the Sugaw Creek Presbyterian Church, Meck-
       lenburg Presbytery, Charlotte, North Carolina. Rock Hill,
       S.C., Record Printing Co., © 1954. 195 p. H L PH R U

2041 McGEE, John Vernon, 1904-
       The empty tomb; proof of life after death. Glendale,
       Calif., G/L Regal Books, © 1968. 128 p. A R

2042 McGEE, John Vernon, 1904-
       Exposition on the book of Esther. Wheaton, Ill., Van
       Kampen Press, © 1951. 76 p. R U

2043 McGEE, John Vernon, 1904-
       The fruit of the sycamore tree, and other sermons.
       Wheaton, Ill., Van Kampen Press, © 1952. 81 p. R

2044   McGEE, John Vernon, 1904-
       How can God exist in three persons? Los Angeles,
       Church of the Open Door, n.d. 23 p.   R

2045   McGEE, John Vernon, 1904-
       In a barley field. Glendale, Calif., G/L Regal Books,
       © 1968. 192 p. On cover: Ruth's romance of redemption.
       1943 and 1954 editions published under title: Ruth: the ro-
       mance of redemption.   R

2046   McGEE, John Vernon, 1904-
       Ruth: the romance of redemption. 2d ed. Wheaton, Ill.,
       Van Kampen Press, 1954. 158 p. Also published as: In a
       barley field.   R

2047   McGEE, John Vernon, 1904-
       The tabernacle: God's portrait of Christ. Wheaton, Ill.,
       Van Kampen Press, n.d. 97 p. Reprinted from Bibliotheca
       Sacra.   R

2048   McGEE, John Vernon, 1904-
       The theology of the tabernacle. n.p., n.d. various pag-
       ings. Reprinted from Bibliotheca Sacra, 1937-38.   C

2049   McGUFFEY, William Holmes, 1800-1873.
       The annotated McGuffey; selections from the McGuffey
       eclectic readers, 1836-1920, [by] Stanley W. Lindberg. New
       York, Van Nostrand Reinhold, © 1976. 358 p.   U

2050   McGUFFEY, William Holmes, 1800-1873.
       ... McGuffey's eclectic primer. Rev. ed. New York,
       American Book Co., © 1909. 64 p.   R

2051   McGUFFEY, William Holmes, 1800-1873.
       McGuffey's first- [sixth] eclectic reader. Rev. ed. New
       York, American Book Co., © 1920-© 1921. 6 v.   H L R

2052   McGUFFEY, William Holmes, 1800-1873.
       McGuffey's new eclectic spelling-book: embracing a pro-
       gressive course of instruction in English orthography and
       orthoepy; including dictation exercises. Electrotype ed.
       Cincinnati, Wilson, Hinkle & Co., © 1865. 144 p.   H ...
       H: Cincinnati; Van Antwerp, [186?]. 138 p.

2053   McGUFFEY, William Holmes, 1800-1873.
       ... McGuffey's new fifth eclectic reader: selected and
       original exercises for schools. Electrotype ed. Cincinnati,
       Sargent, Wilson & Hinkle, © 1857. 336 p.   H ... H R:
       Cincinnati, Van Antwerp, Bragg & Co., © 1866. 338 p. ...
       H: Enl. ed. Cincinnati, Wilson, Hinkle & Co., © 1866 ...
       A: [New York], New American Library, © 1962. 364 p.

2054   McGUFFEY, William Holmes, 1800-1873.

... McGuffey's new fourth eclectic reader: instructive lessons for the young. Enl. ed. Cincinnati, Wilson, Hinkle & Co., © 1866. 242 p. H ... H: New York, American Book Co., © 1896. 256 p.

2055 McGUFFEY, William Holmes, 1800-1873.
McGuffey's new sixth eclectic reader; exercises in rhetorical reading, with introductory rules and examples. Stereotype ed. Cincinnati, Sargent, Wilson & Hinkle, © 1857. 448 p. H ... H: Cincinnati, Winthrop B. Smith & Co., © 1857 ... A: [New York], New American Library, © 1962. 492 p.

2056 McGUFFEY, William Holmes, 1800-1873.
McGuffey's newly revised eclectic fourth reader: containing elegant extracts, in prose and poetry; with rules for reading, and exercises in articulation, defining, &c. Rev. and improved. Permanent stereotype ed. New York, Clark, Austin & Smith, © 1848. 336 p. H

2057 McGUFFEY, William Holmes, 1800-1873.
McGuffey's newly revised rhetorical guide; or fifth reader of the Eclectic series. Containing elegant extracts in prose and poetry: with copious rules and rhetorical exercises. Rev. and improved. Cincinnati, Winthrop B. Smith & Co., [1853]. 480 p. PH

2058 McGUFFEY, William Holmes, 1800-1873.
McGuffey's sixth eclectic reader. Rev. ed. New York, American Book Co., © 1896. 464 p. R

2059 McILWAIN, William Erskine, 1848-1938.
The early planting of Presbyterianism in West Florida. [Pensacola, Fla., Mayes Printing Co.], 1926. 23 p. A C U

2060 McILWAIN, William Erskine, 1848-1938.
Historical sketch of the Presbytery of Mecklenburg, from its organization, October 16th, 1869, to October 1st, 1884; with map of its territory, showing the location of its churches and those of the Associate Reformed Church within its bounds. Charlotte, N.C., Hirst Printing Co., [1884]. 91 p. C U

2061 McILWAINE, Richard, 1834-1913.
Addresses and papers bearing chiefly on education. Richmond, Whittet & Shepperson, © 1908. 184 p. A C H L U

2062 McILWAINE, Richard, 1834-1913.
Beneficiary education. Richmond, Presbyterian Committee of Publication, 1893. 22 p. U

2063 McILWAINE, Richard, 1834-1913.

Hampden-Sidney College, its relation and services to the Presbyterian Church, and to the cause of education and religion: a discourse, preached at the Second Presbyterian Church, Richmond, Virginia, February 5, 1888. n.p., n.d. 18 p.   PH

2064   McILWAINE, Richard, 1834-1913.
Memories of three-score years and ten.   New York, Neale Publishing Co., 1908.   383 p.   A C H PH R U

2065   McILWAINE, Richard, 1834-1913.
Suffrage; an address before the conference of Democratic members of the constitutional convention of Virginia, January 6, 1902.   n.p., n.d.   14 p.   U

2066   McILWAINE, William Andrew, 1893-
An analysis of the Covenant Life Curriculum.   Submitted to the Presbytery of Atlanta at its stated fall meeting, September 26, 1967.   n.p., 1967.   52 p.   C R

2067   McIVER, Malcolm Chester, 1917-
Principles for the development of Christian family education: a leader's guide.   Richmond, CLC Press, © 1963. 47 p.   (The Covenant Life Curriculum.)   C L U

2068   MACK, Edward, 1868-1951.
The Bible story of creation.   n.p., n.d.   15 p.   Reprinted from the Union Seminary Review, April, 1924.   U

2069   MACK, Edward, 1868-1951.
The Christ of the Old Testament.   Studies in the beginnings and growth of messianic prophecy.   Richmond, Presbyterian Committee of Publication, © 1926.   203 p.   A C R ... H L PT U: © 1926.   195 p. ... L: [1932].   203 p. ... R U: [1933].

2070   MACK, Edward, 1868-1951.
The Hebrew looks up to God and gets a religion for mankind.   Richmond, Presbyterian Committee of Publication, 1936.   251 p.   A C H L PT R U

2071   MACK, Edward, 1868-1951.
The office of the deacon: an interpretation of Chapter IV, Section IV, of the form of government, revised, and adopted by the General Assembly in 1922.   Richmond, Presbyterian Committee of Publication, © 1923.   48 p.   C PT U

2072   MACK, Edward, 1868-1951.
Our Presbyterian heritage in eastern Virginia.   A sermon delivered in Schauffler Hall, Union Theological Seminary in Virginia, on February 3, 1924.   n.p., n.d.   10 p.   Reprinted from Union Seminary Review, July, 1924.   H U

2073 MACK, Edward, 1868-1951.
The preacher's Old Testament. London, Fleming H.
Revell Co., © 1923. 158 p. The Stone Lectures, 1923.
A C H L PT R U

2074 *MACK, George H.
One hundred fifty years of Kentucky Presbyterianism,
1802-1952. Sesquicentennial celebration, jointly by the synods of Kentucky, Presbyterian Church, U.S. and U.S.A.
[by George H. Mack and Robert Stuart Sanders]. Danville,
Ky., n.p., 1951. 56 p. H L U

2075 MACK, William, 1807-1879.
Readings for families and vacant churches. Columbia,
Tenn., "Excelsior" News, Book and Job Office, 1876. 64 p.
H

2076 McKAY, Edward James.
The book of Revelation; or, The Apocalypse rightly divided
and interpreted. Raleigh, N.C., Mitchell Printing Co.,
© 1929. 82 p. A

2077 McKAY, Edward James.
The Day of the Lord, based on the Revelation, in verse.
4th ed., rev. and enl. [Raleigh, N.C., Mitchell Printing
Co.], 1954. 64 p. L ... H: 5th ed., rev. and enl.
Dunn, N.C., n.p., 1957. 63 p.

2078 McKAY, Edward James.
Justification by faith; or, An exposition of Galatians 3 and
Romans 3 and 4, to which is added an appendix on the cove-
nants between God and Abraham. Raleigh, N.C., Mitchell
Printing Co., © 1927. 33 p. A U

2079 McKAY, Edward James.
The last things of this age and the coming of our Lord ...
a short treatise, scriptural and comprehensive, for the busy
pastor and layman. Raleigh, N.C., Mitchell Printing Co.,
© 1926. 66 p. A

2080 McKAY, Edward James.
Pleadings and prayer for saved and unsaved in verse.
[Dunn, N.C., Pope Printing Co.], n.d. 12 p. U

2081 *MACKAY, George Leslie.
From far Formosa: the island, its people and missions....
Edited by the Rev. J. A. MacDonald. 2d ed. New York,
Fleming H. Revell Co., 1896. 346 p. PH PT

2082 McKAY, Neill, 1816-1893.
A centenary sermon, delivered before the Presbytery of
Fayetteville, at the Bluff Church, the 18th day of October,
1858. Fayetteville, Presbyterian Office, 1858. 19 p. PT

2083 McKEE, Dean Greer, 1904-
The minister as prophet. Inaugural address as Professor of Biblical Exposition, Columbia Theological Seminary, Monday, May 7, 1962. [Decatur, Ga., Columbia Theological Seminary, 1963]. 25-48 p. Columbia Theological Seminary Bulletin, August, 1963. C H PT R U

2084 McKELWAY, Alexander Jeffery, 1932-
The systematic theology of Paul Tillich, a review and analysis. Richmond, John Knox Press, © 1964. 280 p. C H L PT R U

2085 McKELWAY, Alexander Jeffrey, 1866-1918.
The Scotch-Irish of North Carolina. [Raleigh, W. S. Sherman, 1905]. 27 p. U

2086 MACKENZIE, James Donald, 1924-
Colorful heritage: an informal history of Barbecue Presbyterian Church and Bluff Presbyterian Church. n.p., © 1969. 149 p. H

2087 MACKENZIE, James Donald, 1924-
The Kirkwood story. Kannapolis, N.C., Kirkwood Presbyterian Church, [196?]. unpaged. C U

2088 MACKENZIE, John Anderson Ross, 1927-
Called Christian, named Church. Minneapolis, Minn., Winston Press, © 1972. 64 p. U

2089 MACKENZIE, John Anderson Ross, 1927-
Trying new sandals. Atlanta, John Knox Press, © 1973. 118 p. (The Covenant Life Curriculum.) U ... U: [1975]. 112 p.

2090 MACKENZIE, John Anderson Ross, 1927-
The word in action; the Acts of the Apostles for our time. Richmond, John Knox Press, © 1973. 128 p. (The Covenant Life Curriculum.) U

2091 McKINNON, Arch Cornelius, 1883-1967.
Kapitene of the Congo steamship Lapsley.... Treasures of darkness [by Fannie W. McKinnon. Boston, Christopher Publishing House, © 1968]. 295 p. A H L U

2092 McLAUGHLIN, Henry Woods, 1869-1950.
Christ and the country people. Richmond, Presbyterian Committee of Publication, © 1928. 159 p. A C H L PH PT R U

2093 McLAUGHLIN, Henry Woods, 1869-1950, ed.
The country church and public affairs. New York, The Macmillan Co., 1930. 260 p. A C H L PH U

2094 McLAUGHLIN, Henry Woods, 1869-1950.
The Gospel in action. Richmond, John Knox Press,
© 1944. 135 p. A C H L PT R U

2095 McLAUGHLIN, Henry Woods, 1869-1950.
The new call. Richmond, Presbyterian Committee of
Publication, © 1926. 189 p. A C H L PT R U

2096 McLAUGHLIN, Henry Woods, 1869-1950.
Religious education in the rural church. New York,
Fleming H. Revell Co., © 1932. 220 p. A C H L PT U

2097 McLEAN, James Dunning, 1856-1922.
Bible studies on baptism. Anniston, Ala., G. H. Norwood,
1885. 20 p. U ... PH U: Rev. ed. Richmond, Whittet
& Shepperson, n.d. 29 p.

2098 McLEAN, James Dunning, 1856-1922.
Bible studies on election. Richmond, Whittet & Shepperson, 1889. 60 p. U

2099 McLEAN, James Dunning, 1856-1922.
Bible studies on woman's position and work in the church.
Richmond, Whittet & Shepperson, 1893. 40 p. U

2100 MacLEAN, John Allan, 1891-
The most unforgettable character I've ever met. Richmond, John Knox Press, © 1945. 223 p. A C H L PT U

2101 McLEES, Richard Gustavus, 1864-1956.
Opening doors: my life's story. Weaverville, N.C.,
Southern Presbyterian Journal, 1954. 87 p. A C H R U

2102 McLEOD, William Angus, 1876-1947.
Fullinwider and McFarland, pioneer Texas Presbyterians;
a centennial address ... delivered before the Presbyterian
synods of Texas, U.S.A. and U.S., assembled in joint session in the First Presbyterian Church, Fort Worth, Texas,
September 23, 1931. [Cuero, Tex., Record, 1931]. 18 p.
A H PH PT

2103 McLEOD, William Angus, 1876-1947.
Story of the First Southern Presbyterian Church, Austin,
Texas. n.p., [1939]. 110 p. A C PH PT

2104 McMICHAEL, Jack Brame, 1911-
Congregations without deacons. [Atlanta, Materials Distribution Service, Presbyterian Church in the U.S., 1977].
28 p. L U

2105 McMICHAEL, Jack Brame, 1911-
The new superintendent. Richmond, John Knox Press,
[1950]. 45 p. U ... A C: [1954].

2106 McMICHAEL, Jack Brame, 1911-
    The school of the church; manual. Richmond, CLC Press,
© 1963. 47 p. (The Covenant Life Curriculum.) C L U

2107 McMILLAN, Homer, 1873-1958.
    Near neighbors. Richmond, Presbyterian Committee of
Publication, © 1930. 107 p. A C H L PT R U

2108 McMILLAN, Homer, 1873-1958.
    Other men labored. Richmond, Presbyterian Committee
of Publication, © 1937. 151 p. A C H L PT R U

2109 McMILLAN, Homer, 1873-1958.
    "Unfinished tasks" of the Southern Presbyterian Church.
Richmond, Presbyterian Committee of Publication, © 1922.
192 p. A C H L PT R U

2110 McMILLAN, James Pressley, 1831-1923.
    Presbyterian alienations and separations destructive; an
earnest plea for reunion. n.p., n.d. 8 p. U ... PT:
Rev. ed. n.p., 1919. 7 p.

2111 McMILLAN, Leighton Gaines, 1887-
    Some texts seldom preached on but I have found very use-
ful. [Mobile, Ala., Heiter-Starke Printing Co.], © 1963.
unpaged. C

2112 McMULLEN, John Stuart, 1915-
    Stewardship unlimited. A cooperative text published for
the Cooperative Publication Association. Richmond, John
Knox Press, © 1961. 94 p. A C H L U

2113 McMULLEN, Robert Burns, 1807-1865.
    The difference between Old and New School Presbyterians,
in doctrine and polity. Knoxville, Tenn., The Register
Office, 1854. 27 p. PH

2114 McMULLEN, Robert Burns, 1807-1865.
    A discourse on the death of James Park, Esq., who de-
parted this life on the 19th Sept., 1853. Knoxville, Tenn.,
The Register Office, 1854. 16 p. PH

2115 McMULLEN, Robert Burns, 1807-1865.
    The history of the First Presbyterian Church, in Knoxville,
Tennessee. A discourse delivered by the pastor ... at the
dedication of their new house of worship, March 25th, 1855.
Knoxville, Tenn., John B. G. Kinsloe, 1855. 28 p. PT

2116 McMURRY, Stonewall Jackson, 1862-1946.
    "Future probation," the Presbyterial sermon. Taylor,
Tex., Presbytery of Central Texas, 1922. 7 p. PH

2117 McMURRY, Stonewall Jackson, 1862-1946.

Social service: alumni address at the Austin Presbyterian
Theological Seminary.... Constitution and minutes. Austin,
Tex., n.p., 1914. 19 p. PT

2118 McMURTRY, James Gilmer, 1870-1954.
"The eschatology of the Westminster Confession of Faith."
A doctrinal sermon, by order of Brazos Presbytery, at the
spring meeting, El Campo, Texas, April 17-18, 1951. n.p.,
[1951]. unpaged. PT

2119 McNEILL, Robert Blakely, 1915-1975.
God wills us free: the ordeal of a Southern minister. Introduction by Ralph McGill. New York, Hill and Wang, © 1965.
210 p. A C L PT R U

2120 McNEILL, Robert Blakely, 1915-1975.
Prophet, speak now! Richmond, John Knox Press, © 1961.
92 p. A C H L PT R U

2121 McNEILLY, James Hugh, 1838-1922.
The death of little children. A letter to bereaved parents.
[Richmond, Presbyterian Committee of Publication], n.d.
8 p. U

2122 McNEILLY, James Hugh, 1838-1922.
Religion and slavery; a vindication of the southern churches.
Nashville, Tenn., Publishing House of the M. E. Church,
South, 1911. 88 p. H U

2123 McPHEETERS, William Marcellus, 1854-1935.
The book of Kings: its occasion, theme and purpose.
n.p., n.d. 10 p. C

2124 McPHEETERS, William Marcellus, 1854-1935.
"The book of the twelve prophets, commonly called the
minor": considered as a type. n.p., n.d. 427-542 p.
Reprinted from the Presbyterian Quarterly, July, 1899.
A C

2125 McPHEETERS, William Marcellus, 1854-1935.
Christ as an interpreter of Scripture. n.p., [1900]. 13 p.
Reprinted from the Bible Student, January and April, 1900.
C

2126 McPHEETERS, William Marcellus, 1854-1935.
Columbia Seminary, a noble record of service. [Colum-
bia, S.C.], R. L. Bryan Co., [1901?]. 21 p. C

2127 McPHEETERS, William Marcellus, 1854-1935.
Dr. Briggs higher criticism of the Hexateuch. n.p., n.d.
505-528 p. Reprinted from the Presbyterian Quarterly,
October, 1895. A C

2128 McPHEETERS, William Marcellus, 1854-1935.
      Dr. Driver on the authorship of Isaiah XIII. and XIV.
      Richmond, Whittet & Shepperson, 1894. 25 p. Reprinted
      from the Presbyterian Quarterly, April, 1894. A C PT

2129 McPHEETERS, William Marcellus, 1854-1935.
      The facts in the case of Dr. Hay Watson Smith and Ar-
      kansas Presbytery. Decatur, Ga., Columbia Theological
      Seminary, 1931. 32 p. R U

2130 McPHEETERS, William Marcellus, 1854-1935.
      Facts revealed by the records in the so-called investiga-
      tion of the rumors abroad concerning the soundness in the
      faith of Rev. Dr. Hay Watson Smith. [Decatur, Ga., n.p.,
      1934]. 119 p. A R

2131 McPHEETERS, William Marcellus, 1854-1935.
      A glance at theological encyclopaedia. n.p., n.d. 14 p.
      C

2132 McPHEETERS, William Marcellus, 1854-1935.
      God's ultimatum. [Richmond, Presbyterian Committee of
      Publication], n.d. 4 p. U

2133 McPHEETERS, William Marcellus, 1854-1935.
      The higher criticism: definition and classification. Rich-
      mond, Whittet & Shepperson, 1903. 29 p. Reprinted from
      the Presbyterian Quarterly, July, 1903. C

2134 McPHEETERS, William Marcellus, 1854-1935.
      Interpretation. [Columbia, S.C., R. L. Bryan Co.], n.d.
      35 p. PT

2135 McPHEETERS, William Marcellus, 1854-1935.
      The interpreter's task. n.p., n.d. 4 p. Reprinted
      from the Christian Observer, August 16 and 23, 1905. C

2136 McPHEETERS, William Marcellus, 1854-1935.
      An introduction to Hebrew syntax. n.p., n.d. 26 p.
      A C

2137 McPHEETERS, William Marcellus, 1854-1935.
      The latest criticism and the canon of the Old Testament.
      New York, Funk & Wagnalls Co., [1903?]. 23-28, 114-120 p.
      Reprinted from the Homiletic Review, January and February,
      1903. C

2138 McPHEETERS, William Marcellus, 1854-1935.
      A modern minister's message. [New Orleans, E. S. Up-
      ton Printing Co., 1910?]. 31 p. Paper read at a conference
      at Montreat, N.C., August 18, 1910. C

2139 McPHEETERS, William Marcellus, 1854-1935.

Objections to apostolic authorship, or sanction as the ultimate test of canonicity. n.p., n.d. 26-68 p. Reprinted from the Presbyterian and Reformed Review, January, 1895. A C

2140 McPHEETERS, William Marcellus, 1854-1935.
The question of the authorship of the books of Scripture: a criticism of current views. n.p., n.d. 362-383 p. Reprinted from the Princeton Theological Review, July 1903. C

2141 McPHEETERS, William Marcellus, 1854-1935.
Questions for the junior class: the canon. n.p., n.d. 4 p. A C

2142 McPHEETERS, William Marcellus, 1854-1935.
A recently proposed test of canonicity. Inaugural address on the occasion of his installation as Professor of Biblical Literature in the Theological Seminary at Columbia, S.C., May, 1890. n.p., n.d. 33-55 p. Reprinted from the Presbyterian Quarterly, July, 1890. A C PT

2143 McPHEETERS, William Marcellus, 1854-1935.
A remarkable claim on behalf of the radical criticism. n.p., n.d. 679-693 p. Reprinted from Bibliotheca Sacra, October, 1908. C

2144 McPHEETERS, William Marcellus, 1854-1935.
A reply to a communication of Rev. Dr. Hay Watson Smith, Little Rock, Arkansas, appearing in the Columbia State, October 27, 1929. [Decatur, Ga., n.p., 1930]. 27 p. A R U

2145 McPHEETERS, William Marcellus, 1854-1935.
The science of interpretation and notes on particular introduction. Pamphlets prepared ... for use in classes at Columbia Theological Seminary. n.p., n.d. variously paged. C

2146 McPHEETERS, William Marcellus, 1854-1935.
Some strictures on current conceptions of Biblical criticism. n.p., n.d. 125-146 p. Reprinted from Bibliotheca Sacra, April, 1920. C

2147 McPHEETERS, William Marcellus, 1854-1935.
The spirituality of the church. n.p., n.d. 21 p. Reprinted from a series of articles in the St. Louis Presbyterian reviewing Rev. Dr. S. J. Baird's pamphlet on 'Reunion." C H U

2148 McPHEETERS, William Marcellus, 1854-1935.
Studies in the book of Joel. n.p., n.d. 16 p. C

2149 McPHEETERS, William Marcellus, 1854-1935.
The study of the Bible in the original languages at the
Seminary. n.p., n.d. 542-566 p. Reprinted from the
Presbyterian Quarterly, October, 1891. A C PT

2150 McQUEEN, John Wilber, 1907-1976.
I choose Jesus, [by John W. and Sally McQueen. Richmond, John Knox Press], © 1956. 15 p. U

2151 McQUEEN, John Wilber, 1907-1976.
I want to know about my church, by Chaplain and Mrs.
John W. McQueen. Richmond, John Knox Press, © 1946.
95 p. U

2152 *McQUILKIN, Marguerite.
Always in triumph: the life of Robert C. McQuilkin.
Columbia, S.C., Bible College Bookstore, [1956]. 255 p.
C U

2153 McQUILKIN, Robert Crawford, 1886-1952.
The baptism of the Spirit: shall we seek it? 2d ed.
n.p., 1935. 35 p. Originally published in the Sunday School
Times with the title, "What is Pentecost's message today?"
U

2154 McQUILKIN, Robert Crawford, 1886-1952.
Can we trust the Old Testament? Discussing the meaning
of the miracles, the morals, the judgments, the prophecies,
of the Old Testament, and the "historical view" of the Bible.
Columbia, S.C., Columbia Bible College, [1932]. 53 p. U

2155 McQUILKIN, Robert Crawford, 1886-1952.
Four fundamentals. Fundamental or supplemental? Columbia, S.C., Columbia Bible College, © 1946. 22 p. R U

2156 McQUILKIN, Robert Crawford, 1886-1952.
God's law and God's grace. Grand Rapids, Mich., Wm.
B. Eerdmans Publishing Co., © 1958. 90 p. A U

2157 McQUILKIN, Robert Crawford, 1886-1952.
"Let not your heart be troubled." John Fourteen: chapter
of resurrection life. Columbia, S.C., Columbia Bible College, © 1941. 65 p. H R

2158 McQUILKIN, Robert Crawford, 1886-1952.
"Lord, teach us to pray." How the Lord's Prayer teaches
us to pray. Columbia, S.C., Columbia Bible College,
© 1943. 94 p. R

2159 McQUILKIN, Robert Crawford, 1886-1952.
The message of Romans, an exposition. Grand Rapids,
Mich., Zondervan Publishing House, © 1947. 178 p. R U

2160 McQUILKIN, Robert Crawford, 1886-1952.
Outline and message of Romans. Columbia, S.C., Columbia Bible School, © 1925. 64 p. R

2161 McQUILKIN, Robert Crawford, 1886-1952.
Studying our Lord's parables; a series of studies. Grand
Rapids, Mich., Zondervan Publishing House, 1935. 168 p.
H PT R U

2162 McQUILKIN, Robert Crawford, 1886-1952.
Studying our Lord's parables for yourself. First series.
Columbia, S.C., Columbia Bible School, © 1929. 80 p.
R ... R: second series. © 1933. 112 p.

2163 McQUILKIN, Robert Crawford, 1886-1952.
Victorious life studies. Philadelphia, Christian Life
Literature Fund, © 1918. 104 p. A PT R ... R: Rev.
and enl. ed. © 1918. 128 p.

2164 McQUILKIN, Robert Crawford, 1886-1952.
Victory in Christ; or, Taking God at his word. A personal testimony. Columbia, S.C., Columbia Bible College,
n.d. 51 p. R

2165 MADDOX, Finnis Ewing, 1870-1939.
The passing of medievalism in religion. A series of ser-
mons delivered in First Presbyterian Church, Texarkana,
Ark., issuing in a heresy trial before Ouchita Presbytery,
July 14, 1908. Texarkana, Ark., The Texarkanian, 1908.
77 p. PT

2166 MAHLER, Henry Richard, 1911-
Some problems and opportunities facing the church in Tennessee and the South which have their roots in Presbyterian
history. n.p., [1961]. 12 p. An address delivered at the
meeting of the Synod of Tennessee, May 16, 1961, as a part
of the Centennial observance of the Presbyterian Church in
the United States. H PH U

2167 *MAKEMIE, Francis, 1658-1708.
The life and writings of Francis Makemie. Edited with
an introduction by Boyd S. Schlenther. Philadelphia, Presbyterian Historical Society, 1971. 287 p. A C H L PH
PT U

2168 MALCOLM, Henry Webb, 1934-
Generation of Narcissus. [1st ed.] Boston, Little, Brown,
© 1971. 266 p. A C PH ... C: Japan, Chinchosa, 1973.
238 p. In Japanese.

2169 MALLARD, Robert Quarterman, 1830-1904.
Montevideo-Maybank: some memoirs of a Southern

Christian household in the olden time; or, The family life of the Rev. Charles Colcock Jones, D.D. Richmond, Presbyterian Committee of Publication, © 1898. 87 p. A H PT R U

2170 MALLARD, Robert Quarterman, 1830-1904.
Plantation life before emancipation. Richmond, Whittet & Shepperson, 1892. 237 p. A C H L R U

2171 MALLARD, Robert Quarterman, 1830-1904.
Thy testimonies. Richmond, Presbyterian Committee of Publication, 1893. 45 p. Originally delivered as baccalaureate sermon June 5, 1892, at the Southwestern Presbyterian University, Clarkesville, Tenn. A PT U

2172 MANN, Charles Iverson, 1931-
Ministry to families with teenagers. [Atlanta, Division of National Mission, Presbyterian Church in the U.S., 1977?]. 30 p. U

2173 MARKHAM, Thomas Railey, 1828-1894.
A historical and commemorative discourse, delivered in the Lafayette Presbyterian Church, New Orleans, La., Sabbath, Dec. 19, 1880. New Orleans, Hopkins' Printing Office, 1881. 41 p. PH

2174 MARKHAM, Thomas Railey, 1828-1894.
S. W. P. University. Commencement oration, delivered in Cabinet Hall, June 9, 1886. n.p., n.d. 17 p. PH

2175 MARQUESS, William Hoge, 1854-1921.
The ministry: a challenge and an appeal to Christian young men. Louisville, Ky., Executive Committee of Christian Education and Ministerial Relief, Presbyterian Church in the U.S., n.d. 24 p. U

2176 MARQUESS, William Hoge, 1854-1921.
Prayer for men for the ministry. [Louisville, Ky., Executive Committee of Christian Education and Ministerial Relief, Presbyterian Church in the U.S.], n.d. 15 p. U

2177 MARQUESS, William Hoge, 1854-1921.
Recruiting for the ministry. Louisville, Ky., Executive Committee of Christian Education and Ministerial Relief, Presbyterian Church in the U.S., n.d. 14 p. U

2178 *MARSH, Dwight Whitney, 1823-1896.
The Tennesseean in Persia and Koordistan. Being scenes and incidents in the life of Samuel Audley Rhea. Philadelphia, Presbyterian Board of Publication, © 1869. 381 p. H PH PT

2179 MARSH, Spencer William, 1931-

Edith the Good: the transformation of Edith Bunker from total woman to total person. [1st ed.] New York, Harper & Row, © 1977. 82 p. C PT R U

2180 MARSH, Spencer William, 1931-
God, man, and Archie Bunker. Foreword by Carroll O'Connor. [1st ed.] New York, Harper & Row, © 1975. 104 p. C PT R U ... L: New York, Bantam Books, [1976]. 111 p.

2181 *MARSHALL, Catherine (Wood), 1914-
Friends with God; stories and prayers of the Marshall family. New York, Whittlesey House, [1956]. 48 p. C U

2182 *MARSHALL, Catherine (Wood), 1914-
God loves you; our family's favorite stories and prayers, by Catherine and Peter Marshall. New York, Whittlesey House, [1953]. 48 p. U ... C PT: 2d ed. New York, McGraw-Hill Book Co., © 1967. 59 p.

2183 *MARSHALL, Catherine (Wood), 1914-
A man called Peter: the story of Peter Marshall. New York, McGraw-Hill Book Co., © 1951. 354 p. A C H L PT R U ... PH: Greenwich, Conn., Fawcett Publications, [1964]. 351 p.

2184 *MARSHALL, Catherine (Wood), 1914-
The mystery of the ages, by Catherine and Peter Marshall. Philadelphia, Westminster Press, © 1944. 32 p. PH

2185 *MARSHALL, Catherine (Wood), 1914-
Peter didn't leave a will. New York, United Presbyterian Foundation, [1958]. unpaged. From the book, "To live again." PH

2186 MARSHALL, James Williams, 1882-1964.
The Presbyterian Church in Alabama, a record of the growth of the Presbyterian Church from its beginning in 1811 in the eastern portion of Mississippi territory to the centennial of the Synod of Alabama in 1936.... Robert Strong, editor. Montgomery, Ala., Presbyterian Historical Society of Alabama, 1977. 493 p. A C H PH R U

2187 MARSHALL, Peter, 1902-1949.
Apples of gold: new and inspiring messages.... Selected by Stanley Hendricks. [Kansas City, Mo., Hallmark Cards, Inc.], © 1969. 61 p. H

2188 MARSHALL, Peter, 1902-1949.
The argument of the empty tomb. An address ... delivered ... on November 8th, 1940, in the Arch Street Presbyterian Church, Philadelphia. n.p., n.d. 11 p. PT

2189   MARSHALL, Peter, 1902-1949.
       The exile heart. [1st ed. Washington, D.C.], Peter
Marshall Scottish Memorial Committee, 1949. 157 p. A
compilation of the author's Scottish sermons and addresses.
H PT U ... L U: [2d ed.] 1949 ... C: 3d ed.

2190   MARSHALL, Peter, 1902-1949.
       The first Easter. Edited and with an introduction by
Catherine Marshall. [1st ed.] New York, McGraw-Hill
Book Co., © 1959. 137 p. C H L PH R U

2191   MARSHALL, Peter, 1902-1949.
       The heart of Peter Marshall's faith: two inspirational
messages ... from Mr. Jones, meet the Master. [Westwood,
N.J.], Fleming H. Revell Co., © 1956. 46 p. C L R

2192   MARSHALL, Peter, 1902-1949.
       John Doe, disciple; sermons for the young in spirit.
Edited and with introductions by Catherine Marshall. Preface by Peter John Marshall. New York, McGraw-Hill Book
Co., © 1963. 222 p. Published also as "Under sealed
orders." A C L U

2193   MARSHALL, Peter, 1902-1949.
       Keepers of the springs, and other messages from Mr.
Jones, meet the Master. [Westwood, N.J.], Fleming H.
Revell Co., © 1962. 60 p. C U

2194   MARSHALL, Peter, 1902-1949.
       Let's keep Christmas. [A sermon.] Introduction by
Catherine Marshall. New York, McGraw-Hill Book Co.,
© 1953. unpaged. A C L U

2195   MARSHALL, Peter, 1902-1949.
       Mr. Jones, meet the Master: sermons and prayers.
New York, Fleming H. Revell Co., © 1949. 192 p. A
C L PT U ... H U: Rev. © 1950.

2196   MARSHALL, Peter, 1902-1949.
       Peter Marshall: new and inspiring messages. Selected
by Stanley Hendricks. [Kansas City, Mo.], Hallmark Editions, © 1969. 61 p. Formerly "Apples of gold." U

2197   MARSHALL, Peter, 1902-1949.
       Peter Marshall's lasting prayers, with encouragement to
prayer in the drawings of Jack Hamm. [1st ed.] Anderson,
S.C., Droke House Publishers, © 1969. unpaged. C PT

2198   MARSHALL, Peter, 1902-1949.
       The prayers of Peter Marshall. Edited and with prefaces
by Catherine Marshall. New York, McGraw-Hill Book Co.,
© 1954. 243 p. A C H L PH PT U

2199   MARSHALL, Peter, 1902-1949.
       The prayers of Peter Marshall. Edited and with prefaces
       by Catherine Marshall. Carmel, N.Y., Guideposts Asso-
       ciates, © 1954. 173 p. Bound with: John Doe, disciple.
       Sermons for the young in spirit. Edited and with introduc-
       tions by Catherine Marshall. Preface by Peter John Mar-
       shall. Carmel, N.Y., Guideposts Associates, © 1963.
       187 p.   PT

2200   MARSHALL, Peter, 1902-1949.
       Prayers offered by the chaplain ... at the opening of the
       daily sessions of the Senate of the United States during the
       Eightieth and Eighty-first congresses, 1947-1949. Washing-
       ton, D.C., United States Government Printing Office, 1949.
       97 p. (81st Congress, 1st Session ... Senate Document no.
       86.)   A L PH PT U

2201   MARSHALL, Peter, 1902-1949.
       Prayers. Selections from the prayers offered while chap-
       lain of the United States Senate. New York, Fifth Avenue
       Presbyterian Church, [1949?]. 15 p.   A

2202   MARSHALL, Peter, 1902-1949.
       Sermons.... Washington, D.C., New York Avenue Pres-
       byterian Church, n.d. various pagings. Printed sermons
       bound together.   A U

2203   MARSHALL, Peter, 1902-1949.
       Under sealed orders. Edited and with introductions by
       Catherine Marshall. Preface by Peter John Marshall. Lon-
       don, Hodder and Stoughton, [1971]. 224 p. Published also
       as John Doe, disciple.   C

2204   MARSTON, George W., 1905-
       Are you a biblical Baptist? Philadelphia, Committee on
       Christian Education, Orthodox Presbyterian Church, 1958.
       27 p.   R

2205   MARSTON, George W., 1905-
       The voice of authority. [Nutley, N.J.], Presbyterian and
       Reformed Publishing Co., 1960. 110 p.   PT R U

2206   MARTIN, Arthur Morrison, 1902-
       The Flemington Martins. Columbia, S.C., State Printing
       Co., 1970. 114 p.   H

2207   MARTIN, James Laval, 1838-1922.
       Anti-evolution: Girardeau vs. Woodrow. [Memphis, Tenn.,
       n.p., 1888]. 16 p.   C PT U

2208   MARTIN, James Laval, 1838-1922.
       Campbellism: a testimony. St. Louis, J. T. Smith,
       1893. 12 p.   C PT

2209 MARTIN, James Laval, 1838-1922.
Dr. Girardeau's anti-evolution: the logic of his reply.
Columbia, S.C., Presbyterian Publishing House, 1889. 65 p.
Appendix: From the Christian Observer: Reply to Dr. Martin: What is a miracle? by J. L. Girardeau. A C PT U

2210 MARTIN, James Laval, 1838-1922.
The duty of elders in vacant charges and partially supplied pastorates. [Published originally by request of Elders' and Deacons' Convention, held in connection with the meeting of the Synod of Texas, in Fort Worth, Texas, October 19-20, 1893] n.p., n.d. 16 p. PT U

2211 MARTIN, James Laval, 1838-1922.
"Kronon mikron, " the "little season"--(King James); "A little time"--(R.V.), Revelation 20:3. Originally prepared for the Ministers' Association of Abbeville, S.C. Columbia, S.C., R. L. Bryan Co., 1917. 8 p. PT

2212 MARTIN, Joseph Hamilton, 1825-1887.
The Declaration of Independence: a poem commemorating the one hundredth anniversary of the national birth-day of the United States of America. [New York], The author, 1876. 71 p. C R

2213 MARTIN, Joseph Hamilton, 1825-1887.
The influence, bearing, and effects of Romanism on the civil and religious liberties of our country. New York, n.p., 1844. 47 p. PT

2214 MARTIN, William T., 1921-1956.
The power of an upward look, and other sermons. Tallahassee, Fla., Peninsular Publishing Co., © 1957. 176 p. C H U

2215 MARTINDALE, Charles O'Neale, 1868-1950.
1892 announcement of the YMCA at Columbia, S.C. Columbia, Bryan Printing Co., n.d. 17 p. U

2216 MARTINDALE, Charles O'Neale, 1868-1950.
What it means to be a Christian. Chicago, Neely Printing Co., © 1927. 136 p. A C H L U

2217 MARYOSIP, Michael, 1884-1950.
Why I believe the Bible. Foreword by Thomas W. Currie.
Grand Rapids, Mich., Zondervan Publishing House, © 1937. 136 p. A H L U

2218 MATTHEWS, John Daniel, 1809-1884.
A tribute to the memory of Mrs. Mary Tilford, in a sermon. Lexington, Ky., Office of the Observer and Reporter, 1850. 18 p. PH

2219 MATTHEWS, Mark Allison, 1867-1940.
Building the church. New York, American Tract Society,
© 1940. 193 p. PT U

2220 MATTHEWS, Mark Allison, 1867-1940.
Gospel sword thrusts. New York, Fleming H. Revell Co.,
© 1924. 156 p. A H L R U

2221 MATTHEWS, Mark Allison, 1867-1940.
"In the beginning God--" and other talks. Chicago, Bible
Institute Colportage Ass'n., © 1924. 30 p. PH

2222 MATTHEWS, Mark Allison, 1867-1940.
The seven R's of the full Gospel and other sermons.
Grand Rapids, Mich., Zondervan Publishing House, [1940?].
101 p. L U

2223 MATTHEWS, Mark Allison, 1867-1940.
The victories of faith versus the failures of unbelief. A
sermon preached by the retiring moderator ... before the
125th General Assembly of the Presbyterian Church, U.S.A.,
at Atlanta, Georgia, May 15, 1913. [Philadelphia, Magazine Press], n.d. 15 p. PH

2224 MAURY, Thompson B.
An apology for renouncing the Episcopal ministry. [Louis-
ville, Ky., Davidson & Robinson], 1867. 12 p. PH

2225 MAURY, Thompson B.
"Apostolic succession" the claim of false teachers. An
answer to a sermon published by the Right Rev. William
Green, D.D., Prot. Epis. Bishop of Mississippi. Washington, D.C., Wm. Ballantyne, 1867. 21 p. PH

2226 MAYS, James Luther, 1921-
Amos: a commentary. Philadelphia, Westminster Press,
© 1969. 168 p. (The Old Testament Library.) A C L
PT R ... U: [1976] ... C R U: London, SCM Press,
[1969].

2227 MAYS, James Luther, 1921-
The book of Leviticus. The book of Numbers. Rich-
mond, John Knox Press, © 1963. 143 p. (The Layman's
Bible Commentary, v. 4.) A C H L PT R U

2228 MAYS, James Luther, 1921-
Exegesis as a theological discipline.... Inaugural address
[as Professor of Biblical Interpretation] delivered April 20,
1960, in Schauffler Hall, Union Theological Seminary. Richmond, Union Theological Seminary, n.d. 31 p. A C H
PT R U

2229 MAYS, James Luther, 1921-

Ezekiel, Second Isaiah. Philadelphia, Fortress Press, © 1978. 96 p. (Proclamation Commentaries.) A C L PT R U

2230 MAYS, James Luther, 1921-
Hosea: a commentary. Philadelphia, Westminster Press, © 1969. 190 p. (The Old Testament Library.) A L PT U ... C U: London, SCM Press, [1969].

2231 MAYS, James Luther, 1921-
Micah: a commentary. Philadelphia, Westminster Press, © 1976. 169 p. (The Old Testament Library.) A C L PH PT R U

2232 *MEANS, Robert, -1836.
Sermons, and an essay on the Pentateuch ... with an introduction and a sermon occasioned by his death, by George Howe, Professor of Biblical Literature in the Theol. Sem., Columbia, S.C. Boston, Perkins and Marvin, 1836. 610 p. C H R U

2233 MECKLIN, John Moffatt, 1871-1956.
Democracy and race friction; a study in social ethics. New York, The Macmillan Co., 1914. 273 p. H ... L U: Freeport, N.Y., Books for Libraries Press, [1970].

2234 MECKLIN, John Moffatt, 1871-1956.
An introduction to social ethics: the social conscience in a democracy. London, George Routledge & Sons, 1920. 446 p. PT

2235 MECKLIN, John Moffatt, 1871-1956.
The Ku Klux Klan: a study of the American mind. New York, Harcourt, Brace and Co., © 1924. 244 p. H PT ... A C U: New York, Russell & Russell, 1963.

2236 MECKLIN, John Moffatt, 1871-1956.
My quest for freedom. New York, Charles Scribner's Sons, 1945. 293 p. C PT

2237 MECKLIN, John Moffatt, 1871-1956.
The passing of the saint: a study of a cultural type. Chicago, University of Chicago Press, © 1941. 205 p. L PT U

2238 MECKLIN, John Moffatt, 1871-1956.
Report of the joint committee of inquiry of the American Philosophical Association and the American Psychological Association on the professorship of philosophy and psychology at Lafayette College. n.p., n.d. 67-81 p. Reprinted from the Journal of Philosophy, Psychology and Scientific Methods, January 29, 1914. PT

2239   MECKLIN, John Moffatt, 1871-1956.
        The story of American dissent. [1st ed.] New York,
        Harcourt, Brace and Co., © 1934. 381 p. A C H L PH
        PT R U

2240   MECKLIN, John Moffatt, 1871-1956.
        The survival value of Christianity. New York, Harcourt,
        Brace and Co., © 1926. 260 p. H L PT R

2241   MECKLIN, Robert Wilson, 1843-1914.
        The twin parables; or, The mysteries of the Kingdom of
        God: a series of expository sermons on some of the leading
        parables of our Lord. Richmond, Whittet & Shepperson,
        1892. 135 p. A H U

2242   MEDICINE and religion; strategies of care. Donald W. Shriv-
        er, Jr., editor. Pittsburgh, University of Pittsburgh
        Press, © 1980. 173 p. C L U

2243   MEEKS, Wayne Atherton, 1932-
        Go from your father's house: a college student's intro-
        duction to the Christian faith. Richmond, CLC Press,
        © 1964. 356 p. (The Covenant Life Curriculum.) C R
        U ... L: [1967] ... C R U: Teacher's book. 156 p. ...
        L: [1967].

2244   MEEKS, Wayne Atherton, 1932-
        Jews and Christians in Antioch in the first four centuries
        of the common era, by Wayne A. Meeks and Robert L. Wil-
        ken. Missoula, Mont., Published by Scholars Press for the
        Society of Biblical Literature, © 1978. 127 p. A C L PT
        U

2245   MEEKS, Wayne Atherton, 1932-
        The prophet-king. Moses traditions and the Johannine
        Christology. Leiden, E. J. Brill, 1967. 356 p. (Supple-
        ments to Novum Testamentum. 14.) Thesis--Yale Univer-
        sity, 1965. A C L PT R U

2246   MEEKS, Wayne Atherton, 1932-   ed.
        The writings of St. Paul. [1st ed.] New York, W. W.
        Norton & Co., © 1972. 454 p. A C L PT R U

2247   MELTON, Julius Wemyss, 1933-
        Presbyterian worship in America: changing patterns since
        1787. Richmond, John Knox Press, © 1967. 173 p. A C
        H L PH PT U

2248   MELVIN, Marion Edmund, 1876-1954.
        Royal partnership. New York, Fleming H. Revell Co.,
        © 1926. 87 p. A C H L PH PT R U

2249   MELVIN, Marion Edmund, 1876-1954.

The Royal partnership. Seoul, Korea, Christian Literature Society, 1933. unpaged. Translation into Korean by John C. Crane. U

2250 MEMORIAL addresses on the life and character of Rev. Evander McNair, D.D., delivered at Sardis Church, Cumberland County, N.C., May 28, 1886. Richmond, Whittet & Shepperson, 1886. 48 p. H

2251 MEMORIAL of Rev. E. A. Ramsey, D.D. [Sermon by Rev. J. H. McNeilly, D.D.] n.p., [1898?]. 66 p. H

2252 A MEMORIAL of the late Rev. William H. Adams, for twelve years pastor of the Circular Church, Charleston, S.C. Published by his friends, and members of the congregation. [Charleston, Walker, Evans & Cogswell, 1880]. 64 p. Funeral address by Rev. G. R. Brackett. H PT

2253 MEMORIAL of the Rev. James Park, D.D., for sixty-six years a preacher of the Gospel of our Lord Jesus Christ. Born September 18, 1822; died July 14, 1912. [By J. W. Bachman and J. H. McNeilly.] Nashville, Tenn., Publishing House of the M. E. Church, South, 1912. 38 p. H PH PT

2254 A MEMORIAL of the Rev. John Pinkerton, pastor of the Mossy Creek Presbyterian Church, from November 5, 1853, to May 31st, 1871. [Singer's Glen, Va., Joseph Funks Sons, 1871.] 32 p. PH

2255 MEMORIAL service at Central Presbyterian Church, Washington, D.C., February 10, 1924, in honor of Woodrow Wilson, President of the United States March 4, 1913, to March 4, 1921, a regular attendant at this church. [Washington, D.C., National Capital Press, 1924.] 14 p. Memorial address by Rev. James H. Taylor. H U

2256 MEMORIAL service [for James Turner Leftwich] held in the First Presbyterian Church, Baltimore, Md., Wednesday, March 3rd, 1897, Eight p.m. n.p., n.d. 35 p. H PH

2257 MEMORIAL tablet in honor of the Rev. John H. Rice, D.D. Addresses at the unveiling and dedication, delivered in the chapel of Union Theological Seminary, Va., May 5, 1885, by the Rev. B. M. Smith, D.D., and the Rev. Theodorick Pryor, D.D. Richmond, Whittet & Shepperson, 1885. 18 p. C H PH U

2258 A MEMORIAL to Reverend William Parker Neilson, D.D., pastor, Idlewild Presbyterian Church, May 1921 to May 1925. Prepared under the direction of the session. [Memphis, Tenn., Memphis Linotype Printing Co., 1925?] 30 p. PT

2259 MEMORIALS. Rev. Henry Elias Dosker, D.D., LL.D., L.H.D., Professor of Church History, Louisville Presbyterian Theological Seminary. Died December 23, 1926. n.p., [1927?]. 75 p. Participants included Teunis E. Gouwens, John M. Vander Meulen, Lewis J. Sherrill, Charles R. Hamphill. C H L PT

2260 MEMORIAM of the Rev. Gilbert R. Brackett, D.D., late pastor of the Second Presbyterian Church, Charleston, S.C. Adopted by Charleston Presbytery. Charleston, S.C., Walker, Evans & Cogswell, 1904. 13 p. H PH

2261 MEZA, Herbert, 1922-
The kiss ... the cross ... the tomb ... "Personalities of the passion." Arranged and edited by Bob McKinney. Houston, Tex., St. Stephen Presbyterian Church [1960]. 17 p. U

2262 MEZA, Herbert, 1922-
"... to serve the present age"; a basic Bible study of Christ's mission and the church's mission in the world today. With study guide and discussion questions for individual and group use. Nashville, Tenn., Board of World Missions, Presbyterian Church in the U.S., © 1964. 79 p. "Messages ... presented at the World Mission Conference ... in Montreat, North Carolina, July 30 to August 5, 1964." A R U

2263 MICKEL, Philip Alexander, 1897-1954.
Jochebed's son. Victoria, Va., P. A. Mickel, © 1941. 51 p. A C H

2264 MILES, Robert Whitfield, 1890-1952.
Christians and world order. Louisville, Ky., Joint Committee on Student Work, Westminster Fellowship of Students, [1944?]. 35 p. U

2265 MILES, Robert Whitfield, 1890-1952.
That Frenchman, John Calvin. New York, Fleming H. Revell Co., © 1939. 221 p. A H L PH PT U

2266 MILLER, Arnold W., 1822-1892.
The law of the tithe, and of the free-will offering, and of alms-giving. Columbia, S.C., Presbyterian Publishing House, 1873. 121 p. Republished from the Southern Presbyterian Review, April, 1873. C H

2267 MILLER, Arnold W., 1822-1892.
Memorial sketches of Rev. Robert Hall Morrison, D.D., by Rev. A. W. Miller and Gen. D. H. Hill. Charlotte, N.C., Hirst Printing Co., 1889. 16 p. H

2268 MILLER, Arnold W., 1822-1892.

Report on fraternal relations, presented to the Presbytery of Mecklenburgh, at Mallard Creek Church, May 4, 1883. Charlotte, N.C., Journal-Observer Steam Job Presses, 1883. 24 p.   C

2269 MILLER, Arnold W., 1822-1892.
The restoration of the Jews. Atlanta, Constitution Publishing Co., 1887. 59 p. Reprinted from the Presbyterian Quarterly, July and October, 1887.   U

2270 MILLER, Arnold W., 1822-1892.
The status of the baptized child. The substance of a discourse preached by appointment of the Synod of Virginia, on the 8th of October, 1859, and published at its request. Petersburg, A. F. Crutchfield & Co., 1860. 84 p.   H PH PT

2271 MILLER, Donald George, 1909-
The authority of the Bible. Grand Rapids, Mich., Wm. B. Eerdmans Publishing Co., © 1972. 139 p. First given as the Carson Memorial Lectures, May, 1971, at the First Presbyterian Church, Richmond, Va.   A C H L PT R U

2272 MILLER, Donald George, 1909-
The Christian in a secular world. Scottdale, Pa., Herald Press, © 1969. 61 p. Addresses presented at Eastern Mennonite College, Harrisonburg, Virginia, January 1968.   PT U

2273 MILLER, Donald George, 1909-
Conqueror in chains: a story of the apostle Paul. Philadelphia, Westminster Press, © 1951. 271 p.   A C L PH PT R U

2274 MILLER, Donald George, 1909-
The finality of Jesus Christ in today's world. [Pittsburgh, Pa.], Pittsburgh Theological Seminary, n.d. 98 p.   C H U

2275 MILLER, Donald George, 1909-
Fire in thy mouth. New York, Abingdon Press, © 1954. 160 p.   A C L PT U

2276 MILLER, Donald George, 1909-
The Gospel according to Luke. Richmond, John Knox Press, © 1959. 175 p. (The Layman's Bible Commentary, v. 18.)   A C H L PT R U ... L: [1975].

2277 MILLER, Donald George, 1909-
Live as free men: a study guide on Galatians. [New York], Board of Christian Education, United Presbyterian Church in the U.S.A., © 1964. 53 p.   PH

2278 MILLER, Donald George, 1909-

The nature and mission of the church. Richmond, John Knox Press, © 1957. 134 p. A C H L PT R U ... L: [1959] ... H: [1962].

2279 MILLER, Donald George, 1909-
Neglected emphases in Biblical criticism.... Inaugural address [as Walter H. Robertson Professor of New Testament] delivered June 5, 1945, in Watts Chapel, Union Theological Seminary, Richmond, Virginia. 31 p. Reprinted from the Union Seminary Review, August, 1945. The Union Seminary Bulletin, July, August, September, 1945. A C H PH PT U

2280 MILLER, Donald George, 1909-
The people of God. London, SCM Press, [1959]. 128 p. An abridged version of "The nature and mission of the church." C ... PT U ... L: Naperville, Ill., SCM Book Club [1959].

2281 MILLER, Donald George, 1909-
La piedra que desecharon los edificadores; estudios en la profecia de Isaias, tr. par Alicia McClelland. Atlanta, Ga., Comite sobre obra de la Mujer, Iglesia Presbyteriana en los Estados Unidos, 1949. 64 p. Translation of "The stone which the builders rejected." A U

2282 MILLER, Donald George, 1909-
The stone which the builders rejected. Studies in the prophecy of Isaiah. Atlanta, Committee on Woman's Work, Presbyterian Church in the U.S., © 1946. 64 p. A U

2283 MILLER, Donald George, 1909-
Studia Biblica. I. The book of Genesis. [Richmond], Interpretation, © 1948. 7 ℓ. Reprinted, with permission, by Interpretation. U

2284 MILLER, Donald George, 1909-
The way to Biblical preaching. New York, Abingdon Press, © 1957. 160 p. A C L PT R U

2285 MILLER, Donald George, 1909-
Why serve Christ? [Richmond, Board of Christian Education, Presbyterian Church in the U.S.], n.d. 12 p. U

2286 MILLER, George, 1834-1900.
Missouri's memorable decade, 1860-1870: an historical sketch: personal--political--religious. Columbia, Mo., E. W. Stephens, 1898. 175 p. PH

2287 MILLER, Henry, 1855-1911.
Sketch of Bethesda Church, Lexington Presbytery, Virginia. Richmond, Whittet & Shepperson, 1910. 45 p. PH U

2288 MILLER, John, 1819-1895.
      Are souls immortal? 3d ed. Princeton, N.J., Evangeli-
cal Reform Publication Co., 1887. 178 p. C U

2289 MILLER, John, 1819-1895.
      Commentary on Paul's Epistle to Romans; with an excur-
sus on the famous passage in James (Chap. II.:14-26).
Princeton, N.J., Evangelical Reform Publication Co., 1887.
392 p. C PT U

2290 MILLER, John, 1819-1895.
      The debt, the duty and the hope of the citizen soldiers of
America: a sermon addressed to the military of Frederick
City, November 30th 1843, a day of public thanksgiving.
Frederick, Office of the Examiner, 1843. 15 p. PH PT

2291 MILLER, John, 1819-1895.
      The design of the church, as an index to her real nature
and the true law of her communion. Philadelphia, James M.
Campbell, 1846. 197 p. C H PH PT R

2292 MILLER, John, 1819-1895.
      Fetich in theology; or, Doctrinalism twin to ritualism.
New York, Dodd & Mead, 1874. 261 p. A H PH R U ...
PT: 2d ed. 1875 ... PH PT: 3d ed. Princeton, N.J.,
Evangelical Reform Publication Co., 1887.

2293 MILLER, John, 1819-1895.
      Is God a trinity? 3d ed. Princeton, N.J., n.p., 1922.
152 p. C U

2294 MILLER, John, 1819-1895.
      Metaphysics; or, The science of perception. New York,
Dodd & Mead, © 1875. 402 p. PH PT ... PT: 3d ed.
1904.

2295 MILLER, John, 1819-1895.
      The old church creed. Princeton, N.J., McGinness &
Runyan, 1879. 44 p. PT

2296 MILLER, John, 1819-1895.
      Questions awakened by the Bible. I. Are souls immortal?
II. Was Christ in Adam? III. Is God a trinity? Philadel-
phia, J. B. Lippincott & Co., 1877. 178, 97, 152 p.
PH ... PT: 2d ed. ... PH: 3d ed. Princeton, N.J.,
Evangelical Reform Publication Co., 1887.

2297 MILLER, John, 1819-1895.
      Seven failures of ultra-Calvinism. n.p., n.d. 48-60 p.
From the Cumberland Presbyterian Review, January, 1892.
PT

2298 MILLER, John, 1819-1895.

Theology. Princeton, N.J., Evangelical Reform Publication Co., 1887. 271 p.   C PH PT

2299   MILLER, John, 1819-1895.
Was Christ in Adam? 3d ed.   Princeton, N.J., Evangelical Reform Publication Co., 1887.   97 p.   C U

2300   MILLER, John Reed, 1908-
Sermons.   Jackson, Miss., Evangelical Pulpit Publications, [1979].   3 v.   Contents.--v.1. The anchor of our hope.--v.2. Disciples in disguise.--v.3. Taking heaven by storm.   A C H L PT R U

2301   MILLER, Patrick Dwight, 1900-1974.
The Acts: characteristics of the early church.   Ten studies in the book of Acts of the Apostles for individual or group use.   [New York, Board of Foreign Missions, Board of National Missions, Board of Christian Education, Presbyterian Church in the U.S.A., 1953].   32 p.   PH

2302   MILLER, Patrick Dwight, 1900-1974.
The imperative of home missions.   Richmond, Presbyterian Committee of Publication, © 1931.   101 p.   C H L R U

2303   MILLER, William McElwee, 1892-
The Bahai cause today.   n.p., n.d.   26 p.   Reprinted from the Moslem World, October, 1940.   PH PT

2304   MILLER, William McElwee, 1892-
The Baha'i faith: its history and teachings.   South Pasadena, Calif., William Carey Library, © 1974.   443 p.   C PH PT R U

2305   MILLER, William McElwee, 1892-
Bahaism; its origin, history and teachings.   Introduction by Robert E. Speer.   New York, Fleming H. Revell Co., © 1931.   214 p.   A PT U

2306   MILLER, William McElwee, 1892-
Beliefs and practices of Christians.   (A letter to a friend.)   [4th ed.]   Lahore, Pakistan, Masihi Isha'at Khana, [1975].   80 p.   H

2307   MILLER, William McElwee, 1892-
A Christian's response to Islam.   [Nutley, N.J.], Presbyterian and Reformed Publishing Co., 1976.   178 p.   H PH PT U

2308   MILLER, William McElwee, 1892-
Commentary on the Acts of the Apostles.   Hamadan, Iran, American Presbyterian Mission Press, [1932].   In Persian.   PH

2309 MILLER, William McElwee, 1892-
      History of the ancient church in the empires of Rome and
      Persia. n.p., 1931. 205 p. In Persian. PH

2310 MILLER, William McElwee, 1892-
      History of the Christian church in the Roman empire and
      in Persia. |Leipzig], n.p., 1931. 340 p. In Persian.
      PT

2311 MILLER, William McElwee, 1892-
      Kaliseyi Khuda dar Johan; ya, Tafseer risaleyi arral Polus
      rasul be Corintian. (The church of God in the world; or,
      Commentary on the First Epistle of the apostle Paul to the
      Corinthians, with a new translation from the original Greek
      by William M. Miller and Iraj M. Amini.) n.p., 1953.
      376 p. Title-page and text in Persian. PT

2312 MILLER, William McElwee, 1892- tr.
      Kitabi Hayat; ya, Tafseer Injili Yohanna (The Book of Life;
      or, Commentary on the Gospel of John.) Teheran, Beroheem
      Printing House, 1947. 447 p. Title-page and text in Per-
      sian. PT

2313 MILLER, William McElwee, 1892-
      Tafseer Injili Luqa. (Commentary on the Gospel of
      Luke.).... With a new translation ... with the assistance
      of Ahmad Nakhosteen. [Teheran, Beroheem Printing House],
      1934. 371 p. In Persian. PT

2314 MILLER, William McElwee, 1892-
      Tafseer Kitabi A'mali rasoolan. (Commentary on the book
      of Acts of the Apostles.).... With a new translation ...
      with the assistance of Ahmad Nakhosteen. [Leipzig, A.
      Parees], 1932. 400 p. In Persian. PT

2315 MILLER, William McElwee, 1892-
      Tafseer risaleyi Polus rasul be Rumanian. (Commentary
      on the Epistle of Paul the Apostle to the Romans, by W. M.
      Miller and Ali Nakhosteen.) [Beirut, American Press], 1928.
      182 p. In Persian. PT

2316 MILLER, William McElwee, 1892-
      Tales of Persia: a book for children. Philadelphia, Dor-
      rance & Co., © 1939. 145 p. PT

2317 MILLER, William McElwee, 1892-
      Ten Muslims meet Christ. Grand Rapids, Mich., Wm.
      B. Eerdmans Publishing Co., © 1969. 147 p. A C H L
      PH PT U

2318 MILLER, William McElwee, 1892-
      What is the Baha'i faith? ... an abridgement by William

N. Wysham. [Grand Rapids, Mich.], Wm. B. Eerdmans Publishing Co., © 1977. 151 p. Abridgement of "The Baha'i faith: its history and teachings." A L PT U

2319 MILLER, William McElwee, 1892-
What shall I do to be saved? Isfahan, Nuryehan Press, n.d. 7 p. In Persian. PH

2320 MILLER, William McElwee, 1892-
Your Muslim guest. A practical guide in friendship and witness for Christians who meet Muslims. An open letter from Uncle Bill. Toronto, Ontario, Canada, Fellowship of Faith for Muslims, 1978. 15 p. H

2321 MILLS, Henry Junius, 1876-1918.
Contrary winds and other sermons. Richmond, Presbyterian Committee of Publication, [1919?]. 157 p. A C H L R U

2322 MINISTERING to the elderly: perspectives and opportunities. Edited by John H. Morgan. Preface by Seward Hiltner. Contributions by Helena Znaniecki Lopata, William B. Oglesby [and] Robert D. Wheelock. Wichita, Kan., Institute of Ministry and the Elderly, Kansas Newman College, 1976. 48 ℓ. PT U

2323 MINOR, Harold Whitfield, 1924-
Sex education--the schools and the churches: a study action guide concerned with the issue of sex education and the attacks centered against these programs in the public schools, by Harold W. Minor, Joseph B. Muyskens and Margaret Newell Alexander. [Richmond], John Knox Press, © 1971. 80 p. A H L PH PT U

2324 MINTER, William Ramseur, 1873-1943.
Travel-letters from Palestine and the East. Charlotte, N.C., Presbyterian Standard Publishing Co., 1910. 96 p. A C H R

2325 MISSOURI. University.
... Inauguration of S. S. Laws, LL.D., as President of the University of Missouri, at Columbia, on Wednesday, July 5, 1876. Columbia, Mo., Statesman Book & Job Office Print., 1876. 119 p. U

2326 MITCHELL, Samuel Williamson, 1833-1902.
The baptism question put to rest by the express words of Christ. A plain English Bible-reading on the mode, significance, use and subjects of "Christian baptism." St. Louis, Farris, Smith & Co., n.d. 40 p. U

2327 MITCHELL, William H., -1872.

A farewell discourse, delivered in the First Presbyterian Church, Wetumpka, Ala., on the 28th day of July, 1850. Tuscumbia, William Rollston, "North Alabamian" Office, 1850. 21 p. PH

2328 MITCHELL, William H., -1872.
The influence of missions on people and nations: a discourse preached by the appointment of the Synod of Nashville ... October 4th, 1854. Nashville, J. F. Morgan, 1854. 29 p. PH

2329 MOMENT, Alfred Harrison, 1844-1907.
A nation's funeral dirge. A sermon on the death of President Garfield, in the Spring Street Presbyterian Church, New York City. Newark, N.J., Van Alstyne & Shurts, 1881. 11 p. PH

2330 MOMENT, Alfred Harrison, 1844-1907.
The New York down-town Presbyterian churches. (Preached on Sabbath morning, December 18th, 1881.) n.p., n.d. 27 p. PH

2331 MOMENT, Alfred Harrison, 1844-1907.
Old Spring Street Presbyterian Church, New York City: an historical discourse [on] the sixty-fifth anniversary, December 17th & 18th, 1876. New York, n.p., 1877. 23 p. PH PT

2332 MOMENT, Alfred Harrison, 1844-1907.
The will of God to man and man's duty to God. Richmond, Presbyterian Committee of Publication, n.d. 16 p. U

2333 MONTGOMERY, Samuel M.
A discourse delivered at the last annual commencement in Oakland College. Vicksburg, Marmaduke Shannon, 1847. 20 p. PH

2334 MONTGOMERY, ALA. First Presbyterian Church.
Golden anniversary exercises of the First Presbyterian Church of Montgomery, Ala., February 21st, 1897. [Montgomery?], Brown Printing Co., [1897]. 88 p. Articles by Revs. E. P. Davis, J. R. Burgett, N. L. Anderson, Russell Cecil, A. B. Curry. PH

2335 *MOODY, Dwight Lyman, 1837-1899.
The best of D. L. Moody; sixteen sermons by the great evangelist. Edited by Wilbur M. Smith. Chicago, Moody Press, © 1971. 223 p. PT R

2336 MOORE, Ansley Cunningham, 1903-1973.
Do all things work together for good? n.p., n.d. 15 p. PH

2337   MOORE, Ansley Cunningham, 1903-1973.
        The family turns to God. A sermon preached for the
Southern Radio Conference on the Presbyterian Hour. n.p.,
n.d. 14 p. PH

2338   MOORE, Ansley Cunningham, 1903-1973.
        Here stand Protestants. n.p., n.d. 15 p. PH

2339   MOORE, Ansley Cunningham, 1903-1973.
        "If I sat in the pew." A sermon. n.p., n.d. 8 p.
PH

2340   MOORE, Ansley Cunningham, 1903-1973.
        Let Presbyterians unite! n.p., n.d. 4 p. Reprinted
from the Pulpit, August, 1954. U

2341   MOORE, Ansley Cunningham, 1903-1973.
        So you are a church member! n.p., n.d. 14 p. PH

2342   MOORE, James Wilson, -1874.
        The Bible, a revelation from God: a discourse. Little
Rock, Wm. E. Woodruff, 1831. 28 p. PH

2343   MOORE, James Wilson, -1874.
        Is the Roman Catholic Church the only true church, out
of which none can be saved? Addressed to the Rt. Rev.
Andrew Byrne, Roman Catholic Bishop of Little Rock. n.p.,
n.d. 8 p. PH

2344   MOORE, James Wilson, -1874.
        Remarks on the mode of Christian baptism. Little Rock,
B. J. Borden, 1847. 13 p. PH

2345   MOORE, Park Herrington, 1925-
        History of the Shiloh Presbyterian Church. Grover, N.C.,
Shiloh Presbyterian Church, 1955. 10 p. H

2346   MOORE, Thomas Verner, 1818-1871.
        Adaptation of religion to female character. A discourse
to young ladies, delivered in the First Presbyterian Church,
Richmond, Virginia, February 29th, 1852. Richmond, H. K.
Ellyson, 1852. 13 p. PH

2347   MOORE, Thomas Verner, 1818-1871.
        But a step between man and death. A discourse delivered
at the funeral of Samuel Taylor, Esq., in the First Presbyterian Church, Richmond, Va., Feb. 24th, 1853. Richmond,
Chas. H. Wynne, 1853. 16 p. PH

2348   MOORE, Thomas Verner, 1818-1871.
        The Christian lawyer, or the claims of Christianity on
the legal profession. A discourse delivered at the funeral

of Richard W. Flournoy, Esq., in the First Presbyterian
Church, Richmond, Va., December 1st, 1857. Richmond,
Macfarlane & Fergusson, 1858. 24 p. PH U

2349 MOORE, Thomas Verner, 1818-1871.
A commentary on Haggai and Malachi. [London], Banner
of Truth Trust, 1960. 180 p. "First published along with
commentary on Zechariah under the title 'The prophets of
the restoration.'" C H R

2350 MOORE, Thomas Verner, 1818-1871.
A commentary on Zechariah. London, Banner of Truth
Trust, 1958. 251 p. "First published along with commentaries on Haggai and Malachi under the title 'The prophets
of the restoration.'" A C H L R

2351 MOORE, Thomas Verner, 1818-1871.
The corporate life of the church. A discourse preached
at the opening of the General Assembly of the Presbyterian
Church in the United States, in the Franklin Street Church,
Baltimore, May 21st, 1868. Richmond, Presbyterian Com-
mittee of Publication, © 1868. 36 p. C H PH U

2352 MOORE, Thomas Verner, 1818-1871.
The Culdee Church: or, The historical connection of
modern Presbyterian churches with those of apostolic times,
through the Church of Scotland. Richmond, Presbyterian
Committee of Publication, © 1868. 87 p. Reprinted from
the Central Presbyterian. A C H L PH PT R U

2353 MOORE, Thomas Verner, 1818-1871.
History of the First Presbyterian Church of Helena, Montana. Founded August 1, 1869. Organized June 15, 1872.
With a sketch of the beginning of Presbyterianism in Montana.
n.p., 1898. 29 p. PH

2354 MOORE, Thomas Verner, 1818-1871.
How was Jesus baptized? [Richmond, Presbyterian Committee of Publication], n.d. 4 p. U

2355 MOORE, Thomas Verner, 1818-1871.
God our refuge and strength in this war. A discourse before the congregations of the First and Second Presbyterian
churches, on the day of humiliation, fasting and prayer,
appointed by President Davis, Friday, Nov. 15, 1861. Richmond, W. Hargrave White, 1861. 24 p. H U

2356 MOORE, Thomas Verner, 1818-1871.
Importance of religion to public men. A funeral discourse
on the death of Robert Craig, Esq., of Roanoke.... Preached
... in the First Presbyterian Church, Richmond, Virginia,
January 9, 1853. Richmond, Macfarlane & Fergusson, 1853.
16 p. PH

2357 MOORE, Thomas Verner, 1818-1871.
Inspiration of the scriptures: Morell's theory reviewed.
A lecture on the evidences of Christianity: delivered at the
University of Virginia, November 24, 1850. Richmond,
Colin, Baptist and Nowlan, 1850. 41 p. PH PT

2358 MOORE, Thomas Verner, 1818-1871.
The last days of Jesus; or, The appearances of our Lord
during the forty days between the resurrection and the ascension. Philadelphia, Presbyterian Board of Publication,
© 1858. 300 p. A C H L PH R U

2359 MOORE, Thomas Verner, 1818-1871.
The power and claims of a Calvinistic literature: a sermon on behalf of the Assembly's Board of Publication. Philadelphia, Presbyterian Board of Publication, 1859. 36 p.
(Presbyterian Tracts, no. 232.) H PH U ... PH: 1860.

2360 MOORE, Thomas Verner, 1818-1871.
The prophets of the restoration; or, Haggai, Zechariah,
and Malachi: a new translation, with notes. New York,
Robert Carter and Brothers, 1856. 408 p. A H L PH PT
R U

2361 MOORE, Thomas Verner, 1818-1871.
The relation of Christianity to modern civilization. The
annual address delivered before the General Union Philosophical Society of Dickinson College, Carlisle, Pennsylvania,
July 8, 1846. Philadelphia, T. K. & P. G. Collins, 1846.
32 p. PH PT

2362 MOORE, Thomas Verner, 1818-1871.
Relative influence of presbytery and prelacy on civil and
ecclesiastical liberty. Philadelphia, Presbyterian Board of
Publication, 1845. 31 p. (Presbyterian Tracts.) C H L
PH PT R U

2363 MOORE, Thomas Verner, 1818-1871.
Warning words to young men. A discourse, delivered in
the First Presbyterian Church, Richmond, Virginia, February 29th, 1852. Richmond, H. K. Ellyson, 1852. 16 p.
PH

2364 MOORE, Thomas Verner, 1818-1871.
Young men reminded of the judgment. A sermon on occasion of the funeral of Mr. David Barclay, Jr., delivered in
the First Presbyterian Church, Richmond, Virginia, June 4th,
1848. Richmond, Shepherd and Colin, 1848. 20 p. PH

2365 MOORE, Walter William, 1857-1926.
Appreciations and historical addresses. [Richmond, Presbyterian Committee of Publication, 1914?]. 167 p. Contents. --

Moses Drury Hoge.--Jacob Henry Smith.--The centennial celebration of Union Seminary.--The first fifty years of Union Seminary.--Beginnings and development of the Presbyterian Church in North Carolina.   A C H PH PT R U

2366   MOORE, Walter William, 1857-1926.
Conspectus of geography of the Holy Land. n.p., n.d. 14 ℓ.   U

2367   MOORE, Walter William, 1857-1926.
Correspondence course in Biblical geography. The General Assembly's Training School for Lay Workers. Richmond, Presbyterian Committee of Publication, © 1921. 39 p. PH U

2368   MOORE, Walter William, 1857-1926.
The discovery of Pithom. n.p., n.d. 243-255 p. Reprinted from the Presbyterian Quarterly, April, 1889.   U

2369   MOORE, Walter William, 1857-1926.
The educational value of Presbyterianism. An address delivered at Presbyterian reunion at Penn-Mar, July 25, 1899. Newville, Pa., Star and Enterprise Print., n.d. 24 p. PT U

2370   MOORE, Walter William, 1857-1926.
Epoch-makers of the Old Testament; their messages and their methods. Syllabus of eight lectures. Presented at the seventh annual conference of volunteer workers in city, town and railroad Young Men's Christian Associations, August 5-14, Lake Geneva, Wisconsin. n.p., [1893]. 6 ℓ.   U

2371   MOORE, Walter William, 1857-1926.
Inaugural address ... [as] President of Union Theological Seminary in Virginia. Delivered at the annual commencement, 1905. n.p., n.d. 24 p. Reprinted from the Union Seminary Magazine, Oct.-Nov., 1905.   A PH PT U

2372   MOORE, Walter William, 1857-1926.
The indispensable book. New York, Fleming H. Revell Co., © 1910. 114 p.   A C H L PT R U

2373   MOORE, Walter William, 1857-1926.
The Israel tables of Merneptah. n.p., n.d. 23 p. Reprinted from the Presbyterian Quarterly, January, 1898.   U

2374   MOORE, Walter William, 1857-1926.
Judge George L. Christian; address ... at the memorial service in Schauffler Hall, October 5, 1924. n.p., n.d. 22 p. Reprinted from the Union Seminary Review, October, 1924.   U

2375   MOORE, Walter William, 1857-1926.

The life and letters of Walter W. Moore, second founder and first President of Union Theological Seminary in Virginia, by J. Gray McAllister. Richmond, Union Theological Seminary, 1939. 576 p. A C H L PH PT R U

2376 MOORE, Walter William, 1857-1926.
Memories of Flora Macdonald. n.p., n.d. 16 p. Reprinted from [his] "A year in Europe." U

2377 MOORE, Walter William, 1857-1926.
Montreat. n.p., n.d. 6 p. U

2378 MOORE, Walter William, 1857-1926.
The most valuable service of Davidson College. Remarks ... on the occasion of the visit of the Synod of North Carolina to Davidson College, October 24, 1906. Richmond, Whittet & Shepperson, n.d. 9 p. U

2379 MOORE, Walter William, 1857-1926.
The preparation of the modern minister. New York, Student Young Men's Christian Association, 1909. 28 p. H PH PT U

2380 MOORE, Walter William, 1857-1926.
The Presbyterian Church and education. [Louisville, Ky., Executive Committee of Christian Education and Ministerial Relief, Presbyterian Church in the U.S.], n.d. 4 p. U

2381 MOORE, Walter William, 1857-1926.
A real Boy Scout. Richmond, Presbyterian Committee of Publication, 1920. 53 p. H

2382 MOORE, Walter William, 1857-1926.
Rev. Anthony T. Graybill, D.D. Nashville, Tenn., Executive Committee of Foreign Missions, Presbyterian Church in the U.S., n.d. 8 p. C H U

2383 MOORE, Walter William, 1857-1926.
The seal of the Presbyterian Church in the United States. n.p., n.d. unpaged. U

2384 MOORE, Walter William, 1857-1926.
Supplementary notes on archaeology. Richmond, Whittet & Shepperson, 1891. 19 p. U

2385 MOORE, Walter William, 1857-1926.
Supplementary notes on Exodus. Richmond, Union Theological Seminary, n.d. 40 p. U

2386 MOORE, Walter William, 1857-1926.
Supplementary notes on the poetical books of Scripture and the book of Isaiah. Printed for the use of the students in

Union Theological Seminary of Virginia. Richmond, Whittet & Shepperson, 1913. 93 p. U

2387 MOORE, Walter William, 1857-1926.
Supplementary notes on the Psalms. [Richmond], Union Theological Seminary, n.d. 62 p. Includes notes also on Proverbs, Ecclesiastes, and the Song of Songs. R U

2388 MOORE, Walter William, 1857-1926.
Syllabus of the lectures on the L. P. Stone Foundation for 1897.... (Princeton Theological Seminary, "The beginnings of Hebrew history in the light of recent archaeological research.") n.p., n.d. 4 ℓ. U

2389 MOORE, Walter William, 1857-1926.
The teaching values of the Old Testament, by Walter W. Moore and Edward Mack. General Unit, Number Five, Ten Lessons. Richmond, Presbyterian Committee of Publication, © 1918. 79 p. C H PT R

2390 MOORE, Walter William, 1857-1926.
The teaching values of the Old Testament, by Walter W. Moore and Edward Mack. Trained Workers. 2d year. n.p., n.d. Translation into Japanese. U

2391 MOORE, Walter William, 1857-1926.
The value of the church. New York, Association Press, 1918. 16 p. C PH U

2392 MOORE, Walter William, 1857-1926.
A year in Europe. 2d ed. Richmond, Presbyterian Committee of Publication, 1904. 366 p. C H L R U ... A PT R U: 3d ed. 1905.

2393 MOORE, William D., 1824-1896.
A farewell sermon, delivered in the church of Long Run, October 1st, 1849. Pittsburgh, Johnston and Stockton, 1849. 16 p. PH

2394 MOORE, William D., 1824-1896.
A funeral sermon: preached in the Presbyterian Church of Greensburgh, on Sabbath, 18th January, 1852. Pittsburgh, Shryock & Hacke, 1852. 14 p. PH

2395 MOORE, William D., 1824-1896.
Latitude and longitude. A speech delivered before the Union Literary Society, of Washington College, Pa., on the 27th of September, 1852. Washington, Pa., Reporter Office, 1852. 19 p. H PH

2396 MORGAN, Frank Crossley, 1898-
Habakkuk: analysis. n.p., n.d. unpaged. A

2397 MORGAN, Frank Crossley, 1898-
　　　Haggai, a prophet of correction and comfort. London,
Marshall, Morgan & Scott, n.d. 128 p. First delivered as
a series of sermons in the First Presbyterian Church of
Augusta, Georgia. H PT R U

2398 MORGAN, Frank Crossley, 1898-
　　　The importance of the study of the English Bible. [Lon-
don, Westminster Chapel, The Bookroom], 1949. 15 p.
The Campbell Morgan Memorial Bible Lecture, 1. U

2399 MORGAN, Frank Crossley, 1898-
　　　A Psalm of an old shepherd; a devotional study of Psalm
twenty-three. London, Marshall, Morgan & Scott, n.d.
72 p. A H R U

2400 MORGAN, Gilbert, 1791-1875.
　　　The inaugural address ... [as] President of the Western
University of Pennsylvania. Pittsburgh, E. Lloyd and Co.,
1835. 15 p. PH PT

2401 MORGAN, Howard Moody, ca. 1900-
　　　The word of God through the words of men. [London,
Pickering & Inglis, 1963]. 18 p. The Campbell Morgan
Memorial Lecture, 15. U

2402 MORGAN, Kingsley John, 1895-
　　　The Bible in the life of the missionary ... Westminster
Chapel, Wednesday, 18th July, 1956. Glasgow, Pickering
& Inglis, 1956. 15 p. The Campbell Morgan Memorial
Lecture, 8. H

2403 MORRIS, Robert Hugh, 1876-1942.
　　　An address on some tendencies in present-day educational
methods and aims, and a sermon: Jesus Christ: good man
or God-man. n.p., n.d. 26 p. PH

2404 MORRIS, Robert Hugh, 1876-1942.
　　　"For you ... of me." Preparatory address. n.p., n.d.
17 p. PH

2405 MORRIS, Robert Hugh, 1876-1942.
　　　The power of public opinion. Sermon delivered Sunday
evening, November 24, 1912, in the Central-North Broad
Street Presbyterian Church, Philadelphia. n.p., n.d. 8 p.
PH

2406 MORRIS, Robert Hugh, 1876-1942.
　　　The prince and the pig's gate, and other sermons in story.
New York, Harper & Brothers, 1928. 203 p. L U

2407 MORRIS, Robert Hugh, 1876-1942.

Shepherds of the night watches: a Christmas meditation. n.p., n.d. 14 p. PH

2408 MORRIS, Robert Hugh, 1876-1942.
Sleeping through the sermon, and other discourses. New York, Fleming H. Revell Co., © 1916. 180 p. L PH PT U

2409 MORRIS, Samuel Leslie, 1854-1937.
At our own door; a study of home missions with special reference to the South and West. Richmond, Presbyterian Committee of Publication, © 1904. 304 p. U ... A C H L PT R: New York, Fleming H. Revell Co., © 1904. 258 p. ... C: New York, Young People's Missionary Movement of the United States and Canada.

2410 MORRIS, Samuel Leslie, 1854-1937.
Christianizing Christendom: home mission study. Richmond, Presbyterian Committee of Publication, © 1919. 206 p. A C L R U

2411 MORRIS, Samuel Leslie, 1854-1937.
The country church, its ruin and its remedy. Atlanta, Executive Committee of Home Missions, Presbyterian Church in the U.S., n.d. 23 p. U

2412 MORRIS, Samuel Leslie, 1854-1937.
The drama of Christianity; an interpretation of the Apocalypse. Richmond, Presbyterian Committee of Publication, © 1928. 147 p. A C H L R U

2413 MORRIS, Samuel Leslie, 1854-1937.
The fact of Christianity. [Richmond, Presbyterian Committee of Publication], © 1927. 153 p. The Smyth Lectures, 1925-26. A C H L PT R U

2414 MORRIS, Samuel Leslie, 1854-1937.
Presbyterianism, its principles and practice. Richmond, Presbyterian Committee of Publication, 1922. 177 p. A C H L PH PT R U

2415 MORRIS, Samuel Leslie, 1854-1937.
The records of the Morris family. Atlanta, Hubbard Brothers, n.d. 151 p. H

2416 MORRIS, Samuel Leslie, 1854-1937.
The romance of home missions: home mission study. Richmond, Presbyterian Committee of Publication, [1924]. 257 p. A C H L PT R U

2417 MORRIS, Samuel Leslie, 1854-1937.
Samuel Leslie Morris; an autobiography. Richmond,

Presbyterian Committee of Publication, © 1932. 140 p.   A
C H L PT R U

2418 MORRIS, Samuel Leslie, 1854-1937.
The task that challenges: home mission text book.   Rich-
mond, Presbyterian Committee of Publication, © 1917.   294 p.
A C H L PT R U

2419 MORRISON, Hugh McEwen, 1828-1893.
An appeal to the Presbyterian Church, in behalf of her
theological seminaries, and candidates for the gospel ministry.   Columbia, S.C., I. C. Morgan, 1858.   23 p.   PH

2420 MORRISON, John, 1892-
African mission.   [Nashville, Tenn., Bradley Whitfield],
© 1979.   277 p.   C H

2421 MORRISON, John, 1892-
Beloved physician: Thomas T. Stixrud of Congo.   [Nash-
ville, Tenn., Board of World Missions, Presbyterian Church
in the U.S.], n.d.   15 p.   U

2422 MORRISON, John, 1892-
Mpanda Nshila, "The splitter of paths": the story of
Motte Martin of Africa.   [Nashville, Tenn., Board of World
Missions, Presbyterian Church in the U.S.], n.d.   20 p.
C U

2423 MORRISON, Robert Hall, 1789-1889.
Funeral sermon of the Rev. John Robinson, D.D., late
pastor of Poplar Tent Church, preached at Poplar Tent,
February 22d, 1844.   Charlotte, Office of the Charlotte
Journal, 1844.   16 p.   PH

2424 MORRISON, William McCutchan, 1867-1918.
Baluba-Lulua exercise book.   Luebo, Africa, American
Presbyterian Congo Mission, 1916.   79 p.   H

2425 MORRISON, William McCutchan, 1867-1918.
Bible lessons.   New York, American Tract Society, © 1913.
532 p.   In Baluba.   H

2426 MORRISON, William McCutchan, 1867-1918.
Dictionary of the Tshiluba language (sometimes known as
the Buluba-Lulua, or Luba-Lulua).   Prepared for the Ameri-
can Presbyterian Congo Mission.   Rev. and enl.   Luebo,
Belgian Congo, J. Leighton Wilson Press, 1939.   176 p.
A H U

2427 MORRISON, William McCutchan, 1867-1918.
Grammar and dictionary of the Buluba-Lulua language as
spoken in the upper Kasai and Congo basin; prepared for the

American Presbyterian Congo Mission. New York, American Tract Society, © 1906. 417 p.   A L PT U

2428   MORROW, Thomas, 1808-1885.
A blow at the root of modern infidelity and skepticism; or, Huxleyism analyzed and criticized.   Philadelphia, J. B. Lippincott & Co., 1878. 60 p.   C H

2429   MORTON, John Booker, 1847-1913.
The matter of degrees in the Presbyterian Church.   [Pulaski, Va., B. D. Smith & Brothers], n.d.   4ℓ.   U

2430   MOSELEY, Edward Hilary, 1869-1965.
The cross of gold.   Gainesville, Tex., E. H. Moseley, © 1936.   76 p.   U

2431   MOSELEY, Edward Hilary, 1869-1965.
The Jew and his destiny.   Cleveland, Ohio, Union Gospel Press, © 1931.   96 p.   C ... H: Gainesville, Tex., n.p., © 1931.   71 p. ... A C H R U: [Rev. and enl.]   Berne, Ind., Berne Witness, [1939].   194 p.

2432   MOSELEY, Edward Hilary, 1869-1965.
The prince of this world.   Gainesville, Tex., E. H. Moseley, © 1935.   70 p.   A H U

2433   MOSELEY, John Watkins, 1828-1920.
Joseph and Asenath: a love story.   Richmond, Whittet & Shepperson, © 1907.   95 p.   In verse.   A H U

2434   MOSELEY, John Watkins, 1828-1920.
Samson: a poem.   Richmond, Whittet & Shepperson [1904]   53 p.   H U

2435   MOSELEY, John Watkins, 1866-1937.
The background of the Synod of Oklahoma, U.S.   Duncan, Okla., n.p., 1934.   15 p.   Reprinted from the Union Seminary Review, January, 1934.   A PT

2436   MOSELEY, John Watkins, 1866-1937.
Pan-Presbyterian principles.   Grand Rapids, Mich., Wm. B. Eerdmans Publishing Co., © 1935.   103 p.   A C H L PH PT R U

2437   MOSELEY, John Watkins, 1866-1937.
Presbyterian polity.   n.p., 1936.   22 p.   A paper on ecclesiastical government read as part of the "Diamond Jubilee" program of Mangum Presbytery, Synod of Oklahoma ... April 14-15, 1936.   PH U

2438   MOSELEY, John Watkins, 1866-1937, ed.
A record of missionary meetings held in the Chahta and

Chikesha nations, and Tombigbee Presbytery, from 1825 to 1832. n.p., n.d. 16 p. H

2439 MOUNT, Charles Eric, 1902-
Our 110th anniversary. An address. Versailles, Ky., Versailles Presbyterian Church, 1939. unpaged. H

2440 MOUNT, Charles Eric, 1935-
Conscience and responsibility. Richmond, John Knox Press, © 1969. 191 p. A C H L PT

2441 MOUNT, Charles Eric, 1935-
The feminine factor. Richmond, John Knox Press, © 1973. 190 p. A C H L PT U

2442 MULLIN, Joseph Bartholomew, 1924-
Matters of life and death. [Greensboro, N.C., First Presbyterian Church], n.d. 29 p. L

2443 MURRAY, Ephraim Clark, 1861-1930.
Baptism, the one vital point. Richmond, Presbyterian Committee of Publication, n.d. 12 p. U

2444 MURRAY, Ephraim Clark, 1861-1930.
The pastor's Bible: an analysis of those portions of Holy Scripture pertaining to the various duties of the pastor. Richmond, Presbyterian Committee of Publication, 1888. 207 p. A C H PH R U

2445 MURRAY, James, 1834-1914.
The capacity of Presbyterianism as a form of government for rapid church extension. Richmond, Whittet & Shepperson, 1889. 16 p. U

2446 MURRAY, Joseph James, 1890-1973.
Additions to the Virginia avifauna since 1890. n.p., n.d. 190-200 p. From the Auk, April, 1933. U

2447 MURRAY, Joseph James, 1890-1973.
Children's story sermons for today. Richmond, John Knox Press, © 1945. 151 p. A H U

2448 MURRAY, Joseph James, 1890-1973.
A faith for youth. Richmond, John Knox Press, © 1948. 113 p. C H L R U

2449 MURRAY, Joseph James, 1890-1973.
The faunal zones of the southern Appalachians. n.p., n.d. 67 p. Reprinted from the Virginia Journal of Science, February, March, 1940. U

2450 MURRAY, Joseph James, 1890-1973.

Wild wings. [Richmond, John Knox Press], © 1947.
123 p. H U

2451 MURRAY, Spencer Castles, 1927-
Presbyterians of Old Hickory, a history of First Presbyterian Church, Old Hickory, Tennessee. n.p., 1973. 121 p.
A C H L U

2452 MYERS, Harry White, 1874-1945.
The prisoners' friend. n.p., [Lellyett & Rogers, 1933].
8 p. U

2453 *MYERS, Robert Manson, 1921- ed.
The children of pride; a true story of Georgia and the
Civil War. New Haven, Yale University Press, 1972.
1845 p. "[Selected] from the voluminous family papers of
the Rev. Dr. Charles Colcock Jones (1804-1863), of Liberty
County, Georgia." A C H PH PT R U

2454 *MYERS, Robert Manson, 1921-
A Georgian at Princeton. New York, Harcourt Brace
Jovanovich, © 1976. 365 p. Letters drawn from the family
papers of Charles Colcock Jones. C H PH PT U

2455 NABERS, Charles Haddon, 1889-1968.
Gladness in Christian living; a series of addresses. New
York, Fleming H. Revell Co., © 1931. 94 p. A H L U

2456 NABERS, Charles Haddon, 1889-1968.
"Hear my voice, O God, in prayer"; morning meditations
and prayers over the radio. n.p., n.d. 72 p. U

2457 NABERS, Charles Haddon, 1889-1968.
Mediterranean meditations; radio devotionals. n.p., n.d.
48 p. U

2458 NABERS, Charles Haddon, 1889-1968.
Mediterranean memories. n.p., [Keys Print Co.], 1934.
239 p. H

2459 NABERS, Charles Haddon, 1889-1968.
My morning meditations; a thought and a prayer to bring
God and my soul together. [Greenville, S.C.], n.p., © 1945.
79 p. U

2460 NABERS, Charles Haddon, 1889-1968.
The New Testament correspondence; Bible studies in the
Epistles. n.p., [1928]. 46 p. U

2461 NABERS, Charles Haddon, 1889-1968, ed.
The Southern Presbyterian pulpit: pulpit addresses of the
Presbyterian Church in the United States. New York, Fleming

H. Revell Co., © 1928. 296 p. With brief notices of the
authors: Neal L. Anderson, Andrew W. Blackwood, Robert
F. Campbell, William Crowe, Thomas W. Currie, W. R.
Dobyns, Joseph Dunglinson, R. E. Fry, S. M. Glasgow, J.
H. Henderlite, J. W. Jackson, J. V. Johnson, Harris E.
Kirk, Benj. R. Lacy, Jr., D. Clay Lilly, Walter L. Lingle,
J. S. Lyons, R. H. McCaslin, J. A. McClure, D. H. Og-
den, Henry H. Sweets, Ernest Thompson, James I. Vance,
John M. Vander Meulen, J. G. Venable.   A C H L PT R
U

2462 NABERS, Charles Haddon, 1889-1968.
       Viewpoints; sketches. Pensacola, Fla., [Burrow Press],
       1926. 69 p.   A U

2463 NABERS, Charles Haddon, 1889-1968.
       When Rotary hosts trek Eastward. [Charlotte, N.C.,
       Standard Publishing Co.], © 1928. 156 p.   H

2464 NABERS, Charles Haddon, 1889-1968.
       Youth choosing; Y.M.C.A. talks to men and boys.   Pensa-
       cola, Fla., Mayes Printing Co., 1930. 39 p.   H

2465 NAG HAMMADI Codices.
       The facsimile edition of the Nag Hammadi Codices.   Lei-
       den, E. J. Brill, 1972-   . v. Pref. signed: James M.
       Robinson, Secretary, International Committee for the Nag
       Hammadi Codices.   L PT U

2466 NALL, Robert, 1805-1886.
       The dead of the Synod of Alabama: a discourse.   Mobile,
       Dade, Thompson & Co., 1851. 52 p.   H PH PT

2467 NALL, Robert, 1805-1886.
       A voice from twenty graves: a sermon preached Decem-
       ber 4th, 1853. Mobile, Dade, Thompson & Co., 1854.
       31 p.   H PH PT

2468 NASH, Frederick Kollock, 1813-1861.
       Circumcision and baptism, sacraments of the covenant of
       grace, being a candid consideration of the points at issue be-
       tween Presbyterians and Baptists. Relative to baptism--its
       scope--meaning--mode, and subjects. Fayetteville, N.C.,
       Presbyterian Office, 1859. 79 p.   PH

2469 NEEL, Samuel Monroe, 1841-1921.
       Col. Young's so-called reply. [Kansas City, Mo.], n.d.
       16 p.   U

2470 NEELY, Robert Langdon, 1829-1888.
       Sketches of the Presbytery of the Western District.   Her-
       nando, Miss., F. W. Merrin, 1883. 115 p.   PH

2471 NELSON, Carl Ellis, 1916-
The ABC's of a new venture in church education. n.p.,
n.d. 7 p. PH

2472 NELSON, Carl Ellis, 1916- comp.
Conscience: theological and psychological perspectives.
New York, Newman Press, © 1973. 353 p. A C L PT U

2473 NELSON, Carl Ellis, 1916-
Don't let your conscience be your guide. New York, Paul-
ist Press, © 1978. 109 p. Lectures given as the 1978
Robert F. Jones Lectures in Christian Education at Austin
Presbyterian Theological Seminary. A C L PT R U

2474 NELSON, Carl Ellis, 1916-
Issues facing Christian educators. A report based on the
World Institute on Christian Education meeting in Nairobi,
Kenya, July, 1967. [Geneva], World Council of Christian
Education, [1969]. 39 p. A L PT U

2475 NELSON, Carl Ellis, 1916-
Love and the law; the place of the Ten Commandments in
the Christian faith today. Richmond, John Knox Press,
© 1963. 93 p. A C H L PH R U ... L: [1969].

2476 NELSON, Carl Ellis, 1916-
Using evaluation in theological education. Nashville, Discipleship Resources, © 1975. 121 p. A L PT U

2477 NELSON, Carl Ellis, 1916-
What's right? A study of the Ten Commandments in the
light of the Christian faith. Richmond, CLC Press, © 1966.
80 p. (The Covenant Life Curriculum.) Leaders' booklet
for senior high conference. C L R U

2478 NELSON, Carl Ellis, 1916-
Where faith begins. Richmond, John Knox Press, © 1967.
231 p. The Sprunt Lectures, 1965. A C H L PT R U

2479 NELSON, James Boyce, 1904-1979.
Papa remembers me. [1st ed.] New York, Vantage Press,
© 1957. 117 p. H

2480 NEVILLE, William Gordon, 1855-1907.
Sermons. Richmond, Onward Press, © 1908. 348 p.
A C H R U

2481 The NEW shape of pastoral theology; essays in honor of Seward
Hiltner. Edited by William B. Oglesby, Jr. Nashville
Abingdon Press, © 1969. 383 p. A C L PT R U

2482 NEWLAND, LeRoy Tate, 1885-1969.

Illth or wealth? A series of four Bible studies for the men of the Presbyterian Church, U.S. [Chattanooga, Tenn., General Assembly's Stewardship Committee, Presbyterian Church in the U.S.], © 1924. 48 p. U

2483 NEWLAND, LeRoy Tate, 1885-1969.
So rich a crown: poems of faith. [Atlanta, Gate City Printing], © 1963. 85 p. H

2484 NEWSOME, James DuPre, 1931-
By the waters of Babylon: an introduction to the history and theology of the exile. Atlanta, John Knox Press, © 1979. 176 p. A C L PT R U

2485 NICKLE, Keith Fullerton, 1933-
The collection: a study in Paul's strategy. Naperville, Ill., Alec R. Allenson, [1966]. 176 p. Thesis--Univ. of Basel. A C L PT ... R U: London, SCM Press.

2486 NICKLE, Keith Fullerton, 1933-
The synoptic Gospels: conflict and consensus. Atlanta, John Knox Press, © 1980. 198 p. C H L U

2487 *NICOLASSEN, George Frederick.
The book of Revelation. Richmond, Presbyterian Committee of Publication, [1917]. 67 p. The contents of this book have been derived almost entirely from Rev. J. B. Ramsey's "Spiritual Kingdom." A C H R U

2488 NOTICE of the Rev. John B. Adger's article on the slave trade. Charleston, S.C., Walter, Evans and Co., 1858. 28 p. PH U

2489 OATES, Luther Albertus, 1865-1909.
A sermon preached ... to his congregation the First Presbyterian Church, Bridgton, N.J., November 16th, 1907: the occasion: installation of ruling elders. n.p., n.d. 16 p. PH

2490 OEHLER, James Cornelius, 1857-1941.
Cruise to the Orient. Richmond, Presbyterian Committee of Publication, n.d. 271 p. A H R ... PT: 1907. 273 p.

2491 OGDEN, Dunbar Hunt, 1878-1952.
The heart of Mary. Richmond, Presbyterian Committee of Publication, © 1927. 73 p. A C H L R U

2492 OGDEN, Dunbar Hunt, 1878-1952.
Reunion of the Presbyterian Churches, U.S.A. and U.S. n.p., n.d. 24 p. A C U

2493 OGDEN, Dunbar Hunt, 1878-1952.

Wedding bells. Richmond, John Knox Press, © 1945. 31 p.   C U

2494   OGLESBY, Stuart Roscoe, 1888-1977.
The baby is baptized. Richmond, John Knox Press, © 1942. 22 p.   C R U

2495   OGLESBY, Stuart Roscoe, 1888-1977.
Becoming a member of the Presbyterian Church. Richmond, John Knox Press, 1941. 61 p.   A U ... A L R: [1948] ... C H: [1954] ... U: [1956].

2496   OGLESBY, Stuart Roscoe, 1888-1977.
City church: ministering to millions. Atlanta, Board of Church Extension, Presbyterian Church in the U.S., © 1960. 111 p.   Cover-title: Ministering to millions.   A C H L U

2497   OGLESBY, Stuart Roscoe, 1888-1977.
The light is still shining: the Gospel of John for a troubled world. New York, Fleming H. Revell Co., © 1944. 182 p.   A C R U

2498   OGLESBY, Stuart Roscoe, 1888-1977.
A practising faith: the relation of religious thinking to religious living. New York, Fleming H. Revell Co., © 1948. 157 p.   A C H L R U

2499   OGLESBY, Stuart Roscoe, 1888-1977.
Prayers for all occasions: a book of short prayers for everyday life. Richmond, John Knox Press, © 1940. 187 p. A C H L U

2500   OGLESBY, Stuart Roscoe, 1888-1977.
Presbyterianism in action. How to become a more effective member of the Presbyterian Church. Richmond, John Knox Press, © 1949. 172 p.   A C PH PT R U

2501   OGLESBY, Stuart Roscoe, 1888-1977.
Think on these things. Richmond, John Knox Press, © 1946. 103 p.   A C H L R U

2502   OGLESBY, Stuart Roscoe, 1888-1977.
What is your need? and other sermons. Richmond, John Knox Press, © 1942. 118 p.   A C R U

2503   OGLESBY, Stuart Roscoe, 1888-1977.
You and the Holy Spirit; a neglected New Testament doctrine made personal and practical for everyday life. Richmond, John Knox Press, © 1952. 112 p.   A C H L PT R U

2504   OGLESBY, William Barr, 1916-

Biblical themes for pastoral care. Nashville, Abingdon Press, © 1980. 240 p. A C PT U

2505 OGLESBY, William Barr, 1916-
Pastoral counseling in the theological curriculum.... Inaugural address [as Marthina DeFriece Professor of Pastoral Counseling] delivered March 2, 1954, in Schauffler Hall, Union Theological Seminary. Richmond, Union Theological Seminary, 1954. 19 p. A C R U

2506 OGLESBY, William Barr, 1916-
Referral in pastoral counseling. Englewood Cliffs, N.J., Prentice-Hall, © 1968. 139 p. A C L PT R U ... PT R U: Rev. ed. Nashville, Abingdon, © 1978.

2507 OGLESBY, William Barr, 1916-
With wings as eagles; toward personal maturity. Richmond, CLC Press, © 1966. 234 p. (The Covenant Life Curriculum.) C L U

2508 O'HAIR, John Cowan, 1876-
The dispensational stir; the Presbyterians resolve some other confused theologians. Chicago, n.p., n.d. 32 p. A R

2509 ORMOND, John William, 1919-
Youth entering into covenant: for pastor and session. Richmond, CLC Press, © 1965. 47 p. (The Covenant Life Curriculum.) C ... L: [1967].

2510 ORMOND, John William, 1919-
Youth entering into covenant: for youth. Richmond, CLC Press, © 1965. 48 p. (The Covenant Life Curriculum.) C ... L: [1968].

2511 ORR, William Fridell, 1907-
Great beliefs of the church. Philadelphia, Board of Christian Education, Presbyterian Church in the U.S.A., 1946. 61 p. U

2512 ORTS GONZALES, Juan, 1868-1941.
Americanism, Romanism and Protestantism. Richmond, Presbyterian Committee of Publication, n.d. 13 p. U

2513 ORTS GONZALEZ, Juan, 1868-1941.
The best means to convert Roman Catholics. Richmond, Presbyterian Committee of Publication, n.d. 14 p. U

2514 ORTS GONZALEZ, Juan, 1868-1941.
Do Roman Catholics need the Gospel? Richmond, Presbyterian Committee of Publication, n.d. 16 p. U

2515 ORTS GONZALEZ, Juan, 1868-1941.

El destino de los pueblos ibéricos. 1. ed. Madrid, Libreria Nacional y Extranjera, 1932. 461 p. H

2516 ORTS GONZALEZ, Juan, 1868-1941.
Roman Catholicism capitulating before Protestantism, by G. V. Fradryssa [pseud.]. Translated from the Spanish. Mobile, Ala., Southern Publishing Co., 1908. 359 p. Half-title: A vindication of Christ, by a Catholic priest. A C H L R U

2517 ORTS GONZALEZ, Juan, 1868-1941.
Romanism; the greatest problem now before American Protestants. Address delivered before the conference on home missions at Memphis, Tenn., February, 1913. Richmond, Presbyterian Committee of Publication, n.d. 13 p. U

2518 ORTS GONZALEZ, Juan, 1868-1941.
Shall Roman Catholicism or Protestantism rule? Richmond, Presbyterian Committee of Publication, n.d. 8 p. U

2519 ORTS GONZALEZ, Juan, 1868-1941.
The way to fair play between American Catholics and patriots. Richmond, Presbyterian Committee of Publication, [19-?]. 35 p. U

2520 ORTS GONZALEZ, Juan, 1868-1941.
Why I am a Protestant. Richmond, Presbyterian Committee of Publication, n.d. 17 p. U

2521 OSMAN, John, 1907-1978.
Liberal education for adults and the liberal arts college. n.p., n.d. 10 p. Reprinted from Association of American Colleges Bulletin, March, 1953. U

2522 OSTENSON, Robert James, 1922-
God's happy family. [Miami, Fla., Logoi], © 1972. 95 p. R

2523 OTTS, John Martin Philip, 1837-1901.
At mother's knee. The mother's holy ministry with her children in the home. New York, Fleming H. Revell Co., © 1894. 175 p. H

2524 OTTS, John Martin Philip, 1837-1901.
Christ and the cherubim; or, The ark of the covenant a type of Christ our Saviour.... With an introduction by Francis R. Beattie. Richmond, Presbyterian Committee of Publication, © 1896. 63 p. A C H L PT R U

2525 OTTS, John Martin Philip, 1837-1901.

The fifth gospel; the land where Jesus lived. New York, Fleming H. Revell Co., © 1892. 367 p. H R U

2526 OTTS, John Martin Philip, 1837-1901.
Nicodemus with Jesus; or, Light and life for the dark and dead world. Philadelphia, James S. Claxton, 1867. 230 p. C H R U

2527 OTTS, John Martin Philip, 1837-1901.
Unsettled questions touching the foundations of Christianity. A book for thoughtful young men. New York, Fleming H. Revell Co., © 1893. 169 p. The Davidson College Divinity Lectures, 1893. C H R

2528 OUR THEOLOGIANS speak for Presbyterian reunion. The professors of theology in the four theological seminaries of the Presbyterian Church, U.S. [Kenneth J. Foreman, Felix B. Gear, James I. McCord, John N. Thomas] ... explain why they favor Presbyterian reunion. Charlottesville, Va. Friends of Presbyterian Union, n.d. 6 ℓ. U

2529 OVERHOLSER, James Arthur, 1911-
A contemporary Christian philosophy of religion. Chicago, Henry Regnery Co., © 1964. 214 p. A L PT U

2530 *OWEN, John, 1616-1683.
The glory of Christ. Edited ... by Wilbur M. Smith. Chicago, Moody Press, 1949. 285 p. C L PT R

2531 PAINE, Henry H.
God's people, kept by God's power. A sermon, preached by the appointment of the Presbytery of Montgomery, at Wytheville, Va., September the 13th, 1845. Fincastle, Va., Word & Wilson, 1846. 23 p. PH PT

2532 PAINTER, Henry Martyn, 1827-1893.
The duty of the southern patriot and Christian in the present crisis. A sermon preached in the First Presbyterian Church, Boonville, Mo., on Friday, January 4th, 1861, being the day of the national fast. Boonville, Caldwell & Stahl, 1861. 16 p. PH PT

2533 PAISLEY, Edward Bland, 1890-
Elders and deacons: their office and work. Course for church officers. Manual for teachers. Richmond, Presbyterian Committee of Publication, 1936. 2 pts. A H U

2534 PAISLEY, Henry Lewis, 1873-1961, ed.
Centennial history of Presbyterianism (U.S.) in Arkansas. n.p. [Synod of Arkansas, Presbyterian Church in the U.S.], 1954. 77 p. An up-to-date revision of an earlier work: The history of Presbyterianism in Arkansas. A PH

2535 PALMER, Benjamin Morgan, 1818-1902.
An address at the one hundredth anniversary of the organization of the Nazareth Church and congregation in Spartanburg, S.C. Richmond, Shepperson & Co., 1872. 39 p.
C H

2536 PALMER, Benjamin Morgan, 1818-1902.
An address delivered before the Philomathean & Euphemian
Literary societies, of Erskine College, at the annual com-
mencement, August 9th, 1854. Due West, S.C., Telescope
Office, 1854. 39 p. Running title: The love of truth, the
inspiration of the scholar. C PH ... A: microfilm.

2537 PALMER, Benjamin Morgan, 1818-1902.
An address, delivered to the graduating class of the So.
Ca. Female Collegiate Institute, Barhamville, on the evening
of the 19th June, A.D., 1950. Columbia, S.C., A. S.
Johnston, 1850. 13 p. C

2538 PALMER, Benjamin Morgan, 1818-1902.
The antidote of care. A sermon preached in the First
Presbyterian Church, Columbia, South Carolina, July 29,
1855. Columbia, I. C. Morgan, 1855. 32 p. C PH ...
A: microfilm.

2539 PALMER, Benjamin Morgan, 1818-1902.
Baconianism and the Bible. An address delivered before
the Eumenean and Philanthropic societies of Davidson College,
N.C., August 11, 1852. Columbia, S.C., A. S. Johnston,
1852. 31 p. PH

2540 PALMER, Benjamin Morgan, 1818-1902.
The broken home; or, Lessons in sorrow. New Orleans,
E. S. Upton, © 1890. 166 p. A H R U ... C L PT: 2d
ed. 1891.

2541 PALMER, Benjamin Palmer, 1818-1902.
Christianity and law; or, The claims of religion upon the
legal profession. A discourse upon the occasion of the death
of the late Alfred Hennen, Esq., the patriarch of the New
Orleans bar, delivered in the First Presbyterian Church,
New Orleans, February 27th, 1870. New Orleans, T. H.
Thomason, 1870. 31 p. PH ... A C H PH U: Richmond,
Presbyterian Committee of Publication, © 1871. 41 p.

2542 PALMER, Benjamin Morgan, 1818-1902.
Christianity, the only religion for man. A discourse delivered before the graduating class of the University of North
Carolina, June 4, 1855. Raleigh, "Carolina Cultivator,"
1855. 41 p. PH

2543 PALMER, Benjamin Morgan, 1818-1902.

The claims of the English language. An address delivered before the Phi-Delta and Thalian societies of Oglethorpe University, Georgia, on commencement day, November 10, 1852. Columbia, S.C., I. C. Morgan, 1853. 36 p. C PH

2544 PALMER, Benjamin Morgan, 1818-1902.
Discourse at the dedication of the new church edifice of the Central Presbyterian Church, St. Louis, Mo. (Oct. 1st, 1876). New Orleans, Clark & Hofeline, 1876. 17 p. Running title: The church, the kingdom of truth. C

2545 PALMER, Benjamin Morgan, 1818-1902.
A discourse before the General Assembly of South Carolina, on December 10, 1863, appointed by the legislature as a day of fasting, humiliation and prayer. Columbia, S.C., Charles P. Pelham, 1864. 24 p. C H

2546 PALMER, Benjamin Morgan, 1818-1902.
A discourse commemorative of the life, character, and genius of the late Rev. J. H. Thornwell, D.D., LL.D. Columbia, S.C., Southern Guardian Steampower Press, 1862. 57 p. PH U

2547 PALMER, Benjamin Morgan, 1818-1902.
The family companion; or, Prayers for every morning and evening of the week.... To which is appended, by request, a few sermons. Charleston, Burges & James, 1848. 347 p. H R

2548 PALMER, Benjamin Morgan, 1818-1902.
The family, in its civil and churchly aspects. An essay in two parts. Richmond, Presbyterian Committee of Publication, © 1876. 291 p. Taken from a series of articles originally published in the South Western Presbyterian. A C H L PH PT R U

2549 PALMER, Benjamin Morgan, 1818-1902.
Formation of character. Twelve lectures delivered in the First Presbyterian Church, New Orleans, La. New Orleans, E. S. Upton, © 1889. 222 p. A C H L PT R U

2550 PALMER, Benjamin Morgan, 1818-1902.
Hindrances to union with the church: a letter to an aged friend. Richmond, Presbyterian Committee of Publication, 1891. 19 p. A U

2551 PALMER, Benjamin Morgan, 1818-1902.
Influence of religious belief upon national character. An oration, delivered before the Demosthenian and Phi Kappa societies, of the University of Georgia, August 7, 1845. Athens, Banner Office, 1845. 30 p. C

2552 PALMER, Benjamin Morgan, 1818-1902.

Letter to the Synod of South-Carolina and Georgia, at their sessions in Augusta, in November, 1840. Charleston, S.C., B. Jenkins, 1843. 40 p. C H PH U

2553 PALMER, Benjamin Morgan, 1818-1902.
The life and letters of James Henley Thornwell, D.D., LL.D., ex-President of the South Carolina College, late Professor of Theology in the Theological Seminary at Columbia, S.C. Richmond, Whittet & Shepperson, © 1875. 614 p. A C H L PH PT R U ... C L PH: [New York], Arno Press and the New York Times, 1969 ... H R: London, Banner of Truth Trust, 1974.

2554 PALMER, Benjamin Morgan, 1818-1902.
National responsibility before God. A discourse, delivered on the day of fasting, humiliation and prayer, appointed by the President of the Confederate States of America, June 13, 1861. New Orleans, Price-Current Steam Book and Job Printing Office, 1861. 28 p. PH

2555 PALMER, Benjamin Morgan, 1818-1902.
Never too late. [Richmond, Committee of Publication, n.d.]. 4 p. C U

2556 PALMER, Benjamin Morgan, 1818-1902.
An open letter, prepared by B. M. Palmer, R. K. Smoot, C. R. Vaughan, R. L. Dabney, J. L. Girardeau [and others. New Orleans, E. S. Upton], n.d. 17 p. First page of text: An open letter to the members of the Southern Presbyterian Church. C U

2557 PALMER, Benjamin Morgan, 1818-1902.
"Our historic mission." An address delivered before the Eunomian and Phi-Mu societies of La Grange Synodical College, July 7, 1858. New Orleans, "True Witness" Office, 1859. 32 p. H PH

2558 PALMER, Benjamin Morgan, 1818-1902.
The pastoral letter of 1870, a historical and official document setting forth three "great principles" that "our church has declared in the most solemn and emphatic manner" to be "among the fundamental principles of our organization." Drawn by Dr. B. M. Palmer. Adopted by the General Assembly. n.p., n.d. 17 p. C U

2559 PALMER, Benjamin Morgan, 1818-1902.
The pious physician; or, The claims of religion upon the medical profession. Richmond, Presbyterian Committee of Publication, © 1871. 31 p. A C L PH R U

2560 PALMER, Benjamin Morgan, 1818-1902.
The present crisis and its issues. An address delivered

before the literary societies of Washington and Lee University, Lexington, Va., 27th June, 1872. Baltimore, John Murphy & Co., 1872. 28 p.   C PH

2561   PALMER, Benjamin Morgan, 1818-1902.
The rights of the South defended in the pulpits: by B. M. Palmer, D.D., and W. T. Leacock, D.D., of New Orleans. Mobile, J. Y. Thompson, 1860. 16 p.   H

2562   PALMER, Benjamin Morgan, 1818-1902.
Social dancing inconsistent with a Christian profession and baptismal vows: a sermon, preached in the Presbyterian Church, Columbia, S.C., June 17, 1849. Columbia, Office of the South Carolinian, 1849. 23 p.   C PH

2563   PALMER, Benjamin Morgan, 1818-1902.
The South: her peril and her duty. A discourse, delivered in the First Presbyterian Church, New Orleans, on Thursday, November 29, 1860. New Orleans, True Witness and Sentinel, 1860. 16 p. Thanksgiving sermon.   H U

2564   PALMER, Benjamin Morgan, 1818-1902.
Thanksgiving sermon, delivered at the First Presbyterian Church, New Orleans, on Thursday, December 29, 1860. New York, George F. Nesbitt & Co., 1861. 20 p. Cover-title: Slavery a divine trust. The duty of the South to preserve and perpetuate the institution as it now exists.   PT

2565   PALMER, Benjamin Morgan, 1818-1902.
Theology of prayer, as viewed in the religion of nature and in the system of grace. Richmond, Presbyterian Committee of Publication, 1894.   352 p.   A C H L PH PT R U

2566   PALMER, Benjamin Morgan, 1818-1902.
The threefold fellowship and the threefold assurance: an essay in two parts. Richmond, Presbyterian Committee of Publication, © 1902. 144 p.   A C H L PH PT R U

2567   PALMER, Benjamin Morgan, 1818-1902.
A vindication of secession and the South from the strictures of Rev. R. J. Breckinridge, D.D., LL.D., in the Danville Quarterly Review. Columbia, S.C., Southern Guardian Steam-power Press, 1861. 46 p. From the Southern Presbyterian Review, April, 1861.   PH

2568   PALMER, Benjamin Morgan, 1818-1902.
Warrant and nature of public worship. A discourse delivered at the dedication of the new Presbyterian Church edifice, Columbia, South-Carolina, on Sabbath morning, October 9th, 1853. Columbia, I. C. Morgan, 1853. 41 p.   C PH

2569   PARK, David, 1873-1958.

Missionary methods for missionary committees. Chicago, Fleming H. Revell Co., © 1898. 76 p. H L

2570 PARK, James, 1822-1912.
The history of the First Presbyterian Church, in Knoxville, Tennessee. A discourse ... delivered before the congregation, on Sabbath, July 2, 1876. Knoxville, Ramage & Co., 1876. 29 p. PH PT

2571 PARKER, Harold Marion, 1923-
The alleged union of the Southern Presbyterian Church and Alabama Presbytery of the Associate Reformed Presbyterian Church. n.p., n.d. 29-46 p. Reprinted from the Iliff Review, Winter, 1971. C H PH

2572 PARKER, Harold Marion, 1923-
Artexerxes III Ochus and Psalm 44. n.p., n.d. 152-168 p. Reprinted from the Jewish Quarterly Review, n.s., v. 68, 1977. PH

2573 PARKER, Harold Marion, 1923-
The Independent Presbyterian Church and reunion in the South, 1813-1863. n.p., n.d. 23 p. Reprinted from Journal of Presbyterian History, Summer, 1972. PH R

2574 PARKER, Harold Marion, 1923-
Much wealth and intelligence: the Presbytery of Patapsco. n.p., n.d. 160-174 p. Reprinted from Maryland Historical Magazine, June, 1965. H

2575 PARKER, Harold Marion, 1923-
The New School Presbyterian disruption in North Carolina. [Denver, Iliff School of Theology], 1975. 51-63 p. Reprinted from the Iliff Review, Spring, 1975. PH U

2576 PARKER, Harold Marion, 1923-
A school of the prophets at Maryville. [Nashville, Tenn., Tennessee Historical Quarterly], n.d. 72-90 p. Reprinted from the Tennessee Historical Quarterly. PH R

2577 PARKER, Harold Marion, 1923-
Sermons on the Minor Prophets: preached in Lake City, Colorado, in the summer of 1978. Gunnison, Colo., B & B Printers, 1979. 144 p. L PT U

2578 PARKER, Harold Marion, 1923-
Studies in Southern Presbyterian history. Gunnison, Colo., B & B Printers, 1979. 214 p. A C H L PT R U

2579 PARKER, Harold Marion, 1923-
The Synod of Kentucky, from Old School Assembly to the Southern Church. n.p., [1975]. 23 p. Reprinted from Journal of Presbyterian History, March, 1963. PH R

2580 PARKS, William H.,   -1895 or '96.
Address ... on the question of organic union between the
Presbyterian churches, north and south. St. Louis, Farris,
Smith & Co., 1887. 27 p.   U

2581 PARTEE, Charles Brooks, 1934-
Calvin and classical philosophy. Leiden, E. J. Brill,
1977. 163 p.   A C L R U

2582 *PASCHASIUS RADBERTUS, Saint, Abbot of Corbie, d. ca.
860.
Charlemagne's cousins; contemporary lives of Adalard and
Wala. Translated, with introduction and notes, by Allen Cabaniss. [1st ed. Syracuse, N.Y.], Syracuse University
Press, © 1967. 266 p. Translation of Vita sancti Adalhardi
and Vita Walae seu Epitaphium Arsenii.   A L PT

2583 PASMA, Henry Kay, 1881-1948.
Close-hauled. New York, Frederick A. Stokes Co., 1930.
312 p.   H

2584 PASMA, Henry Kay, 1881-1948.
God's picked young men. Chicago, Bible Institute Colportage Ass'n., © 1925. 96 p.   A L U

2585 PASMA, Henry Kay, 1881-1948.
Things a nation lives by. Richmond, Presbyterian Committee of Publication, © 1924. 179 p.   A H L R U

2586 PATTERSON, Brown Craig, 1865-1953.
Archaeology confirming and illustrating the Bible. Shanghai, Christian Book Room, 1935. In Chinese.   H

2587 PATTERSON, Brown Craig, 1865-1953.
Letters from Suchien, China, [by B. Craig Patterson and
Annie H. Patterson. Suchien, China, 1902]. 18 p.   U

2588 PATTERSON, M. A., ca. 1810-1882, comp.
History of Sandy Grove Presbyterian Church, by M. A.
Patterson and A. D. Carswell. Hoke County, N.C., Mem-
bers of Sandy Grove Church, n.d. 75 p.   H

2589 *PATTERSON, R. Foster, ed.
The best of men: a biography. Tarkio, Mo., Tarkio
Avalanche, 1928. 63 p. Biography of Samuel Jasper Pat-
terson.   H

2590 PATTERSON, Robert Meade, 1888-
Six reasons for total abstinence. Philadelphia, Presbyterian Board of Publication, n.d. 2 p.   U

2591 PATTERSON, Thomas Henry, 1898-

Memorial: David Rolston Bitzer (1902-1938). [Charleston, W.Va., Jarrett Printing Co.], n.d. 4 p. U

2592 PATTON, Franklin, 1820-1895.
The genesis of the Westminster Assembly: or, A brief history of the events and circumstances which occasioned the calling of that venerable assembly of divines and Christian statesmen. A centennial offering to the Sabbath-schools and youth of the Presbyterian Church. Richmond, Presbyterian Committee of Publication, 1889. 83 p. A C H U

2593 *PATTON, S.
A defense of Mr. Wesley and the Methodists, against the hostile attacks of the Rev. F. A. Ross. Knoxville, Tenn., H. & I. E. Barry, 1846. 156 p. PT

2594 *PAULSEN, Friedrich, 1846-1908.
The German universities and university study ... authorized translation by Frank Thilly ... and William W. Elwang. New York, Charles Scribner's Sons, 1906. 451 p. PT U

2595 PAYNE, Charles Montgomery, 1842-1900.
Our church, its faith and order: presented in two discourses delivered in the Second Presbyterian Church of Wilmington, N.C. Wilmington, Jackson & Bell, 1880. 21 p. PH

2596 PAYNE, John Barton, 1922-
Biblical prophecy for today. Grand Rapids, Mich., Baker Book House, © 1978. 93 p. R U

2597 PAYNE, John Barton, 1922-
Encyclopedia of Biblical prophecy; the complete guide to scriptural predictions and their fulfillment. [1st ed.] New York, Harper & Row, © 1973. 754 p. A C L PT R U

2598 PAYNE, John Barton, 1922-
Hebrew vocabularies based on Harper's Hebrew vocabularies. Grand Rapids, Mich., Baker Book House, 1956. 18 ℓ. PT U ... R: 1962.

2599 PAYNE, John Barton, 1922-
The imminent appearing of Christ. Grand Rapids, Mich., Wm. B. Eerdmans Publishing Co., © 1962. 191 p. A C L PT R

2600 PAYNE, John Barton, 1922-
An outline of Hebrew history. Grand Rapids, Mich., Baker Book House, 1954. 257 p. A PT R

2601 PAYNE, John Barton, 1922-
The theology of the older Testament. Grand Rapids, Mich., Zondervan Publishing House, © 1962. 554 p. A C PT R U

2602 PAYNE, John Barton, 1922-
What is a Reformed Presbyterian? Lookout Mountain,
Tenn., Mandate, 1974. 32 p. PH

2603 PEARSON, Robert Gamaliel, 1847-1913.
Evangelistic sermons.... With life sketch by his wife,
Mary Bowen Pearson. [Richmond, Richmond Press], n.d.
241 p. A C H R U

2604 PEARSON, Robert Gamaliel, 1847-1913.
Truth applied, or Bible readings. Nashville, Tenn.,
Cumberland Publishing House, 1889. 244 p. A H ... C
H R: 2d ed. 1890 ... PH R: 3d ed. ... H U: 4th ed.
1892.

2605 PECK, Thomas Ephraim, 1822-1893.
The action of the Assembly of 1879 on worldly amusements.
n.p., n.d. 27 p. Reprinted from the Southern Review,
April, 1880. U

2606 PECK, Thomas Ephraim, 1822-1893.
Herodias and John the Baptist; or, The dance and the mur-
der. A sermon ... delivered in the chapel of Union Theological Seminary, March 12, 1882. Richmond, Presbyterian
Committee of Publication, n.d. 29 p. U

2607 PECK, Thomas Ephraim, 1822-1893.
The Lord's Supper. Richmond, Presbyterian Committee
of Publication, 1882. 53 p. U

2608 PECK, Thomas Ephraim, 1822-1893.
Miscellanies.... Selected and arranged by Rev. T. C.
Johnson. Richmond, Presbyterian Committee of Publication,
1895-1897. 3 v. Biographical sketch of Dr. Peck by Rev.
C. R. Vaughan. A C H L PT R U

2609 PECK, Thomas Ephraim, 1822-1893.
Notes on ecclesiology. Richmond, Presbyterian Commit-
tee of Publication, 1892. 205 p. A C PT R ... C H L
PT U: 2d ed. © 1892. 215 p.

2610 PECK, Thomas Ephraim, 1822-1893.
Notes on the church. Printed by the students of Union
Seminary, Virginia. Exclusively for their own use. Rich-
mond, Baughman Brothers, 1880. 131 p. U

2611 PECK, Thomas Ephraim, 1822-1893.
The wisdom of man versus the power of God. Columbia,
S.C., Presbyterian Publishing House, 1878. 28 p. Reprint-
ed from the Southern Presbyterian Review, October, 1878.
U

2612 PELAN, James, -1863.

Our dangers and their remedies; a sermon preached on Thanksgiving Day. Tiffin City, [Ohio], Tribune Book & Job Office, 1855. 16 p. PH

2613 PENTECOST, George Edward, 1893-1951.
Rabboni; an Easter poem and song service with scenes and characters. Indianapolis, Ind., Meigs Publishing Co., © 1942. 23 p. Includes music. U

2614 PENTECOST, George Edward, 1893-1951.
Song of the winter garden. San Antonio, Tex., The Naylor Co., 1940. 78 p. A book of poems about Texas scenes and Texas people. A H U

2615 PERKINS, Hal Milford, 1860-1937.
Heart-songs, and other poems. [Dallas, Tex., Texas Presbyterian, 1913]. 61 p. H

2616 PERKINS, Richard Franklin, 1928-
Home and family nurture, manual. Richmond, CLC Press, © 1963. 48 p. (The Covenant Life Curriculum.) C L U

2617 PERKINS, Richard Franklin, 1928-
The image of a Christian family. Richmond, CLC Press, © 1964. 108 p. (The Covenant Life Curriculum.) C L R U

2618 PERKINS, Richard Franklin, 1928-
Leader's guide to Christian ethics for modern man. Richmond, John Knox Press, © 1972. 96 p. Contents.--Decisions! by George A. Chauncey.--Rich man poor man, by Donald W. Shriver, Jr.--Foreign policy is your business, by Theodore R. Weber. A C U

2619 PERROW, Maxwell Vermilyea, 1927-
Comunicação Cristã eficiente. n.p., [1965?]. 27 ℓ. A translation into Portuguese of his "Effective Christian communication." L

2620 PERROW, Maxwell Vermilyea, 1927-
Effective Christian communication. Richmond, John Knox Press, © 1962. 47 p. A C H L R U

2621 PERSON, Ralph Erb, 1931-
The mode of theological decision making at the early ecumenical councils: an inquiry into the function of Scripture and tradition at the councils of Nicaea and Ephesus. Basel, Friedrich Reinhardt Kommissionsverlag, 1978. 245 p. Diss.--Univ. of Basel. A C PT

2622 *PERSSON, Per Erik, 1923-
Sacra doctrina; reason and revelation in Aquinas.

Translated by Ross Mackenzie. Philadelphia, Fortress Press, © 1970. 317 p. A U

2623 PETERSEN, Harry Frederick, 1902-1959.
Open my eyes: guides to Bible study. n.p., [1965].
188 p. Title-page and text in Chinese. PT

2624 PETERSON, Eugene Hoiland, 1932-
Five smooth stones for pastoral work. Atlanta, John Knox Press, © 1980. 201 p. A C H L U

2625 PETERSON, Eugene Hoiland, 1932-
Growing up in Christ; a guide for families with adolescents.
Atlanta, John Knox Press, © 1976. 93 p. A H L U

2626 PETERSON, Eugene Hoiland, 1932-
A long obedience in the same direction: discipleship in an instant society. Downers Grove, Ill., InterVarsity Press, © 1980. 197 p. A U

2627 PETERSON, Eugene Hoiland, 1932-
A year with the Psalms: 365 meditations and prayers.
Waco, Tex., Word Books, © 1979. 196 p. U

2628 PETRIE, George Laurens, 1840-1931.
Anniversary address, February 25, 1920 ... on the occasion of his 80th birthday. Published by the officers of this church. Charlottesville, Va., n.p., 1920. 20 p. U

2629 PETRIE, George Laurens, 1840-1931.
Church and state in early Maryland. Baltimore, Johns Hopkins Press, 1892. 50 p. H

2630 PETRIE, George Laurens, 1840-1931.
The days of thy youth, Ecc. 12:1. Baccalaureate sermon, Charlottesville High School. n.p., n.d. unpaged. U

2631 PETRIE, George Laurens, 1840-1931.
Israel's prophets. New York, The Neale Publishing Co., 1912. 243 p. A C H R U

2632 PETRIE, George Laurens, 1840-1931.
Jacob's sons. New York, The Neale Publishing Co., 1910.
229 p. A C H R U

2633 PHARR, Samuel Caldwell, 1825-
A brief essay on the visible church. Charlotte, N.C., Hornets' Nest and True Southron Job Office, 1850. 38 p. PH

2634 PHIFER, Kenneth Galloway, 1915-
A Protestant case for liturgical renewal. Philadelphia, Westminster Press, © 1965. 175 p. A C L R U

2635　PHIFER, Kenneth Galloway, 1915-
　　　　A star is born. [Richmond, John Knox Press], © 1947.
　　　31 p.　U ... L: [1952].

2636　PHIFER, Kenneth Galloway, 1915-
　　　　Tales of human frailty and the gentleness of God.　Atlanta,
　　　John Knox Press, © 1974.　127 p.　A C H L U

2637　PHIFER, William Everette, 1909-
　　　　The cross and great living.　New York, Abingdon-Cokesbury
　　　Press, © 1943.　192 p.　A C H L U

2638　PHILLIPS, Alexander Lacy, 1859-1915.
　　　　A boy and his Bible.　Richmond, Presbyterian Committee
　　　of Publication, © 1903.　15 p.　U

2639　PHILLIPS, Alexander Lacy, 1859-1915.
　　　　The call of the homeland: a study in home missions.
　　　n.p., © 1906.　173 p.　A C H R U ... H PT:　3d ed.,
　　　rev. and enl.　Richmond, Presbyterian Committee of Publica-
　　　tion, 1910.　197 p.

2640　PHILLIPS, Alexander Lacy, 1859-1915.
　　　　A certificate Teacher Training Course covering 54 lessons
　　　or one year's study.　Richmond, Presbyterian Committee of
　　　Publication, © 1908, 191 p.　H ... R: © 1912.

2641　PHILLIPS, Alexander Lacy, 1859-1915.
　　　　The geography of Palestine.... For use in the Sabbath-
　　　school graded course of instruction--junior department, second
　　　and third years.　Richmond, Presbyterian Committee of Pub-
　　　lication, 1904.　57 p.　C U ... H: 1906.　58 p.

2642　PHILLIPS, Alexander Lacy, 1859-1915.
　　　　Hints to leaders of teacher training classes.　Westminster
　　　First Standard Teacher Training Course.　Vol. I.　Rich-
　　　mond, Presbyterian Committee of Publication, 1909.　47 p.
　　　H

2643　PHILLIPS, Alexander Lacy, 1859-1915.
　　　　The Presbyterian Church in the United States and the
　　　colored people. [Birmingham, Roberts & Son, 18-?].　27 p.
　　　A PH

2644　PHILLIPS, Alexander Lacy, 1859-1915.
　　　　Soul winning; the greatest privilege in the world.　Rich-
　　　mond, Presbyterian Committee of Publication, n.d.　12 p.
　　　U

2645　PHILLIPS, Alexander Lacy, 1859-1915.
　　　　Sunday School extension.　Richmond, Presbyterian Com-
　　　mittee of Publication, 1911.　16 p.　U

2646 PHILLIPS, Alexander Lacy, 1859-1915.
The training of the Sabbath-school teacher. Richmond,
Presbyterian Committee of Publication, n.d. 12 p. U

2647 PHILLIPS, Alexander Lacy, 1859-1915, ed.
The Westminster Standard Teacher Training Course.
Standard first course. Approved by the Educational Commit-
tee of the International Sunday School Association, 1908.
Richmond, Presbyterian Committee of Publication, © 1908.
192 p. H ... H U: Rev. and enl. 1914. 191 p.

2648 PHILLIPS, Charles, 1822-1889.
A memoir of the Rev. Elisha Mitchell, D.D., late Professor of chemistry, mineralogy & geology in the University
of North Carolina. Chapel Hill, N.C., J. M. Henderson,
1858. 88 p. H ... U: microfilm.

2649 PHILLIPS, Samuel Knox, 1885-1944.
From a Presbyterian pastor; an address delivered at the
state Baraca-Philathea Convention of North Carolina, Charlotte, N.C., April 15, 1913. n.p., n.d. 61 p. U

2650 PHILLIPS, Samuel Knox, 1885-1944.
Where God classes foreign missions. [Nashville, Tenn.,
Executive Committee of Foreign Missions, Presbyterian
Church in the U.S.], n.d. 16 p. U

2651 PHIPPS, William Eugene, 1930-
Christianity and nationalism in tropical Africa. [Nairobi,
East African Literature Bureau, 1972]. 407-415 p. Off-
print of Pan-African Journal, Winter, 1972. U

2652 PHIPPS, William Eugene, 1930-
Influential theologians on wo/man. [Washington, D.C.],
University Press of America, © 1980. 135 p. A C PT U

2653 PHIPPS, William Eugene, 1930-
Recovering Biblical sensuousness. Philadelphia, Westminster Press, © 1975. 192 p. C L PH PT R U

2654 PHIPPS, William Eugene, 1930-
The sexuality of Jesus: theological and literary perspec-
tives. [1st ed.] New York, Harper & Row, © 1973. 172 p.
A C L PT U

2655 PHIPPS, William Eugene, 1930-
Was Jesus married? The distortion of sexuality in the
Christian tradition. [1st ed.] New York, Harper & Row,
© 1970. 239 p. A C L PT R U

2656 PIERCE, Albert Winthrop, 1872-1964.
From Coquina Beach to coral strand: a sketch of the

progress of the Presbyterian Church, U.S.A., in Florida, from 1824-1927. n.p., n.d. 21 p. PH PT

2657 PIERCE, Albert Winthrop, 1872-1964.
The Presbyterian Church U.S.A. in Florida, 1948. n.p., [1948?]. unpaged. PH

2658 *PIETERS, Albertus, 1869-
A candid examination of the Scofield Bible; a lecture delivered before the Ministerial Association of the Christian Reformed Church at Calvin College, Grand Rapids, Michigan, June 1st, 1938. Swengel (Union Co.), Penna., Bible Truth Depot, n.d. 31 p. C PT U

2659 *PIETERS, Albertus, 1869-
The Scofield Bible. Swengel, Penna., Reiner Publications, 1965. 26 p. R

2660 PING, Charles Jackson, 1930-
Meaningful nonsense. Philadelphia, Westminster Press, © 1966. 143 p. A C L PH U

2661 PIONEER Presbyterianism in Tennessee. Addresses delivered at the Tennessee Exposition on Presbyterian Day, October 28, 1897. Richmond, Presbyterian Committee of Publication, © 1898. 83 p. Contents.--Pioneer Presbyterianism in Tennessee, by C. W. Heiskell.--Rev. Samuel Doak and his successors, by J. W. Bachman.--Presbyterianism and education, by W. W. Moore. A C H L PH PT R U

2662 PISGAH Presbyterian Church, Woodford County, Kentucky, 1784-1940. n.p., n.d. 51 p. Foreword signed by Thomas C. Rhea, minister. H

2663 PITZER, Alexander White, 1834-1927.
The blessed hope of the Lord's return. Washington, D.C., Wm. Ballantyne & Sons, 1904. 87 p. H PH U

2664 PITZER, Alexander White, 1834-1927.
Christ, the teacher of men. Philadelphia, J. B. Lippincott & Co., 1877. 219 p. C R U

2665 PITZER, Alexander White, 1834-1927.
Confidence in Christ; or, Faith that saves. Philadelphia, Presbyterian Board of Publication, © 1888. 108 p. A

2666 PITZER, Alexander White, 1834-1927.
Ecce Deus: essays on the life and doctrine of Jesus Christ. With controversial notes on "Ecce homo." Boston, Roberts Brothers, 1867. 363 p. R

2667 PITZER, Alexander White, 1834-1927.

Ecce Deus-homo; or, The work and kingdom of the Christ of Scripture. Philadelphia, J. B. Lippincott & Co., 1868. 207 p.   H PT U ... C: 1877.

2668   PITZER, Alexander White, 1834-1927.
The final anti-Christ and the cherubim. Roanoke, Va., Stone Printing and Manufacturing Co., n.d. 36 p.   PH

2669   PITZER, Alexander White, 1834-1927.
The manifold ministry of the Holy Spirit. Philadelphia, Presbyterian Board of Publication and Sabbath-school Work, © 1894. 62 p.   C H PH PT R U

2670   PITZER, Alexander White, 1834-1927.
... Missionary aspects of the book of Acts. An address to the Training-School, delivered June 2, 1897. Richmond, Whittet & Shepperson, 1897. 12 p. At head of title: The Assembly's Home and School, at Fredericksburg, Va.   PH

2671   PITZER, Alexander White, 1834-1927.
The new life not the higher life; or, The believer's holiness personal and progressive. Philadelphia, Presbyterian Board of Publication, © 1878. 96 p.   A C H PH PT U

2672   PITZER, Alexander White, 1834-1927.
The origin and work of the Central Presbyterian Church, Washington, D.C. A discourse. Washington, J. F. Sheiry, 1880. 24 p.   PH

2673   PITZER, Alexander White, 1834-1927.
Predestination; a sermon preached from Ephesians I: II ... before the Presbytery of Chesapeake at Aldie, Va., September 7, 1897. Washington, D.C., John F. Sheiry, 1897. 12 p. PH

2674   PITZER, Alexander White, 1834-1927.
Predestination; God's working plan of his universe. Philadelphia, Westminster Press, 1899. 14 p.   PH PT U

2675   PITZER, Alexander White, 1834-1927.
Shall God's house of worship be taxed? The substance of an address at a meeting of ministers and church officers in Washington, D.C. Washington, Wm. Ballantyne, n.d. 7 p. Republished from the Southern Review.   PH

2676   PITZER, Alexander White, 1834-1927.
Will Jesus ever come back to this earth? Salem, Va., Salem Printing and Publishing Co., 1913. 19 p.   PH

2677   PLEUNE, Peter Henry, 1883-1966.
The land of happiness. Richmond, Presbyterian Committee of Publication, © 1929. 128 p.   A H L R U

2678 PLEUNE, Peter Henry, 1883-1966.
The road without a detour. Richmond, Presbyterian Committee of Publication, 1922. 104 p. A C L U

2679 PLEUNE, Peter Henry, 1883-1966.
Some to be pastors. New York, Abingdon-Cokesbury Press, © 1943. 191 p. "War edition." A C L PT R U

2680 PLEUNE, Peter Henry, 1883-1966.
The whereabouts of God. New York, Abingdon-Cokesbury Press, © 1946. 185 p. H L R U

2681 PLUMER, William Swan, 1802-1880.
The afflictions of God's people considered. New York, Board of Publications of the Reformed Protestant Dutch Church, n.d. 12 p. PH

2682 PLUMER, William Swan, 1802-1880.
Angels and men. [Richmond, Presbyterian Committee of Publication], n.d. 8 p. U

2683 PLUMER, William Swan, 1802-1880.
Assurance of grace and salvation: what it is; how to attain it; why more do not enjoy it. Richmond, Presbyterian Committee of Publication, n.d. 34 p. A

2684 PLUMER, William Swan, 1802-1880.
Balm for wounded spirits. Richmond, Presbyterian Committee of Publication, n.d. 70 p. A U

2685 PLUMER, William Swan, 1802-1880.
The beatific vision. New York, Anson D. F. Randolph & Co., © 1878. 93 p. PH

2686 PLUMER, William Swan, 1802-1880.
A beautiful robe. [Richmond, Presbyterian Committee of Publication], n.d. 8 p. U

2687 PLUMER, William Swan, 1802-1880.
The Bible true, and infidelity wicked. New York, American Tract Society, n.d. 79 p. A C H PH PT R ... U: 96 p.

2688 PLUMER, William Swan, 1802-1880.
A call to personal labor as a foreign missionary. n.p., n.d. 16 p. C PT

2689 PLUMER, William Swan, 1802-1880.
Christ is head of the church. Philadelphia, Presbyterian Board of Publication, © 1879. 16 p. PH

2690 PLUMER, William Swan, 1802-1880.

Christ our theme and glory: being the inaugural address ...
as Professor of Didactic and Pastoral Theology in the Western Theological Seminary of the Presbyterian Church at Allegheny City, Pa., October 20, 1854. 2d ed. Philadelphia,
William S. & Alfred Martien, 1855. 35 p. PH

2691 PLUMER, William Swan, 1802-1880.
The Christian. Philadelphia, J. B. Lippincott & Co.,
1878. 146 p. R

2692 PLUMER, William Swan, 1802-1880.
The church and her enemies; or, Practical reflections on
the trials and triumphs of God's afflicted people. Philadelphia, American Baptist Publication Society, © 1856. 124 p.
C

2693 PLUMER, William Swan, 1802-1880.
The cities of refuge. Philadelphia, Presbyterian Board of
Publication, n.d. 11 p. C PH

2694 PLUMER, William Swan, 1802-1880.
Commentary on Paul's Epistle to the Romans. With an
introduction on the life, times, writings, and character of
Paul. New York, Anson D. F. Randolph & Co., 1870.
646 p. A H L PT R U ... C: Edinburgh, W. Oliphant &
Co., n.d. ... C R: Grand Rapids, Mich., Kregel Publications, [1971].

2695 PLUMER, William Swan, 1802-1880.
Commentary on the Epistle of Paul, the apostle, to the
Hebrews. New York, Anson D. F. Randolph & Co., © 1872.
559 p. A C H R U

2696 PLUMER, William Swan, 1802-1880.
The conversion of Dr. Gurley. Philadelphia, Presbyterian
Board of Publication, n.d. 11 p. C PH

2697 PLUMER, William Swan, 1802-1880.
Conviction and conversion. Philadelphia, Presbyterian
Board of Publication, n.d. 11 p. C PH

2698 PLUMER, William Swan, 1802-1880.
Devout meditation, or think on God's name and on all his
works and ways. Philadelphia, Presbyterian Board of Publication, n.d. 16 p. (Presbyterian Tracts, no. 169.) C
H L PH PT R U

2699 PLUMER, William Swan, 1802-1880.
Early impressions revived. Philadelphia, Presbyterian
Board of Publication, n.d. 11 p. PH

2700 PLUMER, William Swan, 1802-1880.

Earnest hours. Richmond, Presbyterian Committee of Publication, © 1869. 333 p. C H PH PT R U

2701 PLUMER, William Swan, 1802-1880.
The fall of our first parents; question no. 15. Bellefonte, Pa., Bellefonte Press, n.d. 6 p. C

2702 PLUMER, William Swan, 1802-1880.
False doctrines and false teachers: how to know them, and how to treat them. Richmond, Presbyterian Committee of Publication, © 1880. 33 p. U

2703 PLUMER, William Swan, 1802-1880.
Farewell letter. To the Central Presbyterian Church, Allegheny, Pa. n.p., 1862. 4 p. H PH

2704 PLUMER, William Swan, 1802-1880.
A friendly letter to a young man. Philadelphia, Presbyterian Board of Publication, n.d. 16 p. PH

2705 PLUMER, William Swan, 1802-1880.
God's purpose of grace. 2d ed. London, Sovereign Grace Union, [1929]. 15 p. PH PT

2706 PLUMER, William Swan, 1802-1880.
The grace of Christ, or sinners saved by unmerited kindness. Philadelphia, Presbyterian Board of Publication, © 1853. 454 p. A C H L PH PT R U

2707 PLUMER, William Swan, 1802-1880.
The great giver. Philadelphia, n.p., n.d. 4 p. PT

2708 PLUMER, William Swan, 1802-1880.
The great race. Philadelphia, Presbyterian Board of Publication, n.d. 11 p. PH

2709 PLUMER, William Swan, 1802-1880.
Hints and helps in pastoral theology. New York, Harper & Brothers, 1874. 381 p. A C H L PH PT R U

2710 PLUMER, William Swan, 1802-1880.
How stands my case with God? A help to self-examination. Philadelphia, Presbyterian Board of Publication, n.d. 28 p. (Presbyterian Tracts, no. 136.) C H L PH PT R U

2711 PLUMER, William Swan, 1802-1880.
How to bring up children. n.p., n.d. 8 p. (Presbyterian Tracts, no. 64.) C H L PH PT R U

2712 PLUMER, William Swan, 1802-1880.
How to use the Bible. n.p., n.d. 28 p. (Presbyterian Tracts, no. 102.) C H L PH PT R U

2713   PLUMER, William Swan, 1802-1880.
       The importance of personal holiness. A farewell address
       to the Presbyterian Church and congregation in Petersburg,
       Va. Shellbanks, Va., Robt. Ricketts, 1834. 11 p.   H PH

2714   PLUMER, William Swan, 1802-1880.
       Inaugural address ... as Professor of Didactic and Polemic
       Theology in the Theological Seminary at Columbia, S.C., in
       the presence and by order of the General Assembly of the
       Presbyterian Church in the United States at Nashville, Tenn.,
       Nov. 26, 1868. Columbia, S.C., Southern Presbyterian Re-
       view, 1868. 16 p.   PH PT

2715   PLUMER, William Swan, 1802-1880.
       The incomprehensibility of God's nature and ways. n.p.,
       n.d. 24 p. First published in the American National Preach-
       er.   C PH PT

2716   PLUMER, William Swan, 1802-1880.
       Jehovah-Jireh: a treatise on providence. Philadelphia,
       J. B. Lippincott & Co., © 1865. 233 p.   C R ... PH
       PT U: 1866 ... R: Richmond, Presbyterian Committee of
       Publication, 1865 ... H U: 1867 ... A PT: 1870 ... C:
       1877.

2717   PLUMER, William Swan, 1802-1880.
       The law of God, as contained in the Ten Commandments,
       explained and enforced. Philadelphia, Presbyterian Board of
       Publication, © 1864. 644 p.   A C H L PH R U

2718   PLUMER, William Swan, 1802-1880.
       The law of the Sabbath still binding, and what it forbids.
       New York, American Tract Society, n.d. 20 p.   C H

2719   PLUMER; William Swan, 1802-1880.
       A letter on the death of a child. Richmond, Presbyterian
       Committee of Publication, n.d. 8 p.   PH U

2720   PLUMER, William Swan, 1802-1880.
       The Lord Jesus Christ, our life, our joy and our glory.
       New York, Board of Publication of the Reformed Protestant
       Dutch Church, n.d. 12 p.   PH

2721   PLUMER, William Swan, 1802-1880.
       The Lord will give grace and glory. n.p., n.d.   4 p.
       (Presbyterian Tracts, no. 93.)   C H L PH PT R U

2722   PLUMER, William Swan, 1802-1880.
       Making haste to be rich. New York, Phillips & Hunt,
       n.d.   4 p.   PT

2723   PLUMER, William Swan, 1802-1880.

Manual for the members of the Presbyterian Church in Petersburg, Virginia. Petersburg, Yancey & Wilson, 1833. 50 p.   A C H

2724   PLUMER, William Swan, 1802-1880.
The martyrdom of Polycarp. Philadelphia, Presbyterian Board of Publication, n.d.   11 p.   PH

2725   PLUMER, William Swan, 1802-1880.
Martyrs and sufferers for the truth. Philadelphia, Presbyterian Board of Publication, [1869].   172 p.   PT

2726   PLUMER, William Swan, 1802-1880.
Missions will succeed: a sermon, preached before the Board of Foreign Missions of the Presbyterian Church, at its meeting in Philadelphia, Pa., May 21, 1843. n.p., n.d. 10 p.   C PH PT

2727   PLUMER, William Swan, 1802-1880.
Naaman the Syrian. Philadelphia, Presbyterian Board of Publication, n.d.   11 p.   PH

2728   PLUMER, William Swan, 1802-1880.
One wrong step. Philadelphia, Presbyterian Board of Publication, n.d.   11 p.   C PH

2729   PLUMER, William Swan, 1802-1880.
The person and sinless character of our Lord Jesus Christ. Richmond, Presbyterian Committee of Publication, © 1876. 127 p.   A C H L PH PT R U

2730   PLUMER, William Swan, 1802-1880.
Plain thoughts about great and good things for little boys and girls. Philadelphia, Presbyterian Board of Publication, © 1849.   122 p.   C PH PT ... C: 124 p.

2731   PLUMER, William Swan, 1802-1880.
Praise and thanksgiving. Philadelphia, Presbyterian Board of Publication, n.d.   11 p.   (Presbyterian Tracts, no. 186.) C H L PH PT R U

2732   PLUMER, William Swan, 1802-1880.
The promises of God; their nature and properties, variety and value. New York, Board of Publication, Reformed Church in America, 1872.   91 p.   A PT ... PH: microfilm.

2733   PLUMER, William Swan, 1802-1880.
Repentance unto life. [Richmond, Presbyterian Committee of Publication], n.d.   4 p.   U

2734   PLUMER, William Swan, 1802-1880.
Revivals of religion. n.p., n.d.   2 p.   U

2735 PLUMER, William Swan, 1802-1880.
        The right temper for a student of God's word. Richmond,
        Presbyterian Committee of Publication, n.d. 16 p.   PH U

2736 PLUMER, William Swan, 1802-1880.
        The rights of conscience. A report presented to the
        General Assembly of the Presbyterian Church in the United
        States of America, May, 1853. Philadelphia, Published by
        request of the Assembly, 1853. 46 p.   PT

2737 PLUMER, William Swan, 1802-1880.
        The rock of our salvation: a treatise respecting the na-
        tures, person, offices, work, sufferings, and glory of Jesus
        Christ. New York, American Tract Society, © 1867. 519 p.
        A C H L PH PT R U

2738 PLUMER, William Swan, 1802-1880.
        Rome against the Bible, and the Bible against Rome; or,
        Pharisaism, Jewish and papal. Philadelphia, American Bap-
        tist Publication Society, © 1854. 129 p.   A C H PH PT R

2739 PLUMER, William Swan, 1802-1880.
        A sad but instructive history. Philadelphia, Presbyterian
        Board of Publication, n.d. 11 p.   PH U

2740 PLUMER, William Swan, 1802-1880.
        The saint and the sinner. Philadelphia, Presbyterian
        Board of Publication, © 1849. 36 p.   C H PH PT U

2741 PLUMER, William Swan, 1802-1880.
        Secret prayer. n.p., n.d. 12 p. (Presbyterian Tracts,
        no. 190.)   C H L PH PT R U

2742 PLUMER, William Swan, 1802-1880.
        Short sermons for the people. New York, American Tract
        Society, [18??]. various pagings.   H R

2743 PLUMER, William Swan, 1802-1880.
        Short sermons to little children.... Written for the Ameri-
        can Sunday-school Union, and revised by the Committee of
        Publication. Philadelphia, American Sunday-school Union,
        © 1848. 123 p.   A C PH PT

2744 PLUMER, William Swan, 1802-1880.
        Sin must die, or the soul must die. Philadelphia, Presby-
        terian Board of Publication, n.d. 12 p. (Presbyterian Tracts,
        no. 85.)   C H L PH PT R U

2745 PLUMER, William Swan, 1802-1880.
        Sins of the tongue, with rules and reasons for avoiding
        them. Philadelphia, Presbyterian Board of Publication, n.d.
        28 p. (Presbyterian Tracts, no. 135.)   C H L PH PT R U

2746   PLUMER, William Swan, 1802-1880.
       Studies in the book of Psalms: being a critical and expo-
sitory commentary, with doctrinal and practical remarks on
the entire Psalter. Philadelphia, J. B. Lippincott & Co.,
1866. 1211 p.   H U ... A C H L PH PT R: 1867 ... U:
1870 ... C R: Psalms. [Edinburgh], Banner of Truth
Trust, [1975].

2747   PLUMER, William Swan, 1802-1880.
       The substance of an argument against the indiscriminate
incorporation of churches and religious societies. Delivered
before the Committee of Courts of Justice of the House of
Delegates of Virginia, on the evening of the 8th of January,
and on subsequent evenings, in A.D. 1846, in reply to James
Lyons and Wm. H. Macfarland, Esqs. Baltimore, Publication Rooms, 1847. 82 p.   C PH PT R

2748   PLUMER, William Swan, 1802-1880.
       Theatrical entertainments. A premium tract. Philadelphia,
American Baptist Publication Society, n.d. 24 p.   PH

2749   PLUMER, William Swan, 1802-1880.
       Thoughts on religious education and early piety. New York,
John S. Taylor, 1836. 113 p.   C H PH

2750   PLUMER, William Swan, 1802-1880.
       Thoughts on the religious instruction of the negroes of this
country. Princeton, N.J., John T. Robinson, 1848. 30 p.
First published in the Princeton Review.   PH

2751   PLUMER, William Swan, 1802-1880.
       To a young man. Philadelphia, n.p., n.d. 16 p. (Pres-
byterian Tracts, no. 129.)   PT

2752   PLUMER, William Swan, 1802-1880.
       To an old disciple. Philadelphia, Presbyterian Board of
Publication, n.d. 12 p. (Presbyterian Tracts, no. 62.)
C H L PH PT R U

2753   PLUMER, William Swan, 1802-1880.
       To an old person who has no hope in Christ. Philadelphia,
Presbyterian Board of Publication, n.d. 8 p. (Presbyterian
Tracts, no. 63.)   C H L PH PT R U

2754   PLUMER, William Swan, 1802-1880.
       The triumph of grace. [Philadelphia, Presbyterian Board
of Publication], n.d. 4 p. (Presbyterian Tracts, no. 224.)
H PH PT R U

2755   PLUMER, William Swan, 1802-1880.
       Truths for the people: or, Several points in theology
plainly stated for beginners. New York, American Tract
Society, © 1875. 227 p.   A H PT R U ... PH: microfilm.

2756 PLUMER, William Swan, 1802-1880.
Two fountains. Philadelphia, Presbyterian Board of Publication, n.d. 11 p. C PH

2757 PLUMER, William Swan, 1802-1880.
The vineyard. Philadelphia, Presbyterian Board of Publication, n.d. 11 p. PH

2758 PLUMER, William Swan, 1802-1880.
Vital godliness: a treatise on experimental and practical
piety. New York, American Tract Society, © 1864. 610 p.
A C H L PH R U

2759 PLUMER, William Swan, 1802-1880.
A Western patriarch. n.p., n.d. 16 p. (Presbyterian
Tracts, no. 89.) C H L PH PT R U

2760 PLUMER, William Swan, 1802-1880.
What think you of Christ? [New York, Board of Publica-
tion of the Reformed Protestant Dutch Church], n.d. 4 p.
PH

2761 PLUMER, William Swan, 1802-1880.
What think you of sin? New York, Phillips & Hunt, n.d.
8 p. PT

2762 PLUMER, William Swan, 1802-1880.
Will you have this Christ? n.p., n.d. 12 p. (Presbyterian Tracts, no. 208.) PT

2763 PLUMER, William Swan, 1802-1880.
A word to the weary. New York, Anson D. F. Randolph
& Co., © 1874. 96 p. PT

2764 PLUMER, William Swan, 1802-1880.
Words of truth and love. Philadelphia, Presbyterian Board
of Publication, © 1867. 126 p. PT

2765 PLUMER, William Swan, 1802-1880.
Young Servin. Philadelphia, Presbyterian Board of Publication, n.d. 11 p. PH

2766 POET, Sylvan Stephen, 1905-
Valdese, N.C. A Waldensian colony in the United States.
[Valdese, The Valdese News], © 1940. 19 p. Prepared in
connection with the Waldensian celebration and the dedication
of the new Sunday School building of the Waldensian Presbyterian Church, February 17th, 1940. H

2767 POLLOCK, Abraham David, 1807-1890.
Laborers in the Gospel harvest: how they are to be forth-
coming in requisite numbers and of the necessary description.

A sermon: preached in High Street Presbyterian Church, Petersburg, Oct. 9th, 1940, at the opening of Hanover Presbytery. Richmond, Peter D. Bernard, 1841. 22 p.   PT

2768 POLLOCK, Abraham David, 1807-1890.
Life in the exode. New York and Baltimore, University Publishing Co., 1872. 609 p.   C H U

2769 PORTER, Abner Addison, 1817-1872.
The church setting up her banners: a discourse delivered at the dedication of the Presbyterian Church, in Selma, Alabama, September 28th, 1851. Selma, Selma Reporter Job Office, [1851]. 16 p.   C

2770 PORTER, Abner Addison, 1817-1872.
On the division of the Presbyterian Church: a lecture, delivered in Austin, Texas, December 5, 1869. Austin, Tex., State Gazette Office, 1870. 19 p.   A H

2771 PORTER, Abner Addison, 1817-1872.
Our danger and duty. A discourse, delivered in the Glebe-street Presbyterian Church, on Friday, December 6th, 1850. Charleston, E. C. Councell, 1850. 16 p.   C

2772 PORTER, Abner Addison, 1817-1872.
A plea for the old, against the new, in education. An address delivered at the close of the annual examination of the Presbyterian high schools, at Greenwood, Abbeville District, S.C., August 2nd, 1850. Charleston, S.C., Walker and James, 1850. 25 p.   C PH

2773 PORTER, David H., 1830-1873.
Religion and the state. A discourse delivered in the First Presbyterian Church, Savannah, Georgia, July 4th, 1858. Savannah, John M. Cooper & Co., 1858. 21 p.   PH

2774 PORTER, George J.,   -1891 or 1892.
Historical discourse delivered in the First Presbyterian Church, Newark, Delaware, July 22, 1876. Philadelphia, Jas. P. Bryan & Co., 1876. 15 p.   PH PT

2775 PORTER, Rufus Kilpatrick, 1827-1869.
Christian duty in the present crisis; the substance of a sermon delivered in the Presbyterian Church in Waynesboro, Ga., Dec. 9, 1860. Savannah, Ga., John M. Cooper & Co., 1860. 20 p.   H PH

2776 PORTER, Rufus Kilpatrick, 1827-1869.
The duties of the eldership. A sermon, preached by appointment of Hopewell Presbytery, at its sessions in Milledgeville, Ga., April 7, 1859. Augusta, Ga., Office of the Constitutionalist, 1859. 20 p.   PH U

2777　PORTERFIELD, Robert E., 1866-1948.
　　　　Presbyterian government, doctrine, sacraments and fruits.
　　　　Kingsville, Tex., Tex.-Mex. Printery, n.d.　41 p.　PH U

2778　POWELL, John Henderson, 1898-
　　　　The Ten Commandments.　New York, The Macmillan Co.,
　　　　1932.　154 p.　Sermons.　A H PT U

2779　*POWER, J. L.
　　　　Address at the unveiling of the monument to Rev. Thomas
　　　　R. Markham, D.D., Metaire Cemetery, New Orleans, May
　　　　20, 1899.　New Orleans, n.p., n.d.　18 p.　H U

2780　PRATT, Charles Henry, 1881-1950.
　　　　"Re-thinking missions." An address.　n.p., n.d.　15 p.
　　　　PH PT

2781　PRATT, Henry Barrington, 1832-1912.
　　　　La Biblia y sus opositores.　Escrito dedicado a los Ro-
　　　　manistas adversarios de la Biblia en jeneral, y al Senor
　　　　José Manuel Groot en particular.　Bogota, Imprenta de
　　　　Gaitan, 1875.　30 p.　PH

2782　PRATT, Henry Barrington, 1832-1912.
　　　　The buried nations of the infant dead; a study in eschatol-
　　　　ogy.　Hackensack, N.J., B. G. Pratt Co., 1911.　158 p.
　　　　A H PT U

2783　PRATT, Henry Barrington, 1832-1912.
　　　　A defence of Presbyterian baptism:　being the substance of
　　　　two addresses on the subjects and mode of Christian baptism,
　　　　delivered in the Presbyterian Church of Hillsboro, N.C.
　　　　Richmond, Vannerson, Shepperson & Graves, 1869.　80 p.
　　　　A C U

2784　PRATT, Henry Barrington, 1832-1912.
　　　　Estudios críticos y aclaratorios sobre la Santa Escritura
　　　　fundados en la versión moderna.　New York, La Sociedad
　　　　Americana de Tratados, 1902-10.　3 v.　A PT

2785　PRATT, Henry Barrington, 1832-1912.
　　　　History of the "Version Moderna" of the Spanish Bible:
　　　　its author and its adversaries.　[Hackensack, N.J., n.p.,
　　　　1911].　31 p.　PH U

2786　PRATT, Henry Barrington, 1832-1912.
　　　　On the length of the sojourn in Egypt.　n.p., n.d.　433-
　　　　442 p.　Reprinted from the Presbyterian Quarterly, July,
　　　　1890.　PT

2787　PRATT, Henry Barrington, 1832-1912.
　　　　Studies on the book of Genesis.　Translated from the

Spanish. Boston, American Tract Society, 1906. 530 p.
A C H R U

2788 PRATT, Henry Barrington, 1832-1912.
Studies on the second advent; ask for the old paths. n.p.,
n.d. 34 p. Reprinted from the Southern Presbyterian, May-
June, 1880. PT U

2789 PRATT, Henry Barrington, 1832-1912.
Studies on the second advent. Second series. n.p., n.d.
26 p. Reprinted from the Christian Observer, January 26 to
March 2, 1881. PT U

2790 PRATT, Henry Barrington, 1832-1912.
The world viewed as the subject of ruin and redemption.
Richmond, Whittet & Shepperson, 1895. 33 p. PT

2791 PRATT, John Wood, 1827-1888.
Given to Christ. A sermon. Louisville, Courier-Journal
Job Printing Co., 1887. 12 p. PT

2792 PRATT, John Wood, 1827-1888.
Given to Christ and other sermons.... With a biographi-
cal sketch of his life and labors. New York, Anson D. F.
Randolph & Co., © 1889. 301 p. A C H PT R U ... C
R: Richmond, Presbyterian Committee of Publication,
© 1889.

2793 PRATT, Nathaniel Alpheus, 1796-1879.
Perils of a dissolution of the union; a discourse, delivered
in the Presbyterian Church, of Roswell, on the day of public
thanksgiving, November 20, 1856. Atlanta, C. R. Hanleiter
& Co., 1856. 21 p. PH

2794 PRESBYTERIAN Church in the U.S.
Assembly songs; for use in evangelistic services, Sabbath
schools, young people's societies, devotional meetings, and
the home. Compiled by J. Ernest Thacker, Geo. A. Fisher,
R. E. Magill. Richmond, Presbyterian Committee of Publication, © 1910. 224 p. A C L PT R U

2795 PRESBYTERIAN Church in the U.S.
Book of hymns and tunes, comprising the Psalms and
hymns for the worship of God, approved by the General Assembly of 1866.... Edited by E. Thompson Baird and
Charles C. Converse. Richmond, Presbyterian Committee
of Publication, © 1874. 409 p. C H PH PT U

2796 PRESBYTERIAN Church in the U.S. Board of Christian
Education.
Social pronouncements of the Presbyterian Church in the
United States; excerpts from statements adopted by the

General Assembly, 1960-1969, edited by George A. Chauncey and Y. Jacqueline Rhoades. [Richmond, n.p., 1969]. 63 p. C R U

2797 PRESBYTERIAN Church in the U.S. Board of Christian Education. Department of Youth Work.
Adventuring the Christian way; guide for quest leaders in pioneer camps. Revised by Arthur M. Field. Richmond, [The author], 1957. 76 p. U

2798 PRESBYTERIAN Church in the U.S. Board of Church Extension.
Building the church. Compiled by the staff of the Board of Church Extension and edited by Patrick D. Miller, Executive Secretary. Atlanta, Dickson's, Inc., © 1958. 93 p. A C H L R U

2799 PRESBYTERIAN Church in the U.S. Board of Women's Work.
The Presbyterian woman's handbook, 1952-53. Yearbook church programs Bible study, [by Joseph M. Gettys. Atlanta, Board of Women's Work, Presbyterian Church in the U.S., 1952?]. 71 p. PH

2800 PRESBYTERIAN Church in the U.S. Board of Women's Work.
Presbyterian woman's workbook, 1960. [Including "Christ, the unifying center," monthly Bible study, by James H. Gailey.] Atlanta, Board of Women's Work, Presbyterian Church in the U.S., n.d. 91 p. C U

2801 PRESBYTERIAN Church in the U.S. Board of Women's Work.
Presbyterian woman's workbook, 1962-63. Monthly Bible study: the Gospel of Matthew, by Mac N. and Anne Turnage. Atlanta, Board of Women's Work, Presbyterian Church in the U.S., © 1962. 104 p. U

2802 PRESBYTERIAN Church in the U.S. Board of Women's Work.
The Psalms, monthly Bible study by Albert Curry Winn. [Presbyterian woman's workbook, 1963-64.] Atlanta, Board of Women's Work, Presbyterian Church in the U.S., © 1963. 104 p. C U

2803 PRESBYTERIAN Church in the U.S. Board of Women's Work.
Presbyterian woman's workbook, 1964-65 ... includes ... Bible study--Ephesians: "Glory in the church," by J. Sherrard Rice. [Atlanta, Board of Women's Work, Presbyterian Church in the U.S., 1963?]. 96 p. U

2804 PRESBYTERIAN Church in the U.S. Board of Women's Work.
Presbyterian woman's workbook, 1965-66. Including Circle Bible study, "The early church in action," by McMaster and Miller. Atlanta, Board of Women's Work, Presbyterian Church in the U.S., 1965. 97 p. Written by Mrs. George

R. (Belle Miller) McMaster and her father, Dr. P. D. Miller.
C U

2805　PRESBYTERIAN Church in the U.S. Board of Women's Work.
　　　"The promise of the new, " workbook 1974-75 [including
　　　monthly Bible studies in Matthew by Dr. James A. Cogs-
　　　well]. Atlanta, General Executive Board, Presbyterian Church
　　　in the U.S., [1974]. 96 p.　H

2806　PRESBYTERIAN Church in the U.S. Executive Committee of
　　　Christian Education and Ministerial Relief.
　　　Our Presbyterian educational institutions ... [by] Henry H.
　　　Sweets. [Louisville, Ky., Executive Committee of Christian
　　　Education and Ministerial Relief], 1914. 206 p.　A H PT U

2807　PRESBYTERIAN Church in the U.S. Executive Committee of
　　　Foreign Missions.
　　　Foundations of world order; the foreign service of the Pres-
　　　byterian Church, U.S., by a missionary from each field, [by
　　　H. Kerr Taylor]. Richmond, John Knox Press, © 1941.
　　　175 p.　A C H L PT R

2808　PRESBYTERIAN Church in the U.S. Executive Committee of
　　　Publication.
　　　The family altar. By order of the General Assembly....
　　　Richmond, [Executive Committee of Publication, 1915?].
　　　128 p. Prefatory note signed: James P. Smith, Chairman.
　　　A C H R U

2809　PRESBYTERIAN Church in the U.S. Executive Committee of
　　　Religious Education and Publication.
　　　Men in the local churches; a unified plan of men's work;
　　　men-of-the-church, men's Bible classes, men's fellowship
　　　clubs, church officers. [Edited by] J. E. Purcell. Rich-
　　　mond, Executive Committee of Religious Education and Pub-
　　　lication, n.d. 60 p.　U

2810　PRESBYTERIAN Church in the U.S. General Assembly.
　　　Calvin memorial addresses, delivered before the General
　　　Assembly of the Presbyterian Church in the United States,
　　　at Savannah, Ga., May, 1909. Richmond, Presbyterian Com-
　　　mittee of Publication, © 1909. 286 p. Contents. --Calvin's
　　　contribution to the Reformation, by Richard C. Reed. --Cal-
　　　vin's contributions to church polity, by Thomas Cary John-
　　　son. --Calvin's doctrine of infant salvation, by R. A. Webb. --
　　　The relation of Calvin and Calvinism to missions, by S. L.
　　　Morris. --How far has original Calvinism been modified by
　　　time?, by Samuel A. King.　A C H L PT R U

2811　PRESBYTERIAN Church in the U.S. General Assembly.
　　　A digest of the acts and proceedings of the General As-
　　　sembly of the Presbyterian Church in the U.S., from its

organization to the Assembly of 1887, inclusive, with certain historical and explanatory notes. By Rev. W. A. Alexander. Richmond, Presbyterian Committee of Publication, 1888. 551 p. A C H L PT U

2812 PRESBYTERIAN Church in the U.S. General Assembly.
A digest of the acts and proceedings of the General Assembly of the Presbyterian Church in the United States, revised down to and including acts of the General Assembly of 1922. By G. F. Nicolassen. Richmond, Presbyterian Committee of Publication, 1923. 1158 p. Cover title: Alexander's digest. C H L PT R U

2813 PRESBYTERIAN Church in the U.S. General Assembly.
A digest of the acts and proceedings of the General Assembly of the Presbyterian Church in the United States, revised down to and including acts of the General Assembly of 1910, by Rev. W. A. Alexander, D.D., and G. F. Nicolassen. Richmond, Presbyterian Committee of Publication, 1911. 780 p. A C H L PH R U

2814 PRESBYTERIAN Church in the U.S. General Assembly.
A digest of the acts and proceedings of the General Assembly of the Presbyterian Church in the United States, 1861-1944. Richmond, Presbyterian Committee of Publication, 1945. 543 p. "... the main body of this Digest consists of material compiled by [Rev. James A.] Millard." A C H L PT U

2815 PRESBYTERIAN Church in the U.S. General Assembly.
Memorial addresses delivered before the General Assembly of 1886, on occasion of the quarter-centennial of the organization of the Southern assembly, in 1861. Richmond, Presbyterian Committee of Publication, 1886. 63 p. Addresses by B. M. Palmer, J. N. Waddel, Jos. R. Wilson. A C H L PH PT U

2816 PRESBYTERIAN Church in the United States. General Assembly.
Memorial volume of the Westminster Assembly. 1647-1897. Containing eleven addresses delivered before the General Assembly of the Presbyterian Church in the United States, at Charlotte, N.C., in May, 1897. In commemoration of the two hundred and fiftieth anniversary of the Westminster Assembly, and of the formation of the Westminster standards. Richmond, Presbyterian Committee of Publication, © 1897. 297 p. Addresses by Henry Alexander White, Robert Price, T. Dwight Witherspoon, Robert L. Dabney, Givens B. Strickler, Eugene Daniel, James D. Tadlock, Moses D. Hoge, Samuel M. Smith, John F. Cannon. Assembly's Editing Committee: Francis R. Beattie, Charles R. Hemphill, Henry V. Escott. A C H L PT R U

2817 PRESBYTERIAN Church in the U.S. General Assembly.
Ministerial directory of the Presbyterian Church, U.S.,
1861-1941, compiled by Rev. E. C. Scott, stated clerk of
the General Assembly. Austin, Tex., Von Boeckmann-Jones
Co., 1942. 826 p. A C H L PH PT R U ... A C H L
PH PT R U: Revised and supplemented, 1942-50. Atlanta,
Hubbard Printing Co., 1950. 798 p. ... A C H L PH PT
R U: 1861-1967. Compiled by Rev. E. D. Witherspoon,
Jr. Doraville, Ga., Foote & Davies, 1967. 648 p. ... A
C H L PH PT R U: 1861-1975. Compiled by Rev. E. D.
Witherspoon, Jr. Atlanta, Darby Printing Co., 1975.
752 p.

2818 PRESBYTERIAN Church in the U.S. General Assembly.
A Presbyterian witness to the nation: a summary of the
public policy statements of the General Assembly of the Pres-
byterian Church in the United States, 1965-1979. Atlanta,
Division of Corporate and Social Mission, General Assembly
Mission Board, Presbyterian Church in the U.S., [1980?].
23 p. Introduction signed by George A. Chauncey and Belle
Miller McMaster. U

2819 PRESBYTERIAN Church in the U.S. General Assembly.
Semi-centennial memorial addresses delivered before the
General Assembly of 1911 at Louisville, Ky., commemorating
the semi-centennial of the organization of the Presbyterian
Church in the U.S. Richmond, Presbyterian Committee of
Publication, 1911. 55 p. Addresses by Henry Alexander
White, Theron H. Rice, Egbert Watson Smith. A C

2820 PRESBYTERIAN Church in the U.S. General Assembly.
Supplement to the Digest of the acts and proceedings of
the General Assembly of the Presbyterian Church in the
United States, published in 1888, bringing the same down to
date. By Rev. W. A. Alexander. Richmond, Presbyterian
Committee of Publication, 1898. 201 p. C H L U

2821 PRESBYTERIAN Church in the U.S. General Assembly. 70th,
Charlottesville, Va., 1930.
Souvenir presented in compliment to George Laurens Petrie,
the sole surviving attendant of that historic assembly which
gave birth to the Presbyterian Church in the U.S., at Augusta, Ga., in the year 1861 ... on the occasion of the
seventieth General Assembly ... Charlottesville, Virginia,
May 30, 1930. [Richmond, Executive Committee of Religious
Education and Publication, 1930]. 12 p. Includes facsimiles
of Thornwell's address, 1861, as well as signatures of sign-
ers. A U

2822 PRESBYTERIAN Church in the U.S. General Assembly. Ad
Interim Committee on Changes in the Confession of Faith.
Dispensationalism and the Confession of Faith. Report of

the Ad Interim Committee on Changes in the Confession of Faith and Catechisms as to whether the type of Bible interpretation known as dispensationalism is in harmony with the Confession of Faith. [F. B. Gear, chairman.] Richmond, Board of Christian Education, Presbyterian Church in the U.S., [1944]. 11 p. A C U

2823 PRESBYTERIAN Church in the U.S. General Assembly. Ad Interim Committee on the Church's Use of Her Ordained Ministry.
Consultation on the church's use of her ordained ministry; [nine] resource papers. [Edited by Kenneth B. Orr. Richmond, n.p., 1972]. 104 p. C L U

2824 PRESBYTERIAN Church in the U.S. Laymen's Missionary Movement. Lynchburg, Va., 1908.
Men and missions. Report of the proceedings of the Laymen's Missionary Movement Conference of the Presbyterian Church in the United States. Synod of Virginia. Held in the First Presbyterian Church, Lynchburg, Virginia, October 13, 14, 1908. Richmond, Whittet & Shepperson, 1908. 125 p. Contents. --The significance of the missionary uprising of men, by Geo. H. Denny. --Quality in service, by Harris E. Kirk. --The present missionary outlook, by J. O. Reavis. --Changed conditions in China, by C. N. Caldwell. --The call of Latin America, by S. R. Gammon. --A voice from the Congo, by Motte Martin. --A man and his money, by D. Clay Lilly. U

2825 PRESBYTERIAN Church in the U.S. Laymen's Missionary Movement. General Convention. 1st, Birmingham, Ala., 1909.
The modern crusade. Addresses and proceedings of the First General Convention of the Laymen's Missionary Movement, Presbyterian Church in the U.S., Birmingham, Ala., February 16-18, 1909. Edited by H. C. Ostrom, secretary. Athens, Ga., Laymen's Missionary Movement, Presbyterian Church in the U.S., © 1909. 318 p. Addresses by S. H. Chester, Motte Martin, J. O. Reavis, D. Clay Lilly, W. R. Dobyns, James I. Vance, James H. Taylor, Egbert W. Smith, T. M. Hunter, Robert Hill, J. M. Wells, A. L. Phillips. A C H L PH R U

2826 PRESBYTERIAN Church in the U.S. Laymen's Missionary Movement. General Convention. 4th, Charlotte, N.C., 1915.
Facing the situation; addresses delivered at the Fourth General Convention of the Laymen's Missionary Movement, Presbyterian Church in the U.S., held in Charlotte, N.C., Feb. 16-18, 1915; Dallas, Texas, Feb. 23-25, 1915. Athens, Ga., Laymen's Missionary Movement, Presbyterian Church in the U.S., [1915]. 376 p. Addresses by Rockwell Brank, Wm. R. Dobyns, Dunbar H. Ogden, D. Clay Lilly, S. H.

Chester, John I. Armstrong, R. T. Coit, H. H. Munroe, J. L. Stuart, Wm. F. Junkin, Stuart Nye Hutchison, R. O. Flinn, Egbert W. Smith. A C H L PT R U

2827   PRESBYTERIAN Church in the U.S. Presbytery of Augusta.
        Calvin quadricentennial addresses before the Presbytery of Augusta at Sparta, Ga., April 8, 1909. Richmond, Whittet & Shepperson [1909]. 56 p. Addresses by J. S. Montgomery, D. W. Brannen, and J. T. Plunkett. PH

2828   PRESBYTERIAN Church in the U.S. Presbytery of Central Texas.
        Revised manual of the Presbytery of Central Texas, compiled by Rev. M. C. Hutton.... Ordered by the presbytery at McGregor, March 30, 1901, and adopted at Wortham, September 27, 1901. n.p., n.d. 91 p. A PH U

2829   PRESBYTERIAN Church in the U.S. Presbytery of Charleston.
        The examination of the Rev. James Woodrow, D.D., by the Charleston Presbytery. Charleston, S.C., Lucas & Richardson, 1890. 12 p. C PH U

2830   PRESBYTERIAN Church in the U.S. Presbytery of Concord.
        Addresses delivered at the sesquicentennial celebration of Concord Presbytery, Bethpage Church, October 16, 1945. Morganton, N.C., n.p., n.d. 15 p. Contents.--Through four eras of Concord's history, by T. H. Spence, Jr.-- Presbyterianism and human freedom, by W. L. Lingle.   U

2831   PRESBYTERIAN Church in the U.S. Presbytery of Eastern Texas.
        History of the Presbytery of Eastern Texas of the Presbyterian Church in the United States. Prepared by Historical Memorials Committee of Presbytery: Rev. S. F. Tenney, chairman, Rev. D. A. McRae, Rev. J. W. McLeod, Rev. F. E. Robbins and Ruling Elder A. S. McNeill. n.p., [1915?]. 52 p. PH

2832   PRESBYTERIAN Church in the U.S. Presbytery of Fayetteville.
        Documents connected with the trial of the Rev. Simeon Colton. Printed by order of Fayetteville Presbytery, for the use of the Synod of North Carolina, at their ensuing sessions; with an appendix containing Mr. Colton's defence, &c. Fayetteville, Edward J. Hale, 1839. 107 p. PH

2833   PRESBYTERIAN Church in the U.S. Presbytery of Montgomery.
        Westminster addresses ... delivered by the direction of the Presbytery of Montgomery, Synod of Virginia, during the last stated meeting of that body ... in Bedford City, Virginia, April 13, 1897. Roanoke, Va., Stone Printing and

Manufacturing Co., 1897. 66 p. Contents.--The Westminster assembly; its genius and its work, by T. W. Hooper.--The spirit of progress in the Westminster symbols, by E. W. MacCorkle.--Some characteristics of Calvinism, by W. C. Campbell.   C H U

2834   PRESBYTERIAN Church in the U.S.   Presbytery of New Orleans.
Beginnings of Presbyterianism in the southwest and in New Orleans.... Selected and published by the Woman's Home Missionary Union, of the Presbytery of New Orleans.   New Orleans, E. S. Upton, 1907.   28 p.   Addresses by B. M. Palmer and H. M. Smith.   PH

2835   PRESBYTERIAN Church in the U.S.   Presbytery of Orange.
Bi-centennial addresses, delivered by Dr. Ernest Trice Thompson.   200th anniversary organization of Orange Presbytery, Hawfields Presbyterian Church, October 22nd, 1970. n.p., n.d.   19 p.   PH

2836   PRESBYTERIAN Church in the U.S.   Synod of Georgia. Executive Committee of Education.
The task of the Presbyterian Church in Georgia.   Edited and published by the Synod's Executive Committee of Education.   n.p., n.d.   217 p.   Contributors are Revs. R. O. Flinn, J. B. Ficklen, E. L. Hill, William Huck, S. L. McCarty, E. R. Leyburn, R. M. Stimson, A. F. Carr, L. G. Henderson, J. E. Purcell, F. K. Sims, Neal L. Anderson, M. M. MacFerrin, H. W. McLaughlin, J. S. Lyons, J. K. Coit.   A C H R

2837   PRESBYTERIAN Church in the U.S.   Synod of Kentucky.
Centennial of Presbyterianism in Kentucky.   Addresses delivered at Harrodsburg, Kentucky, October 12, 1883.   Louisville, Ky., n.p., 1883.   Reprinted, Lexington, Ky., n.p., 1933.   Addresses by J. N. Saunders, L. G. Barbour, T. D. Witherspoon, Moses D. Hoge.   PH

2838   PRESBYTERIAN Church in the U.S.   Synod of Kentucky.
A class book on home missions, issued under the authority of the Executive Committee of Home Missions of the Synod of Kentucky, Presbyterian Church in the United States, March, 1914.   Edited by the Rev. I. Cochrane Hunt.   Lexington, Ky., Transylvania Printing Co., 1914.   263 p.   L

2839   PRESBYTERIAN Church in the U.S.   Synod of Kentucky.
Of our own household, tasks of the Presbyterians in Kentucky.   n.p., Synod of Kentucky, Presbyterian Church in the U.S., 1927.   110 p.   Compiled by a committee composed of Henry H. Sweets, Charles G. Crooks, E. V. Tadlock.   H L

2840   PRESBYTERIAN Church in the U.S.   Synod of Louisiana.

Presbyterian activities in Louisiana; a synopsis for use as a study book by auxiliaries, Sunday Schools, Young people's societies, and others. New Orleans, Louisiana Synod's Board of Education, 1927. 127 p. Prepared by a committee of H. H. Thompson, S. E. McFadden, U. D. Mooney, and George Summey, editor. A H L

2841 PRESBYTERIAN Church in the U.S. Synod of Mississippi.
After fifty years: 1861-1911. Semi-centennial of the Southern Presbyterian Church. Addresses delivered before the Presbytery of Mississippi, meeting at Crystal Springs, April 11-12, 1911. McComb City, Miss., McComb City Journal, n.d. 52 p. Addresses by C. W. Grafton, A. S. Caldwell, J. J. Chisolm, and others. PH

2842 PRESBYTERIAN Church in the U.S. Synod of Mississippi.
Elements of truth. Addresses delivered at Synod's Training School, June 16 to 26, 1914, at Belhaven College, Jackson, Miss., by eminent leaders and workers of the Presbyterian Church. n.p., n.d. 262 p. Contents.--The Christian's hope, by R. A. Webb.--Presbyterian elements in history, by J. S. Foster.--Bird's eye view of the prophets, by A. W. Blackwood.--Evangelism, by Theron H. Rice.--Bible ethics, by C. W. Grafton.--The unlovely Christ, by R. V. Lancaster.--Social service, by L. E. McNair.--Missions: an aggressive missionary campaign, by L. E. McNair.-- Missions: home missions, by A. A. Little. C H R U

2843 PRESBYTERIAN Church in the U.S. Synod of Mississippi.
Elements of truth, volume II. Addresses delivered at Synod's Training School, June 22nd-July 2nd, 1915, at Belhaven College, Jackson, Miss., by eminent workers of the Presbyterian Church. Jackson, Miss., Tucker Printing House, 1915. 243 p. Contents.--The modern mind and Christian service, by R. A. Webb.--Pioneer Presbyterians and their successors in Mississippi, by C. W. Grafton.-- Presbyterian worthies, by John M. Wells. C H R U

2844 PRESBYTERIAN Church in the U.S. Synod of North Carolina.
Centennial addresses, Synod of North Carolina; delivered at Alamance Church, Greensboro, N.C., October 7, 1913. Greensboro, N.C., Synod of North Carolina, Presbyterian Church in the U.S., 1913. 82 p. Addresses by A. W. Crawford, W. W. Moore, Walter L. Lingle, D. I. Craig, H. G. Hill, R. F. Campbell, J. M. Rose. U

2845 PRESBYTERIAN Church in the U.S. Synod of South Carolina.
Centennial addresses, delivered before the Synod of South Carolina in the First Presbyterian Church, Columbia, October 23, 24, 1912, commemorating the birth of the Reverend James Henley Thornwell. Spartanburg, S.C., Band & White, 1913. 52 p. Contents.--Dr. Thornwell as a preacher and a teacher [by] T. H. Law.--Dr. Thornwell as a theologian [by]

Thornton Whaling.--Dr. Thornwell as an ecclesiologist [by]
A. M. Fraser.   A C H PH R U

2846   PRESBYTERIAN Church in the U.S.   Synod of South Carolina.
Historical addresses and commemorative ode, delivered
in the Synod of South Carolina, in Purity Church, Chester,
October 24, 1885, at the centennial celebration of the Pres-
bytery of South Carolina, from which the synod was developed.
Richmond, Whittet & Shepperson, 1886.   86 p.   Participating
were Rev. G. T. Goetchius, Rev. Frontis H. Johnston, Dr.
J. L. Girardeau, Ruling Elder Robert Bingham, and others.
C H PH U

2847   PRESBYTERIAN Church in the U.S.   Synod of Virginia.
Diamond Jubilee addresses at the Synod of Virginia, Presbyterian Church in the United States.   One hundred and forty-
ninth annual session.   [Petersburg, Va., Owen Printing Co.],
1936.   90 p.   Sermons and addresses by Edward Mack, Ernest Trice Thompson, Walter L. Lingle, R. A. Lapsley, Jr.
A C U

2848   PRESBYTERIAN Church in the U.S.   Synod of Virginia.
"The least of these": the beneficences of the Synod of
Virginia.   Compiled and edited by William E. Hudson, D.D.
Richmond, Presbyterian Committee of Publication, © 1926.
152 p.   A H R U

2849   PRESBYTERIAN Church in the U.S.   Synod of Virginia.
The sphere and rights of woman in the church; report
approved by the Synod of Virginia, October 26, 1899.   James
P. Smith, stated clerk.   Richmond, Presbyterian Committee
of Publication, [1899].   16 p.   A U

2850   PRESBYTERIAN Church in the U.S.A.   Presbytery of Balti-
more.
The difficulties of the Presbytery of Baltimore with Mr.
Thomas L. Hamner, and Mr. James G. Hamner, faithfully
exhibited from the records of the presbytery.   Baltimore,
R. J. Matchett, 1842.   8 p.   PH

2851   PRESBYTERIAN Church in the U.S.A.   Presbytery of Pittsburgh.
An appreciation of the Rev. John Franklin Hill, D.D., by
his brethren of the Presbytery of Pittsburgh.   n.p., [1907].
unpaged.   PH

2852   PRESBYTERIAN practice vs. Presbyterian theory, or the judi-
cial case of the Rev. John T. Hendrick, vs. W. H. Marquess: First, Before the Presbyterian Church of Clarksville, Tennessee; Second, Before the Presbytery of Nashville;
and Third, Before the General Assembly of the Presbyterian
Church in the United States.   Nashville, Tenn., John T. S.
Fall, 1849.   72 p.   PH PT

2853 THE PRESENTATION of the portrait of the late Benjamin Rice
Lacy to the state of North Carolina. Held in the House of
Representatives at eleven o'clock in the forenoon, November
the twelfth, nineteen hundred and twenty-nine. [Raleigh,
N.C., Mitchell Printing Co., 1930]. 46 p.   H

2854 PRESTON, Thomas Lewis, 1835-1895.
In memoriam. John Lycan Kirkpatrick, 1813-1885. n.p.,
n.d. 23 p.   H ... U: microfilm.

2855 PRICE, Benjamin Luther, 1867-1928.
John Price the emigrant, Jamestown colony, 1620, with
some of his descendants. Alexandria, La., n.p., [1910].
62 p.   U

2856 PRICE, Francis Wilson, 1895-1974.
As the lightning flashes. Richmond, John Knox Press,
1948. 206 p. The Sprunt Lectures, 1948.   A C H L PH
PT R U

2857 PRICE, Francis Wilson, 1895-1974.
China--twilight or dawn? New York, Friendship Press,
© 1948. 184 p.   A H L PH PT U

2858 PRICE, Francis Wilson, 1895-1974, tr.
Chinese Christian hymns, by Chinese writers, with Chinese tunes. Selected from the Chinese hymn book Hymns of
universal praise. English translations by Frank W. Price.
Richmond, Satterwhite Press, 1953. 23 p.   A PH PT U

2859 PRICE, Francis Wilson, 1895-1974.
Marx meets Christ. Philadelphia, Westminster Press,
© 1957. 176 p.   A C H L PH PT R U

2860 PRICE, Francis Wilson, 1895-1974.
The rural church in China, a survey. [2d ed.] New
York, Agricultural Missions, 1948. 274 p.   A C H L PH
PT U

2861 PRICE, Francis Wilson, 1895-1974.
Specialized research libraries in missions. n.p., n.d.
175-185 p. Reprinted from Library Trends, vol. 9, no. 2.
A PH PT U

2862 PRICE, Francis Wilson, 1895-1974.
We went to West China. [Nashville, Tenn., Executive
Committee of Foreign Missions, Presbyterian Church in the
U.S., 1943]. 30 p.   C

2863 *PRICE, Jacob F.
Speech before the West Lexington Presbytery, on the trial
of Rev. J. C. Stiles, for his agitating, revolutionary and

schismatical course; with an appendix containing the entire
correspondence between Jacob F. Price and Joseph C. Stiles.
Frankfort, Ky., Wm. M. Todd, 1841. 48 p. PH PT U

2864 PRICE, James Ligon, 1915-
Interpreting the New Testament. New York, Holt, Rine-
hart and Winston, © 1961. 572 p. A C L PT R U ... A
C PT U: 2d ed. © 1971. 624 p.

2865 PRICE, Philip Francis, 1864-1954.
The nineties and now. [Nashville, McQuiddy Printing Co.,
1935?]. 8 p. U

2866 PRICE, Philip Francis, 1864-1954, ed.
Our China investment; sixty years of the Southern Presbyterian Church in China, with biographies, autobiographies,
and sketches of all missionaries since the opening of the
work in 1867. Nashville, Tenn., Executive Committee of
Foreign Missions, [Presbyterian Church in the U.S., 1927].
187 p. A C H L PH U

2867 PRICE, Philip Francis, 1864-1954.
Short steps to great truths. A new method for teaching
by easy gradation the Chinese characters and Christian truth
at one and the same time. Hankow, Religious Tract Society,
1933-35. 4 v. Text in Chinese language. H ... U: 1939.

2868 PRICE, Philip Francis, 1864-1954, tr.
Systematic theology; designed for the use of theological
students, by Rev. Chia Yu-ming. Nanking, China, Nanking
Theological Seminary, n.d. In Chinese. H

2869 PRICE, Philip Francis, 1864-1954.
The white harvest fields of the Southern Presbyterian
Church. [Louisville, Ky., Executive Committee of Christian
Education and Ministerial Relief, Presbyterian Church in the
U.S.], n.d. 25 p. U

2870 PRICE, William Thomas, 1830-1921.
Historical sketch of Greenbrier Presbytery. Lewisburg,
W.Va., Greenbrier Independent Print., 1889. 56 p. U

2871 PRICE, William Thomas, 1830-1921.
Historical sketches of Pocahontas County, West Virginia.
Marlinton, W.Va., Price Brothers, 1901. 622 p. H

2872 PRICE, William Thomas, 1830-1921.
With Christ or against him; a biographical sketch. Rich-
mond, Presbyterian Committee of Publication, n.d. unpaged.
U

2873 *PRICE, William Thompson, 1845-1920.

Without scrip or purse; or, "The mountain evangelist,"
George O. Barnes. The history of a consecrated life, the
record of its silent thoughts, and a book of its public utter-
ances. Louisville, Ky., W. T. Price, 1883. 631 p.   C
PH U

2874   PRIMROSE, John W., 1838-1907.
Fellowship. n.p., n.d. 220-237 p. Reprinted from the
Presbyterian Quarterly, April, 1890.   PT

2875   PRIMROSE, John W., 1838-1907.
The Presbyterian Church. Richmond, Presbyterian Com-
mittee of Publication, n.d. 20 p.   PH U ... U: St. Louis,
J. T. Smith Print., n.d. ... U: 2d ed. Wilmington, N.C.,
Jackson & Bell, 1889.   17 p.

2876   PRIMROSE, John W., 1838-1907.
Presbytery--Prelacy. Richmond, Presbyterian Committee
of Publication, n.d.   67 p.   H

2877   PRINCETON Theological Seminary.
Discourses at the inauguration of the Rev. James W. Alexander ... as Professor of Ecclesiastical History and Church
Government in the Theological Seminary at Princeton.   Delivered at Princeton, November 20, 1849, before the directors of the seminary.   New York, Robert Carter & Brothers,
1850.   96 p.   Participants: W. S. Plumer, W. W. Phillips,
J. W. Alexander, and others.   PT

2878   PRITCHARD, Claudius Hornby, 1896-1979.
Living epistles with home mission postmarks.   Atlanta,
Board of Church Extension, Presbyterian Church in the U.S.,
© 1959.   66 p.   A H

2879   PRITCHARD, Claudius Hornby, 1896-1979, ed.
Why stand ye idle? Voices from our home fields.   Richmond, John Knox Press, © 1941.   141 p.   A C H R U

2880   PROUDFOOT, Charles Merrill, 1923-
Diary of a sit-in. Foreword by Frank P. Graham.   Chap-
el Hill, University of North Carolina Press, © 1962.   204 p.
A C L PT U

2881   PROUDFOOT, Charles Merrill, 1923-
Suffering: a Christian understanding.   Philadelphia, Westminster Press, © 1964.   194 p.   C L PH PT U

2882   PRYOR, Theodorick, 1805-1890.
Three sermons on the doctrines of predestination, election,
and final perseverance.   Preached ... in the Brick Church,
at Nottoway Court House, 1841.   Richmond, John B. Martin
& Co., 1842.   50 p.   H PT ... H PH: 2d ed. Richmond,
Ellyson, 1846.   40 p.

2883   PURCELL, Malcolm Lee, 1893-1978.
       A history of the woman's auxiliary of the Presbytery of
       Eastern Texas. [Kingsville, Tex., Tex.-Mex. Printery,
       1941]. 73 p.   A PH

2884   PURVIANCE, James, 1807-1871.
       A sermon on the apostolical succession.   New Orleans,
       William H. Toy, 1843.   28 p.   PH

2885   QUARLES, James Addison, 1837-1907.
       The life of F. T. Kemper, the Christian educator.   New
       York, Burr Printing House, n.d.   492 p.   H PH

2886   QUARLES, James Addison, 1837-1907.
       Our church constitution.   The supremacy of the General
       Assembly.   Its original jurisdiction.   n.p., [1867].   23 p.
       PT

2887   QUARLES, James Addison, 1837-1907.
       Predestination and election: does the Confession of Faith
       present a sound view of them?   Richmond, n.p., 1944.   7 p.
       Reprinted from the Union Seminary Review, February, 1944.
       U

2888   QUINIUS, Henry Willard, 1919-
       The emerging role of the pastor as a church administrator.
       Austin, Tex., Austin Presbyterian Theological Seminary,
       1957.   16 p.   Inaugural address [as Professor of Church Ad-
       ministration] delivered at the formal opening of the fifty-fifth
       year of Austin Presbyterian Theological Seminary.   Austin
       Seminary Bulletin, September, 1957.   A C PT U

2889   RAMSAY, Franklin Pierce, 1856-1926.
       An exposition of the form of government and the rules of
       discipline of the Presbyterian Church in the United States.
       Richmond, Presbyterian Committee of Publication, © 1898.
       298 p.   C H L PH PT U ... A R U: [1899].

2890   RAMSAY, Franklin Pierce, 1856-1926.
       An interpretation of Genesis, including a translation into
       present-day English.   New York, The Neale Publishing Co.,
       1911.   347 p.   A C H PT

2891   RAMSAY, Franklin Pierce, 1856-1926.
       The question; a novel.   New York, The Neale Publishing
       Co., 1909.   178 p.   A H R U

2892   RAMSAY, Franklin Pierce, 1856-1926.
       The virgin birth; a study of the argument, for and against.
       New York, Fleming H. Revell Co., © 1926.   111 p.   A C
       H PT R U

2893   *RAMSAY, J. G.

Historical sketch of Third Creek Church in Rowan County, N.C. ... read at the centennial, May 13th, 1892. Also historical address of Rev. John K. Fleming, at the centennial of the building, July 24th, 1935. Statesville, N.C., Brady Printing Co., 1937. 67 p. H

2894 RAMSAY, John Cummins, 1890-1962.
John Wilbur Chapman, the man, his methods and his message. Boston, Christopher Publishing House, © 1962. 230 p. C H L PH PT R U

2895 RAMSAY, William McDowell, 1922-
The Christ of the earliest Christians. Richmond, John Knox Press, © 1959. 163 p. The author's thesis in shorter and more popular form. A C H L PT R U

2896 RAMSAY, William McDowell, 1922-
The church, a believing fellowship [by] William M. Ramsay [and] John H. Leith. Richmond, CLC Press, © 1965. 224 p. (The Covenant Life Curriculum.) A C L U ... C L U: Leaders' guide. [By] William M. Ramsay [and] Mathews F. Allen, Jr. 96 p.

2897 RAMSAY, William McDowell, 1922-
Cycles and renewal trends in Protestant lay education. Nashville, Abingdon Press, © 1969. 159 p. A C H L PH PT R U

2898 RAMSAY, William McDowell, 1922-
The layman's guide to the New Testament. John Knox Press, © 1981. 273 p. A H L U

2899 RAMSAY, William McDowell, 1922-
The meaning of Jesus Christ. Richmond, CLC Press, © 1964. 199 p. (The Covenant Life Curriculum.) C L R U ... C L R U: Leader's guide. 85 p.

2900 RAMSEY, Harmon Bigelow, 1907-
Mr. Jones goes to Bethlehem. [Richmond, John Knox Press], © 1949. 27 p. H U

2901 RAMSEY, James Beverlin, 1814-1871.
The deaconship; an essay, prepared by appointment of the Synod of Virginia, read before that body at their meeting at Charlottesville, on the 3rd of November, 1858. Richmond, Presbyterian Committee of Publication, n.d. 42 p. U

2902 RAMSEY, James Beverlin, 1814-1871.
"The elders that rule well." A sermon, preached at Lexington, Va., April 4th, 1855, at the opening of Lexington Presbytery. Lexington, Smith & Fuller, 1855. 17 p. H PH PT U ... PH: Lynchburg, Va., Johnson & Treakle,

1857. 26 p. ... A: The eldership. Richmond, Presbyterian Committee of Publication, n.d. 39 p.

2903 RAMSEY, James Beverlin, 1814-1871.
Follow the saints. A memorial of Samuel McCorkle, a ruling elder for thirty-four years of the First Presbyterian Church, of Lynchburg, Va., who died August 6th, 1866. An obituary notice and the sermon addressed to the church in improvement of his death. Lynchburg, Virginian Book and Job Office Print., 1867. 27 p. U

2904 RAMSEY, James Beverlin, 1814-1871.
God's way in the sanctuary remembered. A sermon preached Dec. 23d, 1860, before the congregations of the 1st and 2d Presbyterian churches of Lynchburg, assembled together, in commemoration of the first meeting of the General Assembly of the Church of Scotland, on December 20th, 1560. Lynchburg, J. C. Johnson, 1861. 20 p. PH

2905 RAMSEY, James Beverlin, 1814-1871.
How shall I live? Richmond, Presbyterian Committee of Publication, n.d. 16 p. U

2906 RAMSEY, James Beverlin, 1814-1871.
Questions on Bible doctrine, for the closet, the family, and Bible classes. Richmond, Presbyterian Committee of Publication, 1867. 210 p. C H PH R U ... A H U: © 1869 ... C H PH: 1878.

2907 RAMSEY, James Beverlin, 1814-1871.
Questions on Old Testament history. Revised and extended by Rev. R. L. Dabney. Lynchburg, Bell, Browne & Co., 1879. 114 p. A C H R U

2908 RAMSEY, James Beverlin, 1814-1871.
The spiritual kingdom: an exposition of the first eleven chapters of the book of Revelation.... With an introduction by the Rev. Charles Hodge. Richmond, Presbyterian Committee of Publication, 1873. 518 p. A C H L PH PT R U ... C R: The book of Revelation. [Carlisle, Pa.], Banner of Truth Trust, [1977].

2909 RANKIN, David Cyrus, 1847-1902.
The Congo: a sketch of the country and its missions. Nashville, Tenn., Executive Committee of Foreign Missions, Presbyterian Church in the U.S., 1900. 20 p. PH

2910 RANKIN, Samuel Meek, 1864-1939.
History of Buffalo Presbyterian Church and her people, Greensboro, N.C. [Greensboro, Jos. J. Stone & Co.], n.d. 230 p. A H L PH U

2911 RANKIN, Samuel Meek, 1864-1939.

The Rankin and Wharton families and their genealogy. [Greensboro, N.C., Jos. J. Stone & Co.], n.d. 295 p. H PH U

2912 RATLIFF, Dale Hedrick, 1928-
Bridal beds around the world. n.p., © 1977. 94 p. L

2913 RATLIFF, Dale Hedrick, 1928-
The challenge of Christ; a book of sermons. [1st ed.] New York, Exposition Press, © 1955. 77 p. L

2914 RAUSCHENBERG, Fritz, 1877-1967.
"Why? Man!" New York, Carlton Press, © 1966. 99 p. C

2915 RAYMOND, Moses, 1798-1875.
Bible class lessons. Romney, Va., William Harper, n.d. 13 p. PH

2916 RAYNAL, Charles Edward, 1877-1944.
The tree speaks. Macon, Ga., J. W. Burke Co., 1928. unpaged. Reprinted from American Forests and Forest Life, May, 1928. U

2917 READ, Charles Henry, 1811-1900.
A discourse in behalf of domestic missions, delivered in the United Presbyterian Church, Richmond, Va., May 24, 1857. Richmond, MacFarlane and Fergusson, 1857. 24 p. U

2918 READ, Charles Henry, 1811-1900.
National fast. A discourse delivered on the day of fasting, humiliation and prayer, appointed by the President of the United States, January 4, 1861. Richmond, Ritchie & Dunnavant, 1861. 25 p. PH PT

2919 READ, Charles Henry, 1811-1900.
Ruling elders in the church of Christ. Richmond, Presbyterian Publishing Co., 1883. 33 p. U

2920 READ, Charles Henry, 1811-1900.
Sabbath Schools: their relation to the church and to the obligations of the church in the management of them. Richmond, Presbyterian Committee of Publication, n.d. 12 p. U

2921 READ, Charles Henry, 1811-1900.
The Sabbath. Voice of our standards. [Richmond, Presbyterian Committee of Publication], n.d. 8 p. U

2922 A READER in sociology: Christian perspectives; Charles P. De Santo [and others], editors. Scottdale, Pa., Herald Press, 1980. 736 p. A U

2923 RECONCILIATION in today's world. Edited by Allen O. Miller. Essays by Donald G. Miller, John H. Leith [and others]. Grand Rapids, Mich., Wm. B. Eerdmans Publishing Co., © 1969. 122 p.   A C H L PH PT R U

2924 RECONSIDERATIONS; Roman Catholic/Presbyterian and Reformed theological conversations, 1966-67. Papers presented by Martin Anton Schmidt, John Newton Thomas [and others. New York, World Horizons], © 1967. 157 p.   A L R

2925 RECORD and evidence in the case of the Presbyterian Church in the United States (Rev. Dr. Wm. Adams, voluntary prosecutor) versus James Woodrow. Columbia, S.C., Presbyterian Publishing House, 1888. 16 p.   PT U

2926 RED, William Stuart, 1857-1933.
A history of the Presbyterian Church in Texas. [Austin, Tex., Steck Co.], © 1936. 433 p. Edited by Mrs. W. S. Red and Rev. M. L. Purcell.   A C H L PH PT R U

2927 RED, William Stuart, 1857-1933.
In the court of the General Assembly of the Presbyterian Church in the U.S. W. A. Gillon, et al., complainant, versus Synod of Texas, respondent. Brief for the respondent, by W. S. Red, representative for respondent; J. P. Robertson, associate representative. Houston, Tex., n.p. [1908?]. 10 p.   A

2928 RED, William Stuart, 1857-1933.
The Texas colonists and religion, 1821-1836; a centennial tribute to the Texas patriots who shed their blood that we might enjoy civil and religious liberty. Austin, Tex., E. L. Shettles, © 1924. 149 p.   A H L PH U

2929 *REDDICK, DeWitt Carter, 1904-1980, ed.
Church and campus: Presbyterians look to the future from their historic role in Christian higher education. Richmond, John Knox Press, [1956]. 178 p. Articles by J. J. Murray, R. T. L. Liston, John R. Cunningham, Ernest Trice Thompson, Malcolm C. McIver, Hunter B. Blakely.   A C H L PT R U

2930 REDHEAD, John Agrippa, 1905-
The Christian's calling. A sermon. Washington, D.C., National Presbyterian Church, 1966. 9 p.   PH

2931 REDHEAD, John Agrippa, 1905-
Finding meaning in the Beatitudes. Nashville, Abingdon Press, © 1968. 109 p.   A L PT U

2932 REDHEAD, John Agrippa, 1905-
"For the worship of God." Sermon at the dedication of

the chancel, December 12, 1954. Greensboro, N.C., First Presbyterian Church, [1955?]. unpaged. PH

2933 REDHEAD, John Agrippa, 1905-
Getting to know God and other sermons. Nashville, Abingdon Press, © 1954. 126 p. A C L U

2934 REDHEAD, John Agrippa, 1905-
Guidance from men of God. New York, Abingdon Press, © 1965. 144 p. A C H L PT U

2935 REDHEAD, John Agrippa, 1905-
Learning to have faith. Nashville, Abingdon Press, © 1955. 128 p. C H L PT U

2936 REDHEAD, John Agrippa, 1905-
Let God help you find faith in forgiveness. Atlanta, Board of Church Extension, Presbyterian Church in the U.S., 1955. 12 p. H ... A: tape.

2937 REDHEAD, John Agrippa, 1905-
Letting God help you. New York, Abingdon Press, © 1957. 125 p. A C L PT U

2938 REDHEAD, John Agrippa, 1905-
Living all your life. New York, Abingdon Press, © 1961. 142 p. C H L U

2939 REDHEAD, John Agrippa, 1905-
Putting your faith to work. New York, Abingdon Press, © 1959. 128 p. C L U

2940 REDHEAD, John Agrippa, 1905-
Sermons on Bible characters. New York, Abingdon Press, © 1963. 144 p. A C L R U

2941 REED, Charles Wesley, 1885-1968.
The first hundred and twenty-five years, 1854-1979: First Presbyterian Church, Martinsville, Va. n.p., n.d. 20 p. Contents.--The first hundred years, by Charles W. Reed.-- A history, 1954-1979, by Barbara and Henry Reed; edited by Mary Jane Powell. PH

2942 REED, Gordon Kennedy, 1930-
Christmas--triumph over tragedy. Greenville, S.C., A Press, © 1969. 50 p. R

2943 REED, James Landrum, 1817-1905.
The mode of scriptural baptism demonstrated to be sprinkling. Richmond, Presbyterian Committee of Publication, 1889. 111 p. C H U

2944 REED, Richard Clark, 1851-1925.

As it seemed to me; ten weeks travel in Europe. [Charlotte, N.C., Presbyterian Standard Publishing Co., 1910?]. 85 p. First published in the Presbyterian Standard.   U

2945   REED, Richard Clark, 1851-1925.
Deceivers and their dupes. Richmond, Presbyterian Committee of Publication, © 1900. 35 p.   PT U

2946   REED, Richard Clark, 1851-1925.
The Gospel as taught by Calvin. Richmond, Presbyterian Committee of Publication, n.d. 157 p.   A C H L U ... C
PT R: Jackson, Miss., Presbyterian Reformation Society, n.d.

2947   REED, Richard Clark, 1851-1925.
History of the Presbyterian churches of the world, adapted for use in the class room. Philadelphia, Westminster Press, 1905. 408 p.   A C H L PH PT R U ... PT R: 1915 ...
L PH: 1917 ... C H: 1922 ... C U: 1927.

2948   REED, Richard Clark, 1851-1925.
History of the Southern Presbyterian Church. Charlotte, N.C., n.p., 1923. 23 p.   C

2949   REED, Richard Clark, 1851-1925.
John Knox, his field and work. An address delivered before the General Assembly of the Presbyterian Church in the United States at Fort Worth, Texas, May 21st, 1905. Richmond, Presbyterian Committee of Publication, [1905?]. 32 p.
A C H

2950   REED, Richard Clark, 1851-1925.
Jonathan Edwards. Richmond, Whittet & Shepperson, 1904. 16 p. Reprinted from the Presbyterian Quarterly, January, 1904.   C

2951   REED, Richard Clark, 1851-1925.
Life of Athanasius. Richmond, Presbyterian Committee of Publication, 1904. 41 p.   C H L R U

2952   REED, Richard Clark, 1851-1925.
The Northern assembly. Richmond, Whittet & Shepperson, 1902. 6 p. Reprinted from the Presbyterian Quarterly, October, 1902.   C

2953   REED, Richard Clark, 1851-1925.
Pope Leo XIII. on the validity of Anglican orders. n.p., n.d. 308-324 p. Reprinted from the Presbyterian Quarterly, July, 1897.   C

2954   REED, Richard Clark, 1851-1925.
Presbyterian doctrine. An address delivered before the

Synod of Georgia, and published by request of the synod. Richmond, Presbyterian Committee of Publication, n.d. 24 p.   C H

2955   REED, Richard Clark, 1851-1925.
The relation of church and state. Richmond, Presbyterian Committee of Publication, n.d. 20 p.   U

2956   REED, Richard Clark, 1851-1925.
A sketch of the religious history of the Negroes in the South. n.p., n.d. 175-204 p. Reprinted from the Papers of the American Society of Church History, 2d series, vol. IV, 1914.   C PH

2957   REED, Richard Clark, 1851-1925.
The Vrooman case. [Nashville, Tenn], n.p., n.d. 88-98 p. Reprinted from the Presbyterian Quarterly, January, 1897.   C

2958   REED, Richard Clark, 1851-1925.
What is the Kingdom of God? Richmond, Presbyterian Committee of Publication, © 1922. 146 p.   A C H PT R U ... C H L R U: [2d ed.] Richmond, John Knox Press, [1939]. 117 p.

2959   REID, John Calvin, 1901-
Bird life in Wington; sermonettes for young folk in story form. Grand Rapids, Mich., Wm. B. Eerdmans Publishing Co., 1948. 122 p.   L ... U: 1950 ... C: 1953 ... A U: 1955 ... H: [1963].

2960   REID, John Calvin, 1901-
Frisky finds a treasure. Grand Rapids, Mich., Wm. B. Eerdmans Publishing Co., © 1964. 31 p.   C U

2961   REID, John Calvin, 1901-
The marriage covenant. Richmond, John Knox Press, © 1967. unpaged.   A C H L U

2962   REID, John Calvin, 1901-
On toward the goal: sermons of hope and encouragement. Richmond, John Knox Press, 1949. 159 p.   A C H L R U

2963   REID, John Calvin, 1901-
Parables from nature; earthly stories with a heavenly meaning. The parables of Jesus retold and interpreted for young minds. Grand Rapids, Mich., Wm. B. Eerdmans Publishing Co., 1954. 89 p.   U ... L: [1957] ... C: 1965.

2964   REID, John Calvin, 1901-
Prayer pilgrimage through the Psalms. New York, Abingdon Press, © 1962. 128 p.   A C H L U

2965 REID, John Calvin, 1901-
Reserves of the soul, and other sermons. Richmond,
John Knox Press, © 1942. 156 p.   A H L R U

2966 REID, John Calvin, 1901-
Surprise for Dr. Retriever. Grand Rapids, Mich., Wm.
B. Eerdmans Publishing Co., © 1962. unpaged.   C U

2967 REID, John Calvin, 1901-
War of the birds. Grand Rapids, Mich., Wm. B. Eerdmans Publishing Co., © 1963. unpaged.   C U

2968 REID, John Calvin, 1901-
We knew Jesus: a series of Lenten messages. Grand
Rapids, Mich., Wm. B. Eerdmans Publishing Co., 1954.
148 p.   A C H L PT R U

2969 REID, John Calvin, 1901-
We spoke for God. Grand Rapids, Mich., Wm. B. Eerdmans Publishing Co., © 1967. 122 p.   A L PT R U

2970 REID, John Calvin, 1901-
We wrote the Gospels. Grand Rapids, Mich., Wm. B.
Eerdmans Publishing Co., © 1960. 61 p.   A C H L PH R

2971 REINHOLD, Robert William, 1919-
Diumvuija dia mukanda wa kumudilu wa Petelo, kudi
Muambi Mudaru. [1st ed.] Luluabourg, [Congo], Conseil
des Oeuvres Littéraires en Tshiluba, E.P.C. [and] E.M.C.
81 p.   Commentary on I Peter in Tshiluba.   U

2972 REISNER, Sherwood Hartman, 1920-
God's troublemakers. Nashville, [Board of World Mis-
sions], Presbyterian Church in the U.S., © 1965. 77 p.
Prepared for the Joint Season of Witness, January-March,
1966.   H R U

2973 THE RELATIONSHIPS among the Gospels: an interdisciplinary
dialogue; edited by William O. Walker, Jr.   San Antonio,
Trinity University Press, © 1978. 359 p.   A C L R U

2974 THE RELIGIOUS instruction of our colored population; a pastoral letter from the Presbytery of Tombeckbee to the churches
and people under its care. Columbia, S.C., R. W. Gibbes,
1859. 19 p. Signed by Joseph Bardwell, moderator.   U

2975 REVELEY, Walter Taylor, 1917-
The way of a student. Richmond, CLC Press, © 1963.
63 p. (The Covenant Life Curriculum.)   C U ... L:
[1966].

2976 REV. J. H. ALEXANDER, D.D.   n.p., [1904?].   29 p.   A

celebration of the semi-centennial anniversary of the entrance
into the ministry of Rev. J. H. Alexander, pastor emeritus
(at Kosciusko Presbyterian Church). Participants were Rev.
C. E. Cunningham, Rev. T. L. Haman, Rev. A. H. Mecklin,
Rev. R. J. Beattie, Rev. W. B. Bingham. Includes memorial from the Synod of Mississippi. No title-page.   H

2977   THE REVEREND JOHN MARINUS VANDER MEULEN, D.D.,
LL.D. [Louisville, Ky., Louisville Presbyterian Theological Seminary, 1936]. 147 p.   L

2978   REV. JOSEPH H. HOPPER, 1829-1915. n.p., n.d. unpaged.
H

2979   REV. MOSES D. HOGE: memorial services of Richmond
churches in his memory. Richmond, Whittet & Shepperson, 1899. 54 p.   U

2980   THE REVEREND RICHARD THOMAS GILLESPIE, D.D., LL.D.,
1879-1930. In memoriam. [Decatur, Ga., Columbia Theological Seminary, 1930]. 30 p. Bulletin, Columbia Theological Seminary, November, 1930.   C H R

2981   REYNOLDS, William Davis, 1867-1951, ed.
Universal Bible dictionary, translated into Korean by the
faculty of the Presbyterian Theological Seminary of Korea.
Seoul, Christian Literature Society of Korea, 1927. unpaged.
U

2982   RHEA, Samuel Audley, 1827-1865.
A sermon occasioned by the death of Rev. Edwin H. Crane,
missionary to the Nestorians, preached at Seir, Persia, September 17, 1854. Boston, John P. Jewett and Co., 1855.
23 p.   PH PT

2983   RHODES, Arnold Black, 1913-
Los actos portentosos de Dios. Richmond, CLC Press,
© 1964. 358 p. Translation into Spanish of "The mighty
acts of God."   L

2984   RHODES, Arnold Black, 1913-
The book of Psalms. Richmond, John Knox Press, © 1960.
192 p. (The Layman's Bible Commentary, v. 9.)   A C H
L PT R U ... L: In Japanese. Translated by Ken-ichi Kida.
Tokyo, Board of Publications, The United Church of Christ in
Japan, © 1959. 344 p.

2985   RHODES, Arnold Black, 1913- , ed.
The church faces the isms, [by] the members of the faculty of the Louisville Presbyterian Theological Seminary, Louisville, Kentucky. New York, Abingdon Press, © 1958. 304 p.
Articles by Arnold B. Rhodes, Kenneth J. Foreman, Frank H.

Caldwell, Harry G. Goodykoontz, William A. Benfield, Jr., C. Morton Hanna, and others.   A C L PH PT R U

2986   RHODES, Arnold Black, 1913-
        The mighty acts of God. Richmond, CLC Press, © 1964.
        446 p. (The Covenant Life Curriculum.)   C L PT U ... L:
        [1967]; [1968] ... C L U: Teacher's book. 351 p.

2987   RHODES, Arnold Black, 1913-
        Study and review questions for self-examination in the
        course The mighty acts of God. [Richmond, Board of Chris-
        tian Education, Presbyterian Church in the U.S., 1964?].
        8 p.   U

2988   RHODES, Daniel Durham, 1917-
        A covenant community; a study of the book of Exodus.
        Richmond, John Knox Press, © 1964. 71 p.   A C H L U

2989   RHODES, Daniel Durham, 1917-
        He taught in parables, [by] Daniel D. Rhodes [and] Mathews
        F. Allen, Jr. Richmond, CLC Press, [1966]. 48 p. (The
        Covenant Life Curriculum.)   C L U

2990   RHODES, Paul Simpson, 1876-1956.
        A series of expository sermons on the book of Revelation.
        Pontotoc, Miss., n.p., 1942. 43 p.   C H L

2991   RICE, John Jay, 1886-1972.
        The Presbyterian Church: its origin, organization and in-
        fluence. Richmond, Presbyterian Committee of Publication,
        © 1929. 136 p.   A C H L PH PT R U

2992   RICE, Joseph Sherrard, 1917-
        The commission on Christian witness; to help youth make
        known to others the way of Christ by all they say and do.
        Illustrations by Ruth S. Ensign. Richmond, John Knox Press,
        © 1952. 40 p.   PH U

2993   RICE, Joseph Sherrard, 1917-
        Favorite sermons. Columbia, S.C., First Presbyterian
        Church, [1966]. 97 p.   C

2994   RICE, Joseph Sherrard, 1917-
        Let there be light: a study of the book of Genesis. [At-
        lanta], Board of Women's Work, Presbyterian Church in the
        U.S., n.d. 91 p.   A C H L R U

2995   RICE, Theron Hall, 1867-1922.
        The Bible plan of salvation. n.p., n.d. 4 p.   U

2996   RICE, Theron Hall, 1867-1922.
        The evangelization of the colored race in the United States.

Report to the General Assembly of 1901. [By Theron H.
Rice, R. F. Campbell, and Chas. McKinney]. Richmond,
Presbyterian Committee of Publication, 1901. 34 p.   C U

2997   RICE, Theron Hall, 1867-1922.
The ministry of reconciliation. n.p., n.d.   7 p.   U

2998   RICE, Theron Hall, 1867-1922.
The scriptural relation of woman to the work of the Christian church. n.p., n.d.   29 p.   U

2999   RICHARDS, Charles Malone, 1871-1964.
The baptism of infants and the dedication of children to
the ministry. [Decatur, Ga., Columbia Theological Semi-
nary], 1948. unpaged. Bulletin of Columbia Theological
Seminary, vol. 40, no. 3.   C U

3000   RICHARDS, James McDowell, 1902-
Brothers in black. A sermon preached as retiring moderator before the Presbytery of Atlanta in its one hundred
sixty-ninth stated meeting October 14, 1941, in the West
End Church, Atlanta, Georgia. Printed by order of Presbytery of Atlanta. n.p., n.d.   10 p.   C

3001   RICHARDS, James McDowell, 1902-
Change and the changeless; articles, essays, and sermons.
Decatur, Ga., Columbia Theological Seminary, 1972.   90 p.
A C H L R U

3002   RICHARDS, James McDowell, 1902-
The Christian Sabbath in the twentieth century. n.p., n.d.
unpaged.   H

3003   RICHARDS, James McDowell, 1902-
In memoriam, John Bulow Campbell, business man, philan-
thropist, Christian. [Decatur, Ga., Columbia Theological
Seminary, 1941].   19 p. Bulletin of Columbia Theological
Seminary, vol. 34, no. 2.   C U

3004   RICHARDS, James McDowell, 1902-
In tribute [to Alexander Ramsay Batchelor]. n.p., n.d.
8 p.   U

3005   RICHARDS, James McDowell, 1902-
The meaning of Christmas ... [a sermon preached] Sunday,
December 22, 1946. Atlanta, Radio Committee, Presbyterian
Church in the U.S., 1946.   15 p.   H

3006   RICHARDS, James McDowell, 1902-
On preparation for public prayer. [Richmond, Presbyterian
Outlook], n.d.   4 p. Reprinted from the Presbyterian Out-
look.   U

3007 RICHARDS, James McDowell, 1902-
The Presbyterian Church in Georgia, a centennial address.
Delivered before the Synod of Georgia, Macon, Georgia, September 20, 1944. n.p., n.d. 6 p. C

3008 RICHARDS, John Edwards, 1911-
God's plan of stewardship. Low Moor, Va., Montgomery
Presbytery, 1954. 5 p. H

3009 *RICHARDSON, Agnes Rowland.
The claimed blessing: the story of the lives of the Richardsons in China, 1923-1951. Cincinnati, Ohio, C. J. Krehbiel Co., © 1970. 155 p. "The Richardsons" were Agnes
and "Pete" [Robert Price], and Susan, Bob, Bill and Edgar.
H U

3010 RICHARDSON, Donald William, 1879-1966.
The church in China. Richmond, Presbyterian Committee
of Publication, © 1929. 224 p. A C H L PH R U

3011 RICHARDSON, Donald William, 1879-1966.
[An introduction to the study of the New Testament....
Chinese text written by J. C. Peng ... and Mr. Tao Chung
Liang]. n.p., [1925]. Title-page and text in Chinese. C
PT

3012 RICHARDSON, Donald William, 1879-1966.
The Revelation of Jesus Christ: an interpretation. Richmond, John Knox Press, © 1939. 195 p. A C L PT R
U ... C H L R U: [4th ed. 1957] ... C U: Aletheia ed.
© 1964. 140 p. ... U: 1976. 144 p.

3013 RICHARDSON, Hilary Goode, 1874-
Life and the Book. New York, The Macmillan Co., 1929.
179 p. L PT

3014 RICHARDSON, John Robert, 1901-
The Christian character of General Stonewall Jackson....
Dedicated to the Board of Deacons, First Presbyterian Church,
Alexandria, La. Weaverville, N.C., Southern Presbyterian
Journal, n.d. 20 p. C

3015 RICHARDSON, John Robert, 1901-
Christian economics; studies in the Christian message to the
market place. [Houston, Tex., St. Thomas Press, 1966].
169 p. C R U

3016 RICHARDSON, John Robert, 1901-
The Epistle to the Romans, by John R. Richardson and
Knox Chamblin. Grand Rapids, Baker Book House, 1963.
166 p. C R U ... C R: [1972. In Turnbull, Ralph G.,
ed., Proclaiming the New Testament, v. 2.]

3017   RICHARDSON, John Robert, 1901-
　　　　　Our distinctive Presbyterian emphasis. Weaverville, N.C.,
　　　　Southern Presbyterian Journal, n.d. 12 p.   U

3018   RICHARDSON, Robert Price, 1896-1967.
　　　　　Footprints of a man: the favorite prayers and sermons....
　　　　Prepared by the Richardson Memorial Committee, First Pres-
　　　　byterian Church, Pine Bluff, Arkansas. Pine Bluff, Perdue
　　　　Co., 1968. 90 p.   H

3019   RICHARDSON, William T., 1820-1895.
　　　　　Considerations on the choice of a field for ministerial la-
　　　　bor: annual address before the Society of Alumni of Union
　　　　Theological Seminary, Virginia, May, 1855. [Richmond],
　　　　Richmond Enquirer Book Office, 1855.   PH PT

3020   RICHMOND, Va. Second Presbyterian Church.
　　　　　... Commemoration of forty-five years of service by the
　　　　Rev. Moses Drury Hoge ... as pastor ... [Richmond, Whit-
　　　　tet & Shepperson, 1890]. 143 p. At head of title: 1845-
　　　　1890.   A H PH PT R U

3021   RICHMOND, Va. Second Presbyterian Church.
　　　　　Fifty years a pastor. An account of the observance of
　　　　the semi-centennial anniversary of the installation of Rev.
　　　　Moses Drury Hoge ... in the pastorate of the Second Pres-
　　　　byterian Church.... Richmond, n.p., 1895. 156 p.   A C
　　　　H

3022   RICHMOND, Va. Second Presbyterian Church.
　　　　　Memorials. Rev. Russell Cecil, D.D., pastor.... Died
　　　　June 15, 1925. [Richmond, Second Presbyterian Church],
　　　　n.d. 87 p.   A C H PT U

3023   RIDDLE, David Hunter, 1805-1888.
　　　　　An address, delivered in the Third Presbyterian Church,
　　　　on the Sabbath evening of February 17th, 1839, to the young
　　　　men of the city of Pittsburgh. Pittsburgh, E. B. Fisher &
　　　　Co., 1839. 24 p.   PH

3024   RIDDLE, David Hunter, 1805-1888.
　　　　　The duties of literary men: an address, delivered before
　　　　the Alumni Association of Jefferson College, September 24,
　　　　1834. Pittsburgh, D. and M. Maclean, 1834. 24 p.   PH

3025   RIDDLE, David Hunter, 1805-1888.
　　　　　A farewell letter to Mr. and Mrs. Travelli, missionaries
　　　　to China under the care of the American Board, and sup-
　　　　ported by the Third Presbyterian Church of Pittsburgh, de-
　　　　livered on April 3, 1836. Pittsburgh, William Allinder, Jr.,
　　　　1836. 14 p.   PH

3026   RIDDLE, David Hunter, 1805-1888.

Genuine radicalism! An address before the Goethean and Diagnothian societies of Marshall College, Pa.; delivered on the 26th of September, 1843. Pittsburgh, A. Jaynes, 1843. 23 p. PH PT

3027 RIDDLE, David Hunter, 1805-1888.
The glory and duty of young men. The baccalaureate discourse to the senior class of Jefferson College, 1865. Pittsburgh, O'Neill & Anderson, 1865. 17 p. PH

3028 RIDDLE, David Hunter, 1805-1888.
Ground of confidence in foreign missions. A sermon, preached at Portland, Maine, September 9, 1851, before the American Board of Commissioners for Foreign Missions, at their forty-second annual meeting. Boston, T. R. Marvin, 1851. 34 p. PH PT

3029 RIDDLE, David Hunter, 1805-1888.
The means of peace: a sermon, delivered in the Third Presbyterian Church, Pittsburgh, July 12th, 1846. [Pittsburgh], Johnston & Stockton, 1846. 24 p. PH PT

3030 RIDDLE, David Hunter, 1805-1888.
"The morning cometh"; or, The watchman's voice. A discourse on the day of the national fast. Pittsburgh, A. Jaynes, 1841. 28 p. PH PT

3031 RIDDLE, David Hunter, 1805-1888.
The nation's alternative. A sermon, preached in Providence Hall, before the students of Jefferson College, August 2d, 1840. Pittsburgh, A. Jaynes, 1840. 16 p. H PH

3032 RIDDLE, David Hunter, 1805-1888.
The nation's true glory: the annual address to the senior class of Jefferson College. Delivered in Providence Hall. Pittsburgh, George Parkin, 1845. 21 p. PH

3033 RIDDLE, David Hunter, 1805-1888.
Organic Christianity; or the relation of baptized children to the church. n.p., n.d. 24 p. From the Mercersburg Review, March, 1849. PH PT

3034 RIDDLE, David Hunter, 1805-1888.
Our country for the sake of the world. A sermon in behalf of the American Home Missionary Society, preached in the cities of New York and Brooklyn, May, 1851. New York, Baker, Godwin & Co., 1851. 31 p. PH PT

3035 RIDDLE, David Hunter, 1805-1888.
Our mission: a sermon, delivered at the opening of the General Assembly of the Presbyterian Church in the city of Utica, May 15th, 1851. Utica, R. Northway & Co., 1851. 34 p. PT

3036 RIDDLE, David Hunter, 1805-1888.
Paul: a model. A sermon, delivered by the appointment
of the General Assembly, at the opening of the Synod of
West Pennsylvania, at Meadville, October 17th, 1843. Pittsburgh, A. Jaynes, 1843. 12 p. PH PT

3037 RIDDLE, David Hunter, 1805-1888.
The Pilgrims and their principles: a sermon before the
New England Society of Pittsburgh, on the evening of Decem-
ber 22nd, 1850, in the Third Presbyterian Church. Pittsburgh,
W. S. Haven, 1851. 24 p. H

3038 RIDDLE, David Hunter, 1805-1888.
The Scotch-Irish element of Presbyterianism. A discourse,
delivered before the Presbyterian Historical Society in New
York, and repeated, by request, before the Associate Reformed Synod in Allegheny City. Pittsburgh, John T. Shryock,
1856. 24 p. Reprinted from the Presbyterian Quarterly Review, September, 1856. PH PT

3039 RIDDLE, David Hunter, 1805-1888.
Sound and sanctified scholarship: an address delivered at
the dedication of the new edifice of the Western University of
Pennsylvania, on Tuesday, September 8th, 1846. Pittsburgh,
Commercial Journal Print., 1846. 20 p. PH

3040 RIDDLE, David Hunter, 1805-1888.
"Such a time as this." A sermon, preached in the First
Presbyterian Church, Jersey City, on Thanksgiving Day, Nov.
24, 1859. Jersey City, J. H. Lyon & Co., 1860. 18 p.
PH PT

3041 RIDDLE, David Hunter, 1805-1888.
A voice from heaven: a sermon, commemorative of the
death of Mrs. Mary W. Brown, wife of Rev. Matthew Brown,
D.D., preached in Providence Hall, Canonsburg, May 6, 1838.
Pittsburgh, D. N. White, 1838. 23 p. PH PT

3042 RIDEOUT, Arthur Wilson, 1917-
A short history of the Presbyterian Church in the Synod of
Florida, upon the centennial of the Presbyterian Church, U.S.,
1861-1961. n.p., 1961. 8 p. H PH

3043 RITSCHL, Dietrich, 1929-
Athanasius, versuch einer Interpretation. Zürich, EVZ-
Verlag, © 1964. 74 p. C PT U

3044 RITSCHL, Dietrich, 1929-
Christ our life: the Protestant church at worship and work.
Translated by J. Colin Campbell. Edinburgh, Oliver and
Boyd, 1960. 114 p. Translation of "Vom Leben in der Kirche."
A C PT R U

3045 RITSCHL, Dietrich, 1929-
      The faith and mission of the church. [London], Student
      Christian Movement, [1960?]. 33 p. A

3046 RITSCHL, Dietrich, 1929-
      Hippolytus' conception of deification; remarks on the inter-
      pretation of Refutation X, 34. 388-399 p. Reprinted from
      the Scottish Journal of Theology, December, 1959. A

3047 RITSCHL, Dietrich, 1929-
      Die homiletische Funktion der Gemeinde, zur dogmatischen
      Grundlegung der Predigtlehre. Zollikon, Evangelischer Ver-
      lag, © 1959. 74 p. A C PT U

3048 RITSCHL, Dietrich, 1929-
      Konzepte. Bern, Herbert Lang, 1976. 151 p. Gesam-
      melte Aufsätze: Band I: Patristische Studien. PT

3049 RITSCHL, Dietrich, 1929-
      Memory and hope; an inquiry concerning the presence of
      Christ. New York, The Macmillan Co., © 1967. 237 p.
      A C L PT U

3050 RITSCHL, Dietrich, 1929-
      "Story" als Rohmaterial der Theologie, [by] Dietrich
      Ritschl [and] Hugh O. Jones. [1. Aufl.] München, Chr.
      Kaiser, © 1976. 74 p. L PT U

3051 RITSCHL, Dietrich, 1929-
      A theology of proclamation. Richmond, John Knox Press,
      © 1960. 190 p. A C H L PT R U

3052 RITSCHL, Dietrich, 1929-
      Vom Leben in der Kirche; der Tageslauf der evangelischen
      Gemeinde. Neukirchen Kr. Moers, Buchhandlung des Erzie-
      hungsvereins, [1957]. 109 p. A PT

3053 RIVIERE, William Thurmond, 1893-1973.
      Is the church older than Pentecost? [Richmond], Union
      Seminary Review, 1929. 16 p. Reprinted from the Union
      Seminary Review, January, 1929. C U

3054 RIVIERE, William Thurmond, 1893-1973.
      A pastor looks at Kierkegaard; the man and his philosophy.
      Grand Rapids, Mich., Zondervan Publishing House, © 1941.
      231 p. A C H L PT R U

3055 RIVIERE, William Thurmond, 1893-1973.
      The philosophy underlying Barth's theology. Dallas, Tex.,
      Evangelical Theological College, © 1934. 154-176 p. Re-
      printed from Bibliotheca Sacra, April, 1934. U

3056 ROBERTS, John Kountz, 1906-

A history of the Presbyterian Church, Point Pleasant, W.Va., prepared for the hundredth anniversary, nineteen hundred and thirty-five. n.p., [1935?]. 37 p.   H

3057   ROBERTS, John Kountz, 1906-
       What a Presbyterian believes. Richmond, Presbyterian Committee of Publication, n.d. 6 p.   U ... U: n.p., n.d. 4 ℓ.

3058   ROBERTSON, George Francis, 1853-1938.
       The future of Israel as foretold in the Scriptures. Richmond, Whittet & Shepperson, n.d. 32 p.   PT U

3059   ROBERTSON, George Francis, 1853-1938.
       King John; a tale of the south. Lowell, N.C., Lowell Publishing Co., © 1927. 236 p.   H PT

3060   ROBERTSON, George Francis, 1853-1938.
       A small boy's recollections of the Civil War (War Between the States). Clover, S.C., George F. Robertson, 1932. 116 p.   H R ... A H: © 1935. 122 p.

3061   ROBERTSON, George Francis, 1853-1938.
       Yea, he loved the people. Deut. 33:3. A sermon preached at the Synod of Kentucky in October, 1896. Elizabethtown, Ky., Published by the author, [1896]. unpaged.   PT

3062   ROBERTSON, Jerome Pillow, 1862-1936.
       Hitting the mark in the dark. Richmond, Presbyterian Committee of Publication, n.d. 23 p.   U

3063   ROBERTSON, William W., 1807-1884 or '85.
       Fulton Presbyterian Church: organization and history. A sermon ... in the Presbyterian Church, Fulton, Mo., November 16th, 1876. St. Louis, Presbyterian Publishing Co., 1876. 25 p.   PH

3064   ROBINSON, Charley Boyce, 1899-1976.
       When God's mighty power? Richmond, Presbyterian Committee of Publication, © 1932. 47 p.   A H L PT U

3065   ROBINSON, James McConkey, 1924-   ed.
       The beginnings of dialectic theology. Richmond, John Knox Press, [1968-   ]. v. Vol. 1, pt. 1 translated by Keith R. Crim; pt. 2 translated by Louis De Grazia and Keith R. Crim. A C H L PT R U

3066   ROBINSON, James McConkey, 1924-
       Das Geschichtsverständnis des Markus-Evangeliums. [Aus dem englischen Manuskript ins Deutsche übertragen von Karlfried Frölich.] Zurich, Zwingli-Verlag, 1956. 112 p. Translation of "The problem of history in Mark."   C PT U

3067   ROBINSON, James McConkey, 1924-
      Kerygma und historischer Jesus.   Zurich, Zwingli-Verlag,
      © 1960.   192 p.   Translation of A new quest of the historical
      Jesus, 1959.   A C PT U ... PT: [2. Aufl. 1967].   264 p.

3068   ROBINSON, James McConkey, 1924-   ed.
      The later Heidegger and theology, edited by James M.
      Robinson [and] John B. Cobb, Jr. [1st ed.]   New York,
      Harper & Row, © 1963.   212 p.   A C L PT R U

3069   ROBINSON, James McConkey, 1924-
      Mark's understanding of history.   [Edinburgh, Oliver and
      Boyd], 1956.   17 p.   Off-print from the Scottish Journal of
      Theology, vol. 9, no. 4.   Abstract of dissertation ... Prince-
      ton Theological Seminary.   A U

3070   ROBINSON, James McConkey, 1924-   ed.
      The new hermeneutic, edited by James M. Robinson [and]
      John B. Cobb, Jr. [1st ed.]   New York, Harper & Row,
      © 1964.   243 p.   A C L PT R U

3071   ROBINSON, James McConkey, 1924-
      A new quest of the historical Jesus.   Naperville, Ill.,
      Alec R. Allenson [1959].   128 p.   C L R ... A PT U:
      London, SCM Press ... L: [1961].

3072   ROBINSON, James McConkey, 1924-
      Das Problem des Heiligen Geistes bei Wilhelm Herrmann.
      Druck, Karl Gleiser inhaber der R. Friedrichs Universitats-
      Buchdruckerei Marburg/Lahn, 1952.   102 p.   Inaugural-
      dissertation zur Erlangung der Doktorwürde der theologischen
      Fakultät der Universität Basel.   C PT

3073   ROBINSON, James McConkey, 1924-
      The problem of history in Mark.   Naperville, Ill., Alec
      R. Allenson, [1957].   95 p.   A C L R U ... C L PT:
      London, SCM Press.

3074   ROBINSON, James McConkey, 1924-   ed.
      Theology as history, edited by James M. Robinson [and]
      John B. Cobb, Jr. [1st ed.]   New York, Harper & Row,
      © 1967.   276 p.   A C L PT U

3075   ROBINSON, James McConkey, 1924-
      Trajectories through early Christianity, [by] James M.
      Robinson [and] Helmut Koester.   Philadelphia, Fortress Press,
      © 1971.   297 p.   A C L PT R U ... L: [1979].

3076   ROBINSON, John Joseph, 1822-1894.
      The excellent name; or God in earth, sea and sky.   Two
      sermons delivered in the Presbyterian Church, Eufaula, Ala.,
      February 2d and 9th, 1868.   Macon, Ga., J. W. Burke &
      Co., 1868.   23 p.   PH

3077 ROBINSON, Stuart, 1814-1881.
An appeal to the Christian public, in response to an article entitled "In memoriam: tribute to Rev. Stuart Robinson," in the Danville Review, for March, 1862. Louisville, Ky., Hanna & Co., 1862. 14 p. "From the True Presbyterian, of May 8, 1962." C PH ... U: microfilm.

3078 ROBINSON, Stuart, 1814-1881.
Christ's kingdom on earth: a self-expanding missionary society. A discourse for the Presbyterian Board of Foreign Missions; preached in the First Presbyterian Church, New York, May 6, 1855. New York, Edward O. Jenkins, 1855. 14 p. H PH

3079 ROBINSON, Stuart, 1814-1881.
The church of God as an essential element of the Gospel, and the idea, structure, and functions thereof.... With an appendix, containing the more important symbols of Presbyterian Church government. Philadelphia, Joseph M. Wilson, 1858. 130, 96 p. A C H L PH PT R U

3080 ROBINSON, Stuart, 1814-1881.
Discourses of redemption: as revealed at "sundry times and in divers manners," designed both as Biblical expositions for the people and hints to theological students of a popular method of exhibiting the "divers" revelations through patriarchs, prophets, Jesus, and his apostles. New York, D. Appleton & Co., 1866. 488 p. A PH R U ... L: Toronto, Rollo & Adam ... C L: Louisville, Ky., A. Davidson ... C H L U: 1867 ... H PH U: 2d American ed. Louisville, Ky., Davidson and Robinson, 1867 ... C H L R: 3d American ed. Richmond, Presbyterian Committee of Publication, © 1866 ... A C H L U: 4th American ed. ... H L R: 2d ed. Edinburgh, T & T Clark, 1869.

3081 ROBINSON, Stuart, 1814-1881.
Discourses on the creation, and The Bible its own witness. By Rev. Stuart Robinson, D.D., and Rev. R. L. Dabney, D.D. Memphis, Shotwell & Co., n.d. 181, 27 p. A C H L U ... L: Memphis, Memphis Presbyterian, n.d.

3082 ROBINSON, Stuart, 1814-1881.
The General Assembly of 1854. Philadelphia, Joseph M. Wilson, 1855. 34 p. Reprinted from the Southern Presbyterian Review, January, 1855. C PH PT

3083 ROBINSON, Stuart, 1814-1881.
The infamous perjuries of the "Bureau of military justice" exposed. Letter of Rev. Stuart Robinson to Hon. Mr. Emmons. n.p., n.d. 8 p. PH U

3084 ROBINSON, Stuart, 1814-1881.

The Presbyterian system of government; and the issues between the General Assembly and the Synod of Kentucky.
Louisville, Ky., Harney, Hughes & Co., 1867. 8 p.   PH

3085 ROBINSON, Stuart, 1814-1881.
      The relations of the secular and spiritual power, being the
      substance of a lecture delivered before the Maryland Institute,
      February 1st, 1859. Louisville, Ky., Bradley & Gilbert,
      1859. 26 p.   C PH

3086 ROBINSON, Stuart, 1814-1881.
      Rev. Stuart Robinson to President Lincoln. n.p., 1865.
      8 p.   PH ... H: xeroxed copy.

3087 ROBINSON, Stuart, 1814-1881.
      Slavery as recognized in the Mosaic law. n.p., 1865.
      12 p.   U

3088 ROBINSON, Stuart, 1814-1881.
      Speeches at the great meeting in St. Louis, June 4, 1866,
      by Stuart Robinson and S. R. Wilson, n.p., n.d. 17 p.
      From the St. Louis Republican.   U

3089 ROBINSON, William Childs, 1897-1982.
      Architecture appropriate for Reformed worship: editorials
      from the Southern Presbyterian Journal. [Weaverville, N.C.,
      Southern Presbyterian Journal, 1959]. 22 p.   C

3090 ROBINSON, William Childs, 1897-1982.
      The bodily resurrection of Jesus Christ. Decatur, Ga.,
      Columbia Theological Seminary, 1957. 23 p.   Reprinted
      from Theologische Zeitschrift, 13, 2, 1957. Columbia Theo-
      logical Seminary Bulletin, July, 1957.   A C U

3091 ROBINSON, William Childs, 1897-1982.
      The certainties of the Gospel. Grand Rapids, Mich.,
      Zondervan Publishing House, © 1935. 150 p.   A C H L
      PT R U

3092 ROBINSON, William Childs, 1897-1982.
      Christ--the bread of life. Grand Rapids, Mich., Wm. B.
      Eerdmans Publishing Co., 1950. 190 p.   The Payton Lec-
      tures, Fuller Theological Seminary.   A C H PT R U

3093 ROBINSON, William Childs, 1897-1982.
      Christ--the hope of glory; Christological eschatology.
      Grand Rapids, Mich., Wm. B. Eerdmans Publishing Co.,
      1945. 324 p.   The Sprunt Lectures, 1941.   A C H L PT
      R U

3094 ROBINSON, William Childs, 1897-1982.
      The Christian faith according to the Shorter Catechism.

[Weaverville, N.C., Southern Presbyterian Journal, 1966].
44 p.   C U

3095   ROBINSON, William Childs, 1897-1982.
The church union issue.   [Weaverville, N.C., Southern
Presbyterian Journal].   n.d.   6 ℓ.   U

3096   ROBINSON, William Childs, 1897-1982.
Columbia Theological Seminary and the Southern Presbyterian Church: a study in church history, Presbyterian
polity, missionary enterprise, and religious thought.   [Deca-
tur, Ga., Dennis Lindsey Printing Co.], © 1931.   233 p.
Thesis--Harvard University, 1928.   A C H L PH PT R U

3097   ROBINSON, William Childs, 1897-1982.
Evolution ... is the mirage lifting?   n.p., n.d.   10 p.
Reprinted from the Northwestern Pilot.   C

3098   ROBINSON, William Childs, 1897-1982.
The faith of a soldier.   [2d ed., rev.]   Weaverville, N.C.,
Southern Presbyterian Journal, [1942].   14 p.   Reprinted
from the Southern Presbyterian Journal, August, 1942.   C

3099   ROBINSON, William Childs, 1897-1982.
God incarnate for suffering men.   A word to those who
won the Purple Heart.   The Easter sermon preached at Warm
Springs in the last service attended by our late commander-
in-chief, Franklin Delano Roosevelt.   Weaverville, N.C.,
Southern Presbyterian Journal, [1945].   16 p.   PH

3100   ROBINSON, William Childs, 1897-1982.
God's hand over man's, the mystery of providence.   Delivered at First Presbyterian Church, Charlotte, North Carolina, September 7, 1941.   n.p., n.d.   11 p.   C

3101   ROBINSON, William Childs, 1897-1982.
An interview with Professor Karl Barth.   Decatur, Ga.,
Columbia Theological Seminary, 1938.   8 p.   Bulletin, Co-
lumbia Theological Seminary, November, 1938.   A C U

3102   ROBINSON, William Childs, 1897-1982.
The liberal attack upon the supernatural Christ.   [Weaver-
ville, N.C., Southern Presbyterian Journal], n.d.   8 p.   Reprinted from the Southern Presbyterian Journal, May 1, 1946.
PH U

3103   ROBINSON, William Childs, 1897-1982.
Our Lord: an affirmation of the deity of Christ.   Grand
Rapids, Mich., Wm. B. Eerdmans Publishing Co., © 1937.
239 p.   A C H PT U ... C H L R: 2d ed, rev.   1949.
198 p.

3104   ROBINSON, William Childs, 1897-1982.

The plan of union lacks those tokens which have evidenced God's presence with and favor upon our church. [Weaverville, N.C., Southern Presbyterian Journal], n.d. 8 ℓ. Reprinted from the Southern Presbyterian Journal, October 7, 1953.
U

3105 ROBINSON, William Childs, 1897-1982.
The Reformation: a rediscovery of grace. Grand Rapids, Mich., Wm. B. Eerdmans Publishing Co., © 1962. 189 p.
A C H L PT R U

3106 ROBINSON, William Childs, 1897-1982.
... A re-study of the virgin birth of Christ. God's Son was born of a woman: Mary's son prayed "Abba Father." [Exeter, Eng., Paternoster Press], n.d. 15 p. Reprinted from the Evangelical Quarterly. At head of title: Supplement to the Columbia Theological Seminary Bulletin. C

3107 ROBINSON, William Childs, 1897-1982.
Sparrow, soldier, sailor: not one shall fall without your father (Matthew X:29). Weaverville, N.C., Southern Presbyterian Journal, n.d. 8 p. Reprinted from the Southern Presbyterian Journal, June, 1943. H

3108 ROBINSON, William Childs, 1897-1982.
Summary of the Christian faith according to the Shorter Catechism. [Weaverville, N.C., Southern Presbyterian Journal, 1950]. 44 p. H PT ... C U: 1966.

3109 ROBINSON, William Childs, 1897-1982.
The theocentric theology implicit in the name of the Trinity. Decatur, Ga., Columbia Theological Seminary, 1934. 30 p. Reprinted from the Evangelical Quarterly, July, 1934. Bulletin, Columbia Theological Seminary, October, 1934. A C R U

3110 ROBINSON, William Childs, 1897-1982.
The theology of Jesus and the theology of Paul. Decatur, Ga., Columbia Theological Seminary, 1937. 25 p. Reprinted from the Evangelical Quarterly, October, 1936. Bulletin, Columbia Theological Seminary, February, 1937. C PT U

3111 ROBINSON, William Childs, 1897-1982.
What is Christian faith? Grand Rapids, Mich., Zondervan Publishing House, © 1937. 117 p. A C H PT R U

3112 ROBINSON, William Childs, 1897-1982.
What think ye of Christ? A study in the Christology of the RSV. [Weaverville, N.C., Southern Presbyterian Journal], n.d. 16 p. U

3113 ROBINSON, William Childs, 1897-1982, ed.

Who say ye that I am? Six theses on the deity of Christ, written in competition for the Robert A. Dunn award. Grand Rapids, Mich., Wm. B. Eerdmans Publishing Co., 1949. 173 p. Chapters by Wm. C. Robinson, Jr., Albert N. Wells, George A. Anderson, George Scotchmer, James M. Robinson, Preston Peek Phillips, Jr. C H L PT R U

3114 ROBINSON, William Childs, 1897-1982.
The word of the cross. The 1938 lectures delivered in the Free Church College, Edinburgh. London, Sovereign Grace Union, 1940. 168 p. A C H PT R U ... C: In Korean. Translated by Rev. Kyu Tang Kim. [Korea, Christian Book Association?], n.d. 156 p.

3115 ROBINSON, William Childs, 1922-
The church in the world: "Steward of the mysteries of God." n.p., n.d. 412-417 p. Reprinted from Interpretation, October, 1965. C U

3116 ROBINSON, William Childs, 1922-
Der Weg des Herrn: Studien zur Geschichte und Eschatologie im Lukas-Evangelium. Ein Gespräch mit Hans Conzelmann. Hamburg, Herbert Reich, 1964. 67 p. PT

3117 ROBINSON, William Childs, 1922-
The way of the Lord; a study of history and eschatology in the Gospel of Luke. [Dallas?], n.p., © 1962. 117 p. Translation of "Der Weg des Herrn." C PT R U

3118 ROCHESTER, Adolphus Augustus, 1877-1960.
A. A. Rochester, missionary in the Congo. An autobiography. Atlanta, Committee on Woman's Work, Presbyterian Church in the U.S., [1944]. 32 p. H U

3119 ROCKWELL, Elijah Frink, 1809-1888.
Inaugural address ... [as] Professor of Natural Science, before the Board of Trustees of Davidson College, N.C., August 13, 1851. Salisbury, N.C., J. J. Bruner, 1851. 24 p. C PH

3120 *ROGERS, Ebenezer Platt, 1817-1881.
The doctrine of election; stated, defended and applied in three discourses.... With an introductory essay by Rev. Thomas Smyth. Hartford, Elihu Geer, 1850. 104 p. A C H PH U

3121 *ROGERS, Jack Bartlett.
Case studies in Christ and salvation, by Jack Rogers, Ross Mackenzie [and] Louis Weeks. Philadelphia, Westminster Press, © 1977. 176 p. A H L PH PT U

3122 ROGERS, William Warr, 1926-

Cornell-Brazil project; an experiment in learning, [by] William W. Rogers and Richard Graham. Foreword: Ivan D. Illich. Cuernavaca, Centro Intercultural de Documentación, 1969. 1 v. (various pagings) U

3123 ROLSTON, Holmes, 1900-1977.
The apostle Paul speaks to us today. Atlanta, John Knox Press, [1979]. 188 p. Originally published as Consider Paul. C H PT U

3124 ROLSTON, Holmes, 1900-1977.
The apostle Peter speaks to us today. Atlanta, John Knox Press, © 1977. 99 p. A C H L U

3125 ROLSTON, Holmes, 1900-1977.
The Bible in Christian teaching. Richmond, John Knox Press, © 1962. 104 p. A C H L PT R U ... C H R U: [1966].

3126 ROLSTON, Holmes, 1900-1977.
A conservative looks to Barth and Brunner; an interpretation of Barthian theology. Nashville, Tenn., Cokesbury Press, © 1933. 220 p. A C H L PT R U

3127 ROLSTON, Holmes, 1900-1977.
Consider Paul, apostle of Jesus Christ; revelation and inspiration in the letters of Paul. Richmond, John Knox Press, © 1951. 217 p. Also published as "The apostle Paul speaks to us today." A C H L PT R U

3128 ROLSTON, Holmes, 1900-1977.
Faces about the Christ. Richmond, John Knox Press, © 1959. 215 p. A C H L PT R U ... C: © 1966.

3129 ROLSTON, Holmes, 1900-1977.
The first and second letters of Paul to the Thessalonians. The first and second letters of Paul to Timothy. The letter of Paul to Titus. The letter of Paul to Philemon. Richmond, John Knox Press, © 1963. 131 p. (The Layman's Bible Commentary, v. 23.) A C H L PT R U

3130 ROLSTON, Holmes, 1900-1977.
Personalities around David. Richmond, John Knox Press, © 1968. 144 p. A C H L PT U

3131 ROLSTON, Holmes, 1900-1977.
Personalities around Paul: men and women who helped or hindered the apostle Paul. Richmond, John Knox Press, © 1954. 206 p. A C H L PT U ... R: © 1968.

3132 ROLSTON, Holmes, 1900-1977.
The social message of the apostle Paul. Richmond, John

Knox Press, © 1942. 250 p. The Sprunt Lectures, 1942.
A C H L PT R U

3133 ROLSTON, Holmes, 1900-1977.
Stewardship in the New Testament Church; a study in the
teachings of Saint Paul concerning Christian stewardship.
Richmond, John Knox Press, © 1946. 156 p. A C H PT
R U ... U: 3d ed. 1947 ... A: 4th ed. [1953] ... L PH:
[1956] ... A C H L PT R U: Rev. ed. © 1959. 160 p.

3134 ROLSTON, Holmes, 1900-1977.
The "we knows" of the apostle Paul. Richmond, John
Knox Press, © 1966. 101 p. A C H L PT U

3135 ROLSTON, Holmes, 1932-
The cosmic Christ; themes from Colossians for an expand-
ing world. Richmond, CLC Press, © 1966. 48 p. (The
Covenant Life Curriculum.) C L U

3136 ROLSTON, Holmes, 1932-
John Calvin versus the Westminster Confession. Rich-
mond, John Knox Press, © 1972. 124 p. A C H L PH
PT R U

3137 ROSE, Benjamin Lacy, 1914-
Alexander Rose of Person County, North Carolina, and
his descendants. Richmond, [Ben L. Rose], 1979. 268 p.
H U

3138 ROSE, Benjamin Lacy, 1914-
Baptism by sprinkling. The baptism of infants: its meaning and authority. [Weaverville, N.C., Southern Presbyterian
Journal], n.d. 20, 16 p. Reprinted from the Southern Presbyterian Journal, February 1, 1949, February 1, 1950. U

3139 ROSE, Benjamin Lacy, 1914-
Confirming your call in church, home, and vocation. Richmond, John Knox Press, © 1967. 72 p. A C H L R U

3140 ROSE, Benjamin Lacy, 1914-
God is the sovereign Lord of history. A sermon by Ben
Lacy Rose, Moderator, General Assembly of the Presby-
terian Church in the United States. Preached to St. Andrew
Presbytery, September 21, 1971. n.p., n.d. unpaged.
PH

3141 ROSE, Benjamin Lacy, 1914-
God's love for the world: the message and motive of missions. [Nashville, Tenn., Board of World Missions, Presbyterian Church in the U.S., 1953]. 15 p. Sermon preached
at the World Mission Conference, Montreat, N.C., August 2,
1953. C U

3142 ROSE, Benjamin Lacy, 1914-
      The minister as pastoral director.... Inaugural address
[as the Benjamin Rice Lacy, Jr., Professor of Homiletics
and Pastoral Leadership] delivered November 19, 1957, in
Schauffler Hall, Union Theological Seminary, Richmond, Virginia. Richmond, Union Theological Seminary, 1957. 23 p.
A C H PT R U

3143 ROSE, Benjamin Lacy, 1914-
      Racial segregation in the church. [Richmond, Presbyterian
Outlook], © 1957. 30 p. Reprinted from the Presbyterian
Outlook. C U

3144 ROSE, Benjamin Lacy, 1914- ed.
      The saga of the Red Horse; a short account of the combat
operations in Europe during 1944-45 of the 113th Cavalry
Group, Mechanized. Nijmegen, Holland, G. J. Thieme, n.d.
91 p.   U

3145 ROSE, Benjamin Lacy, 1914-
      What will you do with your life? [Nashville, Tenn., Board
of World Missions, Presbyterian Church in the U.S.], n.d.
4 ℓ.   U

3146 ROSE, John McAden, 1849-1917.
      Address ... delivered at Red Springs, April 24, 1910.
[Charlotte, N.C., Queen City Printing Co.], n.d.   4 ℓ.   U

3147 ROSEBRO, John William, 1847-1912.
      Infant salvation. A sermon, preached before East Hanover
Presbytery. Richmond, Presbyterian Committee of Publication, © 1901. 22 p.   PT

3148 ROSEBRO, John William, 1847-1912.
      Questions on the Book of Church Order. Richmond, Pres-
byterian Committee of Publication, © 1897. 13 p.   U

3149 ROSENBERG, Jacob Herman, 1888-1936.
      Startling fulfillment of the prophecies concerning the Jews
in the last days. Nashville, Tenn., Hebrew Christian Association, © 1917. 6 ℓ.   U

3150 ROSS, Frederick Augustus, 1796-1883.
      Dr. Ross and Bishop Colenso: or the truth restored in re-
gard to polygamy and slavery: by the Rev. Frederick A.
Ross, D.D., of Huntsville, Alabama, and the Right Rev.
John William Colenso, D.D., Lord Bishop of Natal. Philadelphia, Henry B. Ashmead, 1857. 82 p.   PH

3151 ROSS, Frederick Augustus, 1796-1883.
      The doctrine of the direct witness of the Spirit as taught
by the Rev. John Wesley shown to be unscriptural, false,

and of mischievous tendency. Philadelphia, Perkins & Purves, 1846. 108 p. PH

3152 ROSS, Frederick Augustus, 1796-1883.
Position of the Southern Church in relation to slavery as illustrated in a letter ... to Rev. Albert Barnes. New York, John A. Gray, 1857. 23 p. H PH U

3153 ROSS, Frederick Augustus, 1796-1883.
A sermon on intemperance, delivered in the First Presbyterian Church in Knoxville, Tenn., on the evening of the twelfth of October, 1829. Rogersville, Tenn., "Calvinistic Magazine" Office, 1830. 16 p. A PH

3154 ROSS, Frederick Augustus, 1796-1883.
Slavery ordained of God. Philadelphia, J. B. Lippincott & Co., 1857. 186 p. H R ... L PH: 1859 ... C PT U: New York, Negro Universities Press, [1969] ... A L: Miami, Mnemosyne Publishing Co., [1969].

3155 ROSS, William Alfred, 1873-1960.
Estudios en las escrituras del antiguo y del nuevo testimentos. [Mexico, D. F.], Casa de Publicaciones "El Faro," [1955-56]. 3 v. A H

3156 ROSS, William Alfred, 1873-1960.
Realidad historica de Jesus. Version Castellana del ingles. Mexico, D. F., Casa Presbiteriana de Publicaciones, 1940. 252 p. A H

3157 ROSS, William Alfred, 1873-1960.
Sunrise in Aztec land, being an account of the mission work that has been carried on in Mexico since 1874 by the Presbyterian Church in the United States. Richmond, Presbyterian Committee of Publication, 1922. 244 p. A C H PT R U

3158 ROUDEBUSH, George S., 1828-1921.
A plea for a higher education for the women of Mississippi. Jackson, Miss., Clarion Steam Publishing House, 1881. 23 p. PH

3159 RUFFNER, Henry, 1789-1861.
Address to the people of West Virginia; showing that slavery is injurious to the public welfare, and that it may be gradually abolished, without detriment to the rights and interests of slaveholders. By a slaveholder of West Virginia. Lexington, R. C. Noel, 1847. 40 p. H PH

3160 RUFFNER, Henry, 1789-1861.
Centennial address, delivered at the Church of Timberridge, in Rockbridge County, Virginia, October 3rd, 1856. n.p., n.d. 18 p. H

3161 RUFFNER, Henry, 1789-1861.
      A discourse upon the duration of future punishment. Richmond, N. Pollard, 1823. 47 p. H PH PT

3162 RUFFNER, Henry, 1789-1861.
      The fathers of the desert; or, An account of the origin and practice of monkery among heathen nations; its passage into the church; and some wonderful stories of the fathers concerning the primitive monks and hermits. New York, Baker and Scribner, 1850. 2 v. A H PH PT U

3163 RUFFNER, Henry, 1789-1861.
      The predestinarian. A treatise on the decrees of God. Lexington, Va., Valentine M. Mason, 1822. 84 p. PH ... H: 1823. 144 p.

3164 RUFFNER, Henry, 1789-1861.
      Review of the controversy between the Methodists and Presbyterians in central Virginia. Richmond, J. MacFarlan, 1829. 168 p. H U

3165 RUFFNER, Henry, 1789-1861.
      Strictures on a book, entitled, "An apology for the book of Psalms. By Gilbert M'Master." To which will be added, Remarks on a book entitled, "The design and use of the book of Psalms. By Alexander Gordon." Lexington, Va., Valentine M. Mason, 1822. 56 p. C

3166 RUFFNER, Henry, 1789-1861.
      Union speech; delivered at Kanawha Salines, Va., on the fourth of July, 1856. Cincinnati, Applegate & Co., 1856. 16 p. H

3167 RUFFNER, William Henry, 1824-1908.
      Africa's redemption. A discourse on African colonization in its missionary aspects, and in its relation to slavery and abolition. Preached on Sabbath morning, July 4th, 1852, in the Seventh Presbyterian Church, Penn Square, Philadelphia. Philadelphia, William S. Martien, 1852. 48 p. H PH PT

3168 RUFFNER, William Henry, 1824-1908.
      Charity and the clergy: being a review, by a Protestant clergyman, of the "new themes" controversy; together with sundry serious reflections upon the religious press, theological seminaries, ecclesiastical ambition, growth of moderatism, prostitution of the pulpit, and general decay of Christianity. Philadelphia, Lippincott, Grambo & Co., 1853. 208 p. H PH PT

3169 RUFFNER, William Henry, 1824-1908, ed.
      Lectures on the evidences of Christianity, delivered at the University of Virginia, during the session of 1850-1. New

York, Robert Carter & Brothers, 1852. 606 p. Lectures by William S. Plumer, Henry Ruffner, Moses D. Hoge, T. V. Moore, John Miller, B. M. Smith, Stuart Robinson, and others. C H PT R U

3170 RUFFNER, William Henry, 1824-1908.
The public free school system: a series of replies to R. L. Dabney on the subject of the education of the negro and the school system in general. n.p., 1876. 43 p. U

3171 RUFFNER, William Henry, 1824-1908.
A report on Washington territory. New York, Seattle, Lake Shore and Eastern Railway, 1889. 242 p. H

3172 RUMPLE, Jethro, 1827-1906.
The history of Presbyterianism in North Carolina. Richmond, Library of Union Theological Seminary in Virginia, 1966. 349 p. Reprinted from the North Carolina Presbyterian, 1878-1887. A C H L PH R U

3173 RUMPLE, Jethro, 1827-1906.
A history of Rowan County, North Carolina, containing sketches of prominent families and distinguished men, with an appendix. Salisbury, N.C., J. J. Bruner, © 1916. 428 p. H ... H: Salisbury, N.C., Elizabeth Maxwell Steele Chapter, Daughters of the American Revolution, [1929].

3174 *RUSSELL, Margaret T.
The Holy Spirit in the Holy Scriptures, by Margaret T. Russell [and] William C. Robinson. Atlanta, Committee on Woman's Work, Presbyterian Church in the U.S., 1935. 64 p. C H U

3175 SAILES, James Thomas, 1841-1931.
Baptism, its doctrine and mode scripturally presented in a conversation between a Baptist and a Presbyterian. Richmond, Presbyterian Committee of Publication, 1907. 131 p. A H R

3176 SAILES, James Thomas, 1841-1931.
Historical address, delivered at Presbytery at Monroe, La., April 23rd, 1907. n.p., [1907?]. 27 p. H PH

3177 ST. CLAIR, Ray Lawrence, 1896-
We met Jesus. Richmond, John Knox Press, © 1953. 143 p. A C H L R U

3178 *SAMPSON, Francis Smith, 1814-1854.
A critical commentary on the Epistle to the Hebrews.... Edited from the manuscript notes of the author by Robert L. Dabney, D.D. New York, Robert Carter & Brothers, 1856. 475 p. A C H L PH PT R U ... A U: 1857 ... A H: 1866.

3179 SAMUEL NORVELL LAPSLEY, pioneer missionary to the Congo. Nashville, Tenn., Executive Committee of Foreign Missions, Presbyterian Church in the U.S., n.d. 10 p.   U

3180 SANDEN, Oscar Emanuel, 1901-
The Bible in the age of science; or, The correlation of science and religion. Chicago, Moody Press, © 1946. 141 p.   A C R U

3181 SANDEN, Oscar Emanuel, 1901-
Calvin's Institutes of the Christian religion. [San Antonio, Tex., The author, 1939]. 42 p.   A C H PT U

3182 SANDEN, Oscar Emanuel, 1901-
The correlation of science and religion. [San Antonio, Tex., Lone Star Printing Co.], © 1940. 46 p.   R U

3183 SANDEN, Oscar Emanuel, 1901-
Does science support the Scriptures? Foreword by Dr. "Billy" Graham. Grand Rapids, Mich., Zondervan Publishing House, © 1951. 175 p.   A C L

3184 SANDEN, Oscar Emanuel, 1901-
Travels of a viking. [San Antonio, Tex., O. E. Sanden, 1938]. unpaged.   C H

3185 SANDERS, Robert Stuart, 1880-1971.
Annals of the First Presbyterian Church, Lexington, Kentucky, 1784-1959. Louisville, Ky., Dunne Press, 1959. 192 p.   A C H L PH U

3186 SANDERS, Robert Stuart, 1880-1971.
Gleanings from West Lexington Presbytery, 1799-1935; Ebenezer Presbytery, 1820-1935; Lexington-Ebenezer Presbytery, 1935-1950. Lexington, Ky., Lexington-Ebenezer Presbytery, 1952. 66 p.   L PH U

3187 SANDERS, Robert Stuart, 1880-1971.
Historical sketch of Bethel Presbyterian Church in Fayette County, Kentucky, organized in 1787. Lexington, Ky., Bethel Presbyterian Church, 1952. 6 p.   H L

3188 SANDERS, Robert Stuart, 1880-1971.
An historical sketch of Ebenezer Reformed Presbyterian Church, Jessamine County, Kentucky. [1st ed.] Frankfort, Ky., Roberts Printing Co., 1954. 71 p.   L PH U

3189 SANDERS, Robert Stuart, 1880-1971.
An historical sketch of Springfield Presbyterian Church, Bath County, Kentucky. Frankfort, Ky., Roberts Printing Co., 1954. 115 p.   C H L PH U

3190 SANDERS, Robert Stuart, 1880-1971.

History of Louisville Presbyterian Theological Seminary, 1853-1953. [Louisville, Ky.], Louisville Presbyterian Theological Seminary, 1953. 100 p.   A C H L PH PT R U

3191   SANDERS, Robert Stuart, 1880-1971.
History of the Second Presbyterian Church, Lexington, Kentucky, of the United Presbyterian Church in the U.S.A., 1815-1965. Lexington, Second Presbyterian Church, 1965. 242 p.   L PH PT U

3192   SANDERS, Robert Stuart, 1880-1971.
History of Walnut Hill Presbyterian Church (Fayette County, Kentucky). Frankfort, Ky., Kentucky Historical Society, 1956. 88 p.   C H L PH U

3193   SANDERS, Robert Stuart, 1880-1971.
Presbyterianism in Paris and Bourbon County, Kentucky, 1786-1961. Louisville, Ky., Dunne Press, 1961. 275 p.
A C H L PH U

3194   SANDERS, Robert Stuart, 1880-1971.
Presbyterianism in Versailles and Woodford County, Kentucky. Louisville, Ky., Dunne Press, 1963. 220 p.   A C H L PH PT U

3195   SANDERS, Robert Stuart, 1880-1971.
The Reverend Robert Stuart, D.D., 1771-1856, a pioneer in Kentucky Presbyterianism, and his descendants. Louisville, Ky., Dunne Press, 1962. 167 p.   C L PH PT U

3196   SANDERS, Robert Stuart, 1880-1971.
Sketch of Mount Horeb Presbyterian Church, 1827-1952; commemorating the one-hundredth and twenty-fifth anniversary of its founding, and the thirtieth anniversary of the pastorate of Dr. Thomas Wallis Rainey. Lexington, Ky., [Lexington Leader, 1953]. 40 p.   C H L PH U

3197   SAUNDERS, James Newton, 1818-1898.
Memorial upon the life of Rev. Stuart Robinson, D.D. Richmond, Presbyterian Committee of Publication, 1883. 46 p.   A H R U

3198   SAUNDERS, James Newton, 1818-1898.
Memorial upon the life of Rev. Stuart Robinson, D.D. ... before the Synod of Kentucky, October 20, 1882. Louisville, Ky., Courier-Journal Job Rooms, 1883. 29 p.   PH

3199   SAVANNAH, Ga.   First Presbyterian Church.
Dedication of the First Presbyterian Church, Savannah, Ga. Sermon by Rev. B. M. Palmer, D.D., LL.D., of New Orleans. Savannah, Geo. H. Nichols' Steam Power Presses, 1872. 45 p. Added title-page: Christ the builder

of the church. A discourse at the dedication of the new
church edifice ... on the 9th of June, 1872.... C H

3200 SAWTELL, Eli Newton.
A manual for the members of the Second Presbyterian
Church in the city of Louisville, Kentucky. Louisville,
M'Ginnis & Settle, 1833. 52 p. PH ... H: 1927. 45 p.

3201 SAWTELL, Eli Newton.
Plan and proposals for establishing a female seminary, at
Cleveland, Ohio. Boston, Damrell & Moore, 1850. 26 p.
PT

3202 SAWTELL, Eli Newton.
Treasured moments: being a compilation of letters on
various topics, written at different times, and in different
countries, together with notes, incidents of travel, and reminiscences of men and things. London, Robert K. Burt,
1860. 583 p. A PH PT

3203 SAYE, James Hodge, 1808-1892.
Cedar Shoal Church and congregation, Chester, South
Carolina. n.p., n.d. 18 p. H

3204 SAYE, James Hodge, 1808-1892.
A memorial sermon, occasioned by the death of Rev.
Pierpont E. Bishop. Columbia, Robert M. Stokes, 1959.
23 p. PH U

3205 SCANLON, David Howard, 1875-1950, comp.
I am of Ireland: genealogy of the O'Scanlon (Scanlan,
Scanlon) family. [Durham, N.C., n.p., 1938]. 23 p.
PH PT U

3206 SCANLON, David Howard, 1875-1950.
An historical sketch of Shenandoah Normal College, Virginia, 1883-1896. Durham, N.C., Christian Printing Co.,
1941. 24 p. U

3207 SCHAFER, Thomas Anton, 1918-
Jonathan Edward's conception of the church. [Durham,
N.C.], Duke University, 1955. 17 p. Reprinted from
Church History, March, 1955. R

3208 SCHENCK, Lewis Bevens, 1898-
The Presbyterian doctrine of children in the covenant; an
historical study of the significance of infant baptism in the
Presbyterian Church in America. New Haven, Yale University Press, 1940. 188 p. A C H L PH U

3209 SCHMIDT, Martin Anton, 1919-
Gottheit und Trinitaet nach dem Kommentar des Gilbert

Porreta zu Boethius, De Trinitate. Basel, Verlag für Recht und Gesellschaft, 1956. 273 p. PT

3210 SCHMIDT, Martin Anton, 1919-
Prophet und Tempel; eine Studie zum Problem der Gottes-nähe im Alten Testament. Zollikon-Zürich, Evangelischer Verlag, 1948. 276 p. Issued as author's thesis, Basel.
A C PT R U

3211 SCHMIDT, Martin Anton, 1919-
Scholastik, von Martin Anton Schmidt. Kirchliche Kunst im Mittelalter, von Kurt Goldammer. Göttingen, Vanden-hoeck & Ruprecht, © 1969. 68-219 p. A U

3212 *SCHWEITZER, Albert, 1875-1965.
The quest of the historical Jesus; a critical study of its progress from Reimarus to Wrede.... Introduction by James M. Robinson. New York, The Macmillan Co., [1979]. 413 p. L PT U

3213 SCOFIELD, Cyrus Ingerson, 1843-1921.
Addresses on prophecy. New York, A. C. Gaebelein, © 1910. 134 p. A H L R U ... R: Swengel, Bible Truth Depot, 1914.

3214 SCOFIELD, Cyrus Ingerson, 1843-1921.
Barrabas' theory of the atonement. [Harrisburg, Pa., L. & K.], n.d. 4 p. U

3215 SCOFIELD, Cyrus Ingerson, 1843-1921.
Dr. C. I. Scofield's question box. Chicago, Bible Institute Colportage Ass'n., © 1917. 166 p. A C PT R U

3216 SCOFIELD, Cyrus Ingerson, 1843-1921.
Galatians. New York, A. C. Gaebelein, [1903?]. 41 p.
R U

3217 SCOFIELD, Cyrus Ingerson, 1843-1921.
In many pulpits with Dr. C. I. Scofield. New York, Ox-ford University Press, 1922. 317 p. A U ... R: Grand Rapids, Mich., Baker Book House, 1966.

3218 SCOFIELD, Cyrus Ingerson, 1843-1921.
In memoriam Louise Harrison Reily. Born March 31, 1878; with Christ, March 21, 1915. The supreme victory. Harrisburg, Pa., J. Horace McFarland Co., © 1915. 47 p.
PH

3219 SCOFIELD, Cyrus Ingerson, 1843-1921.
The new life in Christ Jesus. Chicago, Bible Institute Colportage Ass'n., © 1915. 117 p. A C H PT R

3220 SCOFIELD, Cyrus Ingerson, 1843-1921.

No room in the inn and other interpretations. Chosen
from the writings of C. I. Scofield ... by Mary Emily Reily.
New York, Oxford University Press, © 1913. 156 p. PT
R

3221 SCOFIELD, Cyrus Ingerson, 1843-1921.
Plain papers on the Holy Spirit. New York, Fleming H.
Revell Co., © 1899. 80 p. L PT R U ... A: [1966] ...
PT: Plain papers on the doctrine of the Holy Spirit. Grand
Rapids, Mich., Baker Book House, [1966].

3222 SCOFIELD, Cyrus Ingerson, 1843-1921.
Rightly dividing the word of truth (2 Tim. 2:15). Being
ten outline studies of the more important divisions of Scrip-
ture. New York, Fleming H. Revell Co., [1907]. 89 p.
A H R ... H L PT R: New York, Loizeauz Brothers, n.d.
95 p. ... C H: Philadelphia, Philadelphia School of the
Bible, [1921]. 97 p. ... R: Westwood, N.J., Fleming H.
Revell Co., n.d. 64 p.

3223 SCOFIELD, Cyrus Ingerson, 1843-1921.
The Scofield Bible Correspondence School. Course of
study. [Dallas? Tex.], n.p., © 1907. 3 v. U ... A: 9th
ed. Chicago, Moody Bible Institute, © 1907 ... R: © 1959.
4 v.

3224 SCOFIELD, Cyrus Ingerson, 1843-1921.
Things new and old: Old and New Testament studies.
New York, Publication Office "Our Hope," © 1920. 323 p.
First published in "Our Hope." R U

3225 SCOFIELD, Cyrus Ingerson, 1843-1921.
The truth about heaven: a lecture. Philadelphia, Philadelphia School of the Bible, © 1916. 32 p. U

3226 SCOFIELD, Cyrus Ingerson, 1843-1921.
The truth about hell: a lecture. Philadelphia, Philadelphia School of the Bible, © 1916. 30 p. U

3227 SCOFIELD, Cyrus Ingerson, 1843-1921.
What do the prophets say? Philadelphia, The Sunday
School Times Co., © 1918. 188 p. A C H PT R U

3228 SCOFIELD, Cyrus Ingerson, 1843-1921.
Where faith sees Christ. New York, Publication Office
"Our Hope," © 1916. 81 p. H

3229 SCOFIELD, Cyrus Ingerson, 1843-1921.
The world's approaching crisis: a lecture. New York,
Publication Office "Our Hope," n.d. 32 p. PT

3230 *SCOTT, J. David.

Wooden crosses, by J. David Scott.... Together with A mission trip to Mexico, by N. S. Cutrer, and The land of the Christless cross, by Stephen B. Williams. Alexandria, La., Good Tidings Press, n.d. 80 p. R

3231 SCOTT, Jack Brown, 1928-
The book of Hosea; a study manual. Grand Rapids, Mich., Baker Book House, © 1971. 86 p. R

3232 SCOTT, Jack Brown, 1928-
God's plan unfolded: a student's introduction to God's written Word, the Old Testament. n.p., [The author], © 1976. 277 p. R ... PT: [Rev. ed.] Wheaton, Ill., Tyndale House, 1977. 384 p.

3233 SENGEL, William Randolph, 1923-
Can these bones live? Pastoral reflections on the Old Presbyterian Meeting House of Alexandria, Virginia, through its first two hundred years. [Kingsport, Tenn., Kingsport Press], © 1973. 98 p. H L PH PT U

3234 SERMONS and charges ... at the installation of the Rev. Charles O'Neale Martindale as the pastor of the Presbyterian Church of Newnan, Coweta County, Georgia ... October 31, 1902. Newnan, S.W. Murray, 1902. 17 p. H U

3235 SERVICES on the occasion of the ordination of the Rev. F. P. Mullally and the installation of Rev. J. H. Thornwell, D.D., and Rev. F. P. Mullally, as co-pastors of the First Presbyterian Church, Columbia, S.C. Sermon by Rev. John L. Girardeau. Charges by Rev. Thomas Smyth, D.D., May 4th, 1860. Published by the congregation. Columbia, Robert M. Stokes, 1860. 44 p. C

3236 THE SESSION of the Presbyterian Church of Clarksville, Tennessee, at the instance of the Rev. J. T. Hendrick, vs. W. H. Marquess. Exposition of the case by W. H. Marquess. Clarkesville, Tenn., Charles Faxon, 1848. 55 p. PH

3237 SETTLE, Paul Gunter, 1935-
Studies in the Shorter Catechism. [Weaverville, N.C., Presbyterian Journal], n.d. unpaged. R

3238 SHAW, Angus Robertson, 1858-1936.
Theology for the people. Richmond, Whittet & Shepperson, 1902. 294 p. A C H L R U

3239 SHAW, William A., 1804-1885.
Benediction of infants and baptism of believers, the only primitive, pure and authoritative organization and order of the church of God, as founded by our Lord Jesus Christ and

his inspired apostles. New York, Published for the author, by Lewis Colby, 1848. 56 p. PT

3240 SHEARER, James William, 1840-1921.
The Bible books. Their names, themes and divisions. n.p., © 1900. unpaged. PT

3241 SHEARER, James William, 1840-1921.
The combination speller. New York, Quison, Blakeman, Taylor & Co., 1874. 168 p. U ... U: Richmond, B. F. Johnson Publishing Co., 1894.

3242 SHEARER, James William, 1840-1921.
The English language made perfectly phonetic by a simple system of diacritical notation. n.p., © 1872. 8 p. PT

3243 SHEARER, James William, 1840-1921.
The pictured outline of the Gospel narrative. St. Louis, n.p., 1900. unpaged. A PT

3244 SHEARER, James William, 1840-1921.
The Shearer-Akers family, combined with "The Bryan line" through the seventh generation; arranged to be continuable indefinitely, both as a genealogy and a picture gallery. [Somerville, N.J., Somerset Messenger], 1915. 171 p. PT U

3245 SHEARER, John Bunyan, 1832-1919.
Bible course syllabus. Richmond, Whittet & Shepperson, 1885-90. 3 v. Vols. 2-3: Clarksville, Tenn., Neblett & Titus, 1885. A H R U ... H: 3d ed. Richmond, B. F. Johnson Publishing Co., 1895.

3246 SHEARER, John Bunyan, 1832-1919.
The canon of Scripture; is it divinely authenticated? Richmond, Whittet & Shepperson, 1893. 13 p. Reprinted from the Presbyterian Quarterly, January, 1893. PT

3247 SHEARER, John Bunyan, 1832-1919.
The Gospel ministry. Richmond, Presbyterian Committee of Publication, 1893. 26 p. A C U

3248 SHEARER, John Bunyan, 1832-1919.
Hebrew institutions, social and civil. Richmond, Presbyterian Committee of Publication, © 1910. 170 p. A C H L PT R U

3249 SHEARER, John Bunyan, 1832-1919.
Modern mysticism; or, The covenants of the spirit, their scope and limitations. Richmond, Presbyterian Committee of Publication, © 1905. 116 p. Davidson College Divinity Lectures, 1905. A C H L PT R U

3250 SHEARER, John Bunyan, 1832-1919.
One hundred brief Bible studies. Richmond, Presbyterian
Committee of Publication, 1912. 229 p. A C H R U

3251 SHEARER, John Bunyan, 1832-1919.
The Presbyteries and the tithe: an analysis of the an-
swers to the Assembly's overture. n.p., n.d. 614-621 p.
Reprinted from the Presbyterian Quarterly, October, 1890.
R

3252 SHEARER, John Bunyan, 1832-1919.
Scientia cum moribus conjuncta; a discussion of the higher
education. Charleston, S.C., Walker, Evans, and Cogswell.
20 p. U

3253 SHEARER, John Bunyan, 1832-1919.
The Scriptures, fundamental facts and features. Richmond,
Presbyterian Committee of Publication, © 1908. 166 p. A
C H PT R U

3254 SHEARER, John Bunyan, 1832-1919.
Selected Old Testament studies. Richmond, Presbyterian
Committee of Publication, © 1909. 223 p. A C H PT R U

3255 SHEARER, John Bunyan, 1832-1919.
The Sermon on the Mount: a study. Richmond, Presby-
terian Committee of Publication, © 1906. 146 p. A C H R
U

3256 SHEARER, John Bunyan, 1832-1919.
Studies in the life of Christ. Richmond, Presbyterian
Committee of Publication, 1907. 172 p. A C H L PT R U

3257 SHEDD, Charles William, 1915-
The best dad is a good lover. Kansas City, Sheed Andrews and McMeel, © 1977. 135 p. C U

3258 SHEDD, Charlie William, 1915-
Celebration in the bedroom, [by] Charlie Shedd, Martha
Shedd. Waco, Tex., Word Books, © 1979. 127 p. L U

3259 SHEDD, Charlie William, 1915-
A dad is for spending time with. Kansas City, Sheed
Andrews and McMeel, © 1978. 136 p. U

3260 SHEDD, Charlie William, 1915-
The exciting church: where people really pray. Waco,
Tex., Word Books, © 1974. 105 p. C PT U ... L:
[1978].

3261 SHEDD, Charlie William, 1915-
The exciting church: where they give their money away.
Waco, Tex., Word Books, © 1975. 88 p. A C L PT U

3262 SHEDD, Charlie William, 1915-
The exciting church: where they really use the Bible.
Waco, Tex., Word Books, © 1975. 122 p.   C PT R U ...
L: [1976].

3263 SHEDD, Charlie William, 1915-
The fat is in your head; a life style to keep it off.   Waco,
Tex., Word Books, © 1972. 122 p.   C L R U

3264 SHEDD, Charlie William, 1915-
Getting through to the wonderful you; a Christian alternative to transcendental meditation.   Old Tappan, N.J., Fleming H. Revell Co., © 1976. 128 p.   A H PT U

3265 SHEDD, Charlie William, 1915-
Grandparents: then God created grandparents and it was
very good. [1st ed.] Garden City, N.Y., Doubleday & Co.,
1976. 140 p.   L U ... A: Boston, G. K. Hall, 1977.
131 p.

3266 SHEDD, Charlie William, 1915-
How to develop a praying church.   New York, Abingdon
Press, © 1964. 111 p.   A L U

3267 SHEDD, Charlie William, 1915-
How to develop a tithing church.   New York, Abingdon
Press, © 1961. 123 p.   A C L PT R U

3268 SHEDD, Charlie William, 1915-
How to know if you're really in love--really in love enough
for marriage.   Kansas City, Sheed Andrews and McMeel,
© 1978. 155 p.   C L U

3269 SHEDD, Charlie William, 1915-
How to stay in love, [by] Charlie and Martha Shedd.   Kansas City, Sheed Andrews and McMeel, © 1980. 153 p.   U

3270 SHEDD, Charlie William, 1915-
Is your family turned on?   Coping with the drug culture.
Waco, Tex., Word Books, © 1971. 148 p.   A U

3271 SHEDD, Charlie William, 1915-
Letters to Karen: on keeping love in marriage.   Nashville, Abingdon Press, © 1965. 159 p.   A C R U

3272 SHEDD, Charlie William, 1915-
Letters to Philip: on how to treat a woman.   Garden
City, N.Y., Doubleday & Co., © 1968. 131 p.   C L R U

3273 SHEDD, Charlie William, 1915-
The pastoral ministry of church officers.   Richmond, John
Knox Press, © 1965. 71 p.   L ... C H R U: [1966] ...
A: Atlanta, John Knox Press, [1974].

3274 SHEDD, Charlie William, 1915-
Pray your weight away. [1st ed.] Philadelphia, J. B.
Lippincott Co., © 1957. 158 p.   C U

3275 SHEDD, Charlie William, 1915-
Promises to Peter; building a bridge from parent to child.
Waco, Tex., Word Books, [1970]. 147 p.   H L R U

3276 SHEDD, Charlie William, 1915-
Smart dads I know. New York, Sheed and Ward, © 1975.
124 p.   A U

3277 SHEDD, Charlie William, 1915-
The stork is dead. Waco, Tex., Word Books, [1968].
127 p.   C R U ... L: [1969].

3278 SHEDD, Charlie William, 1915-
Talk to me! [1st ed.] Garden City, N.Y., Doubleday &
Co., 1975. 105 p.   U

3279 SHEDD, Charlie William, 1915-
Those great big beautiful dollars. [New York, Department
of Interpretation and Stewardship, United Presbyterian Church
in the U.S.A.], © 1965. unpaged. From Letters to Karen.
PH

3280 SHEDD, Charlie William, 1915-
Time for all things; meditations on the Christian manage-
ment of time. New York, Abingdon Press, © 1962. 96 p.
A C H R U

3281 SHEDD, Charlie William, 1915-
Word-focusing--a new way to pray, by Charlie and Martha
Shedd. Nashville, Tenn., The Upper Room, © 1961. 80 p.
U

3282 SHEDD, Charlie William, 1915-
You can be a great parent! Waco, Tex., Word Books,
© 1970. 148 p.   C

3283 SHEPPARD, William Henry, 1865-1927.
Presbyterian pioneers in Congo.... Introduction by Rev.
S. H. Chester. Richmond, Presbyterian Committee of Pub-
lication, [1917]. 157 p.   A C H L PH PT R U ... L:
Pioneers in Congo. Louisville, Ky., Pentecostal Publishing
Co., n.d.

3284 SHEPPERSON, John G., 1814-1894.
Lectures delivered ... before Leesville Lodge, no. 113 ...
1882. [Altavista, Va., Altavista Printing Co., 1967]. 37 p.
Cover title: Memorial of John G. Shepperson; memorial of
H. C. Alexander.   U

3285   *SHERRILL, Helen Hardwicke.
       Interpreting death to children, [by Helen H. Sherrill and
       Lewis J. Sherrill].   Philadelphia, Board of Christian Educa-
       tion, Presbyterian Church in the U.S.A., n.d. unpaged.
       Reprinted from the International Journal of Religious Educa-
       tion.   PH

3286   SHERRILL, Lewis Joseph, 1892-1957.
       Adult education in the church, by Lewis Joseph Sherrill ...
       and John Edwin Purcell.... Richmond, Presbyterian Com-
       mittee of Publication, © 1936. 290 p.   A C H L PH PT
       U ... A C H L R U: Rev. ed. Richmond, John Knox Press,
       1939.

3287   SHERRILL, Lewis Joseph, 1892-1957.
       Becoming a Christian. A manual for communicant classes,
       by Lewis Joseph Sherrill and Helen Hardwicke Sherrill. Rich-
       mond, John Knox Press, 1943. 174 p.   A C H L PH PT R
       U ... U: 1952 ... R: [1966]. 144 p.

3288   SHERRILL, Lewis Joseph, 1892-1957.
       Family and church. New York, Abingdon Press, © 1937.
       266 p.   A C H L U

3289   SHERRILL, Lewis Joseph, 1892-1957.
       Frontiers for youth today. [Louisville, Ky., Executive
       Committee of Christian Education and Ministerial Relief,
       Presbyterian Church in the U.S.], n.d. 11 p.   PH

3290   SHERRILL, Lewis Joseph, 1892-1957.
       The gift of power. New York, The Macmillan Co., 1955.
       203 p.   A C L PH PT R U ... U: 1959 ... U: 1961.

3291   SHERRILL, Lewis Joseph, 1892-1957.
       Guilt and redemption. Richmond, John Knox Press, 1945.
       254 p. The Sprunt Lectures, 1945.   A C H L PT R U ...
       C L PT R U: Rev. ed. © 1957. 255 p. ... L: In Japan-
       ese. Translated by Tokuzo Hiraga and Sanichi Kesen. Tokyo,
       Board of Publication of the Church of Christ in Japan, 1956.

3292   SHERRILL, Lewis Joseph, 1892-1957.
       La infancia: edad de las oportunidades. Buenos Aires,
       Libreria "La Aurora" [1943]. 242 p. Translation into Span-
       ish of his "The opening doors of childhood."   A L

3293   SHERRILL, Lewis Joseph, 1892-1957.
       Lift up your eyes: a report to the churches on the reli-
       gious education re-study. Richmond, John Knox Press,
       © 1949. 175 p.   A C H L PH PT R U

3294   SHERRILL, Lewis Joseph, 1892-1957.
       Looking at your own church; suggestions for study groups

using Lift up your eyes. Richmond, John Knox Press,
© 1949. 23 p. A

3295 SHERRILL, Lewis Joseph, 1892-1957.
The opening doors of childhood. New York, The Macmillan Co., 1939. 193 p. A C H L PH PT R U ... L: 1940.

3296 SHERRILL, Lewis Joseph, 1892-1957.
Presbyterian parochial schools, 1846-1870. New Haven,
Yale University Press, 1932. 261 p. A C H L PH PT R
U ... R: New York, Arno Press, 1969.

3297 SHERRILL, Lewis Joseph, 1892-1957.
The psychology of the Oxford groups movement. Rich-
mond, Presbyterian Committee of Publication, 1933. 34 p.
Reprinted from the Union Seminary Review, October, 1933.
U

3298 SHERRILL, Lewis Joseph, 1892-1957.
Religious education and Presbyterian faith. Richmond,
Presbyterian Committee of Publication, [1929?]. 24 p. A

3299 SHERRILL, Lewis Joseph, 1892-1957.
Religious education in the small church. Philadelphia,
Westminster Press, 1932. 208 p. C H L PH PT R U

3300 SHERRILL, Lewis Joseph, 1892-1957.
The rise of Christian education. New York, The Macmillan Co., 1944. 349 p. A C H L PT R U ... L PH:
[1960].

3301 SHERRILL, Lewis Joseph, 1892-1957.
[The rise of Christian education.... Published for the
Association of Theological Schools in South East Asia by the
Council on Christian Literature for Overseas Chinese, Hong
Kong, © 1944]. 322 p. Title-page and text in Chinese.
L

3302 SHERRILL, Lewis Joseph, 1892-1957.
The struggle of the soul. New York, The Macmillan Co.,
1951. 155 p. The Smyth Lectures, 1950. A C H L PT
U ... U: 1953 ... C U: 1958 ... U: 1961 ... L:
[1963] ... L: In Japanese. [Translated by Sanichi Kesen.
Tokyo, Board of Publication of the United Church in Japan],
© 1951. 239 p.

3303 SHERRILL, Lewis Joseph, 1892-1957.
Understanding children. New York, Abingdon Press,
© 1939. 218 p. A C H L PT R U

3304 *SHERWOOD, Mary Martha (Butt) 1775-1851.
Narratives of Little Henry and his bearer; the amiable

Louisa; and Ann Eliza Williams, [by Rev. William S. Plumer]. New York, American Tract Society, (18-?). 61, 17, 23 p.   U

3305   SHEWMAKER, William Orpheus, 1869-1946.
Pisgah and her people, 1784-1934: a memorial to the past; a testimonial to the present; a reminder to the future. [Lexington, Ky., Commercial Printing Co.], © 1935.   269 p. H L PH PT

3306   SHEWMAKER, William Orpheus, 1869-1946.
The Pisgah book, 1784-1909: a memorial, a lesson, an inspiration.   Pisgah, Woodford County, n.p., 1909.   72 p. PH PT U

3307   SHIPLEY, David Oliver, 1925-
Neither black nor white; the whole church for a broken world.   Waco, Tex., Word Books, © 1971.   164 p.   C L PT R U

3308   SHOTWELL, Albert, 1807-
The duplex hymn and tune book, or selections for praise, for all Christians.   Richmond, Presbyterian Publishing Co., 1883.   244 p.   C PT ... PH: 237 p.

3309   SHOTWELL, Albert, 1807-
Recognition of friends in heaven.   A sermon, preached in the Presbyterian Church, West Point, Ga., March 5, 1854. West Point, Ga., Beacon Office, 1854.   13 p.   PH

3310   SHOTWELL, Albert, 1807-
The Sabbath school: its influence upon our children, our country and our world.   An address delivered to the patrons and friends of Sabbath schools, at a Sabbath school celebration held at Plum Creek on the fourth of July, 1854.   Louisville, J. F. Brennan, 1854.   15 p.   PH

3311   SHOTWELL, Albert, 1807-
Scripture baptism; the mode and subjects, a sermon. [3d ed.] St. Louis, Presbyterian Publishing Co., 1878. 77 p.   PT U

3312   SHRIVER, Donald Woods, 1927-
"The church and its community." Lectures [March 17, 1980] ... at Cliff Temple Baptist Church, Dallas, Texas, in honor of David V. Pittenger, Trinity Presbyterian Church, on his 16th anniversary of ordination.   n.p., n.d.   32 p. H

3313   SHRIVER, Donald Woods, 1927-
How do you do and why: an introduction to Christian ethics.   Richmond, CLC Press, © 1966.   224 p.   (The Covenant

Life Curriculum.) C U ... L: [1969] ... C U: Leaders'
guide. 96 p. ... L: [1969].

3314 SHRIVER, Donald Woods, 1927-
Is there hope for the city? by Donald W. Shriver, Jr.,
and Karl A. Ostrom. Philadelphia, Westminster Press,
© 1977. 204 p. A C L PH PT R U

3315 SHRIVER, Donald Woods, 1927-
Rich man poor man. Richmond, John Knox Press, © 1972.
112 p. A C H L PT U

3316 SHRIVER, Donald Woods, 1927-   ed.
The unsilent South; prophetic preaching in racial crisis.
Richmond, John Knox Press, © 1965. 169 p. Sermons by
John S. Lyles, James [Jimmy Gene] Peck, George A. Chaun-
cey, Richard S. Watt, J. Will Ormond, Robert H. Walkup,
Charles L. Stanford, J. V. Cosby Summerell, Lucius B. Du-
Bose, Carl R. Pritchett, Jefferson P. Rogers, D. P. Mc-
Geachy, III, Paul Tudor Jones, James I. Lowry, Jr., Joe
S. McClure, David H. Currie, Lawrence F. Haygood, Scott
McCormick, Jr. A C H L PH PT R U

3317 SIBLEY, Josiah, 1877-
Pathfinders of the soul country and other sermons for to-
day. New York, Fleming H. Revell Co., © 1918. 209 p.
A C L R

3318 SIBLEY, Julian Scales, 1867-1944.
The climax of revelation. New York, Fleming H. Revell
Co., © 1932. 175 p. A C H L PT R U

3319 SIKES, William Marion, 1875-1941.
The Gospel for the laymen's age. New York, Broadway
Publishing Co., © 1913. 148 p. H

3320 SIMPSON, John David, 1900-
The wounded hand. [Privately printed, 1972]. 46 p.
C R

3321 SINCLAIR, Alexander, 1834-1885.
Funeral sermon preached in the Presbyterian Church,
Sharpsburgh, Penna., on the death of his wife. Pittsburgh,
Jno. T. Shryock, 1856. 13 p. H

3322 SINCLAIR, Alexander, 1834-1885.
Thanksgiving sermon preached in Presbyterian Church at
Six-Mile Creek, Lancaster District, S.C. n.p., 1862. 16 p.
H

3323 SINKS, Perry Wayland, 1851-1940.
In the refiner's fire; the problem of human suffering.

Chicago, Bible Institute Colportage Ass'n., © 1911. 88 p.
R U

3324 SINKS, Perry Wayland, 1851-1940.
Popular amusements and the Christian life. New York,
Fleming H. Revell Co., © 1896. 176 p. R U

3325 SINKS, Perry Wayland, 1851-1940.
The reign of the manuscript. Boston, Richard G. Badger,
© 1917. 176 p. U

3326 SKINNER, James William, 1855-1931.
Evangelism, supreme task of the church. Richmond, Presbyterian Committee of Publication, 1926. 11 p. H

3327 SKINNER, James William, 1855-1931.
Out of the wilderness. Richmond, Presbyterian Committee
of Publication, © 1925. 143 p. A C H R U

3328 *SLUSSER, Dorothy Mallett.
The Jesus of Mark's Gospel, by Dorothy M. Slusser and
Gerald H. Slusser. Philadelphia, Westminster Press, © 1967.
157 p. A L PT R U

3329 *SLUSSER, Dorothy Mallett.
Technology: the God that failed, by Dorothy M. Slusser
and Gerald H. Slusser. Philadelphia, Westminster Press,
© 1971. 169 p. A C L PH PT U

3330 SLUSSER, Gerald Herbert, 1920-
A Christian look at secular society. Philadelphia, Westminster Press, © 1969. 112 p. A C L PT U

3331 SLUSSER, Gerald Herbert, 1920-
A dynamic approach to church education. Philadelphia,
Geneva Press, © 1968. 124 p. A C L PH PT U

3332 SLUSSER, Gerald Herbert, 1920-
The local church in transition: theology, education, and
ministry. Philadelphia, Westminster Press, © 1964. 204 p.
A C L PH R U

3333 *SMARAGDUS, abbot of St. Mihiel, fl. 809-819.
The emperor's monk; contemporary life of Benedict of
Aniane, by Ardo. Translated with an introduction by Allen
Cabaniss. Devon, Arthur H. Stockwell, © 1979. 120 p.
Translation of "Vita Benedicti." L

3334 SMITH, Arthur J.
Without excuse. Chicago, Winona Publishing Co., © 1905.
PH ... C U: [Grand Rapids, Mich.], Zondervan Publishing
House, © 1907. 127 p.

3335 SMITH, Benjamin Mosby, 1811-1893.
An address on the importance and advantage of classical study, delivered before the Graham Philanthropic and Washington Literary societies of Washington College, June, 1849. Lexington, Va., Patton & Burgess, 1849. 16 p.   H U

3336 SMITH, Benjamin Mosby, 1811-1893.
The Bible; a book for the world.   An address delivered before the Cadets' Bible Society of the Virginia Military Institute, May 1st, 1849. New York, John Wiley, 1849. 23 p. PH U

3337 SMITH, Benjamin Mosby, 1811-1893.
The exclusive claims of prelacy, stated and refuted: a discourse, delivered in the Presbyterian Church in Staunton, Friday evening, April 26, 1844.   Staunton, Kenton Harper, 1844. 64 p.   PH PT ... C H L PH PT R U: Philadelphia, Presbyterian Board of Publication, n.d. 35 p. (Presbyterian Tracts.)

3338 SMITH, Benjamin Mosby, 1811-1893.
Family religion, or the domestic relations as regulated by Christian principles.   Philadelphia, Presbyterian Board of Publication, © 1859. 210 p.   A C H PH PT R U

3339 SMITH, Benjamin Mosby, 1811-1893.
An inaugural discourse ... [as] Professor of Oriental Literature in Union Theological Seminary, Prince Edward County, Va., delivered in the seminary chapel, September 12, 1855. Richmond, Richmond Enquirer Book and Job Press, 1855. 39 p.   H PH U

3340 SMITH, Benjamin Mosby, 1811-1893.
Popery fulfilling prophecy. A sermon preached before the Synod of Virginia, October 18, 1850.   Philadelphia, Presbyterian Board of Publication, n.d. 52 p.   PH U

3341 SMITH, Benjamin Mosby, 1811-1893.
Questions on the Gospels.   Vol. I.   Richmond, Presbyterian Committee of Publication, 1868. 196 p.   A H PH R U

3342 SMITH, Benjamin Mosby, 1811-1893.
A sermon occasioned by the death of Chas. T. Edie, who was killed by Edward A. Langhorne, at Hampden Sidney College, Va., January 27, 1857; delivered in the College Church, March 22, 1857.   Petersburg, Va., Express & Job Office, 1857. 17 p.   H PH

3343 SMITH, Benjamin Mosby, 1811-1893.
The testimony of science to the truth of the Bible: an address delivered before the Bible Society of the University

of Virginia, January 27, 1850. Charlottesville, Va., O. S. Allen & Co., 1850. 28 p. H PH U

3344 SMITH, Benjamin Mosby, 1811-1893.
A tribute to the memory of our ancestors. A sermon, occasioned by the death of Gen'l. Robert Porterfield, delivered June 4, 1843. Staunton, Kenton Harper, 1843. 27 p. PH U

3345 SMITH, Edward Everett, 1861-1944.
Four minute sermons. Richmond, Presbyterian Committee of Publication, © 1927. 217 p. A C H L U

3346 *SMITH, Edwin William, 1876-
The life and times of Daniel Lindley (1801-80), missionary to the Zulus, pastor of the Voortrekkers Ubebe Omhlope. London, Epworth Press, [1949]. 456 p. A C L PT U ... C U: New York, Library Publishers, [1952].

3347 SMITH, Egbert Watson, 1862-1944.
Alabama's contribution to foreign missions during 100 years: a challenge to the future.... Address delivered at the centennial of the Synod of Alabama of the Presbyterian Church, at Mobile, Alabama, October 9, 1935, in the Government Street Presbyterian Church. n.p., n.d. 19 p. H

3348 SMITH, Egbert Watson, 1862-1944.
China: essential facts for busy people. Nashville, Tenn., Executive Committee of Foreign Missions, Presbyterian Church in the U.S., 1918. 31 p. H

3349 SMITH, Egbert Watson, 1862-1944.
Christ for Latin America. [Nashville, Tenn., Executive Committee of Foreign Missions, Presbyterian Church in the U.S., 1935?]. 61 p. H R U

3350 SMITH, Egbert Watson, 1862-1944.
The creed of Presbyterians. New York, Baker & Taylor Co., © 1901. 223 p. A C H R U ... C PT: 6th ed. ... PH: 7th ed. 1902 ... H U: Richmond, Presbyterian Committee of Publication, © 1901. 223, 14 p. ... PH: Philadelphia, Board of Christian Education, Presbyterian Church in the U.S.A., 1927 ... A C PH PT R: Richmond, Presbyterian Committee of Publication, © 1931. 96 p. ... A H L R U: Rev. ed. Richmond, John Knox Press, © 1941. 214 p. ... PH: [1960].

3351 SMITH, Egbert Watson, 1862-1944.
The desire of all nations. Garden City, N.Y., Doubleday, Doran & Co., 1928. 193 p. A C H L PH PT R U ... C: 1929 ... R: New York, Richard R. Smith, 1930.

3352 SMITH, Egbert Watson, 1862-1944.

Essential facts about our mission work in Africa. Nashville, Tenn., Executive Committee of Foreign Missions, Presbyterian Church in the U.S., n.d. 24 p. C H

3353 SMITH, Egbert Watson, 1862-1944.
Essential facts about our mission work in Brazil. Nashville, Tenn., Executive Committee of Foreign Missions, Presbyterian Church in the U.S., n.d. 24 p. C

3354 SMITH, Egbert Watson, 1862-1944.
Essential facts about our mission work in China. Nashville, Tenn., Executive Committee of Foreign Missions, Presbyterian Church in the U.S., n.d. 29 p. C

3355 SMITH, Egbert Watson, 1862-1944.
Essential facts about our mission work in Japan. Nashville, Tenn., Executive Committee of Foreign Missions, Presbyterian Church in the U.S., n.d. 32 p. C H

3356 SMITH, Egbert Watson, 1862-1944.
Essential facts about our mission work in Korea. Nashville, Tenn., Executive Committee of Foreign Missions, Presbyterian Church in the U.S., n.d. 15 p. C

3357 SMITH, Egbert Watson, 1862-1944.
The evangelistic pastor. Louisville, Ky., Association of Evangelistic Missions, n.d. 22 p. H ... U: Richmond, Presbyterian Committee of Publication, n.d. 15 p.

3358 SMITH, Egbert Watson, 1862-1944.
From one generation to another. Richmond, John Knox Press, © 1945. 136 p. A C H L PH R U

3359 SMITH, Egbert Watson, 1862-1944.
Kagawa. n.p., n.d. 16 p. U

3360 SMITH, Egbert Watson, 1862-1944.
Lives that challenge. Nashville, Tenn., Executive Committee of Foreign Missions, Presbyterian Church in the U.S., [1937]. 12 p. U

3361 SMITH, Egbert Watson, 1862-1944.
"Mis caminos en Cristo" testimonio de Pablo. Mexico, D.F., Casa Presbiteriana de Publicaciones, 1947. 188 p. Translation into Spanish of his "Paul's ways in Christ." A

3362 SMITH, Egbert Watson, 1862-1944.
Our church's answer in God's call. Nashville, Tenn., Executive Committee of Foreign Missions, Presbyterian Church in the U.S., n.d. 13 p. H

3363 SMITH, Egbert Watson, 1862-1944.

Our missionary Bible. Nashville, Tenn., Executive Committee of Foreign Missions, Presbyterian Church in the U.S., n.d. 6 p. H

3364 SMITH, Egbert Watson, 1862-1944.
Our missionary task, its requirements, progress and urgency. Nashville, Tenn., Executive Committee of Foreign Missions, Presbyterian Church in the U.S., n.d. 12 p. H

3365 SMITH, Egbert Watson, 1862-1944.
The Paul we forget. Nashville, Tenn., Executive Committee of Foreign Missions, Presbyterian Church in the U.S., n.d. 12 p. U

3366 SMITH, Egbert Watson, 1862-1944.
Paul's ways in Christ illustrated and applied. New York, Fleming H. Revell Co., © 1942. 152 p. A C H L R U

3367 SMITH, Egbert Watson, 1862-1944.
Peril and opportunity. Nashville, Tenn., Executive Committee of Foreign Missions, Presbyterian Church in the U.S., n.d. 12 p. H

3368 SMITH, Egbert Watson, 1862-1944.
Present-day Japan. [Nashville, Tenn., Executive Committee of Foreign Missions, Presbyterian Church in the U.S., 1920]. 32 p. H U

3369 SMITH, Egbert Watson, 1862-1944.
The reflex influences of foreign missions. Nashville, Tenn., Executive Committee of Foreign Missions, Presbyterian Church in the U.S., n.d. 12 p. H

3370 SMITH, Harry Edmund, 1928-
Secularization and the university. Foreword by Harvey Cox. Richmond, John Knox Press, © 1968. 172 p. A C H L PT

3371 SMITH, Hay Watson, 1868-1940.
Evolution and intellectual freedom. A compilation of opinions. [Little Rock, Ark., n.p., 1927]. 15 p. PT U

3372 SMITH, Hay Watson, 1868-1940.
Evolution and Presbyterianism. Little Rock, Ark., Allsop and Chapple, 1922. 115 p. A H PT U

3373 SMITH, Hay Watson, 1868-1940.
Prestige and perquisites. Little Rock, Ark., n.p., 1930. 18 p. A C H R

3374 SMITH, Hay Watson, 1868-1940.
Some facts about evolution. [Little Rock, Ark., n.p., 1928]. 23 p. A H

3375 SMITH, J. Kinsey, ca. 1858-1923.
Calvinism and the Presbyterian Church of the twentieth
century: a sermon preached in Fourth Avenue Presbyterian
Church, Louisville, Kentucky ... June 8, 1902. [Louisville,
Nunemacher Press], n.d. 15 p. PT

3376 SMITH, J. Kinsey, ca. 1858-1923.
St. Paul and the gospel of giving. A sermon preached in
the Shadyside Presbyterian Church, of Pittsburgh, Pa., Sunday morning, February 5th, 1905. n.p., Smith Brothers
Co. [1905?]. 25 p. PH

3377 SMITH, Jacob Henry, 1820-1897.
A sermon delivered at Greensboro, N.C. ... on the 5th
Dec. 1861, day appointed for thanksgiving by the governor.
Greensboro, World Office, 1862. 13 p. H

3378 SMITH, James Power, 1837-1923.
Both a king and a father: a sermon preached ... in the
First Presbyterian Church, Montclair, New Jersey, Sunday,
January 23, 1898. n.p., n.d. 12 p. U

3379 SMITH, James Power, 1837-1923.
Brightside idyls every week of the year. Richmond,
Central Presbyterian, © 1904. 143 p. A U

3380 SMITH, James Power, 1837-1923.
Chapel hymns: a selection of church and Sunday School
hymns. Richmond, A. Shotwell, 1881. 95 p. H

3381 SMITH, James Power, 1837-1923.
The Confederate cause and conduct in the War Between
the States. Richmond, n.p., 1907. U

3382 SMITH, James Power, 1837-1923.
General Lee at Gettysburg. A paper read before the
Military Historical Society of Massachusetts on the fourth
of April, 1905. Richmond, R. E. Lee Camp no. 1, Confederate Veterans, 1905. 29 p. U

3383 SMITH, James Power, 1837-1923.
Quit you like men; a sermon preached at the Virginia
Military Institute, June 24th, 1906. Lynchburg, Va., J. P.
Bell Co., [1906]. 11 p. U

3384 SMITH, James Power, 1837-1923.
The religious character of Stonewall Jackson. Delivered
at the inauguration of the Stonewall Jackson Memorial Bui'd-
ing, Virginia Military Institute, June 23d, 1897. Lynchburg,
Va., J. P. Bell Co., 1897. 10 p. C U

3385 SMITH, James Power, 1837-1923.

Stonewall Jackson and Chancellorsville; a paper read before the Military Historical Society of Massachusetts, on the
first of March, 1904. Richmond, R. E. Lee Camp no. 1,
Confederate Veterans, [1904]. 23 p. U

3386 *SMITH, James Ward, 1917- ed.
Religion in American life. Editors: James Ward Smith
and A. Leland Jamison. Princeton, N.J., Princeton University Press, 1961- v. A C H L PH PT R U

3387 SMITH, John Robert, 1910-
The church that stayed: the life and times of Central Pres-
byterian Church in the heart of Atlanta, 1858-1978. [Atlanta,
Atlanta Historical Society], © 1979. 181 p. A C H L PH
PT R U

3388 SMITH, John Robert, 1910-
The Presbyterian task in an urban South. [Atlanta], Board
of Church Extension, Presbyterian Church in the U.S.,
© 1964. 62 p. A C H L PH R U

3389 SMITH, Joseph Addison, 1854-1920.
The challenge of the religion of Christ to the ages. n.p.,
n.d. 10 p. U

3390 SMITH, Morton Howison, 1923-
How is the gold become dim! (Lamentations 4:1) The de-
cline of the Presbyterian Church in the United States, as re-
flected in its Assembly actions. [1st ed.] Jackson, Steering
Committee for a Continuing Presbyterian Church, © 1973.
202 p. A C H R ... C H PT R: [2d ed.] © 1973. 448 p.

3391 SMITH, Morton Howison, 1923-
Reformed evangelism. Clinton, Miss., Multi-Communication
Ministries, © 1975. 32 p. PT R

3392 SMITH, Morton Howison, 1923-
Studies in Southern Presbyterian theology. Amsterdam,
Jacob van Campen, 1962. 367 p. Academisch proefschrift--
Universiteit te Amsterdam. A C H PH R U ... C L PT:
Jackson, Miss., Presbyterian Reformation Society, 1962.

3393 SMITH, Robert Carsall, 1810-1873.
A defence of denominational education. Milledgeville, Ga.,
Federal Union Power Press, 1854. 32 p. H PH

3394 SMITH, Robert Carsall, 1810-1873.
Holiness through faith; light on the way of holiness. Rev.
ed. New York, Anson D. F. Randolph & Co., © 1870.
156 p. PT

3395 SMITH, Robert Perry, 1851-1936.

Experiences in mountain mission work. Richmond, Presbyterian Committee of Publication, 1931. 121 p. A C H U

3396 *SMITH, Rodney, 1860-1947.
Evangelistic talks by Gipsy Smith ... with a foreword by
Rev. James I. Vance. New York, George H. Doran Co.,
© 1922. 170 p. A L PT

3397 SMITH, Samuel Macon, 1851-1910.
Dr. Briggs' confession of faith. n.p., n.d. 138-156 p.
Reprinted from the Presbyterian Quarterly, April, 1896.
PT

3398 SMITH, Samuel Macon, 1851-1910.
The new theology and the old compared. An address de-
livered, by appointment, before the General Assembly of the
Presbyterian Church in the United States, in session at Char-
lotte, North Carolina, May 26, 1897. Richmond, Whittet &
Shepperson, 1897. 36 p. C PT

3399 SMITH, Samuel Macon, 1851-1910.
The pastor in his relations to God. n.p., n.d. 90-101 p.
Reprinted from the Presbyterian Quarterly, January, 1900.
PT

3400 SMITH, Samuel Macon, 1851-1910.
The Presbyterian pastorate. n.p., n.d. 256-261 p. Reprinted from the Presbyterian Quarterly, April, 1889. PT

3401 SMITH, Samuel Macon, 1851-1910.
Some popular misconceptions of Presbyterianism. n.p.,
n.d. 12 p. Reprinted from the Presbyterian Quarterly,
January, 1893. PT

3402 SMITH, Thomas Irvine, 1907-1975.
A soldier's theology. Philadelphia, Dorrance and Co.,
© 1943. 233 p. PT

3403 SMITH, Wade Cothran, 1869-1960.
... "Come and see." A manual of personal evangelism....
For pastors, leaders, men, women, the Sunday school, and
groups of Christian workers. Richmond, Onward Press,
© 1927. 111 p. At head of title: A return to apostolic
evangelism. A C H L R U

3404 SMITH, Wade Cothran, 1869-1960.
Evangelism in the awakened church, practical plans for
home visitation evangelism. Richmond, Executive Committee
of Religious Education, [1933]. 12 p. H PH PT U

3405 SMITH, Wade Cothran, 1869-1960.
Fishers of men. Richmond, Onward Press, © 1923. 22 p.
U

3406 SMITH, Wade Cothran, 1869-1960.
   Lighting fires on family altars. Pittsburgh, Pa., Board
of Administration, United Presbyterian Church, n.d. unpaged.
PH

3407 SMITH, Wade Cothran, 1869-1960.
   The Little Jetts Bible (Old Testament). Boston, W. A.
Wilde Co., © 1942. 213 p. H ... H: New Testament.
© 1944. 232 p.

3408 SMITH, Wade Cothran, 1869-1960.
   The Little Jetts youth talks. Boston, W. A. Wilde Co.,
© 1953. 192 p. H U

3409 SMITH, Wade Cothran, 1869-1960.
   The Little Jetts telling Bible stories for young folks. 2d
ed. Richmond, Wade C. Smith, © 1916. unpaged. H

3410 SMITH, Wade Cothran, 1869-1960.
   New Testament evangelism: "Come and see"--"Go and
tell." A manual of personal work for pastors, leaders, men,
women, the Sunday School and groups of Christian workers.
Richmond, Onward Press, © 1930. 123 p. PT

3411 SMITH, Wade Cothran, 1869-1960.
   On the mark! Getting a fair start in the race of life.
New York, Fleming H. Revell Co., © 1925. 159 p. H

3412 SMITH, Wade Cothran, 1869-1960.
   "Say, fellows--"; fifty practical talks with boys on life's
big issues. New York, Fleming H. Revell Co., © 1921.
173 p. L

3413 SMITH, Wade Cothran, 1869-1960.
   "Venez et voyez!" Manuel d'évangélisation individuelle.
(Traduction R. de Jarnac.) Montpellier, [France], Publications Evangéliques, 1930. 152 p. Translation of "Come and
see." H

3414 SMITH, Wilbur Moorehead, 1894-   comp.
   An annotated bibliography of D. L. Moody. Chicago,
Moody Press, © 1948. 221 p. C PT

3415 SMITH, Wilbur Moorehead, 1894-
   Arno C. Gaebelein: a memoir. New York, Our Hope
Press, [1946?]. 31 p. PT

3416 SMITH, Wilbur Moorehead, 1894-
   Before I forget. Chicago, Moody Press, © 1971. 304 p.
Autobiographical. PH PT R

3417 SMITH, Wilbur Moorehead, 1894-

The Bible and the world today. Scottdale, Pa., Evangelical Fellowship, 1952. 78 p. U

3418 SMITH, Wilbur Moorehead, 1894-
The Bible the foundation of the American republic. A sermon preached in Lafayette Square Presbyterian Church, Baltimore, Md., Sunday evening, June 10th, 1923. n.p., n.d. 22 p. PT

3419 SMITH, Wilbur Moorehead, 1894-
The Biblical doctrine of heaven. [1st ed.] Chicago, Moody Press, © 1968. 317 p. A L PT R U

3420 SMITH, Wilbur Moorehead, 1894-
Biographical and bibliographical foreword to a new edition of the Jamieson, Fausset and Brown Bible commentary, complete and unabridged. Grand Rapids, Mich., Wm. B. Eerdmans Publishing Co., 1945. unpaged. PT

3421 SMITH, Wilbur Moorehead, 1894-
Chats from a minister's library. Boston, W. A. Wilde Co., © 1951. 283 p. A PT R U

3422 SMITH, Wilbur Moorehead, 1894-
Egypt and Israel coming together? Wheaton, Ill., Tyndale House Publishers [1978]. 174 p. L PT

3423 SMITH, Wilbur Moorehead, 1894-
Egypt in Biblical prophecy. Boston, W. A. Wilde Co., © 1957. 256 p. A PT R U

3424 SMITH, Wilbur Moorehead, 1894-
Glorious deliverance by resurrection. Chicago, Moody Press, © 1941. 32 p. R

3425 SMITH, Wilbur Moorehead, 1894-
The glorious revival under King Hezekiah. Rev. reprint ed. Grand Rapids, Mich., Zondervan Publishing House, [1954]. 54 p. A PT R

3426 SMITH, Wilbur Moorehead, 1894-
The Gospel of Mark for men in service. Chicago, Moody Press, © 1944. 92 p. R

3427 SMITH, Wilbur Moorehead, 1894- ed.
Great sermons on the birth of Christ, by celebrated preachers. With biographical sketches and bibliographies. Natick, Mass., W. A. Wilde Co., © 1963. 236 p. L PT R U

3428 SMITH, Wilbur Moorehead, 1894- comp.
Great sermons on the death of Christ, by celebrated preachers. With biographical sketches and bibliographies. Natick, Mass., W. A. Wilde Co., © 1965. 244 p. PT

3429 SMITH, Wilbur Moorehead, 1894- ed.
      Great sermons on the resurrection of Christ, by celebrated
      preachers. With biographical sketches and bibliographies.
      Natick, Mass., W. A. Wilde Co., © 1964. 289 p.   PT R
      U

3430 SMITH, Wilbur Moorehead, 1894-
      Have you considered Him? [A brief for Christianity.
      Downers Grove, Ill., InterVarsity Press, 1976]. 28 p.
      Cover title.   R

3431 SMITH, Wilbur Moorehead, 1894-
      How to study the Bible for the enrichment of the spiritual
      life. With foreword by Robert C. McQuilkin. Philadelphia,
      Revelation, © 1936. 98 p.   PT

3432 SMITH, Wilbur Moorehead, 1894-
      The increasing peril of permitting the dissemination of
      atheistic doctrines on the part of some agencies of the United
      States government. Chicago, Van Kampen Press, © 1947.
      46 p.   PT

3433 SMITH, Wilbur Moorehead, 1894-
      The influence of the first three chapters of Genesis in
      English life and literature. n.p., n.d. 12 p.   PT

3434 SMITH, Wilbur Moorehead, 1894-
      Israeli/Arab conflict, and the Bible. Glendale, Calif.,
      G/L Regal Books, © 1967. 154 p.   PT R

3435 SMITH, Wilbur Moorehead, 1894-
      A list of bibliographies of theological and Biblical litera-
      ture published in Great Britain and America, 1595-1931.
      Coatesville, Pa., n.p., 1931. 62 p.   H L PH PT U

3436 SMITH, Wilbur Moorehead, 1894-
      The minister and the word of God. [Glasgow, Pickering
      & Inglis, 1952]. 19 p. The Campbell Morgan Memorial
      Lecture, 4.   A

3437 SMITH, Wilbur Moorehead, 1894-
      The minister in his study. Chicago, Moody Press, © 1973.
      128 p.   A C PT R U

3438 SMITH, Wilbur Moorehead, 1894-
      A preliminary bibliography for the study of Biblical proph-
      ecy. Boston, W. A. Wilde Co., 1952. 44 p.   PT U

3439 SMITH, Wilbur Moorehead, 1894-
      Profitable Bible study; seven simple methods, with an
      annotated list of the first one hundred best books for the
      Bible student's library. Boston, W. A. Wilde Co., © 1939.

214 p. L PT R U ... C: Rev. ed. 1953. 227 p. ... R: 2d rev. ed. Natick, Mass., W. A. Wilde Co., 1963. 166 p.

3440 SMITH, Wilbur Moorehead, 1894-
The second advent of Christ. Washington, D.C., Christianity Today, n.d. 23 p. R U

3441 SMITH, Wilbur Moorehead, 1894-
Some much needed books in Biblical and theological literature. Dallas, Tex., n.p., 1934. Reprinted from Bibliotheca Sacra, January and April, 1934. PT

3442 SMITH, Wilbur Moorehead, 1894-
The supernaturalness of Christ, can we still believe in it? Boston, Mass., W. A. Wilde Co., 1940. 235 p. R ... PT: 1941 ... L: 1944.

3443 SMITH, Wilbur Moorehead, 1894-
Therefore, stand: a plea for a vigorous apologetic in the present crisis of evangelical Christianity. Boston, W. A. Wilde Co., 1945. 614 p. A C H PT R U ... L: 1949 ... H: Chicago, Moody Press, © 1945.

3444 SMITH, Wilbur Moorehead, 1894-
This atomic age and the Word of God. Boston, W. A. Wilde Co., 1948. 363 p. An expanded version of the author's address The atomic bomb and the Word of God, first published November 1945. C L PT R U

3445 SMITH, Wilbur Moorehead, 1894-
The time periods of prophecy. Philadelphia, American Bible Conference Association, © 1935. 35 p. H PT R

3446 SMITH, Wilbur Moorehead, 1894-
A treasury of books for Bible study. Natick, Mass., W. A. Wilde Co., © 1960. 289 p. L PT R U

3447 SMITH, Wilbur Moorehead, 1894- ed.
A treasury of great sermons on the resurrection of Christ, by celebrated preachers. With biographical sketches and bibliographies. Grand Rapids, Mich., Baker Book House, © 1964. 289 p. Previously published as "Great sermons on the resurrection of Christ." A R ... A: [1971].

3448 SMITH, Wilbur Moorehead, 1894-
A voice from God; the life of Charles E. Fuller, originator of the Old-fashioned Revival Hour. Boston, W. A. Wilde Co., © 1949. 224 p. PT R U

3449 SMITH, Wilbur Moorehead, 1894-
Will H. Houghton: a watchman on the wall. Grand Rapids, Mich., Wm. B. Eerdmans Publishing Co., 1951. 191 p. PT U

3450 SMITH, Wilbur Moorehead, 1894-
The word of God and the life of holiness. Grand Rapids,
Mich., Zondervan Publishing House, [1957]. 95 p. A R

3451 SMITH, Wilbur Moorehead, 1894-
World crises and the prophetic scriptures. Chicago,
Moody Press, 1952. 384 p. L PT R U

3452 SMITH, William Kyle, 1895-
Calvin's ethics of war; a documentary study. Annapolis,
Md., Academic Fellowship, 1972. 166 p. PT U

3453 SMITH, William Sheppard, 1928-
Musical aspects of the New Testament. Amsterdam, W.
ten Have, 1962. 187 p. Academisch proefschrift--Univer-
siteit te Amsterdam. A C H L PT R U

3454 SMOOT, Richmond Kelley, 1836-1905.
Faith, the substance and evidence. Richmond, Presbyterian Committee of Publication, © 1901. 32 p. H PT

3455 SMOOT, Richmond Kelley, 1836-1905.
Parliamentary principles in their application to the courts
of the Presbyterian Church, in sixteen articles.... With an
appendix, containing catechetical analysis and general rules.
Louisville, Webb & Breeding, 1875. 148 p. A C H R

3456 SMYLIE, Theodore Shaw, 1893-
The a b c's of winning men. St. Louis, Frederick Press,
© 1939. 92 p. H L

3457 SMYLIE, Theodore Shaw, 1893-
Taking stock; help for daily living. Richmond, John Knox
Press, © 1965. 128 p. A C H L U

3458 SMYTH, Thomas, 1808-1873.
An address, delivered before a meeting of the Friends of
Sunday-schools, in the Wentworth Street Baptist Church,
Charleston, S.C., on Monday, April 29, 1844. Philadelphia,
American Sunday-school Union, n.d. 8 p. PH

3459 SMYTH, Thomas, 1808-1873.
Autobiographical notes, letters and reflections.... Edited
by his granddaughter, Louisa Cheves Stoney. Charleston,
S.C., Walker, Evans & Cogswell Co., 1914. 784 p. A C
H L PH PT R U

3460 SMYTH, Thomas, 1808-1873.
By whom is the world to be converted? or, Christians
Christ's representatives and agents for the conversion of the
world. Philadelphia, Presbyterian Board of Publication,
© 1856. 108 p. A C H PH PT R U

3461 SMYTH, Thomas, 1808-1873.
Calvin and his enemies. A memoir of the life, character, and principles of Calvin.... New ed., rev. and enl. Philadelphia, Presbyterian Board of Publication, © 1856. 180 p. A C H L PH PT R ... U: New ed. © 1856. 208 p. ... L: [1881] ... PH: [1882].

3462 SMYTH, Thomas, 1808-1873.
Calvin defended: a memoir of the life, character, and principles of Calvin. New ed. Philadelphia, Presbyterian Board of Publication, 1909. 208 p. PH PT

3463 SMYTH, Thomas, 1808-1873.
The character of the late Thomas Chalmers, D.D., LL.D., and the lessons of his life, from personal recollections. Charleston, S.C., Southern Christian Advocate, 1848. 29 p. PH

3464 SMYTH, Thomas, 1808-1873.
Christians Christ's representatives and agents for the conversion of the world, and Self-denying love and liberality essential to Christian character and happiness. New York, Edward O. Jenkins, 1855. 43 p. C PH PT

3465 SMYTH, Thomas, 1808-1873.
The church awakened to her duty and her danger: a sermon preached for the Board of Foreign Missions, of the Presbyterian Church, on Sabbath evening, May 1, 1853, in the church on Fifth Avenue and Nineteenth Street, New York; and also in the Central Church, Philadelphia, on Sabbath evening, May 22, 1853. New York, Mission House, 1853. 24 p. C PH

3466 SMYTH, Thomas, 1808-1873.
Claims of the Christian ministry to an adequate support. Charleston, S.C., B. B. Hussey, 1840. 34 p. C L PH

3467 SMYTH, Thomas, 1808-1873.
The claims of the Free Church of Scotland to the sympathy and assistance of American Christians. Edinburgh, John Johnstone, 1844. 32 p. PH

3468 SMYTH, Thomas, 1808-1873.
Claims of the Presbyterian Church. Charleston, S.C., B. B. Hussey, 1840. 38 p. C L PH PT

3469 SMYTH, Thomas, 1808-1873.
Collections for charitable and religious purposes, a part of the service of God, a means of grace, and therefore, an essential part of Christianity. Charleston, S.C., Walker and James, 1850. 48 p. C H ... PH: 3d ed. 54 p.

3470 SMYTH, Thomas, 1808-1873.

Complete works of Rev. Thomas Smyth, D.D. Edited by
Prof. J. Wm. Flinn, D.D. New ed., with brief notes and
prefaces. Biographical sketch in last volume. Columbia,
S.C., R. L. Bryan Co., 1908-1912. 10 v. Contains repro-
ductions of the original title-pages. After the death of Prof.
Flinn, the editing of the volumes was carried on by his
daughter, Jean Adger Flinn. A C H L PH PT R U

3471 SMYTH, Thomas, 1808-1873.
Conversion and character of Col. William Yeadon. n.p.,
n.d. 24 p. (Presbyterian Tracts, no. 158.) C H L PH
PT R U

3472 SMYTH, Thomas, 1808-1873.
Denominational education in parochial schools and religious
colleges, enforced upon every church by divine authority.
Columbia, S.C., I. C. Morgan, 1849. 32 p. C H PH PT

3473 SMYTH, Thomas, 1808-1873.
Denominational education: its necessity and its practicabil-
ity especially as it regards colleges. An address, delivered
before the Thalian and Phi-Delta societies of Oglethorpe University. Charleston, S.C., B. Jenkins, 1846. 48 p. C
H PH PT

3474 SMYTH, Thomas, 1808-1873.
The design and duty of a church. A sermon delivered in
the Second Presbyterian Church in Charleston (S.C.), on
Sabbath morning, April 1, 1832. Being the twenty-first anniversary of the dedication of that church. Charleston, Observer Office Press, 1832. 25 p. C

3475 SMYTH, Thomas, 1808-1873.
The destined efficiency of juvenile missionary effort.
Charleston, S.C., B. Jenkins, 1847. 32 p. C PH PT

3476 SMYTH, Thomas, 1808-1873.
The duty of interesting children in the missionary cause,
and how this is to be done. Charleston, S.C., B. Jenkins,
1846. 30 p. C H PH PT

3477 SMYTH, Thomas, 1808-1873.
An ecclesiastical catechism of the Presbyterian Church;
for the use of families, Bible-classes, and private members.
Boston, Crocker and Brewster, 1841. 124 p. A PH R
U ... C L PH PT: Charleston, S.C., B. B. Hussey, 1841.
71 p. ... PH PT: 3d ed. New York, Leavitt, Trow & Co.,
1843. 103, 8, 3 p. ... H L U: 6th ed., rev. Richmond,
Presbyterian Committee of Publication, © 1868. 113 p. ...
R: 1871.

3478 SMYTH, Thomas, 1808-1873.

Ecclesiastical republicanism; or the republicanism, liberality, and catholicity of presbytery, in contrast to prelacy and popery. Boston, Crocker and Brewster, 1843. 323 p.   A C H L PH PT R U

3479   SMYTH, Thomas, 1808-1873.
The eldership of the Presbyterian Church. A sermon, preached before the Charleston Union Presbytery, April 4th, 1836. Charleston, S.C., A. E. Miller, 1836. 33 p. C ... C L PH: 2d ed., enl. Charleston, B. B. Hussey, 1840. 39 p.

3480   SMYTH, Thomas, 1808-1873.
The exodus of the Church of Scotland: and the claims of the Free Church of Scotland to the sympathy and assistance of American Christians. Charleston, S.C., B. Jenkins, 1843. 48 p.   C H PH ... C PH PT R U: 2d ed. New York, Leavitt, Trow & Co., 1844. 146 p. ... PH: Edinburgh, Johnstone, 1844. 48 p.

3481   SMYTH, Thomas, 1808-1873.
Faith, the principle of missions. Philadelphia, Presbyterian Board of Publication, © 1857. 70 p.   C H PH ... H L PT R U: 78 p.

3482   SMYTH, Thomas, 1808-1873.
A form of public Christian profession: scriptural, reasonable, and in accordance with the practice of the primitive and other churches. Charleston, S.C., B. B. Hussey, 1840. 47 p.   C L PH PT

3483   SMYTH, Thomas, 1808-1873.
Forms of doxology and benediction; with concluding prayers. Charleston, S.C., B. B. Hussey, n.d. 28 p.   C L PH

3484   SMYTH, Thomas, 1808-1873.
The fundamental doctrines of Christianity, the true and only basis of charity and united Christian effort. A discourse, delivered at Philadelphia, on the twenty-second anniversary of the American Sunday-school Union, May 17, 1846. Philadelphia, American Sunday-school Union, 1846. 39 p.   C PH PT

3485   SMYTH, Thomas, 1808-1873.
The history, character, and results of the Westminster Assembly of Divines. A discourse, in commemoration of the bi-centenary anniversary of that body. New York, Leavitt, Trow, & Co., 1844. 124 p.   C H PH PT R U

3486   SMYTH, Thomas, 1808-1873.
The history of the Second Presbyterian Church, Charleston, S.C. Two discourses delivered in the Second Presbyterian

Church, on the occasion of its twenty-sixth anniversary,
April 3d, 1837. n.p., n.d. 43-98 p. C

3487 SMYTH, Thomas, 1808-1873.
The late Charleston Union Presbytery; the occasion of its
division fairly stated; and the action of Presbytery fully justi-
fied. Charleston, Observer Office Press, 1840. 80 p.
C L PH PT ... U: xeroxed copy.

3488 SMYTH, Thomas, 1808-1873.
The life and character of Calvin, the reformer, reviewed
and defended. Philadelphia, Presbyterian Board of Publication, 1844. 120 p. Cover title: Calvin defended. A C L
PH PT U

3489 SMYTH, Thomas, 1808-1873.
Manual, for the use of the members of the Second Presbyterian Church, Charleston, S.C., prepared under the direction of the church. Charleston, Jenkins & Hussey, 1838.
236 p. A C PH PT R

3490 SMYTH, Thomas, 1808-1873.
Mary not a perpetual virgin, nor the mother of God: but
only a sinner saved by grace, through the worship and mediation of Jesus Christ, her God and our God. Together with
a view of the true position, duty, and liberty of woman,
under the gospel dispensation. Charleston, S.C., B. Jenkins,
1846. 32 p. C PH PT

3491 SMYTH, Thomas, 1808-1873.
The name, nature, and functions, of ruling elders; wherein
it is shown from the testimony of Scripture, the fathers, and
the reformers, that ruling elders are not presbyters or bish-
ops; and that, as representatives of the people, their office
ought to be temporary. With an appendix, on the use of the
title bishop. New York, Mark H. Newman, 1845. 186 p.
A C H L PH PT U

3492 SMYTH, Thomas, 1808-1873.
The nature and claims of Young Men's Christian associa-
tions. Philadelphia, J. B. Lippincott & Co., 1857. 123 p.
C PH PT

3493 SMYTH, Thomas, 1808-1873.
The nature of assurance, Witness of the Spirit, and A call
to the ministry. Columbia, S.C., I. C. Morgan, 1848.
60 p. Reprinted from the Southern Presbyterian Review.
PH

3494 SMYTH, Thomas, 1808-1873.
Obedience, the life of missions. Philadelphia, Presby-
terian Board of Publication, © 1858. 170 p. A C L PH
PT R U

3495 SMYTH, Thomas, 1808-1873.
The office and function of deacons, in relation to those of the pastor and ruling elders, defined and distinguished. Columbia, S.C., I. C. Morgan, 1848. 28 p. PH

3496 SMYTH, Thomas, 1808-1873.
Oration, delivered on the forty-eighth anniversary of the Orphan House, in Charleston, S.C., October 18th, 1837. Charleston, J. S. Burges, 1837. 28 p. C PH PT

3497 SMYTH, Thomas, 1808-1873.
An order for funeral services. Prepared for private use. Boston, Samuel N. Dickinson, 1843. 27 p. C PH

3498 SMYTH, Thomas, 1808-1873.
Pastoral momento. Love waxing cold; and pastoral fidelity consistent with pastoral affection. Two discourses. New York, A. S. Barnes & Co., 1850. 78 p. C PH PT R

3499 SMYTH, Thomas, 1808-1873.
A pattern of mercy and of holiness, exhibited in the conversion and subsequent character of Col. William Yeadon, ruling elder in the Second Presbyterian Church, Charleston, S.C. Charleston, John Russell, 1849. 37 p. C PH U

3500 SMYTH, Thomas, 1808-1873.
The prelatical doctrine of apostolical succession examined, and the Protestant ministry defended against the assumptions of popery and high-churchism, in a series of lectures. Boston, Crocker and Brewster, 1841. 568 p. A C H L PH PT R U

3501 SMYTH, Thomas, 1808-1873.
Presbytery and not prelacy, the scriptural and primitive polity, proved from the testimonies of Scripture; the fathers; the schoolmen; the reformers; and the English and oriental churches. Also the antiquity of presbytery; including an account of the ancient Culdees and of St. Patrick. Boston, Crocker and Brewster, 1843. 568 p. A C H L PH PT U ... PH R: Glasgow, William Collins, 1844. 490 p.

3502 SMYTH, Thomas, 1808-1873.
Prospects of the heathen for eternity. Charleston, Observer Office Press, 1835. 20 p. PT

3503 SMYTH, Thomas, 1808-1873.
The relations of Christianity to war; and the portraiture of a Christian soldier. A discourse delivered on occasion of the first commencement of the Citadel Academy. Charleston, S.C., B. Jenkins, 1847. 33 p. C PH

3504 SMYTH, Thomas, 1808-1873.
The Romish and prelatical rite of confirmation examined,

and proved to be contrary to the Scriptures, and the practice of all the earliest and purest churches, both oriental and western.... With an appendix, on the duty of requiring a public profession of religion. Edinburgh, W. P. Kennedy, 1845. 198 p. A C H R U ... C H PH R: New York, Mark H. Newman, 1845. 213 p.

3505 SMYTH, Thomas, 1808-1873.
The rule and measure of Christian charity. Charleston, S.C., B. Jenkins, 1847. 24 p. PH

3506 SMYTH, Thomas, 1808-1873.
The sin and the curse; or, The union, the true source of disunion, and our duty in the present crisis. A discourse preached on the occasion of the day of humiliation and prayer appointed by the governor of South Carolina, on November 21st, 1860, in the Second Presbyterian Church, Charleston, S.C. Charleston, Evans & Cogswell, 1860. 24 p. C H PH PT

3507 SMYTH, Thomas, 1808-1873.
Solace for bereaved parents: or infants die to live. With a historical account of the doctrine of infant salvation. Charleston, S.C., B. B. Hussey, 1840. 220 p. C ... H: New York, Robert Carter & Brothers, 1846. 314 p. ... PH R U: 1848 ... H PH PT: 1852. 296 p.

3508 SMYTH, Thomas, 1808-1873.
The teachings of the dead. Columbia, S.C., E. H. Britton, 1857. 36 p. PH

3509 SMYTH, Thomas, 1808-1873.
The theatre, a school of religion, manners and morals! Two discourses, delivered on the opening of the new theatre in Charleston. Charleston, S.C., Jenkins & Hussey, 1838. 55 p. C ... C PH PT: 2d ed.

3510 SMYTH, Thomas, 1808-1873.
Tracts on Presbyterianism. Charleston, S.C., B. B. Hussey, 1841. variously paged. Contents. --Claims of the Presbyterian Church. --The eldership of the Presbyterian Church. 2d ed. --A form of public Christian profession. -- Claims of the Christian ministry to an adequate support. -- The late Charleston Union Presbytery. --The ecclesiastical catechism of the Presbyterian Church. --Forms of doxology and benediction; with concluding prayers. C L PH

3511 SMYTH, Thomas, 1808-1873.
The true origin and source of the Mecklenburg and national declaration of independence. Columbia, S.C., I. C. Morgan, 1847. 29 p. Extracted from the Southern Presbyterian Review. PT

3512   SMYTH, Thomas, 1808-1873.
        Two discourses on the occasion of the great fire in Char-
        leston, on Friday night, April 27th, 1838. Delivered in the
        Second Presbyterian Church, on Sabbath, May 6, 1838.
        Charleston, John P. Beile, 1838. 40 p.   C ... C PH PT:
        2d ed.

3513   SMYTH, Thomas, 1808-1873.
        Union to Christ, and to his church; or, The duty and priv-
        ilege of all to believe in Christ, to confess Christ, and to
        become communing members of the church of Christ.   Edin-
        burgh, W. P. Kennedy, 1846. 117 p.   C

3514   SMYTH, Thomas, 1808-1873.
        The unity of the human races proved to be the doctrine of
        Scripture, reason, and science. With a review of the pres-
        ent position and theory of Professor Agassiz. New York,
        George P. Putnam, 1850. 404 p.   C R U ... A H PH:
        Edinburgh, Johnstone and Hunter, 1851. 408 p.

3515   SMYTH, Thomas, 1808-1873.
        The voice of God in calamity: or, reflections on the loss
        of the steam-boat Home, October 9, 1837. A sermon: de-
        livered in the Second Presbyterian Church, Charleston, on
        Sabbath morning, October 22, 1837. Charleston, S.C.,
        Jenkins & Hussey, 1837. 32 p.   C PT ... C PH: 2d
        ed. ... C: 3d ed. ... C H: 4th ed.

3516   SMYTH, Thomas, 1808-1873.
        The well in the valley. Philadelphia, American Sunday-
        school Union, © 1857. 430 p.   C PH ... PT: New and
        rev. ed. © 1860. 412 p.

3517   SMYTH, Thomas, 1808-1873.
        Why do I live? New York, American Tract Society, n.d.
        206 p.   A C H PH PT U

3518   SMYTHE, William Sterling, 1926-1949.
        Two centuries of grace: a history of the Cedar Grove
        Presbyterian Church, 1962. n.p., n.d. 39 p.   PH PT

3519   SNEDECOR, James George, 1855-1916.
        Aspects of our Negro population. Richmond, L. D. Sulli-
        van & Co., 1906. 8 p. Reprinted from the Union Seminary
        Magazine.   U

3520   SNEDECOR, James George, 1855-1916.
        Stillman Institute, Tuscaloosa, Ala.: a phase of home
        missions. Atlanta, Executive Committee of Home Missions,
        Presbyterian Church in the U.S., n.d. 6 p.   U

3521   SOLI Deo gloria; New Testament studies in honor of William

Childs Robinson. Edited by J. McDowell Richards. Richmond, John Knox Press, © 1968. 160 p. Essays by J. McDowell Richards, W. C. Robinson, Jr., J. H. Leith, William Childs Robinson, James M. Robinson, and others. A C H L PT R U

3522 SOMMERVILLE, Charles William, 1867-1938.
Catholic character of the Presbyterian Church. Richmond, Whittet & Shepperson, n.d. 29 p. U

3523 SOMMERVILLE, Charles William, 1867-1938.
The history of Hopewell Presbyterian Church for 175 years from the assigned date of its organization, 1762. [Charlotte, N.C., Observer Printing House, 1939]. 323 p. H U

3524 SOMMERVILLE, Charles William, 1867-1938.
Robert Goodloe Harper. Washington, D.C., The Neale Co., 1899. 41 p. Diss., Ph.D.--Johns Hopkins University. PH

3525 SOMMERVILLE, Charles William, 1867-1938.
Some modern educational tendencies hurtful to the development of the highest ideal of character. An address delivered before the Literary societies of Hampden-Sidney College at the commencement of its 128th session, June 14, 1904. [Petersburg, Frank A. Owen], n.d. 38 p. Reprinted from the Hampden-Sidney Magazine, November, 1904. PH

3526 SOUTH CAROLINA. State Bible Convention.
Proceedings of the State Bible Convention of South Carolina, held at Columbia, Sept. 17 and 18, 1862; with a sermon preached before the convention by the Rev. George Howe, D.D. Columbia, S.C., Southern Guardian Steam-power Press, 1862. 31 p. Title of sermon: "Characteristics of the Bible." C PH

3527 SOUTH CAROLINA. University.
In memoriam, Davidson McDowell Douglas, 1869-1931. Columbia, S.C., Farrell Printing Co., 1932. 68 p. H PT R

3528 SOUTHERN Presbyterian pulpit: a collection of sermons by ministers of the Southern Presbyterian Church. Richmond, Presbyterian Committee of Publication, © 1896. 407 p. Sermons by B. M. Palmer, Moses D. Hoge, J. Henry Smith, Geo. D. Armstrong, J. W. Lupton, John L. Girardeau, J. B. Stratton, R. L. Dabney, J. W. Rosebro, Neander M. Woods, W. U. Murkland, A. W. Pitzer, J. H. Bryson, S. W. Davies, G. R. Brackett, J. R. Burgett, G. B. Strickler, W. N. Scott, John A. Preston, Robert P. Kerr, R. K. Smoot, W. W. Moore, J. F. Cannon, Peyton H. Hoge, James I. Vance, J. R. Howerton, G. L. Petrie, Samuel A. King, C. R. Hemphill, Joseph R. Wilson, T. D. Witherspoon, W. F. V. Bartlett, W. T. Hall. A C H L PH R U

3529 SOUTH-WESTERN Bible Society.
Thirty-first annual report, presented Jan. 16th, 1881,
also, address of B. M. Palmer, D.D., "God's providence
towards the Bible." New Orleans, South-Western Bible Society, 1881. 31 p.   C U

3530 SOUVENIR book of the General Assemblies, Atlanta, Georgia,
May 14-25, 1913. Prepared by Committee on Souvenir
Book, Lucian Lamar Knight, chairman. The Presbyterian
Church in the U.S.A., 125th Assembly; The Presbyterian
Church in the U.S., 53d Assembly; The United Presby-
terian Church of North America, 55th Assembly. Atlanta,
Byrd Printing Co., 1913. 112 p.   PT

3531 SPARROW, Patrick Jones, 1802-1867.
The duty of the educated young men of this country. An
address delivered before the Eumenean and Philanthropick
societies of Davidson College, N.C., July 31st, 1839.
Raleigh, Turner & Hughes, 1839. 32 p.   PH

3532 SPARROW, Patrick Jones, 1802-1867.
The inaugural ... pronounced at his inauguration as Professor of Languages in Davidson College, North Carolina,
August 2, 1838. Philadelphia, William S. Martien, 1838.
24 p.   PH

3533 SPARROW, Patrick Jones, 1802-1867.
The Sabbath: a sermon preached September 11, 1836, in
the Sixth Presbyterian Church, Philadelphia. Philadelphia,
William S. Martien, 1837. 16 p.   PH

3534 SPENCE, Thomas Hugh, 1899-
Catalogues of Presbyterian and Reformed institutions. I.
As historical sources. II. In the Historical Foundation.
Montreat, N.C., Historical Foundation Publications, 1952.
39 p.   A C H L PH PT R U

3535 SPENCE, Thomas Hugh, 1899-
A catechism on the Historical Foundation of the Presby-
terian and Reformed Churches. 1st-5th eds. Montreat,
N.C., Historical Foundation Publications, 1941-44. 6-8 p.
each. H ... A PH: 2d ed. 1941 ....PH: 3d ed. 1941 ...
PH: 5th ed. 1941.

3536 SPENCE, Thomas Hugh, 1899-
A great collection of Presbyterian and Reformed literature.
Montreat, N.C., Historical Foundation Publications, 1944.
8 p.   H

3537 SPENCE, Thomas Hugh, 1899-
The historical Foundation and its treasures. Montreat,
N.C., Historical Foundation Publications, 1956. 174 p.

A C H L PH PT U ... A C H L PH PT R U: Rev. ed.
1960. 171 p.

3538 SPENCE, Thomas Hugh, 1899-
The inns of Christmas. Swannanoa, N.C., Swannanoa
Presbyterian Church, 1951. Christmas hymn with music.
Words by Thomas H. Spence, Jr.; music by Maria E. Spence.
H

3539 SPENCE, Thomas Hugh, 1899-
A memoir of Elizabeth Holman Spence. Montreat, N.C.,
For private distribution, 1978. Printing by Kingsport Press,
Kingsport, Tennessee. 118 p. C H PH U

3540 SPENCE, Thomas Hugh, 1899-
A memoir of Lieutenant Raymond Reid. Concord, N.C.,
Privately printed, 1946. 17 p. H PH U

3541 SPENCE, Thomas Hugh, 1899-
North state refrain. [Kingsville, Tex., Tex.-Mex. Print-
ery], © 1941. 23 p. A H U

3542 SPENCE, Thomas Hugh, 1899-
The Presbyterian congregation on Rocky River. Concord,
N.C., Rocky River Presbyterian Church, 1954. 238 p.
A C H L PH U

3543 SPENCE, Thomas Hugh, 1899-
Rev. Samuel Mills Tenney, D.D., Litt.D., and woman's
work of the Presbyterian and Reformed churches. Montreat,
N.C., Historical Foundation, 1940. unpaged. H PH

3544 SPENCE, Thomas Hugh, 1899-
Sketches of the Westminster Assembly with a bibliography
based on the holdings of the Historical Foundation. Montreat,
N.C., Historical Foundation Publications, 1943. 7 p. H
PH U

3545 SPENCE, Thomas Hugh, 1899-
Southern Presbyterian reviews. n.p., n.d. 16 p. Re-
printed from the Union Seminary Review, February, 1945.
PT U

3546 SPENCE, Thomas Hugh, 1899- comp.
Survey of records and minutes in the Historical Foundation
of the Presbyterian and Reformed Churches. Montreat, N.C.,
Historical Foundation Publications, 1943. 43 p. A H L PH
PT

3547 SPENCE, Thomas Hugh, 1899-
This Christmas, [by] Thomas and Elizabeth Spence. Mon-
treat, N.C., Thomas H. Spence, Jr., © 1970. 1 p. Poem.
PH

3548 SPENCE, Thomas Hugh, 1899-
Tonight to Bethlehem, a Christmas pilgrimage. Montreat,
N.C., n.p., 1946. Folded broadsheet. H U

3549 SPENCE, Thomas Hugh, 1899-
Westward across Nebraska. Hastings, Neb., Democrat
Printing Co., 1939. 85 p. Poems. H PH U

3550 SPRAGENS, John Brewer, 1916-1975.
A leader's guide ... for use with The story of Southern
Presbyterians by T. Watson Street. Richmond, John Knox
Press, © 1960. 29 p. H U

3551 SPRAGENS, John Brewer, 1916-1975.
A leader's guide ... for use with The nature and mission
of the church by Donald G. Miller. Richmond, John Knox
Press, © 1957. 27 p. U

3552 SPROUSE, William Warren, 1888-1954.
The scriptural teaching on eternal punishment. Presbyterial sermon, Lexington Presbytery, September 21, 1937.
n.p., n.d. unpaged. U

3553 SPRUNT, James, 1901-1981.
I believe, sermons on the Apostles' Creed. [Raleigh,
N.C., First Presbyterian Church, 1952]. 79 p. H

3554 SPRUNT, James, 1901-1981.
Messages to homemakers, studies in Deuteronomy. At-
lanta, Board of Women's Work, Presbyterian Church in the
U.S., [1956?]. 55 p. H U

3555 SPRUNT, James, 1901-1981.
"These are written": studies in the Gospel of John. Atlanta, Committee on Woman's Work, Presbyterian Church in
the U.S., © 1949. 76 p. C U

3556 SQUIRES, William Henry Tappey, 1875-1948.
Acadie days: sketches of New Scotland. n.p., [1920].
39 p. PH U

3557 SQUIRES, William Henry Tappey, 1875-1948.
The days of yester-year in colony and commonwealth: a
sketch book of Virginia. Portsmouth, Va., Printcraft Press,
1928. 301 p. H L U

3558 SQUIRES, William Henry Tappey, 1875-1948.
The land of decision. Portsmouth, Va., Printcraft Press,
1931. 402 p. H R U

3559 SQUIRES, William Henry Tappey, 1875-1948.
Peregrine papers; a tale of travel in the Orient. [Rich-
mond, W. H. T. Squires], © 1923. 204, v p. C H R U

3560 SQUIRES, William Henry Tappey, 1875-1948.
The Presbyterian Church in the colony of Virginia, 1562-1788. Richmond, n.p., 1938. 17 p. Reprinted from the Union Seminary Review, October, 1938. H PH U

3561 SQUIRES, William Henry Tappey, 1875-1948.
The rise of the Presbyterian Church in Tidewater Virginia. Norfolk, Va., n.p., [1919?]. 6 p. PH U

3562 SQUIRES, William Henry Tappey, 1875-1948.
Samuel Davies before the king's council for the colony and ancient dominion of Virginia, April 15, 1747. Williamsburg, The Governor's Palace, [1946]. unpaged. An address to the congregation of Holmes Presbyterian Church, April 16, 1946. U

3563 SQUIRES, William Henry Tappey, 1875-1948.
Through centuries three: a short history of the people of Virginia. [1st ed.] Portsmouth, Va., Printcraft Press, 1929. 605 p. H R U

3564 SQUIRES, William Henry Tappey, 1875-1948.
Unleashed at long last; reconstruction in Virginia, April 9, 1865-January 26, 1870. [1st ed.] Portsmouth, Va., Printcraft Press, 1939. 486 p. H R U ... L: New York, Negro Universities Press, [1970].

3565 SQUIRES, William Henry Tappey, 1875-1948.
William Maxwell: a Virginian of ante-bellum days. Richmond, Union Seminary Magazine, n.d. 14 p. PH

3566 STACY, Carlton, Ingersoll, 1866-1945.
The oldest church in the Synod of Georgia. n.p., n.d. 12 p. Waynesboro, Georgia, Presbyterian Church. H PH

3567 STACY, Carlton Ingersoll, 1866-1945.
Seven world movements. n.p., n.d. 9 p. PH

3568 STACY, Carlton Ingersoll, 1866-1945.
The war and the prophets. Toccoa, Ga., Record Printers, n.d. 8 p. Reprinted from the Christian Observer. H

3569 STACY, James, 1830-1912.
Baptism of infants. A sermon preached in the Presbyterian Church, Newnan, Ga., November 1, 1874. Newnan, Ga., Herald Job Office, 1875. 22 p. PH

3570 STACY, James, 1830-1912.
Day of rest: its obligations and advantages. Richmond, Whittet & Shepperson, 1885. 318 p. A C H L R U ... L: 1895.

3571 STACY, James, 1830-1912.
Hand-book of prophecy, containing a brief outline of the prophecies of Daniel and John, together with a critical essay on the second advent. Richmond, Presbyterian Committee of Publication, © 1906. 149 p. A C H L PT R U

3572 STACY, James, 1830-1912.
History of the Midway Congregational Church, Liberty County, Georgia. Newnan, Ga., S. W. Murray, [1899]. 283 p. H ... R: 327 p. ... A C H PH U: [Rev. ed. 1903]. 283 p.

3573 STACY, James, 1830-1912.
History of the Midway Congregational Church, Liberty County, Georgia. [Rev. ed.] Newnan, Ga., S. W. Murray, [1951]. 367, 29, 327 p. With an addenda by Mrs. Elizabeth Walker Quarterman, bringing the history up to date, 1903-1950, and Stacy's "The published records of Midway Church" [Newnan, Murray, 1894]. Separate title-pages. Edited by Albert Lundy Baker. Cover title: History and records of Midway Church. R U

3574 STACY, James, 1830-1912.
A history of the Presbyterian Church in Georgia. [Elberton, Ga., Press of the Star, 1912]. 404 p. Completed and edited, after the author's death, by C. I. Stacy. A C H L PH PT R U

3575 STACY, James, 1830-1912.
The holy Sabbath: its nature, design, and observance. A prize essay. Richmond, Presbyterian Committee of Publication, © 1877. 63 p. A C H L U

3576 STACY, James, 1830-1912.
The Sabbath day. Which day of the week, the seventh or the first: A paper read before Atlanta Presbytery at its conference at Buford, Ga., October 11, 1895, and published at the request of presbytery. n.p., n.d. 12 p. U

3577 STACY, James, 1830-1912.
Water baptism. A sermon preached in the Presbyterian Church, Newnan, Ga., Sept. 1, 1867. Newnan, Herald Job Office, 1868. 16 p. PH

3578 STACY, James, 1830-1912.
Water baptism, a tract. Richmond, Presbyterian Publishing Co., 1882. 103 p. A L U

3579 STAGG, John Weldon, 1864-1915.
Calvin, Twisse and Edwards on the universal salvation of those dying in infancy. Richmond, Presbyterian Committee of Publication, © 1902. 163 p. A C H L PT R U

3580　STAGG, John Weldon, 1864-1915.
　　　　Three maligned theologians: John Calvin, William Twisse,
　　　　and Jonathan Edwards. n.p., n.d. 53 p. Reprinted from
　　　　the Presbyterian Quarterly, January, 1901. PT

3581　STAIR, Frederick Rogers, 1918-
　　　　The Christian in his daily work. [Richmond, Board of
　　　　Christian Education, Presbyterian Church in the U.S., 1956].
　　　　14 p. An address ... to the 1956 Conference on Christian
　　　　Vocation, under the auspices of Union Theological Seminary.
　　　　U

3582　STAPLES, Moses Wilmington, 1827-1892 or '93.
　　　　Presbyterianism in her polity and practice. Defended in
　　　　three discourses ... delivered in Marshall, Texas, February,
　　　　1854. St. Louis, J. K. B. Rice, 1855. 142 p. PT

3583　STATEMENT on issues concerning Presbyterian union. [At-
　　　　lanta, Presbyterian Church in the U.S., 1954]. 44 p.
　　　　Prepared by a special committee of the General Assembly:
　　　　Frank H. Caldwell, Guy T. Gillespie, James A. Jones,
　　　　John R. Richardson. U

3584　STEGALL, Carroll Richard, 1925-
　　　　The modern tongues and healing movement. n.p., n.d.
　　　　43 p. C U ... PH: Atlanta, C. R. Stegall, n.d. 56 p.

3585　STEPHENSON, Philip Daingerfield, 1845-1916.
　　　　The foreign evangelist; an inquiry. Richmond, Whittet &
　　　　Shepperson, 1896. 36 p. U

3586　STEPHENSON, Philip Daingerfield, 1845-1916.
　　　　The woman question. n.p., n.d. 206-228 p. Reprinted
　　　　from the Presbyterian Quarterly, April, 1899. U ... R:
　　　　microfiche.

3587　*STEVENSON, George, 1812-1859.
　　　　The offices of Christ. Abridged from the original work ...
　　　　by William S. Plumer. [Philadelphia], Presbyterian Board of
　　　　Publication, 1840. 150 p. A C L PH PT U ... C H PH:
　　　　[18??]. 143 p.

3588　STEWART, Donald Houston, 1902-
　　　　Prayers; disturbance and transfiguration. [1st ed.] Hicks-
　　　　ville, N.Y., Exposition Press, © 1978. 79 p. L PT

3589　STEWART, John Curtis.
　　　　Substance of a sermon preached ... in the Swananoa Church,
　　　　January 20, 1860. n.p., n.d. 7 p. PH

3590　STILES, Joseph Clay, 1795-1875.
　　　　The Abrahamic covenant and the New Testament church.

Philadelphia, Presbyterian Publication Committee, n.d. 54 p.
H PH PT

3591 STILES, Joseph Clay, 1795-1875.
Address on the life and death of Rev. A. H. H. Boyd,
D.D., of Winchester, Va. Richmond, Charles H. Wynne,
1866. 27 p. U

3592 STILES, Joseph Clay, 1795-1875.
The enquirer, examined and instructed. New York, Wm.
C. Martin, 1867. 35 p. U

3593 STILES, Joseph Clay, 1795-1875.
Future punishment, discussed in a letter to a friend. St.
Louis, n.p., 1868. 60 p. A C U

3594 STILES, Joseph Clay, 1795-1875.
A letter to Alexander Campbell, in reply to an article in
the Millennial Harbinger. Lexington, Ky., Lexington Intelligencer, 1838. 57 p. H PH U

3595 STILES, Joseph Clay, 1795-1875.
Modern reform examined; or, The union of North and
South on the subject of slavery. Philadelphia, J. B. Lippin-
cott & Co., 1857. 310 p. C PH ... H L PT U: 1858.

3596 STILES, Joseph Clay, 1795-1875.
National rectitude, the only true basis of national pros-
perity; an appeal to the Confederate states. Petersburg,
Va., Evangelical Tract Society, 1863. 45 p. U

3597 STILES, Joseph Clay, 1795-1875.
Reply to an article in the June number of the Millennial
Harbinger. Frankfort, Ky., A. G. Hodges, 1838. 55 p.
PH PT

3598 STILES, Joseph Clay, 1795-1875.
A sermon on predestination, preached in Milledgeville,
August, 1826. 2d ed. Charleston, Charleston Observer,
1827. 60 p. C PH ... PH PT: Philadelphia, Young,
1829. 78 p.

3599 STILLMAN, Charles Allen, 1819-1895.
The dead of the Synod of Alabama from 1882 to 1890. A
memorial sermon. Birmingham, Ala., Roberts & Sons,
1891. 16 p. C H PH PT

3600 STILLMAN, Charles Allen, 1819-1895.
The death of the righteous. A sermon preached in the
Presbyterian Church at Gainesville, Ala., on Sunday, Decem-
ber 23, 1855, on the occasion of the death of Dr. Anson
Brackett. New York, R. Craighead, 1856. 16 p. PH

3601 STILLMAN, Charles Allen, 1819-1895.
A discourse, delivered in the Baptist Church, Carlowville, Alabama. Cahawba, Ala., Charles E. Haynes, 1848. 12 p. PH

3602 STILLMAN, Charles Allen, 1819-1895.
Sprinkling and pouring, scriptural modes of baptism: a sermon preached by order of the Presbytery of Tuskaloosa. Montgomery, n.p., 1859. 16 p. PT

3603 STOFFEL, Ernest Lee, 1923-
Believing the impossible before breakfast. Atlanta, John Knox Press, © 1977. 123 p. A C H L PT R U

3604 STOFFEL, Ernest Lee, 1923-
His kingdom is forever. Richmond, John Knox Press, [1956]. 182 p. A C H L PT R U

3605 STOFFEL, Ernest Lee, 1923-
The strong comfort of God. Richmond, John Knox Press, © 1958. 159 p. A C H L PT R U

3606 STONE, Nathan John, 1894-
Answering your questions. Chicago, Moody Press, © 1956. 509 p. L

3607 STONE, Nathan John, 1894-
Names of God in the Old Testament. Chicago, Moody Press, [1944]. 160 p. R U ... A: © 1944. 128 p.

3608 STONE, Robert Hamlin, 1896-1976.
A history of Orange Presbytery, 1770-1970. Greensboro, N.C., [Orange Presbytery], 1970. 430 p. A C H PH PT R U

3609 STRATTON, Joseph Buck, 1815-1903.
Anniversary discourses. 1869--1884--1893. 1. A quarter-century's pastorate. Natchez, Miss. 1869. 2. A forty years pastorate. Natchez, Miss. 1884. 3. Semi-centennial discourses, etc. Natchez, Miss. 1893. Philadelphia, n.p., 1869, 1884 [and] Natchez, n.p., 1894. PT

3610 STRATTON, Joseph Buck, 1815-1903.
Confessing Christ: a manual for inquirers in religion. Philadelphia, Henry B. Ashmead, 1880. 168 p. A C H PT U

3611 STRATTON, Joseph Buck, 1815-1903.
A discourse on the life and character of the Rev. Jeremiah Chamberlain, D.D., late President of Oakland College, delivered at the request of the Board of Directors ... on Thursday, December 18th, 1851. New Orleans, T. Rea, 1852. 19 p. H PT

3612 STRATTON, Joseph Buck, 1815-1903.
Dr. Stratton's report upon beneficiary education, May,
1877. n.p., n.d. 10 p. PT

3613 STRATTON, Joseph Buck, 1815-1903.
The duty of alms-giving. A sermon delivered in the
Presbyterian Church, Natchez. Vidalia, La., "Concordia
Intelligencer," 1847. 17 p. PH

3614 STRATTON, Joseph Buck, 1815-1903, ed.
Extracts from an elder's diary. Richmond, Presbyterian
Committee of Publication, © 1896. 171 p. A H PT R U

3615 STRATTON, Joseph Buck, 1815-1903.
Following Christ. A manual for church-members. Phila-
delphia, Presbyterian Board of Publication, © 1884. 236 p.
A C H PT U

3616 STRATTON, Joseph Buck, 1815-1903.
A forty years pastorate: a sermon preached on the Sab-
bath, January 6, 1884, in the Presbyterian Church, Natchez,
Miss. Philadelphia, J. B. Lippincott & Co., 1884. 73-109 p.
PT

3617 STRATTON, Joseph Buck, 1815-1903.
Hymns to the Holy Spirit. Richmond, Presbyterian Committee of Publication, 1893. 93 p. A C H PT R U

3618 STRATTON, Joseph Buck, 1815-1903.
Memorial of a quarter-century's pastorate. A sermon
preached on the Sabbaths, Jan. 3d and 17th, 1869, in the
Presbyterian Church, Natchez, Miss. Philadelphia, J. B.
Lippincott & Co., 1869. 109 p. H PH PT

3619 STRATTON, Joseph Buck, 1815-1903.
A pastor's valedictory. A selection of early sermons
from the manuscripts of the ... pastor of the Presbyterian
Church, from A. D. 1843 to A. D. 1894, Natchez, Miss.
Natchez, Natchez Printing & Stationery Co., 1899. 328 p.
C H PT R

3620 STRATTON, Joseph Buck, 1815-1903.
The peace-maker. A sermon for the times, preached in
the Presbyterian Church, Natchez, Mississippi, on Sabbath,
the 12th of October, 1856. Natchez, Daily Courier Office,
1856. 13 p. PH

3621 STRATTON, Joseph Buck, 1815-1903.
Piety in youth. A sermon, preached in the Presbyterian
Church, Natchez, on Sabbath, May 11, 1851. Natchez,
Miss., Natchez Courier Book and Job Office, 1851. 18 p.
PT

3622 STRATTON, Joseph Buck, 1815-1903.
      Prayers for the use of the family. Natchez, Miss., n.p.,
      1887. 182 p. H ... A C H R: Prayers for the use of
      families. Richmond, Presbyterian Committee of Publication,
      1888. 185 p.

3623 STRATTON, Joseph Buck, 1815-1903.
      A sermon, for the New Year, preached in the Presby-
      terian Church, Natchez, on Sabbath, Jan. 6, 1856. Natchez,
      Daily Courier Office, 1856. 21 p. H PH PT

3624 STRATTON, Joseph Buck, 1815-1903.
      A sermon preached in the Presbyterian Church, Vicksburg,
      January 20th, 1856, in commemoration of the life and death
      of Rev. Benj. H. Williams. Vicksburg, Vicksburg Whig
      Steam Book and Job Office, 1856. 19 p. PT

3625 STRATTON, Joseph Buck, 1815-1903.
      Truth in the household: a sermon preached by appoint-
      ment before the General Assembly of the Presbyterian Church
      in the United States of America, at Lexington, Kentucky, May
      28, 1857, on behalf of the Assembly's Board of Publication.
      Philadelphia, Presbyterian Board of Publication, 1857. 35 p.
      PH PT

3626 STREET, Thomas Watson, 1916-
      The church and the churches; Christian unity for Christian
      mission. Richmond, CLC Press, © 1965. 48 p. (The
      Covenant Life Curriculum.) C L U

3627 STREET, Thomas Watson, 1916-
      On the growing edge of the church (new dimensions in
      world missions). Richmond, John Knox Press, © 1965.
      128 p. A C H L PH PT R U

3628 STREET, Thomas Watson, 1916-
      The story of Southern Presbyterians. Richmond, John
      Knox Press, © 1960. 134 p. A C H L PH PT R U ...
      L: [1961].

3629 STREET, Thomas Watson, 1916-
      Thomas Smyth: Presbyterian bookman. n.p., [1959].
      14 p. Reprinted from Journal of the Presbyterian Historical
      Society, March, 1959. A U

3630 STRICKLER, Givens Brown, 1840-1913.
      The nature, value and special utility of the catechisms....
      An address delivered before the General Assembly of the
      Southern Presbyterian Church, Charlotte, N.C., May, 1897.
      Richmond, Presbyterian Committee of Publication, 1897.
      116-138 p. C U

3631 STRICKLER, Givens Brown, 1840-1913.

The philosophy of faith.   Richmond, Whittet & Shepperson, 1902.   19 p.   Reprinted from the Presbyterian Quarterly, October, 1902.   C PH U

3632   STRICKLER, Givens Brown, 1840-1913.
Presbyterian doctrines. n.p., n.d.   17 p.   U

3633   STRICKLER, Givens Brown, 1840-1913.
Sermons. New York, Fleming H. Revell Co., © 1910.
273 p. A C H L R U ... C H U: 2d ed. Richmond, Presbyterian Committee of Publication.

3634   STRONG, Robert, 1906-1980.
Critical evaluation of the proposed new Confession of Faith.
[Weaverville, N.C., Presbyterian Journal, 1972]. 20 p.   C

3635   STRONG, Robert, 1906-1980.
Doctrinal sermons; preached in the winter quarter of 1960 in Trinity Presbyterian Church, Montgomery, Alabama. n.p., n.d.   59 p.   H

3636   STRONG, Robert, 1906-1980.
The present relevance of our Confession of Faith. [Weaverville, N.C., Southern Presbyterian Journal, 1959]. 12 p.
Reprinted from the Southern Presbyterian Journal, September 16, 1959.   R

3637   STRONG, Robert, 1906-1980.
Sermons on the Apostles' Creed preached in the winter and spring quarters of 1962 in Trinity Presbyterian Church, Montgomery, Alabama. n.p., n.d.   110 p.   H

3638   STRONG, Robert, 1906-1980.
Sermons on the covenants and on Romans eight. Preached in 1964 and 1965 in Trinity Presbyterian Church, Montgomery, Alabama. n.p., n.d.   156 p.   H R U

3639   STRONG, Robert, 1906-1980.
Sermons on the last things; preached in the winter quarter of 1961 in Trinity Presbyterian Church, Montgomery, Alabama. n.p., n.d.   84 p.   H R

3640   STRONG, Robert, 1906-1980.
Sermons on the order of salvation. Preached mainly in the winter quarter of 1963 in Trinity Presbyterian Church, Montgomery, Alabama. n.p., n.d.   106 p.   H R

3641   STRONG, Robert, 1906-1980.
Sermons on the person and work of Christ. Preached in 1966 in Trinity Presbyterian Church, Montgomery, Alabama.
n.p., n.d.   140 p.   A C R

3642   STRONG, Robert, 1906-1980.

The story of man; sermons preached in 1970 in Trinity Presbyterian Church, Montgomery, Alabama. n.p., n.d. 142 p.   C H L R U

3643 STUART, John Leighton, 1876-1962.
Christianity and Confucianism. New York, International Missionary Council, (19-?). 27 p. A portion of the preliminary draft of notes for the Jerusalem meeting of the International Missionary Council, March 24-April 8, 1928. PT R U

3644 STUART, John Leighton, 1876-1962.
The essentials of New Testament Greek in Chinese [based on Huddilston's The essentials of New Testament Greek]. Shanghai, Presbyterian Mission Press, 1917. 94 p.   U

3645 STUART, John Leighton, 1876-1962.
Fifty years in China; the memoirs of John Leighton Stuart, missionary and ambassador. New York, Random House, © 1954. 346 p.   A C H L PH PT U

3646 STUART, John Leighton, 1876-1962.
The future of missionary education in China. n.p., n.d. unpaged. Reprinted from the Chinese Students' Monthly, April, 1916.   PH

3647 STUART, John Leighton, 1876-1962.
Greek-Chinese-English dictionary of the New Testament. Shanghai, Presbyterian Mission Press, 1918. 238 p.   U

3648 STUART, John Leighton, 1876-1962.
Lectures on modern missions, by J. Leighton Stuart and Rev. G. Y. Chen of Presbyterian Theological Seminary, Nanking. Shanghai, Methodist Publishing House, 1911. 48 ℓ. In Chinese.   U

3649 STUART, Warren Horton, 1879-1961.
Hangchow Christian College. Nashville, Brandon, n.d. unpaged.   PH

3650 STUART, Warren Horton, 1879-1961.
The use of material from China's spiritual inheritance in the Christian education of Chinese youth. A guide and sourcebook for Christian teachers in China. Shanghai, Kwang Hsueh Publishing House, 1932. 93, 202 p. Thesis (Ph.D.)-- Yale University.   C H PH PT U

3651 *SUN, Yat-sen, 1866-1925.
... San min chu i, The three principles of the people.... Translated into English by Frank W. Price. Edited by L. T. Chen. Shanghai, The Commercial Press, 1928. 514 p.   U

3652 SUTCLIFFE, Bernard Bliss, 1872-

Rejoicing in the Lord; notes on the Epistle to the Philippians. Chicago, Bible Institute Colportage Ass'n., © 1925. 54 p. U

3653 *SUTHERLAND, Judith A.
Explorations into faith; a journal; a course for youth preparing to be confirmed/commissioned. Philadelphia, Geneva Press, © 1977. 64 p. With leader's guide by Mac N. and Anne Shaw Turnage. C L PH U

3654 SWALLOW, Isaac Francis, 1873-1942.
The Swallows and Gastons. A family record from the earliest records in American colonies to the present generation. [Perry Mo., Enterprise Print., 1941]. 60 p. H

3655 SWEETS, Henry Hayes, 1872-1952, comp.
Christmas carols for use in churches and Sunday Schools.... [Rev., 4th ed.] Louisville, Ky., Department of Christian Education, Presbyterian Church in the U.S., © 1940. 44 p. C PH PT

3656 SWEETS, Henry Hayes, 1872-1952.
The church and education. Richmond, Presbyterian Committee of Publication, © 1939. 132 p. A C H L PH PT R U

3657 SWEETS, Henry Hayes, 1872-1952.
The church and its students at state institutions of higher education. Louisville, Ky., Department of Christian Education, Presbyterian Church in the U.S., n.d. 87 p. A C PH U

3658 SWEETS, Henry Hayes, 1872-1952.
He laid hold on life; the story of Harry White Myers. [Louisville, Ky., Executive Committee of Christian Education, Presbyterian Church in the U.S.], n.d. 19 p. A PH U

3659 SWEETS, Henry Hayes, 1872-1952.
Our candidates and the supply of ministers. [Louisville, Ky., Executive Committee of Christian Education and Ministerial Relief, Presbyterian Church in the U.S.], n.d. 8 p. U

3660 SWEETS, Henry Hayes, 1872-1952.
Planning the good life. Richmond, Presbyterian Committee of Publication, © 1934. 274 p. A C H L PH PT R U

3661 SWEETS, Henry Hayes, 1872-1952.
The soul of improvement. [Louisville, Ky., Presbyterian Educational Association of the South], n.d. 8 p. U

3662 SWEETS, Henry Hayes, 1872-1952, comp.

Source book for speakers. Louisville, Ky., Ministers' Annuity Fund, Presbyterian Church in the U.S., [1929?]. 136 p. A

3663 SWEETS, Henry Hayes, 1872-1952, comp.
Source book on Christian education as related to the colleges and theological seminaries of the church. Louisville, Ky., Executive Committee of Christian Education and Ministerial Relief, Presbyterian Church in the U.S., 1942. 252 p. A C H L PH PT R U

3664 SWEETS, Henry Hayes, 1872-1952, comp.
Source book on spiritual life and evangelism. Louisville, Ky., Executive Committee of Christian Education, Presbyterian Church in the U.S., 1945. 248 p. A C H L PH PT R U

3665 SWEETS, Henry Hayes, 1872-1952.
Standards of denominational colleges. n.p., n.d. 11 p. Address delivered before the Association of Colleges and Secondary Schools of the Southern States. U

3666 SWETNAM, George Francis, 1904-
Pittsylvania country. New York, Duell, Sloan & Pearce, © 1951. 315 p. PH

3667 SWETNAM, George Francis, 1904-
Understanding the neighbor's faith. Philadelphia, Westminster Book Stores, © 1964. 15 p. (A Living Faith pamphlet.) PH

3668 SWETNAM, George Francis, 1904-
Why I'm Presbyterian. Philadelphia, Westminster Book Stores, © 1964. 11 p. (A Living Faith pamphlet.) PH

3669 SYDENSTRICKER, Absalom, 1852-1931.
Our life and work in China. A private account. Parsons, W.Va., McClain Printing Co., 1978. 54 p. H

3670 SYDENSTRICKER, Hiram Mason, 1858-1914.
The epic of the orient: an original poetic rendering of the book of Job. Hartford, Conn., Student Publishing Co., 1894. 111 p. A U

3671 SYDENSTRICKER, Hiram Mason, 1858-1914.
Nameless immortals. Nashville, Tenn., Publishing House of the M. E. Church, South, 1901. 234 p. "Ten sketches of women of the Bible who came in contact with Christ, but whose names have never been given." R U

3672 TADLOCK, James Doak, 1825-1899.
The early Presbyterian missions in the colonies and states.

Delivered in the chapel of the Theological Seminary at Columbia, S.C., on Mission Day, February 6, 1895. n.p., n.d. unpaged.   C PH U

3673   TALMAGE, Franklin Crane, 1887-1974.
The story of the Presbytery of Atlanta. [Atlanta, Foote & Davies], 1960. 242 p.   A C H L PT U

3674   TALMAGE, Franklin Crane, 1887-1974.
The story of the Synod of Georgia. [Atlanta], n.p., 1961. 123 p.   A C H L R U

3675   TALMAGE, Samuel Kennedy, 1798-1865.
A lecture delivered before the Georgia Historical Society, February 29th and March 4th, 1844. On the subject of education. Savannah, Locke and Davis, 1844. 24 p.   C PH PT U

3676   TALMAGE, Samuel Kennedy, 1798-1865.
Man his brother's keeper: an address delivered in the chapel of the Presbyterian Collegiate Female Institute, at Talladega, Alabama, at the close of the annual examination, August 22d, 1851. Philadelphia, Lippincott, Grambo and Co., 1851. 16 p.   PH

3677   TALMAGE, Samuel Kennedy, 1798-1865.
Man his brother's keeper: an address delivered at the annual commencements of the Wesleyan Female College, Macon, Ga.; the Presbyterian Collegiate Female Institute, Talladega, Ala.; and the Collegiate Seminary for Young Ladies, La Grange, Ga.; during the summer and fall of 1851. 2d ed. Savannah, W. Thorne Williams, 1852. 15 p. PT

3678   TALMAGE, Samuel Kennedy, 1798-1865.
Our Saviour's example: a discourse delivered ... before the students of the La Grange Female Institute, Nov. 28th, 1847. Milledgeville, n.p., 1848. 21 p.   PT

3679   TALMAGE, Samuel Kennedy, 1798-1865.
A proper early training and its priceless value; a discourse in the chapel of the Greensboro Female College, June 23, 1853. Philadelphia, William S. Young, 1853. 24 p. U

3680   TALMAGE, Samuel Kennedy, 1798-1865.
Reasons for public thanksgiving. A discourse delivered before the legislature of Georgia, in the Representative chamber, Milledgeville, on Thanksgiving Day, November 29, 1849. Milledgeville, Southern Recorder Office, 1849. 16 p. PH PT

3681   TAYLOR, Archibald Boggs, 1920-

Three sisters. A one-act play. Zentsuji, Japan, Shikoku
Christian College, n.d. 36 p. L

3682 TAYLOR, George Aiken, 1920-
A sober faith; religion and Alcoholics Anonymous. New
York, The Macmillan Co., 1953. 108 p. A C L PT R
U ... U: 1960.

3683 TAYLOR, Hubert Vance, 1913-
Our singing church: The minister and his music, [by]
Hubert Vance Taylor [and] The minister's responsibility,
[by] John Milton Kelly. [Philadelphia, Board of Christian
Education, Presbyterian Church in the U.S.A.], n.d. 31 p.
Cover title. A C PH U

3684 TAYLOR, Hubert Vance, 1913-
The spirit and the understanding. Inaugural address ...
upon being inducted into the chair of Hymnology and Public
Speech at Columbia Theological Seminary. Delivered in the
chapel of the seminary, Nov. 3, 1955. 25-37 p. Bulletin,
Columbia Theological Seminary, April, 1956. C H

3685 TAYLOR, Hugh Kerr, 1891-1977.
Our church and Madras. [Nashville, Tenn., Executive
Committee of Foreign Missions, Presbyterian Church in the
U.S., 1939]. 22 p. U

3686 TAYLOR, James Henry, 1871-1957.
An address at the tomb of President Woodrow Wilson.
Armistice Day, Sunday, November 11, 1934, Washington,
D.C. n.p., [1934?]. 11 p. H

3687 TAYLOR, James Henry, 1871-1957.
Outlines for Bible study for use of the Young Men's
Christian Association of Washington, D.C. Washington,
Young Men's Christian Association, 1921. 57 p. U

3688 TAYLOR, James Henry, 1871-1957.
Some contributions of Calvinism to thought and life. An
address delivered on the occasion of the bicentennial of the
First (Scotch) Presbyterian Church of Charleston, South
Carolina ... March 1, 1931. n.p., n.d. 24 p. U

3689 TAYLOR, James Henry, 1871-1957.
The spirit of the Huguenots and the maintenance of a great
tradition; address ... on the two hundred and fiftieth anniversary of the landing of the Huguenots. Washington, D.C.,
U.S. Government Printing Office, 1930. 14 p. H U

3690 TAYLOR, James Henry, 1871-1957.
Why I believe in the Bible, in the church, in Christ, in
the incarnation, in the resurrection, in immortality. A

series of sermons in the Central Presbyterian Church, Washington, D.C., February and March, 1937. Washington, n.p., © 1937. 46 p.   C U

3691   TAYLOR, James Henry, 1871-1957.
Woodrow Wilson in church; his membership in the congregation of the Central Presbyterian Church, Washington, D.C., 1913-1924. Charleston, S.C., J. H. Taylor, © 1952. 44 p. A C H L PT U

3692   TAYLOR, John Randolph, 1929-
God loves like that! The theology of James Denny. With a foreword by A. M. Hunter. Richmond, John Knox Press, [1962]. 210 p.   A C H L PT R U ... C: London, SCM Press, [1962].

3693   *TAYLOR, Kenneth Nathaniel.
B C: a digest of the Old Testament. Paraphrase by Kenneth N. Taylor. Compiled by John Calvin Reid. Glendale, Calif., G/L Regal Books, [1971]. 502 p.   R

3694   *TAYLOR, Kenneth Nathaniel.
God and his world: highlights from the Old Testament. Paraphrase by Kenneth N. Taylor. Compiled by John Calvin Reid. Glendale, Calif., G/L Regal Books, [1971]. 502 p. R

3695   *TAYLOR, Margaret Wilson.
My church--General programs for the Women of the Church, Presbyterian Church in the United States, 1953, [by] Margaret and Kerr Taylor. Atlanta, Board of Women's Work, Presbyterian Church in the U.S., 1953. 72 p.   C U

3696   TELFORD, George McAlister, 1883-1954, comp.
Our home task. n.p., Home Mission Committee, Synod of South Carolina, [1927]. 144 p. Home mission study book. H R U

3697   TENNEY, Benjamin Kingsbury, 1889-1952.
Sacrifices ... chosen or thrust upon us. Atlanta, Committee on Stewardship and Finance, Presbyterian Church in the U.S., n.d. unpaged.   PH

3698   TENNEY, Levi, 1823-1907.
History of the Presbytery of Central Texas. Austin, Tex., Eugene von Boeckmann, 1895. 111 p.   C H PH U

3699   TENNEY, Samuel Mills, 1871-1939.
A catechism on the obligation of the East Texas Presbytery. n.p., n.d. 4 p.   PH

3700   TENNEY, Samuel Mills, 1871-1939.

An essay on the public schools of our country. n.p., 1892-93. 18 p. John Hoff essay, 1892-93. PT

3701 TENNEY, Samuel Mills, 1871-1939.
Instructions to historians. Memorial edition to Rev. Samuel Mills Tenney, D.D., LL.D. Atlanta, Committee on Woman's Work, Presbyterian Church in the U.S., [1941]. 12 p. PH U

3702 TENNEY, Samuel Mills, 1871-1939.
Presbyterians: who they are. [Texarkana, Ark.-Tex., Consolidated Printing Co., 1926]. 58 p. A C H L PT U

3703 TENNEY, Samuel Mills, 1871-1939, ed.
Souvenir of the General Assembly of the Presbyterian Church, U.S. [San Antonio, Tex., First Presbyterian Church], 1924. 199 p. Biographical sketches and portraits of leaders. C H PH R U

3704 TENNEY, William Collins, 1873-1956.
... Golden Rule Presbyterian Church, U.S., organized January 15th, 1851, by Rev. M. W. Staples. Elysian Fields, Tex., Golden Rule Presbyterian Church, 1951. 25 p. H

3705 TESTIMONIAL dinner to Dr. Charles Robert Hemphill at the Brown Hotel, Louisville, Friday, June 19, 1925. n.p., n.d. 2 p. H

3706 TEXTS and Testaments: critical essays on the Bible and early church fathers: a volume in honor of Stuart Dickson Currie; edited by W. Eugene March. San Antonio, Trinity University Press, © 1980. 321 p. A L PT U

3707 THOMAS, John Newton, 1903-
Reformed theology and higher education. [Louisville, Ky., Executive Committee of Christian Education and Ministerial Relief, Presbyterian Church in the U.S., 1946]. 23 p. U

3708 THOMAS, John Stanley, 1870-1959.
The pulpit and the people. Wilmington, N.C., Andrew J. Howell, Jr., Press, 1899. 10 p. PT

3709 THOMPSON, Cecil Asbury, 1906-
A digest of the Atlanta school of home visitation evangelism. [Atlanta, n.p., 1947]. 42 p. C U

3710 THOMPSON, Ernest, 1867-1946.
Our church's home mission duty. Atlanta, Executive Committee of Home Missions, Presbyterian Church in the U.S., [1917]. 17 p. U

3711 THOMPSON, Ernest, 1867-1946.

Veto power and other sermons. Charleston, W.Va.,
Tribune Printing Co., n.d. 416 p. C H R U

3712 THOMPSON, Ernest Trice, 1894- ed.
Bases of world order: seminar, Montreat Leadership
School, 1944. Edited by E. T. Thompson, P. H. Car-
michael, K. J. Foreman, Lawrence I. Stell [and others].
Richmond, John Knox Press, © 1945. 121 p. A C H L
PT U

3713 THOMPSON, Ernest Trice, 1894-
The Bible for today. [Richmond, Outlook Publishers],
n.d. 23 p. U

3714 THOMPSON, Ernest Trice, 1894-
Changing emphases in American preaching. Philadelphia,
Westminster Press, © 1943. 234 p. The Stone Lectures
for 1943. A C H L PH PT R U

3715 THOMPSON, Ernest Trice, 1894-
The changing south and the Presbyterian Church in the
United States. Richmond, John Knox Press, © 1950. 221 p.
A C H L PT R U

3716 THOMPSON, Ernest Trice, 1894-
Federal aid for parochial schools. n.p., n.d. 11 p. U

3717 THOMPSON, Ernest Trice, 1894-
The Gospel according to Mark and its meaning for today.
Richmond, John Knox Press, © 1954. 255 p. A C H L
PT R U ... C H U: [Rev. ed.] © 1962.

3718 THOMPSON, Ernest Trice, 1894-
Highlights in the book of Acts. [Richmond, Presbyterian
Outlook Publishers, 1954]. unpaged. Cover title. Reprinted
from the Presbyterian Outlook. A U

3719 THOMPSON, Ernest Trice, 1894-
Highlights of Presbyterian history. [Atlanta, Committee
on Diamond Jubilee, Presbyterian Church in the U.S.], 1936.
7 p. C U

3720 THOMPSON, Ernest Trice, 1894-
Jesus and citizenship. Richmond, John Knox Press,
© 1956. 86 p. H PH R U

3721 THOMPSON, Ernest Trice, 1894-
Love plus knowledge. [Atlanta, Committee on Woman's
Work, Presbyterian Church in the U.S.], n.d. 6 p. U

3722 THOMPSON, Ernest Trice, 1894-
One world, one Lord; studies from the Gospel of Matthew.

Philadelphia, Board of Christian Education, Presbyterian
Church in the U.S.A., © 1947. 40 p. PH U

3723 THOMPSON, Ernest Trice, 1894-
Plenty and want; the responsibility of the church. Nashville, Tenn., Presbyterian Church in the U.S., © 1966.
114 p. H L R U ... C: 2 pts.

3724 THOMPSON, Ernest Trice, 1894-
The Presbyterian Church in the United States. [Rev.]
Richmond, Board of Christian Education, Presbyterian Church
in the U.S., 1961. 6 p. H U

3725 THOMPSON, Ernest Trice, 1894-
Presbyterian missions in the southern United States. Rich-
mond, Presbyterian Committee of Publication, 1934. 281 p.
A C H L PH PT R U

3726 THOMPSON, Ernest Trice, 1894-
Presbyterians in the South. Richmond, John Knox Press,
© 1963-© 1973. 3 v. A C H L PH PT R U

3727 THOMPSON, Ernest Trice, 1894-
The present mission of the church; a sermon delivered at
the opening of the Synod of Virginia. Richmond, Union
Theological Seminary in Virginia, 1941. 9 p. Union Seminary Bulletin, July-Sept., 1941. PH U

3728 THOMPSON, Ernest Trice, 1894-
The Sermon on the Mount and its meaning for today. Richmond, John Knox Press, © 1946. 162 p. A H PT R U ...
C L R U: Rev. ed. [1953]. 128 p. ... A C H U: Rev.
ed. © 1961.

3729 THOMPSON, Ernest Trice, 1894-
The spirituality of the church; a distinctive doctrine of the
Presbyterian Church in the United States. Richmond, John
Knox Press, © 1961. 48 p. A C H L PT R U

3730 THOMPSON, Ernest Trice, 1894-
Studies in the Gospel of Mark. [Richmond, Presbyterian
Outlook, 1953]. 25 ℓ. Reprinted from the Presbyterian Out-
look, 1951. A U

3731 THOMPSON, Ernest Trice, 1894-
The Ten Commandments. [Richmond, Presbyterian Outlook, 1951]. 24 p. Reprinted from the Presbyterian Outlook. A H U

3732 THOMPSON, Ernest Trice, 1894-
Through the ages, a history of the Christian church.
Richmond, CLC Press, © 1965. 447 p. (The Covenant

Life Curriculum.)   A C L PT R U ... A C L PT R U:
Teacher's book.   352 p. ... A: Reformed Church in Ameri-
ca edition.   By Ernest Trice Thompson and Elton M.
Eenigenburg.   [1965].   480 p.

3733   THOMPSON, Ernest Trice, 1894-
Tomorrow's church--tomorrow's world. Richmond, John
Knox Press, © 1960. 128 p.   A C H L PT R U

3734   THOMPSON, Ernest Trice, 1894-
You shall be my witnesses; studies in the Acts of the
Apostles. [Richmond, Board of Christian Education, Pres-
byterian Church in the U.S.], © 1953. 46 p.   U

3735   THOMPSON, Henry Howard,   -1973.
The communicant member. Jackson, Miss., Assembly's
Committee on Evangelism, n.d. 31 p.   H U

3736   *THOMPSON, Thomas Gray.
The oldest church on the Western slope: a history of the
Presbyterian Church, Lake City, Colorado, [by] Thomas Gray
Thompson and Harold M. Parker. Boulder, Colo., Weekley
Enterprises, 1976. 88 p.   L PH PT U

3737   THOMPSON, William Taliaferro, 1886-1964.
An adventure in love; Christian family living. Richmond,
John Knox Press, © 1956. 155 p.   A C H L PT R U ...
C: 1962.

3738   THOMPSON, William Taliaferro, 1886-1964.
Adventures in parenthood; Christian family living. Rich-
mond, John Knox Press, © 1959. 155 p.   A C H L R U ...
H: [1961].

3739   THOMPSON, William Taliaferro, 1886-1964.
Fathers and sons. [Huntington, W.Va., n.p., 1950]. 16 p.
U

3740   THOMPSON, William Taliaferro, 1886-1964.
A prophetic ministry. [Richmond, Union Theological Semi-
nary, 1928]. 12 p. Union Seminary Bulletin, April, May,
June, 1928.   PH PT U

3741   THOMPSON, William Taliaferro, 1886-1964.
Weekday religious education. Richmond, Executive Committee of Religious Education and Publication, Presbyterian
Church in the U.S., 1941. 31 p. Excerpt from the 80th
annual report to the General Assembly.   A U

3742   THOMPSON, William Taliaferro, 1886-1964.
What the church could do for youth in days like these.
[Richmond, John Knox Press], © 1947. 15 p. An address
delivered before the Torch Club of Richmond, Virginia.   U

3743 THOMPSON, Willis, 1887-
Baptism and immersionists. Richmond, Presbyterian Committee of Publication, n.d. 24 p. U

3744 THOMSON, Charles Talbutt, 1858-1926, ed.
Lindsay Hughes Blanton, an appreciation of his life and work. Lexington, Ky., Transylvania Press, 1908. 44 p. H

3745 THOMSON, Charles Talbutt, 1858-1926.
There will be no millennium. Port Gibson, Miss., Reveille Print., n.d. 4 p. U

3746 THORNE, William, 1871-1925.
Five years of home mission work in West Tennessee. n.p., n.d. unpaged. PH

3747 *THORNTON, William M.
John Mayo Pleasants Atkinson, D.D.: a memorial address. Petersburg, Mitchell Manuf'g. Co., 1900. 21 p. H PH PT U

3748 THORNWELL, James Henley, 1812-1862.
Analysis of Butler's analogy, part I. n.p., n.d. 49 p. C

3749 THORNWELL, James Henley, 1812-1862.
... The arguments of Romanists from the infallibility of the church and the testimony of the fathers in behalf of the Apocrypha, discussed and refuted. New York, Leavitt, Trow & Co., 1845. 417 p. At head of title: The apocryphal books of the Old Testament proved to be corrupt additions to the word of God. A C H PH PT R

3750 THORNWELL, James Henley, 1812-1862.
The collected writings of James Henley Thornwell.... Edited by John B. Adger. Richmond, Presbyterian Committee of Publication, 1871-1873. 4 v. Vols. 3-4 edited by John B. Adger and John L. Girardeau. A C H PH PT R ... L U: 1871-1881 ... A C H R U: 1881-1886.

3751 THORNWELL, James Henley, 1812-1862.
Discourses on truth. Delivered in the chapel of the South Carolina College. New York, Robert Carter & Brothers, 1855. 328 p. C H PH ... A PT R U: 1856 ... H R U: 1859 ... C U: 1869.

3752 THORNWELL, James Henley, 1812-1862.
Election and reprobation. Philadelphia, Presbyterian and Reformed Publishing Co., 1961. 97 p. C L U ... A H PT R: Jackson, Miss., Presbyterian Reformation Society, 1961.

3753 THORNWELL, James Henley, 1812-1862.
Exposition and vindication of the revised book of discipline.
Richmond, Shepperson & Co., 1872. 73 p. C H PH PT

3754 THORNWELL, James Henley, 1812-1862.
Hear the South! The state of the country. New York, D.
Appleton and Co., 1861. 32 p. Republished from the South-
ern Presbyterian Review, January, 1861. PH PT

3755 THORNWELL, James Henley, 1812-1862.
Judgements, a call to repentance. A sermon preached by
appointment of the legislature in the hall of House of Representatives ... Saturday, Dec. 9, 1854. Columbia, S.C.,
R. W. Gibbes & Co., 1854. 24 p. C H PH

3756 THORNWELL, James Henley, 1812-1862.
Letter to His Excellency Governor Manning on public in-
struction in South Carolina. Columbia, S.C., R. W. Gibbes
& Co., 1853. 36 p. C PH ... H R: Dr. J. H. Thorn-
well's letter to Governor Manning.... Charleston, S.C.,
News and Courier Book Presses, 1885. 49 p.

3757 THORNWELL, James Henley, 1812-1862.
National sins; a fast day sermon preached in the Presbyterian Church, Columbia, S.C., Wednesday, Nov. 21, 1860.
Columbia, Southern Guardian Steam-power Press, 1860.
42 p. H PH PT

3758 THORNWELL, James Henley, 1812-1862.
The necessity of the atonement. A sermon preached in
the chapel of the South Carolina College, on the 1st day of
December, 1844. Columbia, S.C., Samuel Weir, 1845.
72 p. C H PH PT

3759 THORNWELL, James Henley, 1812-1862.
Our danger and our duty. Columbia, S.C., Southern
Guardian Steam-power Press, 1862. 14 p. H PH

3760 THORNWELL, James Henley, 1812-1862.
Report on the subject of slavery, presented to the Synod
of South Carolina at their sessions in Winnsborough, Novem-
ber 6, 1851, adopted by them and published by their order.
Columbia, S.C., A. S. Johnston, 1852. 16 p. C H PH
PT

3761 THORNWELL, James Henley, 1812-1862.
Review of Paley's moral philosophy. n.p., n.d. 32 p.
C

3762 THORNWELL, James Henley, 1812-1862.
The rights and duties of masters. A sermon preached at
the dedication of a church, erected in Charleston, S.C., for

the benefit and instruction of the coloured population. Charleston, S.C., Walker & James, 1850. 51 p.   C H PH PT

3763   THORNWELL, James Henley, 1812-1862.
The sacrifice of Christ, the type and model of missionary effort. A sermon preached by appointment of the Board of Foreign Missions, before the General Assembly of the Presbyterian Church, in the First Presbyterian Church, New York, Sabbath, May 18, 1856. New York, Mission House, 1856. 32 p.   C PH PT

3764   THORNWELL, James Henley, 1812-1862.
The state of the country. Columbia, S.C., Southern Guardian Steam-power Press, 1861. 32 p. Republished from the Southern Presbyterian Review, January, 1861. Published also under title: Hear the South!   H PH PT

3765   THORNWELL, James Henley, 1812-1862.
Thoughts suited to the present crisis; a sermon, on occasion of the death of Hon. John C. Calhoun, preached in the chapel of the South Carolina College, April 21, 1850. Columbia, S.C., A. S. Johnston, 1850. 45 p.   C H PH PT

3766   THORNWELL, James Henley, 1812-1862.
A tract on the doctrines of election and reprobation. Columbia, Samuel Weir, 1840. 56 p.   C PH PT

3767   THORNWELL, James Henley, 1812-1862.
The vanity and glory of man. A sermon preached in the chapel of the South Carolina College, on the 9th of October, 1842, on occasion of the death of Benjamin R. Maybin, a member of the freshman class. Columbia, Samuel Weir, 1842. 64 p.   C H PH

3768   THORNWELL, James Henley, 1812-1862.
A wedding present more enduring than the ages. Clinton, S.C., Thornwell Orphanage Press, n.d. 12 p.   H U

3769   THORNWELL, James Henley, 1846-1907.
A memorial sketch of William G. Neville, D.D., L.L.D., (President of Presbyterian College of South Carolina). Rock Hill, S.C., London Printery, 1907. 32 p.   C PH

3770   THOROUGHLY furnished. The new Westminster Standard Course for Teacher Training. Second year. (In four parts.) Philadelphia, Westminster Press, 1922. 256, 61 p. Part I is Teaching values of the Old Testament, by Walter W. Moore and Edward Mack.   A H

3771   THREE colloquies on vital matters in religion between D. L. Moody and Dr. Wm. S. Plumer. New York, American Tract Society [1876]. 50 p. Colloquies were held: Dec. 1875, March 1876, May 1876.   R

3772 *THURNEYSEN, Edward, 1888-
The sermon on the mount. Translated by William Childs
Robinson, Sr., with James M. Robinson. Richmond, John
Knox Press, © 1964. 82 p. Translation of "Die Berg-
predigt." A C L PT R U

3773 TIEMANN, William Harold, 1927-
The right to silence; privileged communication and the
pastor. Richmond, John Knox Press, © 1964. 160 p. A
C H L PT R U

3774 *TOMKINS, Anne.
Addresses of Miss Anne E. Tomkins and Mr. William J.
Hoge, before Sumner Division, no. 20, Sons of Temperance,
at Gallatin, Tennessee, on the 22D of May, 1847. Nashville,
J. G. Shepard, 1847. 12 p. PH

3775 TOMKINS, Jerry Robert, 1931- ed.
D-days at Dayton; reflections on the Scopes trial. Baton
Rouge, Louisiana State University Press, 1965. 173 p.
A L PT U

3776 TRADITION and change in Jewish experience. Editor, A.
Leland Jamison. Syracuse, N.Y., Dept of Religion, Syracuse University, 1978. 272 p. A C L PT U

3777 TRAINED workers. The new Standard Teacher Training
Course. Second year. (In four sections). Richmond,
Presbyterian Committee of Publication, © 1918. 335 p.
Section One is The teaching value of the Old Testament,
by Walter W. Moore and Edward Mack. H U

3778 A TRIBUTE to the memory of John McClure. Containing the
resolutions of the session; an obituary notice by A. N. H.
Funeral sermon, delivered at his late residence, Thursday
morning, February 13th, 1873, and memorial discourse,
delivered at the Fairview Presbyterian Church by his pastor, Rev. A. Nelson Hollifield. Philadelphia, Richard
Magee, 1873. 29 p. PH

3779 TRIBUTES to the memory of Rev. Irwin Lamar Cunningham
by Rev. W. H. McCullough [and others]. [Graham, Tex.,
Graham Printing Co.], n.d. 24 p. H

3780 *TRIMBLE, J. G.
Dobyns' day; address given ... on William Ray Dobyns,
D.D., LL.D. Point Lookout, Mo., n.p., n.d. 8 p. H

3781 TROSTLE, John Adams, 1874-1948.
Timber Ridge Presbyterian Church, Rockbridge County,
Virginia.... Handbook and historical sketch. n.p., 1906.
21 p. U

3782 *TRUMBULL, Charles Gallaudet, 1872-1941.
The life story of C. I. Scofield. New York, Oxford University Press, © 1920. 138 p. H R U

3783 TUBBS, Ace Leonard, 1922-
Divorce counseling; a workbook for the couple and their counselor. Danville, Ill., Interstate Printers & Publishers, © 1973. 89 p. C

3784 TUCKER, Grayson Letcher, 1924-
Person-to-person evangelism: a model of sharing God's good news through personal experiences. New York, Program of the United Presbyterian Church in the U.S.A., © 1979. 50 p. C L

3785 TUNYOGI, Andrew Csapo, 1907-
Divine struggle for human salvation: Biblical convictions in their historical setting. [Washington, D.C.], University Press of America, © 1979. 474 p. C R

3786 TUNYOGI, Andrew Csapo, 1907-
The rebellions of Israel. Richmond, John Knox Press, © 1969. 158 p. A C H L PT R U

3787 TURNAGE, Maclyn Neil, 1927-
Explorations into faith; leader's guide. A course for youth preparing to be confirmed/commissioned, by Mac N. and Anne Shaw Turnage. [Philadelphia], Geneva Press, © 1977. 128 p. "Companion piece to Explorations into faith; a journal." L PH U

3788 TURNAGE, Maclyn Neil, 1927-
Leader's guide to Bible studies for modern man, [by] Mac N. and Anne Shaw Turnage. Richmond, John Knox Press, © 1973. 127 p. (The Covenant Life Curriculum.) C L U

3789 TURNAGE, Maclyn Neil, 1927-
Leader's resources for adult communicants' classes, including guide for Toward responsible discipleship [by William B. Ward], by Mac and Anne Turnage. Richmond, John Knox Press, © 1961. 77 p. C H U

3790 TURNAGE, Maclyn Neil, 1927-
More than you dare to ask: the first year of living with cancer, by Mac N. and Anne Shaw Turnage. Atlanta, John Knox Press, © 1976. 114 p. A C H L R U

3791 TURNAGE, Maclyn Neil, 1927-
The mystery of prayer, [by] Mac N. and Anne Shaw Turnage. Richmond, CLC Press, © 1964. 48 p. (The Covenant Life Curriculum.) C U ... L: [1966].

3792 TURNAGE, Maclyn Neil, 1927-

People, families & God: a study guide for participants, by Mac N. and Anne Shaw Turnage. Atlanta, John Knox Press, © 1976. 79 p. A C H L PT R U

3793 TURNAGE, Maclyn Neil, 1927-
Study-action manual on global consciousness, [by] Mac N. and Anne Shaw Turnage. New York, Friendship Press, [1974]. 63 p. U

3794 TURNBULL, Martin Ryerson, 1886-1949.
... Etude personelle de l'évangile selon Saint Marc. (Traduction R. de Jarnac.) Sumeme (Gard), Publications Evangeliques, 1933. 208 p. At head of title: La Bible et l'adult. H

3795 TURNBULL, Martin Ryerson, 1886-1949.
Studying the book of Exodus; a guide to direct you in your own study of the book of Exodus. Richmond, Presbyterian Committee of Publication, © 1925. 110 p. A C H L R U ... U: 2d ed. Richmond, John Knox Press, [1947]. 63 p.

3796 TURNBULL, Martin Ryerson, 1886-1949.
Studying the book of Genesis; a guide to direct you in your own study of the book of Genesis. Richmond, Presbyterian Committee of Publication, © 1924. 120 p. C H U ... R: [1928] ... L: [1935].

3797 TURNBULL, Martin Ryerson, 1886-1949.
Studying the book of Leviticus; a guide to direct you in your own study of the book of Leviticus. Richmond, Presbyterian Committee of Publication, © 1926. 109 p. C H U

3798 TURNBULL, Martin Ryerson, 1886-1949.
Studying the Epistle to the Hebrews; a guide to direct you in your own study of this epistle. Richmond, Presbyterian Committee of Publication, © 1927. 125 p. C H L U ... A: The students handbook. n.d. 32 p. ... C R U: Special teachers' text-book edition. 128 p.

3799 TURNBULL, Martin Ryerson, 1886-1949.
Suggestions for leaders of classes in "Studying the book of Genesis." Richmond, Presbyterian Committee of Publication, n.d. 32 p. H U

3800 TURNER, Herbert Snipes, 1891-1976.
Bethel and her ministers, 1746-1946. n.p., © 1946. 208 p. H U ... H PT: 2d ed. Verona, Va., McClure Print. Co., 1974. 271 p.

3801 TURNER, Herbert Snipes, 1891-1976.
Church in the old fields: Hawfields Presbyterian Church

and community in North Carolina. Chapel Hill, University of
North Carolina Press, © 1962. 297 p. A C H PH U

3802 TURNER, Herbert Snipes, 1891-1976.
The dreamer, Archibald DeBow Murphey, 1777-1832.
[Verona, Va.], McClure Press, © 1971. 259 p. H

3803 TUTTLE, Romulus Morris, 1842-1904.
Tuttle's poems. Dallas, Tex., W. M. Warlick, 1905.
444 p. C H U

3804 TYLER, James W., 1869-1924.
Affusion the only scriptural baptism. Richmond, Presby-
terian Committee of Publication, © 1898. 39 p. PT U ...
U: 2d ed. [1913]. 28 p.

3805 TYLER, James W., 1869-1924.
The southern mountaineer. Atlanta, Executive Committee
of Home Missions, Presbyterian Church in the U.S., [1915].
4 ℓ. U

3806 UNGER, James Kelly, 1893-
Am I a good or bad investment for God? Meridian, Miss.,
J. Kelly Unger, © 1968. 158 p. C R

3807 UNGER, James Kelly, 1893-
The great delusion. Weaverville, N.C., Southern Presby-
terian Journal, 1945. 8 p. Reprinted from the Southern
Presbyterian Journal, March, 1945. PH

3808 UNGER, James Kelly, 1893-
Housekeeping in Korea. n.p., [1932?]. 4 p. U

3809 UNGER, James Kelly, 1893-
Leper work in Korea at Biederwolf home, Soonchun, by
James K. Unger and Robert M. Wilson. n.p., n.d. 24 p.
U

3810 UNGER, James Kelly, 1893-
Peter, before and after the infilling of the Holy Spirit.
Soonchun, Korea, n.p., 1931. 41 p. Sermon on Acts 1:8.
A PT

3811 UNION Theological Seminary in Virginia.
Centennial general catalogue of the trustees, officers,
professors and alumni of Union Theological Seminary in Vir-
ginia, 1807-1907. Edited by Walter W. Moore and Tilden
Scherer. Richmond, Whittet & Shepperson, n.d. 189 p.
A C H PH PT R U

3812 UNION Theological Seminary in Virginia.
Ernest Trice Thompson: an appreciation. Richmond,
Union Theological Seminary, 1964. 52 p. A C PT R U

3813 UNION Theological Seminary in Virginia.
Exercises in connection with the inauguration of the Rev.
Walter W. Moore, D.D., LL.D., as President of Union
Theological Seminary, Richmond, Va., May 9, 1905. Rich-
mond, L. D. Sullivan & Co., [1905?]. 50 p. Participating
were J. W. Rosebro, Egbert W. Smith, Walter W. Moore,
Charles R. Hemphill, Robert Dick Wilson, and others. A
C PT U

3814 UNION Theological Seminary in Virginia.
A general catalog of trustees, officers, professors, and
students of Union Theological Seminary in Virginia, compiled
by Eleanor R. Millard, and A history of Union Theological
Seminary in Virginia, by Ernest Trice Thompson. Balmer
H. Kelly, editor. [Richmond, Union Theological Seminary in
Virginia, 1978?]. 510 p. C H L PH PT U

3815 UNION Theological Seminary in Virginia.
General catalogue of the trustees, officers, professors,
and alumni of Union Theological Seminary in Virginia, 1807-
1924. Edited by Walter W. Moore, William R. Miller, and
John A. Lacy. Richmond, Whittet & Shepperson, 1924.
293 p. A C H L PH PT R U

3816 UNION Theological Seminary in Virginia.
Inauguration of James Archibald Jones as the third Presi-
dent of Union Theological Seminary in Virginia. [Richmond,
Whittet & Shepperson], 1956. unpaged. A C PH PT U

3817 UNION Theological Seminary in Virginia.
Installation of the Rev. J. F. Latimer as Professor of
Ecclesiastical History and Polity, on May 6, 1885. Addresses
of the Rev. H. M. White and of the Rev. Prof. Latimer. Also address of the Rev. J. J. Bullock, D.D., to the graduating
class of 1885. Richmond, Whittet & Shepperson, 1885. 31 p.
C PH U

3818 UNION Theological Seminary in Virginia.
Our Protestant heritage, by members of the faculty of
Union Theological Seminary in Virginia. Richmond, John Knox
Press, © 1948. 224 p. A series of lectures given in 1946.
Contents.--From patriarch and prophet, by John Bright.--
Through history and wisdom, by Balmer H. Kelly.--In the
word incarnate, by Donald G. Miller.--Shaped by the master-
builder, by James E. Bear.--Through growth and decay, by
Ernest Trice Thompson.--Protesting for the truth, by John
Newton Thomas.--A dynamic tradition, by Benjamin Rice
Lacy, Jr. A C H L PH PT R U

3819 UNION Theological Seminary in Virginia.
Septuagesimal celebration of Union Theological Seminary in
Virginia. 1824-1894. Richmond, Whittet & Shepperson, 1894.

76 p.   Participating were W. W. Moore, Robert Burwell,
Moses D. Hoge, C. R. Vaughan, C. C. Hersman, and others.
PT U

3820   UNION Theological Seminary in Virginia.
    Walter W. Moore memorial number.   Richmond, Union
Theological Seminary, 1926.   The Union Seminary Review,
October, 1926.   Articles by Thomas Cary Johnson, Benja-
min Rice Lacy, Jr., A. D. P. Gilmour, James I. Vance,
J. G. McAllister, A. M. Fraser, Frank T. McFaden, Wil-
liam E. Hill, Walter L. Lingle, R. F. Campbell, D. M.
Sweets, C. R. Hemphill, E. W. McCorkle, E. W. Smith,
W. S. Campbell.   H U

3821   UNION Theological Seminary in Virginia.   Bibliographical
lecture.
    Developing lines of theological thought in Germany, by
Martin Noth.   Translated by John Bright.   [Richmond], Union
Theological Seminary in Virginia, 1963.   29 p.   C U

3822   UNION Theological Seminary in Virginia.   Bibliographical
lecture.
    The main lines of development in systematic theology and
Biblical interpretation in Scandinavia, by Gustaf Wingren.
Translated by J. A. Ross Mackenzie.   Richmond, The Li-
brary, Union Theological Seminary in Virginia, 1964.   23 p.
C U

3823   UNION Theological Seminary in Virginia.   Library.
    An index to Sketches of Virginia, historical and biographi-
cal, by William Henry Foote.   Richmond, The Library,
Union Theological Seminary in Virginia, 1966.   52 unnum-
bered pages.   A C H L PH PT R U

3824   THE USE of the Old Testament in the New and other essays;
studies in honor of William Franklin Stinespring.   Edited
by James M. Efird.   Durham, N.C., Duke University
Press, 1972.   332 p.   A C L PT R U

3825   VANCE, James Isaac, 1862-1939.
    Being a preacher: a study of the claims of the Christian
ministry.   New York, Fleming H. Revell Co., © 1923.
171 p.   The Sprunt Lectures, 1923.   A C H L PT R U

3826   VANCE, James Isaac, 1862-1939.
    Christian fundamentals.   Sermon preached in the First
Presbyterian Church, Nashville, Tenn., Sunday, February 3,
1924, and published by the session.   n.p., n.d.   17 p.   U

3827   VANCE, James Isaac, 1862-1939.
    The church and the hour.   [Montreat, N.C., Assembly's
Stewardship Committee, Presbyterian Church in the U.S.],
n.d.   2 ℓ.   U

3828 VANCE, James Isaac, 1862-1939.
Church portals. Richmond, Presbyterian Committee of
Publication, 1895. 145 p. A C H PH R U

3829 VANCE, James Isaac, 1862-1939.
The college girl's religious problems. Sermon preached ...
in the First Presbyterian Church, Nashville, Tenn., Sunday
morning, March 7th, 1926, and published by the session.
n.p., n.d. 16 p. C

3830 VANCE, James Isaac, 1862-1939.
The college of apostles; a study of the twelve. New York,
Fleming H. Revell Co., © 1896. 160 p. H PH R U ...
PT R: © 1935.

3831 VANCE, James Isaac, 1862-1939.
The diet for a sick church. Nashville, Tenn., Executive
Committee of Foreign Missions, Presbyterian Church in the
U.S., n.d. 16 p. U

3832 VANCE, James Isaac, 1862-1939.
The eternal in man. New York, Fleming H. Revell Co.,
© 1907. 240 p. A C H PT R U

3833 VANCE, James Isaac, 1862-1939.
Family worship. n.p., Committee on Evangelistic Work,
Reformed Church in America, 1905. 16 p. PH

3834 VANCE, James Isaac, 1862-1939.
The field is the world. Richmond, Presbyterian Committee
of Publication, © 1930. 164 p. A C H L PH PT R U

3835 VANCE, James Isaac, 1862-1939.
"Forbid him not": messages for our day and time. New
York, Fleming H. Revell Co., © 1925. 201 p. C H L R
U

3836 VANCE, James Isaac, 1862-1939.
Fundamentalism, liberalism, tolerance. Sermon preached
in the First Presbyterian Church, Nashville, Tenn., Sunday,
June 17, 1923, and published by the session. n.p., n.d.
17 p. U

3837 VANCE, James Isaac, 1862-1939.
God's open: sermons that take us out-of-doors. New
York, Fleming H. Revell Co., © 1924. 204 p. A C H L
PT R U

3838 VANCE, James Isaac, 1862-1939.
In the breaking of the bread: a volume of communion ad-
dresses. New York, Fleming H. Revell Co., © 1922. 183 p.
C H L PH PT R U

3839 VANCE, James Isaac, 1862-1939.
John Calvin the citizen. Richmond, Union Theological
Seminary in Virginia, 1935. 7 p. Reprinted from the Union
Seminary Review, October, 1935. A PH

3840 VANCE, James Isaac, 1862-1939.
Let not your heart be troubled: communion addresses.
New York, Fleming H. Revell Co., © 1934. 128 p. H PT
R

3841 VANCE, James Isaac, 1862-1939.
The life of service; some Christian doctrines from Paul's
experience in the Epistle to the Romans. New York, Fleming H. Revell Co., © 1918. 219 p. A H L PT R U

3842 VANCE, James Isaac, 1862-1939.
Life's terminals. New York, Fleming H. Revell Co.,
© 1917. 47 p. A H R U

3843 VANCE, James Isaac, 1862-1939.
Love trails of the long ago. New York, Fleming H.
Revell Co., © 1927. 174 p. A C H L PT R U

3844 VANCE, James Isaac, 1862-1939.
Predestination. A sermon. Richmond, Presbyterian
Committee of Publication, © 1898. 32 p. H PT

3845 VANCE, James Isaac, 1862-1939.
The rise of a soul: a stimulus to personal progress and
development. New York, Fleming H. Revell Co., 1902.
241 p. A C H L PT R U

3846 VANCE, James Isaac, 1862-1939.
Royal manhood. New York, Fleming H. Revell Co.,
1899. 251 p. A C H U ... R: 1903.

3847 VANCE, James Isaac, 1862-1939.
Sermons in argot. New York, Richard R. Smith, 1931.
180 p. A H L PT R U

3848 VANCE, James Isaac, 1862-1939.
The silver on the iron cross. New York, Fleming H.
Revell Co., © 1919. 122 p. H L U

3849 VANCE, James Isaac, 1862-1939.
Simplicity in life. Chicago, Winona Publishing Co.,
© 1903. 38 p. H L PH

3850 VANCE, James Isaac, 1862-1939.
Tendency: the effect of trend and drift in the development of life. New York, Fleming H. Revell Co., © 1910.
247 p. A C H L PT R U

3851 VANCE, James Isaac, 1862-1939.
This dreamer; addresses on achieving faith. New York,
Fleming H. Revell Co., © 1929. 157 p. H L PT R U

3852 VANCE, James Isaac, 1862-1939.
"Thus pray ye." New York, Fleming H. Revell Co.,
© 1935. 90 p. A H PT R

3853 VANCE, James Isaac, 1862-1939.
William the silent. Richmond, Union Theological Semi-
nary in Virginia, 1934. 12 p. Reprinted from the Union
Seminary Review, October, 1934. A H

3854 VANCE, James Isaac, 1862-1939.
Worship God! New York, Fleming H. Revell Co., © 1932.
153 p. A C H PT R U

3855 VANCE, James Isaac, 1862-1939.
The young man foursquare. New York, Fleming H. Revell Co., © 1894. 104 p. A C H PT R

3856 VANCE, James Isaac, 1862-1939.
A young man's makeup. New York, Fleming H. Revell,
Co., © 1904. 150 p. L R ... C: [3d ed.]

3857 VANCE, Joseph Anderson, 1864-1951.
America's future religion. New York, Fleming H. Revell
Co., © 1927. 160 p. A C H L PH PT

3858 VANCE, Joseph Anderson, 1864-1951.
Five reasons. [New York, Evangelism, Board of National
Missions], n.d. 7 p. PH

3859 VANCE, Joseph Anderson, 1864-1951.
The glory way. Bristol, Tenn.-Va., King Printing Co.,
1949. 221 p. PH

3860 VANCE, Joseph Anderson, 1864-1951.
Religion and money. Chicago, Winona Publishing Co.,
© 1903. 40 p. L

3861 VANCE, Joseph Anderson, 1864-1951.
This Christian religion of ours. Sermon by ... retiring
moderator of the General Assembly, Presbyterian Church in
the U.S.A., delivered at Syracuse, New York, May 28, 1936.
Philadelphia, Publicity Department of the General Assembly,
n.d. 19 p. PH

3862 VANCE, Joseph Anderson, 1864-1951.
The upward way. [Bristol, Tenn., King Printing Co.],
1945. 226 p. C PH U

3863 VANCE, Joseph Anderson, 1864-1951.

The way of the cross. New York, Fleming H. Revell Co., © 1935. 62 p. L PH PT R

3864 VANCE, Joseph Anderson, 1864-1951.
The Westminster Assembly and its confession. A sermon, preached to the congregation of the Maryland Avenue Presbyterian Church, Baltimore, Md., Sunday, May 16, 1897. Richmond, Whittet & Shepperson, 1897. 24 p. U

3865 VANCE, Joseph Anderson, 1864-1951.
What is this Christian religion? [New York, Evangelism, Board of National Missions], n.d. 11 p. PH

3866 *VAN COURT, John H.
Review of ecclesiastical proceedings connected with the complaints of Rev. John A. Smylie, against the Presbytery of Louisiana and Synod of Mississippi. Baton Rouge, "Democratic Advocate" Office, 1850. 56, 31 p. Includes minutes of the special meeting of the Presbytery of Louisiana, July 23, 1850. C PH PT

3867 VANDER MEULEN, John Marinus, 1870-1936.
The faith of Christendom: a series of studies on the Apostles' Creed. Richmond, Presbyterian Committee of Publication, 1936. 285 p. A C H L PT R U ... R U: Grand Rapids, Mich., Church Press, 1946.

3868 VANDER MEULEN, John Marinus, 1870-1936.
Getting out of the rough. New York, George H. Doran Co., © 1926. 143 p. A C L U

3869 *VANDER MEULEN, Mary M., comp.
The Reverend John Marinus Vander Meulen, D.D., LL.D. Joined the Church Triumphant June 7, 1936. n.p., 1936. 147 p. PT U

3870 VAN DEVANTER, James Nichols, 1857-1917.
History of the Augusta Church, from 1737 to 1900. Staunton, Va., Ross Printing Co., 1900. 71 p. A C H R U

3871 VAN METER, John Stonestreet, 1845-1904.
That communion wine. Humorous but thoroughly good natured reply to Dr. Witherspoon's reflections upon the Hot Springs communion wine. Little Rock, Ark., Tunnah & Pittard, 1892. 20 p. Reprinted from the Arkansas Presbyterian, September, 1892. PT

3872 *VAN NOPPEN, Charles Leonard, comp.
In memoriam: George Washington Watts. Greensboro, N.C., Privately printed, 1922. 157 p. Contributions by W. W. Moore, E. R. Leyburn, and others. H U

3873 VAN SAUN, Arthur Carlos, 1893-1969.

Replanning the rural church. [Quincy, Pa., Quincy Orphanage Press, 1934]. 178 p. Thesis (Ph.D.)--Pennsyl-
vania State College, 1932. C H

3874 VARDELL, Charles Graves, 1860-1958.
The Annunciation. n.p., n.d. 4 ℓ. A poem. PT U

3875 VASS, Lachlan Cumming, 1831-1896.
Amusements and the Christian life in the primitive church
and in our day. Philadelphia, Presbyterian Board of Publication, © 1884. 91 p. A H L PH U

3876 VASS, Lachlan Cumming, 1831-1896.
History of the Presbyterian Church in New Bern, N.C.,
with a resumé of early ecclesiastical affairs in eastern North
Carolina, and a sketch of the early days of New Bern. Rich-
mond, Whittet & Shepperson, 1886. 196 p. A C H PH PT
U

3877 VAUGHAN, Clement Read, 1827-1911.
The character of the church of Rome, a sermon preached
before the Synod of Virginia, in Lexington, October 26, 1855.
Philadelphia, Presbyterian Board of Publication, 1856. 51 p.
C H PH U

3878 VAUGHAN, Clement Read, 1827-1911.
The deacon's office. Richmond, Presbyterian Committee
of Publication, © 1897. 25 p. U

3879 VAUGHAN, Clement Read, 1827-1911.
Fidelity to the truth. A sermon preached at the opening
of the Synod of Virginia in Charlottesville, Va., Oct. 30th,
1883. Charlottesville, Jeffersonian Publishing Co., 1883.
17 p. U

3880 VAUGHAN, Clement Read, 1827-1911.
The gifts of the Holy Spirit to unbelievers and believers.
Richmond, Presbyterian Committee of Publication, 1894.
415 p. A C H L R U ... PT R: Edinburgh, Banner of
Truth Trust, 1975.

3881 VAUGHAN, Clement Read, 1827-1911.
Organic union. Atlanta, Constitution Publishing Co.,
1887. 38 p. Reprinted from the Presbyterian Quarterly,
October, 1887. U

3882 VAUGHAN, Clement Read, 1827-1911.
The proposed alliance. Richmond, Whittet & Shepperson,
1905. 28 p. Reprinted from the Central Presbyterian. U

3883 VAUGHAN, Clement Read, 1827-1911.
Reply to Dr. S. I. Baird's pamphlet in favor of organic
union. n.p., 1888. 24 p. C H

3884 VAUGHAN, Clement Read, 1827-1911.
Representative government in the church. n.p., n.d.
561-589 p. Reprinted from the Presbyterian Quarterly,
October, 1890. U

3885 VAUGHAN, Clement Read, 1827-1911.
Sermons: apologetic, doctrinal and miscellaneous. Rich-
mond, Presbyterian Committee of Publication, © 1902. 363 p.
A C H L R U

3886 VAUGHAN, Robert Crews, 1919-
A pattern of prayer; seven sermons on the Lord's Prayer.
[Petersburg, Va., Second Presbyterian Church], 1966. 43 p.
U

3887 VAUGHAN, Robert Crews, 1919-
Three messages from Second Presbyterian Church, Peters-
burg, Virginia. [Petersburg, Va., Second Presbyterian
Church, 1970]. 34 p. Cover title: Three Advent sermons.
U

3888 VEDDER, Charles Stuart, 1826-1916.
Huguenot Church of Charleston, S.C., an apostolic and
true church. Charleston, Walker, Evans, & Cogswell, 1880.
32 p. H

3889 VENABLE, Sidney Johnson, 1894-
A practical method in personal evangelism, suggested for
pastors in training personal workers. Atlanta, Assembly's
Committee on Evangelism, [Presbyterian Church in the U.S.],
n.d. 28 p. C U

3890 VERNER, Samuel Phillips, 1873-
Pioneering in central Africa. Richmond, Presbyterian
Committee of Publication, 1903. 500 p. A C H L PH PT
R U

3891 VICK, George Henry, 1912-
The minister and the ministers of tomorrow. [Richmond,
Board of Christian Education, Presbyterian Church in the
U.S.], n.d. unpaged. U

3892 THE VICTORY won: a memorial of the Rev. William J. Hoge,
D.D., late pastor of the Tabb Street Presbyterian Church,
Petersburg, Va., by Moses D. Hoge and Thomas Verner
Moore. Richmond, Presbyterian Committee of Publication,
1864. 16 p. U

3893 VIEHE, Frederick Dana, 1878-1940, comp.
Proof texts to Dabney's theology. Richmond, Union Seminary Publishing Co., © 1901. 350 p. A C L R U

3894 VINSON, John Walker, 1914-

Jack Vinson tells why I became a missionary to Japan.
[Nashville, Tenn., Board of World Missions, Presbyterian
Church in the U.S., 1951?]. 4 p. U

3895 VINSON, Robert Ernest, 1876-1945.
The assembly's budget and how apportioned. Jackson,
Miss., Tucker Printing House, n.d. 16 p. U

3896 VINSON, Thomas Chalmers 1887-1961.
Rev. William McCutchen Morrison, D.D.; a prince among
the great missionaries of modern times. Nashville, Tenn.,
Executive Committee of Foreign Missions, Presbyterian
Church in the U.S., n.d. 8 p. H U

3897 VINSON, Thomas Chalmers, 1887-1961.
William McCutchan Morrison, twenty years in central
Africa. Richmond, Presbyterian Committee of Publication,
1921. 201 p. A C H L PH PT R U

3898 VOSS, Louis, 1856-1936.
The beginnings of Presbyterianism in the Southwest. New
Orleans, Presbyterian Board of Publication of the Synod of
Louisiana, 1923. 50 p. A H PH PT U

3899 VOSS, Louis, 1856-1936.
History of the First Street Presbyterian Church ... read
at its seventy-fifth anniversary. [New Orleans], Presbyterian Board of Publication of the Synod of Louisiana, 1929.
32 p. A C H L PH PT R U

3900 VOSS, Louis, 1856-1936, comp.
Presbyterianism in New Orleans and adjacent points: its
semi-centennial held in 1873, seventy-fifth anniversary of the
organization of New Orleans Presbytery, 1930. Sketches of
individual churches, ministers and ruling elders. [New Or-
leans], Presbyterian Board of Publication of the Synod of
Louisiana, 1931. 416 p. A C H L PH PT R U

3901 WADDEL, John Newton, 1812-1895.
Address, on occasion of laying the foundation of the Pres-
byterial Fem. Col. Institute, at Pontotoc, May 6, 1854.
Holly Springs, "Miss. Times" Cheap Book and Job Office
Print., 1854. 14 p. H

3902 WADDEL, John Newton, 1812-1895.
Address on public education, delivered in the Hall of
Representatives, by joint invitation of the Senate and House
of Representatives, in Jackson, Miss., on the evening of
Wednesday, 25th, October, 1865. Jackson, J. J. Shannon
& Co., 1865. 15 p. H

3903 WADDEL, John Newton, 1812-1895.

Inaugural address, on the nature and advantages of the course of study in institutions of the higher learning; delivered on occasion of the inauguration of the faculty of the University of Mississippi, July 28th, 1866. Natchez, Miss., Daily Courier Book and Job Office, n.d. 28 p. H

3904 WADDEL, John Newton, 1812-1895.
Memorials of academic life: being an historical sketch of the Waddel family, identified through three generations with the history of higher education in the South and Southwest. Richmond, Presbyterian Committee of Publication, 1891. 583 p. A C H L PT R U

3905 WADDEL, John Newton, 1812-1895.
Moral heroism: an oration delivered before the Ciceronian and Phi-Delta societies of Mercer University, Penfield, Georgia, on commencement day, July 28, 1852. Penfield, Banner Office, 1852. 26 p. PT

3906 WADDELL, James Addison, 1817-1905.
Letters to a young Presbyterian. Richmond, Presbyterian Committee of Publication, 1895. 119 p. A H R

3907 WADDELL, James Addison, 1817-1905.
"Uncle Tom's Cabin" reviewed; or, American society vindicated from the aspersions of Mrs. Harriet Beecher Stowe. Raleigh, "Southern Weekly Post," 1852. 68 p. PH

3908 *WADE, Grace Adelaide (Van Duyn), 1883-
Our life story, by Grace Adelaide Van Duyn Wade and Joel Taylor Wade. Chattanooga, Tenn., George C. Hudson Co., 1954. 692 p. A C H L PH U

3909 WADE, Joel Taylor, 1862-1957.
Sermons. [Chattanooga?], n.p., © 1949. 112 p. A C H L U

3910 WAGGETT, John MacPhail, 1884-1969.
Bible landmarks in a changing land.... Introduction by Prof. Ernest Trice Thompson. New York, Fleming H. Revell Co., © 1930. 130 p. A C H PT R U

3911 WAGGETT, John MacPhail, 1884-1969.
Mental, divine and faith healings, their explanation and place. Boston, Richard G. Badger, © 1919. 259 p. PT U

3912 WAGNER, James Benjamin, 1929-
Ascendit ad coelos. The doctrine of the Ascension in the Reformed and Lutheran theology of the period of orthodoxy. Winterthur, P. G. Keller, 1964. 147 p. Diss.--Univ. of Basel. A C PT U

3913 WALDEN, Julius Walker, 1851-1916.
A sermon on the death of President Garfield, preached at Park Presbyterian Church, Dayton, Ohio, Sunday, September 25, 1881. n.p., n.d. 12 p. PH

3914 WALKER, Hugh Kelso, 1861-1949.
Moderator's sermon delivered at opening meeting of General Assembly, Presbyterian Church in the U.S.A., St. Paul, Minnesota, May 23, 1929. Philadelphia, General Assembly's Publicity Dept., 1929. 15 p. PH

3915 WALKER, Hugh Kelso, 1861-1949.
The plain duty of churchmen in the present crisis: is every Presbyterian pulpit as positive as this article on the issue in the coming election? n.p., n.d. 1 p. Reprinted from the Presbyterian Magazine, October, 1928. PH

3916 WALKUP, Robert Lee, 1880-1918.
A catechism on Christian stewardship. Chattanooga, Tenn., General Assembly's Stewardship Committee, Presbyterian Church in the U.S., n.d. 15 p. PH ... PH: Rev. 1922. 16 p.

3917 WALLACE, James Albert, 1810-1880.
History of Williamsburg Church. A discourse delivered on occasion of the 120th anniversary of the Williamsburg Church, July 4th, 1856, Kingstree, S.C. Salisbury, N.C., Bell & James, 1856. 122 p. PH

3918 WALLACE, James Albert, 1810-1880.
Jonah, or the sleeper awakened. Philadelphia, Presbyterian Board of Publication, n.d. 16 p. (Presbyterian Tracts, no. 195.) C H L PH PT R U

3919 WALSH, Clyde Jones, 1888-1947.
Why go to church? A timely question. n.p., n.d. 4 p. U

3920 WALTERS, Carl Franklin, 1934-
I, Mark: a personal encounter: explorations in the earliest Gospel. Atlanta, John Knox Press, © 1980. 142 p. A C H L U

3921 WALTHALL, David Barclay, 1902-
A guide for Presbyterian church schools. Richmond, John Knox Press, © 1951. 80 p. A U ... C: [Rev. ed. 1954] ... C U: [1955] ... L: [1962].

3922 WALTHALL, David Barclay Kirby, 1866-1951.
Everlasting punishment. Richmond, Whittet & Shepperson, n.d. 26 p. U

3923 WALTON, Robert Augustus, 1857-1911.

The Holy Spirit our teacher in prayer; or, The conditions upon which God answers prayer. Chicago, Winona Publishing Co., 1904. 132 p. A L U

3924 *WARD, Carolyn S.
Bible homes and family life today, by Carolyn S. and William B. Ward. Leader's guide (Circle Bible study). Atlanta, Board of Women's Work, Presbyterian Church in the U.S., [1955]. 96 p. H U

3925 WARD, William Bethea, 1912-
After death, what? Richmond, John Knox Press, © 1965. 95 p. A C H L R U

3926 WARD, William Bethea, 1912-
Beliefs that live. Richmond, John Knox Press, © 1963. 126 p. A C H L R U

3927 WARD, William Bethea, 1912-
The divine physician: devotions for the sick. Richmond, John Knox Press, © 1953. unpaged. A C H L U ... C L U: Enl. ed. [1957].

3928 WARD, William Bethea, 1912-
Out of the whirlwind: answers to the problem of suffering from the book of Job. Richmond, John Knox Press, © 1958. 123 p. A C H L PT R U ... C: 1962.

3929 WARD, William Bethea, 1912-
Toward responsible discipleship. Richmond, John Knox Press, © 1960. 86 p. A C H L U

3930 WARD, William Bethea, 1912-
When you're married: a book of devotions for newly married couples. [Richmond, John Knox Press], © 1947. 38 p. U ... C: [1955].

3931 WARDLAW, Thomas DeLacy, 1826-1879.
A discourse on the doctrine of divine providence ... preached in the Presbyterian Church, Cynthiana, Ky. Cincinnati, John D. Thorpe, 1857. 16 p. PH

3932 WARDLAW, Thomas DeLacy, 1826-1879.
Thanksgiving discourse, and the true glory of a nation. Two sermons. Cincinnati, Longley Brothers, 1854. 29, 258-271 p. PH

3933 WARREN, Thomas Brunson, 1921-
History of Marl Bluff Presbyterian Church, Henderson County, Tenn. n.p., n.d. 7 p. H

3934 *WASHBURN, Cephas.

Reminiscences of the Indians.... With a biography of the author by Rev. J. W. Moore, of Arkansas, and an introduction by Rev. J. L. Wilson. Richmond, Presbyterian Committee of Publication, © 1869. 236 p.   PH

3935 WASHBURN, Edmund Emory, 1889-1925.
Foreign work in the Birmingham district. Atlanta, Executive Committee of Home Missions, Presbyterian Church in the U.S., n.d.   3 ℓ.   U

3936 WASHBURN, Hezekiah M., 1884-1972.
A knight in the Congo: God's ambassador in three continents. [Bassett, Va., Printing Corp.], © 1972.   240 p.
C U

3937 WASHINGTON, D.C. Central Presbyterian Church.
Thirty-fourth anniversary (January 19, 1902) of the Central Presbyterian Church, Corner Third and I Streets N.W. Souvenir pamphlet composed of commemorative articles, including the anniversary sermon by Dr. Pitzer. [Washington, D.C.?], Norman T. Elliott Printing Co., [1902?].   38 p.
PH

3938 WATKINS, John Sims, 1844-1930.
A hand-book for ruling elders. Richmond, Presbyterian Committee of Publication, 1895.   128 p.   A H L PH R
U ... L: 2d ed. © 1895.

3939 WATSON, Richard Garland, 1930-
God made me laugh. Wilmington, Del., Cross Publishing, © 1974.   172 p.   Autobiographical.   R

3940 WAYLAND, John Edwin, 1893-
Wholesome truths and wholesome Bible study for all who desire to be Christians. n.p., 1933.   15 p.   U

3941 WEBB, Frank Bell, 1848-1925.
Centennial sermon of Eutaw Church ... at the Synod of Alabama, October 15, 1924. n.p., n.d.   unpaged.   PH

3942 WEBB, Frank Bell, 1848-1925.
The dead of the Synod of Alabama from 1910 to 1920. A memorial sermon. [Magic City, Ala., Magic City Printing Co.], n.d.   18 p.   H PH

3943 WEBB, Robert Alexander, 1856-1919.
Christian salvation: its doctrine and experience. Richmond, Presbyterian Committee of Publication, 1921.   437 p.
2 pts in one vol.   A C H L PT R U

3944 WEBB, Robert Alexander, 1856-1919.
The Christian's hope. Jackson, Miss., Presbyterian School

for Christian Workers, Belhaven College, 1914. 110 p. The Smyth Lectures, 1914. A C H L R U

3945 WEBB, Robert Alexander, 1856-1919.
Jesus the virgin-born. Richmond, Presbyterian Committee of Publication, n.d. 24 p. U

3946 WEBB, Robert Alexander, 1856-1919.
The Reformed doctrine of adoption. Grand Rapids, Mich., Wm. B. Eerdmans Publishing Co., 1947. 188 p. A C H L PT R U

3947 WEBB, Robert Alexander, 1856-1919.
La Salvación cristiana en doctrina y experiencia. Versión al castellano por los Rev. Abraham Fernandez y Santiago O. Sheby. Mexico, D.F., Casa Presbiteriana de Publicaciones, n.d. 472 p. Translation of his "Christian Salvation." A

3948 WEBB, Robert Alexander, 1856-1919.
The theology of infant salvation. Richmond, Presbyterian Committee of Publication, 1907. 330 p. A C H L R U

3949 WEISIGER, Cary Nelson, 1910-
The Epistles of Peter. Grand Rapids, Mich., Baker Book House, 1961. 141 p. H L U

3950 WEISIGER, Cary Nelson, 1910-
The Epistles of Peter. Grand Rapids, Mich., Baker Book House, [1972]. 141 p. (Proclaiming the New Testament, v. 5.; Ralph G. Turnbull, ed.) C R

3951 WEISIGER, Cary Nelson, 1910-
Glimpses of Africa and Asia: sermons on a world tour. n.p., [1955]. 48 p. PH

3952 WEISIGER, Cary Nelson, 1910-
The Gospel of Luke; a study manual. Grand Rapids, Mich., Baker Book House, © 1966. 128 p. R U

3953 WEISIGER, Cary Nelson, 1910-
The Reformed doctrine of sanctification. [Washington, D.C., Christianity Today, 1967]. 23 p. R

3954 *WELCH, Claude.
Religion in the undergraduate curriculum; an analysis and interpretation. With essays contributed by Beverly A. Asbury [and others]. Washington, Association of American Colleges, 1972. 129 p. A C PT U

3955 *WELCH, Mildred.
Edward Lane, 1837-1892. [Nashville, Tenn., Executive Committee of Foreign Missions, Presbyterian Church in the U.S.], n.d. unpaged. H

3956 *WELCH, Mildred.
The shepherd of Floyd. Louisville, Ky., Executive Committee of Christian Education and Ministerial Relief, Presbyterian Church in the U.S., n.d. 4 ℓ. John Kellogg Harris.
U

3957 WELCH, Thomas Rice, 1825-1886.
Half a century. A discourse delivered in the Presbyterian Church at Little Rock, Arkansas, on the 28th of July A.D. 1878, the 50th anniversary of its organization. St. Louis, Presbyterian Publishing Co., 1878. 41 p. H PH PT

3958 WELLFORD, Edwin Taliaferro, 1870-1956.
Crime and cure; a review of this lawless age and the mistrial of Christ. Boston, The Stratford Co., © 1930. 82 p.
A H

3959 WELLFORD, Edwin Taliaferro, 1870-1956.
The lynching of Jesus; a review of the legal aspects of the trial of Christ. Newport News, Va., Franklin Printing Co., 1905. 110 p. H L R U ... PT: 2d ed.

3960 WELLS, Albert Norman, 1922-
The Christian message in a scientific age. Richmond, John Knox Press, © 1962. 160 p. A C H L PT R U

3961 WELLS, Albert Norman, 1922-
Pascal's recovery of man's wholeness. Richmond, John Knox Press, © 1965. 174 p. A C H L PT R U

3962 WELLS, John Miller, 1870-1947.
Southern Presbyterian worthies. Richmond, Presbyterian Committee of Publication, © 1936. 240 p. The Sprunt Lectures, 1936. Lectures on James Henley Thornwell, John Leighton Wilson, Daniel Baker, Moses Drury Hoge, Benjamin Morgan Palmer, Givens Brown Strickler, Walter William Moore. A C H L PT R U

3963 WELLS, John Miller, 1870-1947.
Why are we Presbyterians? Buena Vista, Va., Buena Vista Publishing Co., 1895. 18 p. U

3964 *WERTENBAKER, Green Peyton, 1907-
For God and Texas; the life of P. B. Hill, by Green Peyton [pseud.]. New York, London, Whittlesey House, McGraw-Hill Book Co., © 1947. 201 p. A R U

3965 WESLEY, Thomas Dammes, 1873-1964.
Baptism into Christ or submersion and sprinkling. Richmond, Presbyterian Committee of Publication, n.d. 20 p.
U

3966 WEST, James Durham, 1838-1921.

Making offerings for the poor and other pious uses, as an individual act and as an ordinance of the church, in its relation to reform and retrenchment. Tupelo, Miss., Journal Publishing Co., 1881. 23 p. PH

3967 WEST, James Durham, 1838-1921.
The two systems of creation and providence which reveal God to man through the light of nature and of the Bible. Newton, Miss., C. E. Cunningham, 1913. 208 p. H R

3968 *WESTERHOFF, John H.
McGuffey and his readers: piety, morality, and education in nineteenth-century America. Nashville, Abingdon, © 1978. 206 p. A C H L PT R U

3969 WESTMINSTER Assembly of Divines.
A harmony of the Westminster Presbyterian standards, with explanatory notes, by James Benjamin Green. Richmond, John Knox Press, © 1951. 231 p. A C H L PH PT R U

3970 WESTMINSTER Confession of Faith.
The Westminster Confession of Faith. A new edition, edited by Douglas Kelly, Hugh McClure, and Philip B. Rollinson. [1st ed.] Greenwood, S.C., Attic Press, © 1979. 94 p. H L

3971 WHALING, Thornton, 1858-1938.
The choice of a vocation. Louisville, Ky., Executive Committee of Christian Education and Ministerial Relief, Presbyterian Church in the U.S., n.d. 15 p. U

3972 WHALING, Thornton, 1858-1938.
Jesus and Christian doctrine, Avera Bible Lectures before Trinity College, Durham, N.C., for 1914. Richmond, Presbyterian Committee of Publication, [1915]. 86 p. A C L R U

3973 WHALING, Thornton, 1858-1938.
Our church and education. Richmond, Whittet & Shepperson, 1890. 28 p. Reprinted from the Presbyterian Quarterly, October, 1890. U

3974 WHALING, Thornton, 1858-1938.
Questions on theology. Columbia, S.C., R. L. Bryan Co., 1916. 64 ℓ. A C H L R U

3975 WHALING, Thornton, 1858-1938.
Science and religion today. Chapel Hill, University of North Carolina Press, 1929. 74 p. A C H L PT R U

3976 WHALING, Thornton, 1858-1938.

What the college may do for the denomination. Louisville, Ky., Executive Committee of Christian Education and Ministerial Relief, Presbyterian Church in the U.S., n.d. 14 p. U

3977 WHARTON, Conway Taliaferro, 1890-1953.
The leopard hunts alone; the life and ways of the savages of the Congo and how Christianity was welcomed by them. New York, Fleming H. Revell Co., © 1927. 144 p. A H L U

3978 *WHARTON, Ethel Taylor.
Led in triumph. Illustrations by Claire Randall. [Nashville, Tenn.], Board of World Missions, Presbyterian Church in the U.S., © 1952. 191 p. A C H L PH R U

3979 WHARTON, Lawrence Hay, 1892-1937.
The college campus as a new missionary field. n.p., 1933. 11 p. Reprinted from the Union Seminary Review, April, 1933. U

3980 WHARTON, Lawrence Hay, 1892-1937.
Guideposts for youth: searching for right living. [2d ed.] Edited by DeWitt Reddick. Richmond, John Knox Press, © 1943. 102 p. A C H R U

3981 WHARTON, Lawrence Hay, 1892-1937.
Ten good men. [Louisville, Ky., Committee of Christian Education, Presbyterian Church in the U.S.], n.d. 11 p. PH

3982 WHARTON, Lawrence Hay, 1892-1937.
Weight or wings. [Louisville, Ky., Executive Committee of Christian Education and Ministerial Relief, Presbyterian Church in the U.S.], n.d. 10 p. A

3983 WHARTON, Robert Leslie, 1871-1960.
On the march with Cuba: the story of La Progresiva, Cardenas, Cuba. [New York, Board of National Missions, Presbyterian Church in the U.S.A., 1942]. 21 p. PH

3984 WHARTON, Turner Ashby, 1862-1935.
Then and now; a sketch of the major changes which three score years have wrought in man's attitude toward "the big faith of our fathers." [Sherman, Tex., n.p., 1935]. 109 p. U

3985 WHITE, Charles, 1827-1891.
A discourse delivered ... at Romney, W. Va., on the occasion of the death of Rev. Wm. Henry Foote, D.D., accompanied with remarks by Rev. John A. Scott and Rev. David H. Riddle, D.D., on November 24th, 1869. Baltimore, Innes & Co., [1869?]. 19 p. PH

3986 WHITE, Henry Alexander, 1861-1926.
The gospel of comfort: a historical study of the Epistle to the Hebrews. Richmond, n.p., 1891. 25 p. PT

3987 WHITE, Henry Alexander, 1861-1926.
Jesus the living one: a historical study of John's three visions. Richmond, Whittet & Shepperson, 1891. 181 p. A C H U

3988 WHITE, Henry Alexander, 1861-1926.
The making of South Carolina. New York, Silver, Burdett and Co., © 1906. 344 p. H R ... C: © 1914.

3989 WHITE, Henry Alexander, 1861-1926.
The origin of the Pentateuch in the light of the ancient monuments. Richmond, B. F. Johnson Publishing Co., 1894. 304 p. A C H L PT R U

3990 WHITE, Henry Alexander, 1861-1926.
Robert E. Lee and the Southern Confederacy, 1807-1870. New York, G. P. Putnam's Sons, 1909. 467 p. H PT R U

3991 WHITE, Henry Alexander, 1861-1926.
A school history of the United States. New York, Silver, Burdett & Co., © 1904. 422, 50 p. C R

3992 WHITE, Henry Alexander, 1861-1926.
The Scotch-Irish university of the south: Washington and Lee. n.p., n.d. 24 p. PT U

3993 WHITE, Henry Alexander, 1861-1926.
Southern Presbyterian leaders.... With portrait illustrations. New York, The Neale Publishing Co., 1911. 476 p. Biography and history: chapters on John Holt Rice, Thomas Goulding, George Howe, Aaron W. Leland, John Forrest, Thomas Smyth, Robert Hall Morrison, Daniel Baker, John McElhenny, William Swan Plumer, Charles Colcock Jones, James Henley Thornwell, Benjamin Morgan Palmer, Robert Lewis Dabney, John Leighton Wilson, Jacob Henry Smith, Stuart Robinson, John Newton Waddel, Moses Drury Hoge. A C H L PH PT R U

3994 WHITE, Henry Alexander, 1861-1926.
Stonewall Jackson. Philadelphia, George W. Jacobs & Co., [1909]. 378 p. U

3995 WHITE, Hugh Watt, 1870-1940.
Demonism verified and analyzed. Shanghai, Presbyterian Mission Press, 1922. 155 p. A C H L PH PT R U

3996 WHITE, Hugh Watt, 1870-1940.
Jesus, the missionary; studies in the life of Jesus as the master, the model, the proto-type for all missionaries. On

many scriptures, interpretations are given which have been worked out on the mission field. Shanghai, Presbyterian Mission Press, 1914. 140 p. A H PT U ... C L R: 2d ed. 1916.

3997 WHITE, Hugh Watt, 1870-1940.
Reorganization, the hope of foreign missions. Shanghai, Presbyterian Mission Press, 1917. 42 p. H U

3998 WHITE, Hugh Watt, 1870-1940.
Southern Presbyterians under fire. [Richmond, Presbyterian Committee of Publication, 1928]. 32 p. North Kiangsu mission. A H

3999 WHITE, James Spratt, 1841-1891.
A sermon descriptive of the life and labors of the Rev. William Banks, Tirzah Church, Columbia, S.C. Columbia, Presbyterian Publishing House, 1875. 30 p. H

4000 WHITE, Robert Baker, 1816-1894.
Reason and redemption, or the Gospel as it attests itself. Philadelphia, J. B. Lippincott & Co., 1873. 351 p. A C PT U

4001 WHITE, Robert Baker, 1816-1894.
A sermon, preached before the Alabama Central Sunday School Union, on its first anniversary, at Mount Pleasant Church, Tuscaloosa County, July 27th, 1851. Tuscaloosa, J. W. & J. F. Warren, 1851. 19 p. PH

4002 WHITE, Robert Baker, 1816-1894.
The tabernacles of the Lord: a sermon preached at the dedication of Mount Zion Church, Greene County, Ala., on the 13th of October, 1849. Eutaw, Houston and Nunnelee, 1849. 17 p. PH

4003 WHITE, William Spottswood, 1800-1873.
The African preacher. An authentic narrative. Philadelphia, Presbyterian Board of Publication, © 1849. 139 p. A H PH PT R U

4004 WHITE, William Spottswood, 1800-1873.
4th of July reminiscences and reflections: a sermon: preached in the Presbyterian Church, Charlottesville, July 5th, 1840. Charlottesville, R. C. Noel, 1840. 19 p. PH PT

4005 WHITE, William Spottswood, 1800-1873.
The Gospel ministry, in a series of letters from a father to his sons. Philadelphia, Presbyterian Board of Publication, © 1860. 204 p. A H PH PT U

4006 WHITE, William Spottswood, 1800-1873.

Rev. William S. White, D.D., and his times (1800-1873). An autobiography. Edited by his son, Rev. H. M. White. Richmond, Presbyterian Committee of Publication, 1891. 284 p.   A C H PH R U

4007   WHITE, William Spottswood, 1800-1873.
Sketches of the life of Captain Hugh A. White, of the Stonewall Brigade. By his father. Columbia, S.C., South Carolinian Steam Press, 1864. 124 p.   U

4008   WHITE, William Spottswood, 1800-1873.
Total abstinence. Lexington, Samuel Gillock, 1849. 21 p.   U

4009   WHITELEY, Charles Douglas, 1890-1961.
Reaching upward; or, Man's age-long search for truth. Grand Rapids, Mich., Zondervan Publishing House, © 1937. 182 p.   C H

4010   WHITENER, Henry Carroll, 1885-   tr.
Jesus Christo Tsiianishe: the birth of Jesus Christ. Albuquerque, N.M., National Missions of the Presbyterian Church, U.S.A., n.d. unpaged. Keres Indian text.   PT

4011   WIDMER, Frederick William, 1915-
Christian family education in the local church. Richmond, Board of Christian Education, Presbyterian Church in the U.S., © 1957. 62 p.   A C L U

4012   WIDMER, Frederick William, 1915-
Home and church working together: a study guide for Leadership Course 423b. Richmond, Board of Christian Education, Presbyterian Church in the U.S., © 1958. 42 p.   A C U

4013   WIDMER, Frederick William, 1915-
How home and church can work together. Illustrated by Ruth Ensign. Richmond, John Knox Press, © 1960. 94 p.   A C H L U

4014   WIDMER, Frederick William, 1915-
Living together in Christian homes: a leader's guide for Leadership Course 420b, the Christian Home. Richmond, John Knox Press, © 1956. 52 p.   A C H U

4015   WILDS, Louis Trezevant, 1885-1953.
The Holy Spirit, our spiritual mother. Richmond, John Knox Press, © 1945. 93 p.   C H L U

4016   WILDS, Louis Trezevant, 1885-1953.
On growing old. [Richmond, Executive Committee of Religious Education and Publication, Presbyterian Church in the U.S.], n.d. 7 p.   U

4017 WILDS, Louis Trezevant, 1885-1953.
      Why good people suffer. Richmond, John Knox Press,
      © 1944. 47 p. C H L R U

4018 WILEY, Calvin Henderson, 1819-1887.
      Adventures of old Dan Tucker, and his son Walter; a tale
      of North Carolina. London, Willoughby & Co., [1851].
      222 p. Published in America in 1849 as: Roanoke; or,
      Where is Utopia? U: Microfilm.

4019 WILEY, Calvin Henderson, 1819-1887.
      Alamance Church. A historical address delivered at the
      dedication of its fourth house of worship on October 18th,
      1879. Raleigh, Edwards, Broughton & Co., 1880. 46 p.
      H PH

4020 WILEY, Calvin Henderson, 1819-1887.
      Alamance: the great and final experiment. New York,
      Harper and Brothers, 1847. 151 p. H

4021 WILEY, Calvin Henderson, 1819-1887.
      Life in the South. A companion to Uncle Tom's Cabin.
      Embellished with fourteen beautiful illustrations. Phila-
      delphia, T. B. Peterson, © 1852. 144 p. U: xeroxed
      copy.

4022 WILEY, Calvin Henderson, 1819-1887.
      The North-Carolina reader: containing a history and de-
      scription of North Carolina, selections in prose and verse,
      many of them by eminent citizens of the state, historical and
      chronological tables, and a variety of miscellaneous informa-
      tion and statistics. Philadelphia, Lippincott, Grambo & Co.,
      © 1851. 359 p. H U

4023 WILEY, Calvin Henderson, 1819-1887.
      Report ... on the condition of the University of North
      Carolina. n.p., 1881. 4 p. PT

4024 WILEY, Calvin Henderson, 1819-1887.
      Scriptural views of national trials: or the true road to the
      independence and peace of the Confederate States of America.
      Greensboro, N.C., Sterling, Campbell, & Albright, 1863.
      213 p. H U

4025 WILEY, Calvin Henderson, 1819-1887.
      A sober view of the slavery question: by a citizen of the
      south. n.p., [1847?]. 8 p. H ... U: microfilm.

4026 WILLIAMS, Arthur Hayes, 1932-
      An early Christology; a systematic and exegetical investi-
      gation of the traditions contained in Hebrews, and of the im-
      plications contained in their later neglect. [Mainz], n.p.,
      1971. Diss.--Mainz. A U

4027 *WILLIAMS, David Riddle.
James H. Brookes: a memoir. St. Louis, Buschart
Brothers, 1897. 286 p. H PH R

4028 WILLIAMS, Henry Francis, 1847-1933.
How to use In four continents; suggestions for leaders in
mission study classes. Richmond, Presbyterian Committee
of Publication, n.d. 32 p. U

4029 WILLIAMS, Henry Francis, 1847-1933.
In Brazil. The Brazil mission of the Presbyterian Church
in the United States. Richmond, Presbyterian Committee of
Publication, n.d. 48 p. H

4030 WILLIAMS, Henry Francis, 1847-1933.
In China.... A sketch of the foreign missions of the
Presbyterian Church, U.S., in China. Nashville, Tenn.,
Executive Committee of Foreign Missions, [Presbyterian
Church in the U.S.], n.d. 80 p. A C H

4031 WILLIAMS, Henry Francis, 1847-1933.
In four continents: a sketch of the foreign missions of
the Presbyterian Church, U.S. Richmond, Presbyterian
Committee of Publication, 1910. 230 p. A C H L U ...
H R: 243 p. ... C: 3d ed. 249 p.

4032 WILLIAMS, Henry Francis, 1847-1933.
In seven countries: a sketch of the foreign mission fields
of the Presbyterian Church in the United States. Nashville,
Tenn., Executive Committee of Foreign Missions, (Presbyterian Church in the U.S.), n.d. 99 p. A C U

4033 WILLIAMS, Henry Francis, 1847-1933.
In South America; the Brazil missions of the Presbyterian
Church in the United States. Richmond, Presbyterian Com-
mittee of Publication, n.d. 29 p. A PH

4034 WILLIAMS, Henry Francis, 1847-1933.
In the Congo: the Congo mission of the Presbyterian
Church in the United States. Richmond, Va., Presbyterian
Committee of Publication, n.d. 31 p. R

4035 WILLIAMS, Henry Francis, 1847-1933.
Mexico and Cuba ... mission of the Presbyterian Church
in the United States. Richmond, Presbyterian Committee of
Publication, n.d. 32 p. H

4036 WILLIAMS, Henry Francis, 1847-1933.
7 reasons for mission study. Nashville, Tenn., Executive
Committee of Foreign Missions, Presbyterian Church in the
U.S., n.d. 2 ℓ. U

4037 WILLIAMS, Henry Francis, 1847-1933.

Some objections to mission study. [Nashville, Tenn., Executive Committee of Foreign Missions, Presbyterian Church in the U.S.], n.d. 2 ℓ.   U

4038   WILLIAMS, John Rodman, 1918-
Contemporary existentialism and Christian faith.   Englewood Cliffs, N.J., Prentice-Hall, © 1965. 180 p.   A C H L PH R U

4039   WILLIAMS, John Rodman, 1918-
The era of the Spirit. Plainfield, N.J., Logos International, © 1971. 119 p.   A L PT R U

4040   WILLIAMS, John Rodman, 1918-
The pentecostal reality. Plainfield, N.J., Logos International, © 1972. 109 p.   A C PT R U

4041   WILLIAMS, John Rodman, 1918-
10 teachings. Carol Stream, Ill., Creation House, © 1974. 121 p.   PT U

4042   WILLIAMS, Robert Murphy, 1868-1955.
Williams and Murphy records and related families. Raleigh, N.C., Edwards & Broughton Co., 1949. 369 p.   H

4043   WILLIAMSON, Elbert Madison, 1922-
Message to Theophilus: studies in Luke's Gospel. [Miami, Fla.: LOGOI], © 1972. 157 p.   L U

4044   *WILLIAMSON, Lamar, 1887-
... and a time to laugh; notes from the pen of an untamed iconoclast. Compiled and edited by Jerry R. Tompkins. Camden, Ark., Hurley Co., 1966. 49 p.   Excerpts from sessional records of the First Presbyterian Church of Monticello, Ark., written by Lamar Williamson.   A C U

4045   WILLIAMSON, Lamar, 1926-
God's work of art: images of the church in Ephesians. Richmond, CLC Press, © 1971. 80 p. (The Covenant Life Curriculum.)   C L U

4046   WILLIAMSON, Orin Conway, 1893-1951, comp.
Manual para comulgantes. Chilpancingo, Gro., n.p., 1924. 41 p.   PH

4047   WILLIAMSON, Robert Lewis, 1920-
Effective public prayer. Nashville, Tenn., Broadman Press, © 1960. 152 p.   A L R U

4048   WILSON, Benjamin Frank, 1863-1932.
The Christology of Genesis. n.p., n.d. 212-232 p.   Reprinted from the Presbyterian Quarterly, April, 1889.   H

4049 WILSON, Benjamin Frank, 1863-1932.
Sermon ... at Presbyterian Church, Harrisonburg, Va.,
Sunday evening, March 27th, 1910. n.p., n.d. 12 p. U

4050 WILSON, Carl, 1924-
With Christ in the school of disciple building: a study of
Christ's method of building disciples. Grand Rapids, Mich.,
Zondervan Publishing House, © 1976. 336 p. PT R U

4051 WILSON, Daniel Love, 1849-1892.
Are they lost or saved? What do Presbyterians believe
about those who die in infancy? Pulaski, Tenn., Daniel L.
Love, n.d. 15 p. PT

4052 WILSON, Goodridge Alexander, 1887-1976.
Presbyterian baptism. [Richmond, Executive Committee
of Religious Education and Publication, Presbyterian Church
in the U.S.], n.d. 8 p. U

4053 WILSON, Goodridge Alexander, 1887-1976.
Roosevelts and ranches. Texas Centennial Edition. n.p.,
© 1936. 67 p. U

4054 WILSON, Goodridge Alexander, 1887-1976.
Smyth County history and traditions.... Published in connection with the centennial celebration of Smyth County, Virginia, 1932. [Kingsport, Tenn., Kingsport Press], © 1932.
397 p. H PH U

4055 WILSON, Howard McKnight, 1900-
Great valley patriots: western Virginia in the struggle
for liberty: a Bicentennial project. [Verona, Va.], Mc-
Clure Press, © 1976. 273 p. H U

4056 WILSON, Howard McKnight, 1900-
The Lexington Presbytery heritage. The Presbytery of
Lexington and its churches in the Synod of Virginia, Pres-
byterian Church in the United States. [Verona, Va.], Mc-
Clure Press, © 1971. 510 p. A C L PH PT R U

4057 WILSON, Howard McKnight, 1900-
Presbyterian beginnings in Lower Tidewater Virginia.
[1st ed. Staunton, Va.], © 1973. 57 p. H PH U

4058 WILSON, Howard McKnight, 1900-
The Tinkling Spring, headwater of freedom: a study of
the church and her people, 1732-1952. Fishersville, Va.,
Tinkling Spring and Hermitage Presbyterian churches, 1954.
542 p. A C H L PH PT R U ... H U: [2d ed. 1974].
578 p.

4059 WILSON, John Leighton, 1809-1886.

Address on the duty of personal engagement in the work of foreign missions. Columbia, S.C., Southern Guardian Steam-power Press, 1862. 24 p.   U

4060   WILSON, John Leighton, 1809-1886.
... The agency on white men in missions to western Africa. Boston, The Board, 1848. 27 p. At head of title: American Board of Commissioners for Foreign Missions. C PH

4061   WILSON, John Leighton, 1809-1886.
The foreign slave-trade: can it be revived without violating the most sacred principles of honor, humanity, and religion? n.p., n.d. 20 p. Reprinted from the Southern Presbyterian Review, October, 1859.   H PH PT

4062   WILSON, John Leighton, 1809-1886.
Four propositions sustained against the claims of the American Home Missionary Society. Cincinnati, John L. Wilson, 1831. 19 p.   C

4063   WILSON, John Leighton, 1809-1886.
A grammar of the Mpongwe language, with vocabularies: by the missionaries of the A. B. C. F. M., Gaboon Mission, Western Africa. New York, Snowden & Prall, 1847. 94 p. C

4064   WILSON, John Leighton, 1809-1886.
The great revolt in India: its effects upon the missions of the Presbyterian Board. New York, Printed for the Board of Foreign Missions by Edward O. Jenkins, 1857. 23 p. PT

4065   WILSON, John Leighton, 1809-1886.
Relation and duties of servants and masters. Cincinnati, Isaac Hefley & Co., 1839. 34 p.   PH

4066   WILSON, John Leighton, 1809-1886.
Western Africa: its history, condition, and prospects.... With numerous engravings. New York, Harper and Brothers, 1856. 527 p.   A C H L PH PT R U

4067   WILSON, John Simpson, 1796-1873.
"The dead of the Synod of Georgia." Necrology: or, memorials of deceased ministers who have died during the first twenty years after its organization. Prepared in obedience to the order of the Synod. With a historical introduction. Atlanta, Franklin Printing House, 1869. 377 p.   C H PH R

4068   WILSON, John Simpson, 1796-1873.
Experience of the past should inspire confidence in the future. A discourse on domestic missions, delivered during

the annual sessions of Flint River Presbytery, in the Presbyterian Church, Americus, Georgia, April 3, 1852. Atlanta, Ga., Ware's Book & Job Office, 1852. 34 p. PH

4069 WILSON, John Simpson, 1796-1873.
Woman: her position in society and the means of her elevation: a discourse, preached on Sabbath morning, June 22, 1851, in the Presbyterian Church, Decatur, Georgia. Marietta, Ga., J. G. Campbell, 1851. 23 p. PH

4070 WILSON, Joseph Ruggles, 1825-1903.
Female training. A sermon delivered in the Union Church at Greenesboro, Ga., before the friends of Greenesboro Female College, May 23, 1858. Augusta, Ga., The Chronicle & Sentinel, 1858. 22 p. PH

4071 WILSON, Joseph Ruggles, 1825-1903.
Mutual relation of masters and slaves as taught in the Bible. A discourse, preached in the First Presbyterian Church, Augusta, Georgia, on Sabbath morning, Jan. 6, 1861. Augusta, Ga., The Chronicle & Sentinel, 1861. 20 p. H

4072 WILSON, Joseph Ruggles, 1825-1903.
The true idea of success in life. An address delivered before the Union and Philanthropic societies of Hampden Sidney College, June 10, 1857. Richmond, Chas. H. Wynne, 1857. 30 p. PH

4073 *WILSON, Joshua Lacy, 1774-1846.
Atonement: its necessity, nature and extent, with answers to objections. A sermon ... edited by his son, Samuel R. Wilson. Cincinnati, [Ben Franklin Print.], 1854. 30 p. PH PT

4074 WILSON, Luther Halsey, 1837-1914.
Baptism and the Holy Ghost; or, The ordinance of the Christian Church which signifies, sets forth and seals in symbol the glorious work of the third person of the Trinity in the hearts of the children of men--its mode and subjects and accompanying obligations. St. Louis, Farris, Smith & Co., 1885. 28 p. PH U

4075 WILSON, Luther Halsey, 1837-1914.
The divine and human; or, Foreordination and free-agency as illustrated in predestination and election. Richmond, Presbyterian Committee of Publication, © 1899. 110 p. R U

4076 WILSON, Luther Halsey, 1837-1914.
The lost dream; or, An exposition of the dream of Nebuchadnezzar and other dreams and visions of the book of Daniel. [Dickey? Ga.], n.p., 1906. 240 p. C L PT U

4077 WILSON, Luther Halsey, 1837-1914.
       The pattern of the house; or, A catechism upon the con-
stitution, government, discipline and worship of the Presbyterian Church. Richmond, Presbyterian Committee of Publication, 1893. 50 p.   U

4078 WILSON, Samuel Ramsey, 1818-1886.
       Beecher's slander against Dr. Wilson repelled.   n.p.,
n.d. unpaged.   PT

4079 WILSON, Samuel Ramsey, 1818-1886.
       Blot out the stars and leave the stripes! Why? The
causes and remedies of impending national calamities. An
address by ... [the] pastor of the First Presbyterian Church,
Cincinnati. Cincinnati, Ohio, J. B. Elliott, 1860. 16 p.
H PH PT

4080 WILSON, Samuel Ramsey, 1818-1886.
       Dancing. A discourse on the fashionable amusement of
dancing, delivered in the First Presbyterian Church, Cincinnati, on Sabbath evening, Nov. 26, 1854. Cincinnati, Ben
Franklin Steam Printing, 1854. 31 p.   PH

4081 WILSON, Samuel Ramsey, 1818-1886.
       ... The "declaration and testimony." Drawn by Rev. S.
R. Wilson, D.D., and numerously signed by ministers and
elders in the Synods of Kentucky and Missouri: called forth
by the action of the Old School assembly of 1865 on "The
state of the country." n.p., n.d. 50 p. At head of title:
A memorable historical document: its antecedents and its
outcome.   A C H ... U: 2d ed. By Samuel R. Wilson
and James H. Brookes. n.p., 1865. 27 p.

4082 WILSON, Samuel Ramsey, 1818-1886.
       Discourse delivered at the dedication of the Church of the
Pioneers, in the city of Cincinnati, September 21st, A. D.
1851. Cincinnati, Ohio, n.p., 1851. 35 p.   PH PT

4083 WILSON, Samuel Ramsey, 1818-1886.
       Hymns of the church, ancient and modern, for the use of
all who love to sing the praises of God in Christ, in the
family, the school, or the church; with a discourse on music
as a divine ordinance of worship. Cincinnati, Robert Clarke
& Co., 1872. 124 p.   PT ... U: 2d ed. 1873.

4084 WILSON, Samuel Ramsey, 1818-1886.
       The obligation and importance of Christian assemblies,
with a word to those by whom they are forsaken. Cincinnati,
William Overend & Co., 1856. 35 p.   PH

4085 WILSON, Samuel Ramsey, 1818-1886.
       A Pan-Presbyterian letter. Addressed to Presbyterians
both North and South. [Louisville, Galt House, 1875]. 15 p.   PH

4086 WILSON, Samuel Ramsey, 1818-1886.
Reply to the attack of Rev. R. J. Breckinridge, D.D.,
LL.D., upon the Louisville Presbytery, and defence of the
"Declaration and testimony," made in the Synod of Kentucky,
October 16, A.D. 1865. Louisville, [Ky.], Hanna & Duncan,
1865. 52 p. H L PH PT U

4087 WILSON, Samuel Ramsey, 1818-1886.
A time to dance. Philadelphia, Presbyterian Board of
Publication, n.d. 24 p. (Presbyterian Tracts, no. 172.)
C H L PH PT R U

4088 WILSON, Samuel Ramsey, 1818-1886.
Twelfth Street grave yard and First Presbyterian Church.
n.p., n.d. 7 p. PH

4089 WILSON, Samuel Thomas, 1823-1893.
The Birmingham Presbyterian Church from 1835 to 1876.
A historical discourse preached ... September 10, 1876.
n.p., n.d. 25 p. PH

4090 WILSON, Samuel Thomas, 1823-1893.
The elder. The annual sermon on church polity. Preached
before the Presbytery of Rock River, at Freeport, Oct. 13,
1856. Also preached, by request, before the Synod of Chicago, at Princeton, Oct. 16, 1856. Rock Island, Pershing
& Connelly, 1857. 39 p. PH

4091 WILSON, Samuel Thomas, 1823-1893.
God vs. idols. Bellefonte, Pa., n.p., n.d. 8 p. PT

4092 WILSON, Samuel Thomas, 1823-1893.
The house of God. A sermon preached at the dedication
of the Presbyterian Church at Preemption, Illinois ... Sabbath morning, May 3rd, 1868. Rock Island, Argus Premium
Printing House, 1868. 12 p. PH

4093 WINECOFF, John Eugene Lee, 1863-1953.
The Catholic religion and the Protestant faith. The Bible
vs. the Pope--an argument. Written as a dialogue between
a Protestant and Cardinal Gibbon's book "The faith of our
fathers." Boston, Meador Publishing Co., © 1947. 341 p.
C H PT U

4094 WINECOFF, John Eugene Lee, 1863-1953.
Fair play the Christian way. Boston, Meador Publishing
Co., © 1952. 118 p. H U

4095 WINECOFF, John Eugene Lee, 1863-1953.
False churches and how they got that way. Boston, Meador
Publishing Co., © 1949. 304 p. H U

4096 WINN, Albert Curry, 1921-

The Acts of the Apostles. Richmond, John Knox Press, © 1960. 136 p. (The Layman's Bible Commentary, v. 20.) A C H L PT R U ... U: Large print ed. ... L: Translation into Japanese by Minoru Oonumata. Tokyo, Board of Publications, United Church of Christ in Japan, © 1960. 248 p.

4097 WINN, Albert Curry, 1921-
The Christian sex ideal. A talk based on a study of Genesis 2:18-25; Matthew 19:3-6; I Corinthians 6:9-20; Ephesians 5:21-33, and delivered to the Davidson student body March 18, 1947. n.p., n.d. 14 p. U

4098 WINN, Albert Curry, 1921-
The first manual for church extension; five Bible studies on Acts. [Atlanta, Board of Church Extension, Presbyterian Church in the U.S., 1961]. 26 p. Presented at the Church Extension Conference, Montreat, N.C., August 3-9, 1961. A

4099 WINN, Albert Curry, 1921-
Local church leader's guide to You and your lifework; a Christian choice for youth, written ... in collaboration with the Department of Ministry of the Commission on Higher Education, National Council of the Churches of Christ in the U.S.A. Chicago, Science Research Associates, © 1963. 90 p. L

4100 WINN, Albert Curry, 1921-
Teaching theology in the age of secularity. An address ... on the occasion of his installation as Professor of Doctrinal Theology ... at Louisville Presbyterian Theological Seminary, Louisville, Kentucky, September 7, 1965. n.p., [1965?]. unpaged. C PH

4101 WINN, Albert Curry, 1921-
The two shall be one: a Christian understanding of sex. [Richmond, Board of Christian Education, Presbyterian Church in the U.S.], © 1956. 15 p. U

4102 WINN, Albert Curry, 1921-
The witnessing congregation; three studies in Ephesians on the church's role in God's work of redemption. [Atlanta, Board of Church Extension, Presbyterian Church in the U.S.], n.d. 8 p. U

4103 WINN, Albert Curry, 1921-
The worry & wonder of being human. Richmond, CLC Press, © 1966. 224 p. (The Covenant Life Curriculum.) C L U ... C L U: Leaders' guide. 96 p.

4104 WINN, Albert Curry, 1921-

You and your life work: a Christian choice for youth.
Chicago, Science Research Associates, © 1963. 90 p.
A C L PT U

4105 WINN, Samuel Knox, 1848-1926.
Dangers of Christian Science. Richmond, Presbyterian
Committee of Publication, © 1899. 20 p.   PT U

4106 *WINSTON, E. T.
"Father Stuart" and the Monroe Mission. Meridian, Miss.,
Tell Farmer, 1927. 94 p. "Father Stuart" is Thomas C.
Stuart.   H R

4107 WITHERSPOON, Thomas Dwight, 1836-1898.
An appeal to the baptized children of the church. Richmond,
Presbyterian Committee of Publication, n.d. 121-172 p.
Printed from the plates of "The Children of the covenant."
C

4108 WITHERSPOON, Thomas Dwight, 1836-1898.
Children of the covenant; or the faithfulness of a covenant-
keeping God, illustrated in the lives and deaths of Andrew
Hart, Sarah Ward, and Mary Clarissa, children of the Rev.
A. H. Kerr. Richmond, Presbyterian Committee of Publica-
tion, © 1873. 262 p.   A C H L R U

4109 WITHERSPOON, Thomas Dwight, 1836-1898.
The distinctive doctrines and polity of Presbyterianism.
Address delivered before the two synods of Kentucky at their
joint centennial, held at Harrodsburg, October 12, 1883.
Louisville, Ky., Courier-Journal Job Printing Co., [1883?].
15 p. A C PH PT

4110 WITHERSPOON, Thomas Dwight, 1836-1898.
Romanism. In the light of its most recent and authoritative expositions amongst us. A series of letters, with quota-
tions from original sources hitherto unknown to the general
public. Richmond, Presbyterian Committee of Publication,
[1881]. 159 p.   A C H U

4111 WITHERSPOON, Thomas Dwight, 1836-1898.
A word to Christian parents. Richmond, Presbyterian
Committee of Publication, n.d. 175-220 p.   H U

4112 WITHERSPOON College, Buckhorn, Ky.
The story of Harvey S. Murdoch and the beginning of the
school, hospital, church and homes for children at Buckhorn,
Ky. As told in chapter XIII in a biography of Edward O.
Guerrant, by J. Gray McAllister and Grace Owings Guerrant.
Published in 1950 by Richmond Press, Richmond, Virginia.
Reprinted with permission of the authors for Elmer E. Gab-
bard. 149-157 p.   U

4113 *WOLFF, Hans Walter.
The Old Testament: a guide to its writings. Translated by Keith R. Crim. Philadelphia, Fortress Press, © 1973. 156 p. A L PT U

4114 WOMELDORF, John Andrew, 1911-
The first one hundred years: a brief history of the Princeton Presbyterian Church, Princeton, West Virginia. Our centennial date, 1854-August 5, 1954. n.p., n.d. 25 p. H U

4115 WOOD, Francis Lloyd Ferguson, 1909-1976, ed.
Living echoes: sermons by twelve Georgia Presbyterian ministers. Richmond, John Knox Press, © 1943. 112 p. Sermons by James McDowell Richards, Richard Thomas Gillespie, III, William Marion Elliott, Jr., William Vardaman Gardner, Cecil Asbury Thompson, Vernon Seba Broyles, Jr., John Butt Dickson, Alton Henley Glasure, Sidney Austin Gates, William Franklin Taylor, Jr., John Calvin Reid, Francis Lloyd Ferguson Wood. A C H R U

4116 *WOOD, William T.
Speeches of Hon. Wm. T. Wood and Saml. B. McPheeters, D.D., sustaining a complaint against the Presbytery of St. Louis, before the General Assembly of the Presbyterian Church, met in Newark, N.J., May, 1864. n.p., n.d. 40 p. PT U

4117 WOODALL, William Love, 1908-
Devotions for boys and girls. New York, Association Press, © 1953. 64 p. U ... L: [1957].

4118 WOODALL, William Love, 1908-
100 devotions for boys and girls. New York, Association Press, © 1957. 122 p. A L

4119 WOODALL, William Love, 1908-
Three-minute devotions for boys and girls. New York, Association Press, © 1962. 126 p. A C L R U

4120 WOODALL, William Love, 1908-
William Carey of India. [1st ed.] New York, Pageant Press, © 1951. 101 p. C

4121 WOODBRIDGE, Charles Jahleel, 1902-
The Independent Board for Presbyterian Foreign Missions: a statement as to its organization and program. Philadelphia, the Author, n.d. 7 p. PH PT

4122 WOODBRIDGE, Charles Jahleel, 1902-
Reaping the whirlwind. [Collingswood, N.J., Christian Beacon Press, 1977]. 45 p. PH

4123 WOODBRIDGE, Charles Jahleel, 1902-
Standing on the promises; rich truths from the book of
Acts. Chicago, Moody Press, © 1947. 203 p.   L PT
R ... R: A study of the book of Acts.   Grand Rapids, Mich.,
Baker Book House, © 1955. 151 p.

4124 WOODBRIDGE, Charles Jahleel, 1902-
Tell us, please; answers to life's great questions. [West-
wood, N.J.], Fleming H. Revell Co., © 1958. 127 p.   R
U

4125 WOODBRIDGE, Samuel Isett, 1856-1926.
Fifty years in China; being some account of the history and
conditions in China and of the missions of the Presbyterian
Church in the United States there from 1867 to the present
day.   Richmond, Presbyterian Committee of Publication,
[1919].   231 p.   Introduction by John I. Armstrong.   A C
L PH PT R U

4126 WOODROW, James, 1828-1907.
A defense of true Presbyterianism against two deliverances
of the Augusta Assembly, May, 1886.   By Gillespie [pseud.].
n.p., n.d.   20 p.   A C PH PT

4127 WOODROW, James, 1828-1907.
Dr. James Woodrow as seen by his friends.   Collected
and edited by his daughter, Marion W. Woodrow.   Columbia,
S.C., R. L. Bryan Co., 1909.   973 p.   Contents.--Pt. I,
Character sketches by his former pupils, colleagues, and
associates.--Pt. II, His teachings as contained in his sermons, addresses, editorials, etc.   A C H PH PT R U

4128 WOODROW, James, 1828-1907.
Evolution.   An address delivered May 7th, 1884, before
the Alumni Association of the Columbia Theological Seminary.
Columbia, S.C., Presbyterian Publishing House, 1884.   30 p.
PT U

4129 WOODROW, James, 1828-1907.
An examination of certain assaults on physical science.
Columbia, S.C., Presbyterian Publishing House, 1873.   53 p.
Reprinted from the Southern Presbyterian Review, July,
1873.   C

4130 WOODROW, James, 1828-1907.
"One Lord, one faith, one baptism." The characteristics
or marks of the Holy Catholic Church," and the stumbling-
blocks in the way of those who would enter it.   Sermon
preached before the Synod of South Carolina, at Columbia,
S.C., October 21, 1902.   Columbia, R. L. Bryan Co.,
1902.   24 p.   A ... U: microfilm.

4131 WOODROW, James, 1828-1907.

Professor Woodrow's speech before the Synod of South
Carolina, October 27 and 28, 1884. Columbia, S.C., Pres-
byterian Publishing House, 1885. 65 p. Reprinted from the
Southern Presbyterian Review, January, 1885. A

4132 WOODROW, James, 1828-1907.
"Wherewithal shall a young man cleanse his way?" Bac-
calaureate sermon preached in the chapel of the South Carolina
College, June 27th, 1892. Columbia, S.C., Presbyterian
Publishing House, 1892. 14 p. U: microfilm.

4133 WOODS, David Junkin, 1868-1965.
Our church's youth in state institutions of learning. An
address by ... [the] pastor of the Presbyterian Church at
the Virginia Polytechnic Institute at Blacksburg, Virginia.
Delivered at Montreat, North Carolina, August 5, 1911.
Louisville, Ky., Executive Committee of Christian Education
and Ministerial Relief, Presbyterian Church in the U.S.,
n.d. 7 p. U ... U: 13 p.

4134 WOODS, David Junkin, 1868-1965.
The relation of the Old Testament and the New, and how
this bears on baptism and the family covenant. A sermon
preached during the session of Montgomery Presbytery, at
Peaks Church ... Sept. 4, 1903. n.p., n.d. 16 p. PT
U

4135 WOODS, Edgar, 1827-1910.
Albemarle County in Virginia; giving some account of what
it is by nature, of what it was made by man, and some of
the men who made it. [Charlottesville, Va., The Michie
Co.], © 1901. 412 p. H ... U: Bridgewater, Va., The
Green Bookman, 1932.

4136 WOODS, Edgar, 1827-1910.
Golden apples; or, Fair words for the young. New York,
Robert Carter and Brothers, 1875. 269 p. U ... H: New
York, Worthington Co., 1890.

4137 WOODS, Francis Marion, 1843-1939.
Intemperance, its evils, its causes and its cures. Mar-
tinsburg, [W.Va.], Independent Steam Job Print., 1884. 8 p.
U

4138 WOODS, Henry McKee, 1857-1943, comp.
By way of remembrance. Atlantic City, N.J., World Wide
Revival Prayer Movement, n.d. 110 p. C R

4139 WOODS, Henry McKee, 1857-1943, ed.
A Chinese Bible encyclopedia (Sheng king peh k'o ch'uen
shu) based chiefly on the International Standard Bible Encyclopedia ... with original articles written specially for the

Chinese Bible encyclopedia. Shanghai, The Commercial Press, 1925. 4 v. H U

4140 WOODS, Henry McKee, 1857-1943.
A commentary on the Five Classics, adapted to modern times; I. The book of history; II. The book of poetry. Shanghai, Christian Literature Society for China, 1917. In Chinese. H PT

4141 WOODS, Henry McKee, 1857-1943.
A commentary on the Four Books, adapted to modern times, prepared specially for use in Christian schools and colleges. Shanghai, Christian Literature Society for China, 1914, 1918. In Chinese. H PT ... H: 2d ed. 1922-23.

4142 WOODS, Henry McKee, 1857-1943.
Eight reasons why you ought to believe in foreign missions. [Nashville, Tenn., Executive Committee of Foreign Missions, Presbyterian Church in the U.S.], n.d. 2 ℓ. U

4143 WOODS, Henry McKee, 1857-1943.
Our priceless heritage: a study of Christian doctrine in contrast with Romanism. London, Marshall, Morgan & Scott, [1934]. 204 p. C H L PT U ... A C H L PT R U: 2d ed. Harrisburg, Penna., The Evangelical Press, 1941. 213 p.

4144 WOODS, Henry McKee, 1857-1943.
Robert Lewis Dabney, 1820-1898, prince among theologians and men. A memorial address delivered before West Hanover Presbytery at its fall meeting, 1936, in Stonewall Church, Appomattox County, Virginia, celebrating the Jubilee year of the founding of the Southern Presbyterian Church in 1861. n.p., n.d. unpaged. Reprinted from the Presbyterian of the South, November 9, 1936. A C H R

4145 WOODS, Thomas Edward Peck, 1875-1948.
Bible history--Old Testament: a syllabus for all Bible students. Grand Rapids, Mich., Wm. B. Eerdmans Publishing Co., 1941. 198 p. R

4146 WOODS, Thomas Edward Peck, 1875-1948.
Bible questions; a course of Bible study by means of questions on each chapter. [Chattanooga, Chattanooga Printing and Engraving Co.], © 1930, © 1931. 2 v. H U

4147 WOODS, Thomas Edward Peck, 1875-1948.
For God was with them; some of God's messages through the lives of men and women of the past. Grand Rapids, Mich., Wm. B. Eerdmans Publishing Co., 1939. 150 p. R

4148 WOODS, Thomas Edward Peck, 1875-1948.

The seal of the seven; a blazed trail for Bible readers.
A new analysis of the Bible based on its sevenfold structure
with a brief introduction to each book. Grand Rapids, Mich.,
Wm. B. Eerdmans Publishing Co., © 1938. 181 p. L PT
R U

4149 WOODS, Thomas Edward Peck, 1875-1948.
Studies in the Gospel of Mark; twelve lessons. Chattanooga,
Tenn., Target Printing Co., © 1934. 32 p. A U

4150 WOODS, Thomas Edward Peck, 1875-1948.
Shulammith: a love story which is an interpretation of
"The Song of Songs, which is Solomon's." Grand Rapids,
Mich., Wm. B. Eerdmans Publishing Co., 1940. 72 p. U

4151 WOODS, William Hervey, 1852-1925.
The anteroom and other poems. [Baltimore, Md., Lord
Baltimore Press], © 1911. 158 p. Partly reprinted from
various periodicals. C H U

4152 WOODS, William Hervey, 1852-1925.
The dream of Pilate's wife. [Richmond, Presbyterian
Committee of Publication], © 1922. 24 p. A one-act play.
H U

4153 WOODWORTH, Robert Bell, 1868-1954, ed.
The descendants of Robert and John Poage (pioneer set-
tlers in Augusta County, Va.). A genealogy. Complete ed.
Staunton, Va., McClure Printing Co., 1954. 1372, 5 p.
U

4154 WOODWORTH, Robert Bell, 1868-1954.
A history of the Presbyterian Church in Winchester, Vir-
ginia, 1780-1949, based on official documents ... with the
collaboration of Clifford Duval Grim and Ronald S. Wilson.
Winchester, Pifer Printing Co., 1950. 152 p. H PH PT
U

4155 WOODWORTH, Robert Bell, 1868-1954.
A history of the Presbytery of Winchester (Synod of Vir-
ginia); its rise and growth, ecclesiastical relations, institu-
tions and agencies, churches and ministers, 1719-1945.
Staunton, Va., McClure Printing Co., 1947. 521 p. A H
L PH PT U

4156 WOODWORTH, Robert Bell, 1868-1954.
... The history of Winchester Presbytery (with particular
reference to evangelism) by R. B. Woodworth, D.Sc., and
The men who made history in Winchester Presbytery during
the last 75 years, by Joseph A. McMurray, D.D. Addresses
delivered in the Presbyterian Church, Winchester, Va., September 30, 1936. [Pulaski, Va., B. D. Smith & Brothers],

1936. At head of title: Diamond Jubilee, Presbyterian Church in the United States: organized December 4, 1861. PH U

4157 WOODWORTH, Robert Bell, 1868-1954.
The origin of the Septuagint version. Richmond, Whittet & Shepperson, 1893. 9 p. Reprinted from the Presbyterian Quarterly, July, 1893. U

4158 WOODWORTH, Robert Bell, 1868-1954.
"A peculiar treasure." (Mal. III. 17.) [Burlington, W. Va.], n.p., n.d. 4 p. U

4159 WOODWORTH, Robert Bell, 1868-1954.
The Presbyterial treasury. Chattanooga, Tenn., Assembly's Stewardship Committee, [1926?]. 15 p. Reprinted from the Union Seminary Review, January, 1926. A C U

4160 WORKMAN, William Hay, 1858-1934, comp.
Presbyterian rule, embracing the form of government, rules of discipline, and directory of worship in the Presbyterian Church in the United States ... with the decisions of the General Assembly of the Presbyterian Church in the United States of America. n.p., [W. H. Workman], © 1895. 204 p. C H R ... A H PH R U: Richmond, Presbyterian Committee of Publication, © 1898. 256 p.

4161 *WRIGHT, Alfred, 1788-1853, comp.
Chahta vba isht taloa holisso. Choctaw hymn book. Compiled by Alfred Wright and Cyrus Byington. 9th ed. Richmond, Presbyterian Committee of Publication, n.d. 252 p. U

4162 WRIGHT, Allen, 1826-1885.
Chahta leksikon. A Choctaw in English definition. For the Choctaw academies and schools. 1st ed. St. Louis, Presbyterian Publishing Co., [1880]. 311 p. PH

4163 WRIGHT, Austin Hazen, 1811-1865.
Looking unto Jesus. A sermon, occasioned by the death of Mrs. Martha Ann Rhea, preached at Oroomiah, Persia, October 11, 1857. Boston, T. R. Marvin & Son, 1858. 37 p. H

4164 WRIGHT, Austin Hazen, 1811-1865.
The Saviour's prayer. A discourse, delivered in the Fifth Associate Reformed Presbyterian Church, New-York. New-York, John A. Gray, 1852. 20 p. PH

4165 *WU, Yi-fang, 1893- ed.
China rediscovers her west: a symposium edited by Yi-fang Wu and Frank W. Price. New York, Friendship Press, © 1940. 210 p. H L PH U

4166　WURTS, Edward, 1810-1885.
　　　　The thief on the cross, or the way of salvation by grace,
　　　proved and illustrated from its leading example.　Philadelphia,
　　　Presbyterian Board of Publication, n.d.　16 p.　(Presbyterian
　　　Tracts, no. 231.)　H PH PT R U

4167　WYRICK, Victor Neil, 1928-
　　　　Boundaries unlimited.　Richmond, John Knox Press,
　　　© 1965.　96 p.　A C H L U

4168　WYRICK, Victor Neil, 1928-
　　　　I am.　Nashville, Abingdon Press, © 1966.　80 p.　Poems.
　　　PH

4169　YANDELL, Lunsford Pitts, 1805-1878.
　　　　Proceedings and second annual report of the Kentucky Tem-
　　　perance Society: with an address before the society by Luns-
　　　ford P. Yandell.　Frankfort, Ky., A. G. Hodges, 1832.
　　　24 p.　PH PT

4170　YATES, William Black, 1809-1882.
　　　　An historical sketch of the rise and progress of religious
　　　and moral improvement among seamen, in England and the
　　　United States, with a history of the Port Society of Charles-
　　　ton, S.C.　Charleston, A. J. Burke, 1851.　31 p.　PT

4171　YOHANNON, Isaac Esho, 1864-1918.
　　　　A short sketch of my life.　Petersburg, Va., Frank A.
　　　Owen, 1903.　62 p.　H U

4172　YOU are somebody special, by Bill Cosby [and others]; edited
　　　by Charlie Shedd.　New York, McGraw-Hill Book Co.,
　　　© 1978.　209 p.　U

4173　*YOUNG, Bennett H.
　　　　Dr. S. M. Neel as a wound healer.　[Louisville, Ky.,
　　　n.p., 1906].　14 p.　U

4174　*YOUNG, Bennett H.
　　　　Dr. S. M. Neel, the self-appointed Moses of the Southern
　　　Church.　Being a response to Dr. Neel's article entitled
　　　"Col. Young's so-called reply."　[Louisville, Ky., the Author,
　　　1907].　17 p.　PH PT U

4175　*YOUNG, Bennett H.
　　　　A last shot at blundering Samuel, alias Dr. S. M. Neel.
　　　Louisville, Ky., n.p., [1907].　19 p.　U

4176　*YOUNG, Bennett H.
　　　　Some suggestions touching organic union and the course
　　　of Dr. Francis R. Beattie and the Christian Observer con-
　　　cerning same.　Louisville, Ky., n.p., n.d.　37 p.　U

4177 YOUNG, Daniel P., ca. 1833-1878.
      How children are saved.... Edited by Stuart Robinson.
      Richmond, Presbyterian Committee of Publication, [1878].
      76 p.   C PH U

4178 YOUNG, James Thomas, 1927-
      History of Culdee Presbyterian Church, 1886-1955. Aberdeen, N.C., Dixie Printing Co., 1955. 18 p.   H

4179 ZELUFF, James Daniel, 1930-
      There's algae in the baptismal "fount." Nashville, Abingdon, © 1978. 112 p.   A C L PT R U

4180 ZIVLEY, John Henry, 1824-1905.
      A sermon ... on "The blood of sprinkling." Or, "Sprinkling of the blood of Jesus Christ." San Seba, Tex., Hayworth Printing Co., 1885. 11 p.   PH

4181 ZUR SOZIOLOGIE des Urchristentums: ausgew. Beitrage zum frühchristlichen Gemeinschaftsleben in seiner gesellschaftlichen Umwelt, herausgegeben von Wayne A. Meeks; [aus d. Amerikan, von G. Memmert]. München, Kaiser, 1979. 312 p. Selected articles previously published in various journals.   U

4182   GUTZKE, Manford George, 1896-
       The evangelical Bible teaching of Manford George Gutzke.
    Atlanta, The Bible for You, n.d.   variously paged.   (Plain
    Talk about Bible Truth for Everyday Living.)   Pamphlets:
    All things work together for good.--As for me and my
    house.--The Bible in a nutshell.--Blessed hope.--Bringing
    up the child.--The call to serve.--Called by grace to a life
    of love.--Christ the peacemaker.--The Christian and the
    campus.--Commit thy way.--Count your blessings.--Courage
    for commitment.--Echoes in witnessing.--Effective Christian
    education.--The end of the world.--The fruit of the spirit.--
    Giving thanks always.--Go ... .--God our dwelling.--The
    greater commandment.--The guidance of God.--The Holy
    Spirit.--How to become a Christian.--How can I be forgiven.--
    How can I know the will of God.--How to know the peace of
    God.--How to make a success of the Christian life.--How to
    trust God.--How to understand suffering.--I believe in mir-
    acles.--If you were the only Christian.--In God we trust.--
    Insights into Isaiah.--Insights into James.--Into his marvel-
    ous light.--Introduction to the Bible.--Jonah.--The Kingdom
    of God.--Let not your heart be troubled.--Love thy neigh-
    bor.--Lord... Teach us to pray.--Marks of a real Chris-
    tian.--The meaning of Grace.--The meaning of the Gospel.--
    The message of John.--My brother--Walter Gutzke.--Once
    to die.--Out of darkness, 2 pts.--A plan for Bible study.--
    Praise God... Always.--Praying in the Old Testament.--
    Predestination and election.--The privilege and power of
    prayer.--Profiles of the New Testament.--Profiles of the
    Old Testament.--A prophet like unto me.--Providence in
    preparation.--The reality of angels.--The reality of demons.--
    Reality of heaven.--Reality of hell.--The return of the Lord.--
    The Saviour as seen in the Exodus.--Sing a new song.--Some
    women of the Bible.--Study guide for the fall of the nation.--
    Study guide on Acts.--Study guide on Ephesians.--Study guide
    for I Corinthians.--Study guide for I Peter.--Study guide on
    Galatians.--Study guide on Genesis.--Study guide on Hebrews.--
    Study guide for Job-Ecclesiastes.--Study guide on John, 2
    pts.--Study guide on Mark.--Study guide on Matthew.--Study
    guide to Romans.--Study guide for I Samuel.--Study in love.--
    The superiority of Christ.--Ten testimonies that blessed my
    ministry.--This one called Jesus, 2 pts.--Understanding the
    ways of the Lord, 2 pts.--The virgin birth.--Wells without
    water.--What can Christmas mean, 2 pts.--What Christ thinks

of the Church.--What is American democracy?.--What must
I do?--Why I cannot accept evolution.--Witnesses unto Me.
H

4183 PRESBYTERIAN Church in the U.S. Board of Women's Work.
"The promise of the new," workbook 1974-1975 (including
monthly Bible studies in Matthew by Dr. James A. Cogswell)
Atlanta, General Executive Board, Presbyterian Church in
the U.S., [1974]. 96 p. H

4184 ROBINSON, David Pressly, 1819-1892.
Robinson's sermons ... rewritten and revised by his son,
Rev. G. S. Robinson. Philadelphia, Horting and Snader,
1893. 295 p. H

4185 ROBINSON, James McConkey, 1924-
Scripture and theological method; a Protestant study in sen-
sus plenior. n.p., n.d. 6-27 p. Reprinted from the Catholic Biblical Quarterly, January, 1965. C

4186 SMYTH, Thomas, 1808-1873.
Form for the solemnization of matrimony, according to
the order of the Presbyterian Church. Boston, Crocker and
Brewster, 1841. 12 p. C PH

4187 VANCE, Joseph Anderson, 1864-1951.
The true and the false in Christian Science. Stenographic
report of a sermon delivered at the Hyde Park Presbyterian
Church ... Chicago, Illinois, on the 15th of May, 1904.
Chicago, Winona Publishing Co., © 1904. 24 p. PT

INDEX

A. Ministers of the Presbyterian Church in the United States

Acrey, Oliver Chauncey (1905-   )
    1
Adams, Lane Goldman (1924-   )
    2-3
Adams, Raymond David (1897-1972)
    601
Adams, William (ca. 1836-1896)
    1581, 2925
Adams, William Hooper (1838-1880)
    2252
Adger, John Bailey (1810-1899)
    7-13, 611, 664, 2488, 3750
Aldridge, John William (1929-1976)
    14
Alexander, Eugene (1890-1958) 15
Alexander, Hasell Norwood (1889-
    1968) 16
Alexander, Henry Carrington (1835-
    1894) 17-19, 3284
Alexander, James Harvey (1826-
    1906) 2976
Alexander, Samuel Caldwell (1830-
    1907) 20-26, 1894
Alexander, William Addison (1857-
    1909) 27, 2811-2813, 2820
Alexander, William McFaddin (1861-
    1944) 28
Alexander, William Mortimer
    (1928-   ) 29
Alford, Charles McMillan (1858-
    1921) 30
Allen, Donald Ray (1930-   ) 31
Allen, Elliott Douglas (1874-1964)
    32
Allen, Horace Thaddeus (1933-   )
    33
Allen, James Woodruff (1885-   )
    34-38
Allen, Mathews Franklin (1920-   )
    2896, 2989
Allison, John Lee (1863-1946) 39-
    40
Allsup, Herbert Justin (1884-   ) 41
Alston, Wallace McPherson (1906-)
    42-44
Anderson, Archer E. (1899-   ) 45

Anderson, George Andrew (1916-   )
    3113
Anderson, John Franklin (1920-   )
    46
Anderson, John Gray (1850-1944) 47
Anderson, John Monroe (1821-1879)
    48
Anderson, Neal Larkin (1865-1931)
    49-55, 1570, 2334, 2461, 2836
Anderson, Robert Campbell (1864-
    1955) 56
Anderson, Vernon Andy (1896-   ) 57
Anderson, William Madison (1889-
    1935) 58-60
Appleby, James Mourning (1904-1977)
    61-62
Armistead, Jessie S. see Armistead,
    Jessie Scott (1795-1869)
Armistead, Jessie Scott (1795-1869)
    64, 1793
Armstrong, George Dodd (1813-1899)
    65-88, 3528
Armstrong, John Irvine (1872-1924)
    89, 2826, 4125
Armstrong, Oscar Vance (1876-1941)
    90-91
Arrowood, Charles Flinn (1887-1951)
    458, 887
Arrowood, William Butler (1850-1919)
    92
Asbury, Beverly Allen (1929-   )
    3954
Atkins, Alexander Harrison (1860-
    1933) 93-94
Atkinson, John Mayo Pleasants (1817-
    1883) 97, 3747
Atkinson, Joseph Mayo (1820-1891)
    95-96
Axson, Samuel Edward (1833-1884)
    97-99

Bachman, George Oliver (1854-1939)
    100
Bachman, Jonathan Waverly (1837-
    1924) 2253, 2661

Bullock, James Randolph (1910-   )
461

Bullock, Joseph James (1812-1892)
462, 3817

Bullock, Philip Leslie (1918-   )
463-464

Bullock, Robert Haydon (1913-   )
465, 1026

Bunting, Robert Franklin (1828-
1891) 466-467

Burgett, James Ralston (1830-1900)
470-471, 2334, 3528

Burkhead, Jesse DeWitt (1833-1892)
472

Burney, LeRoy Perry (1897-1955)
473

Burwell, Henry Ward (1865-1941)
527

Burwell, Robert (1802-1895) 3819

Buschgen, Otto William (1885-1948)
475-476

Bush, Monroe (1921-   ) 477

Byington, Cyrus (1793-1868) 479-
480, 4161

Byrd, Samuel Craig (1868-1951)
1578

Cabaniss, Allen see Cabaniss,
James Allen (1911-   )

Cabaniss, James Allen (1911-   )
481-494, 2014, 2582, 3333

Cairns, Fred I. (1907-   ) 495

Calcote, Claude Allen (1896-1956)
496

Caldwell, Alfred Shorter (1848-
1932) 2841

Caldwell, Andrew Harper (1814-
1899) 497-498

Caldwell, Calvin Norris (1861-1937)
2824

Caldwell, Charles Turner (1865-
1965) 499-502

Caldwell, Daniel Templeton (1892-
1952) 503-504

Caldwell, Eugene Craighead (1876-
1931) 505-519, 590

Caldwell, Frank Hill (1902-   )
520, 2985, 3583

Caldwell, John Williamson (1872-
1946) 527

Caldwell, Robert Ernest (1858-
1904) 1573

Caldwell, William (1865-1915) 521

Calhoun, Lawrence Gibson (1899-   )
522

Calhoun, Malcolm Patterson
(1902-   ) 523

Caligan, James Henley (1903-1972)
524

Campbell, Chester McDonald (1889-
1951) 528

Campbell, Duncan Alexander (1805-
1892) 529

Campbell, James Milton (1932-   )
531

Campbell, Robert Fishburne (1858-
1947) 532-536, 2461, 2844, 2996,
3820

Campbell, William Addison (1829-1896)
537-539

Campbell, William Creighton (1850-
1936) 540, 2833

Campbell, William Spencer (1859-1939)
3820

Cannon, John Franklin (1851-1920)
541-542, 2816, 3528

Cannon, Thomas Clarence (1909-   )
543

Carmichael, Patrick Henry (1889-1977)
544-546, 3712

Carr, Archibald Fairly (1868-1958)
2836

Carr, James McLeod (1902-   ) 547-
551

Carse, James Pearce (1932-   ) 552

Carson, Charles Clifton (1870-1944)
553

Carswell, Arthur Dula (1888-1976)
2588

Carter, Hampden C. (1805-1869) 554

Carter, Robert Washington (1858-1903)
555

Cartledge, Groves Harrison (1820-
1899) 556-558

Cartledge, Samuel Antoine (1903-   )
559-564, 565

Cartledge, Samuel Jackson (1864-1940)
558, 565

Cartledge, Thomas Davidson (1860-
1925) 558

Caruthers, Eli Washington (1793-1865)
566-568

Casey, Horace Craig (1903-   ) 572

Cater, Edwin (1813-1882) 573

Cecil, Russell (1853-1925) 574-580,
2334, 3022

Chafer, Lewis Sperry (1871-1952)
583-595

Chafer, Rollin Thomas (1868-1940)
596

Chalmers, Dwight Moody (1899-19,4)
597

Chamberlain, Hiram (1797-1866) 599

Chamberlain, Nelson P. (1818-1869)
600

Cunningham, Thomas McHutchin
(1887-) 728-729

Currie, Armand London (1899-)
731-732

Currie, David Mitchell (1918-)
733, 3316

Currie, Stuart Dickson (1922-1975)
734, 1161-1162, 3706

Currie, Thomas White (1879-1943)
735-738, 2461

Currie, Thomas White (1914-)
730, 739-740, 2217

Curry, Albert Bruce (1852-1939)
741-747, 2334

Dabney, Robert Lewis (1820-1898)
6, 703, 748-784, 946, 1576,
1658, 1660, 1889, 2556, 2816,
2907, 3081, 3170, 3178, 3528,
3893, 3993, 4144

Dallas, James Maxwell (1861-1942)
785

Dana, William Coombs (1810-1880)
786-799

Daniel, Emmett Randolph (1935-)
800

Daniel Eugene (1849-1935) 1579,
2816

Davidson, Robert Franklin (1902-)
803-805

Davies, Samuel Wilson (1834-1916)
3528

Davis, Augustus Lee (1888-1968)
810

Davis, Edward Payson (1851-1937)
2334

Davis, Robert Newton (1818-1871)
2023

Davis, Robert Pickens (1911-)
811-812

Demarest, Gary William (1926-)
813-814

Dendy, Marshall Coleman (1902-)
815-816

Denny, George Hutcheson (1834-
1893) 2824

De Santo, Charles see De Santo,
Charles P. (1923-)

De Santo, Charles P. (1923-)
817-818

Dewitz, Ludwig Richard Max
(1916-) 820-822

Dickson, Andrew Flinn (1825-1879)
823-828

Dickson, John Butt (1909-) 4115

Diehl, Charles Edward (1875-1964)
829

Diehl, George West (1887-1975) 830-
836

Doak, John Keith Whitfield (1814-1891)
838

Doak, Samuel Witherspoon (1785-1864)
839-840, 2661

Dobyns, William Ray (1861-1932) 841-
843, 2461, 2825-2826, 3780

Dodge, David Witherspoon (1887-)
846

Dodge, Richard Daniel (1889-1971)
847

Dodson, Samuel Kendrick (1884-)
848

Doggett, Marshall Wellington (1855-
1941) 849

Donaldson, Newton (ca. 1852-1924)
850-851

Doom, Robert Isaac (1930-) 852-
853

Douglas, Davidson McDowell (1869-
1931) 1584, 3527

Douglas, John (1809-1879) 854-859

Douglass, John Jordan (1875-1940)
860

Downey, William Walton (1849-1889)
861

Doyle, William Bruce (1877-1952) 862

Drummond, James (1856-1927) 863

DuBose, Hampden Coit (1845-1910)
619, 864-868, 1708

DuBose, Henry Wade (1884-1960) 501,
545, 869-870

DuBose, Lucius Beddinger (1932-)
3316

Duckwall, John McCarty (1855-1940)
871-872

Dudley, Harold James (1902-) 873

Duhs, Robert Carl (1924-) 874-876

Dunglinson, Joseph (1880-) 2461

Dupuy, Benjamin Hunter (1845-1926)
877

Eagleton, George Ewing (1831-1899)
878

Eagleton, William (1796-1866) 881-884

Eddins, James Franklin (1876-1942)
888

Edmiston, Alonzo Lmore (1879-1954)
889

Edmonds, Henry Morris (1878-1960)
890-894

Edwards, George Riley (1920-) 895

Efird, James Michael (1932-) 896-
900, 3824

Eggleston, Richard Beverley (1867-
1927) 901

424 / A Presbyterian Bibliography

Gammon, William Jefferson (1876-
1967) 1067
Garber, Paul Leslie (1911-   )
545, 1068-1072, 1403
Gardner, Oscar (1906-1958) 1124
Gardner, William Vardaman (1903-
1970) 4115
Garrett, Willis Edward (1914-   )
1073
Garrison, Joseph Marion (1904-   )
545, 1074-1076
Garrison, Pinkney Jefferson
(1906-   ) 1077
Garth, John Goodall (1871-1952)
1078-1082
Gates, Sidney Austin (1906-1966)
4115
Gauss, Joseph Henry (1855-   )
1083-1084
Gauss, Oscar William (1842-1918)
1085
Gear, Felix Bayard (1899-1982)
545, 1086-1088, 2528, 2822
George, William (1828-1897 or
1898) 1090-1092
Getty, Walter (1882-1969) 1093
Gettys, Joseph Miller (1907-   )
1094-1122, 2799
Ghiselin, Charles (1853-1943) 1123
Gibboney, Charles Haller (1914-   )
1124-1125
Gibbs, John Gamble (1930-   )
1126
Gildersleeve, Benjamin (1791-1875)
1129-1130
Gillespie, Guy Tillman (1885-1958)
3583
Gillespie, Richard Thomas (1879-
1930) 1570, 1575, 2980
Gillespie, Richard Thomas (1909-
1977) 1131, 4115
Gillon, William Albert (1869-1932)
2927
Gilmer, George Hudson (1866-1947)
1132
Gilmour, Abram David Pollock
(1876-1948) 1133, 3820
Girardeau, John Lafayette (1825-
1898) 262, 664, 759, 1134-
1147, 1577, 2207, 2209, 2556,
2846, 3235, 3528, 3750
Glasgow, Samuel McPheeters
(1883-1963) 1148-1158, 2461
Glass, Gilbert (1875-1934) 1160,
1568
Glasure, Alton Henley (1908-   )
4115

Goetchius, George Thomas (1845-1900)
2846
Goff, John (1863-1938) 1165-1169
Gonzales, Juan Orts see Orts Gon-
zales, Juan (1868-1941)
Good, John Walter (1879-1971) 1170
Goodman, Frank Leroy (1900-1968)
1171
Goodpasture, Henry McKennie
(1929-   ) 1172
Goodykoontz, Harry Gordon (1906-   )
1173-1180, 2985
Gordon, Edward Clifford (1842-1922)
1181-1183
Goulding, Francis Robert (1810-1881)
664, 1184
Gouwens, Teunis Earl (1886-1960)
1185-1197, 2259
Grafton, Cornelius Washington (1846-
1934) 488, 2483, 2841-2842
Grafton, Thomas Hancock (1905-   )
1198-1199
Graham, Alfred Thurston (1858-1917)
1200-1202
Graham, Bothwell (1853-1931) 1203-
1204
Graham, Donald Carson (1910-   )
1205
Graham, Henry Tucker (1865-1951)
1206-1212
Graham, James Robert (1824-1914)
1213-1215
Graham, Randolph Watson (1927-   )
1216
Grasty, John Sharshall (1825-1883)
1217-1221
Graves, Frederick Roscoe (1868-
1943) 1222-1223
Graves, Joseph Armstrong (1846-
1915) 1224
Gray, John Hannah (1805-1878) 1225
Gray, William Bristow (1873-1959)
501, 1226-1227
Graybill, Anthony Thomas (1841-1905)
2382
Green, James Benjamin (1871-1967)
1228-1230, 3969
Gregory, Andrew Painter (1867-1955)
1232-1237
Grey, John Hunter (1872-1957) 1238
Gribble, Robert Francis (1890-1970)
1239
Grider, Edgar McLean (1934-   )
1240
Grinnan, Randolph Bryan (1860-1942)
1241, 1429
Grissett, Finley McCorvey (1889-   )
1242

Hendrick, John Thilman (1811-1897 or 1898) see Hendrick, John Thilman (1815-1897 or 1898)

Hendrick, John Thilman (1815-1897 or 1898) 1399, 2852, 3236

Henegar, Edward (1936-) 1400

Henry, Stuart Clark (1914-) 1402-1404

Hensley, Philip Henry, Jr. 1405

Hepburn, Andrew Dousa (1830-1921) 807, 1406

Herndon, John Rankin (1862-1920) 1407

Herron, Charles (1863-1942) 1408-1409

Hersman, Charles Campbell (1838-1924) 3819

Heyer, George Stuart (1930-) 1410

Hiemstra, William Louis (1915-) 1411

Hill, Eugene Lott (1878-1960) 2836

Hill, Halbert Green (1831-1924) 1412-1413, 1427, 2844

Hill, John Franklin (1835-1916) 2851

Hill, Pierre Bernard (1877-1958) 501, 1414-1421, 3964

Hill, Robert (1868-1962) 501, 1422-1423, 2825

Hill, Thomas English (1909-) 1424-1426

Hill, William Edwin (1880-1940) 3820

Hill, William Wallace (1815-1878) 1428

Hills, Edward Freer (1912-) 1430-1433

Hobbie, Francis Wellford (1922-) 1027

Hobson, Benjamin Lewis (1859-1918) 1434

Hodge, Richard Morse (1864-1928) 1435-1439

Hodge, Samuel (1829-1892) 1440

Hodgman, Stephen Alexander (ca. 1808-1887) 1441

Hoffman, Fred Wakefield (1889-1979) 1442

Hoge, Moses Drury (1818-1899) 664, 1443-1453, 1455, 1576, 1583, 2365, 2816, 2837, 2979, 3020-3021, 3169, 3528, 3819, 3892, 3962, 3993

Hoge, Peyton Harrison (1858-1940) 1454-1456, 3528

Hoge, William James (1825-1864) 1457-1459, 1586, 3774, 3892

Hogshead, Alexander Lewis (1816-1880) 1460

Holderby, Andrew Roberdeau (1839-1924) 1461

Holladay, James Minor (1866-1937) 1462

Hollifield, Ambrose Nelson (1851-1901) 1463-1465, 3778

Hollingsworth, Aaron Hayden (1903-) 1466

Hollingsworth, William Franklin (1867-1946) 1467

Holt, David Rice (1925-) 1468

Hooper, Thomas Williamson (1832-1915) 1469-1470, 2833

Hopkins, Henry Harvey (1804-1877) 1471

Hopkins, Martin Armstrong (1889-1964) 234, 1472-1479

Hopper, Joseph (1892-1971) 1480

Hopper, Joseph Barron (1921-) 1481

Hopper, Joseph H. (1829-1915) 2978

Horton, Thomas C. see Horton, Thomas Corwin (ca. 1849-1932)

Horton, Thomas Corwin (ca. 1849-1932) 1482

Hough, Robert Ervin (1874-1965) 1483-1484

Houston, Matthew Hale (1841-1905) 1485-1488

Houston, Samuel Rutherford (1806-1887) 1489-1490

Howard, Charles Morse (-1908) 1492-1493

Howard, George P. see Howard, George Parkinson (1882-)

Howard, George Parkinson (1882-) 1494-1501

Howe, George (1802-1883) 664, 1502-1514, 2232, 3526, 3993

Howell, Andrew Jackson (1869-1947) 1515-1516

Howerton, James Robert (1861-1924) 1517-1518, 3528

Howie, Carl Gordon (1920-) 1519-1530

Howison, Robert Reid (1820-1906) 1531-1533

Hoyt, Henry Francis (1833-1912) 226-227

Hoyt, Nathan (1793-1866) 1534-1536

Hoyt, Thomas A. see Hoyt, Thomas Alexander (1828-1903)

Hoyt, Thomas Alexander (1828-1903) 1537-1539, 1580

Huck, William (1888-) 2836

Hudson, George (1866-1916) 1540

Kadel, William Howard (1913-   )
1710
Kalopothakes, Michael Demetrius
(1825-1911) 1712
Keller, William Chester (1911-   )
1713
Kellersberger, Eugene Roland
(1888-1966) 1714-1716
Kelly, Balmer Hancock (1914-   )
998, 1588, 1717-1719, 3814,
3318
Kennedy, Dennis James (1930-   )
602, 1720-1724
Kennedy, John Joseph (1838-1912)
2023
Kennedy, William Bean (1926-   )
1725-1726
Kerr, Andrew Hart (1812-1883)
4108
Kerr, Edgar Davis (1881-1954) 546
Kerr, James Witherspoon (1820-
1901) 1727-1728
Kerr, Robert Pollok (1850-1923)
1729-1741, 3528
King, Charles Leonidas (1892-   )
501, 1742-1743
King, Samuel Alexander (1834-1918)
1744-1749, 2810, 3528
Kinnaird, Robert Hann (1839-1888)
1577
Kinney, Laurence Forman (1902-
1966) 1750
Kirk, Harris Elliott (1872-1953)
1751-1760, 2461, 2824
Kirkpatrick, John Lycan (1813-
1885) 807, 1761-1763, 2854
Kirkpatrick, Robert White
(1908-   ) 1764-1765
Knight, Lucian Lamar (1868-1933)
1768-1774, 3530
Kraemer, Charles Edgar Stanberry
(1909-   ) 1776
Kuist, Howard Tillman (1895-   )
1777-1791

Lacy, Benjamin Rice (1886-1981)
1584, 1792-1796, 2461, 2853,
3818, 3820
Lacy, Beverly Tucker (1819-1900)
1797
Lacy, Drury (1802-1884) 807,
1798
Lacy, Matthew Lyle (1833-1912)
1029, 1799
Lacy, William Sterling (1842-1899)
809, 1800-1801
Lafferty, John Wilson (1862-1941)
1802

Lambdin, Milton Bennett (1850-1940)
1803
LaMotte, Louis Cossitt (1902-   )
1804
Lancaster, Richard Venable (1863-
1938) 1805, 2842
Landrum, Charles Logan (1900-   )
1806
Lane, Edward (1837-1892) 3955
Lang, Arthur (1886-1923) 1807
Lang, Cecil Herbert (1891-1974) 501,
1124, 1155
Lang, George (1879-1971) 1808
Lapsley, James Norvell (1930-   )
668, 1809-1810
Lapsley, Robert Alberti (1858-1934)
1811-1814
Lapsley, Robert Alberti (1884-1953)
1122, 1815-1822, 2847
Lapsley, Samuel Baxter (1889-1956)
1823-1824
Lapsley, Samuel Norvell (1866-1892)
1003, 1825, 3179, 3978
Latimer, James Fair (1845-1892)
1826, 1899, 3817
Latimer, Robert Milton (1857-1918)
1827
Law, Patrick Redd (1849-1912) 1828
Law, Thomas Hart (1838-1923) 1829,
2845
Lawrence, A. B. (ca. 1787-1862)
1830
Laws, Samuel Spahr (1824-1921) 1831-
1846, 2325
Leavell, William Hayne (1850-1930)
1089, 1847-1848
Leavenworth, Abner Johnson (1803-
1869) 1849
Lee, William States (1793-1875) 1850-
1851
Leftwich, James Turner (1835-1897)
1728, 2256
Legters, Leonard Livingston (1873-   )
1853-1855
Leith, John Haddon (1919-   ) 1856-
1860, 2896, 2923, 3521
Leland, Aaron Whitney (1787-1871)
664, 1861-1865, 3993
Leslie, John Douglass (1860-1935)
1866-1867
Lewis, Frank Bell (1911-1967) 1868
Lewis, Frederick Wheeler (1873-1968)
1869
Lewis, James N. (1809-1887) 1870-
1873
Lewis, John Milligan (1889-1872) 501
Leyburn, Edward Riley (1865-1958)
1874, 2836, 3872

McDill, Joseph Moody (1911-1981)
2016

McDill, Thomas Haldane (1917-   )
1008, 2017-2018

McDonald, Angus (1846-1909) 2019

MacDonald, John Alexander (1853-
1932) 2081

McElhenney, John see McElhenny,
John (1781-1871)

McElhenny, John (1781-1871) 1029,
1799, 2020, 3993

McElroy, Isaac Stuart (1853-1931)
2021-2023

McElroy, Samuel Addison (1860-
1935) 2024-2026

McFadden, Samuel Edgar (1886-   )
2840

McFaden, Frank Talbot (1864-1933)
3820

McFadyen, Henry Richard (1877-
1964) 2027

MacFerrin, Marvin M. (1877-1947)
2836

McGeachy, Archibald Alexander
(1869-1928) 2029

McGeachy, Daniel Patrick (1929-   )
2030-2039, 3316

McGeachy, Neill Roderick (1909-
1979) 2040

McGee, John Vernon (1904-   )
2041-2048

McGuffey, William Holmes (1800-
1873) 1401, 2049-2058, 3968

McIlwain, William Erskine (1848-
1938) 2059-2060

McIlwaine, Richard (1834-1913)
2061-2065

McIlwaine, William Andrew
(1893-   ) 2066

McIver, Daniel Massillon (1864-
1938) 1169

McIver, Malcolm Chester (1917-   )
2067, 2929

Mack, Edward (1868-1951) 2068-
2073, 2389-2390, 2847, 3770,
3777

Mack, William (1807-1879) 2075

McKay, Edward James 2076-2080

McKay, Neill (1816-1893) 2082

McKee, Dean Greer (1904-   )
2083

McKelway, Alexander Jeffery
(1932-   ) 671, 2084

McKelway, Alexander Jeffrey
(1866-1918) 598, 2085

MacKenzie, James Donald (1924-   )
2086-2087

Mackenzie, John Anderson Ross
(1927-   ) 329, 525, 2088-2090,
2622, 3121, 3822

McKinnon, Arch Cornelius (1883-1967)
2091

McKinnon, John Henry (1909-1979)
1598

McLaughlin, Henry Woods (1869-1950)
548, 2092-2096, 2836

McLean, James Dunning (1856-1922)
2097-2099

MacLean, John Allan (1891-   ) 2100

McLees, Richard Gustavus (1864-1956)
2101

McLeod, John Wesley (1853-1926)
2831

McLeod, William Angus (1876-1947)
501, 2102-2103

McMichael, Jack Brame (1911-   )
2104-2106

McMillan, Homer (1873-1958) 2107-
2109

McMillan, James Pressley (1831-1923)
2110

McMillan, Leighton Gaines (1887-   )
2111

McMullen, John Stuart (1915-   )
2112

McMullen, Robert Burns (1807-1865)
2113-2115

McMurray, Joseph Alexander (1866-
1953) 4156

McMurry, Stonewall Jackson (1862-
1946) 2116-2117

McMurtry, James Gilmer (1870-1954)
2118

McNair, Evander (1814-1886) 2250

McNair, Lindsay Evander (1871-1953)
2842

McNeill, Robert Blakely (1915-1975)
523, 2119-2120

McNeilly, James Hugh (1838-1922)
1580, 2121-2122, 2251, 2253

McPhail, George Wilson (1815-1871)
4, 147, 807

McPheeters, Samuel Brown (1819-
1870) 667, 680, 1219, 1567, 4116

McPheeters, William Marcellus
(1854-1935) 1570, 1575, 1578,
2123-2149

McQueen, John Wilber (1907-1976)
2150-2151

McQuilkin, Robert Crawford (1886-
1952) 2152-2164, 3431

McRae, Daniel Abraham (1842-1920)
2831

McSween, John (1888-1964) 1575,
1578

Moore, William D. (1824-1896)
2393-2395
Morgan, Frank Crossley (1898-   )
2396-2399
Morgan, Gilbert (1791-1875) 2400
Morgan, Howard Moody (ca.
1900-   ) 2401
Morgan, Kingsley John (1895-   )
2402
Morris, Robert Hugh (1876-1942)
2403-2408
Morris, Samuel Leslie (1854-
1937) 694, 2409-2418, 2810
Morrison, Hugh McEwen (1828-1893)
2419
Morrison, John (1892-   )
2420-2422
Morrison, Robert Hall (1798-1889)
2023, 2267, 2423, 3993
Morrison, William McCutchan
(1867-1918) 231, 1596, 2424-
2427, 3896-3897, 3978
Morrison, William McCutchon see
Morrison, William McCutchan
(1867-1918)
Morrow, Thomas (1808-1885) 2428
Morton, John Booker (1847-1913)
2429
Moseley, Edward Hilary (1869-
1965) 2430-2432
Moseley, John Watkins (1828-1920)
2433-2434
Moseley, John Watkins (1866-1937)
2435-2438
Mount, Charles Eric (1902-   )
2439
Mount, Charles Eric (1935-   )
2440-2441
Mount, Eric see Mount, Charles
Eric (1935-   )
Mullally, Francis Patrick (ca.
1830-1904) 3235
Mullin, Joseph Bartholomew
(1924-   ) 2442
Munroe, Henry Havener (1877-
1956) 2826
Murkland, William Urwick (1842-
1899) 3528
Murray, Ephraim Clark (1861-
1930) 2443-2444
Murray, James (1834-1914) 2445
Murray, Joseph James (1890-1973)
2446-2450, 2929
Murray, Spencer Castles (1927-   )
159, 2451
Myers, Harry White (1874-1945)
2452, 3658

Nabers, Charles Haddon (1889-1968)
2455-2464
Nall, Robert (1805-1886) 2466-2467
Nash, Frederick Kollock (1813-1861)
2468
Neel, Samuel Monroe (1841-1921)
2469, 4173-4175
Neely, Robert Langdon (1829-1888)
2470
Neilson, William Parker (1879-1925)
2258
Nelson, Carl Ellis (1916-   ) 2471-
2478
Nelson, James Boyce (1904-1979)
2479
Neville, William Gordon (1855-1907)
2480, 3769
Newland, LeRoy Tate (1885-1969)
2482-2483
Newsome, James DuPre (1931-   )
2484
Nickle, Keith Fullerton (1933-   )
2485-2486

Oates, Luther Albertus (1865-1909)
2489
Oehler, James Cornelius (1857-1941)
2490
Ogden, Dunbar Hunt (1878-1952) 2461,
2491-2493, 2826
Oglesby, Stuart Roscoe (1888-1977)
2494-2503
Oglesby, William Barr (1916-   )
2322, 2481, 2504-2507
O'Hair, John Cowan (1876-   ) 2508
Ormond, John William (1919-   )
2509-2510, 3316
Orr, Kenneth Bradley (1933-   ) 2823
Orr, William Fridell (1907-   ) 240,
2511
Orts Gonzalez, Juan (1868-1941) 2512-
2520
Osman, John (1907-1978) 934, 2521
Ostenson, Robert James (1922-   )
2522
Ostrom, Henry Conrad (1876-1937)
2825
Otts, John Martin Philip (1837-1901)
2523-2527
Otts, John Martin Philip (1838-1901)
see Otts, John Martin Philip
(1837-1901)
Overholser, James Arthur (1911-   )
2529

Paine, Henry H. 1128, 2531

Pratt, John Wood (1827-1888) 1460, 2791-2792

Pratt, Nathaniel Alpheus (1796-1879) 2793

Preston, John Alexander (1853-1896) 3528

Preston, Thomas Lewis (1835-1895) 2854

Price, Benjamin Luther (1867-1928) 2855

Price, Francis Wilson (1895-1974) 630, 2856-2862, 3651, 4165

Price, James Ligon (1915-   ) 2864

Price, Philip Francis (1864-1954) 902, 2865-2869

Price, Philip Frank see Price, Philip Francis (1864-1954)

Price, Robert (1830-1916) 2816

Price, William Thomas (1830-1921) 2870-2872

Primrose, John W. (1838-1907) 2874-2876

Pritchard, Claudius Hornby (1896-1979) 2878-2879

Pritchett, Carl Ruffin (1909-   ) 3316

Proudfoot, Charles Merrill (1923-   ) 2880-2881

Proudfoot, Merrill see Proudfoot, Charles Merrill (1923-   )

Pryor, Theodorick (1805-1890) 2257, 2882

Purcell, John Edwin (1884-1950) 2809, 2836, 3286

Purcell, Malcolm Lee (1893-1978) 2883, 2926

Purviance, James (1807-1871) 2884

Quarles, James Addison (1837-1907) 2885-2887

Quinius, Henry Willard (1919-   ) 2888

Ramkey, William Hobday (1915-   ) 1122

Ramsay, Franklin Pierce (1856-1926) 2889-2892

Ramsay, John Cummins (1890-1962) 2894

Ramsay, William McDowell (1922-   ) 1216, 2895-2899

Ramsey, Emmet Alexander (1849-1898) 2251

Ramsey, Harmon Bigelow (1907-   ) 2900

Ramsey, James Beverlin (1814-1871) 2487, 2901-2908

Rankin, David Cyrus (1847-1902) 2909

Rankin, Samuel Meek (1864-1939) 2910-2911

Ratliff, Dale Hedrick (1928-   ) 2912-2913

Rauschenberg, Fritz (1877-1967) 2914

Raymond, Moses (1798-1875) 2915

Raynal, Charles Edward (1877-1944) 2916

Read, Charles Henry (1811-1900) 2917-2921

Reavis, James Overton (1872-1959) 2824-2825

Red, William Stuart (1857-1933) 2926-2928

Redhead, John Agrippa (1905-   ) 2930-2940

Reed, Charles Wesley (1885-1968) 2941

Reed, Gordon Kennedy (1930-   ) 2942

Reed, James Landrum (1817-1905) 2943

Reed, Richard Clark (1851-1925) 1575, 2810, 2944-2958

Reid, John Calvin (1901-   ) 2959-2970, 3693-3694, 4115

Reinhold, Robert William (1919-   ) 2971

Reisner, Sherwood Hartman (1920-   ) 2972

Reveley, Walter Taylor (1917-   ) 2975

Reynolds, William Davis (1867-1951) 2981

Rhea, Samuel Audley (1827-1865) 2178, 2982

Rhea, Thomas Clark Rye (1914-   ) 2662

Rhodes, Arnold Black (1913-   ) 998, 2983-2987

Rhodes, Daniel Durham (1917-   ) 2988-2989

Rhodes, Paul Simpson (1876-1956) 2990

Rice, John Jay (1886-1972) 2991

Rice, Joseph Sherrard (1917-   ) 2803, 2992-2994

Rice, Theron Hall (1867-1922) 2819, 2842, 2995-2998

Richards, Charles Malone (1871-1964) 1584, 2999

Richards, James McDowell (1902-   ) 1578, 3000-3007, 3521, 4115

Scotchmer, George (1916-) 3113

Scott, Eugene Crampton (1889-1972) 2817

Scott, Jack Brown (1928-) 3231-3232

Scott, John Andrew (1820-1895) 3985

Scott, William Nelson (1848-1919) 3528

Sengel, William Randolph (1923-) 3233

Settle, Paul Gunter (1935-) 3237

Shaw, Angus Robertson (1858-1936) 3238

Shaw, William A. (1804-1885) 3239

Shearer, James B. see Shearer, John Bunyan (1832-1919)

Shearer, James W. see Shearer, James William (1840-1921)

Shearer, James William (1840-1921) 236, 3240-3244

Shearer, John Bunyan (1832-1919) 1576, 3245-3256

Shedd, Charlie William (1915-) 3257-3282, 4172

Sheppard, William Henry (1865-1927) 1003, 3283, 3978

Shepperson, John G. (1814-1894) 3284

Sherrill, Lewis Joseph (1892-1957) 2259, 3285-3303

Shewmaker, William Orpheus (1869-1946) 1169, 3305-3306

Shipley, David Oliver (1925-) 3307

Shotwell, Albert (1807-) 3308-3311

Shriver, Donald Woods (1927-) 885, 2242, 2618, 3312-3316

Sibley, Josiah (1877-) 3317

Sibley, Julian Scales (1867-1944) 3318

Sikes, William Marion (1875-1941) 3319

Siler, John Calvin (1876-1952) 546

Simpson, John David (1900-) 3320

Sims, Frank Knight (1873-) 2836

Sinclair, Alexander (1834-1885) 3321-3322

Sinks, Perry Wayland (1851-1940) 3323-3325

Sistar, William Clarence (1904-) 648

Skinner, James William (1855-1931) 3326-3327

Slusser, Gerald Herbert (1920-) 3328-3332

Smith, Arthur J. 3334

Smith, Benjamin Mosby (1811-1893) 947, 962, 1899, 2257, 3169, 3335-3344

Smith, Edward Everett (1861-1944) 3345

Smith, Egbert Watson (1862-1944) 902, 1231, 2028, 2819, 2825-2826, 3347-3369, 3813, 3820

Smith, Harry Edmund (1928-) 168, 3370

Smith, Hay Watson (1868-1940) 446, 608, 2129-2130, 2144, 3371-3374

Smith, Henry Martyn (1828-1894) 664, 2834

Smith, J. Kinsey (ca. 1858-1923) 3375-3376

Smith, Jacob Henry (1820-1897) 1571, 2365, 3377, 3528, 3993

Smith, James Power (1837-1923) 1801, 2849, 3378-3385

Smith, John Robert (1910-) 3387-3388

Smith, Joseph Addison (1854-1920) 3389

Smith, Morton Howison (1923-) 3390-3392

Smith, Robert C. see Smith, Robert Carsall (1810-1873)

Smith, Robert Carsall (1810-1873) 3393-3394

Smith, Robert Perry (1851-1936) 2023, 3395

Smith, Samuel Macon (1851-1910) 2816, 3397-3401

Smith, Thomas Irvine (1907-1975) 3402

Smith, Wade Cothran (1869-1960) 237, 469, 3403-3413

Smith, Wilbur Moorehead (1894-) 468, 928, 1626, 2335, 2530, 3414-3451

Smith, William Kyle (1895-) 3452

Smith, William Sheppard (1928-) 3453

Smoot, Richmond Kelley (1836-1905) 2556, 3454-3455, 3528

Smylie, John Addison (1812-1878 or 1879) 3866

Smylie, Theodore Shaw (1893-) 3456-3457

Smyth, Thomas (1808-1873) 145, 359, 788, 1566, 3120, 3235, 3458-3517, 3629, 3993, 4186

Smythe, William Sterling (1897-1949) 3518

Tenney, Levi (1823-1907) 3698

Tenney, Samuel Fisher (1840-1926) 2831

Tenney, Samuel Mills (1871-1939) 3543, 3699-3703

Tenney, William Collins (1873-1956) 3704

Thacker, James Ernest (1869-1945) 2794

Thomas, John Newton (1903-) 2924, 2528, 3707, 3818

Thomas, John Stanley (1870-1959) 3708

Thompson, Cecil Asbury (1906-) 3709, 4115

Thompson, Ernest (1867-1946) 2461, 3710-3711

Thompson, Ernest Trice (1894-) 464, 913, 1159, 2835, 2847, 2929, 3712-3734, 3812, 3814, 3818, 3910

Thompson, Henry Howard (-1973) 2840, 3735

Thompson, William Taliaferro (1886-1964) 3737-3742

Thompson, Willis (1887-) 3743

Thomson, Charles Talbutt (1858-1926) 3744-3745

Thorne, William (1871-1925) 3746

Thornwell, James Henley (1812-1862) 664, 946, 1068, 2546, 2553, 2821, 2845, 3235, 3748-3768, 3962, 3993

Thornwell, James Henley (1846-1907) 3769

Tiemann, William Harold (1927-) 3773

Tompkins, Jerry Robert (1931-) 3775, 4044

Trostle, John Adams (1874-1948) 3781

Tubbs, Ace Leonard (1922-) 3783

Tucker, Grayson Letcher (1924-) 3784

Tunyogi, Andrew Csapo (1907-) 3785-3786

Turnage, Maclyn Neil (1927-) 2801, 3653, 3787-3793

Turnbull, Martin Ryerson (1886-1949) 3794-3799

Turner, Herbert Snipes (1891-1976) 3800-3802

Tuttle, Romulus Morris (1842-1904) 3803

Tuttle, Romulus Morrison see Tuttle, Romulus Morris (1842-1904)

Tyler, James W. (1869-1924) 3804-3805

Unger, James Kelly (1893-) 3806-3810

Vance, James Isaac (1862-1939) 694, 2461, 2825, 3396, 3528, 3820, 3825-3856

Vance, Joseph Anderson (1864-1951) 3857-3865, 4187

Vander Meulen, John Marinus (1870-1936) 2259, 2461, 2977, 3867-3869

Van Devanter, James Nichols (1857-1917) 3870

Van Meter, John Stonestreet (1845-1904) 3871

Van Saun, Arthur Carlos (1893-1969) 3873

Vardell, Charles Graves (1860-1958) 3874

Vass, Lachlan Cumming (1831-1896) 3875-3876

Vaughan, Clement Read (1827-1911) 314, 538, 758, 2556, 2608, 3819, 3877-3885

Vaughan, Robert Crews (1919-) 3886-3887

Vedder, Charles Stuart (1826-1916 or 1917) 610, 3888

Venable, Joseph Glass (1877-1928) 2461

Venable, Sidney Johnson (1894-) 3889

Verner, Samuel Phillips (1873-) 3890

Vick, George Henry (1912-) 3891

Viehe, Frederick Dana (1878-1940) 3893

Vinson, John Walker (1880-1931) 1335

Vinson, John Walker (1914-) 3894

Vinson, Robert Ernest (1876-1945) 3895

Vinson, Thomas Chalmers (1887-1961) 3896-3897

Voss, Louis (1856-1936) 3898-3900

Waddel, John Newton (1812-1895) 2815, 3901-3905, 3993

Waddell, James Addison (1817-1905) 3906-3907

Wade, Joel Taylor (1862-1957) 3908-3909

Waggett, John MacPhail (1884-1969) 3910-3911

Wilson, Benjamin Frank (1863-1932) 4048-4049

Wilson, Carl (1924-) see Wilson, Carl William (1924-)

Wilson, Carl William (1924-) 4050

Wilson, Daniel Love (1849-1892) 4051

Wilson, Goodridge Alexander (1887-1976) 1124, 4052-4054

Wilson, Howard McKnight (1900-) 4055-4058

Wilson, Hugh (1794-1868) 427, 729

Wilson, John Leighton (1809-1886) 664, 865, 1634, 1929, 3934, 3962, 3993, 4059-4066

Wilson, John Simpson (1796-1873) 4067-4069

Wilson, Joseph Ruggles (1825-1903) 2815, 3528, 4070-4072

Wilson, Lewis Feuilleteau (1804-1873) 729

Wilson, Luther Halsey (1837-1914) 4074-4077

Wilson, Robert Manton (1880-1963) 3809

Wilson, Ronald Samuel (1902-1962) 4154

Wilson, Samuel B. (1783-1869) 1899

Wilson, Samuel Ramsey (1818-1886) 3088, 4073, 4078-4088

Wilson, Samuel Thomas (1823-1893) 4089-4092

Winecoff, John Eugene Lee (1863-1953) 4093-4095

Wingard, George Thomas (1923-) 159

Winn, Albert Curry (1921-) 659, 1944, 2802, 4096-4104

Winn, Samuel Knox (1848-1926) 4105

Witherspoon, Eugene Daniel (1932-) 2817

Witherspoon, Thomas Dwight (1836-1898) 2816, 2837, 3528, 3871, 4107-4111

Womeldorf, John Andrew (1911-) 4114

Wood, Bertram Oliver (1892-) 501

Wood, Francis Lloyd Ferguson (1909-1976) 4115

Woodall, William Love (1908-) 4117-4120

Woodbridge, Charles Jahleel (1902-) 1892, 4121-4124

Woodbridge, Samuel Isett (1856-1926) 604, 4125

Woodrow, James (1828-1907) 961, 1583, 2207, 2829, 2925, 4126-4132

Woods, David Junkin (1868-1965) 4133-4134

Woods, Edgar (1827-1910) 4135-4136

Woods, Francis Marion (1843-1939) 4137

Woods, Henry McKee (1857-1943) 4138-4144

Woods, Neander Montgomery (1844-1910) 3528

Woods, Thomas Edward Peck (1875-1948) 4145-4150

Woods, William Hervey (1852-1925) 4151-4152

Woodson, Marshall Scott (1896-1980) 1582

Woodworth, Robert Bell (1868-1964) 443, 4153-4159

Workman, William Hay (1858-1934) 4160

Wright, Allen (1826-1885) 4162

Wright, Austin Hazen (1811-1865) 4163-4164

Wurts, Edward (1810-1885) 4166

Wyrick, Victor Neil (1928-) 4167-4168

Yandell, Lunsford Pitts (1805-1878) 4169

Yates, William Black (1809-1882) 4170

Yohannon, Isaac Esho (1864-1918) 4171

Young, Daniel P. (ca. 1833-1878) 4177

Young, James Thomas (1927-) 4178

Zeluff, James Daniel (1930-) 4179

Zivley, John Henry (1824-1905) 4180

INDEX

B. Main Entries: Persons not Ministers of the Presbyterian Church
    in the United States; Corporate entries; Pseudonymous Entries

*Not a minister of the Presbyterian Church in the United States

C. SUBJECT INDEX

Addresses 6, 22, 23, 40, 50-51,
60, 65, 71, 87, 103, 130, 133,
146, 148, 152, 252, 254, 306,
310, 343, 358-360, 373, 395,
456, 462, 467, 471, 536, 593,
606-607, 664, 666, 672, 716,
756, 772-773, 789-790, 794,
799, 807, 855, 958, 969, 1134,
1138, 1175, 1263, 1310, 1353,
1408, 1443, 1448-1449, 1458,
1464, 1471, 1490, 1508, 1514,
1537, 1596, 1604, 1681, 1685,
1687, 1808, 1834, 1844, 1862,
1897, 1958, 1983, 2003, 2063,
2117, 2138, 2166, 2173-2174,
2327, 2331, 2342-2343, 2346,
2348, 2351, 2361, 2363, 2365,
2369, 2388, 2395, 2403-2404,
2439, 2455, 2466, 2535-2537,
2539, 2541-2546, 2551, 2554,
2557, 2560, 2563, 2568, 2628,
2649, 2675, 2713, 2747, 2769-
2774, 2793, 2918, 3007, 3019,
3023-3024, 3026-3027, 3038-
3039, 3078, 3085, 3088, 3146,
3160-3161, 3166, 3176, 3225-
3226, 3334-3337, 3343, 3458,
3493, 3496, 3503, 3509, 3512,
3525, 3529, 3531, 3611, 3675-
3680, 3686, 3774, 3818, 3901-
3902, 3905, 3957, 3985, 4019-
4020, 4072, 4082, 4131, 4133,
4164
Adoption 3947
Agnes Scott College, Decatur, Ga.
1058
*Agobard, Saint, abp. of Lyons
(d. 840) 481
Agriculture 889
Alcoholism 1088, 3682
All in the family 2179-2180
*Amalarius, abp. of Treves (9th
cent.) 482
Antichrist 376, 423, 2668
Apostles 1255, 3830
Apostles' creed 870, 1188, 3553,
3867

Apostolic succession 3500
Arkansas 625
Arminianism 438, 1135
Apostasy 424
Art 1410
*Athanasius, Saint, patriarch of Alex-
andria (ca. 297-373) 2951, 3043
Atonement 529, 751-752, 1540, 1833,
3863, 4073
Austin Presbyterian Theological Sem-
inary, Austin, Tex. 739

Bahaism 2303-2305, 2318
Baptism 47, 69, 98, 120-121, 126,
158, 198, 200, 226, 439-441,
497, 554, 603, 647, 655, 673,
881, 1166-1168, 1173, 1230, 1244,
1365, 1370, 1407, 1488, 1599,
1642-1643, 1662, 1729, 1802,
1871, 1883, 1909, 1940, 1943,
2097, 2270, 2326, 2344, 2354,
2443, 2468, 2783, 2943, 3000,
3138, 3175, 3239, 3311, 3577-
3578, 3743, 3804, 3965, 4052
*Barth, Karl (1886-1968) 3055, 3101,
3126
*Beecher, Lyman (1775-1863) 1404
Belief and doubt 1367
Bible--Canon 517, 2139, 2141, 3246
Bible--Commentaries 1626
Bible--Commentaries--O. T. 35-37,
697, 1054, 1520, 1717, 1924-
1925, 1928, 1930, 2226-2227,
2229-2231, 2349-2350, 2984
Bible--Commentaries--N. T. 37, 525,
537, 999, 1241, 1314, 1342, 1382,
1476-1478, 2276-2277, 2289, 2308,
2311-2315, 2694-2695, 3129, 3178
Bible--Criticism, interpretation, etc.
74, 117, 176, 185, 189, 210, 245,
312, 351-352, 425, 560, 596, 639,
674, 677, 689, 736, 749, 787,
842, 848, 897, 900, 933, 938,
940, 998, 1026-1027, 1049, 1164,
1189-1190, 1274, 1277, 1411,
1432, 1512, 1521, 1526, 1555,

---

*Not a minister of the Presbyterian Church in the United States